SO-BKZ-967

OTHER A TO Z GUIDES FROM THE SCARECROW PRESS, INC.

Lao-tzu sculpture (70 cm. high), Indiana limestone, by Saskatoon artist Ed Gibney. *Author's collection.*

The A to Z of Taoism

Julian F. Pas

The A to Z Guide Series, No. 13

The Scarecrow Press, Inc.
Lanham, Maryland • Toronto • Oxford
2006

SCARECROW PRESS, INC.

Published in the United States of America
by Scarecrow Press, Inc.
A wholly owned subsidiary of
The Rowman & Littlefield Publishing Group, Inc.
4501 Forbes Boulevard, Suite 200, Lanham, Maryland 20706
www.scarecrowpress.com

PO Box 317
Oxford
OX2 9RU, UK

The A to Z of Taoism is a revised paperback edition of the *Historical Dictionary of Taoism*, by Julian F. Pas, published by Scarecrow Press in 1998.

British Library Cataloguing in Publication Information Available

Library of Congress Cataloging-in-Publication Data

Pas, Julian F.
   Historical dictionary of Taoism / Julian F. Pas, in cooperation with Man Kam Leung.
      p.   cm.—(Historical dictionaries of religions, philosophies, and movements ; no. 18)
   Includes bibliographical references.
   1. Taoism—History—Dictionaries.   I. Leung, Man Kam.   II. Title.
III. Series.
BL1923.P37 1998
299′.514′03—dc21   97–25780

ISBN 0-8108-5511-9 (pbk. : alk. paper)

*To the many generations of my students of
Taoism at the University of Saskatchewan
and other friends in the Tao
who helped me in my search for the Way.*

Contents

Preface

Taoism is a very complex cultural tradition, which had a deep influence on Chinese ways of thinking and spiritual practice. In the West, Europe and North America, Taoism is best known through translations of the philosophical writings of the *Tao Te Ching* (abbreviated *TTC*) and *Chuang-tzu* (not always properly understood) and through some of its "side products," the martial arts, Chinese medicine, and many of its "pseudo products," the growing number of books titled "The Tao of . . ." authors of which are more motivated by the "Tao of profitmaking" than by the real Tao.

Taoism deserves to be better known in the West. But it must be understood the way it really was or is, not as it is imagined to be. In this volume, I have incorporated mostly secondary information, either from Chinese or western language sources. If one would attempt to walk the Way alone, and find all one's data in primary sources, one lifetime would not be long enough. And there is some urgency in producing a volume on Taoism that is both informative and attractive.

What attracts me the most to Taoism is its philosophy. Taoism as a religion is also colorful, sometimes mysterious, sometimes weird, sometimes senseless. As a religion, it is fascinating to study, but I would not incorporate it into my own life. I do not believe in the stories about "immortals" or Taoist authors who claim that physical immortality is within human reach. That, to me, is an illusion. But in the philosophical writings, I find a rich treasure-house of wisdom that is meaningful in my own life. The *TTC* and the *Chuang-tzu* are "springs" that connect underground with the sources of a "perennial philosophy." And they are free from religious illusion, appealing to the universal human mind, and promote the human capacity for self-transcendence.

Having expressed my own views about Taoism, it is, however, necessary to explain the rationale of this volume, since it includes many items that are part of the Taoist religion. Readers have the right to be informed, and in providing information about many aspects of the Taoist religion, I have tried to be objective and historically correct.

In recent decennia, Taoism has received tremendous scholarly attention, both in the East (China and Japan) and in the West (Europe and

North America). Anna Seidel's "Chronicle of Taoist Studies in the West" (*CEA*, 5, 1989–90) and Franciscus Verellen's state-of-the-art report (*JAS*, 54, 1995: 322–346) are excellent indicators of how much Taoism has gained. Yet, deplorably, there exists as yet no in-depth general survey of the Taoist tradition in a western language. H. Welch's *Parting of the Way* is out of date, and Isabelle Robinet's *Histoire du Taoïsme*, although excellent from a historical viewpoint, does not sufficiently cover the Taoist philosophical tradition and also omits the issue of Taoism in modern times.

The present volume attempts to temporarily fill the gap. In writing the nearly 275 entries, I relied heavily on the expertise of past and present Taoist scholars, sometimes on the work of Chinese scholars, especially on dictionaries and encyclopedias of Taoism published in recent years. I dare not compare this present modest volume with the huge publications in China and Japan. An example is *Encyclopedia of Chinese Taoism* (*Zhonghua Daojiao da cidian*), published in Beijing in 1995, which consists of 2,207 pages in small print and is extremely detailed—obviously meant for Chinese readership. It lists a few hundred contributors. A Japanese volume titled *Dictionary of Taoism* (*Dokyo jiten*), published in Tokyo in 1994, has 1,141 entries, written by 132 contributors.

By contrast, a volume put together by one person, with the assistance of one other, cannot pretend to be a final product. It is, in fact, meant to be a starting point. I hope other scholars of Taoism will respond by sending me their comments and criticisms in order to launch a second edition. I am certain that more entries could be introduced, and that new bibliographic data can be added. I also wish that nonspecialists will give me some feedback: which items they would like to see discussed in greater detail, etc. Indeed, this volume is written especially for nonspecialist, educated readers to use as a reference work. I realize that some entries should be expanded, especially those that discuss aspects of Taoism that are relevant to Westerners today. With the readers' support and suggestions, the second edition should come closer to the ideal reference work.

In the presentation of the entries, I have tried as much as possible to provide names and titles in English, rather than in Chinese. This will help to make this volume less esoteric: An overdose of Chinese terminology would easily overwhelm a nonspecialist reader. Of course, there are exceptions: Particular terms cannot easily be rendered in English and are very often left untranslated. To this group belong such terms as *Tao, Te, Ch'i, Yin-Yang*, etc. Romanizing these terms leaves their rich meaning intact, as long as they are explained sufficiently.

I was fortunate to have the advice and support of quite a few wonderful people. First of all, my longtime colleague Man Kam Leung (history department, University of Saskatchewan) deserves credit for drafting about two dozen entries (mostly historical) and advising me about many other aspects of this book. I also wish to acknowledge the expert advice and support of Norman Girardot, Russell Kirkland, Ma Xiaohong and Chu Ron Guey. Among the nonspecialist lay people (my friends), I'd like to acknowledge the input of Brian Dalsin, Bill Garner, Tonya Kay, Lance Blanchard, and Adele Boychuk.

I am very grateful for my wife Yü-lin's assistance, my son Ed's graphic expertise, and Pauline de Jong's and Audrey Swan's superb word-processing skills, together with their never-failing assistance. The photographs were taken by David Mandeville, whose skill and expertise I greatly admire. I further wish to acknowledge the assistance, advice, and patience of this volume's editor, Jon Woronoff.

Finally, this volume is dedicated to many generations of students of Taoism at the University of Saskatchewan. Although I was their teacher, officially, I wonder who received the greatest benefit. Thank you!

Thanks are finally due to the University of Saskatchewan research unit, which gave me a generous grant to prepare the manuscript.

Note on Spelling

Because the Chinese language does not have an alphabet, several romanization systems have been designed to present the equivalents of Chinese sounds with the help of the western alphabet.

The most commonly used systems today are: the *Wade-Giles* system and the *pinyin* system. The *Wade-Giles* system is the oldest and is still used by the Library of Congress and in many scholarly publications. But the *pinyin* system, devised in China during the 1950s, is becoming more and more acceptable in modern writings (it is the system used in English publications made in China, as well as in the western news media).

In this volume, I prefer the *Wade-Giles* system (with a few exceptions), but in all entry titles, I use both systems, as, for example:

Chang Tao-ling/Zhang Daoling
Tao-te ching/Daodejing
T'ai-chi ch'uan/Taijichuan

The *Wade-Giles* system often uses hyphens in proper names (Chang Tao-ling) or in monosyllabic words that form a unit (such as *T'ai-chi*). These hyphens are omitted in the *pinyin* system: Two or three words are then spelled as units *(Taiji)*, because they are considered to be compounds.

My exceptions to the *Wade-Giles* system concern the use of some diacritics ("umlauts") in such words as *yüan, hsüeh*, etc. Because these diacritics are not necessary, I simply omit them.

Also, words spelled with an initial "i" are changed to "yi" (as in the *pinyin* system): the reason is that terms such as *I ching* are often mispronounced by English speakers. To avoid this, I prefer *Yi ching.*

I don't object to *pinyin* romanization per se, only its intrusion into western languages. The major examples are the spelling of *Taoism, Taoist*, and even *Tao*. Very often these words are spelled *Daoism, Daoist*, and *Dao*, which is not only misleading (leads to mispronunciation), but these words were already accepted into the English and other languages, before the *pinyin* system was introduced. The *pinyin* system should not interfere with other languages. When *Tao* occurs in Chinese words or expressions, the spelling *Dao* is acceptable (like *Daodejing*).

One more observation is important: Throughout the introduction and the dictionary proper, some words appear in **bold**. This means there are other entries in the dictionary that the reader may wish to consult.

Abbreviations

BCE and CE are the abbreviations most often used in this volume and deserve a special note. BCE stands for "before the common era," CE means "of the common era." "Common" means accepted by all, including non-Christians. The traditional abbreviations BC ("before Christ") and AD ("anno Domini" or "in the year of the Lord") are too denominational; moreover, in countries such as China, they are meaningless.

Abbreviations used in the introduction and dictionary

ADC	*Analytic Dictionary of Chinese & Sino-Japanese* (see Karlgren 1923/1973)
b.	born
BCE	before the common era
CE	of the common era
CT	Taoist canon, according to K. Schipper's *Concordance*
d.	died
EB	*Encyclopaedia Britannica*
ER	*Encyclopedia of Religion*, ed. by M. Eliade, 1967
FECED	*Far East Chinese-English Dictionary*, Taipei, 1992
fl.	flourished (refers to the active years of an author)
HCDR	*Harper Collins Dictionary of Religions*, 1995
HNT	*Huai-nan-tzu* (text)
MWT	Ma-wang-tui
PRC	People's Republic of China
r.	reigned (refers to reign period of an emperor or empress)
TPC	*T'ai-p'ing ching (Great Peace Scripture)*
TT	*Tao-tsang* (Taoist Canon)
TTC	*Tao-te ching*

Abbreviations used in the bibliography

AAr	*Asian Art*
AAS	*Association of Asian Studies*

ACQ	*Asian Culture Quarterly*
AM	*Asia Major*
ArA	*Artibus Asiae*
AS	*Asiatische Studien*
BCAS	*Bulletin of Concerned Asian Scholars*
BMFEA	*Bulletin of the Museum of Far Eastern Antiquities*
BSYS	*Bulletin of Sung and Yuan Studies*
BUA	*Bulletin de l'Université de l'Aurore*
BTS	*Buddhist and Taoist Studies,*
	vol. 1 (M. Saso & D. Chappel, eds., 1977)
	vol. 2 (D. Chappell, ed., 1987)
CC	*Chinese Culture* (Taipei)
CEC	*Cahiers d'Etudes Chinoises*
CEA	*Cahiers d'Extrême-Asie*
CF	*Ching Feng*
CS	*Chinese Studies*
CSP	*Chinese Studies in Philosophy*
EB	*Encyclopaedia Britannica*
EC	*Early China*
ER	*Encyclopedia of Religion*
FT	*Facets of Taoism* (Welch & Seidel, eds.)
HHYC:CS	*Han-hsueh yen-chiu: Chinese Studies* (Taipei)
HJAS	*Harvard Journal of Asiatic Studies*
HR	*History of Religions*
IPQ	*International Philosophical Quarterly*
JAAR	*Journal of the American Academy of Religion*
JAH	*Journal of Asian History*
JAOS	*Journal of the American Oriental Society*
JAS	*Journal of Asian Studies*
JCP	*Journal of Chinese Philosophy*
JCR	*Journal of Chinese Religions*
JCS	*Journal of Chinese Studies*
JHI	*Journal for the History of Ideas*
JHKB RAS	*Journal of the Hong Kong Branch, Royal Asiatic Society*
JMS	*Journal of the Mongolia Society*
JNCB RAS	*Journal of the North China Branch, Royal Asiatic Society*
JOS	*Journal of Oriental Studies*
JOSA	*Journal of the Oriental Society of Australia*
JRAS	*Journal of the Royal Asiatic Society*
MS	*Monumenta Serica*
NDGNVO	*Nachrichten der Deutschen Gesellschaft für Natur- und Völkerkunde Ostasiens*
OA	*Oriental Art*
OE	*Oriens Extremus*

PEW	*Philosophy East and West*
RHR	*Revue de l'histoire des religions*
RPOA	*Religion und Philosophie in Ost-Asien* (Naundorf, ed. 1985)
RR	*Review of Religion*
RRCS	*Religion and Ritual in Chinese Society* (A. Wolf, ed., 1974)
RS	*Religious Studies*
RSR	*Religious Studies Review*
RT	*Religious Traditions*
SCEAR	*Studies in Central and East Asian Religions*
SM	*Studia Missionalia*
SSCRB	*Society for the Study of Chinese Religions Bulletin*
SUNY	*State University of New York* (Press)
TMLT	*Taoist Meditation and Longevity Teachings* (L. Kohn, ed., 1989)
TP	*T'oung Pao*
TR	*Taoist Resources*
TS	*T'ang Studies*
TT-RCT	*The Turning of the Tide—Religion in China Today* (J. Pas, ed., 1989)
TTS (1,2)	*Taoist and Tantric Studies, vols. 2 and 3* (M. Strickmann, ed., 1983)
WTB	*Westliche Taoismus-Bibliographie/Western Bibliography of Taoism* (K. Walf, ed., 1992)

Abbreviations of Chinese reference works

CMTT	*Chien-ming Tao-chiao tz'u-tien [Explanatory Dictionary of Taoism]*, by Huang Hai-te & Li Kang-pien. Chengtu: Szechuan University Press, 1991.
CTCT	*Cheng-t'ung Tao-chiao ta tz'u-tien [Encyclopedia of Taoism]* (2 vols.), by Yang Feng-shih. Taipei: Yi-ch'un Publishing Co., 1989.
TCS	*Tao-chiao shou-tz'e [Manual of Taoism]*, edited by Li Yang-cheng. Cheng-chou, China: Ku-chi Publishing Co., 1993.
TCTT-1	*Tao-chiao ta tz'u-tien [Encyclopedia of Taoism]*, by Li Shu-huan, Taipei: Chü-liu Publishing Co., 1979.
TCTT-2	*Tao-chiao ta tz'u-tien [Encyclopedia of Taoism]*, compiled by Kuan Chih-t'ing & Li Yang-cheng. Beijing: Taoist Association of China & Suchou: Taoist Association of Suchou, 1994.

TMSC   *Taiwan miao shen-chuan [Biographies of Taiwan Temple Deities]*, Touliu, Taiwan: Hsin-t'ung Bookstore, 1979.

TPK   *Ta-pai-k'o ch'uan-shu [Great Encyclopedia of China]* (vol. "Religion"). Beijing & Shanghai: Great Encyclopedia of China Publishing Co., 1988.

TTTY   *Tao-tsang t'i-yao [Essentials of the Taoist Canon],* Jen Chi-yü, general editor. Beijing: Social Sciences Publishing Co., 1991.

Table of Chinese Dynasties

SHANG			ca. 1550–ca. 1030 BCE
CHOU	Western Chou	ca. 1030–771	ca 1030–256 BCE
	Eastern Chou	770–256	
	"Spring & Autumn" period	722–481	
	Warring States period	480–222	
CH'IN			221–207
HAN	Former (Western) Han	202BCE–9CE	202 BCE–220 CE
	Hsin	9–23	
	Later (Eastern) Han	25–221	
THREE KINGDOMS	Shu (Han)	221–263	221–265
	Wei	220–265	
	Wu	222–280	
SOUTHERN	Chin	265–316	
(Six Dynasties)	Eastern Chin	317–420	
	Liu Sung	420–479	
	Southern Ch'i	479–502	
and	Liang	502–557	
	Ch'en	557–587	
NORTHERN	Northern Wei (T'o-pa)	386–535	265–581
DYNASTIES	Eastern Wei (T'o-pa)	534–543	
	Western Wei (T'o-pa)	535–554	
	Northern Ch'i	550–577	
	Northern Chou (Hsien-pi)	577–581	
SUI			581–618
T'ANG			618–906
FIVE	Later Liang	907–922	907–960
DYNASTIES	Later T'ang (Turkic)	923–936	
	Later Chin (Turkic)	936–948	
	Latern Han (Turkic)	946–950	
	Later Chou	951–960	
Liao (Khitan Tartars)			907–1125
Hsi-hsia (Tangut Tibetan)			990–1227
SUNG	Northern Sung	960–1126	960–1279
	Southern Sung	1127–1279	
Chin (Jurchen Tartars)			1115–1234
YUAN (Mongols)			1260–1368
MING			1368–1644
CH'ING (Manchus)			1644–1911
REPUBLIC			1912–1949
People's Republic of China (PRC)			1949–
Republic of China (ROC: Taiwan)			1949–

Chronology of Taoist History

Chinese Dynasties B.C.E. (−)	Taoist History		Buddhism & Other Schools in China	
WARRING STATES (−480−222)	−475	Eastern States of Yen and Ch'i belief in "immortals"	−551−479	Confucius
	−350−300	Chuang-tzu (inner chapters)	fl. −479−438	Mo-tzu
	−300−250	Tao-te ching	ca. −371−289	Mencius
	−3rd c.	Chuang-tzu (outer chapters)	fl. −298−238	Hsün-tzu
CH'IN DYNASTY (−221−210) First Emperor	−219	expedition in search for immortality plant (mushroom)	−219	School of Tsou Yen, 3rd c., performs feng and shan sacrifices at Mount T'ai
	−212	calls himself chen-jen ("true, perfected" person)		
			−168	Ma-wang-tui tomb #3 closed (contains silk manuscripts of TTC)
			−145?−90?	Szu-ma Ch'ien, author of Historical Records (Shih-chi)
WESTERN HAN (−206−8 CE) Emperor Wu (r. −141−87)	−139	Huang-Lao Taoism Huai-nan-tzu presented to Emperor Wu by Liu An	−136	Confucianism becomes state doctrine (for education)
	−134	Li Shao-chün sacrifices to Szu-ming		
	−133	Emperor Wu sends fang-shih in search for Immortals	−119	orders sacrifices to be performed to T'ai-yi
			−110	Emperor Wu performs feng and shan sacrifices

C.E.		
EASTERN HAN (+9–220)		
Emperor Hsün (r. 126–144)	105	2nd century: Buddhism starts to enter China invention of paper recorded
	143	Chang Ling visits Szechuan, practices the Tao on Mount Ho-ming; starts Five Bushels of Rice Taoism
		Chang Ling establishes 24 districts
		Great Peace Scripture presented to court
Emperor Huan (r. 146–168)	165	follows Huang-Lao Taoism erects tablet *Lao-tzu ming*
	166	sacrifices to Lao-tzu
Emperor Ling (r. 168–189)	184	T'ai-p'ing Tao in Eastern China Yellow Turban rebellion erupts and is crushed. Three Chang brothers perish.
Emperor Hsien (r. 189–220)	191	Chang Lu organizes theocratic state
		Lao-tzu Hsiang-erh commentary on TTC
	215	Ts'ao Ts'ao attacks and Chang Lu submits
		possible date of Ho-shang kung's *Commentary on TTC*
THREE KINGDOMS (221–264)	222–253	Chih-ch'ien translates some Buddhist scriptures, such as *Pure Land Scripture* (T. 362), and *Pen-yeh ching* (T. 281); they influence Ling-pao scriptures of Ko Ch'ao-fu.
	230	Sun Ch'uan (of Wu kingdom) orders general Wei Wen to search for immortality herbs

Chinese Dynasties		Taoist History	Buddhism & Other Schools in China
WESTERN CHIN (265–317)	277	a disciple of Heavenly Masters Taoism, Ch'en Jui in Yi-chou assumes the title of Heavenly Master. He is executed.	
Emperor Hui (r. 290–306)	288	Wei Hua-ts'un obtains teaching of *Yellow Court Scripture* Taoist Wang Fou "fabricates" *Lao-tzu hua-hu ching* *Yellow Court Scripture* is published	Buddhist response *Zhong-wu lun* (Rectification of Unjustified Criticism) (4th century)
	317	Ko Hung writes his *Pao-p'u-tzu*	
EASTERN CHIN (317–420)			3rd–4th c. Neo-Taoism—dialogue with Buddhism & Confucianism —translation of Buddhist texts by Kumarajiva —Buddhist monk Chih Tun (314–366) writes commentary on *Chuang-tzu*
	364–370	Transcendent Wei Hua-ts'un and others reveal to Yang Hsi the basic scriptures of Shang-ch'ing Taoism.	
	397–402	Ko Ch'ao-fu composes the Ling-pao scriptures	
	399	Sun En's rebellion starts	
	402	Sun En, defeated, commits suicide final years of Eastern Chin: composition of *Tu-jen ching*	

Dynasty / Emperor	Year		
NORTHERN WEI (386–535)	415	K'ou Ch'ien-chih claims to have received title of Heavenly Master, as well as order to reform the corrupt Taoism of the Three Chang	Buddhist Hui-yuan, influenced by Taoism
	423	starts new Heavenly Masters Taoism	
Emperor T'ai-wu (r. 424–452)	424	earliest still existing Taoist image	
	425	emperor invests K'ou as Heavenly Master, new Taoism starts to spread in north	
	432		Buddhist concept of retribution criticized by Ho Ch'eng-t'ien in *Pao-yin lun*
	440	new era called *T'ai-p'ing chen-chün*	
	442	emperor initiated as a Taoist	
	446		suppression of Buddhism
	460		work on Yün-kang caves starts (Buddhist sculpture)
SOUTHERN LIU-SUNG (420–479)	461	Lu Hsiu-ching retires to Mount Lu	
	471	Lu collects Taoist scriptures and publishes first catalogue in three sections (*san-tung*): 1090 scrolls	

Chinese Dynasties	Taoist History	Buddhism & Other Schools in China
SOUTHERN CH'I (479–502)	492 T'ao Hung-ching retires to Mount Mao	
SOUTHERN LIANG (502–557)		500 work on Lung-men caves starts (Buddhist sculpture)
(NORTHERN WEI)	520 Taoist Chiang Pin and Buddhist T'an Wu-tsui debate in court about the priority of their religions	Bodhidharma arrives in China from India (around 520)
NORTHERN CH'I (550–577)	555 Buddhists and Taoists summoned to debate. Taoists defeated, ordered to become Buddhist monks	
NORTHERN CHOU (557–581)	569 court invites Taoists & Buddhists to discuss with 100 officials the meaning of Buddhism and Taoism concerning relative merits of Three Teachings. Emperor decides: Confucianism is first, Taoism second, Buddhism last.	
	574 suppression of Taoism	574 Emperor Wu suppresses Buddhism
	580 restoration of Taoism	580 restoration of Buddhism
T'ANG DYNASTY (618–906) Emperor Kao-tsu (r. 618–627)	618 T'ai-shang Lao-chün's transformation body (hua-shen) appears on Mt. Yang-chiao in Shensi; calls himself ancestor of imperial family	Sui-T'ang dynasties: beginning of golden age of Chinese Buddhism

Emperor	Year	Event	Buddhism
	620	Lao-tzu temple erected on Mt. Yang-chiao, now renamed Lung-chiao	development of Chinese schools: T'ien-t'ai, Hua-yen, Pure Land, Ch'an (Zen) Taoist Fu Yi (554–639) attacks Buddhism in 621 memorial
Emperor T'ai-tsung (r. 627–649)	624	emperor goes to Mt. Chung-nan to worship at Lao-tzu temple. Five Bushels School is transmitted to Korea	
	626	imperial edict to purge Buddhism & Taoism	
	633	imperial edicts: Buddhists & Taoists must honor parents	Hsuan-tsang travels to India (629–645): welcomed back by Emperor T'ai-tsung
	637	Taoists obtain precedence over Buddhists Lao-tzu temple erected in Hao-chou	
Emperor Kao-tsung (r. 650–683)	666	emperor sacrifices to Huang-t'ien Shang-ti on Mt. T'ai gives title to Lao-tzu	
	674	Empress Wu orders all officials to study TTC; TTC becomes primary examination material	
	683	edict to build Taoist monasteries (kuan) in each chou	

Chinese Dynasties		Taoist History	Buddhism & Other Schools in China
Empress Wu Tse-t'ien (r. 684–704)	686	title given to Wang Yuan-chih	Hui-neng (638–713) named sixth patriarch of Ch'an Buddhism, against Shen-hsiu (600–706), the original successor
	690	Buddhists receive precedence over Taoists	
	693	TTC withdrawn as examination material	
Emperor Chung-tsung (r. 705–709)	705	TTC reinstated as examination material	
		edict to build in each chou one Buddhist and one Taoist temple, called chung-hsing, later renamed lung-hsing	
	711	two imperial princesses initiated into Taoism	
Emperor Hsuan-tsung (r. 713–755)	721	emperor receives Taoist master Szu-ma Ch'eng-chen from Mt. T'ien-t'ai, and receives initiation. Has Lao-tzu TTC engraved on tablets in capital's Lung-hsing monastery	
	733	TTC elevated above all scriptures; all officials are ordered to keep a copy at home. Writes a commentary on TTC	
	741	Order to build Hsuan-yuan Huang-ti temple in 2 capitals and all chou; established Ts'ung-hsuan Learning: orders all students to study TTC, Chuang-tzu, Lieh-tzu & Wen-tzu	

			Ma-tsu (709–788), patriarch of Ch'an Buddhism; uses "Taoist" techniques to reach enlightenment
	742	honorary titles are given to four authors, ex. Chuang-tzu is called *Nan-hua chen-jen.* Their writings are called *chen-ching.* In each *chou* is established a doctoral program, with a specialist teacher and 100 students	
	743	Lao-tzu's parents receive honorary titles. Names of temples are changed	
	744	casts bronze images of Yuan-shih T'ien-tsun and places them in K'ai-yuan kuan of each *chou* Princess Yü-chen becomes Taoist priestess (*nü tao-shih*)	
	747	Chang Tao-ling honored with title of *T'ai-shih* (Supreme Teacher); T'ao Hung-ching titled *T'ai-pao* (Supreme Protector)	
	749	Yellow Emperor given honorary titles	
	754	Lao-tzu given honorary titles	
Emperor Su-tsung (r. 756–762)	756	court issues clerical certificates to raise funds for military expenses to put down An Lu-shan rebellion	

Chinese Dynasties		Taoist History		Buddhism & Other Schools in China
			781	Nestorian monument erected in T'ang capital
Emperor Te-tsung (r. 780–804)	796	emperor organizes court debates among Three Teachings		forerunners of Neo-Confucianism: Han Yü (768–824) and Li Ao (d. around 844)
Emperor Hsien-tsung (r. 805–820)	806	Taoist registry office established	806	Manicheism introduced to China by Uighurs
	820	emperor dies of pill poisoning (manufactured by Taoist)		
Emperor Wen-tsung (r. 827–841)	827	emperor organizes court debates among Three Teachings	827	Pai chü-yi writes *Essays on the Three Teachings*
	840	Lao-tzu's birthday fixed on 15th day of 2nd (lunar) month: a national holiday. Summons 81 Taoists to celebrate "golden register fast" in palace; Emperor Wu-tsung receives initiation		
Emperor Wu-tsung (r. 841–846)	846	emperor takes alchemy pills and dies. Hsuan-tsung receives initiation	842–845	great suppression of Buddhism

Dynasty / Emperor	Year	Event		
Emperor Hsuan-tsung (r. 847–859)	859	emperor dies of alchemical poisoning		
Emperor Hsi-tsung (r. 874–889)	884	Chang Tao-ling receives posthumous honors		
SUNG DYNASTY (960–1279)	961	Three Teachings debates are prohibited		
Emperor T'ai-tsu (r. 960–976)		examination imposed on Taoists: those who fail are secularized		
		Taoists and Buddhists are forbidden to study astronomy, *feng-shui*. At court meetings Buddhists have precedence over Taoists		
	976	Summons Chang Shou-chen to perform "golden register *chiao*"		
Emperor T'ai-tsung (r. 976–998)	977	emperor receives Ch'en T'uan in audience		
	981	builds T'ai-yi temple in Su-chou		
	983	builds T'ai-yi temple in capital Kaifeng	983	first complete edition of Buddhist Canon (Szechuan edition)
		secularized Taoist & Buddhist clergy are prohibited from participating in state examinations		
	990	starts compilation of Taoist Canon		
	995	emperor erects a Shang-ch'ing temple in palace		

Buddhism & Other Schools in China

Chinese Dynasties
Emperor Chen-tsung
(r. 998–1022)

Taoist History

1007　Lieh-tzu receives honorary title
1008　"Heavenly Book" descends in capital; Chao-ying palace is erected to house it. Day of "descent" is promoted to national holiday;
again a "Heavenly Book" descends on Mt. T'ai. Sacrifice to Huang-t'ien Shang-ti is performed on Mt. T'ai according to Taoist ritual

1009　*Chai-chiao* rituals performed; Taoist music created in whole country
T'ien-ch'ing kuan are built.
Orders Taoists to collect Taoist Canon
Emperor writes *Record of Holy Ancestor's Descent*

1012　he places in Yü-ch'ing temple holy images of Huang-t'ien

1013　Yü-huang, holy ancestor Chao Hsuan-lang, T'ai-tsu & T'ai-tsung

1014　Yü-huang's worship flourishes
1015　Wang Ch'in-jo writes *Lo-t'ien chiao liturgy* (10 Ch.)
emperor's daughters enter Taoism

	Year	Taoist History	
Emperor Jen-tsung (r. 1023–1064)	1016	24th Heavenly Master Chang Cheng-sui receives title builds Academy for Transmission of Registers on Mt. Lung-hu	
	1019	Wang Ch'in-jo presents new collection of *Tao-tsang* (4,359 scrolls): titled *Pao-wen t'ung-lu*.	
	1030	*Tao-tsang* in 4,565 scrolls compiled by Chang Chün-fang, presented to emperor.	emergence of cosmologists: Chou Tun-yi (1017–73), Shao Yung (1011–77), Chang Tsai (1020–77)
		25th Heavenly Master Chang Ch'ien-yao receives titles. Ch'ang Chün-fang writes *Yun-chi ch'i-ch'ien* in 122 chapters	
	1033	prohibition to build new temples	
	1054	26th Heavenly Master Chang Szu-tsung receives title	
	1060	examination system for Taoist priests set up	
Emperor Ying-tsung (r. 1064–68)	1064	copies of *Tao-tsang* given to five monasteries in Chengtu.	revival of Confucianism: Ch'eng Yi (1033–1108) Ch'eng Hao (1032–1085)
Emperor Shen-tsung (r. 1068–1086)	1080	Taoist candidates must be examined on *TTC, Tu-jen ching, Chuang-tzu*	
	1082	decides that the Department of Sacrifices will confer purple robes and "great teacher" titles	

Chinese Dynasties		Taoist History	Buddhism & Other Schools in China
Emperor Che-tsung (r. 1086–1100)	1091	Ch'en Ching-yuan is ordered to collate (new) *Tao-tsang*	
	1096	empress enters Taoism, receives titles	
Emperor Hui-tsung (r. 1101–1125)	1105	30th Heavenly Master Chang Chi-hsien receives title	
	1105	prohibition to offer joint sacrifices to sacred images of Three Teachings	
	1107	ruling that Taoist priests and nuns have precedence over Buddhist monks and nuns	
	1108	all Taoist monasteries receive imperial copy of golden register rituals. Lin Ling-su ordered to compile Taoist history, scriptures; treated as a teacher	
	1110	emperor sends Taoists to Korea to spread Tao	
	1113	national request for Taoist scriptures	
	1115	establishes 26 Taoist ranks	
	1116	Lin Ling-su receives honorary title	
		Taoist Learning established	

1117	emperor calls himself Taoist monarch; *TTC* renamed	1117	allows Buddhist monks to become Taoists: they are given certificates and purple robe
1118	establishes 26 degrees of Taoist officials; Lao-tzu's birthday on 15th day of 2nd month is defined as *chen-yuan* ("true primordial") festival; announces his *Imperial Commentary on the TTC*; three doctorates established at Taoist Institute (*TTC, Chuang-tzu, Lieh-tzu*)		
		1119	Buddhists are allowed to enter Taoist Institute
1120	Taoist Institute closed		
1126	gold & silver of temples have to be handed to officials		
1133	Buddhism has precedence over Taoism at court		
1138	T'ai-yi Taoism founded by Hsiao Pao-chen		
1140	32nd Heavenly Master Chang Shou-chen receives title		
1142	Great Tao Taoism founded by Liu Te-jen		flourishing of Neo-Confucianism: Chu Hsi (1130–1200) and Ch'eng-yi: School of Principles (*Li Hsueh*)

(SOUTHERN SUNG: 1127–1279)
CHIN DYNASTY (1115–1234)

Chinese Dynasties		Taoist History	Buddhism & Other Schools in China
	1143	10,000 clerical certificates are given to Taoists and Buddhists	
	1159	Wang Che starts cultivation of Tao	
Emperor Hsiao-tsung (r. 1163–1190)	1164	T'ai-shang kan-ying p'ien	
	1167	Ch'uan-chen Taoism founded by Wang Ch'ung-yang	
	1181	Ma Tan-yang performs "Yellow Register chiao"	
	1188	Shih-tsung summons Ch'iu Ch'ang-ch'un	
	1190	decides to have examinations for Taoists & Buddhists every three years. Complete Realization Taoism prohibited. Sun Te-ming edits Ta-Chin hsuan-pu Pao-tsang (Chin Taoist Canon)	
	1191	Taoists are forbidden to communicate with officials of 3rd rank and higher; 32nd patriarch of Shang-ch'ing Taoism, Ch'in Ju-ta, performs "Golden Register chiao"	
	1222	Ch'iu Ch'u-chi visits Genghis Khan in Central Asia	Lu Chiu-yuan (1139–1193) and Wang Yang-ming (1472–1528): School of Mind (Hsin Hsueh)

1223	Ch'iu appointed as supervisor of all Taoists in China
1224	Ch'iu returns to Yen-ching (Beijing), resides in T'ai-chi temple
1227	Genghis changes T'ai-chi temple into Ch'ang-ch'un temple
1229	Ch'uan-chen patriarch Li Chih-ch'ang explains *TTC* to Crown Prince Mongke
1239	35th Heavenly Master Chang K'o-ta receives title
1240	Ch'ung-yang Wan-chou temple constructed
1244	*Hsuan-tu Pao-tsang* completed (7,800 scrolls)
1247	T'ai-yi patriarch, Hsiao Fu-tao, receives title
1255	(first) Taoist defeat during debate at Mongol court (Khubilai Khan). Edict to destroy *Hua-hu scripture* and other spurious texts; prohibition to circulate *Lao-tzu's 81 Transformation Pictures*
1258	second debate between Taoists & Buddhists (Taoists lost again; 237 monasteries returned to Buddhism)

Chinese Dynasties		Taoist History	Buddhism & Other Schools in China
YUAN DYNASTY (1260–1368) Khubilai Khan (r. 1260–94)	1260	T'ai-yi patriarch, Hsiao Chü-shou, receives title	
	1268	Sun Te-fu receives title, appointed to be in charge of *True* Ta-tao School.	
	1276	36th Heavenly Master, Chang Tsung-yen, summoned to court, appointed to supervise Southern Taoism	
	1281	T'ai-yi patriarch, Hsiao Chü-shou, receives seal Goddess Ma-tsu elevated to rank of T'ien-fei (Heavenly Concubine) (third) Taoist defeat during court debate with Buddhism. Taoist scriptures ordered destroyed	
	1285	Khubilai summons Mt. Wu-tang Taoist Yeh Hsi-chen	
	1287	Khubilai performs *chiao* rituals on Mt. Lung-hu, Ko-tsao & Mao ban against Complete	
	1295	Realization Taoism lifted	
	1296	38th Heavenly Master Chang Yü-ts'ai receives title Liu Yü-cha founds Ching-ming Taoism	

1303	God Chen-wu renamed Hsuan-t'ien Ta-ti
1304	Chang Yü-ts'ai named "Lord of Cheng-yi Tao"; receives registers of three mountains
1316	39th Heavenly Master Chang Szu-ch'eng receives title, put in charge of Southern Taoism.
1327	edict that married clergy must be secularized
1329	Ch'uan-chen and Cheng-yi masters perform a *chien-chiao* (dedication ritual) in capital

MING DYNASTY (1368–1644)

Emperor T'ai-tsu (r. 1368–98)

1368	two academies established: Hsuan-chiao yuan, Shan-shih yuan
1370	White Lotus Society proscribed
1373	ruling that court will institute clerical examinations. Each county allowed only one Buddhist or Taoist monastery; others to be destroyed. Women under 40 years not permitted to enter Taoism
1394	Taoists who have wives or lovers may be secularized

Chinese Dynasties		Taoist History		Buddhism & Other Schools in China
Emperor Ch'eng-tsu (r. 1403–25)	1410	44th Heavenly Master receives title, put in charge of Taoist affairs		
	1418	building of new temples on Mt. Wu-tang completed; ruled that those over 20 years may not enter Taoism; clerical certificates issued only every ten years		
Emperor Hsuan-tsung (r. 1426–36)	1445	edition of *Cheng-t'ung Tao-tsang* (5,305 scrolls)		
Emperor Ying-tsung (r. 1436–50)	1456–1506	Beijing's White Cloud Monastery is rebuilt		
	1458	Chang San-feng receives honorary title		
	1566	Emperor Shih-tsung dies of alchemical poisoning		
			1582	Matteo Ricci, Jesuit missionary and scholar, in Macao
	1607	Chang Kuo-hsiang edits *Wan-li hsü Tao-tsang* (Supplement to Taoist Canon) (180 scrolls)		
CH'ING DYNASTY (1644–1911) Emperor K'ang-hsi (r. 1662–1722)	1649	52nd Heavenly Master Chang Ying-ching given title "Great Perfected" (*ta chen-jen*)		

Period	Year	Event
Emperor Ch'ien-lung (r. 1736–95)	1702	Szechuan Taoist Ch'en Ch'ing-chueh goes for audience with Emperor K'ang-hsi; receives title "Perfected of Green Profundity" (pi-tung chen-jen)
	1733	Tao-tsang chi-yao (Compendium of Taoist Canon)
	1747	Cheng-yi patriarch degraded to fifth rank
	1819	Cheng-yi priests no longer invited to imperial audience
	1850–1864	T'ai-p'ing rebellion (Christian inspiration)
	1900	Boxer rebellion
	1904	62nd Heavenly Master Chang Yuan-hsi takes office
	1906	Tao-tsang chi-yao reprinted in Erh-hsien temple, Cheng-tu
	1913	Taoist Association of China established
REPUBLIC (1912–present)	1924	63rd Heavenly Master Chang En-fu takes office
	1924–1929	Taisho edition of Buddhist Canon printed in Tokyo
	1926	Tao-tsang reprinted in Shanghai
	1950	Taoist Association of Taiwan established
	1957	Taoist Association of China established (Tao-chiao hsieh-hui)
	1961	Taoist Association of Hong Kong established

Introduction

Starting on the Way

Taoism is one of the major streams of China's cultural history. Its subtle and mysterious ways have helped to shape the "mind" of China, or perhaps, more accurately, its "soul," i.e., its emotional and intuitive aspects. Its deep influence has been acknowledged in such expressions as "the Taoist in every Chinese"—perhaps one could say "the Taoist in every human." Indeed, Taoism strikes a familiar chord in all those who come into contact with it, and often one hears an initiate say: "There is nothing really new about this Tao; I have always known it implicitly."

Taoism eludes a precise definition. Even today, those who specialize in studying the Tao do not easily agree on its nature and manifestations. In this introductory essay, the complexity of Taoism will be discussed, and new insights into its nature and its various expressions will be formulated. Even though this vision is not necessarily the correct one (in Taoism, there probably is no such thing as absolute truth!), hopefully the discussion will provide all the necessary ingredients for a great banquet. How each reader will cook up a dinner is impossible to predict. "Streams" of wine, however, will not be missing, as the banquet must be enjoyable to be true. Otherwise, it would not be the Tao.

Right from the start, it must be stated that western scholarship has made the distinction between a Taoist school of philosophy and a Taoist religion. How the two "streams" or "branches" relate to each other is still a controversial matter. The distinction between two Taoisms is not just a western device; it is found in the Chinese tradition itself. The Chinese language has two distinct terms for Taoism, for which western equivalents are not easy to find.

The first term is *Tao-chia/Daojia* ("School of the Way," Graham, 1989: 171), a name given by Han scholars when they wanted to systematize the various schools of thought current during the late Warring States period (480–221 BCE). They distinguished *Ju-chia/Rujia* (Confucianism), *Fa-chia/Fajia* (Legalism), *Tao-chia* (Taoism), etc., as various intellectual traditions, or "schools of thought." Under this *Tao-chia* heading, they included the *Tao-te ching* and the *Chuang-tzu* (see below).

1

During that stage of intellectual growth, "Taoism" was just a distinct "school of thought," or, as it was later called, a school of philosophy.

The other term is *Tao-chiao/Daojiao* ("Doctrine of the Way," Graham 1989: 171) currently translated as Taoist Religion. The term probably was coined during the Han period, and used to identify a new religious movement arising in the 2nd century CE with Chang Tao-ling/ Zhang Daoling as founder.

The character *chiao/jiao* of *Tao-chiao* means "[to] teach; teaching, doctrine; instruction; to command, make" (*ADC*, 71), and, thus, *Tao-chiao* literally means "Taoist teaching, Taoist doctrine." It was used to indicate the Taoist religion, probably in imitation of *Fo-chiao*, "Buddhist teaching, Buddhist doctrine," the name given to Buddhism in the 2nd century when it was entering China (see N. Sivin, 1978).

A further extension of the term *chiao* arose during early medieval times, perhaps during the T'ang (618–906 BCE), when Confucianism was linked with Taoism and Buddhism. Together, they were called *san-chiao/sanjiao* or the "Three Teachings," at a time when proponents of a new movement, often called syncretism, started to emphasize the underlying oneness of the three. It is not clear whether these intellectuals understood *chiao* in *san-chiao* in the sense of "teaching" or of "religion." The terms certainly gave occasion to misinterpretation. The Buddhist and Taoist "teachings" were indeed held and propagated by religious bodies. In the late 19th century, the new expression *tsung-chiao/ zongjiao* was created to become the Chinese equivalent of the western term "religion." It further encouraged misunderstanding of *san-chiao*. It was taken for granted that *san-chiao* meant *the* three *religions* of China: Confucianism, Taoism, and Buddhism. This totally wrong translation also caused the most important aspect of Chinese religiosity, the Popular religion, to be ignored and neglected by Chinese and western scholars.

This long digression is necessary to understand that the term *Tao-chiao*, literally meaning "Doctrine of the Way" or "Teaching about the Tao," in fact came to be used to indicate the Taoist Religion. Although more and more western scholars today have started to subscribe to the theory of *one* Taoist body, rather than seeing Taoism as divided, this view needs clarification. The discussion will be taken up in the conclusion.

The Nature of Taoism

In a recent article, L. Thompson summarizes thirteen different answers given by Japanese scholars to the question, "What is Taoism?" (Thompson 1993: 9–22). Since the question was formulated in Japanese, which uses the term *Tao-chiao*, one expects an emphasis on the "religious aspects" of Taoism. Yet among the thirteen voices, several mention the Taoist philosophy as part of *Tao-chiao*. Besides the clearly religious components of the Taoist religion, such as Lao-tzu's divinization, worship of Taoist deities, the Taoist priesthood and monastic life, other aspects are included that are not essentially Taoist and not necessarily religious. This, fairly obviously, causes confusion. Several authors mention ancient popular beliefs and shamanism as the origin and foundation of Taoism. They may be considered somewhat correct, as long as one remembers that the original Heavenly Masters strongly rejected and reacted against unorthodox popular practices, called *kui-tao* (the way of the ghosts).

From this discussion, two principles seem to emerge concerning the nature of Taoism. First, Taoism cannot be strictly identified with a variety of Chinese practices and theories that properly belong to the overall Chinese spiritual world view. In this category fall the theories of Yin-Yang and the Five Agents (or Phases), which are not essentially Taoist but universally Chinese, although Taoism, like Confucianism, adopted them into its own system. Further, excluded from the confines of Taoism are shamanism and mediumistic cults, divination, *feng-shui*, calendar and festivals, and even the areas of outer alchemy, healing, science, technology, and the martial arts. All these areas of study and practice have connections with Taoism, but cannot be bluntly identified with it. Even if they are included in our subsequent discussion, they should not be mistaken as essentially Taoist phenomena.

What, then, is the nature of Taoism? In very general terms, one may call it the Chinese cultural system focusing on the Tao (the Way), but that is too vague to be of any practical use. All Chinese schools discuss the nature of Tao. Taoism is a cultural tradition with several streams, which are sometimes independent, sometimes converging, sometimes separating once more. The sources of these streams are different, even if in the course of their development they occasionally converge, either spontaneously or by human effort.

The streams of Taoism most commonly acknowledged as separate are the Taoist philosophy, the Taoist religion, and the Taoist Immortality Cults. The problem of their mutual relationships will be handled in the conclusion. For now, we accept the existence of these streams, or branches, for a working hypothesis. The analysis of what each stream involves will give us clues for solving the problem of unity as opposed to multiplicity. The nature of Taoism also will be taken up in greater detail at the end of this introduction.

Antecedents and Parallel Developments

Philosophical schools and religious traditions do not arise in a vacuum. Confucius acknowledged his reliance on the past, even though he founded a school of his own. Taoist philosophers and Taoist religious leaders of later times also are indebted to a wide variety of cultural traditions actively vibrant, though not systematized, during the Chou period (1030?-221 BCE). Clear, concise influences, however, remain difficult to pinpoint.

Antecedents of the *Tao-chia* can be found in the cosmological speculations recorded in the *Classic of Change*, or *Yi ching/Yijing*, the ". . . perhaps single most important text in the Chinese philosophical tradition" (Shaughnessy, 1994: 72). Later, the Yin-yang school of Tsou Yen (third century BCE) and the Five Agents/Five Phases Theory either influenced the growth of Taoist philosophical speculation or were at least parallel developments. These would be integrated into Taoism at a later stage, such as in the syncretist stream, of which the *Huai-nan-tzu* is the most mature statement. Antecedents of the *Tao-chiao* (Taoist Religion) are more diffuse, but generally one accepts that shamanism and the search for longevity/immortality had a strong influence on the origin of Han Taoist religion. Almost certainly, some ritual practices and religious concepts of pre-Ch'in times had their effect as well, although partially in a negative way, since the Heavenly Masters school would strongly react against the *kui-tao*, the worship of popular spirits, which they considered to be unorthodox.

Antecedents of *Tao-chia*

Long before the Yin-yang system was fully developed, there already existed a method of divination, introduced by the early Chou, using yarrow or milfoil stalks to obtain "divine" answers to vital questions. Somehow, this gradually led to the discovery of eight graphic symbols or trigrams consisting of three lines called *pa-kua/bagua*, which initially were just eight types of answers obtainable by divination. These eight became the basis of cosmic speculation and are the original building blocks of a Chinese classic, the *Yi ching*, which consists of the eight trigrams multiplied by themselves to form sixty-four symbols, or hexagrams, graphic symbols consisting of six lines. Yin-yang speculation was not part of the original mental background of this technique, but was injected later, so that the *Yi ching* grew into a book of cosmic, ethical, and psychological analysis.

This system's connection with early Taoism is now obvious: The famous saying, "one yin, one yang, that is the Tao" (from an appended text to the *Yi ching*), is a clear expression of this connection.

Besides the *Yi ching*, Taoist philosophers had other sources of inspiration, modifying the Tao into a cosmic concept expressive of an ultimate reality. The concept of Tao itself was available to many different schools, who understood and manipulated it subjectively, such as in the "way" of ruling for the Confucians. Other direct sources of Taoist speculation were the many aphorisms and popular proverbs floating around in society through oral transmission, perhaps created by popular wisdom (as proverbs go) or by individuals (kinds of pre-Taoists) who had their own lineage of disciples.

There may have been other influences at work, but besides and beyond all these factors, there must have been a new type of individual creativity, and these individuals in contact with each other, even living together in an academy sponsored by local rulers. In such an atmosphere, new ideas arose, were discussed, and were sometimes recorded. From the surviving documents of this period (ca. 300 BCE), we realize there was diversity of thought: some believed in the individual search for transcendence and happiness; others felt that something should be done about government and that the Tao should be brought down to the level of the whole country. This difference of opinions and ideals explains the variety of literary compositions in the so-called philosophical writings that have transpired to us (see below).

Parallel with this growth of new ideas, expressed in early Taoist documents, a new school came into being that would deeply affect all other schools of thought: the Naturalist School of Tsou Yen (305–240? BCE), also called the Yin-Yang School. The texts of this school have been lost, but have been integrated into other writings and have recently partially surfaced among the excavated **Ma-wang-tui** manuscripts.

The concepts of yin and yang probably go back to an ancient time period (early Chou?) and gradually snowballed over the centuries. It is a mitigated dualism, according to which yin and yang are two cosmic powers and/or mental categories by which all the phenomena of nature and human life can be interpreted and placed into context. (For a more complete discussion, see **Yin-and-Yang**.)

The five agents theory probably has ancient roots as well, but it was Tsou Yen's genius that combined it with Yin-yang thinking, although the twinning is not always smooth. Five "agents," in the past also called "elements" and today often replaced by "phases," is, like yin-and-yang, based on observation of nature. For an agrarian culture, observation of the four seasons is more acute. Each season has its significance and type of action and, with deeper scrutiny, its own active or dynamic power. Because the four seasons follow a fixed time sequence, correlated to four directions, four basic energies were abstracted and expressed in concrete terms: wood, fire, metal, and water. For some reason a fifth energy was added: earth, different from the others, but very basic and central. These five powers of nature, present in heaven, earth, and humanity (or nature in general) have mutual relationships and interact continuously. Their unceasing action explains all the processes on earth, which interact with heaven. From a different perspective, they can be considered the executors of the yin and yang forces. (For a more complete discussion, see **Five Agents**.)

The twofold theory of Yin-yang and the Five Agents is not uniquely nor specifically Taoist, but has been incorporated into Taoism and Confucianism alike, and was also absorbed by the Popular Religion. It is not presumptuous to say that this naturalistic philosophy constitutes the basic foundation of the Chinese world view. It is most probable, however, that it was elaborated at about the same time as the earliest Taoist writings were recorded. Therefore, its presence in the early *Chuang-tzu* and the *Tao-te ching* is minimal, whereas in the later *Huai-nan-tzu* its influence is very clear.

Antecedents of *Tao-chiao*

During the declining years of the Eastern Han (second century CE), social unrest reached an extreme and gave rise to radical movements (healing cults) both in east and west China. These were the first instances in Chinese history of Taoist institutional religion, and mark the beginning of a long development of the Taoist religion with numerous offshoots.

What were its antecedents? Various influences have been singled out, such as shamanism, the search for immortality, the worldview of Taoist philosophy (especially as in the *Chuang-tzu* and the *Tao-te ching,* hereafter abbreviated *TTC*), and the ancient traditions of popular cults, such as the worship of nature gods. During the early Han, the influence of *fang-shih*/fangshi (magicians? spiritual technocrats?) became more and more prominent and encouraged some emperors to support alchemical research.

Admittedly, the network of influences that stimulated the rise of a Taoist religious institution was extremely complex, yet two basic observations will help clarify the issue. First, the influence of Taoist philosophy should not be exaggerated; secondly, the single most crucial factor must be seen in the scripture, titled **Great Peace Scripture**.

The contribution of Taoist philosophy at the early stage of religious growth was rather minimal. Even if Chang Tao-ling received divine revelations from T'ai-shang Lao-chün, the divinized Lao-tzu, it is not the same as saying that the philosophy itself played an important role in the genesis of Taoist religion. In fact, the two are very different in structure: Taoist philosophy was an elite phenomenon, probably very limited geographically and numerically, and involved political philosophy. The Healing Cults, on the other hand, were social movements, involving large segments of the population, and were worship-oriented, while also striving to realize an ideal political system, based on ideas in the *Great Peace Scripture.*

It is in this scripture, indeed, that one can find the clearest blueprint of the Healing Cults in both east and west: the ideal of a renewed social organization, an era of peace and equality concretely manifested in a theocratic rule, but ultimately based on the Tao and revealed to humans through inspired teachers. An important theme is the close interaction between macrocosm and microcosm, between mind and body, so much so that sickness was seen as a result of moral wrongdoing. One had to repent before one could be healed.

These and other aspects of the Healing Cults are already found in the *Great Peace Scripture*, to which both Chang lineages had access. Even the theme of longevity and, more rarely, of immortality is found in the text. It also stresses the need for meditation and good works.

That other aspects of ancient Chinese culture had their say in the growth of the new movement cannot be denied, but most often these were also incorporated in the *Great Peace Scripture*. What about shamanism? It has been said that the **tao-shih** of the new movement were the successors of the old **fang-shih**. Might they have even replaced the *fang-shih*?

To conclude: It is very clear that the Taoist religious movements of the late Han comprised a distinct new development. This development did not arise in a vacuum, of course, but if there is one all-important influence to be pointed out, it was the *Great Peace Scripture*.

Since, chronologically, the Taoist philosophical writings were produced first (4th to 2nd centuries BCE), long before the first Taoist religious organizations were founded (2nd century CE), the same sequence will be respected hereafter.

The Philosophical Texts: A Taoist Humanism

While the Taoist texts best known in the west are the *Tao-te ching* and the *Chuang-tzu*, the *Lieh-tzu* and *Huai-nan-tzu* are also important, though they do not enjoy so much popularity. Recently a "dark horse" is galloping forward from obscurity: the *Kuan-tzu*, a text partially inspired by Taoism. All these texts will need our attention. Their spiritual message continues to inspire many readers. Because of their mystical overtones (and their occasional inclusion of religious themes) their message easily can be misconstrued as religious. But there exists such a thing as natural mysticism, which can be explained as ecstatic union with the Tao—not in the theistic sense, but as a naturalistic, humanist experience.

Until recently, dating these texts, especially the *TTC* and the *Chuang-tzu*, was difficult and beset with problems. There are few extraneous clues directing one to the time(s) of authorship. Instead, an appeal to internal criteria based on text-redactional studies is promising. Philip Roth has proposed a distinction of three aspects, or perhaps phases, in the development of early Taoism (Roth, 1994; see also Graham, 1981, and LaFargue, 1994).

> The first, or "Individualist," aspect is essentially apolitical and is concerned with individual transformation through inner cultivation placed in the context of a cosmology of the Tao. [*Nei-yeh* part of *Kuan-tzu*; *Chuang-tzu* 1–7]. The second, or Primitivist, aspect adds a political dimension to the first . . . the return to a more simple and basic form of social organization . . . [*TTC* and *Chuang-tzu* 8–11].
> The third and final aspect, the Syncretist, shares the cosmology and inner cultivation theory of the former two, but takes a different direction with its political thought. (Roth, 1994: 6)

With this aspect, a more complex central government is advocated, in accordance with the patterns of heaven and earth. Such a government

> . . . also exhibits a syncretist use of ideas from Confucian, Mohist, and Legalist sources within a Taoist cosmological and political framework. (Roth, 1994: 6–7) [Some Huang-lao texts, *Kuan-tzu*, *Chuang-tzu* 12–15 and 33; *Huai-nan-tzu*]

This new interpretation presents an excellent framework not only for understanding the *TTC* but other early Taoist writings as well. It is possible that the *Kuan-tzu* was the earliest of all Taoist texts, soon followed by, or contemporary with, the inner chapters of the *Chuang-tzu*. The *TTC* traces a growth from Taoist individualism toward a moderate concern with government. The term "primitivist," therefore, is not an ideal characterization of this tendency. There are degrees of "primitivism." For example, Chapter 80 of the *TTC* advocates a radical return to a simple, very "primitive" society, whereas much of the *TTC* preludes the syncretist: moderate government by a sage ruler, who understands the nature and operations of the Tao. Political wisdom, plus insight in the cosmic reality based on spiritual cultivation, is pictured as the best course to "order the world."

Against the trend of placing the *TTC* first in the discussion of Taoist philosophical texts, we shall adopt the order of the three aspects, which may well coincide with chronological stages. In other words, *Chuang-tzu's* inner chapters come first, next the *TTC* and *Chuang-tzu* 8–11, followed by *Chuang-tzu's* remaining chapters, especially 12–14 and 33. Finally, the *Huai-nan tzu* will finish off the discussion. (For the **Kuan-tzu** and **Lieh-tzu,** see their separate entries.)

Chuang-tzu 1–7

Chapters 1–7 of the book *Chuang-tzu*, named after its author **Chuang-tzu** (Master Chuang) or Chuang Chou, are traditionally called the "inner chapters" and are usually ascribed to Chuang-tzu's authorship. While confirming authorship cannot be absolute, the inner chapters must be closer to Chuang-tzu than most of the other parts of the book, which today consists of 33 chapters. In these inner chapters, Chuang-tzu's genius shines. Although part of the text is probably corrupt (especially Chapters 2 and 3) and difficult to understand, most appears to be intact and strikes us as an overwhelming and mind-opening philosophy of life. The style is witty; irony and satire are generously applied, the use of metaphors strikes home a clear message. Chuang-tzu appears both as an ordinary but inspired storyteller and as a radical iconoclast, who smashes social conventional standards and sets up his own standards for individual freedom and transcendence.

For him, the ideal person, whom he often calls c*hen-jen* ("true" person), which means "perfected," "realized," or "authentic," is one who transcends the petty values of ordinary life and soars into the beyond, where he/she finds freedom and happiness. The analogy of the huge bird (Chapter 1) is thought provoking.

Fear of death, at any age, inspires misapprehensions amidst any society. Chuang-tzu says that life and death are two sides of one reality, equally acceptable. Besides, because they are fated, impervious to human manipulation, we better accept the reality of death as we accept the joys of life. He goes one step further: Death is the end of our life, but also the end of our consciousness. There will be transformation, for the creative process goes on and on, but our individual consciousness comes to an end. To accept this is wisdom, to reject it is arrogance. The "true" person accepts life with joy and, when time is up, goes without a fuss. (These ideas are found in Chapter 6). (See also **Immortality**.)

Chuang-tzu shows his genius in his discussion of "truth" (Chapter 2, titled "Seeing the Equality or Relativity of Things and Theories"). Although this chapter has been dreadfully mangled (perhaps it was difficult to understand), some passages yield their ideas unambiguously. Chuang-tzu admits that the Tao has been darkened, and that language has lost its clarity. This disappointment is because of petty minds' self-centered and narrow thinking, and because of flowery rhetoric, empty talk. Therefore, he suspects the infallibility of rational thought and is critical of language, although he does not totally reject it (after all, he taught others and perhaps he wrote!). But the "truth" expressed in words is never absolute. The "real" can be expressed in thousands of different ways and none is absolute; none is without partial truth either. If we accept that, if we consider the Tao as the central axis of the real and of our own knowledge, then *all* things and theories have their place, and even Confucians and Mohists can live in mutual tolerance. That is the only way to prevent absolutist ideologies, which are the most serious danger to individual freedom and social harmony.

Another theme (found in Chapter 3) is "Nurturing Life." To care for the gift of life is to follow its natural course and to use one's vital energy (*ch'i*) sparingly, intelligently. That is the secret of longevity, and Chuang-tzu compares it with the way a skilled butcher uses his knife. He follows the natural anatomy of an ox, but avoids hacking and cutting. His knife is long-lasting. Others, who hack and cut through bones, etc., must replace their knife continuously. It is like wasting one's life energy through careless living.

One final theme selected from the inner chapters refers to Chuang-tzu's views on government (Chapter 4: "The World of Politics"). Chuang-tzu believes it is very difficult and hazardous to be a good advisor to kings. If one uses any approach that the king dislikes, one could be in danger. It is much safer not to serve in government and to be useless. Then one can live long.

Chuang-tzu considers the institution of government, which he witnessed in his own day, as totally irrelevant. Perhaps we would call him an anarchist! Still, there is more meaning than may initially appear. Rulership should be "responsive" (that's in the title of Chapter 7): A good king responds to the needs of the people rather than using the people for his own ends. How does one do that? "Let your mind wander in simplicity, blend your spirit with the vastness . . . leave no room for selfishness, then the world will be governed." (Watson, 1970: 94, and Graham, 1981: 95). The ideal ruler, then, is a mystical, magical presence. Through his own *te,* or charisma, he may cure disease and make harvests grow to maturity. There is no need for a bureaucratic buildup! Here we see Chuang-tzu, the individualist, who believes that the country will be at peace if the king "stays away" to let the people do their own thing. Yet, paradoxically, the king's magical presence will ensure peace and contentment.

(Other themes are: **human perfection**, the **concept of Tao**, the **use of the useless**.)

The *Tao-te ching*

This famous text, better known in the west than the *Chuang-tzu*, is probably the product of a group of scholar-gentlemen, idealists who felt that a person's first duty is to cultivate his own person and only then take up the responsibility of government. This is not unlike the moral-political ideal proposed in the Confucian classic *Great Learning* (*Ta-hsüeh/ Daxue*): The ancients who wished to order the state should first regulate their own family, but even before that cultivate their own person by rectifying their mind and making their will sincere (Chan, 1963: 86). In other words, to engage in political life, a person must be educated and morally perfected. This Confucian parallel was acceptable to early Taoist gentlemen (at that time, the rivalry between the two schools was only just appearing on the horizon). They felt self-cultivation to be the root, government service the fruit, though opinions were not equally shared by all concerning the kind of government to promote.

The *TTC* expresses a stage of thinking beyond what the early *Chuang-tzu* advocated, but there seem to be different gradations in this "primitivist" philosophy. The simplest one is close to the *Chuang-tzu:* no government, no learning. A more developed opinion holds that government is a good thing, if it is executed by a "sage" (*sheng-jen/sheng-ren*) who understands the nature of reality, its underlying Tao, its ways of operating, and, as a result, is able to imitate the Tao's action in his rule. This translates into a laissez-faire style of government, and minimal interference in the lives of the people.

Although the *TTC* strikes us as a poorly organized little treatise (81 short chapters in its present form), it is a gold mine of inspiration. The stimulation of that "familiar chord" explains its lasting appeal and its amazing number of translations. Leaving aside historical and literary problems for now (see **Tao-te ching-The Text**), let us just briefly focus on the major themes we discover in the text: the nature of Tao, its symbols, the government of the sage, and spiritual cultivation. (Each of these themes will be treated in more detail under **Tao-te ching-Themes**.)

First of all, what is the Tao, the "Way"? It is a metaphysical reality, not just a "road" for human beings to follow; it *is* such a road as well, but only as a concrete expression of that supreme reality. In this sense, Tao is more than "nature"—it is the foundation of nature, or nature is only the visible expression of that all-embracing reality. Then, "Tao" is only a word, and words are powerless to express the real. Words are limited, the Tao is limitless. Words are used as indexicals, as pointers; They imply and signify something very deep, very real, beyond the words. What is suggested by words, what is written in between the lines is more important than the lines themselves. But those lines are needed, otherwise there would not be anything between them. Therefore, let us use words with caution.

The true nature of Tao cannot be perfectly grasped for it is invisible, inaudible, untouchable. Yet we see, hear, and touch it all the time. The Tao is also ancient. Existing before all creation, it actually created all things, often expressed as the "ten thousand things." It produced all things, and continues to produce them, until they all return to their roots.

To make abstract theory more appealing, the *TTC* uses various symbols to suggest what the Tao is. It is like water: a life-giving force that is generous without being demanding. Tao is like water in another sense: Water is weak and soft, yet can be extremely powerful and wear down the hardest things, such as rocks. It has the strength of weakness. This connects with other symbols of weakness: woman, mother, the valley, the infant. "Mother" and "woman" in ancient patriarchal societies had little official authority, but through her submissiveness and gentleness she could control the male (in nature, it is often the female of the species who selects her mating partner). Like the valley, humble and lowly in contrast with mountains, the female is a symbol of fertility, a life-giving and nourishing force. Likewise, Tao is the "mother of the ten thousand things." Weak and helpless, a young infant is nonetheless full of vitality, its vital energy is unimpaired, and, being helpless, all its needs are taken care of. Likewise, the Tao appears to be helpless, yet, in fact, it is all-powerful.

In order to bring peace to the world, a would-be ruler must reflect on the nature of Tao and its inherent power, its *te*. He must deeply understand how the Tao operates, and follow the model in his own government. One of the most powerful messages of the *TTC* is the concept of *wu-wei*, literally "nonaction." The Tao appears not to do anything, yet nothing is left undone. In his government, the sage ruler should not act, or acts minimally, yet, paradoxically, the country will be in order. The sage ruler inspires, his presence stimulating the people, but the people do everything themselves. On the contrary, the more laws there are, the more offenses; the more the ruler grabs for himself (in taxes), the harder the people will be to control.

In order to become aware of the secret of sage rule, a ruler must cultivate his own person. Oddly, accumulation of "knowledge" will not do; rather, he must empty himself of mental clutter. Like Tao, which appears to be empty, he will be able to fill everything. Like water, he benefits all beings, without claiming any credit, any return. Empty of himself, he will be humble and kind, and the people will be hardly aware of his existence. Yet, almost magically, his presence will be felt, and his inner power will transform the country.

The above is only a poor analysis of the *TTC*'s message. To penetrate its meaning more deeply, one must be still and listen.

Chuang-tzu 8–10: The Primitivists

We are now entering the "outer chapters" of the *Chuang-tzu* (they cover Chapters 8–22), three of which express the views of the "primitivists." These philosophers, as Graham believes, wrote their essays around 205 BCE, a time of civil war after the collapse of the Ch'in empire. They are "political polemics which defend a Taoist conception of society against the other [post-Ch'in] reviving [and rival] schools . . ." (Graham, 1981: 198).

Their Taoist conception is extremist: moral and aesthetic values are rejected as violations of the original good nature of humanity. The sages are blamed for introducing fake moral prescriptions and, thus, disturbing the peace of the land. Ideally, a country would be small and unsophisticated, not interested in technological advances and warfare; everybody would act morally just by following his own inner good nature. In this ideal situation, along comes the sage, "huffing and puffing" after *jen* (kindness, benevolence), "reaching on tiptoe" for *yi* (righteousness). As a result, doubts arise, and "for the first time, the world is divided" (Watson: 105). Or worse, "whenever sages appear, bandits follow suit" (Watson: 109).

Chuang-tzu's basic critique of the sages is that they introduced external standards of morality, which are totally unnecessary and create doubts and disorder. If human nature and virtue are in perfect shape, there is no need for governing the world. It is the **Yellow Emperor** who first introduced "benevolence and righteousness to meddle with the minds of men" (Watson: 116). Yao and Shun (mythical emperors) followed suit, so that by the time of the Three Dynasties, the world was in chaos. Inborn goodness disappeared, and ethical prescriptions were unable to stop crimes. As a result, the world is full of criminals. It is all the result of meddling with man's mind (paraphrase of Chapter 11; Watson: 114–118). (Hypothetical dates are as follows: Yellow Emperor: 2698–2594 BCE; Yao: 2357–2255 BCE; Shun: 2255–2205 BCE; The Three Dynasties are Hsia, starting in 2205 BCE; Shang, starting in 1520 BCE; Chou, starting in 1030 BCE.)

Chuang-tzu's diatribes against the sages are reminiscent of Chapters 18–19 in the *TTC*, which also derive from a primitivist milieu; his advocacy of a simple lifestyle is echoed in Chapter 80 of the *TTC*, and his rejection of "technology" is beautifully described in *Chuang-tzu*, Chapter 12 (Watson: 134).

Chuang-tzu 12–14 and 33: The Syncretists

Political philosophies advocating rule by moral example, or, on the opposite end, by anarchy and total rejection of government, were not popular among Warring States princes; perhaps they were considered naive, and certainly impractical. Even within the Chuang-tzu school, there appeared proponents of a more realistic approach to government. Graham speculates that the Syncretist group was active between the fall of the Ch'in empire (210 BCE) and the adoption of Confucianism by Han Emperor Wu (around 134 BCE): That is a period of about seventy-five years, when no official state ideology was predominant, except perhaps

Huang-Lao Taoism during the reigns of Emperors Wen (179–157 BCE) and Ching (156–140 BCE).

During this period of competing ideologies, Taoism could not but become more realistic and combine sageliness with competent rulership. The *T'ien-hsia* chapter of the *Chuang-tzu* (Chapter 33) pinpoints it beautifully in a famous expression, "sagely within and kingly without" (Watson: 364). It frankly admits that the "various skills of the hundred schools all have their strong points . . . But none is wholly sufficient, none is universal." (Watson: 364). However, rejecting government completely, as the inner chapters did, is no longer tenable and is rejected (Chapter 15, Watson: 167).

It is possible that the *Chuang-tzu* text as a whole was edited by the Syncretists. (See also ***Chuang-tzu.***)

The *Huai-nan-tzu*: Han Syncretism

The *Huai-nan-tzu*, a text of 21 essays, produced (edited) by the Prince of Huai-nan in 140 BCE and presented by the author to young Emperor Wu in 139 BCE, may well be a product of **Huang-Lao Taoism**. Although its essays were probably written by a group of scholars supported by the court of Huai-nan and cover a variety of topics, there is still a common theme running through them—another example of syncretist political thinking. In order to be an effective ruler, the king must understand the operations of Nature (based on Tao). Tao is primordial but its manifestations in the cosmos must be well grasped so that the sage's government is in accord with the inner workings of the Tao. This is indeed another example of political philosophy advocating inner cultivation (including mind) and political ability. (For more details, see **Huai-nan-tzu.**)

What is most remarkable in all these early Taoist tendencies is that they all operate in a naturalist world order. The supreme principle, the Tao, is a real although mystical presence, but is not treated as a divine being or a creator-god, demanding worship. If "spiritual beings" are recognized (in some texts), they are seen as parts of this natural order, or even as mythical beings, who do not appear to have power over the human world. In other words, we do not find a *religious* world order here, but a naturalistic, *humanistic* one.

Taoist Religious Movements:
From Han to Six Dynasties (206 BCE–581 CE)

The periods of the Han dynasty (Western and Eastern Han), the Chin, and the divided empire (usually called North-South Dynasties or Period of Disunity), was characterized by great intellectual and religious tur-moil. The imperial patronizing of Confucian Learning (starting around 134 BCE) was an important milestone with an incalculable impact on the future growth of Chinese culture. But the collapse of the Han empire (in 210 CE) was likewise extremely significant. Not only did it cause the temporary eclipse of Confucianism, but it also offered Taoism and Buddhism an opportunity to entrench themselves in society and find their own niche of acceptance and efflorescence. For both Taoism and Buddhism, this was indeed a seminal period.

One particular aspect of Taoism that is not well understood so far is the so-called *Huang-Lao Tao*, a rather intellectual stream of Taoist speculation probably connected with the Laoist school, but like other syncretist movements, also incorporating ideas of various other schools, Legalism in particular. As a political system, Legalism was rejected; it had caused too much suffering in the country because of its harsh dictatorship. Yet some of its principles and practices could be used and were incorporated in the new dispensation.

Huang-Lao Taoism, with its elevation of the Yellow Emperor as the model ruler (Huang is short for Huang-ti) and of Lao-tzu as the model royal advisor (Lao is short for Lao-tzu), was not exactly a religious movement, but rather a political philosophy. For a significant period of time, it influenced the early Han rulers, until Emperor Wu reversed the trend. During the Eastern Han, Huang-Lao Taoism was not dead yet, or so it seems, for in 166 CE, Emperor Huan (r. 146–168) offered a sacri-fice to the deified Lao-tzu and to the Buddha. At the same time, the Yellow Emperor cult may have been more or less abandoned. (For de-tails, see **Huang-Lao Taoism**.)

Healing Cult in Eastern China: *Great Peace Taoism*

The Western Han was disturbed by the usurpation of Wang Mang (9–24 CE), who wanted to set up his own dynasty. But in 25 CE, the throne was restored to the Han, and at first there was a period of expansion and tranquility (25–88 CE). After 88 CE, the families of the empresses tried to regain power, while the eunuchs did likewise. This weakened the authority of the imperial government. The result was palace intrigues and struggles for power. In 135, the eunuchs were allowed to adopt sons, which resulted in greater wealth and power. The great families and the literati in the civil service reacted against these abuses. The eunuchs won in 176, but in 189, the gentry recovered; under leadership of Gen. Yuan Shao, over 2,000 eunuchs were massacred.

Government taxes put unbearable burdens on the people. Many peas-ants were forced into banditry. Agriculture was in great trouble due to natural disasters. The time was ripe for messianic expectations, and in both Eastern and Western China, mass movements arose. In the East, "as a result of floods along the lower Yellow River, a vast Messianic movement, Taoist in inspiration, developed on the borders of Shantung and Honan" (Gernet, 1982: 155).

The leaders of this movement were three Chang brothers: Chang Chueh (or Chiao), Chang Liang, and Chang Pao. They established an organization that was military, administrative, and religious. The religious cult symbol was Huang-Lao, their ideology based on the *Great Peace Scripture*. It was a messianic movement striving for a new era, a return to the golden age of the past.

This theocratic state had its own hierarchical structure. The three Chang brothers were the "Lord general of Heaven, Earth, and Men." Their territory included a large area of Eastern China, nine provinces divided into 36 districts, each headed by a *fang* (lit. "magician," but equivalent to "general"). Below them were the *ch'u-shuai* ("great chiefs"), whose role was primarily religious, although law and morality were not separated. Their great festivals were celebrated on the days of the equinoxes and solstices and were conducted by the *fang*. Such assemblies were called "fasts of purification." Because many aspects of their worldview and rituals were very similar to the Taoist movement in Western China, they will be discussed in the following section.

The fate of the Eastern movement, however, was different from its Western counterpart. By 184 CE, the messianic movement had grown into a rebellious force. It is said that the organization had 360,000 supporters under the arms. They were called the "Yellow Turbans" and were attacked by government forces. (See **Yellow Turban Rebellion.**) How and why this rebellion broke out is not clear. A good guess is that the establishment of a theocratic state, rejecting the official government's authority, was in itself seen as an act of open rebellion and needed to be annihilated. The year 184 should have been auspicious for the Taoist movement: It was the beginning of a new 60-year cycle and, therefore, a time for renewal. Unfortunately for the rebels, their three leaders were captured and executed in the same year. The movement did not end but lost its vigor. Its main effect was to weaken the already exhausted Han regime and speed up its downfall.

Healing Cult in Western China: *Five Bushels of Rice Tao*

In Western China, mainly in Szechuan and part of Shensi, a parallel healing cult developed in the middle of the second century CE, initiated by another Chang (not related to the Eastern Changs). This was Chang Ling, who chose for himself the title of "Heavenly Master" (*T'ien-shih*), and who was later recognized as the founder of the Taoist Religion. His name was changed to **Chang *Tao*-ling.**

In this secluded area of China, surrounded by mountain chains and safe from the predominance of a weak imperial administration, Chang Ling's grandson, Chang Lu, set up an independent theocracy. As in the East, it was religious and political at the same time. Members had to pay a fee of five bushels (or pecks) of rice a year. (This was initiated by Chang Ling, who is therefore also called "rice-thief.") Chang Ling, so the legend goes, spent time on some mountains in Szechuan for spiritual cultivation. It is said that Lao-tzu, or better, T'ai-shang Lao-chün, appeared to him and invested him with spiritual authority and a mission to establish a Taoist kingdom. This grew into a healing cult with a church organization similar to the one in Eastern China, although the administrative titles were different. Chang Ling's grandson, Chang Lu, completed his grandfather's work, and from about 185 to 215, this area of China enjoyed independence from the weakened central government. It was a religious and political state, a theocracy. In 215, Chang Lu surrendered to pressure by the military commander of the North, Ts'ao Ts'ao, and, as a result, Taoism became recognized by the state. It is from this rather modest beginning that Heavenly Master Taoism would eventually develop. Chang Tao-ling is nowadays recognized as the founder of (most schools of) the Taoist Religion. He has been described:

> as a thaumaturgist of the highest order, as a compounder of elixirs of life, and as a first-rate exorcist; he was a god-man commanding spirits and gods. He personifies the transformation of ancient Taoist principles and doctrine into a religion with magic, priesthood and hierarchy, under the very auspices of Lao-tze, who appeared before him in person, and commissioned him to carry out that great organization. (J. de Groot, 1908: 138–139)

This short description shows Chang Tao-ling to be a charismatic leader with strong powers of exorcism, a miracle worker, and, more questionably, an alchemist. Tradition ascribes to him the creation of magic **talismans** (still circulating among many Taoist priests today) and the founding of the Heavenly Masters School. Today's leader of Taoism in Taiwan, Chang Yuan-hsien, is believed to be the 64th successor of the founder.

The theocratic Taoist state in Western China was organized along parallel lines with the East. The area was divided into 24 metropoles, each headed by a "libationer" (*chi-chiu*). Libationers were in command of the army troops, and were also responsible for religious instruction; the *TTC* was an important document to be studied. Other officials (junior rank) were called "commander of the perverse" (*chien-ling*). They were in charge of prayer services and the ceremonies of healing.

Crimes were not to be punished, but confessed and atoned for by the performance of good actions. Only after the third time were offenders punished. In any case, sins would sooner or later manifest in sickness—illness was subject to greater sanctions than sin itself. Prisons served to confine sinners and make them reflect on their evil deeds.

The purpose of this theocratic state was not so much to replace the imperial government, but to encourage followers to attain spiritual perfection. Lay people were given titles and rank according to their degree of progress. Beginners were called "sons and daughters of Tao" (*Tao-nan, Tao-nü*). Those of intermediate rank were called *nan-kuan* and *nü-kuan,* whereas the more advanced were "father of Tao" and "mother of Tao" (*Tao-fu, Tao-mu*). Thus all ranks and titles, except "Heavenly Master," were accessible to men and women alike.

Collective ceremonies were held, as in the East, at the beginning of the four seasons. They consisted of "fasting" (*chai*), but also of public confession of sins. The latter were probably held at the three festivals of the *Yuan* ("origin"? "primordial"?), which are principles or Rulers of the Three Realms (*san kuan*): Heaven, Earth and Water. Today these festivals are still held in China on the fifteenth day of the first, seventh, and tenth lunar months.

An extraordinary religious event was the Fast of Mud and Soot, a special ritual of public penance, in which six to 38 persons could participate (described by Maspero, 1981: 385). (See also **Rituals.**) It is an old variation of a revivalist meeting. Another, more puzzling ritual was the **Union of Energies** (*ho ch'i*), sometimes described as "a collective sexual orgy" practiced in some communities.

Historians have speculated about the close similarities between the Eastern and Western healing cults. It is not at all certain that there was mutual influence, because similarities can be explained by both groups' access to the *Great Peace Scripture.* Both Eastern and Western cults followed this scriptural blueprint of an ideal society. Since the Han ruling house was unable to renew itself and the country, reform movements took place in spite of the government and, as in the East, in opposition to it.

Although the Yellow Turban Rebellion failed, it did have some important consequences. It inspired later uprisings, one as late as the 19th century—the T'ai-p'ing Rebellion (1850–1864). It also made all later governments of China cautious and even suspicious of Taoist activities. In fact, many later uprisings were inspired by political-religious conceptions.

What was at first called Five Bushels of Rice Taoism and, in a more dignified way, the Heavenly Masters School, later also became known as Cheng-yi Taoism ("Orthodox Unity"). It is still active today both in the People's Republic of China (PRC) and in Taiwan. (For details, see **Heavenly Masters Taoism.**)

Quest for Longevity/Immortality: Outer and Inner Alchemy

In China, belief in continued existence after this mortal life goes back several millennia. From archaeological discoveries inside excavated royal tombs and the interpretation of their contents, it can hardly be doubted that the Shang people firmly believed in a continuation of life after death. It was nowhere stated that life was conceived as a material existence, or a survival in a sort of *physical* body, but it is an obvious assumption that can be made from the ritual burial practices of the Shang people. Otherwise, the burying of physical objects, food, treasure, chariots, personnel, etc., would not make much sense, because they are not needed in a purely *spiritual* realm of existence.

The Chinese system of belief in a "soul" or "souls" is very complex and fraught with inner difficulties and contradictions (see **soul**). But since prehistoric times there was, at least in ritual practice, a sort of dichotomy; one "soul" would rise to heaven, another "soul" would descend into the grave. This view underwent radical change with the advent of Buddhism, but even today, popular burial practices and the rituals of ancestor cult imply a belief in a multiplicity of "souls." The liturgical tradition of Taoism has adopted this popular view and expresses it in rituals for the dead.

The elite Taoist adept, however, did not share this popular view, and preferred to aspire to an immortal state, living as an **immortal** in a transcendent realm, body and spirit one, not separated (as in death). This happened among a minority of Taoist practitioners, members of the Taoist religion who somehow reversed the life-and-death concept of Taoist philosophers. The *TTC* does not express any belief in life after death, at best it promotes efforts to cultivate longevity (this is for instance found in the commentary by **Ho-shang kung**). The *Chuang-tzu* is even more articulate: Life and death are two states of transformation in the endless processes of the universe. It would be bad taste to demand regeneration as a human being.

How did the idea of physical immortality find its way into Taoism? Most probably through the practice of alchemy—both **outer** and **inner alchemy**. *Outer alchemy* is based on laboratory experiments. It attempts to transform base metals into precious ones, such as gold and silver, or it attempts through various techniques to produce elixirs or pills that confer longevity and even physical immortality. *Inner alchemy*, on the other hand, focuses on the adept's own body physiology and attempts to produce a "seed" of new life or longevity/immortality. Inner alchemy promotes the worship of the gods residing in the body, and promulgates various techniques concerning diet, gymnastics, breathing, meditation, and, sometimes, sexual union. These techniques formulate a recipe for constructing the mysterious seed, the nugget of immortality, within.

When did alchemy first arise in China? It remains a historical riddle, but chances are that it started as early as the Warring States period (480–220 BCE), and was actively engaged in by the school of Tsou Yen (305–240 BCE).

The **First Emperor of China** (r. 221–210 BCE), founder of the Ch'in dynasty, was one of the first to encourage alchemical research. It appears, however, that his dream was to find the "magical mushroom," supposedly growing on some mysterious islands in the eastern ocean.

Han **Emperor Wu** (r.140–86 BCE) was next to support alchemical experimentation. The most famous alchemist, sponsored by Emperor Wu, was **Li Shao-chün,** whose efforts did not have any tangible results, but after him others followed, equally disappointing and occasionally being executed by an irascible emperor.

During the later Han, new efforts were made; outer alchemy was often combined with inner alchemy, but no foolproof pill of immortality was ever produced. Several T'ang emperors continued to dream of deathlessness. In their gullibility, they trusted the alchemists and instead of gaining immortality, they were poisoned and died early.

During the Sung dynasty (960–1279), outer alchemy had practically been discontinued, but more attention was given to the spiritual and physical practices of inner alchemy. (For more details, see **Alchemy, Outer and Inner.**)

New Taoist Revelations: Shang-ch'ing and Ling-pao Schools

After Chang Lu (of the Western Healing Cult) had surrendered to Ts'ao Ts'ao in 215 CE and was pressured to relocate in the capital, it appears that his school of Heavenly Masters spread nationwide. Eventually, after the fall of Loyang in 311 CE, they migrated to the south together with the imperial house and many official families. Although the records are not clear for this episode of Heavenly Masters Taoism, it is stated that they stirred up a new movement in the south. It combined the social-liturgical framework of the Heavenly Masters with southern shamanistic practices. Among the most eminent southern families who adhered to Taoism were the Hsü and Ko families. (**Ko Hung,** 283–343/63 CE, wrote the famous alchemical treatise *Pao-p'u-tzu*; the Hsü received the Shang-ch'ing revelations through **Yang Hsi.**)

While in north China, Taoism had to compete with the ever-growing popularity of Buddhism, in the south two new Taoist movements arose in the fourth century CE that drastically changed the structure of the Taoist religion. Even in the south, Taoism was sensitive to Buddhist influences, as the growth and development of the Ling-pao school demonstrates.

SHANG-CH'ING TAOISM: THE SCHOOL OF GREAT PURITY

This new school of Taoism started with the revelations made to **Yang Hsi** (330–386 CE), a servant of the aristocratic Hsü family in south China during the eastern Chin (317–420 CE). The major revelations that Yang received were made by Lady Wei Hua-ts'un, who died in 334 CE. She had been a **libationer** (*chi-chiu*) in the Heavenly Masters School. This shows that the Heavenly Masters Tao, after the collapse of the Western Chin, had reestablished itself in the south, but was not necessarily comfortable there. The south, indeed, had its own religious tradition, and shamanism seems to have been very strong. The Heavenly Masters rejected several of the southern traditions. They waged a crusade against what they considered to be unorthodox, by destroying popular temples and shrines and reacting against religious customs, such as animal sacrifices. It seems no wonder that their impact on the south was at first minimal, soon to be overshadowed by the newly emerging school of Shang-ch'ing Taoism.

This new movement, starting with Yang Hsi's revelations, began to spread among aristocratic families. It claimed that their own revelations were superior to those of the Heavenly Masters, that they had access to higher heavens, had received new scriptures, and had better methods for spiritual cultivation. Thanks to the coordinating efforts of T'ao Hung-ching, the school gained a good reputation and appealed to the intellectual elite of the south. The new scriptures were in high demand and even encouraged some to steal or plagiarize them. Taoist communities emerged, not quite monastic yet, though it appears that some individuals adopted a celibate lifestyle.

The new school, which eventually settled on **Mount Mao** (and hence has been called Mao Shan Taoism), drastically changed the nature and objectives of traditional Taoism. It moved toward intense internalization and visual meditation. Former aspects of Taoist culture became secondary: physiological exercises, the use of drugs and herbs, and even the ritual practices lost some of their importance. From a community religion, Shang-ch'ing Taoism became an elite phenomenon, bordering on eremitism. Personal cultivation focusing on a new body of revealed scriptures became the standard (Robinet, 1991: 120–128).

Several of the school's patriarchs were invited to and were supported by the imperial court. During the T'ang period (618–906), the Shang-ch'ing's influence was predominant in Taoism. It only started to fade during the 13th and 14th centuries, when the Heavenly Masters rose to eminence again (for details, see **Shang-ch'ing Taoism**).

Among the most important scriptures of this school are the **Huang-t'ing ching** ("Yellow Court Scripture") and the **Ta-tung chen-ching** ("True Scripture of Great Profundity").

LING-PAO TAOISM: THE SCHOOL OF THE NUMINOUS JEWEL

The rise of this second Taoist movement in the south was stimulated by the Shang-ch'ing revelations, as well as by Mahayana Buddhism (see S. Bokenkamp, 1983). It arose at about the same time as the Shang-ch'ing school, based on revelations received by Ko Ch'ao-fu between 397–402 CE, especially those found in the central text, *Ling-pao ching.*

Of this text there was an ancient version dating from the Eastern Han (*Ling-pao wu-fu chen-wen*), but a newer version eventually grew into one of the longest scriptures (*Ling-pao tu-jen ching*, "Ling-pao Scripture of Salvation" in 66 chapters).

The expression *ling-pao* has rich and complex connotations. *Ling* means "sacred, spirit, mysterious, supernatural, numinous" (it is part of the expression *ling-hun*, a common term for "soul") and refers to the divine realm and Heaven. On the other hand, *pao* means "treasure, jewel" and refers to the human realm and earth.

This new Taoist school, partially based on the Heavenly Masters tradition, brought renewal: It amplified the ancient rituals and incorporated some important ideas from Buddhism, especially the concept of universal salvation. It also absorbed some Confucian elements—respect for virtues exemplifies such incorporation.

Ling-pao Taoism has been called "the true father of Taoist liturgy" (Robinet, 1991: 153). It did indeed work out a complex and more systematic elaboration of the Heavenly Masters liturgy. This was mainly the work of **Lu Hsiu-ching**, who developed the Taoist *chai* and *chiao* rituals on the basis of ancient traditions. In this new liturgy, chanting of scriptures became crucial. Another characteristic was the declining role of the laity in the liturgy, in contrast with Heavenly Masters Taoism.

The school introduced a new triad into the Taoist religion: the three *T'ien-tsun* or "Heavenly Venerables or Worthies":

• Yuan-shih t'ien-tsun/Yuanshi tianzun,
  Heavenly Venerable or Worthy of the Original Beginning;
• Ling-pao t'ien-tsun/Lingbao tianzun,
  Heavenly Venerable or Worthy of the Spiritual Jewel;
• Tao-te t'ien-tsun/Daode tianzun,
  Heavenly Venerable or Worthy of Tao and Te (this is the apotheosed Lao-tzu).

These three supreme deities, to be identified with the **Three Pure Ones** (*San-ch'ing*), are perhaps not seen as three distinct "personalities" but as three "hypostases" or transformations of the one original *ch'i*, out of which the universe developed. Scrolls of the three are still used today in Taoist rituals.

Although the Ling-pao school was initially very successful in the south, superior in influence and numbers compared to the Shang-ch'ing school, during the T'ang it was absorbed by Shang-ch'ing Taoism. Its great contribution to Taoism is the re-creation of the liturgy—today all Taoists perform the Ling-pao rituals.

A Taoist Theocracy during the Northern Wei (425–451)

Whereas in southern China Taoism developed into new directions, partially stimulated by the advent of the Heavenly Masters, the fate of Taoism in the north fluctuated between imperial favor and disfavor, as it was affected by the growing influence of Buddhism on the non-Chinese rulers.

> The challenge to classic Chinese civilization was posed most dramatically as a "barbarian" threat, for invaders overran North China and an alien religion, Indian Buddhism, menaced the ideological basis of Chinese society . . . (Fairbank, 1973: 83)

In the north, things were indeed different from the south. Many of the non-Chinese rulers sympathized with the equally non-Chinese Buddhism, and patronized it. Buddhism became dependent on the court and lost some of its autonomy in return for state protection. Rivalry between Taoism and Buddhism continued. A most interesting event was the writing of a satirical attack against Taoism by Chen Luan. A treatise titled **Hsiao-tao lun** was presented by him to Emperor Wu of the Northern Chou in 570 CE, "attacking Taoist mythology, doctrine, ritual and religious practice" (L. Kohn, 1995: 3).

On the other hand, Emperor Wu also "promoted Taoism as the main teaching . . . and sponsored the compilation of the **Wushang biyao** ('Esoteric Essentials of the Most High') . . ." (L. Kohn: 32).

A unique episode was the short-lived revival of Heavenly Masters Taoism by Taoist K'ou Ch'ien-chih during the reign of Emperor T'ai-wu (r. 424–452) of the Northern Wei. This is the only example of a true Taoist "theocracy" being instituted in China. It appears to have been a well-planned strategy put into effect through the cooperation of a Taoist priest, K'ou Ch'ien-chih (365–448), and a Confucian-oriented statesman, Ts'ui Hao (381–450). Each had his own secret agenda; K'ou wished to reestablish the Heavenly Masters School, whereas Ts'ui hoped to restore a Chinese state in north China.

> . . . what drew the two together most intimately was a common dream of a "purified" society, which Ts'ui envisioned as a return to the golden age of Chou feudalism . . . and which K'ou envisioned as a return, through the "chosen people" of the Taoist church, to the primitive simplicity associated with the utopian kingdom of Ta Ch'in . . . (R. Mather, 1979: 112–3)

In order to realize their plans, they supported the new T'o-pa ruler, Emperor T'ai-wu, in his ambition to become the "perfect ruler of Great Peace." In 425, K'ou was officially declared Heavenly Master, thus restoring the broken lineage of Chang Tao-ling and Chang Lu. The state sponsored Taoism throughout the realm by setting up sacrificial shrines (*t'an*) with priests and large monthly celebrations. Meanwhile, as Ts'ui's influence grew, he caused the suppression of Buddhism in 446. This law was rescinded only in 452 by the new Emperor Wen-ch'eng, who made Buddhism his state religion.

The short-lived Taoist theocracy did not have any lasting effects on the religion of the people, nor was the title Heavenly Master transferred to an immediate successor. K'ou Ch'ien-chih, however, is credited with one change in Taoist language: He changed the title of "libationer" (*chi-chiu*) to "gentleman of the Tao" (*tao-shih*), the name still used today for Taoist priests.

Later Taoist Growth

The reunification of China by the Sui (581–618) and T'ang (618–906) dynasties had serious consequences for the further development of Taoism. Of course, Buddhism and Confucianism were also greatly affected. The latter would gradually rise from its lethargy and increase in vigor, because the T'ang court needed the Confucian system of learning to educate the country's young talent and prepare them for civil service. This was a matter of schooling and education. The other two *chiao*, Taoism and Buddhism, had a different function. They were religious institutions, and as such could contribute a great deal to the imperial power base or its legitimation of power.

This concern had been implicitly felt by all preceding dynasties and went as far back as the early Chou, when the Mandate of Heaven (*t'ien-ming/tianming*) was invoked to justify the Chou conquest and their defeat of the Shang rulers. Often in Chinese dynastic history, a rebel overthrew the previous dynasty, and by reason of his success was believed to have received the mandate. However, once firmly entrenched on the dragon throne, more powerful reasons were needed to convince the dynasty itself, as well as the people, that the seize of power was legitimate. The invocation of Heaven's Mandate coincided with the Confucian vision, but once Taoism and Buddhism started to gain spiritual power, they likewise created their own methods of support for the dynasty. In this the two were competitive, for in return for their political-religious support, both Buddhism and Taoism hoped to receive protection and favors from the imperial government. This sort of symbiotic relationship had already started during the period of disunity, especially in Northern

China, occupied by foreign rulers. In exchange for imperial protection and even appointments to official ranks, the Buddhists lost some of their independence. Similarly, the Taoism of K'ou Ch'ien-chih, during the Northern Wei, was an example of Taoism being patronized as well as controlled by the ruling house.

This trend of "mutual benefit" was continued throughout later times. The Sui and T'ang dynasties were pioneers in this regard: Both Taoism and Buddhism had close dealings with the new rulers, but the type of relationship depended greatly on the personal preferences and "tastes" of each emperor.

Sui (581–617) and T'ang (618–907) Periods

The two Sui emperors, Wen-ti and Yang-ti, favored Buddhism as their personal faith, but also supported Taoism. Buddhism was seen as a strong unifying factor because of its deep penetration into the life of the people. Taoism, however, was on the rise, too, and could not be ignored; it got at least minimum court support. The price to be paid by both religious establishments was government control.

When general Yang Chien reunited China (after 360 years of disunity), he became Emperor Wen (r. 581–604). He lifted the Northern Chou ban against Buddhism and Taoism in 580, yet was very dextrous in using the potential of each of the **Three Teachings** to further his political goals. Confucianism lent more credibility to the new dynasty and it also promoted morality and offered training programs for future officials. Taoism received minimal patronage. Although Wen-ti personally disliked Taoist monks, he used them for their calendrical skills and their talent for interpreting omens. He remained, however, suspicious of the subversive force of Taoism and practitioners of black magic. Buddhism, being Wen-ti's personal faith, received strong support. State monasteries were built at the base of the Five Sacred Mountains.

In his personal life, Emperor Wen integrated several Taoist elements. His choice of a new reign title, *k'ai-huang,* was taken from Taoist scriptures. When he built grandiose royal gardens, he included the mysterious islands of the "immortals"—such as P'eng-lai—in layout. On a 100-foot-high gazebo, he enjoyed the company of court ladies, while acting as an immortal. Indeed, like many imperial predecessors, he was very much interested in the secrets of immortality and invited several famous masters to his court.

From the Sui dynastic history (*Sui shu*), one gains some information about the training of Taoist priests (although the school to which they belonged is not mentioned). The training was divided into four stages. After the completion of each stage, candidates received a certificate (*fa-lu*) to state that a particular scripture had been studied, fully comprehended, and could be explained to others. The four scriptures were the *Tao-te ching*, the *San-tung*, the *Tung-hsuan*, and the *Shang-ch'ing*.

Although before the Sui dynasty, Taoism had been growing and created new rituals, deities, and scriptures, it was not yet enjoying great popularity. Not much is known about the Heavenly Masters at this time, but the flourishing of Taoist monastic life was not an indication of Taoist influence on the population. In contrast, Buddhism was much more widespread and would continue to flourish during the T'ang period. At the end of Wen-ti's reign, there were 16 Taoist establishments in the capital, compared to 120 on the Buddhist side. Further, the number of Taoists ordained during Wen-ti's reign was 2,000—230,000 for the Buddhists (A. Wright, 1978: 137).

With the T'ang dynasty, we can imagine the great flourishing of Buddhism, among both the imperial family and the nobility, among both the scholarly world and the people. Important developments were the growth of new Buddhist schools in "Chinese garment": the popular Pure Land devotional movement and the monastic elite school of Ch'an (Zen) Buddhism—perhaps the finest expression of Buddhist-Taoist cross-fertilization.

Among the Tun-huang manuscripts, a large number of Taoist texts have been discovered, testifying to the increased prestige of Taoism, which was partially due to imperial sponsorship. Indeed, Taoism was elevated to an unexpected high rank. It has been said that even before the T'ang dynasty was founded, a Taoist patriarch from Mao Shan, Wang Yuan-chih (528–635), had given the future founder of T'ang, Li Yuan (later to become Kao-tsu, r. 618–626), a secret prophecy of success against the Sui Emperor Yang-ti. This prophecy was said to be based on a revelation from T'ai-shang Lao-chün, the deified Lao-tzu, who stated that the future imperial family, named Li, were in fact his descendants. Once victory had been obtained, the new dynasty did indeed proclaim Lao-tzu as its ancestor. As a result, Taoism gained special status in the realm and would receive a number of special privileges. Patriarch Wang was rewarded for his prophecy: He was the first Taoist monk to receive the purple robe from the emperor. This is another example of political-religious symbiosis. The T'ang imperial family's prestige was boosted enormously, whereas Mao Shan (Shang-ch'ing) Taoism enjoyed the protection of the imperial house (Kubo Noritada, 1977: 219–226).

Imperial patronage of Taoism did not mean, however, that Taoism became the state religion (the Buddhists were too strong to let this happen!). It became part of the imperial family religion, together with the cult of the ancestors. Still, Taoism did get some special privileges. Emperor Kao-tsung (r. 649–683), at first supportive of Buddhism, started to favor Taoism in his later years. He bestowed high titles upon Lao-tzu, and a "network of state-sponsored monastic communities," including Buddhist and Taoist temples, was set up in each prefecture (*Cambridge History* 3–1: 264). In 675, he gave orders to compile the first version of the Taoist scriptures. In 678, the *Tao-te ching* became compulsory study for state examinations (this decree was revoked by Empress Wu in 693).

Rivalry between Buddhism and Taoism continued, and was strong in the countryside. At the court, debates were organized between Buddhism and Taoism (and also Confucianism). In 668, after a bitter debate, the emperor ordered the destruction of the *Conversion of Barbarians Scripture*, "a forged sutra which claimed that the Buddha was in fact the same person as Lao-tzu, and which had been a constant source of irritation" (*Cambridge* 3–1: 965).

Emperor Hsuan-tsung (r. 712–756) stands out as a strong promoter of Taoism. He was "deeply versed in Taoist philosophy of which he became a major patron." In 726, he decided that each household should have a copy of the *TTC*. In 732, he ordered that each prefecture should build a temple in honor of Lao-tzu (*Cambridge* 3–1: 411). In 741, schools were set up to study Taoism. They were part of the state universities.

Among the later T'ang emperors, there was a steady interest in Taoism: Te-tsung (r. 780–804) was attracted to alchemy, as was Wu-tsung (r. 841–846), who took drugs that probably made him lose full control of his faculties (*Cambridge* 3–1: 663). This ended with the severe suppression of Buddhism in 842–845.

Hsuan-tsung (whose name is written with a different character from the above Hsuan-tsung) (r. 847–859) was the fourth emperor in four decades who died of alchemical poisoning.

The T'ang period offers a clear example of the fluctuating fates of Taoism and Buddhism. Buddhism flourished enormously. It seemed to attract the majority of intellectuals to its profound philosophy, while the common people were impressed by its afterlife doctrines, its rich liturgy and its simple approach to salvation. While Taoism was never a serious rival of Buddhism, Confucianism slowly started to make a comeback. Only few Confucian intellectuals are found during the T'ang, but once Confucianism gained momentum, it became a formidable force that would regain its former glory. It succeeded so well because of its absorption of Buddhist and Taoist doctrines and methods of spiritual cultivation.

Some statistics show the relative strength of Taoism and Buddhism. At the height of the T'ang, Taoism had 1,687 monasteries and nunneries, Buddhism had 5,358. In 722, Taoism had 16 establishments in the capital, whereas Buddhism had 91.

The Sung Period (960–1279)

The history of the Sung dynasty somewhat repeats the earlier North-South division of China. Politically it was unstable because China was threatened in the north by various groups of "barbarians," some of whom succeeded in ripping off a large area of the north. (For details concerning this division, see **Chart of Chinese Dynasties**.)

One of the major trends since late T'ang and throughout the Sung was the emergence of Neo-Confucianism as a commanding intellectual force, replacing Buddhism and Taoism. Many Confucians had studied these two schools of thought and now utilized many of their ideas to revive Confucianism and remold it. Confucianism was eclipsed during the period of disunity, but not totally wiped out. It made its comeback during the Sui and T'ang because the reorganized state examination system forced the aspiring intellectuals and bureaucrats to study the Confucian classics. This Confucian revival meant a rejection of the Taoist search for immortality through alchemy and of the Buddhist concern with the supernatural and the afterlife.

> It returned to the ancient Chinese emphasis on mundane social and political matters, particularly ethics, and it reasserted the old agnostic, non-theistic tendencies of Chinese thought. (Fairbank, 1973: 149)

During the Northern Sung, several emperors favored Taoism. The first to do so was T'ai-tsung (r. 976–997), who appreciated the fact that a Taoist priest had predicted his succession to the throne, thus repeating the pattern of the T'ang prophecy. His successor, Chen-tsung (r. 998–1022), patronized Taoism even more. He claimed to have had a dream in which a deity asked him to offer sacrifices in preparation for the receiving of a "Heavenly Script." In 1008, a text came down from Heaven (tied to a kite) praising the emperor and modeled after the *TTC*. Historians see it as an outright fabrication, but much was needed then to improve the lost prestige of the throne after humiliating defeats in the north at the hands of the Khitan people (Liao Dynasty).

Chen-tsung created another myth by naming a Taoist sage, Chao Hsuan-lang, as his ancestor (the Sung emperor's family name was Chao), thus raising the importance of his ancestry (just as the T'ang emperor had done). He continued to worship Lao-tzu, built many Taoist temples, and performed the *feng-shan* sacrifices.

Chen-tsung's abuse of power was exemplifed in his mountain-building, a project that took six years to complete. Originally meant to improve his geomancy and to result in the birth of sons, it grew beyond reason and its price was astronomical:

> Strange stones and rare plants were shipped to the capital from all parts of the country, while upon Mount Ken, lofty peaks and streams abounded,

tens of thousands of plum trees were planted, deer were introduced and numerous pavilions were built. (Yao, 1980: 15)

The strongest patron of Taoism, however, was Hui-tsung (r. 1101–1125), who was called the "Taoist emperor" and supported Taoism at the expense of Buddhism. With 26 Taoist ranks created, Taoist priests and nuns were elevated to higher ranks than the Buddhists. In 1115, he called himself "Patriarchal Taoist Emperor." The next year, Hui-tsung established "Taoist Learning," and created two "doctorates," each for the study of the *Scripture of Internal Medicine*, the *TTC*, the *Chuang-tzu,* and the *Lieh-tzu.*

These measures affected Buddhism and the economy, especially when Hui-tsung started to use state funds for his extravagant building projects. In this he was advised by one of the most controversial Taoist priests of Chinese history, **Lin Ling-su** (d. 1120). He was responsible for the emperor's anti-Buddhist campaigns, and also for persecution of his Taoist rivals. His intrigues backfired: He was exiled in 1120.

All these excesses caused the downfall of the Sung. For a long time, North China was a battlefield between the Chin aggressors and the Sung armies. In 1126, the Sung were defeated and took refuge in the South, where they established themselves as the Southern Sung.

During the Southern Sung, Taoism was not popular. Because of Hui-tsung's former excesses. Taoism was subject to political repression. No emperor of the Southern Sung dared openly support Taoism, but two centers in the South remained active: Lung-hu Shan (Dragon and Tiger Mountain) and Mao Shan. The Taoist religion was favorably accepted by the literati because of the incorporation of Taoist ideas into Neo-Confucianism. In fact, the great masters of Neo-Confucian philosophy had all widely indulged in Buddhism and Taoism.

Overall, the Sung dynasty was a period of great cultural and religious changes, in which Taoism occupied a special position because of its strong imperial patronage. Some of the notable transformations that should be cited are the founding of new Taoist schools, the flowering of **inner alchemy**, and the production of literary works—not only of complete sets of Taoist scriptures but of several very significant Taoist compilations.

New Taoist schools that arose during the Sung are the **Shen-hsiao School**, specializing in thunder magic, and the **T'ien-hsin School**, an offshoot of the Cheng-yi School whose name derived from a new version of the *fu-lu* (talismans and registers) tradition titled "correct method of *t'ien-hsin.*"

During the Southern Sung, while the north of China was ruled by the Chin invaders, three new religious schools (or orders) were founded:

Complete Realization Taoism, Grand Unity Taoism, and **Great Way Taoism**. Only the first one survives today.

Among the important Sung compilations that should be mentioned: *Tao-fa hui-yuan* (Corpus of Taoist Ritual) in 170 chapters (in the Taiwan edition vols. 47–50); *Ling-pao ta-fa* (Great Rituals of Ling-pao Taoism) (in vol. 51); and the often quoted encyclopedic collection *Yün-chi ch'i-ch'ien* (Seven Lots from the Bookbag of Clouds), compiled by Chang Chün-fang in 1028 or 1029.

The Chin (North China) (1115–1235) and Yuan (1206–1368)

Within the great chaos and suffering of the people in the North, new Taoist movements arose, providing "physical and spiritual shelter for the suffering masses" (Yao: 26).

In these times of great stress and hardship, these new Taoist groups arose, partly as a reaction against the foreign rulers, partly to provide services to the people in distress. Three major Taoist organizations were founded in North China under the Jurchen Chin. Although they are usually called "sect" in Western literature (translation of *p'ai*), the term "order" is preferable, since they are comparable to religious orders in Christianity and cannot be considered "sectarian" movements.

GRAND UNITY TAOISM (T'AI-YI TAO)

Grand Unity Taoism was founded around 1138 by Hsiao Pao-chen in Honan, who used the magic powers of talismans in healing. Several patriarchs were patronized by the Chin court and later by the Mongols. They served as imperial advisors.

No works of T'ai-yi origin exist and it is unclear how the school was terminated. There are records of seven patriarchs only; later the school seems to have lost its independent existence and to have been absorbed into Cheng-yi Taoism (this was the new name given to the Heavenly Masters School).

Their teachings appear to be syncretic in nature: On the one hand, they practiced magic healing, on the other hand, they harmonized Taoist and Confucian, and perhaps also Buddhist teachings, stressing yielding, loyalty and trust, and compassion.

GREAT WAY TAOISM (TA TAO, LATER CALLED CHEN TA TAO OR TRUE GREAT WAY)

Its founder was Liu Te-jen, who started his school at the beginning of the Chin (around 1142?). According to legend, one day he met an old man in an oxcart who instructed him in teachings similar to the *TTC*. The basic teachings are summarized in nine precepts (see Yao: 36). Their syncretic nature is obvious: Loyalty, filial piety and sincerity reflect Confucianism; Buddhism can be seen in its ban on killing and its vegetarian diet. Taoist principles are manifest in many practices, such as tranquillity, a simple lifestyle gained through working in the fields, the curving of desires, and oneness with the mundane world.

The Ta-Tao Order did not practice magic healing, but used prayer toward healing and exorcism to expel evil spirits. They had no interest in the methods to reach longevity/immortality.

No writings have been left, but outside information indicates that they had little contact with the ruling dynasties. An important stone inscription was written by Yü-chi: it reflects the great successes of the Northern Taoist orders in general.

After the ninth patriarch, there is no more record. It is assumed that the order declined and disappeared.

COMPLETE REALIZATION TAOISM (CH'UAN-CHEN TAO)
The name of this school has been translated in several ways: "Perfect Realization," "Complete Realization," "Complete Truth." The epithet "complete" is preferable, as *chen* refers to realization, as in *chen-jen*, "realized or perfected person," which is a common Taoist title for sages or immortals.

This school or Taoist order is the most important among the three. Its founder is Wang Che (born around 1101), who changed his life at age 48, when he encountered two "supernatural beings." He is most commonly known as **Wang Ch'ung-yang** (for his biography, see Yao: 41–52).

His teachings are syncretistic, as can be seen in the "fifteen founding principles" collected by Wang's followers (Yao: 73–85) and in the term *san-chiao* (three teachings), which he used for the religious communities he established.

He attracted many followers, seven of whom are known as the **"Seven Perfected."** The best known, and Wang's eventual successor, is **Ch'iu Ch'ang-ch'un.**

Salient points in the teaching of Ch'uan-chen are: its social assistance efforts (to help refugees), its contacts with the intellectuals, its efforts to save Chinese culture during a period of barbarian rule, the emancipation of women, and its publication of the Taoist canon.

In 1216, Ch'iu Ch'ang-ch'un was summoned to court by the Chin emperor, but he refused to go. In 1219, he once again was invited by the Southern Sung emperor—another refusal. Yet in 1219, he accepted the summons of Genghis Khan from Central Asia. Ch'iu was already 72 when he set out for Samarkand. He arrived in 1222.

His meeting with Genghis Khan was successful and Ch'iu returned to China with great honor (Yao: 132–143). He was put in charge of all monastic life in China, and, as a result, the Ch'uan-chen Order prospered and expanded rapidly.

Not long afterward, however, conflicts with Buddhism arose. The Taoists' renewed spread of the *Lao-tzu hua-hu* ("Lao-tzu Converting the Barbarians") forgery and another "blasphemous" work, titled *Book of the 81 Transformations* (of Lao-tzu) were not the major reasons for conflict. The major bone of contention was the Taoist takeover of many previously Buddhist monasteries, deserted during the war years.

A first debate took place in 1255, then another in 1258, under Khubilai Khan, with more than 700 participants: Buddhists, Taoists, and Confucian observers. The Taoists failed to answer the questions put to them and were declared to be the losers. Their punishment was that 17 Taoists had to shave their heads, and that 482 previous Buddhist monasteries, occupied by the Taoists, were to be returned to Buddhism. Moreover, all "forged" books had to be destroyed.

The imperial edicts were not executed with strict rigor. The Buddhists complained and thus, in 1281, a new debate was organized at Khubilai's court. The Taoists were unable to prove the authenticity of their scriptures, except that of the *TTC*. The imperial decision was, once more, to burn the Taoist scriptures, which had been painstakingly collected and published by the Ch'uan-chen Order.

The Ch'uan-chen Taoists continued to flourish for some time, but once China was reunified under the Ming, other Taoist schools, such as the Heavenly Masters School, became more influential.

Today, the Ch'uan-chen Order continues to exist. It remains a monastic order observing the rule of celibacy in contrast with the Heavenly Masters Taoists. In Beijing, one famous temple still exists—the White Cloud Monastery (Pai-yün kuan) —whereas in Taiwan, the Ch'uan-chen Order hardly survives. They still flourish in Hong Kong (B. Tsui, 1991).

The Ming (1368–1644) and Ch'ing (1644–1911) Periods

Taoism was favored by the Ming emperors. Not only did Taoist masters receive high honors and titles, but Taoism exercised a profound social influence during the period.

> True, the Ming period produced no outstanding Taoist philosopher, yet in all of Chinese history Taoism was never more powerful or more pervasive among all social strata than during this time. (Liu Ts'un-yan in de Bary, 1970: 291)

Liu continues to say that Taoists "cultivated intimate friendships with powerful politicians" and that "the political influence of these Taoist priests ramified from the metropolis to every corner of the Ming empire" (Liu: 291).

During the Ch'ing dynasty, Taoist masters were gradually stripped of their authority and rank. For Taoism, as well as for Buddhism, the Ch'ing or Manchu Dynasty was a period of decay and stagnation, which would continue through the republican period.

The Heavenly Masters School had gained a favorite position during the Mongol regime and was eager to keep it (H. Welch: 156). In 1368, Chang Cheng-ch'ang visited the Ming court and was confirmed in his status. In 1383, a new Taoist control office was set up (*Tao-lu szu*) to supervise Taoist activities throughout the empire. Taoists were divided into two groups: *Cheng-yi* (or Heavenly Masters) and *Ch'üan-chen*.

Emperor Shih-tsung (r. 1522–1567) is perhaps the last emperor to patronize Taoism. A Taoist priest was appointed as tutor of the heir apparent in 1524.

During the Ch'ing period, Taoism was in decline. The Ch'ing rulers preferred the Buddhist lamas, who were apparently better qualified to perform magic. Only two emperors, Yung-cheng (r. 1723–1735) and Chia-ch'ing (r. 1796–1820), showed some interest in Taoism. Other rulers tried to reduce the number of Taoist priests (and Buddhist monks, as well).

The K'ang-hsi emperor (r. 1662–1722), at the end of his long rule, became very skeptical of the Taoist claims of immortality: "They have no shame . . ." he stated, but they become old and die like anybody else.

> . . . when a commoner in Chiangnan offered me a book of his that claimed to contain secrets of immortality through alchemy, I ordered it thrown back at him. (J. Spence, 1974: 101–2)

Still, he believed in the good results of tranquility gained through sitting in quietness, Taoist fashion (Spence: 106–7).

During K'ang-hsi's reign, the Jesuits were active in China, including in the capital, and made a strong impression of scholarship on many Chinese intellectuals. K'ang-hsi scorned them (in his diary) however, as much as the Buddhists and Taoists for "some of their words were no different from the wild and improper teachings of Buddhists and Taoists, and why should they be treated differently?" (Spence: 84).

The famous Emperor Ch'ien-lung (r. 1736–1796) issued an edict in 1739 that fairly well represents the attitude of Ch'ing emperors in general. Buddhist and Taoist clergy were considered to be parasites, not only for failing to contribute food or clothing to society but for relying on the labor of others for their own living (K. Ch'en, 1964: 453–4).

Further government restrictions, imposed on the Buddhist clergy, also applied to Taoism (Ch'en: 453). The assumed reason for these restrictive laws was the decay of the priesthood:

> Whatever the size of the samgha, one point is clear: moral and spiritual decadence was universal. Too many clerics entered the order not for the spiritual message of the Buddha or for religious discipline, but mainly to gain a livelihood. All too often they were the ones who failed to succeed in society or who wanted to escape from society because of some crimes committed. (Ch'en: 452–3)

During the 19th century, China was forced to allow Christian missionaries to preach in their country due to treaties imposed upon China after the Opium Wars of 1842 and especially of 1857–58. As a result, missionary activity increased enormously throughout the 19th century and the first half of the 20th century. Several Christian missionaries wrote gloomy reports about the condition of the Buddhist and Taoist clergy, thus creating a stereotype of ignorance, corruption, laziness, and superstitious activities (see H. Welch, 1968: 222ff). This was all partially true, but did not present a complete picture. In remote monasteries, perhaps never visited by those Christian writers, a minority of Buddhist monks and Taoist priests lived in isolation and practiced their spiritual programs in great earnest.

Later Western authors have rectified this unbalanced and unfair perception (examples are Reichelt, Prip-Møller, and Goullart).

Taoism in Modern Times

As during imperial times, the fate of religion in China was greatly affected by the enormous changes that shook the country. The beginning of the republic in 1912 can be seen as a new starting point. From 1949 (communist victory over the nationalists), developments were different on the mainland than in Taiwan, which became the stronghold of the nationalists.

In mainland China (the People's Republic of China or PRC), the Marxist leadership did not believe in the validity of religion. Yet from the start, they included "freedom of religious belief" in their new constitution. Religion is thus tolerated, but "superstition" is very different. Superstitious practices, which had constituted the livelihood of many Taoist priests, were outlawed. Besides, Taoism did not prove to be of any diplomatic importance, unlike Buddhism, which therefore received more government consideration.

Already in the years of the new republic, some Taoists attempted to set up Taoist organizations. In 1912, a Central Association of Taoism was established, but it was only local (Peking) and was founded by the

Complete Realization Order. In the same year, the Cheng-yi Taoists set up their own General Taoist Assembly of the Republic of China. Another local group was founded in 1932: the Chinese Taoist Association.

After World War II, Shanghai Taoists had plans for the revival of Taoism. In 1947, they established the Shanghai Municipal Taoist Association, with Taoists Chang En-po (63rd Heavenly Master) and Chen Ying-ming (1880–1969) as leaders. The latter became very active in spreading Taoist culture through a journal called *Yang-shan*.

After the PRC had been established, the national Taoist Association was founded in 1957, and in 1961, they defined their objectives: to study the history of Taoism, publish journals, and set up training programs for young candidates. But the "Ten Years of Chaos" (1966–77) stopped all efforts. All religious organizations suffered immensely. Temples and churches were destroyed, or at least closed down, or were used as auxiliary space by the government. It was a time of great suffering for all religious practitioners, exposed to the fanaticism of the "Red Guards," who left trails of destruction everywhere.

Only since 1978 has there been a comeback (see J. Pas, 1989). Religious associations have been restored, such as the Taoist Association of China, with its headquarters in the White Cloud Monastery in Beijing.

By 1986, 21 key monasteries had been returned to the Taoists, and since 1990, training programs for new candidates were organized not only in Beijing but also in Shanghai and Chengtu. Rituals were revived, and the academic study of Taoism became more respectable.

Despite these efforts for renewal and survival, some pessimism still remains as to the fate of Taoism in the future. In a 1995 issue of *China Study Journal*, Taoism is seen as a "dying religion" (following an article in the Hong Kong *South China Morning Post*, December 16, 1995). One symptom of the decline is singled out—the smaller number of pilgrims who went up to Mount Wu-tang (Wudangshan) on the god's birthday. Instead of 30,000 expected visitors, only a few thousand showed up.

Other voices are moderately optimistic and hope that the gap in recruiting new clergy (from 1949 to 1979) can still be filled. Yet Taoism lags behind Buddhism. According to official statistics, Taoism counts 600 temples and monasteries while Buddhism has 9,500. Taoism counts 6,000 priests and nuns, while Buddhism has 170,000 (*China Study Journal* 10–3, 1995: 31).

The major difficulty that Taoism faces in the PRC is the flimsy official identification of Taoism with "feudal superstition." Superstition includes agelong folk religion practices, such as fortune-telling, geomancy, palmistry, and even mediumship. These are considered different from acceptable *religious* practices, and are forbidden. But government regulations against superstition leave the door wide open for government officials to harass and boycott other, *legal* Taoist practices (see A. Seidel, 1989–90: 285–286).

In China, two major Taoist schools are active; the Ch'üan-chen Order (monastic) and the Heavenly Masters School, whose ancient headquarters on Lung-hu Shan (Dragon and Tiger Mountain) are presently being restored.

In Taiwan, the situation has been very different. No Taoist monastic life has been preserved (except for a recent new beginning: Taoist priestesses in Kaohsiung). All Taoists are householders ("fire-dwellers"), and their profession has been traditionally transmitted to their sons.

The 64th successor of Chang Tao-ling lives in Taiwan and seems to (or tries to) control most of the Taiwan Taoists, especially those of his own order—the Heavenly Masters or Cheng-yi Taoists. They are popularly called **"blackhead" Taoists,** because in their rituals they wear a black hat with a gold pin, in contrast to the **"redhead" Taoists,** who wear a red headband. The redheads are popular practitioners—probably a carryover from ancient shamanism.

Today, the services of Taoist priests are in great demand in Taiwan. Many temples organize special **cosmic renewal festivals** to purify the community and pray for divine blessings. Taoists are hired by the temple, while the temple committee runs temple affairs.

Other centers of significant Chinese settlement, such as Hong Kong, Singapore, and Malaysia, also have witnessed a revival of Taoist activity. It appears that the laity have become more involved (Taiwan, Hong Kong). Lay people study the Taoist texts and gather on a regular basis to chant the scriptures. Taoist spirituality is not the monopoly of the priests. Besides, the Taoist clergy has rather limited training. They become apprentices at a young age, go through practical, on-the-spot training (instruments, writing, assisting in rituals, chanting), and once they can master the liturgy, they are ordained. But there is nothing like a seminary training available to them, at least not in Taiwan. On the mainland, however, Taoist monasteries provide some training and spiritual discipline for their young recruits. In other words, Taoism is still very much alive and although it still has a long way to go, some pessimistic forecasters such as H. Welch have proved to be mistaken.

> Today, after centuries of decay, the [Taoist] church has reached the end of the road. The sixty-third Celestial Master will probably be the last. The White Cloud Temple and a few others may be preserved as cultural monuments with a handful of priests as caretakers, but their religious function is over . . . (Welch, 1957: 156–7)

In the West, Taoism has captured the attention of many. The philosophical writings stir the greatest interest, but many related areas, such as Taoist meditation, inner alchemy and the "martial arts" also are actively pursued. In the academic world, new aspects of the Taoist religious tradition have made us aware of the rich Taoist liturgical heritage. A great number of scholars from China and Japan to Europe and North America are actively engaged in the study of Taoism.

Taoism and Chinese Culture

In the *TTC*, there is a set of paradoxical aphorisms about what appears to be, as opposed to what really is: "Great achievements are as if deficient . . . great fullness is as if empty . . ." (Chapter 45). "Superior virtue/power appears as non-virtue/power; therefore there is [real] virtue/power" (Chapter 38). This is an excellent assessment of Taoism and its role in the long history of Chinese civilization. It has been a strong and staying force in Chinese cultural history, while often appearing as weak and helpless.

Several analogies can be used to illustrate the profound influence of the Taoist tradition on China's cultural development (of course we here naively assume that Taoism is a unified system, whereas, in fact, it is not that clear. See below). One analogy is the symbol of two currents in a river, a second is the contrast between establishment and counterculture. A third analogy is found in the application of Yin-Yang philosophy. These three analogies are slightly different, yet have much in common—they are three images of one reality.

Rivers have two kinds of currents: those on the surface, and those deeper down. In Chinese history, Confucianism represents the surface current. Officially sponsored, it was the most visible and the most acceptable norm of thinking and behavior. However, the undercurrents of a river are also very real. Though invisibly contained on the riverbed, they are an image of the deeper levels of human society (and of the human psyche, as well). These two levels interact in mysterious ways. The surface may be calm, but the deeper currents may be in motion and treacherous (and surprise unaware swimmers), or the surface may be in turmoil, while the lower levels are calm and undisturbed.

The analogy of official as opposed to unofficial culture has been noticed. If Confucianism can be compared to "establishment" and its set of values, Taoism fits easily into the pattern of "counter-culture." Official values are represented by government, the world of big business, education and church, all dictating how one should think and behave in a socially acceptable way. Counterculture embraces the opposite, the failure to go along officially, and includes various ways of dropping out, the rejection of established tradition, and experimentation with new, sometimes wild and esoteric ideas (drugs, sexual freedom, new art forms, etc.). In counterculture, one feels no longer bound to perform and be successful; it is acceptable to do one's own thing, even if it leads to "failure" (this discussion is a paraphrase of Ellwood, 1982: 168–169).

The analogy of yin and yang is also very suggestive. Confucianism is symbolized by yang; Taoism by yin. Whereas yang is strong, domineering, creative, and aggressive (qualities that apply to Confucianism), yin is weak, submissive, nurturing, and yielding (clearly applicable to Taoism). Yet, just as the universe consists of yin and yang, in continuous tension but in ultimate harmony, Chinese society cannot exist without its yin-yang balance. Since in each person there is yin and yang, there is something of a Confucian and something of a Taoist in every Chinese. This has been marvelously expressed by a Chinese scholar:

> A Chinese intellectual may outwardly be a Confucianist, but at the bottom he is a Taoist . . . We are socially Confucian and individually Taoist.
>
> There is such a thing as a personality in solitude as distinguished from personality in association . . . Consciously, we are Confucianists, but deep down in the obscure subconscious, we feel with alternate fear and joy the blatant Taoist in us all. We fear because we believe we *should be* Confucians *in toto*. We rejoice because we know we *are* not. (T.C. Lin 1940–41: 211)

Recognizing, in principle, Taoist influence upon Chinese culture, is there any way of pinpointing concrete examples of such an influence? There is, but we must keep in mind that there has been a complex network of interactions and that isolating Taoism as one particular component is perhaps artificial and misleading. With this caution, it is possible to isolate particular areas of Taoist influence on Chinese cultural history. These areas refer to the Chinese view of life (or aspects of the "Chinese character"), the fine arts, science and technology, philosophy and religion, political rule, and the "martial arts."

The Chinese view of life is based on oneness with nature and includes the acceptance of fate, acceptance of life and death as predetermined and natural phases in the transformation of the cosmos, and resignation to the inevitable, even if many people secretly hope there is immortality, or at least a chance for reincarnation (but that would be due to Buddhist influence). Expressed in a different way, the Taoist input would inspire people to go along with the flow, to take things easy, not to worry about what cannot be helped. Yet at the same time, few peoples are so active and enterprising as the Chinese, so prepared to "cheat" fate, or to get around it.

Taoists are also said to be nonconformists, rebels and anarchists, hating conventions. That is certainly true for some, but as a people, the

Chinese are rather gregarious, finding safety in their families or groups, rather uncertain about standing out. That is another paradox.

Taoist *influence on the arts* has been often recognized, but it is difficult to isolate it from the overall Chinese spirit. One factor, more Taoist than anything else, is Chinese love of nature, expressed over and over in their poetry and landscape painting. Oneness with nature is at its best here; no words are wasted on it, but it is implicit in concrete images and symbols. Landscape is one of the favorite topics of Chinese painting, but its theme differs from western styles; it embodies the Chinese principles of oneness of heaven and earth with humanity, or the oneness of the macrocosm with the microcosm. Most paintings show scenery, mountains and water, and vegetation, but usually there is a human presence in it, however small and insignificant it may be. Humans do not dominate the landscape, they are a humble part of it. Very often, landscapes express serenity, because somewhere hidden among the trees or bamboo plants, there is a hut or cottage with a hermit sitting in quiet meditation, or playing the lute, or drinking wine with a friend. A Taoist recluse? Or perhaps an ex-Confucian turned Taoist in failure? Whatever the case, the sense of oneness between the recluse and surrounding nature is intense. This was marvelously expressed by a 17th-century art critic, Wang Kai (ca. 1679):

> In landscape painting . . . a figure should seem to be contemplating the mountain; the mountain, in turn, should seem to be bending over and watching the figure. A lute player plucking his instrument should appear also to be listening to the moon, while the moon, calm and still, appears to be listening to the notes of the lute. Figures should in fact be depicted in such a way that people looking at a painting wish they could change places with them. (*Arts of China:* 205)

Discussion of Taoism and its impact on art can fill volumes. But one final observation is a must. Chinese painting is different from most other styles in its simplicity, its "emptiness." Canvasses or scrolls are not crammed with figures and paint or ink. Most of the space is empty—it is like "being" in "nonbeing." Whatever figures appear stand out against a backdrop of emptiness. There is room for moving around, there is room for imagination in the viewer's mind. This is strongly reminiscent of a well-known passage in the *TTC*:

> "Thirty spokes converge on one hub,
> but it is the empty space
> that makes a carriage functional (useful)
> . . .
> Indeed what "is" has its benefit,
> what "is not" has its function. (Chapter 11)

That is to say that a carriage is put together by assembling a number of materials: Without them, there is no vehicle. But it is its empty space that makes the vehicle useful: It may carry people or things to various destinations.

On a different level, "emptiness" in painting has its function, almost as much as what is actually depicted.

Taoism has its "magic finger" in other art forms as well—architecture and landscaping spontaneously come to mind. Who can forget the Taoist-inspired islands and mountains of the immortals constructed by Sui Emperor Wen and Sung Emperor Hui-tsung, who brought ruin to the empire? The cultivation of miniature trees (*bonzai* in Japanese) and the representation of the Eight Immortals (and other sages) in sculpture and other folkloristic media are further expressions of Taoist inspiration. It must be admitted, however, that Buddhist sculpture has always been much more abundant than Taoist sculpture.

Taoist *contributions to science and technology* are significant, although in the past too many medals have been pinned on the wrong breasts. This means: Not all scientific discoveries in China should be credited to Taoism. It is far from certain, for example, that external alchemy and Chinese traditional medicine are the result of specifically Taoist experimentation. The earliest Chinese alchemists known in history were called *fang-shih* (magicians) and were not Taoists. Chinese medicine, with its various branches (acupuncture, moxibustion, herbal medicine, pulse reading, etc.), is not a clear product of Taoist masters. But it is also true that many alchemists and practitioners of medicine were indeed Taoists, who therefore deserve some credit for the advancement of medicine and alchemy and its concomitant sciences: botany, chemistry, metallurgy, physiology, geography, astronomy, sexology, etc. (More information on this is found in J. Needham's impressive set of volumes: *Science and Civilization in China*. But also see N. Sivin, 1978.)

A delightful story is told in Chapter 5 of the *Lieh-tzu* (dating at the latest from the third century CE): the first recorded "heart transplant" in history. It is the story of a Chinese doctor who operated on two patients, each of whom had the wrong kind of "heart" for their "temperament." Under sedation, he exchanged their hearts and changed their lives (Graham 1960: 106–107). Appearing in a Taoist work, it is suggested that this doctor was indeed a Taoist.

Philosophy and religion have most unambiguously been affected by Taoism; we already know that there is a Taoist philosophy and a Taoist religion. But we have to go beyond the obvious. Taoism has affected Chinese philosophy and religion beyond its own boundaries. Although inspired and challenged by Buddhism in its early history, Taoism in return moved Buddhism to new heights of growth. Buddhism was a "foreign" import (both Confucianists and Taoists would remind them forever!), while Taoism was a native product—an enviable position for outside competitors.

Buddhism was eventually successful in adapting itself to the Chinese culture scene. When it started to take root in Chinese soil, it attracted many literati who had been trained in either classical culture (Confucianism) or in Taoism. Chih-tun and Hui-yuan are examples of "eminent monks" who were Taoists "converted" to Buddhism. During the North-South division, the newly emerging Taoist schools (Mao-shan, Ling-pao) had been incorporating many ideas from the Taoist philosophical tradition. Some of these ideas must have infiltrated Buddhism, for during the T'ang period we see the gradual emergence of a new Buddhist school—the *Ch'an* or meditation school (Japanese *Zen*). This tradition is being studied in great detail by modern scholars. But one thing is certain: this new Buddhism is of Chinese vintage, produced by a mixing of two quality wines.

The story does not end here: Ch'an became very successful in China, and was particularly attractive to intellectuals. When Buddhism started to decline (after the suppression of 842–845 and the subsequent Huang Ch'ao rebellion 875–884), Confucian-oriented literati found inspiration in Ch'an Buddhism. The final result of a long search for revival was the growth of what westerners call "Neo-Confucianism." Through Ch'an, this new school embodied a strong dose of Taoist concepts and spiritual practices, so much so that today many scholars call this new brand of Confucian learning a "religion," which is overstating the case. It is more accurate to call it a "spiritual culture."

Many Chinese literati of late imperial China did not emphasize the differences of the "three teachings" (*san-chiao*), but their basic unity. This was perhaps a simplification of things, but also shows how much all three systems had mutually interacted. Taoism was certainly a source of great inspiration in this process of "syncretism."

The relationships between *Taoism and the Chinese government* have not been easy over the centuries, with numerous complicated interactions between the two poles. On the one hand, Taoism supported the state, in particular some imperial families (T'ang, Sung, and the Northern Wei) and, in return, received honors, economic advantages (building of temples), and overall imperial patronage. Some famous monks were invited to court and served as imperial advisors or as tutors of imperial princes. This occurred especially during the T'ang and Sung eras, but was repeated by the Chin (Jurchen) rulers in North China. Genghis Khan summoned Ch'uan-chen monk **Ch'iu Ch'u-chi** to his encampment in Central Asia, and although he could not offer any drugs for immortality, Genghis was impressed by the good advice he received and sent Ch'iu back to China with honor and new powers.

On the other hand, the relationship between the imperial government and the Taoist establishment has sometimes been strenuous. One of the earliest examples of Taoist antigovernment activity is the **Yellow Turban** uprising (184 CE). It did not overthrow the ruling Han house, but weakened it enough that it did not survive for a long time. This kind of uprising would be repeated many times in later history. During the Period of Disunity, a new myth arose about a future messianic figure named Li Hung, who would come and restore a reign of peace on earth. This was more an outflow of popular Taoism, not approved of by the Taoist establishment. Several uprisings occurred that were suppressed by the government. The T'ang claim of being descended from Lao-tzu (last name was Li) must also be understood in the same messianic context (A. Seidel, 1969/70).

This sequence of sporadic uprisings made Taoism rather suspect in the eyes of any subsequent government. It had always been the official state doctrine that the rulers had the monopoly of worship, and although Taoism and Buddhism were mostly tolerated, the government watched them carefully, hoping to stave off anti-government activities.

Secret societies plotting the overthrow of corrupt dynasties have been a particular characteristic of Chinese political history. Some were successful and received the mandate, but in most cases they were defeated and the leaders executed. Taoist ideology had a role in this, but Buddhism (at least popular Buddhism) likewise often engaged in revolt. A detailed history of secret societies would fill several volumes. However, most of these secret societies were syncretistic, combining concepts of Taoist and Buddhist origin with aspects of the overall popular religion. They were particularly active in times of social unrest, often caused by political abuse or incompetence and economic disasters.

The polar relationship between government and Taoism (and religion in general) continued after the republic was established in 1912.

Finally, a word about *Taoism and the martial arts*. There has been a proliferation of techniques, loosely grouped together as "martial arts," but consisting of widely divergent practices. It is an overstatement to generalize and call them all "Taoist." Some have been inspired by Taoist principles, others are probably of Buddhist origin, but they also could be considered generally "Chinese," incorporating a variety of influences.

In a wide sense, martial arts include a variety of body exercises in which the unity of body-mind is always maintained. One may distinguish **gymnastics** (*tao-yin*), which focuses on individual exercises, and the martial arts in a stricter sense. Some techniques can be considered gentle: *t'ai-chi-ch'uan/taijichuan* and *ch'i-kung/qigong*. Others are not so gentle, but aim at self-defense such as *kung-fu* (and techniques developed in Japan, including *judo, aikido,* and *kendo*). Finally, some techniques may be considered aggressive or offensive and originated in

Japan, such as *karate;* or Korea such as *taekwando.* (See separate entries for *tao-yin, t'ai-chi-ch'uan, ch'i-kung.*)

The history of the origin and development of these various techniques is not always clear, but there is unmistakable evidence that some types of gymnastics for health were already practiced in the second century BCE. There also is a strong belief that *t'ai-chi-ch'uan* was created by a Taoist priest living on Mount Wu-tang (in Hupei province) during the 14th century. (See **Chang San-feng.**)

What all these techniques have in common are the two following characteristics: First, they are intended to promote a person's well-being (including safety from attack) and longevity. Keeping the body-mind continuum healthy and vital is the best preventive medicine. Second, the emphasis is always on body-mind unity. Brute force is not sufficient to overcome an attacker, one must be mentally concentrated. As recent studies point out, body and mind are ultimately one. "The body is essentially fluid and so is the mind. Beings are not solid, material entities, but are highly differentiated combinations of energy" (Ishida in L. Kohn, 1989: 68).

Unity versus Multiplicity

Whether Taoism is one or many remains an ongoing question, one which may never be solved. Answers vary, depending on one's personal understanding of a complex tradition, and are influenced by many factors, including one's exposure to various aspects of Taoism, as well as by missing some other important aspects. Perhaps it is just a matter of interpretation.

But let's first explain the problem, next discuss some of the solutions that have been proposed, and, finally, present an interpretation that does not pretend to be totally new, but has some merit of originality.

The Problem. At least two major "branches" or "streams" of Taoism have been distinguished: "philosophical Taoism" and "religious Taoism." We should abolish this terminology once and for all and use instead "Taoist philosophy" and "Taoist religion." By analogy, nobody talks about "philosophical Buddhism" and "religious Buddhism," whereas "Buddhist philosophy" and "Buddhist religion" are quite acceptable terms. For the same reason, one should avoid terms such as "liturgical Taoism," "mystical Taoism" or "monastic Taoism" and rather use "Taoist liturgy," "Taoist mysticism," "Taoist monasticism." It is remarkable that Taoism (that old rebel!) is unlike other religions in its genesis and development. In other religious traditions—for example, Buddhism, Christianity, and Islam—there is at first a prophet, an enlightened teacher who spreads his message and inspires the birth of a community of followers. The message is at first remembered and orally transmitted, and eventually recorded in scriptures. This is still the stage of simple religion. But once the movement is solidified, great minds start to build various systems of "theology," which are rational (philosophical) elaborations of the original revelation. In Buddhism appeared Abhidharma treatises and numerous schools of philosophy, all contending and claiming to interpret the Buddha's message. In Christianity appeared an incredible number of apologists, church fathers and theologians, and, likewise, in Islam, a great number of scholars built up rational systematizations of Mohammed's revelation, first deposited in the Koran. This may be a simplification of history, but the essential pattern is that first there is a religious message and a religious community accepting the message, then there is a "philosophical" (rational) elaboration of the message.

In the case of Taoism, the reverse happened: There was first a group of thinkers, or even several groups, who proposed a certain philosophy of government in various modalities. This philosophy was at first not very systematized and it had nothing to do with any sort of religious cult. It was a humanistic blueprint for an ideal laissez-faire government, to ensure harmony in the world.

It was only 400 or 500 years later that a religious movement arose, which at first had nothing in common with the old school of Taoist thought, except perhaps the person of Lao-tzu, who had gone through a thorough process of transformation and had become deified, but not by the original thinkers themselves. That religious movement was radically different from the earlier "schools" of Taoist thought. There were charismatic leaders, claiming to have received revelations. They organized their members into religious units, performed rituals of worship, penance and healing, and were helping to establish a utopian state on earth with the promise of eternal life in the hereafter. Worship of T'ai-shang Lao-chün and other deities was central.

This description of two movements, one philosophical-political, one religious-political, emphasizes their differences. One could, and often does, seek out similarities, but these probably date from a later period when the original distinctions became blurred, so that the issue was no longer obvious.

A gradual absorption took place, a rereading and reinterpretation of Taoist philosophical concepts to enrich the new religious world view. The appropriation of the *TTC* itself by the Heavenly Masters School was a significant operation. This text, produced for the inspiration of political rulers, was reinterpreted in a religious sense. Of course, since the *TTC* contains great instructions for spiritual cultivation, these aspects could be easily "converted" and be given a religious orientation. Nevertheless, the distortion is noticeable.

In China, two terms have been coined to differentiate between the two movements: *Tao-chia* and *Tao-chiao* (see above under "Starting on the Way"). *Tao-chia* appeared first, a practical term the Han used to group a number of philosophical texts discussing the *Tao*. Here, *chia* means "school of thought." The term *Tao-chiao* was created later, and although *chiao* does not per se mean "religion" but "teaching," it was soon used to indicate the Taoist religious movement, in contrast with other groups, such as *Fo-chiao*, the (newly arrived) Buddhist religion.

Today's Chinese specialists are not in mutual agreement about the relationship between *Tao-chia* and *Tao-chiao*. It is significant that many books produced in recent years have *Tao-chiao* in their title, and do not discuss Taoist philosophy at all. (See works by Ch'ing Hsi-tai, Ren Jiyu, etc.) In encyclopedias of Taoism (*Tao-chiao ta tz'u-tien*) we do find many entries of Taoist philosophy, but it would be impossible to find a Chinese term that includes both religion and philosophy. A similar situation exists in western languages: the term "Taoism" is ambiguous. To make one's intention clear, one must specify and create new terms; "Taoist philosophy" and "Taoist religion" remain the two best terms.

Proposed Solutions. What have modern scholars proposed as a solution? There are two opposite groups. First, those who make a clear distinction between Tao-*chia* and Tao-*chiao*, and, more recently, those who see beyond the distinctions, or even ignore them, to discover a basic unity.

The strongest proponent of multiple Taoism was H. Creel (1956/ 1970), who probably coined the term "philosophic" Taoism and inspired the term "religious" Taoism, a vocabulary that, unfortunately, still haunts modern scholarship:

> In my opinion philosophic Taoism (including both the "contemplative" and the "purposive" aspects) and Hsien Taoism not only were never identical; their associations, even, have been minimal. (Creel 1970: 11)

Creel divides Taoism into two distinct branches. One, he decides, is philosophic and can be broken down under the categories of "contemplative" and "purposive." The *TTC* and the *Chuang-tzu* represent each subdivision, respectively. The second branch is called Hsien Taoism, which is the cult of immortality, the striving for *hsien*ship. Missing from this listing is the Taoist religion, starting with the Heavenly Masters in the second century CE, which cannot be simply identified with "Hsien Taoism." Creel's imperfect division still had a strong influence on later scholarship, and for a long time his distinction of two kinds of Taoism was generally accepted. It did, in fact almost coincide with the Chinese distinction of *Tao-chia* and *Tao-chiao*.

What Creel overlooked was the reality of a Taoist priesthood and their rituals, and the existence of a body of scriptures (*Tao-Tsang*). Still, somehow Creel's view is not dead yet. M. Strickmann, for one, states that:

> . . . the two opposing faces of Taoism, philosophical and religious . . . in reality represent two such disparate phenomena that they do not admit of meaningful comparison. (1979: 166)

He proposes to reserve the word *Taoist* "only in referring to those who recognize the historical position of Chang Tao-ling . . ." (165).

This solution is fraught with difficulties and does not find favor with modern specialists, who prefer to emphasize the unity in Taoism as:

> . . . a single cultural system. This position is especially held by scholars who have done the most intensive study of Taoist history and literature, particularly the diverse array of materials preserved in the Chinese Taoist canon . . . (*HCDR,* 1995: 1054)

On the other hand, those who have done fieldwork and have seen Taoism in action have also been struck by the discrepancies between the ritual tradition and the more intellectual aspects of the philosophical tradition. There is, in other words, a real dilemma when it comes to properly "naming" the tradition. A recent review article provided a good analysis of the current situation, but the final estimate remains inconclusive (C. Bell, 1993).

A New Proposal. How to solve the dilemma? There are some principles that shed light on this darkness, illuminating directions toward a solution.

First of all, can Taoism be defined "in terms of some principles of inner coherence . . ."? (C. Bell: 189). In view of the discussion in the body of this introduction, it does not seem likely. What unites all branches, all types of Taoism, is perhaps only a name: *Tao.* That does not help at all. One must analyze the intentionality, the purpose, of each aspect of Taoism. What is its objective? What are the means of reaching it? If one "listens" carefully, some answers will be suggested. They can be supported by historical evidence, by analysis of texts, by observation of social realities.

The answer that comes to mind most clearly is that the various branches of Taoism have distinct orientations, distinct intentionalities, and are based on two basically different worldviews: One may call them Taoist *naturalism* and Taoist *theism.* They are like two strands running through the tradition, sometimes quite distinct, sometimes overlapping, but essentially different.

In Taoist *naturalism*, there is no personal creator god, but an impersonal creative force, named Tao for the sake of convenience. There are spiritual beings in the universe, but no divine beings to be worshipped. Without a belief in a continued existence after death, there are still strongly held spiritual values. This is the worldview of the Taoist philosophers Lao-tzu, Chuang-tzu, Huai-nan-tzu, and even Huang-Lao Taoism. Its goal is to bring humanity, under sage rulership, in tune with the cosmos. The social goal is to bring order to the world, and the personal goal is natural mysticism, oneness with the ultimate Tao, freedom and joy.

Taoist *theism*, on the other hand, requires belief in and the worship of a deity (one or many, or later as a triad). There are gods in the cosmos, as well as gods in the human body, from whom meditation secures help. There is belief in salvation, either as an "immortal" in paradise (for a very small elite only) or some sort of eternal life, not clearly formulated (for the masses).

There is a gray area, a no-man's land, in between, where distinctions are not so clearly perceived, where the two worldviews may overlap in the subconsciousness of the adept and in his/her conscious practices. It is, for instance, difficult to place alchemy in this scheme. "Inner" alchemy is mostly theistic (the support of the inner gods is essential), but "outer" alchemy could be just a naturalist attempt to prolong life and to produce, in a quasi-scientific way, pills or elixirs to continue life indefinitely.

This distinction of two strands, two intentionalities, in Taoism helps to alleviate the dilemma. What remains a riddle is why many Taoist practitioners, even today, and many scholars of Taoism emphasize the oneness of the Taoist "body." One can easily see major parts in a body, such as head, abdomen, limbs, yet we all know that these disjointed parts comprise an organic unity. In the case of Taoism, this metaphor is not so clear, unless we call Taoism a schizophrenic entity, torn between different directions. One reason why Taoist religionists prefer to call Taoism a "unified cultural system" is that Taoist religious literature is coated in philosophical terminology. Whereas Chuang-tzu's mystical language can be easily adopted and given religious significance, it does not make his mysticism theistic. Chuang-tzu's is essentially a naturalist mysticism; union with the Tao is not like union with a personal divine being! Further, admittedly, the *TTC* contains many quasi-mystical passages and emphasizes spiritual cultivation as a means to good rulership, but this does not make the *TTC* a religious document. It is, however, easy to see how the meaning of the text can be reinterpreted in a religious sense. In other words, the religious writers of later ages have "converted" the philosophical texts of early Taoism into religious documents. The distinction between the two became blurred, but if we focus on their basic intentionality, we must admit that they are on two separate levels.

Taoism as a unified system, it seems, only exists in the minds of Taoist adepts and scholars, though it is a matter of interpretation. To use a comparative analogy: If a devoted Christian believes in reincarnation, it is only a subjective synthesis, it does not mean that Christianity and Buddhism are a "unified cultural system." Another analogy is perhaps even sharper: We all know the essential difference between a meat diet and a protein-rich bean curd diet. But some Chinese Buddhists are very talented at making "meat" dishes out of bean curd. Although it may be deceptive, it does not take away the basic difference between the two.

To conclude: As long as naturalism and theism are being confused, the problem of Taoism cannot be solved. This is only a concrete application of the confusion that exists concerning the *nature of religion*. *Religion* is theistic; it deals with divine beings, however they are conceived, and is expressed by acts of worship. Its opposite is *spiritual culture*; it is humanistic and strives for the realization of human perfection, without reliance on divine agents. It is based on *self-effort*, in contrast with *religion*, which relies on *other power*. The cause of confusion is that the two often overlap, most commonly in one direction; those who practice religion usually also practice spiritual culture, although in a different mind frame.

If one keeps this distinction in mind, other problems may be solved as well. Early Buddhism, the teaching of Gautama, was not religious, it was spiritual culture. Buddhism became religious with the "deification" of the Buddha. For Buddhism, as well as for the early Jains, praying to the gods was of no help whatsoever—the gods themselves needed emancipation. Going one step further: Confucianism, always considered to be a humanist doctrine, is indeed also a spiritual culture. But just because Confucians meditate, one cannot call them religious practitioners. They remain in the sphere of naturalism. *Tao* means "road, way, or path," and "Taoism" is a word that implies a doctrine of the way. But there is more than one way to the top of the mountain. Besides, there is more than one mountaintop.

Once Again: The Nature of Taoism

This is partially a recapitulation of what has already been discussed, but goes one step further: It is a final statement about the essence of Taoism.

As was said before, in very general terms Taoism is a cultural system focusing on the Tao, the Way. Meanwhile, one has discovered that there are at least two "Ways": a *naturalist* and a *theistic* Way. Each has its own intentionality (purpose, objective) and its own methods for reaching it. One could object and say, "This is all theory, a matter of dry definition." Well, yes and no; clear distinctions are necessary and useful, but in real life they are often deceptive. Here the definitions are analyzed, and what anyone does with them is a matter of personal decision. In other words, it is perhaps possible to walk on two "ways." This is what many religious believers actually do. They believe in theism and they also follow the principles of naturalism. The former presupposes the latter, but not *vice versa*. A religious-oriented person worships deities, believes in a salvation and an afterlife, but also accepts humanistic principles (a code of ethics) and naturalist goals in life (freedom, happiness, physical love, economics, and physical well-being). In fact, many religious people pray to their gods just for those earthly blessings.

A naturalist-oriented person does not worship any gods, does not demand a continued existence after this life; he/she is happy with a fulfilling earthly existence, which includes both material comfort and a spiritual dimension.

The above can easily be applied to Taoism. If asked the question "What is Taoism?" one could and should say Taoism is a system of the "Way," but there are at least "two ways." The first one is *naturalism, humanism*. When this system was first devised and developed, its intention was to understand the nature of reality (*Tao*), to adjust one's life to it, and to apply it in ruling the country. This is the *Tao-chia*: the way of insight applied to government. This kind of Taoism hardly became a social reality, it was a "school of thought," not an organized body. As a way of governing, it was never put to use (only partially and very rarely, because rulers did not like to follow *wu-wei* principles). In our modern world, this "way" is still attractive for many; the popularity of the *TTC* and the *Chuang-tzu* proves it. But it has become a "way" for personal spiritual growth, not a "way" applied in government. The Chinese government often acts in diametrical opposition to Taoist principles. Still, this kind of Taoism is *universal* and exerts a lasting attraction.

The second kind of Taoism is *theism*, a full-fledged religious system with deities to worship, holy scriptures, a priesthood to perform rituals, temples, monastic life, and all the paraphernalia of religion, embodied in social reality. This is Taoism that is *particular* (not universal), a part of the overall system of the Chinese religious tradition, yet somehow distinct from it, because it is *elitist*—and it is that in two ways. First, it is elitist because the priests of Taoism are not part of the popular religion per se, although they often interact with it. Their services are required whenever communities or individuals wish to pray to their deities to obtain this-worldly blessings. The priests have their own esoteric tools of the trade: scriptures, which the common people do not understand, and various techniques to implore blessings from gods and goddesses. This Taoism focuses on the liturgy.

Second, Taoism is elitist in its monastic life. Monks and nuns live a celibate life in seclusion, are basically concerned with their own spiritual perfection. They meditate, read the scriptures, perform some kinds of martial arts (mostly *ch'i-kung* and *t'ai-chi ch'uan*), and follow an ascetic lifestyle, hoping to attain longevity and possibly to become an "immortal." This lifestyle was once embodied in *Shang-ch'ing Taoism*, and was taken over by the *Ch'uan-chen* order, which still exists today.

The distinction between these two elite Taoisms can be effectively compared with Roman Catholic practices. There are "secular" priests who serve congregations and perform the Christian liturgy, and "monastics," priests (monks) and nuns who live in community and seclusion. Their goal is to reach Christian perfection, mainly by observing three vows: poverty, chastity, and obedience. In actual fact, the two classes of practitioners sometimes overlap: Some monastics also can be in charge of parish communities. In general, however, the Christian model is very similar to the Taoist situation.

Taoist theism is particular to China and to Chinese communities elsewhere in the world. Its goals and methods are culture-bound, and so not particularly meaningful to Westerners. Still, these Taoists have elicited the interest and attention of cultural anthropologists and historians of religion as an intellectual pursuit. Some aspects of their tradition can also be singled out and adopted by Westerners and more or less integrated into a different, even non-Taoist lifestyle. Diet, martial arts, and techniques of meditation are the most popular aspects derived from Taoism that appeal to a Western audience.

If a Westerner, a convinced Christian, is sometimes able to incorporate Buddhist elements into his/her Christian worldview without psychological conflict, so likewise can Taoist elements enrich a Western way of living. The most promising in that respect are the writings of the Taoist philosophers, which are universal and eternal. The world should be grateful to China not only for teaching us the secrets of "bean curd" but for its invaluable gift of Lao-tzu and Chuang-tzu.

Dictionary

A

ALCHEMY. The etymology indicates a double origin: *al* is Arabic, *chem* is European; it has the same root as "chemistry." The term was coined in the 12th century. Originally, alchemy related to astrology: They both represent attempts to discover man's relationship to the cosmos and to gain benefits from it. Strictly speaking, alchemy is usually defined as "the pseudo-science which concerns attempts to transform base metals such as lead or copper into silver or gold" (Leicester, 1973: 535). Such a definition, however, is too narrow, since alchemists have not limited their efforts to mere metallurgy, but went far beyond this scope, transferring their aim to the higher level of mysticism: "In fact, alchemy may be called the art of the transmutations of the soul" (Burchard, 1967 & 1971: 23).

In China, both these aspects are important. Whereas the former one, the metallurgical experiments and transformations, are called *wai-tan* ("external," outer or "operative" alchemy), the latter, or mystical-spiritual practices to reach longevity-immortality, are called *nei-tan* ("internal" or inner alchemy).

It is possible that the two types of alchemy began together. As N. Sivin says, a number of important adepts follow the ***Kinship of the Three*** "in seeing external, internal, and sexual alchemy as aspects of a single process" (Sivin, 1987, *ER* 1: 189). However, if one remembers that *Kinship* dates only from the second century CE, whereas "operative" alchemy was already practiced during the late Warring States period and the Former Han, one may wonder about the validity of Sivin's argument.

It appears that the classical age of external alchemy was from the second to the eighth century CE, whereas internal alchemy made its breakthrough from the sixth century and flourished especially during the Sung and Yuan periods.

Because the two techniques are very different, they will be treated separately. (See **Outer Alchemy** and **Inner Alchemy**.)

ANIMAL SYMBOLISM. Chinese culture loves the use of symbolism: animals, plants, objects, colors, etc., are often used in art and literature to represent values, ideas, and ideals. This is true for Chinese culture generally, but also for Taoism. Here, Taoist animal symbols are briefly explained (see also **Plant Symbolism**): They are the crane, the dragon, the tortoise, the cicada.

• *Crane*: a symbol of longevity, a frequent motif in Chinese popular art. Crane and pine are often combined. For the Taoists, the crane is the mythical mount of Lao-tzu and of other immortals. Among four kinds of cranes: black, yellow, white and blue, the black cranes live the longest, more than 600 years (see C. Williams, 1977: 101).

• *Dragon*: one of the four "numinous" (*ling*) or mythical animals, the other three are the phoenix, the tortoise, and the unicorn. The dragon in East Asia is an auspicious animal (in contrast with the West, where it represents evil, satanic forces). The dragon is not only a symbol, it is also a deity. Several dragon-kings live in the oceans, other dragons live in the cloudy sky and in the rivers. They control water and rain and, hence, are responsible for seasonal rainfall and bountiful harvests. Dragon lore in China and Japan is extensive.

Concrete symbols of dragons are found in Chinese temples (dragon-columns) and on walls (nine-dragon wall in Beijing), on Taoist ritual garments, and formerly on imperial embroidered garments. The emperor's throne was called "dragon throne."

• *Tortoise*: this is a multifaceted animal. In old mythology, the tortoise or turtle was considered an ominous and sacred animal. Its carapace was used in divination (see *Chuang-tzu* anecdote, Watson, 1970: 298–299); occasionally, it was worshipped, as in the ancestral temple of another Chuang-tzu anecdote (Watson: 187–188). Its reputation for wisdom was based on its old age and its symbolic body shape: The upper carapace was round (oval), representing heaven; its lower plastron was square, representing earth. This was interpreted as being able to mediate and carry messages between the human world and the gods or spirits.

In sculpture, the tortoise is often seen as the pedestal for stone tablets and statues. This custom has ancient roots in mythology, reminding of the goddess Nü-kua, who cut off the legs of a turtle and used them as a foundation for the earth.

The turtle is also seen as a lewd and man-seducing animal. However, its blood, concocted in a soup, is recommended to cure some illnesses (lack of vitality). In some temples, there are turtle ponds with hundreds of them, bred for this purpose (ex., the City God temple in Taichung, Central Taiwan).

• *Cicada*: an amazing insect, because it has been observed that the larva, after maturing, disappears in the ground and stays there 17 years before it emerges as a full-grown insect. Then it soars up into the sky. It thus became a symbol of immortality. During Han times, the Chinese people hoped to reach "*post-mortem* immortality" (release of the body to be reunited with the spirit, by bureaucratic decree). For that reason it was important to keep the body intact and prevent corruption. Han aristocracy used jade plugs to seal the corpse's orifices, but a more common custom was to place a "jade cicada" in the person's mouth, in the belief that it would confer resurrection (B. Till, 1986: 23–24). (See also **Body Liberation**.) Today "jade cicadas" are very popular as pendants and as collectors' items.

The above four symbols are shared by all Chinese, but crane and cicada are more prominent in Taoist lore. The *Chuang-tzu* uses an amazing number of animal analogies to illustrate his views.

ARTS OF THE BEDCHAMBER See SEXUALITY

ASCETICISM (ascetic lifestyle, ascetic practices). *Webster's Dictionary* defines asceticism as "the religious doctrine that one can reach a higher spiritual state by rigorous self-discipline and self-denial." This is a more accurate definition than the one found in the Harper Collins *Dictionary of Religion*, which defines asceticism as "the renunciation of physical pleasures or other forms of bodily self-denial as a means of spiritual development" (*HCDR* 1995: 77). The superiority of the former definition lies in the fact that it does not single out "physical pleasures" and "bodily self-denial," but leaves it broad enough to include other aspects of self-denial that relate to mind and emotion. Asceticism is indeed not restricted to the physical body. For instance the type of ascetic lifestyle found in the Catholic Church expressed in taking three religious vows (poverty, chastity, obedience) are kinds of self-denial that renounce mental-emotional desires as much as physical cravings. The vow of chastity, like abstinence from marriage in other religions, is a denial of sexual pleasures, but also means giving up emotional needs of love and affection (spouse, children, family). The vow of poverty means accepting a lifestyle without personal ownership, but also includes the humiliation of depending on the generosity of others, even to the extreme humiliation of begging for one's daily food. The vow of obedience involves the humiliation of doing someone else's will, even if one cannot accept the reason or appropriateness of a particular action.

Ascetic lifestyles are found in most religious traditions, but in various degrees. It is usually the expression of a philosophical (or theological) view about the body-soul relationship, which in extreme cases can go as far as hatred for the body seen as a prison of the soul. In such situations, ascetic practices can be very harsh. All needs of the body are suppressed, and one can barely survive: no clothing, hardly any food, no social ties, no dwelling place, etc., as one finds among some groups of Jains in India.

The Buddha preferred the middle way between indulgence of the senses and extreme hatred of the body. He experienced that spiritual progress is impossible if one is almost starved to death.

In Taoism, there is no unified theory or practice in this regard. Asceticism is more stressed among monastic Taoists than among the "fire dwellers" (the married clergy, such as the Heavenly Masters). There are amusing stories about some Taoist priests overindulging in alcohol, and although this is an individual choice, many Taoist priests are meat eaters.

In a monastic setting, the scenario is different. The lifestyle of monks and nuns is geared toward spiritual perfection, and asceticism has its role in it. Besides abstention from marriage, there are also rules about **diet**. Some groups of Taoists would abstain from the "five grains," from meat and alcohol, and follow a diet of bare survival. Their main attention was on meditation and inner vision of the in-dwelling deities. A restricted diet was believed to help them progress faster spiritually than in normal conditions.

The Taoist monastic order that was committed most definitely to asceticism was **Complete Realization Taoism**. It appears to have been a decision that founder **Wang Che** imposed on his followers:

Taoism as practiced by the Ch'uan-chen masters was a full-scale rejection of the selfish seeking of worldly benefits and pleasures in favor of diligent and arduous training in pursuit of Immortal-hood [Immortal-*hsien*]. (S. Eskildsen, 1990: 171)

In order to become Perfected Men and to prove to themselves and others that they had indeed succeeded in doing so, they had to toil and suffer in ways that exceeded the normal human capacity. (Eskildsen: 170)

Chinese society in general does not approve of such extremes. Ch'uan-chen masters, going out to beg for food, had often to endure ridicule and even violence (this is in contrast with India, where ascetics are honored). Even Ch'an Buddhists realized the difference of attitude between India and China; rather than begging for their food, they preferred earning their livelihood by manual labor.

From the agelong experiences of various religions, two conclusions can be drawn. First, a moderate degree of asceticism and self-denial enhances spiritual progress: No one can meditate with a full stomach and with uncontrolled sexual desires in their mind. But the body should not be seen as the soul's enemy: Care for the body is important, as Taoism clearly demonstrates. Hatred for the body is misguided; after all, the physical body's ultimate destiny is to be spiritualized, not to be destroyed. (See also **Diet**.)

B

BAMBOO See PLANT SYMBOLISM

BIG DIPPER or **NORTHERN BUSHEL** (*Pei-tou/Beidou*). Although an important constellation in Taoist religious speculation, there appears to be no consensus about its exact role. The Big Dipper, also called Great Bear (*ursa major*) appears to be more important than the Small Dipper (*ursa minor*), although it is in the latter that the pole star is located, and this star's eminence is supreme in Taoism.

The Big Dipper is a group of seven stars (often of nine stars, since two are dark, invisible stars, yet influential) that play an important role in Taoist cosmology and spirituality. It has been described as ". . . the center of the celestial administration of human destinies and it functions as a sort of life-giving center of the universe" (P. Anderson 1990: 25). It has been said that the stars of the Northern Dipper "record men's actions, both good and evil, and according to one's virtuous deeds or sins, they add to or cut off a portion of his life" (Werner, 1969: 369).

The stars most worshipped are those of the Triple Happiness (*sanfu*): *fu-lu-shou* (happiness, career, long life), but that is a more popular tradition.

It is said in some texts that Lao-tzu (deified) has his residence in the Big Dipper. On the other hand, the pole star, considered to be the center of the sky, but belonging to the Small Dipper, is seen as the residence of the god T'ai-yi.

BIOGRAPHIES OF IMMORTALS (*Lieh-hsien chuan/Liexianzhuan*). A collection of about 70 biographies, or rather hagiographies, of Taoist "saints" (sages, immortals, or transcendents). Traditionally, this small volume is attributed to Liu Hsiang (77–6 BCE), a scholar of the Former Han, a relative of Liu An, prince of Huai-nan. For reasons of inner criticism, Liu Hsiang's authorship appears to be impossible, but the question is rather irrelevant, because the text as it is now is not the original. An early version or versions of the collection existed already during the Later Han (first century CE), but the text was fixed only after it was incorporated into the Sung edition of the Taoist Canon (1019 CE) and partially in *Yün-chi ch'i-ch'ien* (1025). It is included in the Ming Canon (*CT* 294; *TT* 138).

The collection does not contain real biographies of sages, but just a few anecdotes of each person, one or two rather interesting stories. Most of the personalities treated are only known through this collection. This literary genre of hagiographic biographies served as a model for later authors, especially *Shen-hsien chuan* (**Biographies of Spirit Immortals**) with which it should not be confused. (For a full discussion and French translation of the text, see M. Kaltenmark, 1953.)

There appears to exist another collection of legendary stories with the same title, *Lieh-hsien chuan*, but dating only from the Yuan period (1206–1368 CE). This volume contains the stories of 55 immortals (illustrated with woodcuts) among whom figure the famous **Eight Immortals** (see P. Yetts, 1916).

BIOGRAPHIES OF SPIRIT-IMMORTALS (*Shen-hsien chuan/Shen-xianzhuan*). A collection of legendary Taoist biographies (or hagiographies) originally attributed to Ko Hung (263–343). His collection was lost, then reconstructed during the sixth century. L. Kohn (1993) contains translations of several stories, such as "The Master with the Yellow Pupils," "The Lady of Great Mystery," "Liu An and the Eight Worthies" (290–296), and "The Life of Shen Hsi" (326–328).

The *Shen-hsien chuan* is the second early collection of hagiographic stories of Taoist sages, following the model of *Biographies of Immortals*.

BLACKHEAD TAOIST (Wu-t'ou Tao-shih). The Taoist ritual tradition of southern China (Fukien province and Taiwan) makes a distinction between two types of Taoist "priests," based on the color of their ritual headdress. The distinction, however, goes beyond the colors and involves the nature of the ritual services each group is entitled to perform.

Blackhead Taoists are so called because during their liturgy they wear a black cap (hat) with a gold pin on top, in contrast with the **Redhead Taoists**, who just wear a red scarf or turban draped around their forehead. Whereas the Blackhead priests are the "orthodox" or officially ordained ritualists, mostly in the lineage of the Heavenly Masters School, the Redhead masters are popular performers, who also perform "unorthodox" or black magic rituals when the need arises.

The legal distinction between the two kinds of Taoists is not clearly defined, yet in general one may say that

> the major differences are that Black-Head Taoists are literate, their rituals are usually written in classical Chinese prose, and the ritual manual is always open on the altar as the liturgy is read . . . In contrast, Red-

Head Taoists are often illiterate, their rituals are usually in seven-sylla-
ble per line verse, and the liturgy is recited from memory. (A. Cohen,
1992: 187)

Training, ordination and ritual repertoire of the two kinds are also
different (see **Priesthood**). The major difference as regards ritual repertoire is that the Blackhead Taoists are trained and entitled to perform the solemn liturgy of Renewal (*chiao*), including the "ritual of
universal salvation," from which the Redhead Taoists are excluded.
But Blackheads also perform so-called "shamanistic" rituals, the
proper field of the Redhead Taoists (see **Shamans**). A complete study
of the topic is still missing, and there appears to be much overlap of
functions between the two. It is often said that the Blackhead priests
perform the rituals for the dead, while the Redhead masters specialize
in rituals for the living. This is a crude and mostly incorrect assessment. The liturgy of Renewal is mainly for the living, and Redhead
masters are often seen performing rituals to appease the dead (as in
the well-known Tung-yueh chien or Eastern Peak temple in Tainan,
southern Taiwan). In other words, the overlap of functions is quite
obvious and the competition is very real. Some Taoist masters occasionally hire Redhead Taoists to assist them or perform Redhead rituals on their own. (See also **Redhead Taoist**. For further study, see K.
Schipper, 1985; Saso, 1970 and 1974; Cohen, 1992.)

BLESSED SPOTS See GROTTO-HEAVENS

BODY LIBERATION (*Shih-chieh/Shijie*). The expression "body liberation" has to do with the Taoist ideal of becoming an immortal, or
a transcendent (*hsien*). It is a difficult concept, sometimes misrepre-
sented or interpreted in a way too vague to be intelligible. It has to do
with the Taoist aspiration of gaining physical immortality, and is similar to the concept of resurrection. To make things clear, these concepts must be carefully defined.

First of all, "body liberation" (usually translated by others as "liberation or deliverance from the corpse") is one of three methods to
become an immortal (*hsien*). There is a superior way and an inferior
way. The superior way means that the human candidate does not die
but directly ascends to heaven, usually "in broad daylight." Only
those who have perfected themselves to the utmost reach this supreme
degree. Spirit and body, the whole person is transferred from a mortal
state to an immortal one, not passing through the medium of death.
There are, in Taoist literature, exceptional cases of this highest state
of being. These persons are said to join the divine hierarchy of the

Taoist heavens. There are two subgrades in this category: heavenly and earthly immortals.

The inferior way is very different: the candidate passes through the medium of death, some sources say of apparent death, because the ultimate state of perfection or purification was not achieved during life. But soon after death, the body is revived, transformed, and the candidate becomes an immortal, body and spirit united, and lives forever in some earthly paradise, far remote from human civilization.

Looking at the Chinese terms separately, one finds that *shih* usually means "corpse, dead body," but occasionally also "body." The term *chieh* is more complex: It can mean "to divide, separate, disperse . . . to detach, deliver"; also, "to loosen, dissolve, explain." In Buddhism it has sometimes the extra meaning of "emancipation, liberation." Although the compound is already found in the first century CE, before Buddhism had any influence in China, it probably meant something different at that time. Under the influence of Buddhism, the Taoist meaning could have shifted and the concept of liberation, emancipation could have been superimposed on the earlier meaning.

What exactly was the earlier meaning? Three considerations will be helpful: first, as D. Harper mentions, in the *Shih-chi*, the expression *hsing-chieh* (*xingjie*) occurs "in connection with the [*hsien*] cult during the reign of the First [Ch'in Emperor] . . ." (Harper, 1994: 27). It is also found in a Ma-wang-tui medical manuscript, where it

> . . . signifies the end result of the cultivation regimen, when the practitioner's body becomes spirit-like and he is no longer bound to mundane existence . . . In this context I translate [*hsing-chieh*] as "release of the form" (not "*from* the form"), meaning that the refined body is freed from constraints and lives as the spirits. (Harper: 27)

Second, the first occurrence of the term *shih-chieh* is found in **Wang Ch'ung's** *Lun-heng* (first century CE). He explains *shih-chieh* as a transformation comparable to a cicada's that leaves its pupa behind (Harper: 25). This analogy will need further scrutiny.

But first, a third consideration is in order: In her first-rate research of Han tomb inscriptions, A. Seidel has brought to light new data that clarify a number of former hypotheses and even will cause drastic changes in our understanding of Han religion. Until recently, it was believed that at death the dual soul, *hun* and *p'o*, separate, the former rising to heaven, the latter descending into the grave with the corpse. However,

> . . . The funerary texts make it quite clear that the *hun* as well as the *p'o* components of man, his whole social persona and individual being,

must descend under the earth while his body becomes the prey of the demons of putrefaction. (Seidel, 1987: 230)

Unless appeased and controlled, the disembodied "souls" become demons and create dangers for the living. The Long before the arrival of Buddhism, long before the Taoist religion flourished, Chinese society had already construed fairly elaborate ideas about a netherworld, structured as a bureaucracy with the supreme god T'ian-Ti (Heavenly Emperor) in overall charge, and lower officials in his service. The living could communicate with the netherworld authorities by means of some legal procedures (A. Cedzich, 1993).

When the Taoist religion rose to eminence in the second century CE, one of the reasons for its success "was no doubt the fact that they proposed a way out of the dilemma of physical death." What is more, they eventually came to devise means to save even those who had already become wretched demonic shades (Seidel, 1987: 230). The former relates to the superior immortals, already mentioned. The latter group refers to Taoist believers, members of the Heavenly Masters community, whose merits had been outstanding. The earthly Taoist administration could issue petitions, addressed to the netherworld authorities, to

. . . release forthwith the *hun* and *p'o* spirits of so-and-so, *to return his corpse to him and reassemble his bones* . . . and let him ascend and join celestial officialdom in the Land of Harmony and Joy. (Seidel: 233–4)

This is indeed a case of "body liberation," accomplished by bureaucratic order. Implicit in the whole scenario is the conclusion that even such happening is exceptional. To state that the goal of institutional Taoist religion is the attainment of physical immortality is an incorrect assessment.

Bureaucratic petitions to the netherworld were already being issued during the Warring States period, as one case of "resurrection" in 297 BCE shows (Harper, 1994: 13.ff). When Taoism adopted the procedure, it changed the focus somehow: Instead of reviving a dead person, he/she was "liberated" or "set free, released" and transferred to a state of immortality in the Taoist heavens. This probably was the basis for an extension of this process: "body liberation," practiced by Taoist seekers of immortality. They did not rely on official documents, but on their own spiritual cultivation.

Since their purification was not complete, they would first die a natural death, and after some indefinite period of time, their body would "ascend" (leave the coffin) and be united with their spirit to become an "earthly immortal" (*ti-hsien*), in contrast with the superior "heavenly immortal" (*t'ien-hsien*). This is the process commonly called *shih-chieh*, body liberation. In view of the above analysis, the expression *shih-chieh* cannot mean "liberation *from* the body," but must be translated as liberation *of* or *through* the body.

The term "from" would indicate that the spirit is freed from the physical body (reminiscent of the Christian view that the "soul" is imprisoned in the body and needs to be freed). In the Taoist case, the body itself is transformed, purified (posthumously) in such a way that it now becomes worthy to be rejoined with the spirit. This is very similar to "resurrection," which, in a Christian context, signifies the revival of the deceased body and its reunion with the soul. The parallelism goes even further: As the gospel narrates, Jesus' tomb was found empty, except for a piece of clothing in which his body had been wrapped. In the Taoist case, when the master's coffin is opened, there is some article left behind: a sandal or a sword or a piece of clothing. But the body has disappeared, it has been transformed.

The analogy already mentioned of the cicada is eloquent: After the pupa has been transformed, the "new" insect emerges and rises to the sky, leaving behind the outer skin of the old body. The cicada has not been freed from the pupa, it only emerged new from the old skin. "Liberation *from* the corpse" would imply that the spirit of the Taoist adept leaves the body behind in the grave. But that is not the case: The body is transformed and joins the spirit, and, as in the case of the cicada, only an "outer shell" or some external objects are left in the coffin to make it clear that the body has disappeared. It has joined the spirit to enjoy physical immortality. (See also **Immortal**; **Resurrection**.)

BODY-MIND-SOUL. Many practices recommended in the Taoist religion are intended to transform, in various ways, this mortal human body into an immortal one. **Outer** and **inner alchemy** are attempts in that direction.

In the Chinese tradition of Taoism and traditional medicine, body and mind are seen as a continuum, a unity, perhaps with two manifestations, but basically one. How the "soul" theory fits into that framework is not so clear (see **soul**). It was believed that human beings have two basic vital principles or souls; as long as they stay united with the physical body, there is life. Death is their separation.

The Taoists believed that it was possible to stop and even reverse the process of aging and death by special practices. They believed that the physical body could somehow be refined, spiritualized. Or they use the metaphor of a new embryo being generated in one's body; this embryo can be nourished and developed and, at death, this new person is the immortal body-mind unit, the immortal or transcendent that leaves the old shell behind (many Taoists would not see this as a metaphor, but understand it literally).

This basic unity view of body and mind is an insight that has started to make some inroads into Western thinking. In China, it already has a long history.

Looking at it from a different angle, the Taoists considered the body as a microcosm, a miniature of the cosmos at large, or macrocosm. This is deeply implied in the **Five Agents Theory**, and also in the symbolism that sees the human body as a landscape. The Taoists have actually drawn pictures of such a transformed body (reproductions of this remarkable drawing made into stone rubbings are found in K. Schipper (1982: 143), but not in the English translation and in L. Kohn (1993: 177). It represents an abstract image of a human body in which all the body parts are aspects of a landscape, augmented with symbolic figures, human or animal, representing the "veins" of energy coursing through the body.

This picture also can be seen as a concrete expression of *ch'i* (vital energy) which is believed to run through a human body as well as through the physical geography. In the latter case, it is the foundation of the Chinese practice of *feng-shui* ("wind and water") or geomancy. (See also *ch'i*. For more bibliographic references, see A. Seidel, 1989–90: 258–259.)

BOOK OF CHANGES See *YI CHING*

BREATH See *CH'I*

BREATHING EXERCISES. In the Taoist religion several terms occur, that in different ways, all express the idea and the goal of "nourishing" (*yang*) or strengthening the life force, the physical body, the spirit. (See also *yang-sheng*; *yang hsing* - nature; *yang hsing* - physical body; *yang-ch'i*; *yang-shen*.) Although some of the practices do not have any religious value and are purely physiological (diet, gymnastics, sexuality, breathing exercises) (see Maspero, 1971/1981: 445), they can be harnessed in the pursuit of the religious goal of longevity (*ch'ang-sheng*, a term that is often translated as "eternal" life, but that may be questionable).

One of the practices mentioned, breathing, appears to be crucial in spiritual cultivation: Not only Taoists but also the Hindus and Buddhists give a central place to breathing exercises. It is one of the preparations for concentration, but also can be an independent meditation exercise (even outside a religious context). In Taoism, it is very much recommended, and variations exist, such as "embryonic" breathing, and guiding the *ch'i* throughout the body. There is, however, a caution: *ch'i* can mean "breath" (inhalation and exhalation of air), but often it is more than that; it can mean "energy, vitality," etc. Taoist authors are not always careful to maintain the distinction and slip from one meaning into another, thus creating confusion.

A pioneering study in the methods of nourishing one's vital energies was done by H. Maspero in 1937. He realized that the physiological effects obtained were all in conformity with the principles of Chinese medicine.

By studying the Taoist Canon, Maspero discovered that at first Taoist practitioners only knew what they call "external breath," but that during the T'ang and later, they became more precise and made a distinction between outer and inner breath. The former is acquired by normal breathing, but it was recommended to "stop breath" or "hold the breath" for as long as possible, from three counts to five, seven, nine and 12; then, on a more advanced level, to 120 counts. Once one could hold the breath for 1,000 counts, one was close to immortality.

With the discovery of the internal breath, this scenario changed. Stopping the breath was discouraged. It was more important to cultivate the inner breath, which was identified with the original breath (*yuan-ch'i*) received at birth. This breath was inside the body and its circulation within was considered very important. One could either "guide" the breath wherever one wanted it to go, especially to particular organs affected by illness, or one could "refine" the breath and let it circulate freely without conscious interference.

Circulating the inner breath was called "embryonic respiration" (*t'ai-hsi*): "Its aim was to recreate the embryo's breathing in the mother's womb (Maspero: 459). It was believed that this practice would lead to immortality.

This is, in a very simplified way, the Taoist view of "breathing" and its effects on spiritual cultivation (for a full discussion, see Maspero: 445–554). A few comments seem necessary. As was already mentioned, the whole matter becomes nebulous and confusing if one shifts from one understanding of *ch'i* into another. "Breath" and "vitality, or vital energy" are two distinct realities. One may wonder how the Taoist views fit in with our present knowledge of physiology. First of all, "breathing" is inhaling air, which contains oxygen and is transmitted, via the lungs, into the bloodstream. The blood circulates oxygen to all parts of the body. Breathing also means exhaling the "bad" air, saturated with carbon dioxide, back into the atmosphere. It is obvious that this whole process of breathing is beneficial, even absolutely necessary for the body's health.

When the Taoists discuss "circulating the interior breath," it is more likely they use *ch'i* in the sense of energy. Embryonic breathing is not real breathing: The embryo receives nutrients from the mother, but there is no respiration. This "breath," then, is more symbolic or means "vitality." Similarly, when an adept practices "embryonic breathing," it makes more sense to understand it as a voluntary circulation of energy in the body via the energy channels (meridians) discussed in Chinese medicine. These are just a few remarks, cautioning one to be critical. There is a need for more exploration of this topic by specialists, both practitioners with personal experience and scientifically trained people. Breathing exercises are indeed important, but nebulous language can create dangers. If the Taoist concepts and practices have a scientific foundation, they could and should be expressed in clear, scientific language.

BUDDHISM AND TAOISM: Mutual Relationships. Although laypeople in China and elsewhere are mostly not aware of the great doctrinal differences between Buddhism and Taoism ("Don't all religions teach the same: do good, avoid evil?"), their differences in worldview are very deep, very realistic. This applies to both the Taoist philosophy and the Taoist religion, although especially in the latter, mutual absorption of concepts and practices has somehow softened the sharp edges of friction. Moreover, the innate Chinese sense of harmony and compromise has resulted in mutual tolerance and a spirit of coexistence.

Whereas today a spirit of mutual acceptance and tolerance prevails, this was not at all the case during early medieval times. Buddhists and Taoists sometimes supported and copied each other, but more often they clashed on account of doctrinal differences and of competition for imperial patronage. Their relationship through the centuries can be summarized under four headings, loosely connected with time periods: naive acceptance and dialogue; rivalry, competition, and mutual attacks; absorption; coexistence and tolerance. Of course, not all Buddhists nor all Taoists were involved in all of these relationships: Such a generalization would be an historical mistake. Mutual attacks by some coincided with mutual appreciation by others.

• *Naive Acceptance and Dialogue.* At first, Buddhism was misunderstood as another branch of Taoism. The earliest scriptures translated into Chinese deal with topics close to the heart of the Taoists: spiritual yoga, meditation, wisdom (*prajna*). Buddhism entered China during the decline of the Han, and together with Taoism benefited from the weakness of Confucianism, which was further discredited by the collapse of the Han dynasty. Early Buddhist translators used Taoist terminology to express their own concepts, and discussions of similarity in meaning were common (see **Ko Yi**). Philosophical dialogue between Buddhists and Chinese literati resulted in comparing Buddhist ontology with Taoist concepts of nonbeing; the Buddhist *prajna* texts particularly attracted the interest of Chinese literati, whereas Buddhist monks studied the Taoist writings *TTC* and *Chuang-tzu* (see **Neo-Taoism**).

• *Rivalry, Competition, Attacks.* Once a better understanding of the new religion and their early successes was gained, a new relationship developed. Taoists saw Buddhism as a competitive force that had to be curbed. A mythical story was created to prove the superiority of Taoism: The *hua-hu* (or "Conversion of the Barbarians") myth, claiming that Lao-tzu left China by the western border and reappeared in India as the Buddha, angered the Buddhists and created a spirit of antagonism, especially when, around 300 CE, the legend was written down in the *Hua-hu ching* (***Conversion of the Barbarians Scripture***). The Buddhists turned to counterattacks, claiming that both Lao-tzu and Confucius were followers of the Buddha and were sent to China to awaken the people (see E. Zürcher, 1959: 308–9).

When the Northern Chou Emperor Wu considered adopting Taoism as his state orthodoxy, which would serve as a unifying force in the country, the scholar Zhen Luan, in 570, wrote a strong protest treatise (***Laughing at the Tao***) saying it would not work! (See L. Kohn, 1995.)

The controversies between Buddhists and Taoists continued throughout the T'ang: each religion was vying for imperial favor and protection. Occasionally, Confucians would join in and attack Buddhism as a foreign import, not suited to the Chinese way of life (see L. Kohn 1995: 34–41). Accusations against Buddhism included their lack of filial piety, because they practiced celibacy and did not produce heirs for their ancestors; their parasitic lifestyle, because they did not work for a living; and their growing economic wealth (see K. Ch'en, 1964).

During the reign of Sung Emperor Hui-tsung (r. 1101–1125), Taoism was especially favored, whereas Buddhism became the target of actively adverse policy. A number of Buddhist temples were transformed into Taoist monasteries, and Buddhist monks were encouraged to become Taoist priests. There was, however, no outright suppression of Buddhism, as had happened during the T'ang in 842–845, rather a subtle strategy was adopted to sinify the "alien" religion (M. Strickmann, 1979: 346–348).

The *Hua-hu* controversy resurfaced during the Yuan (Mongol) dynasty: Debates took place between Taoists and Buddhists at the court of Khubilai Khan in 1255, 1258, and 1281. By imperial order, all Taoist scriptures had to be burned except the *TTC* (see **Introduction**).

During the late imperial period, especially the Ch'ing dynasty, rivalries between the two religions were no longer as vivid, although Lamaism was favored by the court, Buddhism was in decline, and so was Taoism. In their misery, the two became more friendly to each other.

• *Mutual Absorption* takes us back to the time of the Southern dynasties. The Taoist religion, especially the Ling-pao School, borrowed heavily from the Buddhists: scriptures, doctrines, rituals, temples, and, during the Jurchen Chin, monastic life. The Buddhist views of the afterlife, including the doctrine of karma and reincarnation, and the belief in paradises and hells, were assimilated into Taoism, as well as into the Popular religion (see also **Soul**).

On the other hand, Taoism had its impact on Buddhism as well: the most eloquent example is the emergence of a new school of Buddhism, distinctly Chinese: the Ch'an (Zen) or Meditation School. Ch'an is the genial combination of the Buddhist principle of enlightenment and the Taoist intuitive, nonverbal approach to understanding. The early interest of Buddhist masters in Taoist philosophy bears its fruit in this transformation of Buddhism. The Chinese genius of absorption and new creation is seen here at its best. One of its major characteristics is "wordless teaching" and teaching by paradox. To cite only one example of a parallel:

> An interview between a Buddhist master and a monk:
> "What is the path?"
> "Everyday life is the path."
> "Can it be studied?"
> "If you try to study, you will be far away from it . . ."
> (Reps, 1961: 105)

> A parallel Chuang-tzu story:
> "Is it possible to possess the Way?"
> "You don't even have possession of your own body,
> how could you possibly gain possession of the Way?"
> (Watson: 238)

Even with the mutually influencing processes, Buddhism and Taoism remained themselves, kept their own identity. Their basic worldviews and goals to be attained remained distinct, even if some of their practices and a number of paraphernalia looked similar, at least to an outsider.

• *Coexistence and Tolerance.* In late imperial times, and during the republic, Buddhists and Taoists shared the general contempt of the Chinese intelligentsia and, since the 19th century, the criticism and ridicule of Western observers, especially Christian missionaries. That was greatly due to bias, although the spiritual and intellectual caliber of both the Taoist and Buddhist clergy was mostly of low quality. In remote monasteries, however, spiritual life flourished, unknown by most foreign observers. Among Taoists and Buddhists, there was a spirit of mutual acceptance. Some reports mention the mutual hospitality among their monasteries. An excellent example is narrated by Peter Goullart: A Taoist abbot invited Buddhist monks to his monastery for a sumptuous banquet (P. Goullart, 1961: 50–51). Today, Buddhists and Taoists each continue in their own traditions, but a spirit of coexistence has smoothed their relationships. They both are under the same state control (in the PRC) or are supported by the population at large (as in Taiwan). It does not mean that there is no more rivalry. Economics and reputation occasionally still cause friction, as in the case of the Ch'ing-shui (central Taiwan) **Cosmic Renewal Festival** in the 1980s. Although the temple is in fact a community temple, the major deity is Kuan-yin, which is originally a Buddhist cult object. Therefore, the temple committee decided to invite Buddhist monks to perform the *chiao* rituals after the temple had been rebuilt, rather than the Taoists, who are the traditional specialists of this celebration. Taoist priests of the area were very upset, but their protest did not move the committee to change its mind.

Such smaller conflicts will arise now and then, but, otherwise, a spirit of mutual respect prevails, especially among the monastic Taoists and Buddhists (see P. Goullart, 1961: 52–59).

C

CALABASH See PLANT SYMBOLISM

CHAI/ZHAI (Purification Fast). The great cosmic renewal festivals of modern Taoism, called *chiao*, are always a combination of *chai* and *chiao*, simply defined as a purification fast followed by offerings and prayers. In ancient times, the two were not necessarily combined. *Chai* were held by numerous rulers as preparation before a sacrifice, and when the Heavenly Masters School was founded in the second century CE, it adopted a number of ancient ritual practices, making them their own, while creating new ones.

It seems that in ancient China, *chai* was a rite of purification of body and mind as preparation for sacrificial offerings. In order to approach the deities, humans had to purify themselves: The mind had to be calmed and freed from desire, the body had to be cleansed by fasting, especially by abstention from meat and liquor, and by sexual continence. The body had to be washed by bathing, and clean or new clothes had to be worn to appear before the deities. These were all preparations made by the chief sacrificer. Various officials would take care of the external conditions of a sacrifice, such as selecting the right victims and sacrificial offerings.

In early Taoism, *chai* rituals developed into new directions. Two new types were created: the "fast of mud and soot" (*t'u-t'an chai*) and the "yellow register fast" (*huang-lu chai*). H. Maspero has written an extensive report on the former (Maspero, 1971/1981: 381–386). It was a sort of purification of the adept from moral transgressions, a rite of confession and penance, that occasionally grew into revival-type wild parties with ecstatic dancing and loud screaming. Mud and soot were rubbed onto the body, a sign of repentance, in order to obtain forgiveness from moral guilt. Such events were followed by a vegetarian banquet, which has inspired some authors to define *chai* as a religious banquet.

The "yellow register" *chai* was a ritual for the benefit of the deceased. The Taoists believed that by acting ethically, an adept could gain special merit and be able to liberate his ancestors from hell up to the seventh generation. The Taoist community would organize special rituals for the salvation of all the deceased.

In later times, Taoism developed new rituals called *chai*. **Lu Hsiu-ching** and **T'ao Hung-ching** are among the masters who reorganized the liturgy; their reforms had a longlasting effect on Taoist ritual, and are still influential today. An example of new *chai* rituals is found in a text from the T'ang period: *Chai-chieh lu* (literally "Fast and Moral Prescriptions Register"). It has been specially studied by R. Malek (1985), who reports that it contains two listings of *chai*: a list of six kinds, and another of twelve kinds (Malek: 178–180). But besides these special lists, the book further discusses other types of *chai* in a less organized way. Malek has thus listed 54 kinds of *chai*, which he briefly describes (181–225). Some are ordinary rituals to be performed during solstices and equinoxes or during particular months. Some *chai* appear to be more important, such as the "golden register fast" and the "yellow register fast."

• *Chin-lu chai* ("golden register fast") is one of the most popular Taoist rituals and was performed "to guarantee the welfare of the imperial house" (M. Strickmann 1978, quoted by Malek: 189). It is probably that its function has been broadened during later T'ang times to include healing of disease and prevention of natural catastrophes.

• *Huang-lu chai* ("yellow register fast"), also a well-known ritual that is performed to liberate the deceased from the netherworld. At first, during the T'ang period, it consisted of prayers for rain, later as prevention of pestilence and for victory over one's enemies. But the major objective was the release of the dead by performing penance on their behalf, and by buying jade and silk, to reconcile the spirits of the netherworld (Malek: 200–204).

• *San-yuan chai* ("three primordials fast"), consisted of confession rituals of one's personal wrongdoings. It alludes to the *san-yuan* and the **Three Officials**, rulers of heaven, earth and water, to whom the Heavenly Masters Taoists of the second century CE already confessed their moral transgressions.

CHAI/ZHAI and ***CHIAO/JIAO*** (or *Chai-chiao*). A very important, central event in the Taoist liturgy is the celebration of *chai* and *chiao*. The two can be separated but are often combined in actual practice, especially since Sung and Yuan times. Contemporary usage of the word *chiao*, celebrated by communities in China, Taiwan, Hong Kong etc., includes *chai* as part of the whole.

In a very simple way, *chai* refers to fasting and purification. In early Heavenly Masters Taoism, *chai* rituals were performed as an atonement for evil-doing: a rite of purification to obtain divine forgiveness. Likewise, in a very simple way, *chiao* refers to sacrificial offerings to the spirit world. For that reason, the expression *chai-chiao* indicates the true chronology of events: first, purification, next, sacrificial offering. It implies that in order to present oneself before the deities with offerings and prayers, one must be spiritually cleansed or morally (as well as physically) pure. (In the Roman Catholic tradition, there is a parallel: Before receiving the Eucharist, one should—ideally—purify oneself through confession.)

The performance of *chai* and *chiao* are a crucial part of the Taoist liturgical repertoire. Already during Sung and Yuan times (if not earlier), emperors asked renowned Taoist priests to perform these grand rituals on their behalf or on behalf of the whole population. The tradition survives today. Reports on *chiao* rituals in Hong Kong and China, and especially in Taiwan, have been published. They have become grandiose affairs, in which the whole local community participates (see **Cosmic Renewal Festival**).

CHANG/ZHANG BROTHERS (or the Three Changs). They were the three leaders of **Great Peace Taoism** (*T'ai-p'ing Tao*), which flourished in the middle of the second century CE in eastern China. Their names are Chang Chueh, Chang Liang, and Chang Pao, who claimed to be the representatives of the Three Powers: heaven, earth, and mankind.

They started a healing cult and organized their territory into a theocratic state: Religious, political, and military powers were all combined in the same individuals. The movement was inspired by

Huang-Lao Taoism and, more particularly, by an early Taoist text, *Great Peace Scripture* (*T'ai-p'ing ching*).

In 184 CE, the movement turned into an open rebellion against the state. (See also **Yellow Turban Rebellion**. About its organization and rituals, see **Great Peace Taoism**.)

CHANG CHUEH/ZHANG JUE (d. 184 CE). He was the oldest of the three Chang brothers who founded the *T'ai-p'ing* (Great Peace) movement in Eastern China in the middle of the Later Han dynasty. In the year 184 CE, the originally religio-political movement turned rebellious, called the **Yellow Turbans**, and came into conflict with the imperial government. Chang Chueh died of illness, and his two brothers were captured and executed in 184. This was the end of a grandiose dream to bring about a millennial period of peace and equality.

Very likely, Chang Chueh's religious organization developed from **Huang-Lao Taoism**, which first appeared in the state of Ch'i during the middle of the Warring States period (475–221 BCE), but also was greatly indebted to the *T'ai-p'ing ching*.

CHANG HENG/ZHANG HENG. He was the son of Chang (Tao-) ling and succeeded his father as the second Heavenly Master at the end of the Han dynasty. Later Taoist followers called him "Hereditary Master."

According to a legend, he is said to have "risen to heaven in broad daylight" and become an immortal in 179 CE, during the reign of Han Emperor Ling (r. 168–188).

As leader of the Heavenly Masters School, his role was not significant; his son, **Chang Lu**, played a more powerful role (*CMTT*: 118–9).

CHANG HSIU/ZHANG XIU. This is a different Chang from the Three Chang Brothers in the east, and from the Three Generations of Changs in the west. He was a Taoist from the end of the Han dynasty. Maspero called him the leader of the Western Yellow Turban movement, who joined the eastern rebellion in 184, but was defeated.

However, the sources are not clear about his exact identity: leader of the Western Yellow Turbans is one identity, but it is also said that:

> Besides being a successful warlord, he had been running a health cult of his own and had acquired the title of "wizard-shaman." (H. Welch, 1957: 115)

In the *Latter Han History* it is said that his followers had to pay five bushels of rice as a tax, and so he was called the "Five Bushels of Rice Teacher."

The relationships between the various groups of Taoist organizations are unclear. Maspero says that **Chang Lu** killed Chang Hsiu and replaced him (1971/81: 375). Welch states that Chang Lu was at first helped by Chang Hsiu, but when Lu realized that Hsiu's new "health cult represented an improvement on his own . . . he proceeded to take it over. He had Chang Hsiu executed" (Welch: 116).

From these confused reports, it seems possible that Chang Hsiu was the intermediary between eastern and western health cults. He was the one who introduced the system of libationers, the five bushels of rice tax, and rituals of confession to the **Three Officials.** Then it must be that Chang Tao-ling's movement came later, and, eventually, through Chang Lu, absorbed the organization of Chang Hsiu (see also **Chang Lu**).

CHANG KUO-LAO/ZHANG GUOLAO (*Emblem*: Bamboo tube with two rods). One of the **Eight Immortals.** He was a recluse living during the seventh and eighth centuries CE. He possessed supernatural powers of magic, such as rendering himself invisible. Pressed by Empress Wu of the T'ang, he agreed to go to court but "at the gate of the Temple of the Jealous Woman" he died and his body began to decay (Werner, 1969: 346). Soon afterward, he was seen again in the mountains. He used to ride a white mule covering immense distances. Often, he is depicted as riding the mule backward. When he arrived at his destination, he would roll up the mule and put it in his sleeve; when he wished to resume his travels, he squirted some water on it and the animal at once reappeared. Emperor Ming Huang wished to attach him to his court; but Chang could not give up his wandering life. On the second summons from court, he disappeared and entered the realm of immortals without suffering bodily dissolution.

CHANG LU/ZHANG LU. The grandson of Chang Tao-ling and third Heavenly Master during the late second and early third century. He built on the work of his grandfather and father, and expanded his organization by setting up a theocratic state in the region of Han-chung (which included part of Szechuan and Shensi provinces). His "kingdom" combined political, religious, and military authority.

It is not clear how much he was indebted to a similar cult organized by **Chang Hsiu** in western China. For a while the two Changs cooperated, until Hsiu was seen as a rival, and was assassinated by Lu (about 190 CE).

Chang Lu ruled over Han-chung for about 30 years (185–215 CE). He divided his "kingdom" into 24 districts, headed by **libationers** (*chi-chiu*): They took care of the needs of the people, especially their spiritual needs. Confession of moral misdeeds was one of the crucial rituals. In this all these late Han movements are alike: Disease is seen as a result of "sin" or moral transgression. Therefore, to be healed, one first had to confess to the Three Officials (or Agents). Written statements were sent to each of them, on a mountaintop for Heaven, buried in the ground for Earth, and submerged in water for Water. "The festival of the Three Agents, San-kuan, seems to have been in the beginning peculiar to Chang Lu's sect" (Maspero, 1971/81: 380). It spread throughout the whole Chinese world and was adopted universally during the third and fourth centuries.

Another feature of Chang Lu's system was the establishment of "lodges (inns) of righteousness" (*yi-she*), for use by travelers. They could stay there up to three nights with free accommodation and food. In general, life in Han-chung was peaceful for about 30 years, probably not only due to Chang Lu's charisma, but also because of the central government's weakness. After the fall of the Han, with the emergence of the Three Kingdoms, the Wei kingdom of the North, under military rule of Ts'ao Ts'ao, started to assert itself. When Ts'ao attacked Han-chung in 215, Chang Lu decided to submit to superior power and was generously rewarded for it.

"Ts'ao Ts'ao heaped honors upon him, bestowed upon him the title of General Tamer-of-the-South, raised him to the rank of marquis . . ." (Maspero: 374) and officially recognized Chang's organization as a legal religious body (without any political authority, of course). Thus, in contrast with the eastern T'ai-p'ing movement, which ended in rebellion and proscription, the western movement of Chang Tao-ling and his successors found its niche in Chinese life and would start on a long history, which continues today (it appears there have been interruptions, however).

This shows, once again, that in China, religion is a political matter. Chang Lu would also find out. He was "requested" to move to the Wei capital with thousands of followers: There, he could be more easily "supervised" by the Wei government. Later, after Wei and the western Chin, many outstanding members of the Heavenly Masters Tao would move to the south, following the court in exile.

Chang Lu has been credited with one of the oldest commentaries on the *TTC*: ***Lao-tzu Hsiang-er chu***. The text had been lost for a long time, but was recovered among the Tun-huang manuscripts.

CHANG PO-TUAN/ZHANG BODUAN (984–1082). A Taoist priest and scholar of the Northern Sung, who was later considered to be the founding patriarch of the **Southern School** of Inner Alchemy. He was a native of T'ien-t'ai in present-day Chekiang. From a young age, he was eager to study and immersed himself in the scriptures of the Three Teachings so that, in the end, he became a specialist in criminal law, bibliography, medicine, divination, strategy, astronomy, geography, and good or bad luck predictions. He served several decades as a government official.

But seeing through the nonsubstantiality of reputation, wealth, and career, his mind (and heart) was focused on the "road to P'eng-lai" and the immortals: hereupon he burned all the documents in the office. For this transgression, he was sent to the south in exile.

During the years 1064–67, he served under Lu Hsien in Kweilin, in charge of important documents. After Lu Hsien was transferred to Chengtu (in 1069), Chang followed him and met a transcendent who transmitted to him secret instructions on the cultivation of inner alchemy. His understanding was fast and deep. He died in 1082 and left behind a famous text titled *Essay on Understanding Reality* (*Wu-chen p'ien*), which explains the principles of inner alchemy. His views were very syncretistic, combining Confucian and Buddhist theories with his Taoist worldview: "Although there are three teachings, the Way(s) is (are) ultimately one."

Chang advocated the dual cultivation of nature and life, but believed that one should first focus on life, only later on nature. This is in contrast with the views of **Wang Che**, founder of Complete Realization Taoism.

Chang's *Wu-chen p'ien* has been reviewed by several later authors; his text is included in the Taoist Canon (*CT* 263; *TT* 122–131). It has greatly influenced later Taoism. An English translation was written by T. Cleary in 1987. (See also L. Kohn, 1993: 313–319.)

CHANG SAN-FENG/ZHANG SANFONG. A famous Taoist from the Yuan and Ming dynasties. One of his major "legendary" contributions was the creation of the *T'ai-chi ch'uan* system, but there is no historical evidence to support this. Indeed, an impressive network of legends has been built around this figure, but "we know next to nothing about Chang San-feng's historical existence and his thought" (A. Seidel, in de Bary, 1970: 484).

Popular legends were created around him, because he was a "holy eccentric," and perhaps more important, his advice was sought by Ming emperors, who did not succeed in luring him to their palace. But that did not stop them from bestowing honorable titles on him; he was even canonized by Emperor Ying-tsung (r. 1457–1465) in 1459.

Chang San-feng was a "wandering Taoist": It is believed that he spent many years on the Wu-tang mountains (in Hupei), and later traveled to Chengtu (in Szechuan). It is very likely that he was promoted as the creator of *T'ai-chi ch'uan* because Mt. Wu-tang was the cult center of the martial deity Chen-wu or Dark Warrior (also called

Hsuan-t'ien Ta-ti), "who revealed the military skill of boxing to San-feng in a dream" (Seidel: 506).

Other credits given to Chang were that he was "The Master of Sexual Practices" and a deity of a spirit medium cult. He was also nominated as a minor "god of riches," which is almost ludicrous, because he practiced a simple lifestyle to the extreme.

The dates of his life are not known, but he had the makings of an immortal in his own personality: His hagiographies describe him "as exceedingly tall (seven feet); looking as if he had the longevity of a turtle and the immortality of a crane. He had enormous eyes and ears, a beard bristling like the blades of halberds . . . he could sleep in the snow without catching cold, could eat huge quantities of food at one sitting or fast for months, and could climb mountains as if flying" (Seidel: 485). No wonder he is still remembered today.

CHANG SHENG/ZHANG SHENG. He was the son of **Chang Lu,** and became the fourth Heavenly Master. After Chang Lu's surrender to the aggression of Ts'ao Ts'ao in 215 CE, he and his family were forced to move to the Wei capital. Chang Sheng was enfeoffed.

According to legend, he moved to Mount Lung-hu during the years 307–312 of the Western Chin, but there is no historical evidence to support this. The Heavenly Masters' move to Lung-hu Shan is dated much later (perhaps during the T'ang era).

Another legend states that he succeeded in producing an alchemical pill and, as a result, became an immortal of the third class: through **body liberation** (*shih-chieh*).

The Mongol court gave him an honorary title in 1341. (*CMTT*: 119)

CHANG TAO-LING/ZHANG DAOLING. He is the acclaimed founder of the **Heavenly Masters** School of Taoism (*T'ien-shih Tao*). Although his biography has been overlaid with legend, it is accepted that he was a historical person, living in the first two centuries CE. His dates are given as 34–156 CE. He founded a movement called "Five Bushels of Rice Taoism" (*Wu-tou-mi tao*), as new members were told to contribute five bushels of rice as a membership fee. Official sources call him, in derision, "rice thief."

In contemporary religious art, Chang Tao-ling is represented as a powerful, charismatic personality with frightening eyes and a black face. He is a strong exorcist who scares evil spirits away. He created talismans for healing and exorcism that are still used by Taoist priests today. Chang Tao-ling talismans show him brandishing a sword and seated on a tiger. His seal of office is placed near him.

Whether his traditional biography is historically reliable has been questioned. But contemporary sources relate the following as factual information.

Born in 34 CE in what is today Chekiang, from an early age he was interested in spiritual matters, studying the *TTC* as well as astronomy and geomancy. He enrolled in an institute of higher learning, where he studied the Chinese classics. Later, he moved to the land of Shu (today's Szechuan), where he cultivated the Tao on Mount Ho-ming and where he wrote a book in 24 chapters. Tradition has it that he received revelations from **Lao-tzu** himself, most importantly secrets for healing disease. He worshipped the deified Lao-tzu as T'ai-shang Lao-chün (Lord Lao Most High) and chose the *TTC* as his basic scripture.

Whether he was invested by Lao-tzu as a new religious leader is not certain, but he called himself "Teacher of the Three Heavens, (*San-t'ien fa-shih*), Perfected [Sage] of Orthodox Unity (*cheng-yi chen-jen*)." Because of his healing and exorcistic powers, he strongly influenced the people, attracted numerous disciples, and organized a theocratic state in Szechuan. (See **Heavenly Masters School**). He invested his followers' ample contributions in alchemical ingredients and set out to produce the pill of immortality. Legend says that he succeeded: With two of his closest disciples, he rose to heaven in broad daylight, thus becoming an immortal.

His grandson, **Chang Lu**, continued to rule his theocratic state until 215 CE, when he submitted to political and military pressure and surrendered to Ts'ao Ts'ao. His great-grandson, Chang Sheng, moved to **Mount Lung-hu** (Dragon-and-Tiger Mountain) between the years 307–317. This mountain has remained the center of the school; its temples and buildings are being restored today.

CHAOS (*Hun-tun/Hundun*). Chaos is a mythical theme related to "creation." As such it is not very prominent in the Chinese classics, but has a place of eminence in Taoism. In the *TTC* and the **Chuang-tzu**, as well as in the *Huai-nan-tzu*, there are several passages referring to chaos as a state of the universe before the origin of heaven and earth, and although not fully developed, these passages refer to a possible ancient myth that has been lost in subsequent literature. It is only later, in several scriptures of the Taoist religion, that creation of the world out of original chaos is fully discussed.

> . . . in early Taoist texts . . . the mythical *hun-tun* can be identified with the ultimate principle of the Tao as the rhythmic source and ground of life . . . (N. Girardot, *ER* 3: 217)

A clear allusion to a primitive state of chaos is found in the *TTC* (Chapter 25: 1, 3–4):

> There was something undifferentiated and yet complete,
> which existed before heaven and earth . . .
> It may be considered the mother of the universe.
> I do not know its name; I call it Tao.
>   (Chan, 1963: 152)

Heaven and earth are our physical universe, born out of chaos, that was not yet fully developed, but contained all the "seeds," or potentialities, of future differentiated beings. Chaos then has a very positive meaning, although it must be said that chaos cannot stay chaos forever. It must develop all its potentials. This is expressed in other Taoist texts, such as the *Huai-nan-tzu*, which likes to speculate on how the world must have come into being:

> Heaven and Earth inchoate and unformed: The Great Inception [or chaos]
> The [Tao] begins in the nebulous void.
> The nebulous void produces spacetime.
> Spacetime produces primordial [*ch'i*]
> [*Ch'i*] divides; the light and pure forms Heaven,
> the heavy and turbid forms Earth. (J. Major, 1993: 25)

Several interesting conclusions can be drawn from this: There is no mention of a creator-god, a personal being who brings order to chaos (as in the *Genesis* story of the Bible). The transition from chaos to an ordered universe is a spontaneous transformation, the Tao operating out of its own inner compulsion.

Two kinds of *ch'i* or energetic powers issued from the original chaos: What the Taoists call "heaven" and "earth" are two products of *ch'i* and, because of their common origin, are both spiritual-material (the distinction is actually not made, but has important consequences in the philosophy of the cosmos).

This speculation about the coming into existence of the cosmos reflects a rather simplistic understanding of reality—in particular the sharp distinction between "light" and "heavy" elements in our cosmos are naive and unscientific. But then, cosmological speculation needs not be scientific.

The *Chuang-tzu* has preserved the remains of a cosmogonic myth (Chapter 7, Watson, 1970: 97) in an anecdote about *hun-tun* (another name for "chaos"). His friends had noticed that *Hun-tun* did not have any openings in his body, so they decided to bore him some. On the seventh day Hun-tun died ("bored to death"). This mythical leftover seems to project a negative light on the nature of civilization, and is perhaps an example of Taoism's negative attitude toward culture and learning, as if chaos is better than growth.

In the Taoist religion, the theme of chaos giving birth to creation is further developed. But here a personified Tao, the Venerable Lord, appears to be the grand initiator of creation. In L. Kohn's translation of a text dating perhaps from the T'ang dynasty, she describes the various stages of creation: Out of a "Barren Nonbeing" which "transformed hundreds of millions of times . . ." emerged the "Vast Prime," then "Coagulated Prime," then "Great Antecedence" (during which stage human beings appeared); then came "Grand Initiation," next "Grand Immaculate" (*T'ai-su*, better rendered as "Grand Simplicity" or "Plainness"). Only after that came "Chaos." What happened then and later is a strange mix of fantasy and symbolism, not easily made sense of (see L. Kohn, 1993: 35–43). It is also not clear why "chaos" made its appearance after human beings and animals had emerged.

CHEN-KAO See *DECLARATIONS OF THE PERFECTED*

CH'EN T'UAN/CHEN TUAN (871–989). A well-known Taoist from Chen Yuan/Zhen Yuan in Honan province. During the Later T'ang period (930–933), he attempted to pass the civil service examinations, but was not successful. He then retired to **Mount Wu-tang** and became a recluse. He practiced breathing exercises and abstained from food for over 20 years. However, he drank several glasses of wine every day.

Emperor Shih-tsung (r. 955–959) of the Later Chou dynasty summoned him to court and inquired about the secrets of **alchemy** and **immortality**. Ch'en answered that the emperor should pay more attention to good government instead. Invited to serve in his administration, Ch'en turned down the offer, yet received the honorary title "Mr. White Cloud."

It was alleged that he often went into a long sleep, lasting more than a hundred days. This was one of his methods of spiritual cultivation. Hence, he was known as the "Sleeping Recluse."

During the reign of Sung Emperor T'ai-tsung (r. 927–997) he went to the capital and advised the emperor to choose men of talent in his administration and to keep away ministers of ill repute; further, to reduce the high taxes imposed on the people, and to give substantial rewards to the military. The emperor greatly valued his advice and honored him with the title of Mr. Hsi-yi/Xiyi ("*aspiring* after Po-*yi*," a famous recluse of ancient times).

Ch'en T'uan was an expert on the *Yi ching*, which he had studied for many years. In his commentaries, he emphasized the use of diagrams. He had a strong influence on Neo-Confucianist thought. It has been said that Chou Tun-yi's (1017–1073) famous *T'ai-chi* (Supreme

Ultimate) diagram was based on Ch'en T'uan's *Wu-chi* (Ultimateless) diagram. (See *TR* 2.1, 1990.)

CHEN-WU TA-TI See HSUAN-T'IEN SHANG-TI

CH'ENG-HUANG SHEN See CITY GOD

CHENG-YI/ZHENG1 TAOISM. The name of a School of Taoism, translated as "Orthodox Unity School." It coincides with **Heavenly Masters Taoism,** at least starting with the Yuan (Mongol) dynasty (1260–1368).

Indeed, in 1304, Yuan Emperor Ch'eng-tsung (r. 1295–1308) invested the 38th Heavenly Master, Chang Yü-ts'ai, with the title of "Master (or Leader) of Orthodox Unity" (*Cheng-yi chiao-chu*). From then on, the Lung-hu School (Heavenly Masters Taoism) was renamed Cheng-yi Tao.

This imperial decision had some precedents. Previously, Emperor Shih-tsu (Khubilai Khan) (r. 1260–94) had sent a secret messenger to Mount Lung-hu to interview the 35th Heavenly Master, Chang K'o-ta, in order to cast an oracle about the unification of the country. The answer was that after 20 years, the country would be unified. Later, Khubilai summoned the 36th Heavenly Master, Chang Tsung-yen, to his court. He put him in charge of all southern Taoism, gave him a silver seal, and honored him with a title *chen-jen* (perfected). All later Heavenly Masters were called *chen-jen* by the Mongol court. They inherited the registers (*fu-lu*) of Mount Ko-tsao, Mount Lung-hu, and Mount Mao, and administered Taoism south of the (Yang-tse) river (*chiang-nan*).

Yuan Emperor Wu-tsung (r. 1308–12) gave posthumous honorary titles to Chang Heng and Chang Lu, calling them "perfected lords" (*chen-chün*). His successor, Emperor Shun (r. 1333–41), extended the title to all Heavenly Masters from the fourth, Chang Sheng, to the thirty-fourth. Especially honored was the 38th successor, already mentioned, who received titles and a golden seal. It is then obvious that the Mongol court favored and patronized the Cheng-yi School, which flourished as a result. Most of the Taoist temples and monasteries in the south were under their control. The Cheng-yi Taoists were allowed to have their own home shrines (offices), were not forbidden to marry, and were not ordered to live in monasteries. Their rules of discipline were not as strict as those of Complete Realization Taoism. From the Yuan period until the present time, the Complete Realization School and the Cheng-yi School are the two major Taoist organizations.

It is thus quite clear that Heavenly Masters Taoism and Cheng-yi

Taoism refer to the same school. The name *Cheng-yi* started to be used during the Yuan period. However, there seems to be some historical reason why *cheng-yi* was selected. When **Chang Tao-ling** was still in spiritual seclusion in Szechuan, he claimed that T'ai-shang Lao-chün had transmitted to him the "correct teachings of the Three Heavens" (*san-t'ien cheng-fa*) and had given him the titles "Teacher of the Three Heavens" (*san-t'ien fa-shih*), and "Realized Man of Orthodox Unity" (*cheng-yi chen-jen*) (*CMTT*: 118). Perhaps this latter title lingered on in the Taoist tradition, only to surface again during the Yuan period (*CMTT*: 15). (See also **Heavenly Masters Taoism**.)

CH'I/QI (Breath, Vital Energy). A central concept in Taoist philosophical speculation, anthropology, and spiritual practices, as well as in Neo-Confucian metaphysics.

The etymology of the character is significant: the upper part and radical means "air, vapor, steam," while the lower part means "rice." Thus the basic meaning of *ch'i* indicates steam arising from cooking rice. By extension, it came to mean "breath" (which in winter is very similar to steam). Because in many cultures "breath" signifies "life," a further extension became understandable: "vital spirit, vitality, vital breath, life energy, vital force."

As the concept *ch'i* developed, it took on two fundamentally different dimensions: a cosmic dimension and an individual dimension. In this respect, it has parallels in other traditions: The same vital principles or energy course through both the cosmos and individual beings:

> The same concept exists in the Indian tradition as *prana*, in the Greek tradition as *pneuma*, in the Latin tradition as *spiritus*, and in the Hebrew tradition as *ruah*. (V. Mair, 1990: 137)

In the ***Huai-nan-tzu***, *ch'i* is the creative force that generated the universe. From an initial state of chaos, spacetime developed that produced the primordial *ch'i*. Out of this primordial *ch'i*, yang *ch'i* and yin *ch'i* came forth, dividing into heaven and earth (J. Major, 1993: 62). All of the later 10,000 beings were produced by heaven and earth, and thus contain yin and yang energies in their very being. This analysis clearly shows the double nature or dimension of *ch'i* (as it also explains the ultimate oneness of all beings).

In Neo-Confucianism, especially in the work of Chu Hsi, the same word *ch'i* is used in a cosmic dimension, but very different from Taoism: It is part of the dichotomy of *li* (principle) and *ch'i* (primary "matter"). All beings are constituted by *li* and *ch'i*: *li* is their essential nature, a sort of blueprint; *ch'i* makes the actual embodiment of *li* possible in concrete beings. It is because of possible defects in *ch'i* that nature is subject to imperfections.

Ch'i, as the "breath of life" in all living beings, is a particularization of cosmic energy. Life is the coming together of vital energies; death is their scattering (*Chuang-tzu*, Chapter 22—Watson, 1970: 235). At birth, each living being is endowed with a certain amount of *ch'i* (*yuan-ch'i*), as well as with *ching* and *shen* (see **Three Primary Vitalities**); when it runs out or is cut off in midstream, death ensues (compare with a car filled with gas; when the gas tank is empty, the motor "dies"). The Taoists, however, believe that if one follows the right practices, the level of *ch'i* can be renewed, replenished, restored. Then, longevity and even immortality can be reached,

> . . . for energy is the life force and the Taoist loves life. To be alive is good; to be more alive is better; to be always alive is best. Hence the Taoist immortality cults. (H. Smith, 1994: 130)

(For methods of cultivating the *ch'i*, see **Breathing Exercises**; see also **Inner Alchemy** and **Ch'i-kung**).

CH'I-CHEN See SEVEN PERFECTED

CHI-CHIU See LIBATIONER

CH'I-KUNG/QIGONG (Translated as "work of the *ch'i*" or "working the energy"). A series of physical health practices, performed either in motion or in stillness. Although manifestly a set of outer body movements, they also imply breath regulation and concentration of the mind.

These exercises are rooted in ancient practices and are not specifically or essentially Taoist. They are not even essentially religious in nature and could be performed purely for health reasons (similar to yoga exercises). However, *ch'i-kung* has some connections with Taoism, especially with inner alchemy.

In recent years, *ch'i-kung* has become extremely popular in China, even overshadowing *t'ai-chi ch'uan*, with which it has some similarities. Many publications (in Chinese) have hit the market. It appears that modern authors emphasize the nonreligious aspects of *ch'i-kung* to keep it free from irrational and superstitious elements. Instead, they stress the scientific side of the practice.

In a recent study by Kunio Miura, it is said that *ch'i-kung* can be divided according to martial practice and health practice. The latter is subdivided into two groups: techniques applied to others (laying on of hands, massage, acupuncture, chiropractice), and those applied to oneself (either without body movement or with movement). Those practices requiring movement are comparable to *t'ai-chi ch'uan* in that there are established sets of movements, which one has to learn by heart. Because *ch'i-kung* centers on breathing exercises, the health benefits can be astounding. But, as K. Miura states:

> The modern age of science and technology has brought changes in the understanding, description, and evaluation of the practices. Transcendence or immortality is out of the question. Spirit or spirits don't play any significant role anymore. Trance states are discouraged, since traditional ways of understanding and controlling them have been lost. Scientific man shies from the supernatural. The *qi* itself is no longer the primordial creative power of the universe, but merely one force among others, somewhat like electricity. The gods are dethroned, the cosmos is made measurable, and man remains strictly within the confines of the known. (K. Miura, in L. Kohn, 1989: 357)

Whereas Western medicine remains skeptical of the scientific value of *ch'i-kung* (and traditional Chinese medicine in general), religious practitioners may deplore the "disregard of the sacred" and the loss of basic cosmology and theory out of which *ch'i-kung* developed. (For more details, see the informative article by K. Miura, in L. Kohn, 1989: 331–362.)

CHIAO See COSMIC RENEWAL FESTIVAL

CH'IN SHIH HUANG-TI See FIRST EMPEROR OF CHINA

CHIN-TAN P'AI See GOLD CINNABAR TAOISM

CHING/JING (Seminal fluid, seminal energy). It is one of the **Three Primordial Vitalities** (*san-yuan*) with which each human being (and animal) is born. The etymology of the character *ching* indicates the refined part of rice as its basic meaning; its extended meaning refers to the most subtle part in something, in a physical body. In the human body, it refers, broadly speaking, to the various fluid secretions: saliva, gastric juices, sweat, male semen. In a narrower sense, it refers only to sexual or seminal secretions, a body's "essence par excellence."

Since saliva and seminal fluid are the principal aspects of *ching*, they must be strengthened and accumulated. Production of saliva and its swallowing down is encouraged; it is called "liquor of immortality."

In terms of Yin-yang philosophy, *ching* (liquid) is the body's yin element; *ch'i* (aerial) is its yang element. Through cultivation, the two must be unified. (See also *ch'i*.)

CHING/JING (Scripture). Has a variety of meanings that partially over-lap with "classic," "authoritative writing." The earliest use in Chi-nese refers to the "Five or Six Classics," often called "Confucian" classics, but this is not entirely correct, because they were not created by Confucius, nor exclusively used in Confucian learning. In any case, the five or six books were invested with authority, they are "ca-nonical" writings, although their authority is not based on revelations. They are the Book of Odes (*Shih ching/shijing*), the Book of Histori-cal Documents (*Shu ching/shujing*), the Book of Changes (*Yi ching/yijing*), the Book of Ritual (*Li ching/lijing*), the Spring-and-Autumn Annals (*Ch'un-ch'iu/cunqiu*), and the now lost Book of Music (*Yueh ching/yuejing*). Confucius may have used earlier versions of these texts in his own teaching. The earliest texts of Taoism, the philosophi-cal writings of Lao-tzu and Chuang-tzu, were originally not called *ching*. They received this title only during the T'ang dynasty, when Taoism was sponsored by some emperors.

When Buddhism spread to China, their many sutras were translated as *ching*, and much later, the Christian scriptures, as well as the Mus-lim Koran, were named *ching* (the "Holy Bible" became *Sheng-ching;* the Koran, *Ku-lan ching*).

Many of the writings of the Taoist religion carry the word *ching* in their title, and a great number of them are believed to have been re-vealed by divine beings. A great many were not revealed but com-posed by human authors, whose names and dates are often known to us.

CH'ING-CHING CHING See *PURITY AND TRANQUILLITY SCRIP-TURE*

CH'ING-T'AN See PURE CONVERSATION

CH'ING-WEI/QINGWEI SCHOOL ("Pure Tenuity" or "Clarified Tenuity"). A school of Taoism founded by a woman at the end of the T'ang period, about 900. It has also been called a school of Tantric Taoism (M. Saso, 1978: 11), whose magic derives from Mount Mao and Mount Hua (western peak). The school combined inner **alchemy** and the use of talismans-registers (*fu-lu*), which it claimed proceeded from Yuan-shih T'ien-tsun, residing in the Ch'ing-wei heaven.

The school developed widely during the Sung dynasty; it had many followers. Its goals are similar to those of the **Shen-hsiao School**, but it uses different methods. A number of its "thunder techniques" are included in the great Taoist compendium, *Tao-fa hui-yuan* ("Corpus of Taoist Ritual") (*CT* 1220, *TT* 884–941). The school's "thunder methods" are their special focus. Following the Mao Shan meditative tradition,

> . . . the power of thunder is stored in the five central organs and in the gall bladder. From the gall bladder, it lights the alchemical furnace within the microcosm, that is, the lower cinnabar field in the belly of man. (Saso: 237)

Through this kind of meditation, thunder is summoned to purify the inner organs. This is inner alchemy, but the power of thunder can also be used to cure disease and to counteract the effects of black magic. (See J. Boltz, 1987: 38–41.)

CH'IU CH'U-CHI/QIU CHUJI (1148–1227), also named Ch'ang-ch'un-tzu/Changchunzi. At first a direct disciple of Ch'uan-chen founder **Wang Che,** he became the school's second patriarch and founded his own branch, named Lung-men p'ai ("Dragon Gate Sect").

A native of Shantung province, he lost his parents when still very young. At age 19, he left his adoptive family and became a Taoist. In 1168, he met Wang Che and became his disciple. After Wang passed away in 1170, Ch'iu became for six years a recluse in Shansi province, next moved to Lung-men mountain, also in the same province, where he stayed for seven more years. He attracted many followers through his ascetic lifestyle and won the admiration of scholars by his literary works. His reputation spread gradually.

In 1188, he was summoned to the capital of Peking by Chin Emperor Shih-tsung (r. 1162–1189), where he obtained a friendly reception.

With the rise of Mongol power, Shantung became a strategic area contested by three powers: the Mongols, the Sung, and the Chin. At the time, Ch'iu lived as a recluse in Ch'i-hsia (Shantung) and was courted by many. Both the Sung and the Chin wanted him to be on their side, but Ch'iu refused to commit himself to either. But when Genghis Khan (1162–1227), during his expedition in Central Asia, sent an envoy to summon Ch'iu in 1219, Ch'iu obliged. He realized that Mongol power was rising and would probably rule China in the future; Genghis' invitation could not be ignored. In 1220, Ch'iu, already 72 years old, set out on the journey with 18 disciples. After much hardship, his party reached the Hindu Kush ("Snow Mountains") in April 1222, where Genghis Khan's headquarters were located.

Ch'iu had several audiences with the Mongol leader, and found him receptive to many of his ideas. Since a war was going on, Ch'iu advised the Khan to restraint in killing: this was a basic requirement for someone who wished to rule the world. Asked about rulership, Ch'iu answered that worship of heaven and the love of one's subjects were the cardinal virtues. Asked whether he possessed the elixir of immortality, Ch'iu said "no," but claimed to know how to achieve longevity. The secret was to purify one's mind, to reduce desires, and to practice sexual moderation.

Genghis was pleased with the advice and called Ch'iu an "immortal" (*shen-hsien*). Ch'iu returned in 1223, after being invested by Genghis with the charge of all Taoist clergy in China. As a result, the Ch'uan-chen order flourished. Ch'iu settled in the White Cloud Monastery in Peking, where he died in 1227. His journey to Central Asia was recorded by a disciple. (See Waley, 1931.) Ch'iu is still worshipped as a patriarch and patron saint of the Lung-men branch of Ch'uan-chen Taoism.

CHOU See TALISMANS

CH'U TEXTS (*Ch'u Tz'u/Chuci*). A collection of poetic songs from the state of Ch'u: a large southern state during the Chou dynasty. It was defeated by the state of Ch'in in 223 BCE, and annexed to the Ch'in empire.

This collection is the second oldest anthology of ancient Chinese poetry (modeled after the more than 300-poem collection, titled *Shih ching,* "Classic of Odes," one of the five Chinese classics). It contains more than 70 poems, several grouped into cycles of nine. Originally, about half were attributed to Ch'ü Yuan, a statesman and poet from the fourth century BCE. When the king rejected his counsel, Ch'ü went into exile and ended his life by jumping into the Mi-lo river. Several of the poems express anger at the king and feelings of desperation.

The monograph by D. Hawkes (1959) provides a sound analysis, plus translation of all the poems. It appears that the collection was put together during the second century CE by Wang Yi. But Ch'ü Yuan's authorship must be restricted: many others imitated the genre during the three centuries following Ch'ü's death in the fourth century BCE.

The Ch'u texts are discussed here because of their connection with Taoism. Hawkes discovered Taoist influence in several poems. But more often, the poems reflect the religious ideas of the south, centering around ancestor cult, animism, and shamanism. Some express the ecstatic practices of Ch'u religion. *Li Sao* ("On Encountering Sorrow") is a good example: It describes escape from human misery, and journey into the supernatural world (Hawkes: 22). Ch'ü Yuan was the first to use this theme, but many later imitators were inspired by it. Ch'ü himself probably found the theme in the recitals of Ch'u shamans, journeying to the lands of the spirits.

Another famous poem is *Yuan Yu* ("Far-Off Journey"). Hawkes calls it "a Taoist answer to *Li Sao*" (Hawkes: 81). In this case, in contrast with *Li Sao*, the celestial journey does not end in despair but in triumphant fulfillment. Hawkes finds here references to yoga techniques and Han Taoist hagiology. *Hsi Shih* ("Sorrow for Truth Betrayed") is another song strongly influenced by beliefs of Han Taoism.

Although Ch'ü Yuan was a contemporary of Chuang-tzu, there is hardly any concrete evidence of his influence on the Ch'u texts, except in a negative way. Chuang-tzu (in Chapter 4 and elsewhere) advises against taking up government positions: The fickleness of kings is something dreadful. One may be in favor one day, rejected or even executed the next day. It is better to be useless and live out one's years. In many of the songs, the same theme is expressed in verses of anger, disappointment, disbelief, and despair, because rejection by the king, often due to jealousy, slander, and flattery, is exactly what happened. It drove several of the poets to despair and perhaps suicide.

Overall the Ch'u collection of songs testify to the religious spirit of the South. During the Six Dynasties period, this kind of religious experience (ecstatic shamanism) blended with the newly introduced Taoism of the Heavenly Masters School to inspire a new type of Taoism in the Great Purity and Ling-pao movements.

CHU-KO LIANG/ZHUGE LIANG. A legendary Taoist military strategist from the Three Kingdoms period in the service of Liu Pei, descendant of the Han imperial house, and ruler of southwest China, Shu (Szechuan). His marvelous exploits in the wars against the two rival kingdoms (Wei in the North, and Wu in the South) are narrated in the popular novel *Romance of the Three Kingdoms.*

He has been deified as K'ung-ming Hsien-shih (First Teacher K'ung-Ming), but his worship is not as important as his popularity as a national hero. No temples have been reported in Taiwan, although he is one of a divine "quartet": the Four "Lord-Benefactors" (see also **Director of Destiny**). His image is occasionally found in secondary shrines.

CH'UAN-CHEN TAOISM See COMPLETE REALIZATION SCHOOL

CHUANG-LIN HSU TAO-TSANG/ZHUANGLIN XU DAOZANG. A collection of Taoist ritual manuals currently in use in northern Taiwan, collected and edited by Michael Saso. It contains 25 volumes, published by Ch'eng-wen Publishing, Taipei, 1975. All the texts are in calligraphy. The title Chuang-Lin refers to the Chuang and Lin families from the city of Hsinchu in northern Taiwan, who made their manuscripts available for reproduction. Except for the introduction in volume 1 (pages 1–33), which is in English, the bulk of the set consists of Chinese texts, only useful to Taoist practitioners and specialist scholars of Taoism.

The collection consists of four sections, following the particular type of ritual in which the texts are used:

- *Gold Registers* (*chin-lu*), texts used during the Cosmic Renewal Festival: 50 texts (vol. 1–14);
- *Yellow Registers* (*huang-lu*), manuals used during the rituals for the dead, funerals: 19 texts (vol. 15–18);
- *Esoteric Texts* (*wen-chien* and *mi-chueh*), texts explaining the esoteric rubrics of "orthodox Taoist ritual": 10 texts (vol. 19–20);
- *Shen-hsiao* or *Lü Shan* texts, used by the Redhead Taoists: 25 texts (vol. 21–25).

In total, the collection contains 104 texts.

What is interesting here is that the Chuang-Lin collection, used by Taoist families of "orthodox" Taoism, still includes the "small rites" of the "unorthodox" Redhead Taoists. It shows that the ritual repertoire of Blackhead Taoists overlaps with that of their competitors, which makes it almost impossible to uphold the often repeated principle that Blackheads perform rituals for the dead, while Redheads perform the liturgy for the living.

One final comment seems appropriate: Although no comparative study has been made so far to check whether the texts in this collection (especially parts 1–3) are also included in the Taoist Canon, there is a strong suspicion that most are indeed in the official Taoist Canon. If that is correct, the title *Hsü Tao-tsang* ("Supplement to the *Tao-tsang*") is not well chosen and sounds, in fact, rather pretentious. Instead, the collection could have been titled: "Ritual Manuals of the Chuang-Lin Families."

CHUANG-TZU/ZHUANGZI: THE PERSON. The Taoist author named Chuang-tzu ("Master Chuang"), whose personal name is Chuang Chou/Zhuang Zhou, is estimated to have lived in the fourth century BCE, between 399 and 295 BCE (as Wing-tsit Chan, 1963, suggests). He was probably a contemporary of the Confucian scholar Mencius, although their writings do not mention any mutual acquaintance.

Chuang-tzu was a native of a place called Meng, situated in today's Honan province, at that time part of the state of Sung. This state did not have much political clout, but its mark of distinction was that here the descendants of the defeated Shang dynasty were enfeoffed "in order that they might carry on the sacrifices to their illustrious ancestors" (B. Watson, 1970: 1–2). Chuang-tzu's connection with the Sung state would explain the background of his thinking: "skepticism and mystical detachment" (Watson: 2), so much in contrast with the more optimistic vision of Confucianism.

From his writings, especially the "Seven Inner Chapters," Chuang-tzu appears as a brilliant thinker, an ironical mind, an iconoclast even, who smiles at the narrow-minded concepts and customs of society. Although the text attributed to him may be corrupt in some places, his message of transcendence and freedom comes through clearly and strongly.

His personality also shines bright through the inclusion of several biographic anecdotes: They cannot be given strict historical credit, but they "smell" like the work of his close associates or disciples and probably reflect true life situations. They put some meat on the meager skeleton of historical evidence.

Several anecdotal stories relate Chuang-tzu's relationship with Hui-tzu, a master who belonged to the School of Logic. Although they were good friends and excellently matched opponents in philosophic dispute, Chuang-tzu disliked logic and distrusted language, too often abused. The anecdotes are delightful "short" stories of dialogues between Master Chuang and Master Hui, and give us a lively image of Chuang-tzu's technique of argument. To quote just one example from Chapter 17, titled "Autumn Floods": The two masters were strolling along the Hao River, when Chuang-tzu noticed a school of fish down in the water. "See how these minnows swim around as they please!" he said. "That is what fish really enjoy!" Hui-tzu, skeptical in his logic responds: "You are not a fish; how do you know what fish enjoy?" Chuang-tzu said, "You are not me, how do you know I don't know . . ." Hui-tzu agreed, but was not convinced: "I admit I don't know what you know, but it still proves that you don't know what fish enjoy!" Chuang-tzu then said: "Let's get back to your original question: You asked me how [whence] I know what fish enjoy—so you already implied that I knew it. Well, I know it from standing here along the river." (paraphrase of Watson: 188–9).

Here we see the deep difference of knowing things logically or through immediate intuition. Chuang-tzu is an intuitive thinker, who frustrates the logical mind but keeps delighting those who trust their own basic instincts and intuitions.

(For other amusing anecdotes on the "use of the useless," see Chapter 1, Watson: 34–35; on "government," see Chapter 17—Watson: 187–8.)

CHUANG-TZU/ZHUANGZI: **THE TEXT.** The transmitted text, edited by "Neo-Taoist" philosopher **Kuo-hsiang** (d. 312 CE) consists of three sections: the so-called inner chapters (Chapters 1–7), possibly written by Chuang-tzu himself; the "outer chapters" (Chapters 8–22); and the "miscellaneous chapters" (Chapters 23–33). It is probable that Kuo-hsiang cut out part of the existing text and gave the titles to each chapter, which we still know today. But many historical and literary questions remained unsolved until modern scholarship started to tackle the problem. No external evidence exists about the time of composition, nor about the actual authorship. It has been assumed that the *TTC* was older than the *Chuang-tzu*, and one still finds senseless statements in scholarly works that Chuang-tzu was a student of Lao-tzu. This is ludicrous. The "inner chapters" were certainly written before the *TTC*, possibly by the master himself, but in any case by someone close to him, like a direct disciple. The other chapters have been written at various times. A. Graham has made an intensive study of the text and has proposed approximate dates for the different "streams" of thought present in the 33 chapters (Graham, 1981: 27–28):

- Chapters 1–7: Chuang-tzu's own writings (4th c. BCE);
- Chapters 8–10, half of 11: primitivist stream (about 205 BCE);
- Chapters 11 (2nd half), 12–14 & 33: syncretist stream (2nd c. BCE);
- Chapters 28–31: "Yangist miscellany" (see **Yang Chu**), (about 200 BCE).

Other chapters are partially assigned to particular streams, but no exact dates are offered:

- Chapters 15–16 (a Chinese source dates them between Ch'in and Han);
- Chapters 17–22: school of Chuang-tzu;
- Chapters 23–27 & 32: "rag bag" (heterogeneous and fragmented).

Graham's analysis is mainly based on inner criticism: What we summarily call the *Chuang-tzu* does not have a predominant inner consistency. There are obviously different streams of thought present, so that today we realize that the whole collection of essays was written over a few centuries, between Chuang-tzu's own time (perhaps from around 340–320 BCE) and when his school or related schools flourished (perhaps until about 150 BCE). The date 150 BCE is tentative: It is the time of Han Emperor Wu's rise to power and his adoption of Confucianism as the state orthodoxy. That would certainly influence the fate of Taoism.

Another consideration that few *Chuang-tzu* specialists have proposed so far may indirectly throw light on the composition of some chapters. It is the way in which the various authors depict Confucius. The 33 chapters of the Chuang-tzu are usually subdivided into separate episodes, sometimes stories or anecdotes, theoretic discussions, or dialogues. They are clearly separated, although not numbered. (For instance, in Chapter 14, there are seven episodes, in Chapter 23, there are 12, etc.)

When focusing on those chapters in which Confucius or an immediate disciple appears, we get a great surprise: In the whole book, there are 46 such episodes spread over the three sections ("inner": 9; "outer": 25; misc.: 12). This does not yet include other chapters in which Confucian principles are criticized without naming them. What is more astounding as well as puzzling, however, is the way in which the sage is portrayed: Sometimes he is attacked, ridiculed, or criticized as a bombast or ignorant bore, sometimes Confucius admired skilled persons (who embody some Taoist principle); in other places, he is instructed by **Lao Tan** (Lao-tzu) because he has not yet quite "got it"; and finally, in over a dozen episodes, he appears as an enlightened Taoist sage, discussing Taoist principles as brilliantly as if he were Lao Tan himself.

One wonders about the rationale behind these various presentations. One speculation is that the different depictions may be connected with different time periods. At first, Confucius was not a great competitor with Taoism, but as time went on, the schools accentuated their differences and may have become rivals to gain official favor; finally, once Confucianism became enshrined as the official learning, it may have become dangerous to criticize Confucius. It was politically safer to praise him as a great sage. This interpretation is worthwhile to pursue and may or may not confirm earlier presumptions about dating the *Chuang-tzu.*

Whatever transpires about authorships and dates, it is beyond doubt that Chuang-tzu was a brilliant thinker and attracted other bright minds, who continued the master's teaching. In many of the later chapters (such as Chapters 17 and 22) we find jewels of literary composition, even if some of those chapters have been "butchered" by later editors. The final Chapter 33 presents a brilliant overview of the philosophical schools competing at the time. The expression "sagely within and kingly without" (Watson, 1970: 364) is a masterful slogan characterizing the syncretist author, who perhaps was also the final editor of the book before Kuo Hsiang totally revised it.

CHUANG-TZU/ZHUANGZI: **THEMES.** To read the *Chuang-tzu* is an enriching experience, a discovery of literary genius as well as of deep spirituality. The book is like a fascinating landscape painting, both realistic and abstract, both obvious and full of hidden meanings. The longer one looks, the more discoveries one makes. It is difficult, therefore, to express the basic *Chuang-tzu* themes in just a few pages.

In general, the *Chuang-tzu* is quite different from the *TTC.* Even if they talk about similar concepts (the Tao, the sage, nonaction, etc.) they move on different levels: The *TTC* advocates spiritual practices and a deep understanding of the *Tao* in order to become an enlightened sage-ruler. The *Chuang-tzu* is not interested in bureaucratic government: Life is too interesting to waste on politics! He inspires mystical transcendence, joyful freedom, freedom from the boundaries and restrictions imposed on us, not by nature, but by narrow-minded human societies (this is the contrast between what is "of heaven" and what is "of man"). These restrictions imposed on us are like a cage preventing us from flying up into open space and being fully ourselves. To avoid the traps of society, fly high enough.

The sage of *Chuang-tzu* is multifaceted. Above all, he *scorns the values of a mediocre society.* As the huge mythical bird (Chapter 1), he soars above the clouds beyond the limited space of little birds. Small understanding cannot fathom great understanding. To use another analogy, small people are like frogs in a deep well, reveling in the lowly enjoyments of their mudpool, but incapable of understanding life in the wide ocean. (See also **Human Perfection**.)

Chuang-tzu appears to be a skeptic, he *does not overly trust language,* certainly not as something absolute. It has only relative value because, although it is meant to express what is "true" or to communicate ideas, it is often abused and divides. There is too much empty language, which means nothing, yet appears to be smart and eloquent. Language leads to positions that contradict each other; it divides people instead of bringing them together.

Why is that? It is because what people perceive as truth is made into absolute truth. From the standpoint of the Tao (Transcendent Being), human values, including truth value, have only relative validity. Chuang-tzu uses a beautiful analogy to explain this (Chapter 2). He talks about the music of earth, the music of man, the music of heaven. The music of the earth is when the wind blows in holes and cavities of mountains and trees: It generates roaring, screeching, gasping, crying, howling (Watson: 36), as if an army of demented is on the move. Yet, with the wind as music master, there is a oneness of sound with all particular sounds blending together. Similarly, the music of man consists of a great orchestra with many different instruments, but the baton of the musical director creates harmony, where otherwise, if each plays his/her own tune, there would be cacophony and chaos. As a group, each plays his/her own part, and the result is meaningful and delightful.

However, with the music of heaven, there is a difference. Heaven "breathes" through the minds of all people. Yet everyone thinks differently (three people, four opinions!), and when emotions get involved, the result is disastrous. Here too there should be a unifying principle, but it is hard to find. As a result, societies are in chaos, because opinions or partial truths are taken for absolute and complete. This leads to intolerance, hatred, prejudice, discrimination, suppression, dictatorship, exploitation, even persecution. The world does not need this.

Looked at in the light of heaven, one should realize that the Tao is like the axis of all things and opinions (the title of Chapter 2 is the "relativity of all things and opinions"). There is no absolute expression of truth in any particular statement. All opinions and convictions are necessarily relative and incomplete. Fighting with words and arguments is nonsense. Within the greater light of Tao as central axis, all things and opinions find their place as partial expressions of the real. That is the wholeness of the Tao, which leads to the harmony of minds and peaceful coexistence.

> Tao as *Reality* is one and absolute;
> what we *know* of it cannot be absolute.

A simple yet deeply meaningful anecdote concludes Chapter 2: the famous "butterfly dream" (Watson: 49). In his dream, Chuang-tzu becomes a butterfly, happily fluttering around. When he "wakes up," he is Chuang-tzu again . . . or is he? Dream and reality are fluid, easily transforming into one another. (The dream motif occurs frequently in both the *Chuang-tzu* and the *Lieh-tzu.)*

Caring for life (Chapter 3) is an important motif in the *Chuang-tzu.* Life is a precious gift and should be nurtured; it must be enjoyed to the fullest, always in moderation. Once time is up, the gift should be returned without a grudge. Some people abuse their life energies: they are like butchers who hack when cutting up a dead ox. Their knife does not stay sharp for long. The sage goes along with the flow of life, but does not "hack," does not exhaust his life force. After watching Cook Ting cut up an ox, his Lord exclaims: I have now learned how to care for life! (Watson: 50–51).

A corollary of this episode is that *Chuang-tzu* does not advocate efforts to prolong life beyond what is heaven-given and less so efforts to reach immortality.

Indeed, *acceptance of death* or *submission to fate* are a theme very dear to *Chuang-tzu* (Chapter 6 and many others). Life and death are fated, they rotate in perfect order, just like the four seasons. Life is a gift, to be appreciated, but when the allotted time is up, it should be returned without any fuss.

The sage understands the higher reality of the life processes; here, too, his insight transcends the mediocre mind of most. It is not the individual who is important, but the eternal "play" of the Tao, creating, destroying, and creating again. As individuals, appearing somewhere from nowhere, we are on the stage for a short while, and then must get off; the life cycle goes on. This is reality: Because it is fated and irreversible, it is wise for us to accept it with joy. Life will be more joyful without the scare of death. (Related anecdotes in the *Chuang-tzu,* besides Chapter 6, are in Chapter 3, Watson: 52–53; Chapter 18, Watson: 191–2, when Chuang-tzu's wife died; Chapter 18, Watson: 193–4, story of the skull.)

Chuang-tzu's cynical views on the *world of politics* are well-known. Would-be ministers and royal advisers take heed: Rulers cannot be trusted. Two of the inner chapters discuss the matter of government: Chapters 4 and 7. The theme of Chapter 4 is a warning: It is very difficult to be a good advisor to kings. If one uses any approach that the king dislikes, one could be in danger. It is safer not to serve in government and to be useless, that ensures long life. In episode 3, a realistic analogy is proposed: how to deal with tigers (in a zoo). Go along with the tiger's wishes, to a point. To oppose them completely is dangerous, but so is going along. Other analogies are about "useless" old trees (see below) and "useless" people: crippled Shu is a "reject" of society, but is able to live well and be cared for. How much better is "crippled virtue"!

Chapter 7 discusses *responsive rulership*. Although this title promises a treatise on the Taoist way of government, there is not much to support the title. Episode 3 best reflects Chuang-tzu's views, when he lets "Nameless" give this advice:

> let your mind wander in simplicity,
> blend your spirit with the vastness,
> follow along with things the way they are
> and make no room for personal views—
> then the world will be governed. (Watson: 94)

If no personal considerations of gain or power interfere, or, in a more positive way, if a ruler lets his people live their lives in spontaneity, then the empire will be in order of its own accord. That is the meaning of being "responsive," to be in correspondence with all beings. (The famous story of Chuang-tzu rejecting a government offer is in Chapter 17, Watson: 187–8.)

A corollary to Chuang-tzu's view on government is his almost playful introduction of the *Use of the Useless,* a theme occurring several times in Chapter 4 and elsewhere. His favorite analogy is the "useless" tree: Because its wood cannot be used for anything or (in another case) because it bears no edible fruit, nobody is going to hurt it. It will be able to live out its allotted life span in tranquillity and become huge and provide shade so as to become a resting place for people and animals. (Reminiscent of "sacred" old trees even today, often growing near the shrines of the earth-spirit.)

Useless trees, useless people, useless "words" too! That is what Hui-tzu accused Chuang-tzu of. But the answer was scattering Hui-tzu's logic: A person stands only on a small spot at one time; if one cuts away all the surrounding earth, would it still be of any use? "No," Hui-tzu admits. "It is obvious, then," said Chuang-tzu, "that the useless has its use" (Chapter 26, Watson: 299).

Chuang-tzu's words remain "useful" for us today: They help us to accept our mortality, while yet trying to reach a happy and free life.

CHUNG-LI CH'UAN/ZHONGLI CHUAN (Emblem: fan). He is one of the **Eight Immortals**, also called Han Chung-li, since it is believed that he lived during the Han dynasty.

He is represented as a bearded, corpulent, bare-bellied old man of pleasant disposition. According to legend, he was a military commander during Chou times. Defeated in battle, he withdrew from the service and started to practice alchemy. He was instrumental in convincing Lü Tung-pin to follow the quest for immortality. Together they may have appeared to Wang Che, founder of Ch'uan-chen Taoism.

Many legends narrate his connections with alchemy and his subsequent ascension to heaven on the back of a heavenly stork. Since he became a god, he appeared on earth several times as heaven's messenger (Werner 1969: 345).

CICADA See ANIMAL SYMBOLISM

CITY GOD (Ch'eng-huang shen/Chenghuangshen). His Chinese name literally means "God of walls and moats," "God of Ramparts and Ditches," or god of the defense structure surrounding ancient Chinese cities. Walls and moats are a symbol for the city itself, and, hence, the city god is the spiritual authority ("spirit-mayor") of each city. As such, he is a "multiple deity," which means that it is a function, a rank, just like a mayor in the human realm. Each spirit is a different person, during imperial times often appointed by the imperial court, who wanted to reward meritorious gentlemen after they died.

Taoism has claimed this god as its own, but like the spirit of the soil, he was once a popular deity, during later imperial times also patronized by the government as the spirit-world colleague of the civic magistrate: The latter is the *yang* official, the city god the *yin* official. They are jointly responsible for the well-being of the city.

The origin of his worship goes back to prehistoric (legendary) times, but records are not clear. His worship was at first a projection of the people's belief that, like other places, the city walls were inhabited by a spirit, whose responsibility it was to protect the people inside the walls. In later times, his cult spread so that every city in China had its own city god. Some emperors bestowed various ranks and titles on them, such as king, duke, marquis, or count. The appointment of particular city gods was made either by the people themselves or by the imperial government and was sometimes sanctioned by the Heavenly Master of Taoism.

The City God's duties were many:

> . . . he acts as governor, judge, magistrate, tax-collector, and coroner, and has a retinue of secretaries and attendants. He controls the demons of the district, and can compel them to release his territory from drought and plagues. (Werner 1969: 49)

Another important function of this deity is his responsibility to conduct the souls of the recently dead through the scenery of the netherworld and deliver them to the courts of hell (purgatory) for judgment. In this work, he is assisted by two extraordinary personalities: "Ox-head" (*niu-t'ou*) and "Horse-face" (*ma-mien*), and another pair of spirit-secretaries: "White Old Gentleman" (*Pai lao-yeh*), and "Black Old Gentleman" (*Hei lao-yeh*). One other assistant is "Judge" (*P'an-kuan*); they all help the city god make an initial assessment of the deceased and deliver a report to the netherworld officials. In some city god temples, one sees instruments of torture (for evil-doers) on display and a huge abacus fixed to the wall to warn worshippers about their future "calculation" of merits and demerits. In several temples of the city god, one finds depictions of the Ten Courts of Hell, sometimes on painted scrolls or frescoes, sometimes engraved on the walls: They likewise serve as warnings to the people to refrain from evil.

> By thus governing man's soul after death, the cult of Ch'eng-huang influenced man's conscience through deterrence, just as the temporal government controlled man's conduct through fear of the law. (Yang 1970: 157)

Moreover,

> The system of appointing spirits of deceased officials to the office of Ch'eng-huang once more points toward the inculcation into the people's minds of the idea that there was no escape whatsoever from the ethico-political order, for the human officials who had ruled them in this world were the same ones appointed as Ch'eng-huang to govern them after death. (Yang: 158)

Even in the 20th century, many city god temples remained in China. In Taiwan, they are still very popular places of worship, especially the temple in Taichung city. The god's birthday is celebrated on the 15th of the sixth lunar month.

COMMUNITY. There is no specific Chinese term to express the concept of community with regard to Taoism. For Buddhism, there is the term *sangha* (which includes four groups of followers: monks, nuns, laymen, laywomen), comparable to the Christian term *ecclesia* (church). Although there have always been Taoist believers, clerics, and lay people, there is not a term to tie them all together; there are only terms that emphasize particular groups (*p'ai, tsung, tao,* etc.) (see also **Schools**).

Is it because there never was a Taoist community? No, it is a fact that in some periods of Chinese history there were religious communities, well established and flourishing. But it was not a lasting phenomenon, certainly not in the same sense as the Buddhist *sangha.*

Before proceeding, one should understand the term "community." *Webster's* lists eight meanings, but very few apply in our case: The second, and possibly the first, are most appropriate. The first meaning applies more suitably to the Chinese Popular Religion: "all the people living in a particular district, city, etc." This refers to a geographically determined number of households, bound together by social, economic, religious, cultural, and recreational interactions. The Chinese popular religion is such a phenomenon: It is practiced by the local communities, each independent from its neighbor, yet linked regionally and nationally because they all share a common worldview and practice common rituals (with local differences). Taoism does not, and rarely did, display this kind of community life.

The second meaning (in *Webster's*) has a better chance of applying to Taoism: "a group of people living together as a smaller social unit within a larger one, and having interests, works, etc., in common." In this sense, the term would apply to Taoist monastic orders, whose members live "in community" (monasteries) and share the same ideals of "theology" and lifestyle. But this only applies to elite groups and does not come anywhere close to a "national" community.

Therefore, the views expressed by some Taoist specialists are subject to doubt and criticism. M. Strickmann (in Seidel & Welch, 1979: 166) speaks of Taoism as "China's indigenous *higher religion*" (italics added). A. Seidel (1990) nominates Taoism as "the unofficial *high religion* of China." (In F. Baldrian-Hussein's French translation of 1995, the title has been modified as "nonofficial religion of China.") In a similar vein of reasoning, J. Lagerwey talks about the "*national* religion of the T'ang and of the Sung, even of the Ming . . ." (1987: xii). This way of "interpreting" the real presence of Taoism in Chinese history is rather hyperbolic. Taoism never was the national religion of China, at best the favorite personal religion of some emperors (Hsuan-tsung during the T'ang, Hui-tsung during the Sung). If they had had more time, they might have tried to make Taoism a national belief, but the "community" of the people never took to Taoism as their unique religious option. They had their own community beliefs and practices, which, at times, absorbed Taoist elements, along with elements from Buddhism.

Does it then make sense to postulate the existence of a "Taoist Religious Community"? (This is the title of a long article by J. Lagerwey, very instructive in its details, but more a summary of Taoist history than a treatment of "community." See *ER* 14: 306–317).

To answer this question, one must first of all observe that there never was nor is such a thing as a (national) Taoist community. There have been *temporary* regional Taoist communities, especially during the Later Han: **Heavenly Masters Taoism** and the **Great Peace Taoism**. But the official promotion of Taoism by some T'ang and Sung emperors did not convert Taoism into a national "high religion." Those emperors patronized Taoism for political reasons, and there is no way to know how the people (the community) reacted to this imperial patronage. The most likely explanation is to accept that the people absorbed elements of Taoism into their own "community" beliefs and practices, and nothing more. For that reason one often hears about "popular Taoism," which either points to Taoist elements within the overall community religion, or a sort of specialized personnel (Redhead Taoists, *fa-shih*), who perform rituals on behalf of the community.

The self-identity of Taoist communities has been fluctuating through the centuries. In modern times, Taoism remains either an elite phenomenon (such as in monastic Taoism) or lives on the periphery of society, in towns and villages where Taoist masters (mostly of the Heavenly Masters or Cheng-yi brand) operate. But, as Maspero observes, as a separate religion, Taoism is quasi-extinct:

> ... today, even though certain Taoist ideas still hold a great place in the Chinese mind, which they contributed to shaping, one can say that if this religion still has temples and monks it has hardly any believers. (Maspero, 1971/1981: 441)

If one may talk about a "high religion" of China, it is not Taoism, nor Buddhism; it is what may more suitably be called the "communal religion" of China, practiced not only by the common folks, but by the country's elite as well. This communal religion is not opposed to Taoism, indeed Taoist priests take care of the spiritual needs of the community, although they do not control it. (See also **Popular Religion and Taoism**.)

COMPLETE REALIZATION SCHOOL (Ch'uan-chen/Chuanzhen School). A Taoist monastic order founded in North China during the occupation by the Jurchen Chin (while South China was ruled by the Southern Sung) around 1160 CE. Its founder was **Wang Che** (1112–1170), who soon after his own spiritual conversion at age 48 gathered disciples who were later called the "Seven Patriarchs," or "**Seven Perfected** of the Northern School."

The name *Ch'uan-chen* is not easy to translate: *ch'uan* means "whole, total, complete, perfect," and *chen* means, literally "truth," but in the Taoist context it refers to spiritual realization, as in the expression *chen-jen*—realized or perfected person, transcendent being, an epithet for immortals and sages. In view of this Taoist connotation, *ch'uan-chen* may be best rendered by "complete realization" or similar terms. The idea of "completeness" may be the result of this school's syncretistic tendency, which is one of their major distinctive traits. By "complete" they meant "perfect and complete realization" since it is the result of the combined doctrines and disciplines of the **Three Teachings** (Confucianism, Taoism, Buddhism). It is indeed known that founder Wang emphasized the study of three scriptures: the *Confucian Classic of Filial Piety* (*Hsiao ching*), the Taoist *TTC*, and the Buddhist *Heart Sutra* (one of the *prajnaparamita* scriptures). Because of this syncretism, some scholars believe that the Ch'uan-chen School was originally not a Taoist organization; only subsequently it was given that appellation.

Although strongly influenced by Ch'an Buddhism, which at that time flourished in China, still Ch'uan-chen's major goal was spiritual cultivation in order to reach the state of the immortal (*chen-jen*): That is certainly Taoist in nature. Their lifestyle was monastic, they practiced celibacy and a very simple ascetic way of life. Wang Che devised ten commandments. If one disobeyed those, punishments varied. In five cases, expulsion followed: to transgress national laws; stealing; to cause disturbance; indulgence in liquor, sex, wealth, anger, and eating strong-smelling roots; finally, to be villainous, treacherous, jealous, etc. (Yao, 1980: 87–88). Punishments for minor offenses included fasting, burning incense, renewing oil in the lamps, serving tea, and worship.

Although asceticism in Taoism was not invented by the Ch'uan-chen school, "it seems very likely that [they] took it to extremes previously unrealized" (Eskildsen, 1990: 163). This meant for them a "complete rejection of everyday comforts" and an ideal of "pure poverty" (Eskildsen: 164). It also meant begging for food and being content with one small bowl of rice gruel in the morning and a large bowl of rice noodles at noon. Neither fruit nor spicy vegetables were allowed.

Founder Wang did not hesitate to use violence to punish reluctant members of his group. There is a story that once disciple Ma (future patriarch) was beaten by Wang for an act of disobedience: "The [master] became furious and beat me continually until dawn" (Eskildsen: 168). The same disciple Ma, after the master's death ". . . wore clothes made of paper and hemp. He ate coarse food. In the severe cold of mid-winter he exposed his body and went barefoot" (Quoted by Eskildsen: 178).

Continuing in the line of founder Wang, Ma wrote:

> As for *Tao*, I consider no-mind as the substance, and no-speech as its function, weakness and yielding as its root, purity and clarity as its foundation. Be moderate in eating and drinking, shut off thoughts and worries, sit in meditation to regulate your breathing, sleep peacefully to nourish your vital energy (*ch'i*) . . . emotions will dissolve into emptiness, the spirit will become tranquil to the highest degree. Even if you do not leave your residence, you will reach the mysterious *Tao*. (From Chen Yuan, 1941: chapter 2. Translated by M.K. Leung and J. Pas)

It has been hypothesized by Chen Yuan and others that Ch'uan-chen Taoism and other schools founded in the same period were established as a literati device to avoid serving the barbarian (Chin) government and as a method to preserve Chinese culture, threatened by foreign invasions. This hypothesis is not generally accepted, but it is a fact that Ch'uan-chen Taoism contributed to the stabilization of northern China during a period of warfare and unrest. Among their contributions are their efforts to stop massacre by the invaders and to maintain culture among the masses. Moreover, they compiled and edited a new edition of the **Taoist Canon** (*Tao Tsang*) in 1192 and promoted membership of women in their order. It is unfortunate that under the Mongol rule of Khubilai Khan, the Taoist Canon was destroyed and many texts were lost forever.

Although eventually eclipsed by Heavenly Masters Taoism, the Ch'uan-chen order has survived until today, especially in one of its subdivisions, the Lung-men branch. Its famous monastery in Beijing, the White Cloud Monastery, is the organizational center of the Taoist Association of China. This monastery is also one of the few training schools for young Taoists. Other Ch'uan-chen priests are still active in Hong Kong. (For details, see Yao Tao-chung, 1980; B. Tsui, 1991. See also **Wang Che**; the **Seven Perfected**.)

CONFUCIANISM AND TAOISM. The relationship between the two "native daughters" of the ancient Chinese "matrix" have not been as stormy as between Taoism and Buddhism, the "adopted" daughter, arriving on the Chinese scene in the second century CE. (See **Buddhism and Taoism**.) In general, the relationship between Confucianism and Taoism has already been briefly discussed in the **Introduction** (see **Taoism and Chinese Culture**); here we must try to be more specific. Two concrete situations will be examined in which the two schools interacted with each other: first, before the establishment of Confucianism as the state doctrine; next, the often assumed influence of Taoism on the later renewal of Confucianism, in Western studies called Neo-Confucianism. A third period of interaction falls in between, time-wise, but the information is scarce: It will only be briefly discussed.

Taoism and Confucianism during the Warring States and the Han periods. It was about 134 BCE when Han Emperor Wu officially adopted Confucianism as the state doctrine, which meant that all future candidates for state employment had to study the ancient Five Classics (*wu ching*) and the "Four Books" of Confucianism in preparation for state examinations. Once this decision had been made, it was the end of a period of uncertainty, during which Taoism and Confucianism, two rival schools, attempted to receive imperial sponsorship. Taoism, under the name of Huang-Lao Taoism, had been the chosen philosophy of emperors before Emperor Wu, but now the roles were reversed. That may be the reason why the figure of Confucius in the *Chuang-tzu* appears in so many different *gestalten*: sometimes he is ridiculed or criticized, in other passages he is praised and portrayed as a real Taoist sage. These variables in presentation are partially due to the diverse authorships of the *Chuang-tzu* chapters, but also reflect, indirectly, the political climate of the time of composition. Before Confucianism was enthroned, it was safe to criticize and ridicule Confucius; but once Confucianism became officially sponsored, such language may be dangerous. In other words, in the early period of relationships between the schools, there is certainly some rivalry and competition for official favor, but there is no bitterness.

During the period of north-south division, especially after the exodus of many literati to the south, it appears that there was some dialogue between the schools. Buddhism contributed to the exchange of ideas as well, but between Taoists and Confucians, many of whom had lost their position in government, there was a healthy interaction, especially in the area of philosophy. It is not clear whether adepts of the Taoist religion participated in the dialogue. (See, for example, the **Seven Sages of the Bamboo Grove.**)

• A crucial period of interaction between Confucianism and Taoism was the time before Confucianism reached its peak of development during the Sung; this is called in Western literature Neo-Confucianism. During the T'ang dynasty already some Confucian-minded individuals started to stir and gradually prepared for a revival. Several T'ang emperors favored either Taoism or Buddhism, but they all relied on Confucianism as the backbone for the education of their intellectual elite. During the T'ang, several schools of Buddhist philosophy flourished and attracted many of the best minds in the empire. Buddhism had a great impact on the Taoist religion, but Taoism, as well, influenced Buddhism, especially in the formation of Ch'an (Zen) Buddhism as a native expression of the Buddhist tradition.

Since both Buddhism and Taoism flourished, Confucians felt they should learn from them and perhaps borrow from them some of their major attractions. A whole row of Confucian scholars were instrumental in this process of renewal, which reached its first peak in the synthesis of Chu Hsi (1130–1200). In Western studies of this period, it is usually recognized that the Confucian revival was partly due to the adoption of Buddhist and Taoist ideas and practices, but rarely does one find concrete examples of this process. Where exactly does one find them? There is a need for a thorough examination, but here only a few pointers will be proposed.

What Confucian scholars felt they lacked in their own system was a metaphysics and a program of spiritual cultivation. These were seen as among the major attractions of Buddhism and Taoism. However, they rejected the overall direction of these two as too unrealistic (the world seen as an illusion by Buddhism) and based on fantasy and useless mystical speculation (by Taoism).

The Confucian revival started with Chou Tun-yi (1017–1073), who began a wave of cosmological exploration by using the diagram of the **Supreme Ultimate** cherished by the Taoists:

. . . what he did was to assimilate the Taoist element of non-being to Confucian thought, but in so doing, he discarded the fantasy and mysticism of Taoism. (Chan, 1963: 460)

Other philosopher-cosmologists, such as Chang Tsai (1020–1077), discussed creation and evolution in terms of *ch'i*, which he identified with the Supreme Ultimate. Although he built up his own system of thought, one feels that it somehow parallels the Taoist vision, developed during the Southern Dynasties. When he says that "stillness and purity characterize the original state of material force [*ch'i*]" (Chang: 510), it comes very close to what the Taoist *Purity and Tranquillity Scripture* is all about. Although influenced by Buddhism and Taoism, this new wave of philosophers also criticized these systems. All Neo-Confucians stress the need for social involvement: They blame Buddhists and also Taoists for their "escape from social responsibility and selfish desire for personal salvation" (Chan: 516). Moreover, as Chang Tsai said:

Buddhists do not investigate principle to the utmost [a Confucian concern]. They consider everything to be the result of subjective illusion. Chuang Tzu did understand principle, but when he went to its utmost, he also considered things to be a dream. (Chan: 517)

When the new Confucianism reached its highest point of development in Chu Hsi, one once again can feel a subtle network of influences operating. Like others before him, he was both dependent on Buddhism and Taoism, while he also criticized their ultimate intentionality, which he considered world-rejecting. Confucians long before Chu Hsi used to blame Taoist recluses for escaping social responsibility. What did he find useful in Buddhism and Taoism, however? It is possible that Chu Hsi's basic doctrine, the distinction of *ch'i* (basic, undifferentiated matter) and *li* (principle or nature of things) was inspired by the Buddhist distinction between *li* and *shih* (principle and "actuality," as developed in the Hua-yen School of Buddhism).

All the above are hints and speculation; there is a need for detailed detective work to discover the complex network of influences. But one practical innovation common to most Neo-Confucians is their emphasis on the need for meditation. They called it "quiet-sitting" (*ching-tso*), a means of spiritual self-cultivation. The technique itself may have been inspired by either Taoist or Buddhist models (*tso-wang* or *tso-ch'an/zazen*), yet their objectives were very different. For the Confucians, meditation was a means to still the mind, to calm one's desires, with the ultimate goal of action in the world; for Buddhists the end goal was enlightenment (which Confucians considered a negative value); for the Taoists the objective was immortality, but it also was very private, individualistic, and, ultimately, selfish.

This discussion, once again, is not finished, barely just started. But whatever the mechanics of the influencing process have been, the fact of influencing has been recognized, and one also can understand a common conviction of many Chinese literati: "the Three Teachings are ultimately one" (*san-chiao kui-yi*).

CONVERSION OF BARBARIANS SCRIPTURE (*Hua-hu ching/Huahujing*). A controversial Taoist text, first written around 300, during the Western Chin (265–317), supposedly by a Taoist libationer, Wang Fou. This is an important document from a historical perspective, because it highlights the growing rivalry between Taoist religionists and the newcomers of Buddhism. At first, Buddhism had been received with sympathy by the Chinese, since it seemed just to be a variety of Taoism. As time went on, it was realized that Buddhism was very different: Then it became a rival of Taoism, and although the Taoist religion absorbed many aspects of the new religion, the rivalry at times was sharp and bitter.

In the *Hua-hu scripture*, an old tradition was taken up and enlarged. It had been stated in the *Historical Documents* (*Shih-chi*) by Szu-ma Ch'ien (about 90 BCE) that Lao-tzu left China from the western border and was never heard of again. The *Conversion* story now declared that Lao-tzu in fact went to India and reappeared there as the Buddha to convert the "barbarians" (all non-Chinese were considered barbarians!). That meant that Taoism was older (and therefore more respectable) than Buddhism, and that the Buddha was inferior to Lao-tzu.

This story is totally apocryphal, based on fantasy, and, as the Buddhists would claim, written to slander their religion. T'ang Emperors Kao-tsung (r. 649–683) and Chung-tsung (r. 705–710) issued edicts to stop the controversy, but during the Mongol rule, the matter emerged again. In 1281, an imperial order was issued to destroy all the spurious scriptures (forgeries) of the Taoist Canon: that included the *Hua-hu ching* and all other Taoist texts, except the *TTC*. As a result, the *Hua-hu ching* was lost and was not included in the Ming edition of the *Tao-tsang*.

A T'ang copy has been discovered among the Tun-huang manuscripts, but it is not the same as the original by Wang Fou. (For further discussion, see L. Kohn, 1995, Introduction. See also **Buddhism and Taoism,** and *Laughing at the Tao*.)

COSMIC RENEWAL FESTIVAL (*Chiao/Jiao*). The greatest, most splendid, elaborate, and colorful of all the ritual events taking place in a Chinese community today is the *chiao* celebration, variously translated as "rite of cosmic renewal," "rites of community renewal," "great propitiatory rites," or, simply, "offering." As it is being celebrated in contemporary Chinese communities, it is a "joint venture" in which local communities and the Taoist priesthood (rarely Buddhist monks) participate. The organizational aspects are handled by the community temple, the specific rituals are performed by Taoist priests, the so-called Blackhead Taoists, because the popular Taoists, the "Redheads," are not entitled to handle the highly esoteric rituals.

The *chiao* already has much history: There are references to this ritual in the *Shuo-wen* and some of the dynastic histories and chronicles. (It must be distinguished from another royal sacrifice, also romanized as *chiao*, but a different character meaning a sacrifice performed in the suburbs since ancient times.) Traditionally, *chiao* was often combined with *chai/zhai*, as in the expression *chai-chiao*.

Since the beginning of scholarly interest in the ritual tradition of Taoism, the *chiao* has been subject of several studies: two monographs (Saso 1972; Lagerwey 1986) and several articles (Liu). More intense research is needed to give this important ritual all the attention it deserves.

Hereafter, three aspects of the *chiao* will be discussed: its basic meaning and objectives; the community's contribution or organizational aspects; the specialized Taoist rituals. Sources of information are twofold: published reports and studies; fieldwork observations.

Because of the rapid economic expansion in Taiwan within the last few decades, there has been an intense revival of temple construction and ritual celebrations in all communities. In China, there has been a revival of a different kind: The greater freedom allowed by the government in the area of religious practice has stimulated the return to a number of dormant traditions, with the *chiao* among them. *Chiao* celebrations in the province of Fukien have been observed and reported in journals (K. Dean in *CEA* 2, 1986). In Hong Kong as well, there has been a revival and multiplication of the *chiao*, and reports have been published (Tanaka, in Pas, 1989: 271–298). It appears that underneath the visible differences of detail, there is a similarity in basic structure and a similarity of purpose. Further research will be most exciting. The temples themselves are helping today's researchers: Many temples have published illustrated report booklets of their own *chiao*. Pride and competition between temples bring these documents to a high level of sophistication.

• Meaning and Objectives of the *Chiao* Festival

Unfortunately the temple reports often do not discuss the nature and significance of the *chiao*. These we find in the more scholarly publications.

The basic significance of the *chiao* as it is celebrated today is the renewal of the community. Originally, it took place at the transition between an old sixty-year cycle and a new one. Today, this time schedule is not often adhered to: some temples in Hong Kong have it every ten years, and the frequency in Taiwan temples has also increased with greater economic prosperity. Few cases in which the sixty-year cycle has been maintained have been reported: The Kaohsiung (southern Taiwan) *San-feng kung* (Three Phoenixes Temple) in 1978 had not had a *chiao* for 59 years. Another example is the *Tai-ho kung* (Temple of Supreme Harmony) in Kuan-hsi (Hsinchu county) in 1971: 73 years had elapsed.

There are different types of *chiao* celebrations: Most common is *chien-chiao* ("construction *chiao*"), taking place after the building of a new temple or the reconstruction, renovation, or redecoration of an old temple has been completed. Other kinds are celebrations of thanksgiving, or rituals to exorcise the spirits of disease, especially of epidemics. One of the most famous of this kind is the "plague expulsion ritual" performed every three years in the southern Taiwan town of Tungkang (Pingtung county), during which the "plague spirits" are ritually expulsed on a boat to rid the community of their nefarious influences. What all the various types of *chiao* have in common is a request for "peace" (*p'ing-an*) so that the community may live without threats or dangers.

Renewal of the community is desirable, if not necessary, after a sixty-year cycle has ended or when a new temple has been built. Repentance of misdeeds ("sins"), purification of individuals, as well as the community as a whole, are necessary conditions for the opening up of the heavenly sluices of blessings needed to start a new cycle. These blessings consist in bestowal of health and fertility, removal of epidemics and catastrophes by fire or water (floods), and overall prosperity of the whole community.

The *chiao* rituals are thus a set of magico-religious ritual actions performed by Taoist priests to ensure that the new cycle of time will be blessed by the highest powers above (the Taoist Triad), who control the creative powers of the universe. Through their rituals, the Taoists feel confident that they can bring down the divine energy from above to renew and revitalize the community, after all impurities and bad old energies have been removed through the people's own efforts and ritual confession, as well as through the chanting of the canons of repentance by the Taoists.

Similar to the meaning of sacrifice in other religions, the whole process of the *chiao* lies in the belief that the correct performance of the rituals will maintain creation in existence.

• *Chiao* Organization: Local Community

The decision to hold a *chiao* festival is made by the people themselves. Each community temple (in Taiwan) appoints a board of directors on a yearly basis; they make decisions with regard to temple activities, such as building, renovating, and holding regular temple festivities. They also control the temple finances.

Once the decision to hold a *chiao* has been made—this depends on each temple's history and tradition—a lucky date is chosen by fortune-tellers or a local medium, and the whole community is then set in motion to start with the preparations, usually one year ahead of time, in larger temples, even earlier.

The temple board strikes committees to be responsible for the multiple activities involved. Under the leadership of a general planning committee, there may be up to a dozen subcommittees to coordinate the event, in charge, respectively, of finances, equipment, temple grounds, rituals, reception, food services, travel, traffic, etc. (At the Kaohsiung *chiao* in 1978, there were 130 committee members serving on 14 committees.)

A Taoist master must be contacted to take charge of the rituals. Very likely, several candidates are invited to submit their fee structure, and the committees on rituals and finances make their selection. The head priest (*tao-chang/daozhang*), once appointed, contacts and hires his assistants, at least four priests and four or five musicians. Large temples hire up to 12 or 14 assistant priests. But this is all decided between the temple committee and the head priest.

Once the officiating master has been appointed, the organizing committee will meet with him to set up a concrete time schedule, which includes the Taoist rituals, but also community activities, such as processions, building of shrines (*t'an*), visits from neighboring temples, and the *p'u-tu* ritual (rite of "universal salvation"). The finance committee plays, of course, a crucial role. The celebration of a *chiao* is very expensive, as can be discovered from the published temple records. Construction works and the priests' salaries are among the largest expenditures. Revenues are made by taxing each household living within the temple boundaries. Prominent members of the community are given special titles and have to pay extraordinary donations for the honor. (Their contributions are also listed in the temple records.) Another source of income is the "leasing" of small spots occupied by "visiting deities" from other temples. For the occasion, special shelves are built inside the temple, away from the center, which becomes the sacred area. These shelves are occupied by statues brought over from other temples for this occasion: They are entitled to witness the sacred rituals and gain spiritual power from it. But there is a price to pay, according to size and location of each spot. In some temples, the number of visiting deities may run in the thousands.

Preparations for the renewal festival become hectic as the date of commencement approaches. The whole community is involved: All the work is done by volunteers and the spirit of cooperation is admirable (excepting, of course, all kinds of petty rivalries and disagreements). It is an occasion for the community to renew its social ties, to gain prestige in the outside world, and to prepare itself for a prosperous new cycle.

• Taoist *Chiao* rituals

Although in ancient times a *chiao* could last up to 50 days, or even longer, the most common pattern today is either a three-day or a five-day event (*san-ch'ao* or *wu-ch'ao*), with sometimes two days added in the beginning for the exorcism of *fire* and *water*: two extremely important powers in human societies, which are mostly benevolent, but can also become dangerous and destructive. Fires and floods (typhoons) are believed to be controlled by divine spirits, who must be pacified at the start of a new era.

Whether a temple decides to choose a three-day or a five-day celebration depends on its size and economic strength. Whatever the choice may be, there are some basic rituals that must always take place, although the timing of each rite may be different from school to school, from master to master. Here are some of the major Taoist rituals occurring during a *chiao:*

- *Announcement to the Spirits* (*fa-piao*) and Invitation (*ch'ing-shen*): The spirits (deities of heaven, earth, and water) are informed about the upcoming renewal festival and are invited to descend and to participate.
- *Purification of the Sacred Area*: While all the temple doors are closed (except for one service entrance), the temple must be purified. There are several rites of purification or exorcism, performed by the master with the sprinkling of holy water, the writing of sacred talismans in the air, the brandishing of a ritual sword, and the enactment of an evil spirit "stealing" the incense burner of the gods. A more popular, and spectacular, method is the performance by a stage actor impersonating Chung K'ui, the "devil catcher."
- *Consecration of New Fire* (*fen-teng*): Usually on the first or second evening, newly struck fire is brought inside the temple and offered to the three highest deities. This is reminiscent of an ancient pre-Taoist rite: seasonal renewal of fire and water.
- *Planting of Five Talismans:* A magico-religious act, in which the master through interior meditation draws the cosmic life-giving

forces of "prior" heaven into his own body, and implants them into the microcosm of the community. This is one of the most crucial rites of the festival.

- *Audience with the Tao*: From day two on, three audiences with the three supreme deities take place; morning, noon, and evening. The master "ascending" to the heavens channels the divine powers in himself and implants them into the community.
- *Recitation of the Scriptures*: Depending of the length of the *chiao*, several scriptures are chanted or recited. The canons of repentance, the scripture of salvation (*tu-jen ching*), and the Jade Emperor scripture are among the most significant.
- *Invitation of the Hungry Ghosts and Final Banquet*: All the ghosts from far and near are invited to attend a sumptuous banquet at the end of the festival. They are notified by lanterns hung high up on bamboo poles (land ghosts) and by the floating of lanterns on a nearby river or the sea (water ghosts). Each family brings food dishes for display on tables set up on the temple square or a neighboring field: It is a spectacular sight. Many pigs and goats are slaughtered and placed on wooden frames for the offering.

  In the evening, the Taoist priests come out to bless the offerings and to chant scriptures of salvation with the hope that many ghosts will be "put to rest" and gain a happy reincarnation. In ancient times, this *p'u-tu* banquet could become a wild affair with hundreds of beggars competing for the food offerings after the ceremony. (See G. MacKay, 1895: 129–131.)

The festival ends with sending the deities back to their respective heavens and with a grandiose banquet for the living, organized by caterers for the benefit (and at the expense) of individual families on the last day.

The above description only offers a general outline of the *chiao* celebration: An extensive monograph of description and interpretation would be most desirable.

CRANE See ANIMAL SYMBOLISM

D

DANCE. The relationship between dance and religious ritual is very strong. Among the best examples today are probably Indian temple dances, Thai dances, and dances of Tibetan Buddhism. But dances have developed independently as well, although traces of their relationship with ritual are still very suggestive.

In China, dance and ritual have often been closely connected. One example, actually the only remnant of the ancient state cult, is the celebration of Confucius' birthday, nowadays fixed on September 28. During the ritual, there is a performance of a "feather dance" executed by young boys dressed in yellow silk robes.

In Taoism, dance is still a part of the liturgy. But it is not performed by specialized dancing groups. The Taoist master himself, together with four or six assistants, performs some dance-like rituals during the Cosmic Renewal Festival.

- *Steps of Yü*: A solo dance-like performance by the Taoist head-priest.
- *Renewal of Light (fen-teng)*: After the new light has been brought into the temple, and each of the Taoists has his candle (or torch) lit, there is a ritual dance all around the altar.
- *Noon Offering*: A special ritual during which nine precious gifts are offered to the Taoist triad (they include jewelry, flowers, tea, etc.). This is an elegant dance-like performance, beautiful to watch as, one by one, those gifts are first presented by a layperson, then by the Taoist priests, to the supreme gods of Prior Heaven.

In "popular" Taoism (Redhead Taoists), more of the ancient dance traditions may have survived. This topic deserves more intense fieldwork investigation.

DARK LEARNING See MYSTERY LEARNING

DECLARATIONS OF THE PERFECTED (*Chen-kao/Zhengao*). A Taoist collection of essays, composed by **T'ao Hung-ching** (around 492 CE) on **Mount Mao** (Mao Shan). This work contains "discontinuous portions of the revealed materials [Shang-ch'ing revelations], auricular instructions and fragmentary poetic effusions dictated to **Yang [Hsi]** by his celestial visitors" (Strickmann, 1977: 4).

The book (*CT* 1016; *TT* 637–640) is divided into 20 chapters, of which Chapters 1–16 contain revelations made to Yang; then follow letters, memoranda, records of dreams. T'ao's own commentaries go along with the texts. In the final chapters, T'ao provides important information about the manuscripts he personally collected, ending with a genealogy of the Hsü family, Yang Hsi's patrons.

The *Chen-kao* is therefore a unique source of information about the original Shang-ch'ing scriptures, about T'ao's own activities and forms:

> . . . an imposing body of documents, of certain date and origin, granting a unique historical perspective of a century and a half in the development of Taoism in Southeast China. (Strickmann: 5)

DIET. As in most spiritual traditions, in the Taoist religion diet is one of the basic disciplines of the adept. It has two aspects: Positively, a proper diet strengthens one's health and nourishes one's *ch'i*; negatively, abstention from certain foods prevents evil influences to affect one's physical and spiritual well-being. The positive aspect is diet in the proper sense; the second aspect, abstention, is more closely related to fasting.

In most spiritual traditions, fasting is more emphasized than proper diet, but the rationale for fasting varies. In Hinduism, believers abstain from beef because the cow is considered a sacred symbol. Moreover, Hinduism and Buddhism both believe in the essential identity of all "sentient beings," therefore abstaining from eating meat is a natural consequence of the belief system. The Roman Catholic Church used to impose a six-week fast, including abstaining from meat two days a week, but except for the idea of penance and self-denial, no further rationale was given.

In Taoism, abstention from meat eating was not universal, except that the Buddhist custom had affected most other Chinese. In monastic Taoism, however, meat consumption was discouraged or even forbidden. The rationale was different from Buddhist concepts. Engaged in spiritual practices and meditation, monastic Taoists believed in the presence of deities inside the body (see **Three Ones**): these deities loathed the smell of meat. The adept had to abstain for this reason. Maybe there is a link here with older Taoist religious practices: The Heavenly masters in the second century CE criticized and forbade "blood" sacrifices, or offerings of slaughtered animals. This was seen as an excessive cult, unorthodox, only practiced by the ignorant masses. The Taoists believed that the gods detested those blood sacrifices.

It appears, then, that Taoist monastics abstained from eating meat, not for "theological" reasons (as the Buddhists) nor for reasons of hygienic diet, but simply for practical considerations: to please the indwelling gods and ensure their continuing presence in the adept.

When it comes to diet or food habits, the Taoists were even more radical: They disapproved of the consumption of the five cereals that would block the internal organs and feed the **Three Worms** living in the three fields of cinnabar (*tan-t'ien*). Drinking liquor was also forbidden, not because alcohol intoxicates and obscures one's reason, but because the inner gods detest its smell.

As a result, a healthy Taoist diet was rather limited in possibilities and strictly vegetarian; it

> was not without its painful moments. Without grains and meat, whoever practices it is undernourished; and the Taoist authors admit that at the beginning one may have numerous troubles, some of them general (vertigo, weakness, sleepiness, difficulties in moving), others local (diarrhea, constipation, and so on). Nevertheless they advise persevering, insisting that . . . the body . . . feels better [than before]: more calm and more at ease . . . (Maspero, 1971/1981: 335)

Although some vegetarian foods (fruit, vegetables, mushrooms) were approved, the ideal was to dispense with all solid food. The best nourishment was believed to come from swallowing saliva and "feeding on breath," to make it circulate through all the parts of one's body. Such a "poor" diet could be enriched with drugs and minerals.

This ideal diet was hardly suitable for beginners (and totally unsuitable for common people who had to do a lot of physical labor!), but even beginners should try to balance their diet, and take food in moderation. Food should be well cooked, not strongly flavored, not conserved but fresh. "If one is hungry, one eats—but never to satiation. Thus we establish a balanced diet" (L. Kohn, 1993: 83). (See also **Asceticism**.)

DIRECTOR OF DESTINY (Szu-ming/Siming). Name of a god worshipped by the Taoists, as well as by the popular tradition under the name of Kitchen God, God of the Stove or Hearth.

The origin of Szu-ming's worship is unclear: As kitchen god he is mentioned in the *Analects* of Confucius (Chapter 3: 13), going back to the fifth century BCE. In this role, he may have been a popular adaptation of the ancient God of Fire, a nature deity, whose worship has been identified with Yen Ti, mythical emperor of prehistoric times. (See also **Nature Deities**.)

Under the name of Szu-ming, Controller or Director of Destiny, he was worshipped by shamans and magicians during the fourth and third centuries BCE, later adopted by the alchemists as the god who controls the alchemical fire (or furnace). He was introduced by alchemist **Li Shao-chün** to the imperial court of Han Emperor Wu, who was encouraged to sacrifice to Szu-ming to enhance his quest for immortality. The god of the alchemists was adopted by Taoism: His function as Controller of Destiny was most essential because it was believed that he decided on the length of life of all human beings.

During the period of the Five Dynasties, texts were written about inner visualization of the gods living in the human body. The god Szu-ming was said to dwell in one of the nine palaces in the upper "field of cinnabar," called "Palace of the Moving Pearl":

> He keeps the register of merits and demerits for the upper section. Those who commit sins will have their life shortened; for those who do good deeds, death is deferred and life is lengthened. The Director of Destiny presents a request to the Great One [*T'ai-yi*], asking him to increase or diminish the number of years established at birth for each man. (Maspero, 1971/1981: 350–351)

It is therefore very important for the Taoist adept to be on good terms with Szu-ming. On the popular level, too, his worship as God of the Stove (or Kitchen God) was very important. Although of lowly rank in the popular pantheon, his influence on the supreme deity is essential:

> This deity has power over the lives of the members of each family under his supervision, distributes riches and poverty at will, and makes an annual report to the Supreme Being on the conduct of the family during the year . . . (Werner, 1969: 519)

Since the Sung dynasty, his worship was universal in China. He had his niche in every kitchen, or a print was pasted on the wall. Near year's end, the old picture was removed, a sacrifice of sweets was offered to him before he took off to heaven for his annual report to the **Jade Emperor**. Sweets and honey would induce him to speak only "sweet words" up there. He returned from heaven soon after the New Year, and a new image was then pasted on the kitchen wall.

"There are more than 40 different stories of the origin of the kitchen god, and of the men deified to take this responsible position" (Werner: 520). His birthday is on the third day of the eighth lunar month. (For more details, see Werner: 518–521; Welch, 1957: *passim.*)

In Taiwan today, he is still worshipped as a home deity, but also in the more solemn role of Szu-ming in temples dedicated to three, four, or five "Lord-Benefactors" (*En-chu/Enzhu*). The three are: **Kuan-sheng Ti-chün**, **Fu-yu Ti-chün**, and Szu-ming Chen-chün. There are 16 temples dedicated to their joint worship. The group of four, adds "First Teacher" K'ung-ming (**Chu-Ke Liang** deified). The group of five adds **Wang Ling-kuan** and "Original Teacher" **Yueh-fei**. Five temples in Taiwan enshrine the five "Lord-Benefactors," but many other temples have their images installed on secondary altars (*TMSC*: 76–78).

DISCOURSE ON SITTING-AND-FORGETTING (*Tso-wang lun/ Zuowanglun*). A Taoist treatise on meditation, written by T'ang master Szu-ma Ch'eng-chen/Sima Chengzhen (647–735), a prolific author and 12th patriarch of Shang-ch'ing or Mao Shan Taoism (the *Tso-wang lun* is included in the *T'ai-hsuan* section of the Taoist Canon: *CT* 1036, *TT* 704).

During the T'ang dynasty, meditation practices started to flourish in Taoism, especially within the Shang-ch'ing or Mao Shan School. This school focused on internal spirituality and rather than relying on ritualism and alchemy, practiced meditation and inner vision of the gods in order to reach the state of transcendence (*hsien*).

There was much interaction with Buddhism, a tradition for which meditation was paramount. Taoism adopted some of the Buddhist techniques, but their methods remained essentially Taoist. In a similar way, Buddhism adopted some Taoist methods and created their own brand of Chinese Buddhism in the Ch'an school (see **Meditation**).

The title *Tso-wang lun* (literally "Sit-and-Forget Discourse") clearly alludes to Chapter 6 of the *Chuang-tzu*, in which Yen Hui tells his master Confucius that he can now "sit down and forget everything" (Watson, 1970: 90). This means that, while the body remains still and calm, the mind has emptied itself of all concepts and subjectivity and is absorbed in the reality of *Tao*. In this treatise, Master Szu-ma proposes seven steps in the meditative process, which he believes will ultimately lead to absorption in the *Tao*.

Following L. Kohn's discussion and translation (Kohn, 1987-a), here is a short presentation of the seven stages:

- *Respect and Faith* stresses a state of mind needed at the outset: trust in the method, freedom from doubt.
- *Interception of Karma* explains the need to withdraw from ordinary life and leave all business outside. At least temporarily, the mind must be free from all worldly affairs and concerns.
- *Taming the Mind* brings home the urgent necessity of stilling the mind and reaching a state of "blind concentration." Only then can the mind be directed to its goal, in analogy with oxen and horses tamed and used by humans.
- *Detachment of Affairs* goes even further by urging the inner separation from society and total detachment from worldly achievements.
- *True Observation* (*chen-kuan*) introduces the first stage of meditation, but rather than visualizing inner gods (*kuan*), it involves concentration on one's situation, and a coming to grips with it.
- *Intent Concentration* leads the adept to "the first foothold of the Tao," which means "perfect serenity on the inside and a 'heav-

enly light' radiating on the outside" (Kohn: 37). It is like tranquillity and wisdom.
* *Realizing the Tao* explains how the mind is gradually emptied
and united with the reality of *Tao*.

From this short analysis, it is clear that the *Tso-wang lun* is a very
practical and pedagogic instrument of instruction: All the essential
conditions and techniques for a gradually attained mystical union are
presented clearly. Its influence on Taoism and later on Neo-Confucianism is understandable. (For a detailed discussion, see L. Kohn,
1987-a.)

DIVINE EMPYREAN SCHOOL See SHEN-HSIAO TAOISM

DOOR GODS (Door Spirits) (*Men-shen/Menshen*). This pair of modest, low-ranking deities are not specifically of Taoist affiliation, but
belong to the universal Chinese communal religion. Yet, the Taoists
as well as the Buddhists have incorporated them into their own pantheon, particularly as guardian spirits of the temple gates. Their
painted images are found universally on temple doors, whether they
are Taoist, Buddhist, popular, or even ancestral halls. The temple door
gods are usually painted extra large, mostly like martial heroes, holding weapons and looking fierce. That is in order to frighten away evil
spirits who would otherwise enter the temple premises and desecrate
it.
    But most commonly, the door gods are associated with private
homes. The traditional entrance to a Chinese home was a door consisting of two wings, hence the door gods always come in pairs.
    Their origin goes back to prehistoric times and is particularly con-
nected with the Yellow Emperor. A new dimension was added during
the T'ang dynasty, when Emperor T'ai-tsung (r. 627–649) was disturbed in his palace at night by demonic brick-throwing. He became
seriously ill. Two generals offered to stand on guard at the door so
that the demons dared not approach. The emperor then recovered. But
instead of asking his generals to continue their night watch, images
of the two were painted on the doors, with the same effect. This device was widely copied by the people and is still being practiced
today. On New Year's day, paper prints of the two spirits are pasted
on the external door panels of private homes to ensure protection
from evil spirits.

> The gods are almost always portrayed in military uniform, helmeted,
> and clad in full armor, with little flags on their shoulders [insignia of a
> military commander], armed with a saber or halberd and, in order to

frighten the demons still more, they are given ferocious countenances and big beards. (Maspero, 1971/1981: 116)

Although the T'ang generals had personal names—Ch'in Shu-pao/ Qin Shubao and Hu Ching-te/Hu Jingde (alternatively, Weichi K'ung/ Weichi Gong and Ch'in Ch'iung/Qin Qiong)—one finds other names as well as local variations throughout China. However, popular genius has made more adjustments. Official families, who did not wish their sons to engage in a military career, substituted the generals with officials in civil mandarin costume.

The most recent transformation has been noticed in the People's Republic of China: Although all expressions of ancient beliefs and customs were radically forbidden during the Period of Chaos (1966–77), they started to revive in the early '80s. In 1985, several villages were spotted in Szechuan and Hupei where almost all houses had pasted paper images of the door gods. What was remarkable was the "ideological" adjustment: Cadre families (party members) had posters hailing Marxism or socialism instead of the "old" gods. Several posters portrayed new door spirits, even female amazons, or sometimes, more in tune with the party's antireligion stand, just faces of happy children. In Taiwan, the tradition of old continues, but the paper prints are more sophisticated and of good quality paper, in tune with the economic prosperity.

(For more details, see Maspero, 1971/81; Werner, 1969: 311–312; Pas, 1989: 175–180. A large selection of beautiful color reproductions of door gods can be seen in *The Art of the Traditional Chinese New Year Print*, published by the National Central Library, Taipei, 1991.)

DRAGON See ANIMAL SYMBOLISM

"DRAGON THROW" (*T'ou-lung/Toulong*). A less well-known ancient Taoist ritual, performed by Taoist priests on behalf of the ruling emperor. The "dragon throw" rite used to be incorporated into the more general celebration of the yearly *chai/zhai* and *chiao/jiao* ceremony at the site of a sacred mountain.

Its purpose was to send messages to some of the highest Taoist deities, the Three Supreme Officials (**San-kuan**) in order to ask for their blessings. It was executed in a special way: Taoist priests would throw small tablets of jade, engraved with prayers, tied to a "golden dragon" into one of the sacred mountains' *tung-t'ien*. Chavannes translated *tung-t'ien* as "palace or residence qualified as profound and mysterious." It is an abbreviation of *tung-kung*. In this context, *tung* does not mean cave or grotto, but profound or mysterious. A *tung-t'ien* is a "profound celestial place," the residence of a deity who presides over a celestial region or celestial place (*t'ien*).

One may assume that in Taoist descriptions *tung-t'ien* is often identified with celestial caves situated on mountains, because as a noun *tung* also means cave, grotto, cavern. In fact, the *tung-t'ien* are located on famous mountains and, during the rite of the "dragon throw," the tablets-cum-dragons were thrown into the subterranean residences of famous mountains.

A book by T'ang Taoist **Tu Kuang-t'ing**, described as "a true religious geography of the empire," contains discussions of the five peaks, ten *tung-t'ien*, five regulating mountains, four seas, five watercourses, 36 hermitages, 36 more *tung-t'ien*, and 72 *fu-ti* (Chavannes: 129).

The rite of the "dragon throw" is connected with the 36 *tung-t'ien*, which probably date from the T'ang dynasty, and the rite itself dates from the same period. It was still practiced during the Sung dynasty: The "throw" is said to have been performed several times during the yearly *chai* and *chiao* rituals. Emperor Jen-tsung thought many of these places were not easily accessible and were too much trouble to execute. He decided to cut down their number to 20.

The tablets are said to have measured $1'2''$ in length, $2^4/_{10}''$ wide, and $^2/_{10}''$ thick. For state ceremonies, they were made of jade; in less important instances, of hibiscus or cypress wood. To the tablets a gold dragon was attached: This dragon was charged to take the tablet to the residences of the *san-yuan* (or *san-kuan*).

In modern times, the rite of the "dragon throw" is not performed. (For details, see Ed. Chavannes, 1919.)

E

EARTHLY BRANCHES (*Ti-chih/Dizhi*). As heaven has its ten **Heavenly Stems**, earth has its 12 branches. Together, they are used to mark time and for the divination of future events.

As markers of time, the 12 branches, like the ten stems, are just numerical symbols similar to our Arabic numerals. But they were used by the Chinese as equivalents to our dating system. For example, the year I-1 is identical to the first year of a 60-year cycle (the Roman numerals represent the ten stems, whereas the Arabic numerals represent the 12 branches). For example, the year 1984 was the first year of a new 60-year cycle: it was represented by I-1; therefore 1985 was represented by II-2, etc. After 60 changes, when the year was X-12, a new 60-year cycle started.

It is interesting to notice that the ancient Chinese had a dual system for counting or measuring time: ten stems (based on the myth of ten suns?) and 12 branches (based on the 12 lunations, approximately, occurring in one solar year).

Besides their use as time markers, the 12 branches also served as indicators of good or bad luck in the popular tradition. But their value as omens depended on the **five agents** coinciding with each year, not just on the cyclical characters.

ECOLOGY. This is a contemporary issue that did not consciously affect the ancients, although problems did occasionally arise, as when huge demands for construction timber caused deforestation and soil erosion in North China.

But being a more modern problem, it is almost ludicrous to search for scriptural statements regarding ecological principles. Yet, written or nonwritten attitudes toward earth, creation, including animate and inanimate beings, are definitely part of various cultural or religious traditions. These can be considered the basis from which ecological principles can be extracted.

Of all traditions that we are aware of today, only two provide an ideological framework that favors and encourages ecological responsibility: the native traditions of North America and Taoism. More than any other system, these two consider human beings as part of a cosmic whole, and not necessarily even the most important part. Both regard nature as a mother who gives birth to and nourishes her children, gives of herself without calculation. That, in turn, leads to an attitude of respect for Mother Nature, especially Mother Earth: One does not exploit and hurt one's mother and endanger her life by various kinds of abuses.

In modern times, ecology has become an urgent problem, and the causes may vary, but human greed aided by technology certainly is one of the more important factors. In Taoist philosophical writings, there is an urgent warning not to indulge in technology. Better to keep life simple with the basic needs satisfied. That is especially the tendency of the "primitivists," as exemplified in the *TTC*, Chapter 80, and in Chapters 8–11 of the **Chuang-tzu**. In *Chuang-tzu*, Chapter 12 (Watson: 134), there is the marvelous anecdote about a "well sweep," a machine devised for watering the fields before spring planting. Rather than carrying water in pitchers by hand, a frustratingly slow process, the well sweep can "In one day . . . water a hundred fields, demanding very little effort and producing excellent results . . ." (Watson: 134).

When Tzu-kung, a disciple of Confucius, tried to convince an old man to try to use it, the man got angry, and said with a sneer:

I've heard my teacher say, where there are machines, there are bound to be machine worries; where there are machine worries, there are bound to be machine hearts. With a machine heart in your breast, you've spoiled what was pure and simple; and without the pure and simple, the life of the spirit knows no rest. Where the life of the spirit knows no rest, the Way will cease to buoy you up. It's not that I don't know about your machine—I would be ashamed to use it! (Watson: 134)

It is not so much a matter of rejecting technology for a Taoist, it is a question of one's "heart" becoming like a machine, and with it the threat of converting society into a "forest of machines," that is, the danger of treating humans like machines or objects, rather than free spiritual beings. That is the ultimate poison of overdeveloped technology, as we see happening in 20th-century society.

The *Lieh-tzu* offers another charming anecdote that stimulates reflection (see **Lieh-tzu: Themes**). A poor man went to consult a very rich one about methods to accumulate wealth. "I am good at stealing," said the rich man, but the poor man misunderstood. He started to break into houses and commit robberies until he was caught and jailed. After his term was over, he returned to the rich man to complain, only to discover that the rich man's way of stealing was not what he had imagined. Here is the rich man's response:

Alas! . . . Have you erred so far from the true Way of stealing? Let me explain. I have heard it said: "heaven has its seasons, earth has its benefits." I rob heaven and earth of their seasonal benefits, the clouds and rain of their irrigating floods, the mountains and marshes of their products, in order to grow my crops, plant my seed, raise my walls, build my house. I steal birds and animals from the land, fish and turtles from the water. All this is stealing; for crops and seed, clay and wood, birds and animals, fish and turtles, are all begotten by heaven, and how can they become my possessions? Yet I suffer no retribution for robbing heaven. On the other hand, precious things such as gold and jade, and commodities such as grain and silk, are collected by men, and how can we claim that it is heaven which provides them? When you steal them, why should you resent being found guilty? (A. Graham, 1960: 30–31)

Although the word "stealing" is used in a hyperbolic way, the principle implied is that one should take from nature in moderation, to satisfy one's needs, but not to accumulate superfluous wealth. Once again, the principle of simplicity in lifestyle is advocated and, as the *TTC* already expressed: display of wealth encourages robbers to come forward. Even more, extreme development of technology and its subsequent social wealth for some will lead to "overstealing" from nature and damaging it in the end. This attitude of humility, humans portrayed as "thieves," should put a stop to overexploiting our planet.

EIGHT IMMORTALS (*Pa-hsien/baxian*). The Eight Immortals are a group of semihistorical, semilegendary figures prominent in Taoism as well as in the popular religion and folklore of China.

In the Taoist tradition, a great number of **Immortals** occur: Their legendary lives are narrated in books, such as the *Lieh-hsien chuan/ Liexianzhuan* (see Kaltenmark, 1953).

In popular Taoist lore, eight immortals have been selected as eminent exemplars of world-transcendent, freely wandering sages, who reached their state of human perfection through various practices such as meditation, an ascetic life, and alchemy. Although in literature and art Taoist immortals are often depicted without any personal attributes, rather as stereotyped images of what an immortal is thought to be, a great number also appear with distinct personalities, with personal characteristics and emblems. The Eight Immortals are such a group: Each of them is clearly recognizable, in a way similar to Christian saints, who can be easily identified by their iconographic characteristics.

Since late imperial times, the cult of the Eight Immortals became an important national phenomenon. The number "eight" was chosen because of earlier sets of eight sages existed, and because eight is seen as a perfect number. One can think of the "eight diagrams" (*pa-kua/bagua*) and eight directions as important examples of numerology.

Why these particular eight were selected from among a vast number of candidates remains a mystery. But their selection does not appear to be a random combination: "Here we have old and young, male and female, rich and honoured, and poor and humble" (Yetts 1922: 399). Although the number eight certainly reflects a Chinese interest, the choice of particular sages may have followed a Buddhist model. In Buddhism, 16 sages had been selected as ideals of sainthood; they are the 16 *arhats* (*lo-han*) and which were later amplified to 18, and are still very often seen in Chinese temples of the Popular religion (especially in Taiwan). Another model may have been the Buddhist figure of Chi-kung/Jigong, a legendary monk who became an idealized symbol of eccentricity. Although he was reputed to break most of his monastic vows, he was a charismatic healer and miracle worker who helped the common people in sickness and misery. Thought of as a "mad monk," he was extremely popular and is still very much so today in the Taiwanese folk cult. Chi-kung is very likely the closest parallel to the Taoist Eight Immortals, who also excelled through their eccentricity, some even through their craziness.

Here are the names of the Eight Immortals (for each of them there is a separate entry): **Chung-li Ch'uan/Zhongli Quan; Ho Hsien-ku/ He Xiangu; Chang Kuo(-lao)/Zhang Guo(lao); Lü Tung-pin/Lü Dongbin; Han Hsiang-tzu/Han Xiangzi; Ts'ao Kuo-chiu/Cao Guojiu; Li T'ieh-kuai/Li Tiekuai; Lan Ts'ai-ho/Lan Caiho**. The order of naming is not fixed; greatest importance is usually given to Lü and Li.

The selection of eight immortals as a definite group did not occur earlier than the Yuan (Mongol) dynasty (1260–1368). But the exact "when?" and "why?" are unknown. Some historic individuals go back to the T'ang dynasty. Others, rather legendary, belong to Han times. Lü Tung-pin is given the strongest historical background, but numerous legends have changed his biography into hagiography. Chung-li Ch'uan, Han Hsiang-tzu, and Chang Kuo-lao may also have been historical personalities, but for the other four, there is no reliable historic evidence.

Their stories are told in a collection about legendary Taoist figures, *Lieh hsien chuan/Liexian zhuan*, an illustrated compilation of 55 "biographies" by a Taoist of the Yuan period, Huan-ch'u/Huanchu. (This collection has the same title as the above mentioned *Lieh hsien chuan* attributed to Liu Hsiang of the first century BCE, but is a totally different work.)

One of the major factors in the popularization of the Eight Immortals was the influence of popular drama, novels, folk stories, and the spread of woodblock printing.

Representations of the Eight Immortals in art and folklore are extremely popular and diversified. Although individual members appear already in Sung times (for example, a Sung bronze mirror shows Chung-li Ch'üan and Lü Tung-pin) as a group of eight, they do not go back beyond Ming times. But ever since, their popularity and success rate have been going crescendo. Their images appear on porcelain, embroidery, fans, painting, in wood carving, bronze, and ivory and in other popular art forms. One famous and often recurring representation is "The Eight Immortals Crossing the Ocean"; it is the story of the eight on their journey to the residence of the **Queen Mother of the West**. They are sitting on a dragon boat carrying them across the ocean to offer their birthday congratulations to the goddess. A variation of this story tells that the eight, having decided to cross the ocean together, each dropped their emblem on the waves: It turned into a magic vehicle carrying them across.

Large embroideries of the eight immortals with a ninth figure at the center, the spirit of longevity, have become central decorations in modern religious rituals. "In village temples, the altar is covered with a length of fabric on which the Immortals are shown as a group" (Eberhard, 1986: 150).

Over time, the eight have become good luck symbols: As a result, large embroideries are hung up at the homes of groom and bride on their wedding day (this is still a current Taiwan custom). Moreover, the eight often appear in stories of romance as performers of miraculous feats, and as symbols of perfect, idealized happiness. Perhaps they reflect human nostalgia for perfect happiness.

EIGHT TRIGRAMS (*Pa-kua/Bagua*). These are eight graphic symbols, each composed of three lines, either a whole line _____ or a broken line ___ ___. Originally they probably were just records of divination results, each line noting down the result of one consultation. Answers were either "lucky" or "unlucky," which was determined by odd or even numbers of a randomly picked bundle of milfoil stalks. "Lucky" results (odd numbers) were expressed by a single line _____; "unlucky" results (even numbers) were symbolized by a *double* line: ___ ___. If a consultation was repeated three times (which was acceptable because only once was doubtful; twice repeated could be a stalemate), there was a possible array of only eight results, graphically expressed in the eight following symbols (or *trigrams*, which means graphic symbols of three lines):

In a later stage of development, other meanings were superimposed on them. From simple graphics, they received philosophic (cosmic), social, and psychological dimensions. They are the basic building blocks of the classic *Yi ching* (*Book of Changes*). They are also used in *feng-shui* (geomancy) and in Taoist ritual (see **Lo River Writing** and **River Chart**). They are, in the Popular religious tradition of China, a powerful talisman to protect one's home or one's person. But they are cherished by the Taoists as well (see also **Hexagrams**).

EMBRYONIC RESPIRATION See BREATHING EXERCISES

EMPEROR WU (Han Wu-ti) (r. 140–87 BCE). He was the fourth emperor of the Former Han Dynasty (202 BCE–9 CE). Besides being a powerful ruler, he had an interest in Taoism and hoped to obtain the secrets of immortality.

During Emperor Wu's reign, the power of the Han Dynasty reached its zenith. He gradually wiped out the independent princedoms inside the country, and gathered more and more power in the central government. From 127 to 119 BCE, he waged a series of wars against the Hsiung-nu people (the "Huns"), and thus secured the northern frontiers of China. In 138 BCE, he had sent Chang Ch'ien (d. 114 BCE) to the western regions (present Sinkiang and Russian Central Asia) looking for allies against the Hsiung-nu. Chang's mission broadened the Chinese geographical and intellectual world; one of the results was the establishment of the "silk route" and silk trade both with Central Asia and with India. China's power expanded in all directions.

In 134 BCE, Emperor Wu made Confucianism the state orthodoxy: provincial schools and a national university at the capital were established for the education of students in the Confucian classics.

He also founded state monopolies of salt, iron, liquor, and coinage. His government controlled and regulated commercial life.

With regard to Taoism, Emperor Wu is remembered for his addiction to the search for immortality. He repeatedly fell victim to the deceptions and follies of *fang-shih* (alchemist-magicians), who promised that they would transmute cinnabar into gold. Drinking utensils made from this alchemical gold would eventually lead to immortality. Because the *fang-shih* promised to realize two cherished dreams of mankind, wealth and immortality, Emperor Wu continued his support of the *fang-shih*, many of whom came to enjoy high honors and wealth. However, when they failed to deliver the expected results, they were often executed.

The first *fang-shih* who gained the emperor's trust was **Li Shao-Chün**, who claimed to have met the Immortal An Ch'i-sheng on one of the far away islands in the eastern ocean. The emperor sent out search parties to find the mysterious islands, but in vain.

After Li, Shao Wong (d. 119 BCE) took over his position and claimed that he could summon the spirit of Emperor Wu's late consort, Lady Wang, a favorite concubine. The emperor trusted him and elevated him to the rank of general. He persuaded the emperor to build the Kan-ch'uan palace, in which there was a pavilion platform with various kinds of utensils for sacrifice, used to welcome the arrival of immortals and spirits. However, because this never happened, Shao Wong was executed.

Several years later, a colleague of Shao Wong named Luan Ta (d. 112 BCE) once again claimed to possess the secrets for manufacturing alchemical gold and further claimed that he could stop the flooding of the Yellow River, that he could produce the elixir of life, and was able to make the immortals appear. Within a short time, he too was ennobled and made into a general. Once more, his claims were found to be false, and he was executed.

In 113 BCE, an ancient sacrificial cauldron (*ting*) was discovered in Shansi. A *fang-shih* named Kung-sun Ch'ing convinced Emperor

Wu with the story of the Yellow Emperor's ascent to heaven. He claimed that, after the Yellow Emperor had manufactured this vessel, a dragon appeared and took the emperor, together with more than 70 ministers and concubines, up to heaven in daylight to become immortals. Emperor Wu was greatly impressed. Kung-sun advised to build more sacrificial sites and palaces throughout the country, and to improve the road system in order to facilitate and welcome the appearance of immortals.

In 110 BCE, Emperor Wu went up to Mount T'ai in Shantung to offer the sacrifices *feng* and *shan* to heaven and earth, to prepare for the arrival of immortals. Throughout his long reign, he toured the country, visiting famous mountains and the coastal areas of the east, always with the hope of encountering the immortals. Mission after mission was sent out overseas to search for the land of the immortals. Shortly before his death, he realized that death was the common fate of all, even of an uncommon person like himself. He then issued an order to abandon all the projects involving the search for the immortals and immortality.

Waking up too late from his foolish dream, Emperor Wu had drained the national treasury. At the end of his reign, the country was bankrupt. In 89 BCE, he showed his regrets by putting an end to his foreign "adventures" and domestic "follies." This decision gave his dynasty and the people a period of recovery and saved the dynasty from destruction.

However, the great lure of the secrets of immortality continued to attract many and laid the foundation for the development of Taoist alchemy. The dream of "eternal youth" proved to be enduring, but remained elusive.

EPITOME OF THE TAOIST CANON (*Tao-tsang chi-yao/Daozang jiyao*). This is a supplement to the **Taoist Canon**, although originally it was meant to be an "epitome" of the *Tao-tsang*. Indeed, in its first edition it contained 173 titles that were already included in the *Tao-tsang*.

This collection has been edited and augmented several times: The most widely available today was edited by Ho Lung-hsiang and P'eng Han-jan in Chengtu, Szechuan, at the Erh-hsien an (Temple of the Two Immortals) in 1906. This latest compilation has added several new works written in Szechuan.

A *Guide to the Tao-tsang Chi-yao* has been compiled by W. Chen: It contains a total of 308 titles. Modern reprints in circulation were published in Taipei in 1971 and 1977 (see Chen, 1987; J. Boltz, 1987).

ESSENTIALS OF SUPREME SECRETS (*Wu-shang pi-yao/Wushang biyao*). The earliest still surviving compendium of Taoist texts, compiled on order of Emperor Wu of the Northern Chou (Toba) (r. 561–577). It is an invaluable source of information about early Taoist scriptures, because it is "entirely composed of Taoist text citations" (Lagerwey, 1981: 1) from scriptures antedating the T'ang dynasty. It has been included in the Taoist Canon (*CT* 1138, *TT* 768–779) and consists of 100 chapters.

(For a complete discussion of the text, see J. Lagerwey, 1981. The introduction, pages 1–48, provides an excellent historical background.)

ETHICS. All religious and humanist systems propose a code of ethical prescriptions to their followers. Taoism is no exception, although it has been sometimes said that the Taoist philosophers, *TTC* and *Chuang-tzu*, reject all standards and values or consider them relative at best. That is a misinterpretation and needs rectification. In the Taoist religion, ethical rules were very important:

> . . . the establishment of ethical standards and their justification and enforcement were a central element of Taoism from its inception. (T. Kleeman, 1991: 163)

This statement refers obviously to the Taoist religion. It will be discussed in some detail after the ethical position of the Taoist philosophers has been explored.

• *Ethical Values in the **TTC** and **Chuang-tzu***. The *TTC*, written for the inspiration of sage rulers, contains a fair amount of ethical guidelines on how to govern a country. The ideal ruler, a *sheng-jen* or "sage," follows the model of the Tao itself. The Tao operates spontaneously, effortlessly, without any selfish motivations, etc. (see ***wu-wei***). Only this kind of superior ethics enables the ruler to attain his goals: bringing order to the country and realizing his personal objective of oneness with the Tao. Only in a derived sense does the *TTC* inspire ethical principles to follow in daily life. The greatest, richest, yet nonsuffocating ethical rule consists in *wu-wei* and all of its applications. There is also a stream of apparently anti-ethical principles noticeable in the *TTC* (Chapters 18–19; 5). This is indeed a discordant voice in the text, which originated in a rather conservative wing of Taoism and has been called "primitivist." This stream also appears in some *Chuang-tzu* chapters.

The primitivist view considers all externally imposed ethical rules as offensive against the inborn nature of human beings. Specifically, in the *TTC*, Confucian ethics are criticized; The ethical ideals of humaneness (*jen*), righteousness (*yi*), and propriety (*li*), all emphasized in the Confucian system, are rejected as violating human nature, and as signs of the decline of Tao. In Chapter 5, it is stated quite bluntly that heaven and earth (the cosmos) are not guided by *jen* (humaneness), neither is the sage. They do not act according to those artificially imposed standards.

The primitivist chapters of the *Chuang-tzu* (Chapters 8–10) are even more critical of ethical values "preached" by the sages. Although Confucianism is not named, it is clear that it is the target of *Chuang-tzu*'s iconoclasm.

Does *Chuang-tzu* reject all ethical values as irrelevant? Not at all. But true and authentic human perfection goes beyond the petty ideals of ordinary society. The sage, or the "realized person," transcends those and embodies ethical values that go far beyond them. This is not easy for "small minds" to understand! (See also **Introduction: Philosophical Texts**.)

• The *Taoist Religion*, in its various branches, has always stressed ethical rules and warned offenders against moral transgressions. To avoid being struck by disease, or in order to be healed, repentance was imposed as a necessary condition. Moreover, good works were considered to be absolute requirements to reach immortality or longevity. If the total of one's good actions fell short when compared with one's evil deeds, life would be shortened accordingly.

In setting up moral codes, Taoism was influenced by Confucian ethics and by Buddhist codes of discipline, as well as by the universally accepted Chinese belief in the unity of heaven, earth and humanity. As heaven grants emperors the mandate to rule, it also responds to the moral conduct of all individuals. Virtuous behavior will be rewarded, evil actions will be punished.

Various schools of Taoism set up their own standards of moral behavior. The early Heavenly Masters encouraged good works (such as socially useful projects: building roads, repairing bridges, etc.) as a way to atone for moral misdeeds.

Among those Taoists who strove for immortality, including Shangch'ing Taoism, rules and regulations were imposed to curb evil tendencies, to control one's thought and behavior. Good actions were "weighed" against evil actions; the balance would be a deciding factor in one's future destiny. This was especially expressed in "ledgers of good and evil deeds," which lend a quasimagical quality to moral behavior. Numerical values were assigned "to good and evil acts so that one might roughly compute one's own standing in the registers of life" (Kleeman, 1991: 164).

The ***Pao-p'u-tzu*** "contains a detailed exposition of ethical standards and their enforcement, and this account influenced much later speculation." (Kleeman: 164)

It is claimed that the body of each adept houses "secret agents" who report to heaven about the adept's wrongdoings and good deeds. These agents are either the **"Three Worms,"** the **Director of Destiny**, or the God of the Stove, who ascend periodically to heaven to submit their reports. As a result, an adept's lifespan can be either shortened or lengthened.

In imitation of Buddhism, the Taoists also established codes of ethical rules, such as the five precepts, the eight and ten precepts, and other numerical categories. The group of ten appears the most important and includes prohibitions of rebellion (against one's parents and superiors; against the government), of harming others, of having sexual relations with one's relatives, of talking evil about the Taoist doctrine, of profaning the holy places of Taoism, etc.

The degree of rigorousness depends on each school. Whereas the Complete Realization School is very demanding (it imposes celibacy and a vegetarian diet), the Heavenly Masters are more relaxed in their code; their priests are allowed to marry, and eating meat or drinking wine are not prohibited.

In general, Taoist lay people follow five precepts, similar to those of Buddhism, and are persuaded to act ethically, because good actions will have their certain reward, while evil actions will have their necessary punishment. Of this basic law of "cause and effect" (Buddhist style), they are continuously reminded by popular scriptures, such as the *Treatise on Action and Retribution* (*Kan-ying p'ien*).

As in Buddhism, the expression "receiving the precepts" (*shou-chieh*) signified one's formal initiation into Taoism, either as a cleric or as a layperson. (For an excellent survey of Taoist discipline, see T. Kleeman's article, "Taoist Ethics," 1991: 162–194.)

EXORCISM. It literally means "ritual expulsion of demons or of evil spirits from an individual or place" (*HCDR*: 352). It also could refer to the ritual purification of a person or place, with the implied intention of ridding a person or place of impersonal evil forces. In the Taoist context, exorcism serves an important function. Although cases of demon possession are very exceptional, they do occur once in a while, but exorcism of places is more frequent. Purification of the temple is one of the regular rites scheduled during the **Cosmic Renewal Festival**, whereas purification of homes or other buildings occurs only when the need arises: that is, when people believe that evil forces have entrenched themselves in their home.

First, a few words about individual exorcism. Demon possession and its exorcism is encountered in other religions besides Taoism. In Christianity, exorcism used to be a part of the baptism ritual, but other cases of possession may occur after baptism and need the special attention of priests-exorcists. Because in the Chinese tradition belief in good spirits (deities or *shen*) and in evil ones (*kui*) is taken for granted, states of possession occur regularly. Mostly, they are by good spirits, such as in mediumistic seances, when men or women, even young persons, are temporarily possessed by a deity, who uses their bodily faculties to advise clients about various situations or problems in life. Mediumism is very much alive today in Taiwan, Hong Kong, Singapore, etc., and is perhaps a remnant of ancient shamanism.

A case of demon possession is narrated by Peter Goullart, who was an eyewitness to a ritual of exorcism taking place in a Taoist temple (the date of the event is not mentioned, but the book was published in 1961). It was a dramatic event: a struggle of wills between the Taoist abbot and the possessed man, controlled by two demons. The Taoist concentrated deeply and issued orders to leave the man, but the demons fought back ferociously until, after many hours (on the third day of exorcism), they capitulated and left the man's body. The abbot's vital energy (*ch'i*) was totally exhausted, and, as a result, his life span would be shortened, like that of many other abbots, whose photographs were displayed in a temple room: They all died young as a result of their commitment to save people from evil possession (P. Goullart, 1961: 83–90. See also L. Thompson, 1979, 3rd ed.: 32–33, which has a condensed version of Goullart's story).

Ritual purification of a temple is dramatically enacted during the *chiao* festival. It may occur in several forms, either performed by a Taoist master or by a stage actor, impersonating the official devil catcher Chung K'ui. The first instance occurs on the regular agenda of the *chiao*: One of the Taoist master's acolytes dresses up as a demon, wearing a devil mask. He appears in the sacred area of the temple, searching for something and somersaulting. Then he steals the small incense burner, which belongs to the gods. This is sacrilege! Then the master appears with grandiose gestures, brandishing his ritual sword. He succeeds in "killing" the demon and returning the incense burner to the gods. This little drama, enlivened by frantic drum beatings and firecrackers, symbolizes the purification of the temple and restoring it to its pristine purity and sacredness.

When a stage actor, as Chung K'ui, performs the rite, it is even more dramatic. He descends from the stage, set up opposite the temple, and walks in grandiose strides toward the temple. Long "snakes" of firecrackers are set off everywhere on the temple square. Chung K'ui proceeds to the temple, enters it brandishing his magic sword, and kills all the demons. Thus, the temple is purified. This dramatic exorcism is possibly a remnant of ancient shamanistic ritual.

One final way of exorcistic purification is by "smoking out" the evil spirit. A large container filled with oil is heated up over a coal fire. Then liquor or water is poured on the boiling oil by a Taoist priest. It creates huge flames and clouds of smoke, which are believed to drive out all evil forces from the temple (or other buildings). Belief in the importance of ritual purity is a characteristic of Chinese religion.

F

FA-SHIH See REDHEAD TAOIST

FAN See REVERSAL

FANG-SHIH/FANGSHI. The name of a spiritual practitioner in Han and pre-Han times, which is difficult to translate, partially because his exact functions are not fully known to us. Most often the term "magician" is used. The dictionary does not help much to clarify the idea of a *fang*: 13 meanings are listed in *FECED*, of which two or three are perhaps applicable—"a prescription, recipe"; "occultism"; and "method, a way." Perhaps these gentlemen (*shih*) had something to do with medical prescriptions or, more likely, they were practitioners of occult arts; indeed the dictionary translates *fang-shih* as "occultist" or "alchemist." The latter very likely offers the best clue: *Fang-shih* were indeed among the earliest practitioners of alchemy, and alchemy was then considered an occult art.

> As used throughout the Han and Six Dynasties, *fang-shih* was more an imputation than a classification, and as an imputation it was usually pejorative. Those who were called *fang-shih* belonged to a larger community of practitioners of medicine, divination, and magic . . . (K. De-Woskin, 1981: 79)

It is reported that before 200 BCE, *fang-shih* ("magicians") appeared along the northeast coast of China and transmitted the arts of Tsou Yen. They "practiced the Tao of recipes and immortality (*fang hsien tao*)" (Welch, 1957: 96). Perhaps L. Kohn's paraphrase of *fang-shih* as "magico-technicians" is an excellent choice, because it emphasizes their expert technical skills, while leaving the area of their expertise open (Kohn, 1995: 40).

With the development of **Heavenly Masters Taoism,** the *fang-shih* seem to disappear. It is said that they were replaced by *tao-shih,* "gentlemen of the Tao." Yet, as DeWoskin demonstrates, they remained active throughout the Six Dynasties period. (See K. De-Woskin, 1981 and 1983.)

FANG-SHU See SEXUALITY

FASTING See DIET

FEMINIST PERSPECTIVES. Like ecology, feminism is a contemporary issue, but woman's position in society, or society's attitudes toward women, is an ancient problem. Here the focus, of course, is on Taoism and Taoist attitudes toward women in a Chinese cultural context. In general, ancient religions did not have a high regard for women.

> Like Judaism and Christianity, Buddhism is an overwhelmingly male-created institution dominated by a patriarchal power structure. As a consequence of this male dominance, the feminine is frequently associated with the secular, powerless, profane, and imperfect. (D. Paul, 1979: xiii)

Much of this statement applies to China. Confucianism did not regard women highly and the prevailing social attitude, not necessarily Confucian but generally Chinese, placed women in a lower social condition than men. Women were subjected to the authority of males all through life: as young girls to their father, as married to their husbands, in old age to their sons. Women did not enjoy the same privileges as men, including access to education, power of economic decision-making, overall independence. In general, Chinese religion went along with this prevailing social climate, and even tended to strengthen social prejudices. Buddhism, and somehow Taoism as well, accepted as a matter of fact that females were of an inferior essence due to karma incurred in previous lives. Once this karma was wiped out, they would be eligible to be reborn as males. (This was originally a Buddhist concept, but taken over by Taoism and the Popular religion.)

Taoism was different from other systems and did not follow along completely with the prevailing value system. It is important, however, to distinguish between theory and practice. That distinction applies to other religions as well, for example, in Christianity, men and women are of equal dignity, theoretically; in practice, however, not at all! In Taoism, the theory places women on a very high pedestal; in actual practice, there is no complete equality, but the situation is better than in most other systems. These two distinct areas of theory and practice must be further explored.

On the level of theory, the *Tao-te ching* values the dignity of the female, of the mother. Tao is compared to the female, not to the male. The female conquers male aggressiveness through stillness, yielding; like Tao, she embodies fertility and life-nurturing qualities. That is the theory. Did those who wrote the *TTC* apply these principles in their own lives? We don't know. But some modern voices are skeptical:

> The *Tao-te ching* contains many statements praising non-interference, yielding, lowliness, and the virtues of water, all of them conventionally regarded as showing appreciation for the "feminine" side of existence, but of course all these virtues are simply expressions of what men would like women to be . . . [It] does not mean that one thinks highly of women . . ." (Overmyer, 1991: 92)

Whether Overmyer's assessment is fully valid or not is hard to say, but in actual practice, the Taoist organized institution of the second century CE treated women as equals of men in all but one level of hierarchy: the highest rank of Heavenly Master. But the lower ranks were all accessible to women. (See also **Heavenly Masters Taoism.**)

During the medieval period, women were entitled to enter into religious life. There were several princesses of the T'ang who gained a reputation of eminent virtue and scholarship. The Taoist master Tu Kuang-t'ing, around 900 CE, compiled a collection of 28 biographies of Taoist women saints, who lived from the Han through the T'ang period (S. Cahill, 1990: 23). Remarkable though these stories are, they also show the great difficulties those women had to overcome to realize their goal of spiritual life. Society had other expectations for them: Women belong to families and must produce the next generation in their husbands' families. A woman who chose not to marry and have children was eyed with suspicion, unless she was in poor health or was "widowed" before the wedding took place.

One of the new schools of Taoism founded during the foreign Chin rule (1115–1235) was Complete Realization (Ch'uan-chen) Taoism. One of its major characteristics, besides an ascetic lifestyle and a syncretistic tendency, was its concern for women membership. Among the seven disciples of founder Wang Che was one woman. Like the others, she founded her own branch. The new school attracted women, because Taoism, unlike Confucianism, which did not welcome females into its educational system, gave women a chance to be educated. Some of them gained a high reputation of learning and spiritual achievement.

What happened to women in Taoism in later times is not clear. When Taoism, as well as Buddhism, declined during the Manchu dynasty, little is heard of women Taoists rising to prominence. Overall, women's roles were much stronger in the Popular religion (as shamanesses or trance mediums) and in sectarian movements.

In recent times, women once again have access to religious professionalism, at least in the Complete Realization School in China. In Taiwan, the **Heavenly Masters** and **"Redhead" Taoists** seem to be all male. The only exhilarating exception is the Tao-te yuan in the southern city of Kaohsiung. In this temple, a group of Taoist priestesses live in community maintaining a celibate lifestyle. They actively spread Taoism and Taoist spirituality within the community.

The future of women in Taoism is a matter of speculation. Their status will greatly depend on the overall status of women in society. In China, there is much more gender equality today than there ever was, but women's participation in Taoism will not just be a matter of equality, but of incentive. The road is open, but to become a Taoist nun (or a Buddhist nun) may always be a choice made by few.

Beyond talking about legal issues, Taoism emphasizes that woman really rules the world in a deeper sense. For what we all need in a harsh (masculine?) world is tenderness, gentleness, nurturing, loving, and spiritual healing, and woman is best qualified to offer these gifts to the world. This is much more important than the "unreal" world of power politics, poverty, and oppression.

FENG and **SHAN** **SACRIFICES.** A double set of sacrificial rituals performed in ancient times by some emperors, who felt confident enough to believe they had received heaven's mandate to rule. The terms *feng* and *shan* are not easy to translate, although "wind" and "mountain" (as in *HCDR* 1995: 360) are certainly incorrect. *Feng* indicates "altar mound" or elevation (a suitable location to sacrifice to heaven), whereas *shan* (same character as *ch'an* or *zen*, but pronounced differently) indicates level ground (appropriate location to sacrifice to earth).

Emperors well established and confident would perform these sacrifices to announce their mandate to the spiritual realm of heaven and earth, and possibly to thank Heaven for bestowing the mandate. Several mythical rulers are believed to have performed *feng* and *shan* sacrifices, especially the **Yellow Emperor.** In historic times, the First Emperor of Ch'in had the presumption to do the same in 219 BCE, but was not able to keep the mandate for his successors. His action has been criticized in *Historical Documents* as presumptuous.

One of the most famous cases is Han Emperor Wu, whose *feng* and *shan* sacrifices took place in 110 BCE. First the *feng* ritual took place at the foot of Mount T'ai (and a second time on the mountaintop), and next, the *shan* took place at Mount Su-jan in Liang-fu (also reported in *Historical Documents*). Although these rituals were actions of the imperial state cult without any specific Taoist significance, in the case of Emperor Wu, Taoist ideas may have been involved. He had been encouraged by his *fang-shih* to perform these sacrifices after he had visualized the immortals on the island of P'eng-lai. As a result, he would become an immortal just as the Yellow Emperor in ancient times. Emperor Wu's dream, however, did not materialize. (See B. Watson, 1971, II: 13–69.)

The sacrifices have been performed several times by later emperors of the Han, T'ang, Sung, Ming, and Ch'ing dynasties, but there hardly seems to be any connection with Taoism. They were rituals of the state cult.

FIELDS OF CINNABAR See *TAN-T'IEN*

FIRST EMPEROR OF CHINA (Ch'in shih huang-ti/Qinshihuangdi) (259–210 BCE). He was the first emperor of China, who unified the country into an immense centralized empire and founded the Ch'in dynasty. (The English word "China" is derived from "Ch'in.")

When he ascended the throne of the state of Ch'in as a young man of thirteen, the Ch'in state power was already on the rise. He chose an able and ruthless man as prime minister, Li Szu/Li Si (d. 208), and chose the Legalism of Han Fei-tzu as state doctrine. The two, plus the young king's own determination, were critical factors in the conquest of all rival states. Between 230 and 221 BCE, Ch'in was successful in destroying and annexing all other states and proclaimed his new empire.

During his twelve years on the throne, he introduced many changes that outlasted his dynasty. He divided the country into commanderies (*chün/jun*) and prefectures (*hsien/xian*) and appointed officials to run them. He unified and standardized weights, measures, and currency; established a uniform writing system and a body of laws. To solidify his own power, he abolished the hereditary aristocracy in the former rival kingdoms and moved many of these potential opponents to his capital of Hsien-yang/Xianyang (in the province of Shensi). To prevent all possible opposition among the intellectuals, he exercised thought control and censored books. One of his actions fiercely criticized by later scholars is his destruction of all books considered politically detrimental to his regime (in 211 BCE). Those scholars, all together 460, who objected and criticized the government were buried alive.

Following legalist doctrines to the extreme, he was able, for a time, to control the people by rewards and harsh punishments.

The first emperor also undertook a series of huge engineering projects: a national network of roads, a chain of palaces in the capital, and his own mausoleum (now one of the most splendid tourist attractions near the modern city of Xi'an). He further strengthened the northern defense line against barbarian invasions by linking up the defense walls built by the former states of Chao, Yen, and Ch'in. This huge project became known as the Great Wall of China, a 2,500 km. defense corridor stretching from Kansu in the west to Liaoning in the east. All these engineering projects probably engaged about 15 percent of the total population. This overtaxation of human, economic, and natural resources eventually led to the downfall of the Ch'in dynasty, when the first emperor passed away in 210 BCE.

Although the first emperor was an able, though ruthless, general and administrator, he is also known for his quasi-Taoist beliefs in the drug of immortality, beliefs verging on superstition. Obsessed with a desire for immortality, he toured the country five times, not only to offer sacrifices to the spirits of mountains and rivers and to demonstrate his new dynasty's glory and power, but also to find experts able to give him the secret of eternal life. During his eastern tour to the coast, he conducted a series of interviews with local magicians (*fang-shih*), who informed him of the existence of three mysterious islands of immortals located in the eastern oceans: P'eng-lai/Penglai (the best known), Fang Chang/Fangzhang and Ying Chou/Yingzhou. On these islands, the *fang-shih* claimed, grew the mushroom of immortality (*ling-chih*) and lived many immortals in a state of happiness. Reports brought back from these islands said that everything on these islands, including animals, was white colored. The immortals' palaces were built of gold and silver.

The first emperor was obsessed with these mythical stories and sent several missions to find them and bring back the magic mushroom. But his efforts did not meet with success. Wasting energy and resources, they just sped up the fall of his dynasty. When he died during his eastern trip in 210 BCE, there was a conspiracy against his son, Fu Su, who had not been informed of his father's death. A subsequent power struggle in court completed the collapse of the Ch'in empire. Eventually, a new dynasty, the Han, would take over the mandate.

FIVE AGENTS SYSTEM (*Wu-hsing/Wuxing*). This is a philosophical system integrated into the *Yin-Yang* worldview: in simple terms, *yin* and *yang*, as primordial powers of the cosmos, operate through five agencies, five powers, five kinds of activity. Formerly often translated as "five elements" (which is misleading, because they are "active" powers, not "dead" elements), a more modern term, on its way to general acceptance is "five phases." Yet, this translation too is inadequate: "phases" emphasizes the time sequence in which these five are active, but time is not the major consideration. The inner essence of the five is better indicated by "agents" or "phasic agents": active powers that are active in rotation. A more rare translation is "five powers."

THE FIVE AGENTS

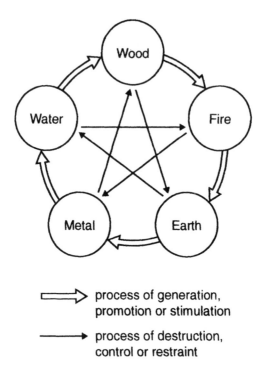

process of generation, promotion or stimulation

process of destruction, control or restraint

Just like yin and yang, the five agents system is not specifically Taoist. But it has been incorporated into Taoism, as well as into Confucianism. To understand all aspects of Taoism, the **Yin-Yang Worldview** and the Five Agents System have to be taken into account.

The origin of the Five Agents is as elusive as the origin of *Yin-Yang*. In the beginning the two were not combined. It is the School of Naturalism, with **Tsou Yen**, that came up with the ingenious idea to "marry" the two systems. Although their union is rather artificial, it works, especially when one considers that those five powers of nature are not unchanging entities. They rotate in time with the seasons and with the years, each of them having a *yang* or strong phase, and a *yin* or weak phase. After an agent has grown weak, it is overcome and replaced by the next one, all in a fixed order or sequence.

Other philosophical traditions have come to similar observations concerning the constitution of reality. The ancient Greeks, and later the Buddhists (and Hindus), analyzed reality by discerning "four elements": fire and water (these are universal), earth, and air or either wind or ether. The Chinese system is exceptional in that it has included unusual components; besides fire and water and earth, they thought of wood and metal as powerful agencies of nature. The rationale is not clear, but the choice of these five has a definite link with the observation of nature, in particular the rotation of the seasons.

Another, or complementary, explanation is that the Five Agents had a strong connection with alchemy within the School of Tsou-yen. Then the choice of wood and metal made good sense: "Wood" was the indispensable source of heat in the alchemical furnace; "metal" (in Chinese it is the same characters as "gold") was the basic stuff to experiment with and (as gold) the end product of experimentation.

By the time of Tsou-yen, the choice of "five" as a sacred number had become universal (five sacred mountains, five Confucian virtues, etc., had replaced the former four). Applied to the agents, a fifth had to be added, although it created a problem: How to coordinate five with four seasons and four directions? A solution was found by placing "earth" in the center (although its corresponding season remained a problem). The final arrangement of the Five Agents and their correlates was very ingenious, as the table indicates.

Five Agents

wood	east	spring	green
fire	south	summer	red
earth	center		yellow
metal	west	fall	white
water	north	winter	black

As each agent works seasonally, in rotation in a definite sequence, it was equivalent to saying that each agent "produces" the next one (just as spring "produces" summer). Moreover, a different type of relationship was also seen as prominent: Some agents work against others. This double set of relationships is quite important to explain natural and human phenomena: in the *positive* set, wood produces fire; fire produces earth; earth produces metal; metal produces water; water produces wood. The word "produce" means "to generate, promote, stimulate." There is also a set of *negative* relationships, in which agents defeat each other. There is conflict, control, even destruction. This order or sequence is as follows: Wood defeats earth, earth defeats water, water defeats fire, fire defeats metal, metal defeats wood.

This double set is an interpretation of what one observes in nature, in the history of individuals and of nations. Applied to the calendar or rotation of the years, each year is assigned an agent: first in its strong or *yang* phase; next in its weak or *yin* phase; then it is followed by the next agent in the positive sequence, etc.

The intimate rapport between human beings and nature is very well expressed in this scheme; it is another illustration of the oneness of the cosmos and humanity, and serves as a basis for reflection and meditation.

In *spring*, the power of wood is dominant. This expresses new birth, generation, the revival of growth after winter. It is water that stimulates this growth. Spring is related to the east, where the sun is seen to rise; its color is green, as a symbol of vegetation.

In *summer*, the power of fire takes over, stimulated by wood. Indeed, fire easily arises in forests through thunderstorms. Summer is the time of heat, which brings life to its peak. It is related to the south, and its color is red.

In *fall*, the power of metal is in control. Metals are found inside the earth. In other words, earth generates metal. It is linked to the west; its color is white (this is probably based on "white gold" as the representative of all metals). It is the time of maturing and harvesting, when metal implements are needed.

In *winter*, finally, the power of water takes over. It is not easy to see how metal produces water, but water is related to winter and to the north. Its color is black, which has many mythical connotations, such as the Northern Darkness. Water also appears in the form of snow and ice.

Although this scheme of rotation of seasons-agents is a useful device to explain changes in the universe, it must not be thought that any of the Five Agents was active exclusively at any given time. All five were active all the time, but only one was predominant. After an agent had exhausted its strength, it gave way to the next one in line.

Tied to the seasons, this scheme also explains and justifies human activity throughout the agricultural year: Spring is the time of sowing and planting; summer the time of growth and weeding; fall the time of harvest; winter the time for storing and rest. The Chinese Spring Festival (which used to be called New Year) came at the end of winter, when there was still leisure and time for celebration, before action in the fields would be resumed.

If one looks at the four seasons as a microcycle, they become symbols of life times (macrocycle). Spring is the time of youth and growth (when one is still "green"?); summer means adulthood and maturity, married life and career; fall is the time of old age (with "gold in the bank"?); winter is return to one's root, decay and death.

An important application of the Five Agents system has to do with Taoist meditation. The Shang-ch'ing School attached great importance to the visualization of the Five Viscera (five internal organs), seen as correspondences with the Five Agents.

> . . . within the human body, the viscera are both the location and privileged form of the expression of [the Five Agents or Powers]. The Powers are active everywhere in the body—each according to its own mode, its own means of action . . . and its own time . . . the viscera are the points of concentration or nodes which integrate the other bodily parts according to a rule determined by the relationship of the Five Agents-Powers and the viscera. (Robinet, 1979/1993: 61–62)

The Five Agents System had other interesting applications to human life and destiny. Each year is under the influence of one agent, but so are month, day, and hour of day. These are the "four pillars" of life (or "eight characters," because each pillar was expressed in two cyclical characters). These "four pillars" constitute each individual's horoscope, the year, month, day, and hour of birth influence one's life's destiny. It still is one of the functions of Taoist priests to advise young people about the suitability of a marriage alliance, because the "four pillars" of each party have to be checked for compatibility. This has nothing to do with the twelve cyclic animals (which are a funny folkloric custom), but with the five agents and their mutual relationships. (See also *Yin-Yang* **Worldview**.)

FIVE PHASES See FIVE AGENTS SYSTEM

FIVE SACRED MOUNTAINS (Five Sacred Peaks, or "Marchmounts") (*Wu-yueh/Wuywe*). Sometimes described as Taoist mountains, this appellation is incorrect. These five mountains are part of the overall geographic culture of China, and were already highly esteemed and worshipped before the formation of Taoism. It is true, however, that they play a role in Taoism as well, as several of these mountain peaks have become sites of famous Taoist temples. Besides these, the Taoists had their own specific mountains as well. (See also **Mountains**.)

In recent publications, one often encounters the term "marchmount," a term coined by Ed Schafer, who found "sacred mountain" a somewhat awkward equivalent, especially in translation of poetry. His version was based "on the ancient belief that these numinous mountains stood at the four extremities of the habitable world, the marches of man's proper domain, the limits of the ritual tour of the Son of Heaven" (Schafer, 1977: 6). The word "march" indeed can signify "a boundary, a border or frontier" (*Webster's*), but it is probably better to keep "marchmount" limited to poetry, as Schafer's argument about "extremities" is not fully convincing. In ordinary prose, "marchmount" is rather cumbersome.

Originally there were only four sacred peaks, but with the rise of the Five Agents theory, another one, in the center, was added. It is believed that the mountains and their directions were established at a time when Loyang was China's capital: otherwise, the western mountain, Hua-shan, would not have been situated in the east.

Worship of the "four" mountains is already very old: Emperor Shun is said to have visited his empire and sacrificed to Shang-ti on the four mountains (mentioned in the *Book of Documents* or *Shu ching*). Later emperors gave special titles and assigned functions to the mountain deities believed to reside there. Moreover, because it was believed that those mountain spirits must feel sad and melancholy, the Sung Emperor Chen-tsung (r. 998–1022) gave them female companions with the title of empress.

But before that, T'ang emperors had temples constructed at the foot of each mountain. The Eastern Peak was elevated to the rank of "president," because it was in the direction of the rising sun (see table below).

All throughout history, temples have been constructed on the mountains, both of Taoist and Buddhist affiliation, but also of the State Cult and the Popular religion. In a monograph on T'ai-shan, E. Chavannes lists and describes 252 temples and pavilions that he visited on the mountain during two research trips, in 1891 and 1907 (Chavannes 1910). Other mountains, like Hua-shan, less accessible, were a favorite site for Taoist practitioners and centers for training in meditation and martial arts (Deng, 1987).

Table: Five Sacred Mountains

Direction	Mountain	Location	Deity's Duties
East	T'ai-shan	T'ai-an fu Shantung	Distribution of goods and ranks. Fixing times of birth and death.
South	Heng-shan	Heng-chou fu Hunan	Rules heavenly bodies that influence existence; earthly properties, acts of fish, dragons, scaled water animals.
West	Hua-shan	Tung-chou fu Shansi	Distributions of goods, lands, marshes, watercourses, hills, canals, mountains, forests, etc.
North	Heng-shan	Ta-t'ung fu Shensi	Ruler of five metals, their fusion and furnace; all winged and hairy animals, etc.

Center	Sung-shan	Honan fu Honan	Particular formation of great rivers, all species of tigers, leopards, and running animals, snakes, reptiles, etc.

(Ch. de Harlez, 1893: 112–117)

FIVE TALISMANS (SCRIPTURE) (*Wu-fu hsü/Wufuxu*). A Taoist text, one of the earliest scriptures of the Ling-pao School. Its full title is *T'ai-shang ling-pao wu-fu hsü* (*CT* 338; *TT* 183). Although the present text dates from the fifth century CE, it is believed that its oldest parts go back to the Eastern Han and are based on magical writings of that period. It includes

> . . . a variety of magical and mystical longevity techniques, to a large part based on a cosmology that correlates celestial, mundane, and human phenomena . . . (T. Yamada, in L. Kohn, 1989: 99–100)

The text discusses dietetics as one important method to gain immortality. Another method is meditation, preferably practiced in a mountain setting. That explains the inclusion of the Five Talismans in the final chapter, which give the title to the text as a whole. Entering mountains was considered to be potentially dangerous; the talismans are for protection against evil, but are also "active helpers in the search for immortality . . ." (Yamada: 117).

(For a more detailed analysis, see Yamada, in Kohn, 1989: 99–124.)

FU See REVERSAL and RETURN; FU-LU

FU-LU ("Register"). The expression *fu-lu* consists of two characters, which together indicate Taoist registers, but, used separately, can have different meanings. This applies especially to *fu*, which by itself refers to **talismans**.

The expression dates from the second century CE Heavenly Masters School. When Chang Tao-ling divided his realm into 24 administrative units, he appointed male and female officers for each of them, named "libationers" (*chi-chiu*), "chosen from among the Elders and charged with the responsibility of the sacrifices" (K. Schipper, 1982/ 1993: 63). These libationers received a *fu* and a *lu* as official documents of their initiation and empowerment. These *fu* combined made up the 24 energies within the "Diagram of the Orthodox One of the Twenty-Four energies" (Schipper: 63). It is not clearly indicated that these *fu* are the same or the prototypes of the later *fu*, talismans, so popular from the Six Dynasties on.

A *lu* or register was also given to those who had received the *fu*. It contained all the powers given to the adept and put at his disposal "a small corpse of lesser gods whom he could mentally invoke and call on by name to protect him" (Schipper: 64).

So from the start, *fu* and *lu* were different in nature, but bestowed simultaneously at initiation. *Fu* was more of a graphic symbol (*t'u*), whereas a *lu* was a list of gods whom the Taoist could call down for assistance.

It appears that the meaning and contents of *fu-lu* have changed over time. *Fu* (talismans) became an independent Taoist (and Popular and Buddhist) magic art; *lu* grew in complexity, which was already fore-shadowed in Han times. Even then, registers were graded: the lowest for children guaranteed protection of a single general. At age twelve, the protective deities were increased to ten, at the age of marriage, to 75 (Schipper: 64). With time, each school developed its own registers, because the pantheons were not identical. But a common trait is the correct use of the *lu*:

> In order to perform ritual properly, the Taoist was required to memorize these spirits' appearance, clothing, secret names, and even the sort of perfume used on their apparel. In the performance of public ritual as well as in private meditation, the vision was to be formed in the mind of the adept with immense care that every detail . . . was complete and accurate. (M. Saso, 1978: 35)

In Chinese language, the term *fu-lu p'ai* (fu-lu school) is often used to refer to this particular Taoist method. In fact, there is no organized body of this name; it is a ritual method that can be and has been adopted by various schools (see **School**).

FU-TI See GROTTO-HEAVENS AND BLESSED SPOTS

FU-YU TI-CHÜN See LÜ TUNG-PIN

G

GHOST See "SOUL"

GOD OF THE SOIL or Earth-Spirit (*T'u-ti kung/Tudigong*. Another name is *Fu-te cheng-shen/Fude zhengshen*, literally, "Correct Spirit of the Power of Happiness"). Not essentially a Taoist deity, but shared with the Communal religion, he is the protector of small geographic areas, such as hamlets, city districts, or even privately owned land. Most likely a "descendant" of ancient fertility gods, he is believed to ensure rich harvests (in modern iconography, he is holding a gold ingot in one hand), but is also some sort of "rural policeman" of the spirit world. Whenever a person in his constituency dies, his guards will take his/her soul and conduct it to the temple of the **City God**, his immediate superior, whence it will be escorted to the netherworld.

The cult of the Earth-Spirit is still very strong in such Chinese areas as Taiwan and Hong Kong. In Taiwan, his temples count in the thousands, mostly small roadside shrines, a few feet high, very soberly decorated. Other shrines are placed very auspiciously at the center of community life and preferably in the shadow of a huge, old tree (where a tree-spirit resides). In recent times, Taiwanese people have rebuilt hundreds of these modest shrines, and made them very colorful, with ceramic tiles and glazed roofs. It represents the economic prosperity of recent years.

Some older Earth-Spirit temples, especially in major cities, continue to play an important role in the life of the surrounding community. These temples, in contrast with thousands of others, have been officially registered at the city hall and are, functionally, small community temples.

In some temples, one finds images of the Earth-spirit's wife (*T'u-ti-p'o/Tudipo*), because, like many other gods of the Chinese pantheon, the Earth-Spirit lives a "human" life, with consort and family.

Perhaps unexpectedly, one finds smaller clay images of the Earth-Spirit on grave sites, usually on the side, almost unnoticeable. The rationale is that the god is master of the tomb site, and his good graces must be implored and obtained so that the "soul" of the person buried there may rest undisturbed and protected from evil forces.

GOLD CINNABAR TAOISM (*Chin-tan* or *Tan-ting P'ai*). A Taoist technique that is not a school in the proper sense, but a method that can be shared by various schools; a practical synonym for **alchemy**, in its double meaning.

The expression *chin-tan* is sometimes translated as "golden elixir" or "golden pill," but that is not accurate (what would be the meaning of a golden pill anyway?). It seems better to see *chin* and *tan* as two concrete nouns: *gold* and *cinnabar* (two goals to be achieved) that together, constitute an abstract noun, like alchemy.

The roots of alchemy go back to ancient times and had to do with striving for immortality and becoming a spirit-immortal (*shen-hsien*). The writings of **Wei Po-yang** and **Ko Hung** strongly influenced the movement.

At first, during the North-South dynasties until Sui and T'ang, the emphasis was on **outer alchemy**; from the Sung and Yuan periods on, **inner alchemy**.

The results of alchemical practices were the development of scientific research methods (proto-chemistry), and the creation of techniques for long life ("nourishing life," *yang-sheng*) and **ch'i-kung.**

GOURD See PLANT SYMBOLISM

GRAND UNITY TAOISM (*T'ai-yi Tao/Taiyi Dao*). One of the three schools of Taoism established in Northern China during the Jurchen Chin dynasty, after the Sung court had moved south. Its founder was Hsiao Pao-chen/Xiao Baozhen, who established his school in about 1138.

The name *T'ai-yi* has two possible origins: It either refers to the school's transmission of *T'ai-yi* (Supreme One) and *San-yuan* (Three Originals) registers or takes the concept of pure Oneness of the original *ch'i* as its basic theory.

Soon after its start, the Grand Unity School became quite popular, attracting a great number of followers. It built T'ai-yi halls in Ch'ao-chou and Chen-ting. Its fame reached the imperial court. In 1149, Chin Emperor Hsi-tsung (r. 1135–1149) invited founder Hsiao to his palace to heal the empress's illness. He gave the title *T'ai-yi wan-shou kuan* to his T'ai-yi hall. Several patriarchs were patronized by the Chin and later by the Mongol court.

In 1274, Yuan Emperor Shih-tsu (Khubilai Khan) ordered the construction of T'ai-yi temples in the two capitals and put the fifth patriarch, Hsiao Chü-shou, in charge of sacrifices. In 1315, Emperor Jen-tsung (r. 1312–1321) ordered three patriarchs (i.e., the seventh patriarch of T'ai-yi, the Cheng-yi patriarch Chang Liu-sun and Complete Realization patriarch Sun Te-yi) to celebrate a great golden register *chiao* ritual in Ta-tu's (today's Beijing) Ch'ang-ch'un kung (Eternal Spring Temple).

The T'ai-yi School existed for about 200 years, until the end of the Yuan dynasty. After the seventh patriarch, there are no more historical documents; its continuation remains doubtful. It was possibly absorbed into Cheng-yi Taoism.

The school emphasized *fu-lu* (talismans and registers) and *chai-chiao* (fasting and sacrificial offerings), similar to Cheng-yi Taoism. They used *fu-lu* for healing and exorcism, and used *chai-chiao* to pray for rain or to stop rain. Besides serving the people, its patriarchs often performed the golden register great *chiao* for the benefit of the imperial court. It is the only *fu-lu* school among the three northern schools.

The T'ai-yi School imposed the rule of celibacy on its members, in contrast with the Cheng-yi School. During the Yuan period, it was influenced by the Neo-Confucian "School of Principle" (*li-hsueh*); as a result, it focused on the (Confucian) virtues of loyalty-trust; and filial piety-kindness, thus embodying a spirit of syncretism (*MDC*: 22).

Patriarchs of T'ai-yi Taoism (the founder ordered all his successors to change their last name to Hsiao):
1. Hsiao Pao-chen (d. 1166)
2. Hsiao Tao-hsi (d. 1182)
3. Hsiao Chih-ch'ung (1150–1216)
4. Hsiao Fu-tao (great-grandson of founder) (d. 1252)
5. Hsiao Chü-shou (1220–1280)
6. Hsiao Ch'uan-yu (patriarch in 1281; d. 1318?)
7. Hsiao T'ien-yu

GREAT PEACE (EQUALITY) SCRIPTURE (*T'ai-p'ing Ching/ Taipingjing*) (Abbreviated *TPC*). It is the earliest scripture of the Taoist religious movement and became the theoretical basis of the T'ai-p'ing Tao in the second century CE. Although written by several hands over a period of time, it contains most of the elements of later Taoism, including chapters on meditation and immortality. Its central message is that heaven is sending a Heavenly Master (*T'ien-shih*) to restore peace in the world.

The extant *Tao-tsang* version is titled *T'ai-p'ing ching* (*CT* 1101, *TT* 746–755; in Taiwan edition, vol. 40). However, it is believed (and recorded) that earlier versions existed, each having a slightly different title:

- *T'ien-kuan li pao-yuan T'ai-p'ing ching,* in 12 chapters, presented to Han Emperor Ch'eng (r. 32–7 BCE) by Kan Chung-k'o from the eastern state of Ch'i.
- *T'ai-p'ing ch'ing-ling shu,* in 170 chapters, presented to Emperor Shun (r. 126–144 CE) by Kung Ch'ung, who said he had received it from his master, **Yü Chi** (or Kan Chi).
- *T'ai-p'ing tung-chi ching,* in 144 chapters, revealed to Chang Ling (Tao-ling) by T'ai-shang Lao-chün.

How much the extant canonical text has inherited from the earlier versions is not known, but it is accepted that it contains ancient parts that predate the healing cults of the second century CE.

It is also fairly certain that old version number two influenced Taoist leader Chang Chüeh in the east, and old version number three had a great impact on Chang Tao-ling in the West. Indeed, the scripture contains the blueprint for a renewed era of great peace, to be realized by a renewed government on the basis of sound religious beliefs and practices. It is, in a new dress, the combination of good rulership and sageliness. Perhaps its effect on the dynasty was minimal, and because the middle of the second century CE saw a deteriorating situation, the new ideology inspired men of action who attempted to inaugurate the promised era of peace without, and even against, the government.

The concept of *t'ai-p'ing* had an ancient history and is found in several of the classics. The rulers of high antiquity, the only ones who ever established great peace, governed through *wu-wei*, and satisfied three basic needs of the people: food, union of the sexes, and clothing. The scripture reveals that the great peace will return to the earth in the near future, but some conditions must be fulfilled: a return to the essential (*yuan-ch'i/yuanqi*) through exercises of spiritual concentration (*shou-yi*, "retaining the One") and other methods to obtain longevity, as well as the practice of morality and good government.

This basic insight makes the *TPC* "a religious book which teaches a doctrine of salvation" (Kaltenmark, 1979: 24). Strangely for a Western reader, this book must be transmitted to a prince of high virtue. For this purpose, heaven periodically sends sages (*sheng-jen*), or sage teachers (*sheng-shih*), to earth to transmit its teachings to the ruler. In other words, one sees here the seeds of theocratic rule.

There is a strong emphasis on moral obligations, one of the most urgent ones being the duty to share. This does not only mean the circulation of material possessions, but also of spiritual treasures and experience. For instance, those who have "accumulated the Tao and refuse to share it with others commit a heavy sin, which will harm the sinners as well as their descendants." The same, of course, applies to the sharing of material goods. "Thus, on all levels—spiritual, material, economic, and, it must be added, physiological—things have to circulate: This is what the Tao and life consist of." (Kaltenmark: 35).

Further, four kinds of evil conduct are denounced: to lack in filial piety, not to procreate, to eat manure and urine, to beg. This is most likely a hidden attack against Buddhism (Kaltenmark: 35).

Other moral prescriptions are: prohibition of alcohol; infanticide (especially of daughters), which causes a shortage of available women, because each man should have two wives (yang is odd, yin is even); rejection of chastity.

The ideal of long life is strongly promoted, but is only possible in a time of *T'ai-p'ing*. There are different allotments of life expectancy: 80, 100, 120 years. Beyond that, only exceptionally can one go beyond this limit and become an immortal. There are, of course, conditions: One must live morally; one must meditate on the One (*shou-yi*) and reflect upon one's sins, which are the cause of disease; one must practice various kinds of hygiene, including diet and breathing;

and one may use medicinal substances for health, and use talismans for curing disease. Also, some aspects of (Chinese) medicine are recommended: moxa, acupuncture, pulse taking. And, finally, music is seen as promoting good health: the five tones have their good effects on the five inner organs (Kaltenmark: 41–44).

The overall ideology of the *TPC* reflects much of classical (philosophical) Taoism, but also foreshadows important aspects of later Taoist religion. Classical ideas are the yin-yang structure of the universe and the triad of heaven, earth and man. But above all, it is Tao that controls all changes in the universe. This universe, as macrocosm, is inherent in human beings and society, the microcosm. Great Peace (and Equality) can only be achieved if these two worlds interact through the mediation of an enlightened and virtuous ruler.

GREAT PEACE TAOISM (*T'ai-p'ing Tao/Taipingdao*). A Taoist utopian movement that was very popular in the middle of the second century CE. It spread into eight eastern provinces of China at the end of the Han dynasty. Its founder, the eldest of Three **Chang Brothers**, Chang Chueh, claimed to have received the revelation that a new era of Great Peace and Equality was about to arrive. It would replace the Han government and inaugurate a paradise on earth. It was believed that this would start in the year 184 CE, the first year of a new 60-year cycle.

Chang Chueh and his brothers Chang Liang and Chang Pao started to preach their vision and attracted numberless followers. They sent out preachers to the eight provinces of eastern China, and within just over ten years, their converts numbered in the tens of thousands. They had

> . . . something like 360,000 adherents. Such figures imply massive conversions. This rapid burgeoning can only be explained through an unleashing of religious enthusiasm. (Maspero, 1971/1981: 379)

The Chang brothers divided their territory into 36 districts, each of which was headed by a *fang* (a regional authority): *ta-fang* or great *fang*, who had more than 10,000 subjects; and *hsiao-fang* or lesser *fang*, with 6,000 to 8,000 subjects. The title *fang* is obviously reminiscent of *fang-shih*, and Maspero thinks it might have been a reference to "magician" (Maspero: 375). Under the *fang*'s authority was a rank of lower officials, named "great chiefs" (*ch'ü-shuai*), assisting them in the organization of the communities.

The Chang brothers themselves were the top leaders: they chose high-ranking titles for themselves, claiming to be representatives of the Three Powers: heaven, earth, mankind. Chang Chueh, as supreme leader, took the title of General Lord-Heaven (*T'ien-kung chiang-chün*), whereas the younger brothers were General Lord-Earth (*Ti-kung chiang-chün*) and General Lord-Mankind (*Jen-kung chiang-chün*).

These titles clearly indicate the basic religious nature of their organization. But their rituals give a clearer picture of what their religious goals were. In order to prepare for the New Era of Great Peace, people had to convert truly and to purify themselves through confession of their faults:

> In their doctrine sudden death or illness was the consequence of sin: protection could be had by public confession of faults and by washing them away through the "charmed water" [*fu-shui*] which the chief of the community gave penitents to drink. At equinoctial festivals, warrior amulets were distributed to defend against maleficent demons. (Maspero: 291)

By the year 184, religious enthusiasm and revolutionary spirit reached a climax. The movement turned rebellious and hoped to overthrow the Han empire (see also **Yellow Turban Rebellion**). But Chang Chueh apparently had no talent as a military commander and his uprising failed. What happened to his communities after 184 is not clear.

But while they were flourishing, the Chang brothers instituted a great number of rituals, both for the living and for the dead. Some disappeared soon after the Yellow Turbans' defeat, others were later reformed by **K'ou Ch'ien-chih** and **T'ao Hung-ching**. (For comparison and contrast, see also **Heavenly Masters Taoism**, a similar movement flourishing in western China.)

GREAT PROFUNDITY SCRIPTURE (*Ta-tung ching/Dadongjing*). One of the basic scriptures of Shang-ch'ing or Mao Shan Taoism. Although originally it was the very first text of the first *tung* (*tung-chen* section) of the Taoist Canon, in the Ming edition of today it is number six (*CT* 6, *TT* 16–17). The reason for this change is the extreme importance attached to a *Ling-pao* scripture, **Salvation Scripture** (*Tu-jen ching*), by the Sung court. They placed this text in the Sung edition of the Canon before all other scriptures, taking precedence over the *Great Profundity* scripture.

Sacred myth tells that this text was originally transmitted to the Queen Mother of the West before the world existed. The book ". . . was eventually revealed to **Lady Wei**, who transmitted it to her disciple, **Yang Hsi**. It constitutes the core of the Great Purity revelation" (Robinet, 1979/1993: 98).

The book deals with recitation taking place while the gods dwelling in the body are being visualized. The body is indeed seen as a sacred realm, animated and divinized by the inhabiting deities. Important among them are 39 guardian spirits, all individually named, who protect the "gates of death": They

> . . . close up the bodily orifices to make the body into a hermetically closed world which will then function as the receptacle and dwelling place of the gods . . ." (Robinet: 103)

The essence of the visualization recommended in the text is the joining together of the body and the indwelling spirits. Next, union must be established between these inner spirits and the corresponding deities of heaven. Then, "the body is spiritualized and unites with what we would call the Spirit" (Robinet: 104).

(For a more complete discussion of the *Great Profundity Scripture*, see Robinet, 1979/1993: 97–117.)

GREAT PURITY SCHOOL See SHANG-CH'ING TAOISM

GREAT WAY TAOISM (*Ta-tao chiao/Dadaojiao*), later called "True" Great Way Taoism (*Chen/zhen Ta-tao chiao*). One of the three new schools founded in northern China during the Jurchen Chin rule, after the Sung court had reestablished itself in the south.

Its founder was Liu Te-jen/Liu Deren, a native of Loling in Ts'ang-chou, born in 1122. One winter day in 1142, while waiting for the breaking of dawn, he met an old man as if in a dream. This old man, with a white beard and white eyebrows, was riding an oxcart. He stopped and transmitted to Liu the mysteries of the dark and wonderful Tao. Then he left again. That was the beginning of the Ta-tao order.

The new school was characterized by its monastic (celibate) lifestyle, emphasizing a simple way of living, a combination of manual labor (one should till the soil for one's food) with spiritual practices. Liu Te-jen expressed this ideal in nine rules of discipline:

- Look at all beings as at yourself; do not harbor feelings of hatred nor the intention of hurting others.
- Be loyal to your ruler, filial to your parents, sincere toward your fellow men; in speech avoid flowery and evil language.
- Rid yourself of lustful conduct and preserve purity.
- Stay away from power, be satisfied with a humble position and poverty; cultivate the fields to grow your own food; keep only as much income as necessary for your needs.

- Do not gamble or take risks; do not steal.
- Do not drink alcohol, do not eat meat; be happy with simple food and simple clothing.
- Empty your mind and soften your will: "darken your light and become one with the dust" (*TTC,* Chapter 4).
- Do not be overbearing; be modest and respect others.
- Know that contentment is not a disgrace; if you know when to stop, you will not come to grief.

    (Translated from Chen Yuan. *Nan-Sung ch'u ho-pei hsin Tao-chiao k'ao.*)

It is interesting to note that this lifestyle, combining meditative life, ascetic practices, and manual labor, resembles both the Chinese way of Ch'an (Zen) Buddhism and, at the opposite pole of the prism, the monastic institution of Christian monks, such as the Benedictines.

When the Ta-tao school started to acquire a reputation and spread far and wide, it attracted the attention of the ruling house, both of the Chin and of the Mongol court. After his death, founder Liu received the honorary title of "perfected" (*chen-jen*). His leadership was entrusted to the second, third, and fourth patriarch, until 1229. In that year, for reasons not clearly documented, Chin Emperor Ai-tsung (r. 1224–34) suspended the Ta-tao order so that, for several decennia, it went into hiding and spread its teaching secretly. Of this episode, there are no historical documents.

During the reign of Yuan (Mongol) Emperor Hsien-tsung (r. 1251–60), when the fifth patriarch was in charge, the Ta-tao order once again obtained the ruler's trust and received official support. That is when its name was changed to *True Ta-tao.* The patriarch received imperial honors, such as the title of *chen-jen*, and honorary garments for himself and 30 of its members. The sixth patriarch was appointed in 1268 by Khubilai Khan as official superintendent of the whole order. Since this imperial patronage continued, the order started flourishing in the whole country, from north to south, from east to west.

After the Mongol period, the Ta-tao order declined and left the "stage of history." Perhaps it was absorbed into Complete Realization Taoism.

What this school of Taoism focused on was not the arts of inner alchemy to become a "flying immortal," but tranquillity and prayer. It did not worship spiritual beings, and to cure people's illnesses, it did not rely on talismans. Their way was "silent prayer and [cultivation of] emptiness," a life of celibacy and asceticism.

At first, their temples were called "*an*" and their tombs "*t'a,*" following the Buddhist custom. This shows that Buddhism was one of their sources of inspiration.

Most of the information on the Ta-tao order of Taoism is found in various writings from the Yuan and Ming periods, as well as in certain stone inscriptions, recorded by Chen Yuan (*CMTT*: 22–23).

Patriarchs of (True) Great Way Taoism
1. Liu Te-jen (1122–1180)
2. Ch'en Shih-cheng (d. 1194)
3. Chang Hsin-chen (1163–1218)
4. Mao Hsi-tsung (1185–1223)
5. Li Hsi-ch'eng (name of order changed to Chen Ta-tao) (1181–1259)
6. Sun Te-fu (1217–1273)
7. Li Te-ho (d. 1284)
8. Yueh Te-wen (1234–1299)
9. Chang Chih-ch'ing (or Ch'ing-chih)
10. (unknown)
11. Cheng Chin-yuan (1267–1307)

GROTTO-HEAVENS and **BLESSED SPOTS** (*Tung-t'ien/Tongtian* and *Fu-ti/Fudi*). According to Taoism, there is a sacred geography inherent in the physical contours of the landscape. Mountain peaks and great rivers especially are seen as invisible centers of energy, vitalizing all living beings. Besides these, there are particular spots of energy, believed to be inhabited by spirits and gods. This lore is ancient and predates Taoism and Buddhism. But during the Six Dynasties period, this "sacred geography" was described in the **Chen-kao**. It was further elaborated by **Tu Kuang-t'ing** during T'ang times. He recorded and named first ten (great) "grotto-heavens" (*tung-t'ien*), then a further 36 (smaller) *tung-t'ien*, and finally 72 "blessed spots." Together with mountains, these are like a network of power stations all through the imperial realm.

That mountains are endowed with supernatural power is a universal phenomenon and has great psychological relevance (see also **Mountains**). The reason mountain caves (grottoes, caverns) are also considered sacred is not so obvious. There are a number of hypotheses: Caves are often occupied by wild carnivores and inspire fear; or they are dens of bandit gangs, who hide their treasure in them; they are also believed to be dwelling places of gods and especially mountain gods. Another reason is that caves attracted religious practitioners who wished to live in isolation and solitude; they were an ideal base for meditators and ascetics. In Buddhism, there has been a long tradition of cave-dwellers, often living in community. In Afghanistan there are the Bamiyan grottoes. In China's province of Sinkiang, fifth century Buddhist caves have been discovered recently in Kizil, north of the Taklimakan Desert, within the T'ien-shan range (*National Geographic* 189, April 1996: 52–63). On the crossroads to Central Asia, there are the still existing **Tun-huang** caves, for centuries a deposit of an unknown Buddhist library, only discovered around 1900, a rich treasure house of Buddhist art (frescoes and sculpture). Other famous Buddhist caves are located near Ta-t'ung in North China (Yün-kang caves) and near Lo-yang (Lung-men caves). There are more examples, all of which have their antecedents in the older and famous cave-monasteries of India.

This extraordinary phenomenon in religious geography shows that mountain caves have fascinated spiritual practitioners over the centuries: Not only did they find shelter and isolation there, the presence of spiritual energy was very real for them. No wonder the Taoists were also attracted to them, although no Taoist monastic community is known to ever have lived in a cave complex as the Buddhists did.

Why and based on what criteria did the Taoists create their 10 and 36 and 72 special places of sacred energy? The rationale of selection is not known and must be examined for each case in the written documents of local history. But we can still analyze the meaning of *tung-t'ien* and *fu-ti* within the Taoist worldview.

Tung-t'ien is a strange compound. *Tung* can mean "cave, grotto," but also means "profound, mysterious"; *t'ien* means "heaven." One would normally expect an adjective before a noun, so that *tung* should be considered an adjective. If that assumption is correct, *tung-t'ien* would mean "mysterious, profound heaven," but the use of *tung* and the fact that these heavens were located in mountains gives *tung* an extra nuance of "grotto," or "mysterious heaven linked with a grotto" (see also **Dragon Throw**).

Behind the term there hides a Taoist view that special mountain caves not only house spirits and transcendents (*hsien*), they are mysteriously linked to heavenly residences:

> Many of these and other sacred places were believed to be interconnected by a system of mysterious underground passages. The grotto-heavens were in part offices of the celestial bureaucracy, in part self-contained worlds with sun, moon, and stars, rivers, parks and palaces . . . (R. Birnbaum, 1989–90: 124–125)

Because of the spirits and gods dwelling in those grottoes, their entrance is believed to issue vital energy and thus assist cave-dwellers in their spiritual quest. They are controlled by transcendents appointed by Shang-ti.

Here is the list of the *ten great grotto-heavens*:

1. Wang-wu cave (Shansi)
2. Wei-yü (Chekiang)
3. Hsi-ch'eng (Szechuan?)
4. Hsi-hsuan (Shensi?)
5. Ch'ing-ch'eng (Szechuan)
6. Ch'ih-ch'eng (Chekiang)
7. Lou-fu (Kuangtung)
8. Chü-ch'ü (Mount Mao) (Kiangsu)
9. Lin-wu (Kiangsu)
10. K'uo-ts'ang (Chekiang)

The small grotto-heavens, 36 in number, are also considered to be governed by transcendents appointed by heaven. Some of them are located on the famous sacred mountains: Mount T'ai, Mount Heng, Mount Hua, Mount Sung, Mount Omei, etc.

The 72 Blessed Spots (*Fu-ti*, literally "places of happiness"), located on famous mountains as well, are also administered by realized transcendents (*chen-jen*) upon orders from Shang-ti. Their names, as well as those of the grotto-heavens, are all listed in the Sung mini encyclopedia **Yün-chi ch'i-ch'ien**.

GYMNASTICS (*Tao-yin*). Among the various practices that Taoism recommends to promote good health and, ultimately, long life and immortality, some are more spiritual, others more physical. The two, however, cannot be completely separated.

Since ancient times, gymnastics was practiced to promote good health. But the term "gymnastics" does not coincide with the modern word for it, such as it is performed during the Olympic games. In the Chinese context, gymnastics is an exercise of the body similar to yoga, without putting the body to great strain. A useful definition says that:

> "Gymnastics" means physical exercises for the purpose of expelling all evil breath from the limbs, the joints, and the bones of the body. In its stead, healthy, good energy or breath is to be preserved . . . Grinding the teeth and massaging oneself are also part of the practice of gymnastics. (Y. Sakade in L. Kohn, 1989: 8)

Its ancient origin has been demonstrated by the discovery of a manuscript found in the Ma-wang-tui tomb, dating from the middle of the second century BCE. This manuscript consists of a text, illustrated with a chart of drawings of various body exercises. Even older than this manuscript is a text in the *Chuang-tzu*, where the author somehow ridicules those gentlemen keen on longevity who practice *tao-yin*. For *Chuang-tzu*, this is inferior to inner meditation.

Although gymnastics developed before Taoism, it was eventually integrated into the Taoist system by the Shang-ch'ing School as a complementary technique to promote health. Since it was recommended to combine gymnastics with circulation of energy (*ch'i*) this was seen as very beneficial to the health of body and mind. Not only was it preventative medicine, but because it could help stimulate the circulation of *ch'i* inside the body, it was considered an effective way to promote health and longevity.

An example of the healing power of gymnastics is found in the biography of Hua T'o, a medical doctor in the service of Ts'ao Ts'ao of the kingdom of Wei (Three Kingdoms period).

> The body needs a certain amount of movement . . . This is why Taoists practice gymnastics . . . I myself have developed a series of exercises which I name the Five Animals Pattern. The five animals are the tiger, the deer, the bear, the monkey, and the bird. The practice of the Pattern aids the elimination of diseases and increases the functioning of the lesser members. (Quoted by C. Despeux, in L. Kohn, 1989: 242)

Indeed, if the value of *tao-yin* is assessed as compared to *ch'i* circulation, one may consider the following quote:

> Those who are able to circulate the [*ch'i*] can perfect the inside of their bodies, those who are good at doing gymnastic exercises can cure all ailments of the limbs. (Despeux: 258)

Without describing the actual exercises, one can still be struck by the similarity between *tao-yin* and ***t'ai-ch'i ch'uan***: The physical-emotional effects are very similar. Another related practice is ***ch'i-kung***, which has developed tremendously in China in recent times.

(For more information about gymnastics, see C. Despeux, in L. Kohn, 1989: 225–261.)

H

HAN HSIANG-TZU/HAN XIANGZI (*Emblem*: the flute). One of the Eight Immortals. He is said to be a grand-nephew of the famous T'ang scholar and statesman Han Yü. He was also a favorite disciple of Lü Tung-p'in, who carried him up to a numinous peach tree. While he fell down from its branches, he suddenly became an immortal.

He wandered about in the country, playing his flute, attracting birds and wild animals by his sweet music. He did not know the value of money, and, if given any, scattered it around on the ground.

HEAVEN (*T'ien/Tian*). A basic concept both in Chinese philosophy and in popular culture. The term is found in all schools of Chinese thought (Confucianism, Taoism, Mohism, Legalism, Naturalism), but with a great variety of meanings. Here, the Taoist understanding of heaven must be specially examined, but an elementary analysis of what the Confucian school understood by it is useful for the sake of comparison.

In general, Confucianism understands heaven as the supreme moral authority that controls human history: the fate of dynasties and the fate of all individuals. Heaven gives its "mandate" to rule to a virtuous king and removes it if the ruler turns out to be unworthy. Heaven also decides about the fate of individuals. Whether heaven is conceived as personal or not seems to be irrelevant (it is not a Chinese concern!), but heaven seems to have human-like qualities, at least in some Confucian writings (*Analects* and *Mencius*). In Hsün-tzu, heaven is totally impersonal, almost a synonym of Nature, and operates naturally, spontaneously, almost blindly, without any feelings for the well-being of humans. It is very close to the Taoist concept of Tao, except that Tao is more abstract, more transcendent. An eminent modern Chinese philosopher, Fung Yu-lan, states that *T'ien* (heaven) appears in Chinese writings with five different meanings: physical heaven or sky; a ruling or presiding *T'ien*; a fatalistic *T'ien* (or *ming*, fate); a naturalistic *T'ien* (nature); an ethical *T'ien* or moral principle in the universe (Fung Y.-l./Bodde, 1952 I: 31).

Perhaps one could say that for the Taoists heaven, in the sense of nature, is the visible manifestation or creation of the invisible, absolutely transcendent and unknowable **Tao**.

In this sense, nature, is "what is natural," given at the outset, or inborn in humans and animals. The Taoist texts often speak of heaven in contrast to what has been man-made. What heaven provides is spontaneous, natural, healthy; what man adds to it, or superimposes on it, is often not spontaneous, is artificial and unhealthy.

The *TTC* already observes that human society creates standards ("values"?) that are not inherent in things. Striking examples are the sense of beauty and the sense of goodness. They are not inherent in the things as they are, they are put there by human evaluation. If humans discern some person as beautiful, the concept of ugliness is born. But in nature (heaven), there is no such discrimination. The same applies to the concept of (moral) goodness or evil: it is created by society as a norm for living in harmony, and often it is appropriate, but often it is not.

In the *Chuang-tzu*, the contrast between "natural" (heaven) and the "man-made" is an often recurring theme.

> . . . the Heavenly is on the inside, the human is on the outside. Virtue resides in the Heavenly. Understand the actions of Heaven and man, base yourself upon Heaven . . . and then . . . you may return to the essential and speak of the ultimate. (Chapter 17, Watson, 1970: 182–3)

What is from "heaven" is our essential nature with all its potentialities for inner development; what is from "man" are the demands and expectations placed on us because of socially, artificially created values. While most people accept these external values almost automatically, because of social pressure, they do not necessarily suit everybody. There always are individuals who prefer to be non-conformists because they sense there is a more authentic way of living.

HEAVEN-AND-EARTH (*T'ien-Ti/Tiandi*). All Chinese schools of thought, including the Taoists, discuss the concept of heaven-and-earth, its creative-generative energies, its power to affect the lives of humans and of societies.

From a language viewpoint, "heaven" and "earth" are two concrete terms, which together form an abstract, equivalent to our notion of "universe, cosmos." (Chinese language often recurs to the combination of two concrete terms to make an abstract, since there are few abstract notions available. Other examples are *fu-mu*: *fu* is father, *mu* is mother, *fu-mu* means "parents"; and *to-shao*: *to* means "much"; *shao* means "little"; *to-shao* means "how much?").

Apart from its abstract meaning, *T'ien-Ti* or cosmos, the two terms may sometimes also be understood as separate concepts: *T'ien* has its own meaning as "heaven" or heavenly dome covering the earth; and *Ti* may be the planet earth that is the dwelling place of all things. (Because on its own, *T'ien* or heaven has very rich connotations, there is a separate entry for it. See **Heaven**.)

Ancient cosmological concepts in China are very remarkable. J. Needham has described them in his vol. 3 (Needham, 1959: III, 210–224). The most archaic view of the cosmos is the Theory of the Hemispherical Dome or Heavenly Cover (*Kai-t'ien* theory). The heavens were imagined as a hemispherical cover, resting on the ocean, above and around the earth, which in turn was imagined as a bowl turned upside down. Heaven was round, the earth square (if looked at from above), but its surface was rounded, sloping down. The heavenly cover turned around, the earth remained still. Sun, moon, and planets had their own independent movements in the sky, but all other stars were fixed, with the pole star in the very center.

The other theories explained by Needham are the Celestial Sphere Theory (*Hun-t'ien*) and the Infinite Empty Space Theory (*Hsüan-yeh*). The former imagined the universe like an egg; the latter speculated that the heavenly bodies and the earth are floating in infinite space, but not seen as concentric.

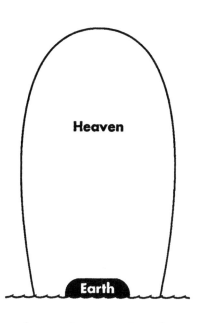

The Heavenly Dome theory was apparently the most current in ancient times, and echoes of it are found in Taoist writings. The *TTC* (Chapter 32) discusses the One, or Oneness, and says that if heaven had not obtained the One, it would soon "crack" or "be rent." This image makes sense if one keeps in mind that the heavenly cover is compared to a huge bowl or a huge tent.

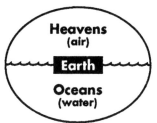

Since heaven-and-earth (H-and-E) are identical with the cosmos, or the universe, it is obvious that H-and-E have no feelings. It is just a physical reality, in which all creatures live their own lives, but must cope for themselves. Heaven especially is not considered to be a spiritual being that cares for living things. It only provides an environment in which life can develop. Humans (and all animals) must look after themselves and thus create harmony with H-and-E. This is clearly implied in the expression heaven, earth, mankind (*T'ien-Ti-Jen/Tiandiren*).

In this context, the enigmatic verses of the *TTC* (Chapter 5: 1) become clearly intelligible:

> Heaven-and-Earth are not "humane,"
> It treats all beings as straw dogs.

"Straw dogs" were used as temporary supports in animal sacrifices. Once the ritual was finished, they were burned and discarded.

In the same sense, all living beings come to life, flourish, and leave the scene again: "return to their roots" (Chapter 16: 3). Even the cosmos, which had a beginning, is not "eternal": it will come to an end eventually, even if it is "long-lived" (Chapter 7: 1). (Also see **Heaven; Heaven-Earth-Mankind**.)

HEAVEN-EARTH-MANKIND (*T'ien-Ti-Jen/Tiandiren*). These are the so-called Three Powers (*san-ts'ai/sancai*), which, through their mutual interactions, bring order and civilization to the world.

That there is an intimate, active relationship between heaven-and-earth (our physical universe) and mankind is a universally accepted doctrine of Chinese thought: All schools subscribe to it and explain it in their own terms. The "Great Norm," a chapter in the classic *Book of History* or *Shu ching*, already expresses this view early during the Chou dynasty. A modern commentator writes as follows:

> This document . . . encompasses early Chinese ideas about the interrelationship of nature, the cultivation of personal life, government, retribution, and a central principle, the Supreme Standard. Heaven, Earth, and man are correlated, preparing for the later development of the doctrine of the unity of man and Nature that was to dominate the course of Chinese history. (W.t. Chan, 1963: 10)

Later on, the Confucian scholar Hsün-tzu (third century BCE) puts it very succinctly: "Heaven has its seasons, earth has its wealth, and man has his government. This is how they are able to form a triad" (Chan: 117). The Han Confucian synthesizer, Tung Chung-shu (about 179–104 BCE), elevating the position and dignity of humans above other creatures, states that

> Heaven is characterized by the power to create and spread things, Earth is characterized by its power to transform, and man is characterized by moral principles. (Chan: 280)

> . . . we can see that man is distinct from other creatures and forms a trinity with Heaven and Earth. (Chan: 281)

This deep conviction of heaven-earth-mankind being a trinity, which through their interactions and mutual influences bring harmony and create culture, is not just a Confucian belief, it is also essentially Taoist. As is explained elsewhere (see **Heaven-and-Earth**), heaven-and-earth are two concrete terms that make up an abstract, the cosmos, the universe, or nature (the visible manifestation of *Tao*). Whereas for Taoism, nature is not "humane" (has no feelings of affection for its creatures) and is "impartial" (Chapter 79: 5), it provides a foundation for human action, in which life can thrive and find its fulfillment. The roles of heaven and earth are different, yet each contributes to the overall well-being of humanity. Humans must, however, avail themselves of the rich potential given and create their own environment, in accord with the intrinsic principles of nature's operations. In some contexts, heaven-and-earth are replaced by *Tao* and *Te*, which are more distinctly Taoist notions, but they can be quasi-synonyms:

> Tao gives them life,
> Virtue nurses them.
> Matter shapes them.
> Environment perfects them (Chapter 51: 1–2, Wu: 71)

Whereas Tao is the origin of all life, its power ("virtue") gives nourishment. This is like saying that heaven-and-earth create the myriad beings and give them their livelihood. "Matter" and "environment" are more related to earth and its treasures stored in rivers, mountains and fields. This is a commonsense statement holding that heaven (the atmosphere, with sun and rain especially) and earth (with all its products and "raw materials") provide all living things with the potential of nourishment and full development.

But the relationship between humans and the cosmos cannot be one of exploitation, but one of humble and grateful respect. If humans go beyond this limit, heaven-and-earth will react with signs of warning (see **Ecology**). This "Reciprocity of Heaven and Man" is well expressed in Chapter 3 of the Huai-nan-tzu: (but "heaven" must be understood as heaven-and-earth):

The natures of the rulers of men penetrate to Heaven on high.
Thus, if there are punishments and cruelty, there will be whirlwinds;
If there are wrongful ordinances, there will be plagues of devouring
    insects.
If there are unjust executions, the land will redden with drought.
If (lawful) commands are not accepted, there will be great excess of rain.
The four seasons are the officers of Heaven.
The sun and moon are the agents of Heaven.
The stars and planets mark the appointed times of Heaven.
Rainbows and comets are the portents of Heaven. (J. Major, 1993: 67)

HEAVENLY MASTERS TAOISM (*T'ien-shih Tao/Tianshi Dao*). The first Taoist religious organization, established by Chang Tao-ling in the middle of the second century CE. Because member families had to contribute a tax of five bushels (pecks) of rice per year to the organization, the movement was also called Five Bushels of Rice Taoism

(*Wu-tou-mi tao*). Chang was derided in official history as "Rice Thief." (For a short biographical sketch of Chang Ling, later renamed Chang Tao-ling, see also **Chang Tao-ling**.)

It is remarkable that two similar Taoist movements originated about the same time: one in the east of China, one in the west. It is probable that there was mutual influence, but besides probabilities, there is no hard evidence. Even though the surnames of the founders of both was Chang, there was no family relationship. (For details concerning the eastern movement, see also **T'ai-p'ing Taoism**.)

During a period of political and social unrest, with natural disasters aggravating the economic condition of the people, the time was felt to be ripe for a major upheaval, a sort of messianic cataclysm, that would overthrow the dynasty and bring about a time of millenarian peace and prosperity. Because of the Han dynasty's weakness due to inner corruption, Chang was able to establish himself in the mountainous recesses of Szechuan and part of Shensi and organize a politico-religious cult, similar to the eastern *T'ai-p'ing Tao*. Claiming to have received revelations from T'ai-shang Lao-chün, the divinized Lao-tzu, he called himself Heavenly (or Celestial) Master, echoing expectations expressed in the *T'ai-p'ing ching* (*Great Peace Scripture*).

His organization was a kind of theocracy: Political rule effected by religious leaders. Chang divided his territory into 24 districts, each administered by functionaries, who had 240 spirit armies under their command. The whole organization somehow imitated the Han bureaucratic structure, but went beyond political administration and most of all served the spiritual needs of the membership. Various communal rituals took place periodically, especially on the days of the solstices and equinoxes. A major focus of the organization was on healing. They viewed sickness as the result of evil deeds; therefore, to get healed, it was necessary to confess one's misdeeds and obtain forgiveness. A rather dramatic way of confession was to write one's evil deeds together with prayers for forgiveness on three slips of paper and address them to the **Three Officials** (*san-kuan*), rulers of heaven, earth, and water.

The founder, Chang Tao-ling, was renowned for his powers of exorcism and wrote talismans for protection and forgiveness. Today, Taoist priests still use his models of talismans in various rituals, private and public.

Among the most "spectacular" communal rituals, one should mention the Fast of Mud and Soot (see **CHAI/ZHAI**), taking place occasionally. Its goal was to repent one's moral transgressions, to ward off disease, and to pray for happiness and long life. It was like a revivalist event in which enthusiastic participants smeared themselves with soot and mud and engaged in ecstatic and wild motions, throwing themselves on the ground, "rolling about in all directions, covering [their] faces with dirt and lamenting" (Maspero, 1971/1981: 385). (See also **Ritual**.)

Another famous ceremony was the "union of *ch'i*" (*ho-ch'i*), a sexual celebration also meant to be a "deliverance from sins" (Maspero: 386). (See **Union of Energies**.)

The Heavenly Masters School, established by Chang Tao-ling, was continued by his son, Chang Heng, and solidified by his grandson, Chang Lu. (These three are sometimes called the "Three Changs" but should not be confused with the three Chang brothers from the East, who founded the T'ai-p'ing Tao and eventually started the Yellow Turban Revolt.) Chang Lu maintained his theocratic state until 215 CE, when he surrendered to the military pressure from the northern general-warlord Ts'ao Ts'ao. He was honored and supported by the general, but forced to leave Szechuan, together with several tens of thousands of believers, and settle around the capital, "thus placing them under the close scrutiny of his government" (Kobayashi, 1992: 17).

The situation of the Heavenly Masters School after their move is not clear. On the one hand, it is said that many powerful families converted, yet on the other hand, during the Wei kingdom (220–264) ". . . the parishes and with them the entire organization of the early church collapsed, bringing the institution of spiritual officialdom to the verge of total destruction" (Kobayashi: 18).

During the western Chin (265–317), the school was probably limited to the north (Shansi) and the southwest (Szechuan). It is only after 317, when the court started its exile to the south, and many northern aristocrats as well as Taoists fled southward, that the Heavenly Masters established themselves in southern China and gradually made new converts. But it appears that at first their position was not prestigious. Could it be that the southern aristocrats resented the influx of northern preachers, or were they criticized for their unusual ritual practices, especially the "Union of Energies"? Besides the guesswork, there is evidence that the school was not highly respected: The first catalogue of Taoist scriptures, made by Lu Hsiu-ching in 471, did not include any works originating within the Heavenly Masters School.

It was only at the end of the Liu-Sung period (420–479) and the subsequent Liang dynasty (502–557) that the situation started to change, and "around 480, the basic order had been restored and the church administration was showing signs of stabilization" (Kobayashi: 33). When the Taoist Canon was augmented toward the end of the sixth century, the Heavenly Masters scriptures were appended in the fourth supplement. This period of the Six Dynasties was a time of great inspiration for the Heavenly Masters School: Many new scriptures were produced, probably under the stimulation of the Shang-ch'ing and Ling-pao traditions.

In the north, there was one instance of Heavenly Masters revival: the Taoist master **K'ou Ch'ien-chih** (who called himself Heavenly Master) was instrumental in establishing a Taoist state religion, during the years of the Northern Wei. But it is doubtful that it was related to the Heavenly Masters School, except by his title; and he had no heir to continue after him. The Heavenly Masters, on the other hand, claim to have continued the line of transmission since Chang Tao-ling. But their history from the Six Dynasties on is not clear, and when they start to reemerge during the Sung period, there seem to be many gaps in the hereditary transmission.

All through later imperial history, the Heavenly Masters remained very active; some eminent masters received honorary titles from the court, until the Ch'ing (Manchu) dynasty came to power and did not give them any strong support. That was a period of decline for Heavenly Masters Taoism. But they have survived their hardships, and today they are still active in China and in Taiwan. They serve the local communities through their highly specialized liturgy, of which the rituals of the Cosmic Renewal Festival are the most brilliant and colorful, while also very esoteric. (See also **Priesthood, Cosmic Renewal Festival**.)

HEAVENLY MIND SCHOOL See T'IEN-HSIN TAOISM

HEAVENLY STEMS (*T'ien-kan/Tiangan*). "Stems" and "branches" are mutually complementary. In the Chinese tradition shared by Taoism, the stems and branches have a dual function: first as "markers" of time; second, as instruments of divination.

As markers of time, the *ten stems* are combined with the *twelve branches* to date years, months, days, and hours of day. (It is important to read the complementary entry of **Earthly Branches**). If we use Roman numerals I to X to identify the 10 heavenly stems, and Arabic numerals for the 12 earthly branches, then we would have the following:

I-1 would be year one (first year of a cycle);
II-2 would then be year two of a cycle.

When it comes to X, the year would be X-10, but the next year would be I again, with 11 as its mate: I-11. If one continues in that way, one ends up with a 60-year cycle.

The most ancient use of the cyclical symbols dates from the Shang dynasty. They were used to measure time: A week consisted of ten days. Later on, the symbols were used to indicate years and, still later, for months and the hours of the day.

A practical application refers to a popular tradition of China: A person's horoscope depended on his "eight characters" (a combination of stems and branches for the year, month, day, and hour of birth), and even today, people consult Taoist priests to advise them about the horoscopic compatibility of marriage partners.

The Heavenly Stems have no particular value unless they are studied in combination with the **Earthly Branches**. They are sets of 10 and 12 characters, respectively, used as numerals.

HEAVENLY VENERABLE See T'IEN-TSUN

HEAVENLY VENERABLE OF TAO AND POWER See TAO-TE T'IEN-TSUN

HEAVENLY VENERABLE OF THE FIRST ORIGIN See YUAN-SHIH T'IEN-TSUN

HEAVENLY VENERABLE OF THE NUMINOUS TREASURE See LING-PAO T'IEN-TSUN

HEAVENLY WORTHY See T'IEN-TSUN

HEXAGRAMS. There are 64 hexagrams constituting the core of the Chinese classic *Yi ching* (*Book of Changes*). To understand their origin and meaning, one must first look into the **Eight Trigrams** (*pakua*).

If the Eight Trigrams are multiplied by themselves (each of the eight placed on top of all the others), the result is 64 symbols or hexagrams, which means graphic symbols consisting of six lines.

In the *Yi ching*, each hexagram has a particular meaning or expresses a particular life situation or cosmic event. By throwing three coins six times in a row, one is able to obtain a hexagram, which is considered to be relevant to a question asked or a situation in one's life.

HO-CH'I See SEXUALITY

HO HSIEN-KU/HE XIANGU (Emblem: bamboo ladle or lotus). One of the Eight Immortals, in fact, the only female among them. Represented as a beautiful maiden, she vowed herself to a life of virginity.

An encounter with Lü Tung-pin, who saved her from a malignant demon, set her on the road to spiritual practice. In a different account, Lü gave her a peach to eat, after which she was never hungry again.

Summoned to the T'ang court by Empress Wu, she disappeared suddenly and became an immortal.

HO-SHANG KUNG/HESHANG GONG (Lit. "Old Gentleman by the River"). Although "Ho-shang kung" refers to a person about whom not much is known, one usually thinks about the text attributed to him: the *Ho-shang kung Commentary on the Tao-te ching*. It is one of the earliest commentaries ever written, but opinions are divided as to exact dating. Some scholars argue that it dates from between the late fifth and early sixth century, because one of the major themes, they say, is the striving for immortality, which is seen as a later goal pursued by the Taoist practitioners of the Southern Dynasties. Yet, it appears that the commentary does not focus so much on immortality as on "nourishing life" or the attainment of longevity, a Taoist practice of an earlier period.

The other view is that the commentary was more likely written during the later Han period (first or second century CE). The issue has not been resolved. It is, however, clear that the *Ho-shang kung* text explains the *TTC* in terms of self-cultivation and government of the state, themes indeed dear to the *TTC* and the Huang-Lao School. (For a translation of the text, see E. Erkes, 1958; for a thorough analysis and theories about dating, see A. Chan, 1991.)

HO-T'U See RIVER CHART

HOLD ON TO ONENESS (*pao-yi/baoyi*). This is a concept that stirred the interest of Taoist religious practitioners and became a focal point in their meditative practice. The starting point, however, lies in the *TTC*, Chapter 10: 1. This is a difficult passage, controversial, in fact, and has been translated in widely divergent ways. A few examples:

> Can you keep the spirit and embrace the One [*pao-yi*] without departing from them? (Chan, 1963: 144)
> Can you keep the unquiet physical-soul from straying, hold fast to the Unity, and never quit it? (Waley, 1958: 153)
> By clinging to the One with both your spiritual and physical souls, can you prevent them from becoming divorced? (Duyvendak, 1954: 36)
> In bringing your spiritual and bodily souls to embrace the One, can you ever depart from it? (E. Chen, 1989: 78)
> In nourishing the soul and embracing the One—can you do it without letting them leave? (R. Henricks, 1989: 206)

When "carrying your soul," embracing the One Thing, can you be un-
divided? (M. LaFargue, 1992: 60)
While you cultivate the soul and embrace unity, can you keep them
from separating? (V. Mair, 1990: 69)

This is obviously an obscure verse, and the translators struggled
between translating and interpreting: There is no other choice. Comparing the translations and studying the Chinese text, the following
emerges: First, part 2 of the verse clearly implies a separation. Of
what? Of two principles or, rather, two "souls." It was an early Chinese belief that human beings were endowed with two souls: a *hun* or
yang soul and a *p'o* or yin soul (see also **soul**). If the two separate,
death follows. So here is the question: Can you prevent your two
souls from separating? Therefore, part 1 of the verse must reflect that:
Pao-yi means "to hold together." The characters in front must then
mean *hun* and *p'o* (as Duyvendak and Chen clearly state).

Pao-yi, in this exegesis, then means to "hold together" the two
souls of one's personality and to stay alive (until old age?). The following verses all ask a question about similar difficulties, and each
answer expected seems to refer to something very difficult to realize.
Only a sage would be able to do it.

Holding together in oneness the two souls is the same as to maintain, to hold on to, the oneness of one's vital principles. But, taken
out of context, one can easily understand how *pao-yi* could have given
rise to new interpretations. In other chapters of the *TTC*, the One
appears again, but with different connotations. Only once more does
pao-yi reappear: Chapter 22: 4:

The sage holds on to Oneness
and becomes the model of the world.

In two more locations, the One may be a synonym of Tao. In Chapter 39, all beings in the universe "obtained Oneness," and thus became empowered, each in its own way. The best-known passage,
however, is in Chapter 42: 1–2:

Tao gave birth to (produced) the One,
The One gave birth to (produced) Two, etc.

It has been argued that verse 1 is an interpolation (Duyvendak,
1954): Tao does not "produce" Oneness, it is the principle of Oneness.

As has been explained in the **Introduction**, the *TTC* is not a religious text: Tao, or the One, is an abstract principle, the supreme
ground of Being. When Tao later on became personified and deified,

the expression *pao-yi* was transformed into a religious experience. From natural mysticism, it was changed into religious mysticism. However, because Taoism has a pantheistic orientation, this One is also the true inner self: The outer one, the Tao, is not different from the inner self of the Taoist adept. Then to hold on to Oneness (*pao-yi*) is only to maintain one's self-identity and keep it grounded in the One, the Tao. (See also K. Schipper, 1982/1993: 130–132.)

HSI-SHENG CHING See *WESTERN ASCENSION SCRIPTURE*

HSI WANG-MU See QUEEN MOTHER OF THE WEST

HSIANG-ERH COMMENTARY See *LAO-TZU HSIANG-ERH CHU*

HSIAO-TAO LUN See *LAUGHING AT THE TAO*

HSIEN/XIAN ("Immortal," "Perfected," "Transcendent," all used as nouns). In Taoism, nothing appears to be simple, but few concepts are as elusive as what is seen as the ideal Taoist realized state: *hsien* (or *hsien*ship). To reach this state of perfection is the goal of Taoist religion (the goal expressed in the Taoist philosophical writings is different: see **Human Perfection**).

Before Taoism adopted this ideal of transcendent perfection, it was already part of the popular tradition: this has transpired from funeral texts found in Han tombs. What the people's expectations were, however, is not clear. It is likely that they hoped for what A. Seidel has called "post-mortem" **immortality**: This would involve a bureaucratic decision to restore the deceased's body and reunite it with the soul, to live in heaven forever. It is also probable that the Heavenly Masters School adopted this ideal for its own loyal adepts; some believe that such a hope for immortality explains the school's great success in the late Han.

Meanwhile, **alchemy**, outer and inner, had appeared on the stage. The adept's goal was to reach physical longevity, and hopefully physical immortality (although sometimes it looks more like immortality of the soul only). The ideal of becoming a *hsien*, an "immortal," became the major goal of Six Dynasties Taoism, especially within the newly established Shang-ch'ing School.

What is a *hsien*? As N. Girardot defines it:

A *hsien* is a human being . . . who—by assiduously following various spiritual . . . and physical . . . practices, or sometimes by fortuitous happenstance—has attained a unique mode of holy existence that is permanently in harmony with the ultimate life rhythm of the Tao. Because of this integration with universal life, the *hsien* continues to live for cycles of cosmic time equivalent to hundreds of thousands of normal human years, roaming about . . . on mountains and in deep grottoes . . . or in the starry mansions of the heavens. (*ER* 6: 475)

The twofold area of the *hsien's* residence, mountains and heavens, points to the two kinds of immortals that were believed to exist; yet a third category was added, so that in all there were three groups of *hsien*, as Ko Hung mentions in his *Pao-p'u-tzu*. The superior group are the *t'ien-hsien* or heavenly immortals, who were able to rise to heaven in broad daylight, to become members of the heavenly administration; the second group are the *ti-hsien*, earthly immortals, less perfect, yet transcendent beings, who dwell in mountains and forests; finally, there are immortals who did not reach perfection on earth yet, but some time after death (real or apparent) qualified for the position. There is no special name given to them, but their achievement is indicated by the process: **body liberation**. This is not an easy concept to understand.

This triple division raises many questions: It seems to leave no room for those perfected beings who are believed to have developed the "spirit embryo" inside their own body. To which group do they belong? A further question is whether to become a *hsien* is a matter of technique, or whether intense spiritual cultivation and strict ethical integrity are required as well. It seems that the tradition favors the latter method, yet there are cases reported in the literature (legendary, one must assume) in which pure technique seems to be all that's necessary—especially intake of alchemical elixirs or pills. The legend about Huai-nan-tzu supports such a view; even the dogs and chickens who got hold of the alchemical drugs rose to heaven as immortals. In the spiritual tradition of Shang-ch'ing Taoism, this seems impossible; to become an immortal at all requires long years of effort and moral purification.

What, then, are the methods for becoming a *hsien*? They are numerous and sometimes very complex. They usually require full-time attention. Basically, two types can be distinguished, although this distinction is probably artificial, in view of the Chinese unitary view of body-and-mind (soul). But for the sake of convenience, one can discuss *spiritual* practices and *physical* practices (Girardot: 475).

- *Spiritual Practices* involve meditation, concentration, inner visualization (*nei-kuan*), holding on to Oneness, up to the point of mystical experience. They are closely linked with **inner alchemy**.
- *Physical Practices* include **breathing exercises** (for example,

"embryonic breathing"), dietary restrictions, gymnastics, sexual union (for instance **"union of energies"**), alchemical drugs (**outer alchemy**), liturgical rituals.

An adept, hoping to reach the state of a *hsien*, has a choice of practices. If he attempts to do everything, he may not become an immortal but a lunatic! But as a general requirement, he/she must act ethically, observe various precepts, because immoral acts would be counterproductive and shorten his/her natural lifespan.

Whether all the efforts (and sweating!) of Taoist adepts have been successful or not is impossible to ascertain. No reliable report of a *hsien* manifesting itself to humanity is available, in spite of the many legends embroidered around them. They are certainly an interesting literary theme, but so are the numerous stories about ghosts and vampires, which can hardly be taken as historical evidence.

The old Taoist masters (**Lao-tzu, Chuang-tzu,** etc.) did not hope for immortality; the Confucians believed in immortality of merits, achievements, and family line, and the Buddhists had the patience not to demand eternal life after just one lifetime. Were the Taoists successful? Longevity was probably a reachable goal, but of true physical immortality reached through these esoteric practices, there is no evidence at all. Su Tung-po (1036–1101), one of China's finest poets, as well as a statesman of high status, was interested in alchemy, but remained skeptical. He would have liked to meet someone who had actually never died. Although since childhood he had heard stories about "immortals," he found that sages died just like anyone else:

> I am beginning to wonder whether such immortals ever existed, or whether they do exist but are not seen by the people. Or are we all mistaken? Is it not possible that the stories in the ancient books about Taoists who never died are just . . . exaggerated by the writers? (Lin Yutang, 1947: 245)

Taoism is often seen as a religion of "salvation." It is not always clear what this means, but when it is stated that the common goal of the Taoist religion was to reach (physical) immortality, that is inaccurate. The Heavenly Masters promised eternal life to some of their adepts, but this was an unusual (and exceptional) process. If one chooses the harder path of full-time spiritual practice, it will take years of intense effort to have one's name transferred to the Book of Life. Only an elite among the elite is successful. Finally, as Yü Ying-shih observed: Not even one in a million is able to ascend to heaven in broad daylight (Yü, 1964: 112). The common people who followed

Taoism (today there are very few of them), placed their hope on a future life along Buddhist parameters: to be freed from punishment in hell, to be assigned a favorable reincarnation, that is "eternal life."

HSING-MING See NATURE AND LIFE

HSUAN-HSUEH See MYSTERY LEARNING

HSUAN-T'IEN SHANG-TI/XUANTIAN SHANGDI ("Supreme Emperor of Dark Heaven"). Also called Chen-wu Ta-ti/Zhenwu Dadi ("Great Emperor Perfected Martial"). He is a Taoist deity with a national cult in China since Ming times (see also **Mount Wu-tang**), where he is commonly known as Chen-wu Ta-ti; in Taiwan, his usual name is Hsuan-t'ien Shang-ti.

His cult had an ancient origin, ". . . the sole survivor in living religion of the spirits who in high antiquity ruled the four quarters of the universe" (L. Thompson, 1995; 59).

According to a legend, he was sent down to earth by the **Jade Emperor** to subdue an army of demon-kings ravaging the universe. He won the battle and captured all the demons who were cast down in the abysses of hell. Among them were a turtle and a serpent, serving the Lord of Demons (see Werner, 1969: 178). In modern iconography, Hsuan-t'ien Shang-ti is represented as seated on a throne, his feet resting on a turtle and a serpent, reminiscent of his victory over evil powers.

His worship is very strong in Taiwan: Almost 400 temples are dedicated to him. He often "descends into the pen" of spirit-writing mediums. His birthday is celebrated on the third day of the third lunar month (see *TMSC*: 284–312).

HUA-HU CHING See *CONVERSION OF BARBARIANS SCRIPTURE*

HUAI-NAN-TZU/HUAINANZI: THE PERSON. Literal meaning is "Master of Huai-nan," whose personal name was Liu An (180–122 BCE). He was the prince of Huai-nan, a small kingdom in eastern China, south of the Huai River, where he attracted a large retinue of scholar-gentlemen to his court.

Liu An was the grandson of Liu Pang, founder of the Han dynasty who was later known as Kao-tsu or Kao Ti (r. 206–195 BCE).

Liu An's father, Liu Ch'ang, plotted against the court, but as it was discovered, committed suicide in 174 BCE. Liu An, however, was still ennobled as a marquis of Fou-ling and later promoted to prince of Huai-nan, in present Anhwei province.

Like his father, Liu An fostered political ambitions: During the

Rebellion of Seven Kingdoms (in 154 BCE), he considered joining the rebel princes against Emperor Ching (r. 156–141 BCE). However, his plan was rejected by his chief minister, who had been appointed by the central government.

In 139 BCE, Liu An went to the capital to visit his nephew, the young Emperor Wu (r. 140–86 BCE), and presented to him his new book, to be called the *Huai-nan-tzu.* Liu An might have hoped that the young emperor would choose Taoism as the guiding philosophy of his rule. In fact, however, Emperor Wu preferred Confucianism, which was declared to be state doctrine in or around 136 BCE.

In 122 BCE, Liu An was accused by his grandson of plotting against the throne. This accusation was perhaps motivated by the grandson's anger, as his father had not been awarded the title of marquis, but was given a fiefdom instead. Afraid of facing the consequences of the accusation, Liu An committed suicide (in 122 BCE). His wife and heir-apparent were later executed and several thousands of people perished as a result of this event.

Later Taoist mystification has replaced the suicide story by a more attractive legend: Liu An had been informed that a government delegation was on its way to arrest him, to be tried for treason. Since he had experimented with **alchemy** for a long time and had found the secret of immortality, he and his family and all domestic animals took the alchemical pill and together rose to heaven in clear daylight. A more grandiose ending for a famous philosopher!

HUAI-NAN-TZU/HUANANZI: THE TEXT. A collection of 21 essays, edited in the second century BCE by the prince of Huai-nan (or Huai-nan-tzu), whose name was Liu An. The title of this volume is known either as *Huai-nan hung-lieh* ("Great Light of Huai-nan") or simply as the *Huai-nan-tzu* (abbreviated as *HNT*).

Liu An (180–122 BCE) had high political ambitions that remained unsatisfied. It is perhaps as a compensation that he gathered a numerous crowd of scholarly gentlemen at his court: This was another way to establish a grandiose reputation. Whatever his motivation, the book of 21 essays that he left behind is today a rich source of information about the intellectual worldview of the early Han:

> [It] offers to the reader a kind of summary of contemporary knowledge on astronomy and geography, zoology and botany, government and military strategy, customs and rites, myth and history . . ." (C. LeBlanc & R. Mathieu, 1992: xvi)

Because of its "mixed" nature, the *HNT* was not identified as a "Taoist" work, but placed under the category of "miscellaneous."

But several chapters are strictly Taoist, and the other chapters, although covering some non-Taoist subjects, are still composed within a framework of Taoist thinking. For a long time, the *HNT* has been neglected by both Chinese and western scholars. In his *Source Book of Chinese Philosophy*, Wing-tsit Chan (1963) devotes only three-and-a-half pages to it, giving it credit solely for "keeping the fire of Taoism burning and [helping] to make possible the emergence of **Neo-Taoism**" (Chan: 305).

For a long time, the only (partial) translation of the *HNT* was the one by Morgan (1933), but this translation is no longer considered satisfactory. In more recent years, an explosion of interest has produced various books and articles with partial translations and interpretations, and a full translation is now in preparation (see table).

Table of Modern Text Studies and Translations of *HNT*

Author/Trans.	Date	Chapter(s)	Language of translation
E. Morgan	1933	1, 2, 7, 8, 12, 13, 15, 19	English
E. Kraft	1957–58	1, 2	German
B. Wallacker	1962	11	English
J. Major	1973	4	English
C. Larre	1982	7	French
R. Ames	1983	9	English
C. LeBlanc	1985	6	English
C. Larre, I. Robinet, E. Rochat de la Vallée	1993	1, 7, 11, 13, 18, 21 (part)	French
C. LeBlanc & R. Mathieu	1992		French (not a translation)
J. Major	1983	3, 4, 5	English
C. LeBlanc & R. Mathieu	(in prep.)	21 chapters	French

Although at first glance the subject matter of the *HNT* appears to be disorganized, there is a deep underlying unity hidden in it, perhaps due to the editorial talent of Liu An himself, who must have chosen the best essays produced by the best minds in his circle. Later historians said many literati flocked to Liu An's court, perhaps even thousands. Whatever their number, only eight are mentioned by name as contributors to the *HNT* volume.

Today's text retains only 21 of the original 61 chapters. There were at first 32 outer and 8 middle essays, all lost; the 21 remaining ones are called "inner chapters" and have been strongly influenced by Taoism, especially by the *TTC* and the *Chuang-tzu*, although other schools of thought, Confucianism, Legalism, the Yin-yang/Five Agents School, are also well represented. This makes the *HNT* an eclectic composition, with a predominant Taoist preference.

Liu An and his associates wrote the book for a double purpose: First, on a personal level, it gives advice on how to obtain happiness and avoid misfortune, how to nourish life and achieve longevity. In that respect, it follows the *Chuang-tzu* and parts of the *TTC*, in which personal cultivation is recommended. Second, on the social level, it presents a blueprint for and a set of visions of a stable society and the empire, based on Taoist views and evaluations of the rise and fall of past kingdoms and dynasties. In a wider perspective, it tries to fathom the secret workings of the universe and the interrelationships between human destiny and natural phenoma or forces of nature. (See also **Huai-nan-tzu: Themes.** For a detailed critical text study, see H. Roth, 1992.)

HUAI-NAN-TZU/HUAINANZI: **THEMES.** Although for a long time neglected and underestimated as a "miscellaneous" product of early Han thought, the *Huai-nan-tzu* (*HNT*) has become for scholars today a gold mine of information about intellectual speculation during the late Warring States and the early Han periods. Admittedly syncretistic, the 21 essays inform us about the Taoist worldview, inspired by the *TTC* and *Chuang-tzu*, about natural philosophy with speculations on the cosmos, its "creation" (self-creation) and cycles, about military strategy and the art of ruling a country Taoist style. The common ground of these and other speculations is the Huang-Lao philosophy, which had produced a special view of government: ". . . a theory of statecraft according to which the enlightened ruler could align his own actions with those of the universe and rule in accord with natural rhythms and harmonies" (J. Major, 1993: 1).

The *HNT* has become a favorite topic of sinology today. Its revival is partially due to the Ma-wang-tui manuscript discovery, which placed Huang-Lao Taoism in the very center of scholarly attention. Many partial studies of the *HNT* have been published in recent years. Here, a selection of only a few themes will be made, in the hope that a full translation plus commentary on the 21 essays will become available in the near future.

The themes to be discussed here are cosmology, resonance, and the art of rulership.

First *Han cosmology*: it is covered in essays three, four and five of the *HNT*. After essays one and two, which analyze the nature of Tao, here we find speculations about how the cosmos originated and how it operates. *Ch'i* is at the inception of "creation":

> The [Tao] began in the Nebulous Void
> The Nebulous Void produced spacetime;
> Spacetime produced the primordial [ch'i]. (Major: 62)

Out of the original *ch'i*, heaven and earth developed: Heaven was pure and right, earth heavy and turbid. Their joined essences produced yin and yang:

> To Heaven belong the sun, moon, stars and planets;
> To Earth belong waters and floods, dust and soil. (Major: 62)

The origin of mankind is not included in this cosmogony. The essay continues with the operations of heaven (stars, planets, etc.) and earth (the seasons, etc.), all in great detail.

Although this is a mythical story (purely speculative) it is basically naturalistic. There is no creator god, and even if the existence of "divine spirits" is acknowledged, they are like everything else, born out of the same original *ch'i.*

> . . . in the cosmological chapters of the Huainanzi, the gods play a role that seems curiously divorced from religious faith . . .
>
> There is no hint in [*HNT*] 3 and 4 of prayers to any of these divinities, or of the likelihood that they could intervene on behalf of humans to affect the nonhuman world in any way . . . (Major: 47–48)

Chapter 4 of the *HNT* is a treatise on topography: a description of the world as it was known in Han times, including all the living things and how they interact with the environment. Chapter 5 discusses seasonal rules; it

> . . . belongs to a genre of early Chinese almanacs that give astronomical, stem-branch and five phase correlations for each of the twelve months and prescribe appropriate ritual and administrative behavior for the ruler throughout the year . . . (Major: 217)

The concept of "resonance" (*kan-ying*) is found in essay six of the *HNT.* For a Western reader, the great number of seemingly unrelated stories is disconcerting, until one discovers the great idea behind them: In nature and history, all things are related. "They are the result and manifestation of mutual resonance between different parts of the universe" (LeBlanc, 1985: 110). The example often quoted is that if one strikes a particular note on one instrument, the corresponding note on another instrument responds and vibrates.

Moreover ". . . human beings, inasmuch as they are one with *Tao*, are 'agents' of mutual resonance and 'make things happen'. They participate fully in the creative transformation of the *Tao*" (LeBlanc: 110).

This theory of mutual response of humans and nature, also known as the system of correspondences, is found nowhere in antiquity but here in Taoism. It is a grandiose scheme of the oneness (wholeness) of the universe, to which humanity must submit for its own preservation. It parallels the modern scientific concept of the basic unity of matter-energy.

Chapter 9 focuses on the "art of rulership," one of the major concerns of Huang-Lao Taoism. The Chinese title *chu-shu* suggests that ruling a country is an "art," a "special technique," which must and can be learned, but must be based on self-cultivation of spirit and moral character. A great emphasis is placed on **wu-wei**, not taking any (undue, unnatural) action, because all beings know how to act on their own accord, spontaneously, naturally, and should not be provoked into unnatural action. Echoing some passages in the *TTC*, the *HNT* states:

> The sage governs easily . . .
> He is benevolent without giving,
> he is trusted with speaking,
> he gets without seeking
> he accomplishes without doing.
> (Section 3 of Chapter 9, R. Ames, 1983: 171)

Like in the *TTC*, the ruler, who must be an enlightened person, a sage, must have the necessary qualifications for ruling, but rather than merely intellectual and political skills, he must possess proper virtues: uprightness, integrity, and justice; frugality and moderation; concern for the well-being of all; and a keen sense of timeliness, which, in other words, means that he must understand the workings of the universe, the proper actions to take in all seasons, which is very much related to the system of correspondences discussed in Chapter 6.

Although only three themes have been chosen here, it is already quite obvious that the philosophy of the *HNT* is not just Taoist; it incorporates many pan-Chinese values and concepts, and even opens up to other systems of thought. It is indeed syncretistic and had the Han bibliophiles confused so that they catalogued the work as "miscellaneous." Today, it is being realized that the *HNT* deserves better!

HUANG-LAO CHÜN/HUANGLAOJUN ("Lord Huang-Lao"). The name of what appears to be a "composite" deity (combination of

Huang-ti or the **Yellow Emperor,** and **Lao-tzu**), unless the title should be read differently, as Huang Lao-chün, Venerable Lord Huang (as in **T'ai-shang Lao-chün**).

Huang-Lao Chün is a deified form of Lao-tzu (plus the Yellow Emperor?). His worship appears to have been prevalent during the second half of the second century CE. Han Emperor Huan (r. 147–167), in 165 CE "sanctioned a sacrifice to the god Lao-tzu in a temple at the latter's reputed birthplace. Several months later, he made Huang-lao the object of the annual *chiao* sacrifice in the capital. "The . . . installation of Huang-lao at the *chiao* was clearly a sign of his growing importance" (H. Roth, *ER* 6: 483). (This *chiao* is the traditional suburban sacrifice dating from Chou times, and should not be confused with the later *chiao* of renewal. The two characters are different.)

If this Huang-Lao Chün is the cult figure of **Huang Lao Taoism,** his cult must have ancient roots and go back to the third century BCE. But at that point, he was not yet deified, only the elevated "twin hero" (Yellow Emperor and Lao-tzu) of the Huang-Lao School, which was a political-religious movement flourishing among members of the Chi-hsia Academy in the state of Ch'i. (See also **Huang-Lao Taoism.** For details, see H. Roth, *ER* 6: 483–4.)

HUANG-LAO TAOISM. A Taoist movement, at first philosophical-political, that later seems to have developed into a religious messianic movement.

As a philosophical-political movement, it may have been active as early as the fourth century BCE, in the eastern coastal area of China, within the Chi-hsia Academy of the state of Ch'i. Its name is a contraction of *Huang*-ti (**Yellow Emperor**) and *Lao*-tzu (unless Huang-Lao refers to one single cult object: "Venerable Huang[-ti]" or **Huang-Lao Chün**). If the former hypothesis is correct, it implies that this school had a double cult object: Huang-ti was seen as the ideal sage ruler, who became so successful just because he implemented the advice given by the sage-philosopher Lao-tzu. (This creates a problem, though. If *Lao* in the compound Huang-Lao stands for Lao-tzu, it is hardly possible that such a movement could have arisen in the fourth century: The *TTC* was written only around 250 BCE and, in it, the Yellow Emperor is not mentioned.)

After the collapse of the Ch'in empire (210 BCE), Huang-Lao Taoism reasserted itself. It was favored by some of the early Han emperors, under the influence of their imperial consorts. It also was very active under the sponsorship of Liu An, king of Huai-nan, who gathered hundreds of scholars at his court and produced a volume of 21 essays titled the *Huai-nan-tzu*. The popularity of Huang-Lao thinking is also proven by the discovery of several Huang-Lao manuscripts, found in the **Ma-wang-tui** tomb in the early 1970s.

When Han Emperor Wu (r. 140–87 BCE) chose to adopt Confucianism as his state ideology in or around 136 BCE, Taoist influence was eclipsed, but the movement changed its direction and resurfaced in the early centuries CE.

Indeed, it was transformed into a religious-messianic movement, in which the figure of **Lao-tzu Deified** became the central focus. This process of deification was enhanced by the Heavenly Masters School, but must also have become strong among the population in general. It even reached the imperial court, as the **Lao-tzu Inscription** of 165 CE testifies. However, it is probable that in this later phase of Huang-Lao Taoism, the figure of Huang-ti had receded to the background. Lao-tzu's image as a messianic savior figure had practically eclipsed the Yellow Emperor.

The **T'ai-p'ing Tao** of east China, on the other hand, appears to have endorsed the worship of the Yellow Emperor. This whole movement is an interesting episode in Chinese history and, in particular, Taoist history, but needs more study. It already has attracted the attention of a good number of Han specialists.

HUANG-TI See YELLOW EMPEROR

HUANG-T'ING CHING See *YELLOW COURT SCRIPTURE*

HUMAN PERFECTION. In all religious traditions we find concepts of ultimate realization, of highest human perfection. The terms used are widely different, but more so is the meaning or content of each term. The early Buddhist ideal of *arhat* is different from the Christian *saint* and stands in contrast to the later Buddhist concept of *bodhisattva*.

The Taoists use a variety of terminology to express what they mean by "perfect" human being. Most commonly used is *sheng-jen/shengren*, but other common forms are ***hsien***/xian (immortal), *chen-jen/zhenren, shen-jen/shenren, chih-jen/zhiren,* and *ch'eng-jen/chengren.*

First of all, what is the meaning of *sheng-jen*? It is most commonly translated as "sage," but occasionally one comes across "saint" or "sacred man." An exact equivalent is hard to find; moreover, a term is only a general indicator, and one needs an analysis of the term's content to make it understandable. *Sheng-jen* is about the only term for "sage" found in the *TTC* but it also appears in the *Chuang-tzu* and other Taoist writings. It is also the term found in Confucian texts to express their concept of "sage." In Confucian writings, *sheng-jen* refers to mythical heroes, sage-kings of the past, or to the ideal of human perfection. In the *Analects* of Confucius, there are only two references (7:25 and 7:33), translated as "divine sage" (Waley, 1938: 128, 130), although the addition of "divine" is questionable; it is not inherent in the concept of *sheng-jen*. Mencius holds that all human beings are equal, have an inborn goodness as natural endowment, and are all able to become sages. In the Confucian tradition, sagehood is the utmost of human perfection, one step beyond Confucius' ideal of "superior person," yet still within the boundaries of human nature. Sagehood implies both moral perfection and great intelligence. Sages are the natural rulers of the country.

The Taoist concept is likewise naturalistic: The sage in the *TTC* is a model of Taoist "virtue," spiritually cultivated and intelligent enough to let the people live without interference. He is endowed with the power (*te*) of Tao, which means also "virtue" and "charisma," the power of radiating authority. To a sage ruler everyone submits freely, not forced by fear of physical strength, but by the power of wisdom, goodness, and authority combined.

Many verses in the *TTC* discuss the sage: very often he is named *sheng-jen*, often the idea is only implied. But essentially, the sage is one who has a deep understanding of the Tao, of the Tao's operation in the world, and follows that example in his own government. By "holding on to Oneness [Tao], the sage becomes the model of the world" (Chapter 22:4). By following the model of the cosmos (heaven-and-earth), which is selfless and eternal, the sage is humble and does not pursue personal interests; yet, paradoxically, finds fulfillment of all his goals (Chapter 7:4–6). In his action, he is actionless (*wu-wei*): that is, he does not act contrary to what is natural, or "manages his affairs without ado" (Chapter 2:9, Wu, 1961: 5). He does not dwell on his own merits. Like the cosmos, which gives birth to all things and nurtures them without claiming anything in return, the sage is selfless: He encourages and stimulates, but lets people free. "Is it not because he is selfless that his self is realized?" (Chapter 7:6, Wu: 9).

Just as nature does not speak, the sage "teaches without words" (Chapter 2:9), being aware that "those who know do not speak, and those who speak do not know" (Chapter 56:1).

All this is hard to accomplish even for a sage-ruler: He is a lonely man, "forlorn as one who has no home to return to" (Chapter 20:8, Wu: 27). Summarizing the *TTC's* views of the sage, his most essential characteristic is that he "does not act, yet nothing is left undone" (Chapter 48: 3). That is why it is said that the best ruler is he of whose existence the people are barely aware (Chapter 17:1). Working behind the scene, the ruler is yet there.

In the *Chuang-tzu*, there is a difference: there is no need at all for anyone to rule the country! The sage of the *TTC* is committed to the human realm, the *Chuang-tzu* sage transcends it. *Chuang-tzu's* concept of the ideal person is not as simple and straightforward as that in the *TTC*. He uses various terms, which in view of the multiple authorship should not surprise us. The various terms may partially overlap. Most common are *sheng-jen* and *chen-jen*. *Chuang-tzu's sheng -jen*, translated as "sage" by Watson and Graham, appears many times (in almost 40 passages). He appears as a person of superior intelligence; he does not discriminate against others but lets the ten thousand things be what they are, because he transcends the narrow-minded world of things and opinions and "wanders beyond the dust and grime" (Chapter 2, Watson: 46). As the huge mythical bird, he travels far beyond the boundaries of space, "wanders in the realm where things cannot get away from him, and all things are preserved" (Chapter 6, Watson: 81):

> . . . To spend little effort and achieve big results—that is the Way of the sage. Now it seems that this isn't so. He who holds fast to the Way is complete in Virtue; being complete in Virtue, he is complete in body; being complete in body, he is complete in spirit [*shen*]; and to be complete in spirit is the Way of the Sage. (Chapter 12, Watson: 135)

The sage is thus complete in virtue (*te*), his body and spirit are complete and in harmony, moreover

> A man of true brightness and purity who can enter into simplicity [*su*], give body to his inborn nature, and embrace his spirit [*pao-shen*], and in this way wander through the everyday world—if you had met one like that, you would have had real cause for astonishment. (Chapter 12, Watson: 136)

This is still the original Chuang-tzu's concept of the sage (*sheng-jen*). In a later strand, we find the combination of two strands: inner and outer.

Empty, still, limpid, silent, inactive are qualities of heaven-and-earth. The sage follows this model, and is worthy to be the ruler of the world. Yet heaven-and-earth are also active: They generate and nourish all living beings. The ideal is the combination of both (this is the view of the later Chuang-tzu school): "In stillness, you will be a sage, in action, a king" (Chapter 13, Watson: 143).

Inner or outer, or both combined, the *sage* is in union with heaven-and-earth, or with what is natural. His virtue is complete and his spirit unimpaired (Watson: 168). He does not follow the action plans of others, who are overconcerned about life in society or who care for their physical health and longevity more than for anything else. The sage attains longevity without the gymnastic exercises of *tao-yin* (Watson: 168) and does not seem to care about physical immortality. Life-and-death is the cycle decided by heaven.

Other characteristics of *Chuang-tzu*'s *sheng-jen* prepare for later religious ideas and even prelude Ch'an concepts: The sage teaches without words (repeated after the *TTC*) (Chapter 22, Watson: 235) and does not rely on learning and eloquence: "Breadth of learning does not necessarily mean knowledge; eloquence does not necessarily mean wisdom . . ." (Chapter 22, Watson: 239).

As the above analysis shows, Chuang-tzu's sage has several faces, depending on who wrote the particular chapters. But then, besides *sheng-jen*, other terms are used throughout the text and it is not clear whether they are meant as synonyms. The best known passage is this:

> the Perfect Man [*chih-jen*] has no self;
> the Holy Man [*shen-jen*] has no merit;
> the Sage [*sheng-jen*] has no fame. (Chapter 1, Watson: 32)

By contrast, Graham translates the three terms as "utmost man," "daemonic man," and "sage" (1981: 45).

What Chuang-tzu means by each term exactly is uncertain, but in this context, it is most likely that the three terms are understood as synonyms, since the perfect sage has given up all notion of "self" or "selfishness," all desire for "achievement" or "reputation." The perfect sage is not known and does not set any store by what are in fact externals.

Rendering *shen-jen* by "holy man" or "daemonic man" is questionable. The term *shen* sometimes refers to "deity, ancestral spirit," but here more probably means "spiritual" person, someone who is guided by spiritual values or the spiritual essence of human nature.

A well-known passage describes what a *shen-jen* is: It refers to the "holy man" living on the Ku-she mountain, who combines in his person characteristics of a Taoist mystic (later called "immortal") and the traditional shaman, who travels to the spirit world and cures disease (see Chapter 1, Watson: 33). This image is somehow different from the *sheng-jen*, in that the "holy man" completely transcends the human world, lives in a separate reality, yet is able to influence the well-being of this world. Is that perhaps Chuang-tzu's own concept of the ruler: totally rejecting human bureaucratic government, he brings order to the world through his mere magic presence.

The term *chih-jen*, translated as "perfect man" (Watson) and "utmost man" (Graham), occurs about a dozen times in the *Chuang-tzu*. The character *chih* by itself means to "go to, arrive at, reach, unto, to . . . utmost, in the highest degree" (Karlgren, 1973: 345). Applied to *chih-jen*, the compound refers to a person who has reached the utmost or highest degree of human perfection, one who looks on fame and reputation "as so many handcuffs and fetters" (Chapter 5, Watson: 72), who "uses his mind like a mirror—going after nothing, welcoming nothing, responding but not storing" (Chapter 7, Watson: 97). Or, as Gate Keeper Yin was told by Lieh-tzu, the Perfect Man

> may . . . wander where the ten thousand things have their end and beginning, unify his nature, nourish his breath, unite his virtue, and thereby communicate with that which creates all things. A man like this guards what belongs to Heaven and keeps it whole. His spirit has no flaw, so how can things enter in and get at him? (Chapter 19, Watson: 198)

What about the "true man" (*chen-jen*)? This is a term that gained strong currency in the later Taoist religion and often became a title placed after a name or translated as "perfected (one)" or "transcendent," as in the book title **Chen-kao** (*Declarations of the Perfected*). In *Chuang-tzu*, it does not have this specialized meaning yet and, from its description, it appears to be very close to "perfect man" (*chih-jen*) or "spirit-man" (*shen-jen*).

> The True Man of ancient times slept without dreaming and woke without care . . . his breath came from deep inside . . .
> The True Man of ancient times knew nothing of loving life, knew nothing of hating death . . . (Chapter 6, Watson: 77–78)

The analysis of the "true man" continues, and ends with this: "When man and Heaven do not defeat each other, then we may be said to have the True Man" (Watson: 80). In other words; the "true" person understands and accepts whatever "heaven" decides. Heaven is what is natural, it is the cosmic process, which one should accept in humble resignation. This is oneness with the Tao.

The most frequently occurring terms to designate the Taoist ideal of human perfection have been mentioned: *sheng-jen, chih-jen, shen-jen,* and *chen-jen*. Rarely still other words are used, such as *ch'eng-jen* or "complete man" (Watson: 259–260), or "man of great completion" (Watson: 214), "man of virtue" (Watson: 72, 127), "gentleman of complete virtue" (Watson: 221), or simply "great man" (Watson: 124, 178–9, 235).

Further analysis may throw light on these epithets, but the obvious conclusion is twofold: First, the ideal person in the *Chuang-tzu* is one who has transcended the common limitations of humans, who has deep insight into the reality of Tao and the cosmos, who wanders in the beyond to the utmost boundaries of the cosmos, and who acts and speaks sometimes in eccentric ways. In the second place, there is not even once an allusion or direct mention of a supernatural force (divine beings) as the source of human perfection. Taoism here is a self-quest, not a process helped by divine grace. Once again, this is humanism, not supernaturalism. But it is a deeply spiritual path nonetheless.

In the *Huai-nan-tzu*, the figure of the sage (*sheng-jen*) or the "perfected" (*chen-jen*) follows the patterns expressed in the *TTC* and the *Chuang-tzu*. To cite just one example from Chapter 7:

> The one who is called the True Man (*chen-jen*) is naturally one with Tao; he has as if not having; he is full as if empty; he dwells in unity without knowing duality, governs his inner person and ignores the external. He clearly knows Grand Simplicity (*t'ai-su*); and without ado, he returns to the uncarved block (*p'u*) [wholeness]; he incorporates the Root, embraces the divine, and frolics between heaven and earth. (I. Robinet, 1993: 42)

It would be hardly possible to summarize the Taoist view of the ideal human being, the sage, the perfected or transcendent. For later religious ideals of perfect being, see the entry **Hsien**. But by contrasting the Taoist ideal with other traditions, one will have a better insight into the unique nature of the Taoist sage. In Confucianism, to recover one's original nature and become a sage is within the realm of possibility, but the emphasis is on moral perfection, and the goal is to become a perfect ruler, after the model of the ancient sage-kings. In Buddhism, the emphasis is on enlightenment, which involves a complete understanding of reality (including one's own nature) and overcoming of the moral fetters of ignorance, hatred, and desire. In Mahayana Buddhism, there is an added objective: compassion besides wisdom, so as to make heroic efforts toward the salvation of all other beings. In Christianity, the ideal is sainthood: with the help of divine grace, to become Christ-like and to practice all virtues to a heroic degree. Although the golden rule of loving one's neighbor as oneself is theoretically the criterium of one's love for God, many saints of the past were not always interested in the actual exercise of charity. While sainthood was promoted as the human ideal, those who claimed to experience the divine through mystical trance were often regarded with suspicion. In Christianity, as in Islam, to be a mystic could be dangerous to one's safety.

It is now clear that Christian sainthood is probably most different from the Taoist ideal; to translate *sheng-jen* by "saint" is misleading, because "saint" has strong overtones of the Christian ideal of union with the divine.

HUN See "SOUL"

HUNG-T'OU TAO-SHIH See REDHEAD TAOIST

HUN-TUN See CHAOS

I

I CHING See *YI CHING*

IMMORTAL See *HSIEN*

IMMORTALITY. One of the major issues in every religious tradition is the concept of "life after death." In China, this issue did not receive a uniform solution, each of the "Three Teachings" (**san-chiao**) had its own theory. In summary, one could state that Confucianism was skeptical and agnostic about the notion of the afterlife, although the ancestor cult was positively encouraged. Buddhism contributed a whole new vista to the Chinese otherworldly perspectives, and Taoism proposed several options, according to the *TTC*, the *Chuang-tzu*, the alchemists, and the Taoist institutional religion.

Neither the *TTC* nor the *Chuang-tzu* posit immortality as a goal to achieve. In the alchemical branch, on the other hand, longevity and hopefully immortality are believed to be a possible and desirable goal. In the Taoist institutional religion, the emphasis is on attaining this-worldly happiness, which can be achieved through ritual means. However, as was the case with the Popular religion, Buddhist views and ideals were added to it and merged with the original Taoist concept. The result of this mixing up of different outlooks has certainly confused the whole issue. Here, we should try to unravel the various strands of the tradition (see also the Taoist views of the **soul**).

First of all, is there any evidence of belief in immortality in the *TTC*? This short text combines a whole spectrum of themes, but the idea of life after death is not one of them. As much as possible, we must try to penetrate to the original author's intent. Chapter 7 says that heaven-and-earth (the physical universe) is long lasting because it was not "born." What is unborn does not die. All the myriad creatures, by contrast, are "born" or produced and, therefore, will come to their end, as Chapter 16 states.

> While the myriad beings stir and strive,
> I contemplate their return.
> Indeed, the numerous beings

All return to their root.

Some passages (such as Chapter 50: 6–11) are ambiguous in that they project the possibility of deathlessness, for at least some rare persons, probably the "immortals" (*hsien*). But it is more likely that "longevity" was meant here.

One verse in particular has created a controversy in the past: Chapter 33:5. The common way of translating it was something like: "Who dies but does not perish has longevity." There is an inherent contradiction between "die" and "not die," and whatever one does to manipulate the text does not really help. The Ma-wang-tui manuscripts have shed new light on it and now the meaning is perfectly clear: "Who dies but is not forgotten has longevity."

This new reading is based on a different Chinese character: Instead of *wang* ("to die"), there is another character *wang* (same as "to die" with "heart, mind" radical, which means "to forget"). It is probable that the line is a sort of popular proverb, or an aphorism, perhaps akin to Confucian thinking; immortality is understood as permanence of a good reputation, being remembered for one's merits and continuation of the family in one's offspring.

The *Chuang-tzu* deals with the question of life after death in much greater detail than the *Lao-tzu*. His many passages on death are among the most beautiful of the whole book, perhaps the most meaningful of all literature. Life and death are from heaven, i.e., nature. They are fated. Humans cannot do anything about their eventual occurrence. While unenlightened people resent fate and fear death, the true sage accepts it and sees it as part of the process of the transformation of things:

> The True Man of ancient times knew nothing of loving life, knew nothing of hating death. He emerged without delight, he went back without a fuss. He came briskly, he went briskly, and that was all. He didn't forget where he began, he didn't try to find out where he would end. He received something and took pleasure in it; he forgot about it and handed it back again. (Chapter 6, Watson: 78)

In another passage, he compares life and death with the continuous succession of day and night, with the continuous cycle of the seasons: a natural process that we should accept graciously, because we cannot stop it anyway. Perhaps the most beautiful expression of this simple and inexorable "fact of life" is:

> The Great Clod [earth] burdens me with form, labors me with life, eases me in old age, and rests me in death. So if I think well of my life, for the same reason I must think well of my death. (Chapter 6, Watson: 80)

If life and death are fated and unavoidable, what happens after death? Is there a sparkle of hope at least of some survival? That is for most humans the crucial reason to be religious: They fear that death is the absolute end and, if not, the terrors of torture in hell are a paralyzing force. For Chuang-tzu, there is no hell; death is the end of a minicycle (an individual existence), but the maxicycle, the creative process of the universe, goes on forever.

Two anecdotes in *the Chuang-tzu* illustrate this; both are stories about old gentlemen who became close friends in the shared knowledge that ". . . life and death, existence and annihilation, are all a single body" (Chapter 6, Watson: 84). When one of them fell ill and became deformed, he laughed at himself: "The Creator [Creative Force] is making me all crookedy like this! My back sticks up like a hunchback and my vital organs are on top of me . . . [Yet he remained] calm at heart and unconcerned" (Chapter 6, Watson: 84). Then he started speculating what his body would be transformed into: a rooster, a crossbow pellet, or cartwheels? In the other story, one of the old men says to his dying friend: "How marvelous the Creator is! What is he going to make of you next? Where is he going to send you? Will he make you into a rat's liver? Will he make you into a bug's arm? (Chapter 6, Watson: 85). Amusing speculation, but testimony of a cheerful acceptance of death, implying the dissolution of personal consciousness by merging with the infinite stream of creative potentiality.

Death is thus seen as the end of our individuality, our personal consciousness. What human beings usually think of as the animal kingdom also applies to themselves. There is no continuity after death, only reabsorption into the matrix of creation. This is in perfect agreement with what Chuang-tzu said in an earlier passage: "The Perfect Man (*chi-jen*) has no self" (Chapter 1, Watson: 32).

Chuang-tzu stresses this point when he compared the Creative Force with a skillful smith casting metal objects ". . . if the metal should leap up and say: 'I insist on being made into a Mo-yeh' [equivalent of Excalibur], he would surely regard it as very inauspicious metal indeed" (Chapter 6, Watson: 85). Similarly, humans cannot demand to be made into human beings again. Heaven and earth are a great furnace of creativity, creating and recreating without end. All beings coming out of the furnace return to it after only a short while, but the process goes on. Because Taoism often uses the analogy of water, one can add a new one (not found in the texts, though): Each being, human or other, is like a tiny drop of water, coming out of the ocean and, within seconds, returning to it. Would a drop dare to demand eternity?

For the views of the alchemists on longevity or immortality, see *hsien* and **alchemy**. It seems that the goal of Taoist practitioners was to prolong life and hopefully to reach the state of physical immortality in the end. Yet, this was a very elite ideal, beyond the reach of ordinary human beings.

Also complex is the case of the Taoist religion. In contrast with the views of the popular religion, and yet in some respects similar to it, the Taoist religion focuses on this-worldly happiness. At least this appears from the structure of the Taoist rituals, performed by the Heavenly Master Taoists. Their major ritual celebration, the **Cosmic Renewal Festival**, or *chiao/jiao*, is meant to bring down the blessings from the highest deities and to secure good fortune for the community in times to come. The added purpose of liberating the ancestral spirits from the netherworld appears to be a pre-Taoist but elite aspiration. But overall, although this is a paradoxical situation, the focus is not on immortality but on a blessed mortal existence. Then again, the case is different in monastic Taoism, where the goal is to become a *hsien*.

INCENSE. The offering of incense (by burning) is an almost universal practice in religious rituals. In China in particular, burning incense is an essential part of worship in all religious traditions, including Taoism. The origin of the custom has not been discovered, but there is a strong suspicion that it was introduced to China with Buddhism.

In the Taoist liturgy, incense is used in different ways: One lights *incense sticks* (in popular descriptions they are called "joss sticks") and, while bowing toward the divine images and raising the hands three times, one presents them to these deities as an offering. Then they are placed in an incense burner on the altar. During special rituals, such as the Cosmic Renewal Festival, large (thick) incense sticks are used: One of the Taoist assistants distributes them to the attending laypeople, who hold them in their hands (or in special incense holders) for the duration of the ritual.

In the Popular religion, incense sticks are used in a similar way: When devotees go to the temple, they purchase a package of incense and "spirit-money" and offer the incense to the gods, first to heaven (T'ien-kung), next to the major deity of the temple, finally, to all the subsidiary deities on side altars. In the ancestor cult, incense sticks are offered every day at the home shrine—at least that is the ideal practice.

Then there is also *incense powder*: a fine yellowish dust made from sandalwood and other aromatic plants. During rituals, powder is put inside incense burners, on top of burning coal. It burns up slowly, but the smell is extremely pleasing (in Taiwan, this kind of incense is very expensive, and there are different grades of quality). More rarely, one sees the burning of small chips of *aromatic wood* used as incense.

One could say that offering incense is one of the essential aspects of Chinese religion. It is not so much meant as a means of purification (there are other methods for that, such as producing clouds of smoke), but as an offering to the divine personnel that is pleasing and inclines them to be generous.

Incense is also an important aspect of the Christian liturgy, especially in the Greek Orthodox and Roman Catholic traditions. It would be worthwhile to investigate its origins; maybe Persia or India are the lands of origin. From there it may have spread both East and West.

INNER ALCHEMY (*Nei-tan/neidan*). Inner or internal alchemy has been called "proto-biochemistry." In contrast with outer alchemy, "operations" take place inside one's own body:

> The Chinese adept of the "inner elixir" . . . believed that by doing things with one's own body, a physiological medicine of longevity and even immortality could be prepared within it. (J. Needham V, 5: 23)

To "do things with one's own body" includes a variety of practices on the spiritual-mystical level: meditation, guiding and circulating one's *ch'i* (energy, breath) throughout one's body, but also worship of the deities residing in one's body. Diet is not an essential aspect of *nei-tan*, but rather a condition; so is moral behavior, because the indwelling spirits would report to heaven about an adept's moral misbehavior, and this would be counterproductive as it results in shortening one's lifespan. Gymnastics and *ch'i-kung* can be helpful as auxiliary practices, but do not constitute the essence of *nei-tan*.

This body of spiritual techniques is not alchemy proper. However, because it developed out of *wai-tan* and was probably practiced in combination with it, alchemical language was used to describe its processes. As in the case of the second-century treatise *Ts'an-t'ung-ch'i* (**Kinship of the Three**), alchemical language often became very ambiguous, so that commentators are divided about the text's intention: Does it describe *wai-tan* or *nei-tan*?

If outer alchemy aims at purification of various materials to produce life-prolonging medicine, inner alchemy aims at the purification or refinement of the adept's body-mind unit, also hoping to conquer death and attain the state of immortal *hsien*-ship, but the means of attaining it were not necessarily agreed upon by all:

> . . . some seeing the end of meditation as the physical and spiritual transformation of man into an immortal, a godlike being with an indestructible spiritual body infusing and illuminating the physical body.

Others saw it as the transformation of man into a new spiritual state through the mind, a mind made new, reborn into its original state of unity with the Tao, a mind of pure luminosity which could light the entire cosmos. (J. Berling, 1980: 94)

This conception of inner alchemy has strong affinities with Indian and Tibetan yogas. Whether there have been historical influences in either direction is still not settled. But the Taoist yoga of inner alchemy is distinctly Chinese in that it is based on the Yin-Yang World-view and the Five Agents Theory. It uses in particular the basic trigrams of the *Yi ching*: *ch'ien* ☰ and *k'un* ☷, representing heaven and earth on the cosmic level, the cauldron (furnace) on the alchemical level, and the body on the human level. Two other trigrams are equally important: *li* ☲ and *k'an* ☵, representing fire and water and, in alchemy, also lead and mercury. Inner alchemy consists of uniting the opposites inside one's own body, in the "cauldron" of one's own body by a process of spiritual refinement that will ultimately produce a spiritualized body that is incorruptible and has many transcendent powers (I. Robinet, 1986: 383).

This view of alchemy is different from its Western counterpart: In mystical theology, the focus of spiritual practice is also on "purification" of the soul, but the body is not an integral part of the process. The body, as in dualistic systems, is rather the adversary.

Inner alchemy, as it gradually developed, started to focus on two distinct aspects of a human being: *nature* and *life*.

Nature (*hsing*) is what constitutes a human being; it is the source of human faculties, including the spirit (*shen*). Life (*ming*) is the actual sum total of all one's vital energies, which make nature come alive. It includes the three primary vitalities, which give real existence to what otherwise would be an abstraction, nature. Through cultivation of the three vitalities, a Taoist adept is able to reverse the natural flow of energy dissipation and return "to the non-differentiated state at the beginning of creation, that which antedated heaven . . . Through this re-creation, the Taoist became physically and spiritually identified with the underlying cosmic unity of the Tao" (Berling: 95–96). (See also **hsien**, **outer alchemy**, **alchemy**, **Three Primary Vitalities**.)

Procedures/Techniques Used in Nei-Tan
Whoever aspired to becoming an "accomplished person," a *chen-jen* or a *hsien*, had a rigorous program of spiritual practices and procedures available. They are not all equally necessary: An adept had some choice. Some procedures, however, were essential. Needham

(II: 143–152) lists six techniques: respiratory techniques (see **Breathing Exercises**); heliotherapeutic techniques (exposure to sun rays, or to moon rays for women); gymnastic techniques (see **Gymnastics**); sexual techniques (see **Sexuality**; **Union of Energies**); alchemical and pharmaceutical techniques; dietary techniques (see **Diet**).

An auxiliary procedure, optional to some degree, was the use of alchemical pills. More important, recommended together with breathing and sexual techniques, was the conservation of bodily fluids, especially saliva and semen.

To conclude: Even if some of these concepts and practices strike a Western reader as weird and out of this world, it cannot be denied that their impact on a serious adept could be surprising. Even if immortality, claimed or pretended, remains questionable, the spiritual program of inner alchemy and its various concomitant practices were often instrumental in obtaining a long and healthy life. That cannot be underestimated.

J

JADE EMPEROR (*Yü-huang Ta-ti/Yuhuang Dadi*). The supreme deity of popular Taoism and of the Chinese community religion. This god's rise to eminence only started with the Sung dynasty. Emperor Chentsung (r. 998–1022) had suffered defeat at the hands of the northern Liao invaders in 1004. To boost his image, a story was created that the Jade Emperor would send down "divine revelations." Indeed, in 1008 "heavenly scriptures" descended from heaven and were received with great pomp and solemnity. From this time, the prestige of Yü-huang Ta-ti became second to none.

During the southern dynasties, his position had been much less elevated. In the pantheon system devised by T'ao Hung-ching, two names of gods appear, similar to the Jade Emperor: Yü-huang Taochün and Kao-shang Yü-ti, but they are not placed in a high position. It is only during the T'ang that the god Yü-huang started to become popular. A scripture from T'ang or Sung times describes his birth and life story. When the need for a special revelation arose during the Sung period, Yü-huang was an acceptable candidate used by the imperial court for its own objectives. Grandiose new titles were given to the deity and, although among the Taoists the Three Pure Ones (*San Ch'ing*) are still supreme, the Jade Emperor became the highest deity of the Popular religion. He is the head of the divine hierarchy and controls the whole heavenly administration. Every year, he checks the performance of each staff member and metes out rewards (promotions) and punishments (demotions) accordingly.

In Taiwan today, there are several temples in which he is the main deity; in other temples, a special shrine to him is on the highest temple floor, symbolically expressing his supreme status. The common people usually refer to him as *T'ien-kung* ("Mr. Heaven" or "Venerable Heaven"). His birthday is celebrated on the ninth day of the first lunar month.

JADE EMPEROR SCRIPTURE (*Yü-huang ching/Yuhuangjing*). A Taoist scripture. The author and date of composition are not known. Yet it is one of the very important texts recited or chanted in the Taoist liturgy today, a must during the **Cosmic Renewal Festival** (*chiao*). It is included in the first section of the Taoist Canon (*tung-chen*) under the complete title *Kao-shang Yü-huang pen-hsing chi-ching* (*CT* 10; *TT* 23).

It is said that this text is an imitation of the Buddhist scripture *Fo pen-hsing chi-ching* (T. 680), translated into Chinese by Jnanagupta in 487 CE. It has been speculated that a Taoist from the T'ang dynasty wrote it during the reign of Emperor Hsuan-tsung (r. 713–755).

The text consists of three "scrolls" (*chuan*) in five chapters (*p'in*). It narrates how the Heavenly Worthy of the Original Beginning in Ch'ing-wei Heaven preached the unique *ling-pao* method of purity and tranquillity. It also narrates the story of the spiritual cultivation of the Jade Emperor (Yü-huang): In ancient times, there was a kingdom of great bright splendor and wonderful happiness. In a dream, the queen saw T'ai-shang Tao-chün holding a baby and giving it to her. After she woke up, she was pregnant, and gave birth to a prince. After he succeeded to the throne, he gave up his position and entered the mountains to cultivate the Way for 3,200 *kalpas* (a *kalpa* is a fabulous period of time). He became a "golden immortal." Awakened to the correct method of the "great vehicle," he spent another 100,000 kalpas, then became Yü-ti, the Jade Emperor (*TTTY*: 13).

JUJUBE See PLANT SYMBOLISM

K

KINSHIP OF THE THREE (*Ts'an-t'ung ch'i/Cantongqi*). The earliest still existing text on **alchemy**, attributed to **Wei Po-yang** (fl. 100–170 CE), dated about 142 CE.

The meaning of the title has been often discussed and could refer to the three areas of Taoist concern, as J. Needham explains:

> . . . the theory of the *Book of Changes*, which in a broader sense includes those of the Yin and the Yang as well as the Five [Agents],

the philosophical teachings of Taoism, and the processes of alchemy. (Needham: V, 3: 52)

The text is obscure and has given rise to numerous commentaries, roughly falling into two categories: those who claim that the book talks about **outer alchemy**, and their opponents, who believe it deals with **inner alchemy**, a dichotomy comparable to the western duality of practical versus allegorical-mystical alchemy (Needham V, 3: 57).

The proto-scientific spirit of the work is obvious: Needham quotes two texts, which clearly state the need for using the proper materials and the correct techniques, rather than to hope for miracles. Sexual symbolism is often used to illustrate the proper blending of materials (Needham: 68–69, 71).

Wei Po-yang's influence on later philosophers and alchemists has been extremely powerful: it gave alchemy new directions, but also limited its scope of experimentation. The use of mercury and lead as the main sources of elixir would cause many cases of poisoning.

. . . indeed it is possible that many of the most brilliant and creative alchemists fell victim to their own experiments by taking dangerous elixirs. (Needham: 74)

The elusive language used was a factor that obstructed the easy spread of alchemy and was probably deliberate, for self-protection and in order to prevent the secrets from being communicated to unworthy amateurs. (See Needham V, 3: 50–75; see also **Outer Alchemy.**)

KITCHEN GOD See DIRECTOR OF DESTINY

KO CH'AO-FU/GE CHAOFU. A Taoist of the late fourth and early fifth century, the actual author of the **Ling-pao Scriptures**. He was a grand-nephew of **Ko Hung**. The scriptures he composed number about 50. Ko Ch'ao-fu claimed that they had been obtained from an immortal by Ko Hsuan, Ko Hung's uncle. Later, the transmission lineage was reconstructed as follows: Ko Hsuan → Ko Hung → Ko Ch'ao-fu → Lu Hsiu-ching → T'ao Hung-ching. It was T'ao who first made the triple division of the Taoist Canon: Shang-ch'ing Scriptures, Ling-pao Scriptures, San-huang Scriptures.

Besides being the real author of the Ling-pao corpus, not much is known about the life and personality of Ko Ch'ao-fu. He was a syncretistic writer who had access to the Shang-ch'ing collection of scriptures and also was very much influenced by some Buddhist texts, which had circulated in southern China.

KO HSUAN/GE XUAN (164–244). An alchemist during the Three Kingdoms period. He was a native of Tan-yang, Chü-jung, in present-day Kiangsu province. According to the *Pao-p'u-tzu*, written by his nephew, **Ko Hung**, he received his training from Tso Tz'u, a famous alchemist of the period, who also gave him several alchemical writings, such as *T'ai-ch'ing tan-ching* ("Alchemy Scripture of Grand Purity") and others. These texts were later transmitted to Cheng Yin (d. 302), then finally to Ko Hung. Recent scholarship has pointed out this transmission lineage, which later came to be known as the Tan-ting (Alchemy) School of Taoism.

Because Ko Hsuan once resided on **Mount Ko-tsao** in Kiangsi, a school named Ko-tsao School developed there: they worshipped Ko Hsuan as their founder. The later **Ling-pao School** also venerated him as their founding patriarch, because **Ko Ch'ao-fu** claimed that the Ling-pao scriptures had been transmitted to him by Ko Hsuan.

Many legends surround this famous personality. It was said that he was able to fast for long stretches of time without feeling hungry; that he was able to cure disease and to control the coming and going of spiritual beings. He was an expert in Taoist magic and talismans. He is also known as Ko Hsien-ong (Venerable Immortal Ko).

KO HUNG/GE HONG (283–343/63 CE). A famous author and alchemist of the Eastern Chin dynasty (317–420), usually considered to be a Taoist. This attribution must be qualified, however, since he was also a strong proponent of Confucian social-political thinking. His literary name was Pao-p'u-tzu (the Master who holds on to Wholeness), hence the book he wrote has also been called *Pao-p'u-tzu/ Baopuzi*.

He was a native of Tan-yang in present-day Kiangsu province, a nephew of **Ko Hsuan**/Ge Xuan (164–244), a Taoist alchemist of the Three Kingdoms period. When he was young, he was very poor, but intelligent and eager to study. He often went to the mountains to cut wood, which he sold as fuel so that he could afford to buy writing materials. As an adult, he was well versed in the Confucian classics, historical, and philosophical writings. He was known as an expert in Confucianism, yet he was also attracted to the arts of immortality and instructed in it by Cheng Yin (d. 302), a well-known alchemist.

In 303, he was appointed as a military officer and in this function was instrumental in the suppression of the Shih Ping rebellion. After the rebels' defeat, Ko resigned from the military and wanted to go to Loyang to look for Taoist texts. Because of the chaotic situation in the north at that time, he had to give up his plan and instead accepted his friend Chi Han's invitation to go south. His friend was the governor of Canton, and Ko joined his staff. When Chi was assassinated soon afterward, Ko was stranded in Canton, but decided to stay anyway. During this Canton episode, Ko experienced the instability of a political career and started to devote his time and efforts to studying and writing. Later, he returned to his home in Tan-yang.

In 317, he completed the *Pao-p'u-tzu*. Although the government offered him several high positions, he declined on the grounds of getting old. He wanted to search for the elixir of life through alchemical experiments. When he heard that cinnabar, a basic alchemical ingredient, was produced in northern Vietnam, he asked to be appointed magistrate of Kou-lou county. But when he reached Canton with his family, he was detained by the governor and not allowed to go any further. Forced to comply, Ko stayed on nearby **Mount Lou-fu**, where he continued his writing and his alchemical experiments. He passed away there in 343 or 363.

Ko hung was a versatile scholar who authored several books. His best-known work, *Pao-p'u-tzu,* contains 70 chapters: 20 inner chapters and 50 outer chapters. The former deal with immortals, medical prescriptions, and drugs, the configuration and transformation of spiritual beings, methods of nourishing and prolonging life and how to avoid disasters. These inner chapters summarize all the theories on immortals since the Warring States period. They also describe a theoretical system on the concept of the immortal. Founded on the alchemical legacy of **Wei Po-yang**, it outlines a summation and synthesis of all the alchemical theories of the Wei and Chin periods. In those 20 chapters, 282 texts on immortals and talismans are listed and evaluated. This is indeed very valuable as a source of information on Chinese **alchemy** up to the Eastern Chin period, and as a source for studying the intellectual currents of the Wei-Chin periods. Moreover, important concepts, such as Tao, Oneness (*yi*), and Mystery (*hsuan*), are analyzed, and the possibility of becoming an immortal (*hsien*) is strongly defended.

The 50 outer chapters contain Ko Hung's social and political views, implying that he saw himself as a Taoist in his inner being, while acting as a Confucian in his social life. It is the combination or reconciliation of his immortality concepts with Confucian social obligations. This reconciliation was not purely artificial: For him, the Confucian virtues of loyalty, filial piety, humaneness, and trust were basic conditions to achieve (Taoist) immortality.

As to his method for achieving immortality, Ko combined inner cultivation with outer nourishment. The inner part included breathing exercises and sexual practices; the outer part consisted of taking drugs and alchemical elixirs.

Although Ko Hung was both a Taoist and a Confucian, he was an important figure in the further development of Taoism. He transformed Taoism from being a movement for the masses to one of individual practice and personal choice in the search for immortality.

KO YI/GEYI ("Matching Meanings"). Refers to a method of textual hermeneutics and exegesis practiced for a short period of time (fourth century CE) when Buddhism started to adjust itself to the intellectual climate of China. Buddhist ideology had created its own very technical concepts and philosophical interpretations, which had no exact equivalents in Chinese language. Yet, in order to make its message understandable to a Chinese audience, Buddhism had to use Chinese terms. With the help of analogous terms and concepts found in the Chinese classical literature and more so in Taoism, they tried to explain the new Buddhist ideology. Tao-an and Hui-yuan and others used this technique. But Tao-an soon realized that it was more harmful than helpful and abandoned the method. With the arrival of Kumarajiva (401 CE), who devised better translation techniques, the *ko-yi* practice was abandoned. (See E. Zürcher, 1959: 184, 187; K. Ch'en, 1964: 68.)

K'OU CH'IEN-CHIH/KOU QIANZHI (365–448). A Taoist priest during the Northern Wei dynasty (386–534). He was a native of Chang-ping, Shangku (present-day Beijing), and claimed to have descended from an aristocratic family of the Later Han dynasty.

From an early age, he was attracted to Taoism and studied the teachings of **Chang Lu**, but was unable to grasp their subtleties. Later, together with Ch'eng Kung-hsing, he went to Mount Sung, where he studied Taoism for seven years. Ch'eng allegedly was a Taoist immortal and a well-known mathematician. K'ou's reputation gradually spread. He started to reform the Heavenly Masters School, which he claimed had been corrupted by the three Changs (Chang Ling, Chang Heng, and Chang Lu). He also claimed that T'ai-shang Lao-chün (Lao-tzu deified) had descended on Mount Sung, conferred upon him the title of Heavenly Master, and had given him a sacred text in 20 chapters dealing with talismans, breathing exercises, and other practices. He decidedly wanted to abolish the sexual ritual of *ho-ch'i* (union of energies), as well as do away with the imposed taxation of five bushels of rice. K'ou maintained that the religious practices of Taoism should concentrate on social etiquette and manners, in combination with the taking of medicinal drugs and the observation of mental discipline as effective ways toward salvation. This shows that K'ou had in mind to restore Heavenly Masters Taoism by raising it to the level of the higher classes of society and transforming it from a popular movement to a religious establishment, submissive to the political authority of the Northern Wei.

Eight years later, he claimed to have received new revelations, this time by the appearance of Li P'u-wen, the great-great-grandson of Lao-tzu. K'ou claimed that Li had personally given him a text in 60 chapters: the *True Scripture of Registers and Charts* (*Lu-t'u chen-ching*). Moreover, Li P'u-wen instructed him in the skills of summoning spiritual beings and practicing alchemy. Li also ordered K'ou to assist Wei Emperor T'ai-wu, whom he called "True Ruler of Great Peace" (T'ai-p'ing chen-chün).

With the assistance of Ts'ui Hao, a high court official, K'ou went to P'ing-ch'eng, the Northern Wei capital (present-day Ta-t'ung in Shansi) and presented various Taoist texts to the emperor. With the emperor's support, he built a new sacrificial site in the capital: a building of five floors, which he himself had designed. The emperor followed K'ou's advice and changed his reign title to *T'ai-p'ing chen-chün*. Initiated into the order by K'ou personally, he became a Taoist emperor-priest, and K'ou became the imperial teacher. The Northern School of Heavenly Master Taoism became an upper-class religion, infused with Confucian concepts, and emphasis on social relationships and obligations, such as filial piety and loyalty.

Probably due to K'ou and especially the Confucian minister Ts'ui Hao, starting in 445, Buddhism suffered suppression during the reign of T'ai-wu. K'ou Ch'ien-chih died in 448 during the high tide of suppression. Ts'ui Hao was executed in 450, and two years later, in 452, Emperor T'ai-wu was assassinated. With the enthronement of the new emperor, Buddhism regained its freedom, whereas Taoism went into gradual decline. It is doubtful whether this short episode of Taoist glory had any lasting effects.

KUAN See TEMPLES

KUAN-KUNG See KUAN-TI

KUAN-SHENG TI-CHÜN See KUAN-TI

KUAN-TI/GUANDI or **KUAN-KUNG/GUANGONG**. One of the most popular gods of Chinese religion, properly belonging to the Communal religion, but also claimed by Taoism as one of its own, although the state religion, during imperial times, promoted his cult with great efforts: He was considered for all citizens to be a model of civic virtues, especially loyalty and courage. This makes Kuan-kung a very intriguing deity indeed.

A more formal and dignified title, found today in sectarian movements, is Kuan-sheng Ti-chün/Guansheng Dijun (Holy Emperor Lord Kuan). Other names are Wen-heng Ti-chün, Fu-mo Ta-ti, Hsieh-t'ien

Ta-ti, En-chu kung ("Lord Benefactor"). It is interesting to note that none of these titles indicates that Kuan-kung was worshipped as "God of War," although this is the most common epithet found in Western literature. He is a martial god all right, very brave and strong in war, but not a god of war as such.

Kuan-kung was a historical figure named Kuan Yü. He lived during the period of Three Kingdoms (220–265 CE). After the collapse of the Han dynasty, he and two other eminent warriors: Liu Pei, throne pretendant and Chang Fei, a general, swore an oath of mutual loyalty in the "peach garden." They would remain loyal to each other throughout their life and made great efforts to restore the Han dynasty. Kuan Yü was eventually captured by the southern armies and executed. After his death, a cult arose and legends flourished.

> His character and exploits were popularized in the great work of histori-
> cal fiction entitled *The Romance of the Three Kingdoms*, written during
> the fourteenth century. The extraordinary success of this novel . . . was
> spread among the entire populace through the medium of the storytell-
> ers and the stage. (L. Thompson, 1996: 59)

Being a popular deified martial hero, his worship was strongly promoted by the imperial court: His temple "became an integral part of every major Chinese community" (Yang, 1970: 159), often built at government expense, since this god symbolized and actively encouraged ". . . the civic values of loyalty, righteousness, and devoted support for the legitimate political power" (Yang: 160).

For the community, however, Kuan-kung served other functions.

> He was worshipped by merchants as a god of wealth and of fidelity in
> business contracts, by common people as a curer of disease, by soldiers
> as their patron god, and by many local communities as the chief protec-
> tive deity against calamities and destruction. (Yang: 159)

Because of his popularity, Kuan-kung's image is still often found today in temples, private homes, shops, and restaurants. Characteristically, he has a red face and wears a long beautiful beard, of which he was very proud. Several temples are dedicated to *Wen* and *Wu* (example: the Wen-Wu temple on Hollywood Road in Hong Kong): *Wen* means culture, literature, and is represented by such gods as **Wen-ch'ang Ti-chün**; *Wu* means martial, and Kuan-kung is the martial hero par excellence.

In modern sectarian movements, Kuan-kung, or rather Kuan-sheng Ti-chün, is especially revered as one of the major patron deities of automatic writing. Many temples are dedicated to him in Taiwan, and devotees gather there several times a week to ask for divine messages.

It is the belief of these groups that Kuan-sheng Ti-chün has succeeded in the role of the **Jade Emperor** or Yü-huang Ta-ti, and is now the supreme deity of the pantheon.

In Taiwan, there are important centers of Kuan-kung worship in temples of Tainan, Changhua, Hsinchu, Hsinchuang, Taipei and San-hsia, as well as on the outskirts of Taichung (Ta-k'eng) at the newly built, grandiose temple Sheng-shou kung. The god's birthday is celebrated on the 13th of the fifth lunar month.

KUAN-TZU/GUANZI. A collection of essays dating from the Warring States and Han periods, attributed to Kuan-tzu, a minister of the state of Ch'i who died in 645 BCE. Kuan-tzu (Master Kuan), whose personal name was Kuan Chung, probably did not personally write any of the essays, but because he had the reputation of a model minister, it is not surprising that his name was chosen by whoever edited the collection at a later time.

A recent study and partial translation of the text (A. Rickett, 1985) suggests multiple authorship. The core of the present work ("proto-Kuan-tzu") is said to date from about 250 BCE. It "originated with the Jixia [Chi-hsia] Academy founded by King Xuan [Hsuan] of Qi [Ch'i] . . . in about 302 BCE, and additional materials were gradually added until its final shape was determined in about 26 BCE" (Rickett: 15).

The *Kuan-tzu* is one of the oldest and largest pre-Han and early Han works that have survived. Its content indicates a variety of sources and authors involved in it: Not only does it deal with political, social, and economic theory, it also combines various schools of thought, such as Confucianism, Legalism, and Taoism. It discusses yin-yang theory, military strategy, and Huang-Lao philosophy. Some essays may even derive from the school of Huai-nan-tzu.

From the viewpoint of Taoism, it is most interesting to see how various schools of thought are interwoven into a new synthesis. It is syncretism in action, not surprising when the variety of contributing authors is considered.

KUI See "SOUL"

K'UI-HSING/KUIXING. A star-god transformed into the Taoist god of literature, worshipped for success in the imperial examinations, usually placed on the left of **Wen-ch'ang Ti-chün**.

There is some uncertainty about his actual identity: Sometimes he is considered as the chief star of the Big Dipper, other times as the four stars in the bowl of the Dipper.

The character *k'ui* is enigmatic: The left part represents *kui* (ghost) and on the right is *tou*, meaning "dipper, bushel." Most likely it is an artificially composed graphic, and so is the god's iconographic representation: a stylized form of the character *kui*, with a face and limbs added. In the right hand he holds a writing brush, and in his left a bushel (*tou*). This is very interesting and unusual and betrays its purely stellar origin, for which no "human" figure was available.

KUO HSIANG/GUO XIANG (d. 312 CE). A well-known Neo-Taoist philosopher from the Western Chin dynasty (265–316), most famous for his still-existing commentary on the *Chuang-tzu* (translated by Fung Yu-lan, 1933/1964).

He was a native of present-day Loyang in Honan province. He served as a high government official. According to his biography in the *Chin Dynastic History* (*Chin-shu*), he was a talented and precocious young man. He loved the *Tao-te ching* and the *Chuang-tzu* and was skillful in "pure conversation" (*ch'ing-t'an/qingtan*). Wan Yen (256–311), another famous Neo-Taoist, compared Kuo Hsiang's intellectual abilities to the inexhaustible waters in a flowing river. His contemporaries placed him on the same intellectual rank as **Wang Pi** (226–249).

Kuo Hsiang is mainly known for his commentary on the *Chuang-tzu*. Yet, there is some controversy about whether it was Kuo's own work, or whether he plagiarized Hsiang Hsiu's (227?–272) previous commentary. Sometimes, scholars refer to the work as the Hsiang-Kuo commentary.

Kuo Hsiang elaborated the idea of *tzu-jan* (self-so, natural) and its self-transformations. All things in the universe transform themselves without any external force. He rejected the idea of Tao as Non-Being as the origin of all things. He also considered human ethics and institutions important in society, thus rejecting Chuang-tzu's contempt for social obligations. To follow one's nature is not contradictory with observing moral and social duties: Both are complementary; whoever is capable of combining both naturalness and social involvement is a true sage. He is not someone who "folds his arms and sits in silence in the midst of some mountain forest . . . Confucius, and not Lao Tzu or Chuang Tzu, was such a sage" (Chan, 1963: 317–8).

Jen Chi-yu and others state that Kuo Hsiang's thought is the final synthesis of Neo-Taoist philosophy (in *Historical Development of Chinese Philosophy*, vol. 3. Beijing, 1988—in Chinese). It is indeed a synthesis of Taoist and Confucian thinking.

L

LADY WEI HUA-TS'UN (252–334). During life, she was a **libationer** in Heavenly Masters Taoism. About 30 years after her death, she appeared to **Yang Hsi** together with other "transcendents" (or "perfected immortals") to reveal to him the scriptures of Shang-ch'ing Taoism. The nocturnal visits lasted from 364 to 370. She is considered to be the first patriarch of Shang-ch'ing or Mao Shan Taoism.

LAN TS'AI-HO/LAN CAIHE (*Emblem*: flower basket). One of the **Eight Immortals**, sometimes regarded as a woman or even a hermaphrodite. Today, he would probably be recognized as a homosexual or transvestite. "Though he was a man, he could not understand how to be a man." (Werner, 1969: 346).

He is represented in a blue gown, with one foot shod and the other bare, waving a wand as he/she wandered begging through the streets. He chanted a doggerel verse, which denounced this fleeting life and its elusive pleasures. Like other legendary immortals, he was an eccentric, called the "mountebank" of the immortals. In a Sung period description, it is said that he ". . . liked to lie on the snow, and from his body issued a steam-like vapor . . . He was habitually drunk, singing while he walked . . . [and making] people laugh till they rolled on the ground. . . . His songs were many, not always intelligible but always full of ideas of immortality. He would string the coins he received with a long cord, which he trailed behind him as he walked. He would give some of them to the poor or spend them in the tavern. He traveled all over the country and he kept himself always young. On one occasion, he was drinking in a tavern when he heard the sound of a flute and reed-organ. He suddenly took off from the ground, mounted a crane, and disappeared into the clouds, meanwhile throwing down his clothing, a boot, his girdle, and castanets" (Lai, 1972: 5, 7).

LAO TAN/LAO DAN. Another name for Lao-tzu in Szu-ma Ch'ien's *Shih chi* (*Historical Records*). It is Lao-tzu's name most often encountered in the *Chuang-tzu*, in which Lao Tan has frequent discussions with Confucius, such as, for example, the fascinating dialogue between the two narrated in Chapter 21 (Watson, 1970: 224–227). (See also **Li Erh**.)

LAO-TZU/LAOZI ("Old Master"). The name given to the assumed author of the ***Tao-te ching***. It is not a real name, rather a title, or perhaps a nickname. This indicates that his true name was not known. It is quite possible that the *TTC* was the joint work of a group of anonymous gentlemen, who used the name Lao-tzu to hide their own identities.

Yet traditionally, the *TTC* has been attributed to Lao-tzu. This started with Szu-ma Ch'ien's *Shi-chi* (*Historical Records*), written about 90 BCE. It contains the first biography of Lao-tzu, named Li Erh or Li Tan. But this is more than a biography. It is a legendary narrative and contains even the mythical story of Lao-tzu's miraculous birth. His mother had conceived him after seeing a falling star, but she gave birth to him some 62 years later (the name *lao tzu* can also be translated as "old son").

Lao-tzu served as an official of the archives in the Chou capital. During that time, Confucius, who was about 20 years his junior, went to consult him on *li* (rituals). Lao-tzu became disgusted with court life and, seeing the decline of the Chou kingdom, decided to leave. He mounted an ox and traveled to the West. But before leaving China, the western border pass-keeper, Yin Hsi, urged him to write down his ideas and this became a text of 5,000 words about *Tao* and *Te* (*TTC*). Thereupon, Lao-tzu left and was never seen again. Nobody knows what happened to him. (See also E.M. Chen, 1989: 4–14.)

This is about the substance of the Lao-tzu legend. Certainly not much to go by! The later Taoists would create more legends and myths for apologetic reasons, as well as part of their "theological" speculations. (See also **Lao-tzu Deified, Lao-tzu Inscription,** and **Conversion of Barbarians Scripture.**)

LAO-TZU DEIFIED. Several entries discuss the phenomenon of Lao-tzu's apotheosis from a merely human "wise" philosopher to a supernatural being and, ultimately, to the personification of the Transcendent Tao. The present entry ties the various data together into a sketch of the historical process of this transformation. It is hypothetical, because there are gaps in our knowledge. But it is safe enough to distinguish several stages in the development of the Lao-tzu cult.

• *Lao-tzu as a human teacher and author.* Lao-tzu's name as author of the ***Tao-te ching*** was not immediately recognized, but in the *Shih-chi* (about 90 BCE) he is clearly presented as its author, who wrote the short treatise at the request of the border guardian Yin-hsi. The name "Lao-tzu" is most likely not a real name but a symbolic name hiding the identity of the true author(s). In any case, in the early phase, Lao-tzu is considered a human sage-philosopher who, like other authors, expressed his (their?) views on how a country should ideally be governed.

• *Lao-tzu as counselor to kings.* This is a new image of the Old Teacher as it was projected in the school named **Huang-Lao Taoism**. In this context, the cult of Lao-tzu and the Yellow Emperor were combined into one: The Yellow Emperor was the sage king, who ruled effectively, following Lao-tzu's advice on correct policy. There is, however, a doubt about the identity of *Huang-Lao*. It could be that it reflects the cult of Huang-ti only. The word *Lao* in this expression is ambiguous; it could be an honorific title meaning "venerable" ("old" was respectable). If Lao-tzu was not yet known as author of the *TTC* whenever Huang-Lao Taoism started, it is not likely that he would be the object of a cult yet.

• *Lao-tzu as legendary hero.* The first evidence of legend-building dates from about 90 BCE: Szu-ma Ch'ien's biography of Lao-tzu in the *Shih-chi* is rather a hagiography, and its details about a supernatural "virginal" birth and unusual phenomena cannot be taken as historical facts. It opened the road, however, to further mystification.

• *T'ai-shang Lao-chün.* From Szu-ma's story until the middle of the second century CE, there is a gap of more than 200 years, during which a gradual deification process must have taken place. For the founder of Heavenly Masters Taoism, Lao-tzu was a divine being, who revealed himself to Chang Tao-ling in order to save the world.

• *Savior and creator.* About the same time, Lao-tzu deified was also worshipped officially. The **Lao-tzu Inscription** (165 CE) gives clear evidence of belief in Lao-tzu (or in Huang-Lao Chün?) as the divine Lord, creator of the universe, who descends to earth in times of crisis and impending disaster to save humanity. His worship is both official and popular, but for two different purposes: Emperor Huan hoped Lao-tzu's descent would save the dynasty from extinction; the people (and the Yellow Turbans) hoped Lao-tzu would help them overthrow the dynasty and inaugurate a state of universal peace.

• *Lao-tzu and Huang-Lao Chün.* Usually "Huang-Lao Chün" is understood as the dual figures of *Huang*-Ti (Yellow Emperor) and *Lao*-tzu. But it is possible that the name only means "Venerable Yellow [Emperor]." In any case, during the second century CE, either as a dual or a single deity, Huang-Lao Chün has been elevated to the highest level of supreme being. His cult may have continued until it was eclipsed by the rise of new Taoist triads.

• After the defeat of the Yellow Turbans (184 CE), belief in Lao-tzu as a supergod continued. Due to controversies with Buddhism, now seen as a rival religion that attracted many Chinese (see also **Buddhism** and **Taoism**), Taoist imagination and techniques of self-defense created new myths about the prehistory of Lao-tzu. Texts such as ***Lao-tzu hua-hu ching*** and *Lao-tzu pien-hua ching* were concrete evidence of a new concept of Lao-tzu deified. Yet, the very idea of multiple reincarnations itself may have been formulated under the influence of the Buddhist prototype.

• *Lao-tzu as member of a new triad.* During the Southern Dynasties, T'ao Hung-ching and others were instrumental in "restructuring" the Taoist pantheon. In the final creation, Lao-tzu deified became the third member of the new triad of **Three Heavenly Worthies** (*T'ien-tsun*).

• *Lao-tzu as supreme deity.* Keeping the title of the Heavenly Masters Taoists, T'ai-shang Lao-chün, Lao-tzu kept his place of autonomy as supreme being in various scriptures as late as the T'ang period. (See **T'ai-shang Lao-chün** for details.)

In today's Taoist religious worship, the figure of the deified Lao-tzu is most commonly seen in the context of the Three Heavenly Worthies (or Three Pure Ones). More rarely, one can see images of a sole Lao-tzu, not as part of the triad. His iconographic features are not clearly those of a supreme deity. More commonly, he is represented as a human figure, a sage, either seated or riding the "old ox." Some of these images date from the T'ang dynasty or are copies of old prototypes.

LAO-TZU HSIANG-ERH CHU/LAOZI XIANGER ZHU. One of the earliest commentaries on the *TTC*, perhaps dating from the second century CE. Lost for a long time, part of the text has been discovered among the Tun-huang manuscript collection of Sir Aurel Stein (1862–1943), Hungarian-British archaeologist and geographer. The text has been published with annotations by Jao Tsung-yi (1959 and 1991). Jao attributed the commentary to either **Chang Tao-ling** or, more probably, to his grandson, **Chang-Lu.** But the question remains whether the *Hsiang-erh* commentary is dependent on the Ho-shang kung commentary or vice versa (see A. Chan, 1991: 109–118).

If the authorship of Chang Lu is accepted, it would indicate that the *TTC* was an important sacred text among the early Heavenly Masters' followers. The significance of the *TTC* was changed from a philosophical text (addressed to rulers of the country) to a religious scripture. Some of its major concepts correspond with ideas found in the *Great Peace Scripture* (*T'ai-p'ing ching*), but, more importantly, the person of Lao-tzu, the assumed author of the *TTC*, and the concept of Tao are deified and presented as objects of worship and of obedience. Lao-tzu is transformed into **T'ai-shang Lao-chün**, the embodiment of Tao.

Whereas the *TTC* criticizes and dismisses the (Confucian) virtues of humaneness (*jen*), righteousness (*yi*), and filial piety (*hsiao*), in this commentary, these virtues are emphasized and stressed as important keys toward a smooth functioning of society. There is further elaboration of new ideas, such as the concept of longevity and the cult of the immortals. It means that this old philosophical essay has been transformed into the blueprint of a new "theological" system. Members of the Heavenly Masters Tao were urged to read and recite the text as a source of inspiration in their spiritual life.

LAO-TZU INSCRIPTION (*Lao-tzu ming/Laoziming*). This is a stone inscription dating from 165 CE, during the end of the Han dynasty. The text of this inscription was composed by a local official, named Pien Shao. It is the first textual evidence about the official cult of a deified Lao-tzu. The occasion of its composition was the imperially sponsored sacrifice to Lao-tzu in 165, performed by two eunuchs. The following year, 166 CE, Emperor Huan (r. 147–168) himself performed a sacrifice in honor of Lao-tzu in his imperial palace in Lo-yang. But the text of the inscription goes far beyond recording an historical event; it expresses a new "theology" of Lao-tzu deified.

The deification of Lao-tzu was not an officially sponsored phenomenon, but rather an expression of the Popular religion, and perhaps more importantly, of the Heavenly Masters School, where his cultic name was **T'ai-shang Lao-chün**. It is most interesting that Lao-tzu's cult was taken over (or shared) by the court. The underlying reason was probably the belief in Lao-tzu's many incarnations of the past, when the empire was in crisis. In 165 CE, a crisis was indeed brewing, and the emperor hoped that Lao-tzu would descend again and save the dynasty.

A detailed study of the *Lao-tzu Inscription* has been made by A. Seidel in her monograph of 1969. In her paraphrase of the text, four parts are discussed:

• The first part describes the early career of Lao-tzu and is basically a restatement of details found in the *Shih-chi*.

• In the second part, "Lao-tzu is a cosmic deity, coexisting with primordial chaos and the beginning of the Universe; he dwells in the center of heaven—in the Big Dipper—where he establishes communication between Heaven and Earth" (Seidel: 44). Lao-tzu is also the Realized Man, who had reached his state through Taoist cultivation.

• In part three, the circumstances of the erection of the tablet are explained: Emperor Huan, who had applied himself to physiological practices and the study of the wisdom of the Yellow Emperor, had seen Lao-tzu in a dream. This made him decide to offer sacrifices.

The author, letting his own rationalist sentiments express themselves, also plays down the supernatural stature of Lao-tzu. He sees in Lao-tzu's divinity a symbolic expression of faith, rather than true reality.

• Part four contains the text itself (the former parts were merely introductory) (Seidel: 43–45. A full translation of the main text, written in verse, is found on pages 60–73).

This inscription is an important document in the development of the Lao-tzu cult. It shows how far the official and popular Lao-tzu concept has distanced itself from the old view of Lao-tzu as a human teacher of ideal government.

It is clear from Pien's inscription that by the late Han, Lao-tzu was viewed as a cosmic force capable of multiple reincarnations in the role of preceptor to the ruling elite. The messianic purpose of his descent became the single most important theme in Lao-tzu's divinization, one that subsequently served all classes of Chinese society, from emperor to revolutionary. (J. Boltz, *ER* 8: 456)

(See also **Lao-tzu Deified.**)

LAO-TZU MING See *LAO-TZU INSCRIPTION*

LAO-TZU PIEN-HUA CHING See *TRANSFORMATIONS OF LAO-TZU SCRIPTURE*

LAUGHING AT THE TAO. Title of a polemical text, *Hsiao Tao lun/ Xiaodao lun*, written by the official Chen Luan/Zhen Luan in 570 CE. It was presented to Emperor Wu of the short-lived Northern Chou dynasty (557–581), who fostered the dream of re-unifying the whole of China into one empire. To realize his plan, he was well aware of the need for a unifying worldview:

He searched for an "equalization of the three teachings," a worldview that would, in combination with the ancient rites of the Zhou, give his state the stability necessary for the conquest and reorganization of all China. (L. Kohn 1995: 30)

Both Buddhists and Taoists believed their own system of thought was most suitable to serve the country. Although Emperor Wu first followed Buddhism, in 567 he was initiated as a Taoist and started to promote Taoism as the main teaching. Buddhist protest soon followed. In the *Hsiao Tao lun*, author Chen Luan ridiculed Taoism as unable to serve the emperor's goals:

Taoism can't do this job. It's too confused, too disorganized, too immoral, too dishonest, and too much at odds with the Confucian tradition. It is a plagiate and poor imitation of Buddhism . . . it does not lead anywhere. (L. Kohn: 32)

The emperor's reaction to the treatise was not favorable. Although he had commissioned Chen Luan to write it, once it was received and discussed with his court officials, he was displeased and burned it.

The title *Hsiao Tao lun* is probably a play on words alluding to a passage in the *TTC*: ". . . when an inferior gentleman hears about the Tao, he has a big laugh!" (Chapter 41).

To prove his point of Taoist inferiority as compared to Buddhism, Chen Luan cites a large number of Taoist scriptures and ritual texts (a total of 42), and points out the inner contradictions of the system to conclude that Taoism is "foolish, treacherous, rebellious, unworthy, and immoral" (Kohn: 45. For a full translation of *Hsiao Tao lun*, see Kohn: 47–156).

The debate between **Buddhism** and **Taoism** remained inconclusive. However, angered by Buddhist criticism of imperial decisions, Emperor Wu in 574 issued a decree by which Buddhism was to be suppressed. Feeling that Taoism was not better than its competitors, the emperor included Taoism in the decree. It lasted until 578, when Emperor Wu died and was succeeded by a more lenient ruler (Ch'en, 1964: 190–194).

LI ERH. Another name given to Lao-tzu, based on Szu-ma Ch'ien's *Shih-chi* (*Historical Records*) of the second century BCE. Because Lao-tzu's assumed family name was Li, it played an important role in later history (see **Li Hung**), especially when the T'ang emperors, whose family name was also Li, accepted the myth that Lao-tzu was their own ancestor. (See also **Lao Tan**.)

LI HUNG/LI HONG. Originally the name of a person who in 324 CE claimed that there was a prophecy predicting he would become king. Together with his elder brother, Li T'o, they established a faith-healing cult in the areas of Kiangsu and Honan. Because of their rebellious aspirations, both were executed.

This Li Hung was not the first person named Li involved in messianic expectations. The family name Li was connected with **Lao-tzu**, who was believed to have returned to earth periodically to restore peace, or to be the sage advisor to rulers.

The name Li Hung became popular all through the Southern Dynasties. There was a Taoist belief that Lao-tzu himself, after returning from his "Conversion of the Barbarians," reappeared during the Western Han under the name Li Hung.

But later, the connection of Lao-tzu with Li Hung was discontinued. Official Taoism (the Heavenly Masters) condemned the popular revolt movements, but the people, the peasants, in times of political instability and unrest, fostered the hope that Li Hung would return and bring about a time of Great Peace, along the lines of the *Great Peace Scripture*. It is very likely that the founder of the T'ang dynasty, Li Yuan, considered himself the fulfillment of messianic expectations. The T'ang rulers did indeed adopt the belief that they were descendants of Lao-tzu (Li Erh).

The Shang-ch'ing School, however, which had strong links with the T'ang ruling house, transformed the political-religious aspirations of rebel movements into an exclusively religious vision: The divine ruler reigns as emperor in heaven with his heavenly hierarchy.

After the T'ang period, Li Hung resurfaced at least once more, in 1112, in a new rebellion, but he failed and was executed.

In summary, the image of Li Hung evokes an important but not well-known aspect of Taoist history: popular messianic expectations of a utopian state of political-religious Great Peace on earth. (This entry is based on the pioneering article of A. Seidel, 1969–70.)

LI SHAO-CHÜN/ LI SHAOJUN. A well-known *fang-shih* of the Former Han Dynasty (206 BCE–8 CE), from Lin-tzu in Shantung. He was an expert in medicine, especially in medical prescriptions. During the reign of Emperor Wu (r. 140–87 BCE), he won the emperor's favor by his claim of possessing the secrets of **alchemy**. He also claimed to have met the immortal An Ch'i-sheng/An Qisheng during one of his sea excursions. Consequently, Emperor Wu sent out several expeditions to find the Islands of the Blessed (**P'eng-lai**) and supported Li's experiments for gold manufacturing. When Li died without producing any results, the emperor believed he had merely left the world to become an immortal. In later legends, Li was made into a Taoist immortal, as a third-century book describes in this anecdote:

> When Li Shao-chün was near departing, emperor Wu dreamed that he was climbing mount Sung with him. Halfway up, a messenger riding upon a dragon and carrying his insignia of office in hand descended from a cloud and said: "The Great One, *T'ai-yi*, begs Shao-chün to come." The emperor awoke and said to those around him: "According to what I have just dreamt, Shao-chün is going to leave me." Several days later Shao-chün said that he was ill and died. A long time afterwards, the emperor ordered that his coffin be opened: no body was there; only clothes and cap remained. (Maspero, 1971/1981: 320)

Emperor Wu then supported others to continue Li's experiments, based on Li's recorded formulas. From then on, the court was flooded with *fang-shih* from the eastern coastal regions of Yen and Ch'i, all claiming to possess the secrets of immortality and gold-making.

LI T'IEH-KUAI/LI TIEGUAI (*Emblem*: gourd and crutch). One of the **Eight Immortals**, perhaps the most colorful among them. But in popular art, he looks ugly and deformed, a cripple who leans on an iron staff. Hence, his common name of Iron Crutch Li.

Most likely, this is a purely legendary character, but it is always possible that there is some historical basis. One tradition states that originally he was a man of good stature and appearance, who from early youth devoted himself to spiritual practices. He lived in the mountains for over 40 years, often so absorbed in meditation that he would forget food and sleep. Because he had the same family name as **Lao-tzu** (Li Erh), Lao-tzu often descended to earth to instruct him in the emptiness of all earthly things. It also happened that he visited Lao-tzu in the heavens. On these occasions, his *hun* soul would journey, while his *p'o* soul remained with the body, leaving it as if in a coma. His servant stayed by him until the master's return. It once happened that Li's instructions were to cremate his body if he had not returned after seven days. On the sixth day, the servant was summoned home urgently to visit his dying mother. Torn between two loyalties, he decided to cremate his master's body and went home. The next day, when Li's soul returned and could not recover his own body, he entered into the corpse of a beggar who had just died. That explains his ugly and crippled appearance in iconography.

He had a reputation for reviving the dead and curing illness. In the gourd on his back, he kept various medicines and at night he would reduce his physical shape and enter the gourd to sleep. Li is worshipped by pharmacists, who used to paint his image on their signboards.

LIBATIONER (*Chi-chiu/Jijiu*). An official rank in the early administration of **Heavenly Masters Taoism**. Their responsibility was to instruct the believers and to administer their district, as well as to conduct religious ceremonies. Men and women were eligible for this position, as well as for other ranks in the Heavenly Masters School. One famous libationer was **Lady Wei Hua-ts'un**, who about 30 years after her death appeared to **Yang Hsi** and revealed to him a number of Shang-ch'ing scriptures.

LIEH-HSIEN CHUAN See *BIOGRAPHIES OF IMMORTALS*

LIEH-TZU/LIEZI: THE PERSON. The name of a Taoist author who possibly is just a mythical or a legendary figure. The only problem is that there is a book titled *Lieh-tzu*, which seems to indicate that perhaps there once was such a person. That, of course, is not a good enough reason to accept his existence. If someone collected a number of Taoist essays and wanted to "borrow" someone's name, Lieh-tzu was a good choice. His name occurs quite frequently in the book

Chuang-tzu, and the *Lieh-tzu* volume repeats a great deal of Chuang-tzu materials. There is thus a definite affinity between the two collections.

In Chapter 1 of the *Chuang-tzu*, Lieh-tzu can ride the wind and soar into space. In Chapter 7, he introduces a shaman to his teacher, Hu-tzu, and is so shocked by the encounter that he rushes back home and stays there for three years. In Chapter 18, Lieh-tzu finds a skull along the roadside. In Chapter 21, he learns about the archery of a non-archer. In Chapter 28, he lives in poverty, yet refuses to accept food donations from his lord. In Chapter 32, he has become a true sage, attracting many followers, but is rebuked for it by the practitioner of nonarchery.

All these anecdotes are more legendary than historical, yet they show that Lieh-tzu had gained some reputation in Chuang-tzu's circle and was worthy enough to be chosen as the author of a collection of Chuang-tzu-like essays.

***LIEH-TZU/LIEZI*: THE TEXT.** Although the historicity of Lieh-tzu as a person is doubtful, it is a fact that there is a volume of essays bearing his name. Opinions are divided as to its time of composition: 600 and 300 BCE have been proposed. But today the general opinion of Chinese scholars favors a later date, like 300 CE. That would place the text within a time frame of Taoist revival, called "**Neo-Taoism.**"

The book is composed of eight chapters, containing anecdotes, discussions and dialogues, much like in the *Chuang-tzu*, to which it is obviously indebted. Indeed the *Lieh-tzu* repeats a number of episodes already included in the *Chuang-tzu*. This seems to indicate that a number of materials are much older than the third century CE. But one should not blindly accept that *Lieh-tzu* passages found in the *Chuang-tzu* are necessarily copied by *Lieh-tzu*. Could it not be the other way around, especially when we remember that Kuo Hsiang (d. 312) did the final editing? One good example is the dream discussion found in Chuang-tzu's Chapter 2 (Watson: 47–48): it is out of place there, whereas in Lieh-tzu Chapter 3, it fits in perfectly well: the topic of the chapter is reality and dreaming and wondering whether life is not an illusion.

The eight chapters are each grouped around a certain topic, indicated in the title: "Heaven's Gifts," "The Yellow Emperor," etc. Chapter 7, titled "**Yang Chu**" does not really belong here: it is too overly hedonist in character and is not Taoist in spirit. Yet it has its own charm and attractiveness.

If one takes exception to Chapter 7 as being interpolated, it is quite possible that the number seven of the authentic chapters was copied from *Chuang-tzu*'s "inner chapters."

A complete English translation of the *Lieh-tzu*, with commentaries, has been written by A.C. Graham (1960).

LIEH-TZU/LIEZI: THEMES. As A.C. Graham says in the introduction to his translation ". . . the *Lieh-tzu* has the merit of being by far the most easily intelligible of the classics of Taoism" (Graham 1960: 1). If that is correct, it does not mean that Chinese specialists have a great appreciation for the book. W. Chan, for instance, calls it "negative Taoism" (but this assessment is mainly based on the **Yang Chu** chapter). However, he does not find much good to say about the *Lieh-tzu*. In it

> . . . the Taoist doctrine of inaction, i.e., taking no artificial action, has degenerated into a complete abandonment of effort. Spontaneity is confused with resignation. And the Taoist doctrine of nourishing one's nature is forgotten. Perhaps the only constructive aspect is the strong sense of skepticism, which, as is the case of Wang Ch'ung (27–100?), did help to set the Chinese mind free from dogmas and traditions.
>
> (Chan, 1963: 309)

This rather negative evaluation is comparable to the one made by another modern Chinese philosopher, well known in the West. Fung Yu-lan sees in the *Lieh-tzu* "numerous expressions of a philosophy of materialism and mechanism . . ." (Fung, 1953: II, 191), which are, for him, "illustrations of the dictum that 'Heaven and Earth are not benevolent' " [*TTC*, Chapter 5]. Natural changes and human activities are equally mechanistic in their operation, and there is no such thing as divine or human freedom, divine or human purpose (Fung: II, 194).

This is probably all beside the point. Lieh-tzu, although indebted to the *Chuang-tzu*, has his own originality and sparkling genius. His style is similar to *Chuang-tzu's* in the use of parables, anecdotal and mythical stories, and amusing events. But behind all this superficial lightheadedness and apparent humor, there is a deep-going concern with real problems of life, which it attempts to solve Taoist fashion. As Graham interprets, *Lieh-tzu* discusses reconciliation with death (Chapter 1), the Taoist principle of action (Chapter 2), the difficulty of differentiating between dream and reality (Chapter 3), the futility of Confucian faith in knowledge (Chapter 4), man's ignorance of his own limitations and Taoist delight in the extraordinary (Chapter 5), the problem of fate or destiny in contrast to human freedom (Chapter 6), and the failure of absolute moral standards (Chapter 8). The Yang Chu chapter (Chapter 7) is rather an interpolation.

Chinese philosophy and Taoism in particular state that our universe was generated out of primordial energy, *ch'i*, solidifying and dissolving, expanding and contracting. This is a continuous process in which all beings participate. Humans, too, are products of this *ch'i*: "birth and death of an individual are merely episodes in the endless transformations of *ch'i*" (Graham, 1960: 15). Life must be enjoyed; death must be accepted with equanimity:

> Death is a return to where we set out from when we were born . . . How do I know that life and death are not as good as each other? How do I know that it is not a delusion to crave anxiously for life? How do I know that present death would not be better than my past life? (Chapter 1, Graham: 25)

Among the "Gifts of Heaven" are all the products that the earth makes grow for consumption by the living. *Lieh-tzu* calls it "stealing": robbing heaven and earth of their seasonal benefits; stealing animals from the land, fish from the water, etc. (Graham: 30). Once a man, misunderstanding the meaning of "stealing," was caught and put in jail: an amusing story with a deeper message. (See also **Ecology**.)

Another precious gift is our own body (actually also "stolen" from the yin and yang energies): We do not own it

> It is a shape lent to you by heaven and earth. Your life is not your possession; it is harmony between your forces, granted for a time by heaven and earth. (Chapter 1, Graham: 29)

This contains another deep message with wide ramifications: respect for our own life, and the lives of others; nonownership of our children and grandchildren. Taoist *wu-wei* is not necessarily an easy practice!

The Taoist principle of action is based on naturalness, unselfconsciousness. To follow the Tao is ". . . a capacity for dealing effortlessly with external things." The swimmer in the whirlpool below a waterfall does not drown: He is at ease in the water; the cicada catcher is oblivious to all else except cicadas, and very few escape him. Applied to human behavior, there is a story of an innkeeper who had two concubines. The uglier one was his favorite; the beautiful one was too conscious of her beauty and thus lost it (Chapter 2, Graham: 52). These anecdotes are mostly duplicates from the *Chuang-tzu*.

How to perceive reality is another favorite theme in the *Lieh-tzu*. It relates to *Chuang-tzu*'s second chapter, with the "butterfly dream" and "love of life as a delusion" as common anecdotes.

> How do I know that the love of life is not a delusion? . . . How do I know that the dead do not regret that they ever prayed for life? We drink

wine in our dreams, and at dawn shed tears; we shed tears in our dreams, and at dawn go hunting. While we dream, we do not know we are dreaming, and in the middle of a dream interpret a dream within it; not until we wake do we know we were dreaming. Only at the ultimate awakening shall we know that this is the ultimate dream. (Chapter 3, Graham: 58; for the parallel passage in the *Chuang-tzu*, see Watson: 47)

This "dream story" seems to imply that there is conscious life after death, but this could as well be another dream.

Lieh-tzu emphasizes the practical impossibility of knowing what is real and what is unreal: The real may appear as unreal, and the unreal is imagined as real. Sometimes people prefer to live in a dream as an escape from reality, as in the story of a servant who had a horrible life in the daytime, but dreamed at night he was a lord, living in great comfort (Chapter 3, Graham: 68–69).

Another amusing story is about a man who found a deer in the forest. Entangled in dreams, the case becomes complicated. Taken to court, the judges themselves are confused. Dream and reality fuse into each other (Chapter 3, Graham: 69–70).

The *Lieh-tzu* is delightful reading and provides—in a casual and humorous way—hints at solving some of the deeper problems of human existence; the problem of freedom and fate, or "Endeavor and Destiny" (Chapter 6) is another theme that is worth reflecting on. To end with another analysis by A. C. Graham:

> The Western reader of this book, struck first of all by its naive delight in the irrational and marvelous, may well feel that no way of thought could be more alien to the climate of twentieth-century science. Looking more closely, he may be surprised to discover that Taoism coincides with the scientific world-view at just those points where the latter most disturbs Westerners rooted in the Christian tradition—the littleness of man in a vast universe; the inhuman Tao, which all things follow without purpose and indifferent to human needs; the transience of life, the impossibility of knowing what comes after death; unending change in which the possibility of progress is not even conceived; the relativity of values; a fatalism very close to determinism, even a suggestion that the human organism operates like a machine. (Graham: 12–13)

LIN CHAO-EN/LIN ZHAO'EN (1517–1598). A famous scholar of the Ming period who, as a young man, studied the classics and prepared for a career in the imperial administration. But in his early thirties, he gave up his political ambitions and instead started to search for spiritual realization. "He turned to all three traditions . . . and found them all wanting" (J. Berling, 1980: 68). Yet, he found a mysterious teacher who started him on the right path, and eventually set up his own school. Although basically a Confucian, he also appreciated the values of Taoism and Buddhism, thus establishing a syncretistic movement that bridged the differences between the three teachings. He had many followers, among the literati as well as among the common people. He repaired temples of all three traditions, and wrote commentaries on Buddhist and Taoist texts. He was called "Master of the Three Teachings." After his death, his numerous disciples continued his teaching.

> For him . . . the sage represented a dual model: the sagely ruler who devoted himself to public service and the aid of the people, and the transmitter of the Way who could rectify the minds of the people. (Berling: 237)

Although J. Berling believes that he was essentially a Confucian teaching the Confucian Way, the above quotation shows that his idea of sagehood was also essentially Taoist, as it is expressed in the *Tao-te ching*.

(For a detailed study, see J. Berling's monograph, 1980.)

LIN LING-SU (1075–1119). A Taoist priest at the end of the Northern Sung dynasty. He was a native of Wen-chou in present-day Chekiang. At a young age, he entered the Buddhist order, but could not endure his master's physical abuse. He left the Buddhist monastery and became a Taoist.

In 1116, he was recommended to Sung Emperor Hui-tsung (r. 1101–1125). Once he gained the emperor's attention, Lin was able to play the diplomatic game and court the emperor's favor. He proclaimed Hui-tsung as the earthly incarnation of the god Shen-hsiao Chen-wang (True King of the Divine Empyrean), as well as the Emperor of Eternal Life, and the eldest son of the Heavenly Emperor (T'ien-ti). Lin Ling-su claimed that he was originally a minister in the Courts of Heaven, sent down to earth to assist the emperor. Consequently, he received the honorary name *Ling-su* (Numinous Simplicity), and was asked to propagate to the general public the story of how the eldest son of the Heavenly Emperor had descended to the world to rule the Sung empire.

Lin encouraged the emperor to convert Buddhist monasteries into Taoist temples, and Buddhist religious titles into Taoist ones. During his four years in the capital of Kaifeng, Lin's charisma attracted a large following, but his various ventures cost the Sung treasury a tremendous fortune. Eventually, he angered the emperor in 1119, when he refused to negotiate safe passage for the crown prince. Disgraced, he was exiled to his home city, where he died in the same year.

The Lin Ling-su episode reflects the deepening political, economic, and social crisis facing the Northern Sung dynasty during its last years of existence. Perhaps the court used a figure like Lin to justify its own incompetence. The Northern Sung collapsed in 1126, and for a long time thereafter, Taoism was not in favor. (See also **Shen-hsiao Taoism**.)

LING-HUN See "SOUL"

LING-PAO/LINGBAO. This expression refers to three distinct entities: first, **Ling-pao scriptures**; second, the Ling-pao "school" or tradition; third, the third member of the Supreme Taoist triad, Ling-pao **T'ien-tsun**. (See also **Ling-pao Tradition**.)

Although these three items are discussed as separate entries, the term *ling-pao* itself has not been analyzed yet. The term *ling* means "spiritual, mystical, transcendent, numinous" and refers to the transcendent divine realm. The term *pao* means "treasure, jewel" and refers to the earthly realm. Combined, the expression *ling-pao* refers to the realms of heaven and earth, in their sacred dimension. But more particularly, there is a vast network of meanings, which have to do with spiritual treasures on earth, the origin of which is in transcendent heaven. That includes symbols, charts, talismans, and scriptures originating with divine beings, but given to humans as tokens of authority and spiritual powers. They have thus a sacramental effectiveness that authorizes kings to rule and empowers spiritual practitioners to draw on the vast cosmic reservoir of divine power to help humanity in its efforts toward salvation.

Ling-pao has a strong connection with Taoist scriptures. Its first appearance was in one of the oldest texts: *Ling-pao wu-fu ching* (*Ling-pao Five Talismans Scripture*). A tradition says that these five had been revealed to the sage Yü as a means to control the floods. Without any effort and in no time, Yü succeeded and then, as he was ordered, went to hide the talismans in a mountain cave. The connection between talismans (*fu*) and scripture (*ching*) is very close: Scriptures are believed to be extensions of basic talismanic diagrams and are, like the *fu* themselves, endowed with spiritual power.

Like all other tokens of supernatural origin, such as charts (**River Chart, Yellow River Writing**), talismans and scriptures are like earthly incarnations of divine power. The double term *ling* and *pao* indicates this dual nature. Originating in heaven (*ling*), they are communicated to human beings on earth (*pao*), where they become signs and efficacious instruments of spiritual power. (Major source of information: M. Kaltenmark, 1960.)

The term *ling* by itself occurs frequently in religious literature. It signifies "spiritual potency" and is most often applied to the deities of the Popular religion. If a god or goddess possesses *ling*, its worship will increase; if the *ling* decays, the worship also will decrease and disappear. The *ling* of deities seems to correspond with the *ch'i* (vital energy) of human beings.

LING-PAO/LINGBAO SCRIPTURES. A collection of Taoist scriptures written by **Ko Ch'ao-fu** (a grand-nephew of **Ko Hung**) around 397–402 CE in the south. Ko Ch'ao-fu claimed that these scriptures had been revealed to his ancestor, **Ko Hsuan** (who was Ko Hung's uncle). The Ling-pao scriptures, which focus on liturgy, became the basis of the second division of the **Taoist Canon**, as well as the starting point of a new Taoist school: **Ling-pao Taoism.**

The sources of the Ling-pao scriptures are threefold: the Shang-ch'ing corpus, the older religious traditions of South China, and some scriptures from Buddhism. Ko Ch'ao-fu lived in Chü-jung in the neighborhood of the Hsü family and had easy access to the Shang-ch'ing scriptures. He was also familiar with some of the oldest Chinese translations of Buddhist texts, especially those translated by Chih Ch'ien. S. Bokenkamp's seminal article on the Ling-pao scriptures points out very concrete examples of Buddhist influence, such as the Pure Land text *Sukhavati-vyuha*, the ten Buddhist precepts, and the 12 supreme vows. (See S. Bokenkamp, in Strickmann, 1983: 461–478.)

LING-PAO/LINGBAO TRADITION. Refers to a Taoist movement, almost like a "school of thought and practice," but not necessarily an independent organization. This movement was based on a body of texts, the **Ling-pao Scriptures**, composed by **Ko Ch'ao-fu** around 397–402 CE, soon after the Shang-ch'ing scriptures had been received in revelation. The *Ling-pao* Scriptures were probably written with the purpose of surpassing the Shang-ch'ing corpus, in a spirit of competition, and to show the eminent status of the Ko family (of which Ko Hsuan and Ko Hung were eminent ancestors).

Whether the Ling-pao tradition occasioned the foundation of an organized school, with its own priesthood and temples, is not at all certain. I. Robinet (1991) does not mention a school in that sense, and in Chinese the movement is called *Ling-pao p'ai*, similar to *Shang-ch'ing p'ai*, in contrast with Mao Shan *tsung*. Is it possible that both Ling-pao and Shang-ch'ing originally refer to scripture collections, without a social organization, whereas Mao Shan *tsung*, the Mao Shan *School*, was the organized structure that took the Shang-ch'ing corpus as the basis of its religious practice? If that is a correct assumption, it would explain several riddles, one of which is the ambiguous status of **Lu Hsiu-ching**. He is said to belong to the Ling-pao school, yet he was also a patriarch of Shang-ch'ing Taoism. The above distinction would eliminate the problem.

Even if the Ling-pao corpus did not give rise to an independent Taoist organization (such as the Heavenly Masters School), it is almost certain that there was a loose association of literati, and possibly of Taoist priests (of the Heavenly Masters Tao), who cherished the new scriptures and took them as the basis of spiritual practice and/or ritual performance.

After Lu Hsiu-ching, the records on a Ling-pao "school" are not clear. That supports the thesis that Ling-pao is a scriptural tradition, not an organized social body. Yet Ling-pao's influence was very decisive in the formulation of all later Taoist liturgy. Many of their scriptures are still used today by Cheng-yi (Heavenly Masters) Taoist priests.

LING-PAO T'IEN-TSUN/LINGBAO TIANZUN (Heavenly Venerable of the Numinous Treasure). Title of the second highest deity of Taoism, within the triad of **T'ien-tsun**, Heavenly Venerables, also called **Three Pure Ones**.

His full name is Shang-ch'ing (High Purity) Ling-pao T'ien-tsun or T'ai-shang Tao-chün (Supreme Lord of the Tao).

Like the first member of the trinity, Ling-pao T'ien-tsun is most likely a mythical creation or a projection of an idea, rather than a true deity in the ordinary sense (such as **nature deities** or deified human personalities). Perhaps his creation as a deity was occasioned by the existence of the *Ling-pao* corpus of scriptures. He is indeed also called Master of the *Tung-hsuan* [division of the Canon].

He is always worshipped in the company of the Three Heavenly Venerables or Three Pure Ones. He is seated to the left of Yuan-shih T'ien-tsun; in his hand he holds the Supreme Ultimate image, or a *ju-yi* scepter (*CMTT*: 71–72; see also **T'ien-tsun**).

LITERATURE. The topic Taoist Literature is rather immense both in time and in themes, as well as genres. The latter, genres in Taoist literature, have been briefly indicated in the entry **Taoist Canon**. The most important texts, at least from a Westerner's point of view, have been all discussed under separate entries. And in the **Introduction**, a distinction has been made between the texts of a *philosophical nature* and those generated by the *Taoist religious tradition*. Therefore, a detailed separate analysis is not called for.

Those who wish to have more detailed information, especially about texts not included here, may consult J. Boltz's excellent *Survey* (1987), or else hold their breath for the long-awaited publication of the *Tao-tsang* Project (*Projet Tao-tsang*) (started in 1979), a comprehensive survey of the Taoist Canon prepared by a team of European scholars under the direction of K. Schipper. This grand enterprise aims at compiling "an analytic and descriptive catalogue of the Taoist Canon, with the following data for each work: (1) a physical description of the text, (2) a translation and explanation of the title, (3) precise information on the history and transmission of the text, and (4) a summary of the contents" (J. Boltz, 1987: 13).

Meanwhile, a survey article by M. Strickmann (*EB* 1974) is still useful, but J. Boltz's article in *ER* 14 is more complete and up-to-date.

LITURGY See RITUAL

LIU HAI-CH'AN/LIU HAICHAN. A famous Taoist priest of the Five Dynasties period (907–960). He was a native of Yen-shan (today's Beijing). During the Liao rule (a foreign dynasty ruling part of China from 907 till 1119), he passed the civil examination and obtained the *chin-shih* literary degree. He served as prime minister to Liu Shou-kuang, ruler of Yen.

He loved to discuss philosophical topics, such as nature (*hsing*) and life (*ming*), and was impressed by the writings of Huang-Lao Taoism. There is a story that one day he met a Taoist who called himself Cheng-yang tzu (Master of Orthodox Yang). He asked Liu to get him ten coppers and ten eggs. He piled them up on the table. Liu could not restrain himself from yelling, "How dangerous!" The Taoist said, smiling: "The position of a prime minister is much more dangerous!" Liu was suddenly awakened. He gave away his family wealth, gave up his position, left his wife and children, left home, and went wandering. He called himself "Sea Toad" (*hai-ch'an*), and wholeheartedly started self-cultivation. He often traveled between Mount Hua and Mount Chung-nan, and eventually became an immortal. The Complete Realization School considered him as one of their five founding patriarchs.

In the Chinese folk tradition, there are many stories about him and a "golden toad," which is seen as a symbol of good fortune (*MDC*: 133).

LO RIVER WRITING (*Lo-shu/Loshu*). A cosmological diagram that mythology claims to have been revealed to Yü the Great, mythic sage and culture hero, when a giant turtle emerged from the Lo River. On its back, he found the "magic square," which helped him to control the floods ravaging China and make the country ready for agriculture.

From this writing, King Wen, founder of the Chou dynasty, is said

4	9	2
3	5	7
8	1	6

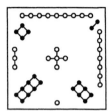

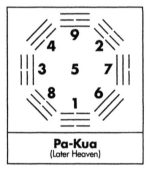

Pa-Kua
(Later Heaven)

to have devised the new ("Later Heaven") arrangement of the eight *Yi ching* trigrams, which is the one actually used in the *Yi ching*, as well as in geomancy. (See also **River Chart.**)

Adopted by the Taoist priests, the Lo River Writing has become an interesting symbol and ritual instrument. It represents the floor plan within the sacred area (*t'an*) of the temple where Taoist liturgy is being performed, as, for example, during the **Cosmic Renewal Festival**:

The chief cantor takes the solemn memorial, during orthodox ritual, and dances the steps of Yü after the model of the *Lo-shu*. He travels from 1 to 9 in the magic square, that is, from earth to heaven, presenting the memorial to the heavenly emperors. Then, reversing the dance steps, he returns to earth, bearing the rescript that brings blessings to the visible world of men. With the greatest reverence, the Taoist Master receives back the rescript and dances a triumphant *Yü-pu* (steps of Yü) modeled after the *Ho-t'u.* (Saso, 1978: 412–3)

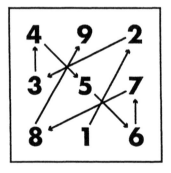

(See also **Steps of Yü**.)

LO-SHU See LO RIVER WRITING

LORD HUANG-LAO See HUANG-LAO CHÜN

LU HSIU-CHING/LU XIUJING (406–477). A Taoist priest and scholar during the southern Liu Sung Dynasty (420–479). A native of present-day Wu-hsing county in Chekiang province, he came from a powerful aristocratic family.

In his youth, he studied Confucianism, but was also interested in Taoism and its paraphernalia, such as magic, divination, and prophecy. In adulthood, he turned his intellectual energies toward Taoism, in search of tranquillity. He left home and lived as a recluse in some mountain areas. Later, he toured all the famous mountains in search of the whereabouts of the immortals, while also collecting valuable Taoist texts. He traveled extensively, south to Hunan and Kuangtung, and west to **Mount Ch'ing-ch'eng** and Mount O-mei, in Szechuan.

In 453, he was invited to the palace by Emperor Wen of the Liu Sung Dynasty to discuss Taoism. When the emperor was killed by his own two sons in that year, he left the capital in disgust and traveled to the south.

In 461, he established a Taoist monastery on **Mount Lu**, where he lived a quiet, reclusive life. But in 467, he was again invited to the capital in Chien-kang (near present-day Nanjing) by Emperor Ming (r. 465–472). He then lived on Mount T'ien-yin, north of the capital. It was during this period that he collated and edited all the Taoist texts he had gathered, dividing them into three categories (*san-tung*). (See also **Taoist Canon**.) He published his catalogue in 471, entitled *San-tung ching-shu mu-lu*.

Lu advocated that spiritual cultivation should include three areas: ritual performance, chanting of texts, and mental discipline. He compiled and edited over 100 texts on Taoist ritual. He also adapted many key Buddhist concepts, such as *karma*, retribution, and the transmigration of souls, integrating them into his Taoist writings, and thus enriching Taoist doctrine.

To summarize, Lu Hsiu-ching made some major contributions to Taoism. He standardized Taoist rituals; he collected and edited the Taoist scriptures and designed the first catalogue, dividing it into the three sections that would remain the standard model for later times; finally, he adopted Buddhist ideas into Taoism, especially in the *Ling-pao* tradition.

His efforts gave early Taoism, which had so far been mainly a folk religion, increased scholarship and respectability.

Lu Hsiu-ching was the seventh patriarch of **Shang-ch'ing Taoism.**

LÜ SHAN TAOISM. A school of Taoism found mostly in southern China (Fukien and Taiwan) to which the **Redhead Taoists** belong. Another name is Three Matrons (San-nai) sect, named after three legendary shamaness-like ladies, who may have been associated with Mount Lü in Liaoning province.

> The sect is identified in the popular mind with the "Gate of Hell"; the term Lü Shan refers to the place in the cosmos through which the demonic forces attack the world of the living. The ritual role of the Lü Shan Taoists is to capture the demons and send them back to the world of darkness." (M. Saso, 1978: 60)

Although Lü Shan or Redhead Taoists do not enjoy the esteem of their Blackhead colleagues, their powerful magic is respected.

LÜ TUNG-PIN/LÜ DONGBIN (*Emblem*: Sword and flywhisk). Lü Tung-pin is one of the **Eight Immortals,** often represented as leader or most prominent among them. He is a complex personality because, besides being a popular sage, he also is venerated as one of the Complete Realization School patriarchs and became an important patron saint in modern automatic writing cults.

It is generally accepted that he was a historic figure, born in 755 during the T'ang dynasty in a family of officials. His name was Lü Yen/Yan. Other traditions place him after the T'ang, during the Five Dynasties Period (907–960): History and legend are difficult to separate in the later biographies; the earliest account dates from the Sung period.

There are two traditions of his "conversion" to Taoism. One story narrates that, during a visit to the capital Ch'ang-an, he met **Chung-li Ch'uan,** who instructed him in the arts of alchemy, but subjected him first to ten trials. Lü passed them successfully and then received magic powers and a magic sword, in order to stay evil spirits.

The other story holds that Lü met Chung-li Ch'uan in an inn, heating up some wine. Falling asleep, Lü had a dream: He became a very high official of the state, had a successful career, but was finally accused of serious wrongdoings and sent into exile. His family was exterminated. Waking up, the wine was not hot yet. But these few minutes of dreaming ("rice-wine dream") made him see through the emptiness of success and honor. He gave up his ambition of an official

守人員靈　守人始元　守人德道

Supreme Taoist Triad or Trinity: Three Heavenly Venerables or Worthies (T'ien-tsun). (Painting by Taiwan artist Ch'en Wan-ch'uan, used by permission.)

Chang Tao-ling protective talisman (*fu*). *Author's collection.*

Chang Tao-ling with two assistants. (Painting by Taiwan artist Ch'en Wan-ch'uan, used by permission.)

The Jade Emperor or Yü-huang Ta-ti, higher deity of Taoism and supreme deity of the Chinese Popular Religion. (Painting by Taiwan artist Ch'en Wan-ch'uan, used by permission.)

The Queen Mother of the West, one of the earliest Taoist deities. (Painting by Taiwan artist Ch'en Wan-ch'uan, used by permission.)

Director of Destiny (Szu-ming) and Kitchen God (Tsao-chün). *Author's collection.*

God of the Locality, God of Soil, Earth Spirit (T'u-ti-kung). *Author's collection.*

Two of the Eight Immortals (25 cm. high), ivory, twentieth century, Hong Kong. Left: Chang Kuo-lao. Right: Chung-li Ch'uan. *Author's collection.*

Two of the Eight Immortals (25 cm. high), ivory, twentieth century, Hong Kong. Left: Li T'ieh-kuai. Right: Han Hsiang-tzu. *Author's collection.*

Two of the Eight Immortals (25 cm. high), ivory, twentieth century, Hong Kong. Left: Ts'ao Kuo-chiu. Right: Ho Hsien-ku.

Two of the Eight Immortals (25 cm. high), ivory, twentieth century, Hong Kong. Left:
Lan Ts'ai-ho. Right: Lü Tung-pin.

Taoist Master (Tao-chang) Ch'en Jung-sheng, from Taiwan, reads a document during the Cosmic Renewal Festival (Tainan, November 1994). *Photo: Julian Pas.*

Local laypeople representing the community are in attendance during the Cosmic Renewal Festival. *Photo: Julian Pas.*

Taoist Master Ch'en Jung-sheng wearing the *tao-p'ao* (gown of the Tao) during the Cosmic Renewal Festival. *Photo: Julian Pas.*

As assistant priest reads a sacred document during *chiao* festival. *Photo: Julian Pas.*

道問子孔

道問子老向子孔

Confucius visits Lao-tzu to learn about ritual according to an ancient legend. (Drawing by Taiwan artist Ch'en Wan-ch'uan,

career and decided to follow Chung-li. Initiated into the Taoist mysteries, he became an immortal.

Behind the legend there hides perhaps the historic fact that Lü failed in the state examinations and followed what the Popular tradition recommended: When successful, become a Confucian; when you fail, become a Taoist.

Another legend states that Lü and Chung-li appeared to Ch'uan-chen founder Wang Che: This initiated Wang's conversion; as a result, Lü is worshipped by this school as one of their founding patriarchs, named Lü-tsu/Lüzu. In Taoist temples today, he is called Ch'un-yang (Pure Yang), a title conferred on him during the Yuan period. In modern temples of the Popular religion and sectarian movements, he is usually called by the second part of the same Yuan title: Fu-yu Ti-chün/Fuyou Dijun (Imperial Lord Protector). He often figures among three or five lord protectors or lord benefactors (en-chu/enzhu) and is thus associated with Lord Kuan (Kuan-ti) or Kuang-sheng Ti-chün.

There are many other legends about Lü Tung-pin. One of the ten ordeals "relates how one day he was drinking in a wine shop and showed no signs of paying. Finally, instead of paying, he painted two dancing cranes on the wall of the inn." That spread the inn's reputation, attracting many customers. "When the debt was paid, however, the cranes detached themselves from the wall and flew away" (Eberhard, 1986: 170).

Other legends, not found in the Ch'uan-chen records but dating from Ming times, narrate Lü's encounters with prostitutes, even his unsuccessful efforts to seduce the Bodhisattva Kuan-yin. As a result of this misadventure, he is sometimes portrayed as jealous of young lovers. The famous mountain temple south of Taipei, Chih-nan kung (where Lü is enshrined as the major deity), attracts huge crowds of worshippers. But few young couples dare to visit it, fearing that the jealous Lü might break up their relationship.

The same temple attracts worshippers who have personal problems. It is believed that when they pray at Lü's shrine in the daytime and stay overnight in the temple's hostel, Lü will solve their problem during a dream. (This is an example of dream divination. See R. Smith 1991: 245–257.)

In the divination writing cults, Patriarch Lü or Lü-tsu is portrayed as a more serious deity who "descends into the pen" to bring to earth his teachings, in order to edify the faithful and convert the world. In this context, his cult is almost as important as that of Kuan-kung (Kuan-sheng Ti-chün).

LUNG-MEN TAOISM ("Dragon Gate" Taoism). The best-known branch school of Complete Realization (Ch'uan-chen) Taoism, founded by a disciple of Wang Che, **Ch'iu Ch'u-chi** (1148–1227). Summoned by Genghis Khan, he made the long trek to Samarkand (Central Asia) in 1221. Returning with great honor, he became one of the most famous religious figures of his time. It made Complete Realization Taoism the most popular school, until conflicts with Buddhism arose during the reign of Khubilai Khan.

The Lung-men branch school stresses purification of the mind and curbing of desires as the basis of Taoist cultivation; it holds that if "one thought does not arise, that is freedom; if the mind is free from affairs, that is spiritual perfection" (*CMTT*: 24–25).

The seventh patriarch, Wang Ch'ang-yueh, held initiation rituals six times at the White Cloud Monastery (Beijing). His lectures were later edited by disciples under the title *Mind Method of Lung-men* (*Lung-men hsin-fa*).

Today, Lung-men Taoism is the strongest branch of the Complete Realization School.

M

MA-TSU/MAZU (Also named *T'ien-shang Sheng-mu/Tianshang Shengmu* or "Holy Mother in Heaven"). She is one of the most popular goddesses of the Chinese Community Religion, sometimes inaccurately considered a Taoist deity. Ma-tsu exemplifies the mother goddess typology found in many other religions: in South China, she is often compared, and worshipped together, with Kuan-yin, the "Goddess of Compassion," derived from Buddhism. Common people also see Ma-tsu and Kuan-yin as Chinese equivalents to the Virgin Mary.

The worship of Ma-tsu is based on a mixture of historical facts and legends. Traditionally, it is believed that she was born on the island of Mei-chou (Fukien province) between 900 and 1000 CE. At a young age, she had already shown signs of attraction to a spiritual life and had decided not to get married. Legend has it that once she rescued her father and brothers in a storm, and this sign of extraordinary power gave rise to more legends.

After her death at age 28, her cult started to spread, at first very slowly. But once people experienced her supernatural help, especially in dangers on the ocean, her fame started to spread and eventually reached the imperial court.

In 1155, she was decreed Princess of Supernatural Favour; in 1192 she became Queen; in 1198, Holy Queen and in 1278, Kublai Khan decreed her Queen of Heaven . . . subordinate only to the Jade Emperor . . . The first Ch'ing Emperor raised her from Imperial Concubine to Imperial Consort. (J. Chamberlain, 1983: 100)

From protectress on the ocean, Ma-tsu has become a more universal deity, assisting worshippers in all kinds of difficulties. She is one of the most popular deities in Taiwan today: over 400 temples are dedicated to her. Her birthday, on the 23rd of the third lunar month, attracts huge crowds of pilgrims to the Peikang temple (Yünlin County) and other famous Ma-tsu temples. Her cult is being revitalized in her native province of Fukien.

MA-WANG-TUI/MAWANGDUI. Name of a small village near Changsha, Hunan province, where a Han tomb was excavated in 1972–73. It is the grave of the son of the marquis of Tai, buried in 168 BCE. This nobleman's grave contained a rich collection of funerary artifacts, including a large number of texts, some of which had been lost.

> As far as Chinese religious and intellectual history is concerned, the most significant of these discoveries is that of the ancient manuscripts written on silk, which Chinese scholars and archaeologists call *po-shu* or "**Silk Manuscripts**." (Jan, 1977: 65)

Two of those manuscripts are the oldest versions of the *TTC*, but there are, among the 51 items identified, other texts and materials that are very significant for our understanding of Han culture.

> There are texts on medical theories and practices, texts on Yin and Yang and the Five Elements (or "Phases"), texts on political philosophy, and texts on astronomy and astrology. (Henricks, 1989: xiii)

Of great importance, too, is the discovery of the *Four Classics of the Yellow Emperor*, previously unknown. They belong to the **Huang-Lao School** and present

> . . . a view of good government which combines practical Confucian and Legalist principles with Taoist metaphysics and psychology. (Henricks: xiv)

The findings of the Ma-wang-tui tomb are now gradually being studied and analyzed. The *TTC* versions have been translated and published, and all in all, these new data will certainly enrich our understanding of early Han culture.

MAGIC FORMULAS See TALISMANS

MAGIC MUSHROOM See PLANT SYMBOLISM

MAO SHAN TAOISM See SHANG-CH'ING TAOISM

MARTIAL ARTS. It is a paradox to discuss "martial" things in the context of Taoism. The word "martial" means (following *Webster's*) "of, or suitable for war; showing a readiness or eagerness to fight; warlike," etc. This invests the expression "martial arts" with a questionable qualification of "warlike skills," which one would not expect in Taoist spirituality. But there is a difference: Those warrior combat skills can be "transformed into spiritual disciplines" (*HCDR*: 686). Indeed, several kinds of martial arts grew out of Taoist or Buddhist monasteries. Because monks used to travel frequently to search for spiritual leaders, but were not allowed to carry arms, the learning of self-defense techniques was of vital importance. This also applied to common people who wanted to travel and needed self-protection.

For spirit-oriented people, however, martial arts emphasize spiritual values as much as physical power and fitness. Development of mind power and self-discipline were a natural result of the martial arts, and this in turn would be very helpful during the practice of **meditation**. According to legend, Bodhidharma, who arrived in China around 520 CE and started the Ch'an (Zen) movement, initiated physical exercises, named *kung-fu*, as an antidote for his student-monks who sat in meditation for many hours a day.

Some of the major martial art forms are kung-fu (Chinese), karate or "empty-hand," judo or "way of softness" (Japanese), and tae kwan do (Korean). None of these techniques uses any weapons, but only rely on the power of arms, legs, and body as a whole. A "soft" form of martial arts is *t'ai-chi ch'uan* (China), which has become very popular in China and in the West.

MATCHING MEANINGS See *KO YI*

MEDITATION. Most Asian spiritual traditions stress the importance of meditation in the pursuit of whatever they consider to be the ultimate perfection or final goal, whether it is called enlightenment, emancipation, total realization, etc. In religions of salvation, the emphasis is rather on faith, divine grace, prayer, redemption, etc., but the practice of meditation is not excluded. In the Christian tradition, the contemplative life is upheld as the model lifestyle, although it is only suitable to a small minority.

In general, the term *meditation* includes a great range of practices, from breathing exercises, concentration, visualization, deep meditation, and higher contemplation to mystical ecstasy. All these forms, and more, are found within Taoism, as they also exist in Buddhism. In China, the two traditions have indeed adopted principles and practices from each other, and it is probable that some of their methods are identical, while only the object of attention and the goal to be pursued are different.

A very wide range of Western publications are available on Buddhist meditation, from Hinayana practices (focusing on "tranquillity" and "insight") to Ch'an or Zen methods used in East Asia. The Taoist tradition is not so well represented, yet, indirectly, because the Ch'an practice owes part of its methodology to Taoist concepts, some credits are due to Taoism.

The philosophical texts *TTC* and *Chuang-tzu* do not deal with meditation techniques per se, but contain several passages that allude to it, as well as terminology, later adopted and developed by new schools of Taoism, especially the Shang-ch'ing School. In the *TTC*, there is the expression *shou-yi* (hold on to "oneness"), later transformed into a meditation method called "Holding the Three Ones" (see also **Three Ones**). There are also clear allusions to meditation practices, such as: "attain extreme emptiness; hold on to genuine quietude" (Chapter 16: 1). Even clearer is this passage:

Stop the apertures, Close the door;
Blunt the sharp, Untie the entangled;
Harmonize the bright, Make identical the dust.
This is called the mystical identity.
(Chapter 56: 2–5—Chen, 1989: 188)

The *Chuang-tzu* has introduced terminology that later religious practitioners have taken over and infused with new meaning: *tso-wang* ("sit-and-forget"), "the fasting of the mind," to be like "dead ashes," and like a "withered tree," all refer to states of meditation and mystical trance.

It is within the Shang-ch'ing (Mao Shan) School that meditation was developed to the highest degree. The emphasis is on inner visualization and on contemplation. But first a few words about concentration as a preliminary to meditation.

Concentration is the exercise of focusing the mind's attention on a single object. It is a learning process by which external objects and distractions are consciously removed from one's mental "screen," so as to remain single-mindedly attentive to the chosen object. One can concentrate on physical objects (as the Buddhists recommend for beginners), even on one's own breathing. Taoists also recommend concentration on particular body areas, such as the navel *tan-t'ien*, or the spot between the eyebrows, or the spot between one's breasts. These exercises are meant to help the practitioner become focused, to become "grounded," and to reach a state of tranquillity. Once one has learned how to concentrate, meditation through inner visualization becomes easier.

The method of "Holding the Three Ones" (*shou san-yi*) was developed in the fourth century. It consists of inner concentration whereby the adept first brings down to a position above his head the seven stars of the Big Dipper. The Three Ones then step out of the Dipper stars, which are their residential palaces, and are invited to enter into the three energy fields (*tan-t'ien*) of the adept's body. By constantly concentrating on them they become clearly visible in a permanent way and immortality can be reached (P. Andersen, 1980).

Two treatises from the T'ang dynasty discuss meditation in some detail, in particular the physical and mental activities to be undertaken. They were written by the famous Mao-shan master Szu-ma Ch'eng-chen and titled *T'ien-yin-tzu* and *Tso-wang-lun* ("Treatise on Sitting in Forgetfulness"). (See L. Kohn, 1987 and 1987; also, L. Kohn and Sakade, 1989.)

Drawing on these various texts, it is possible to summarize the major steps of Taoist meditation in five stages.

• *Stage 1:* Stilling the body. One must choose a quiet place, and a suitable time of day to meditate. The best period, when the *yang* force is on the rise, is from 11 p.m. till 1 a.m., but other time periods are also acceptable. The body must adopt the correct posture (in common with Buddhist practice) and follow particular rules. To still the body, breathing must be regular and slow; focusing on it helps one to calm down and get ready for the next stage, which follows imperceptibly.

• *Stage 2:* Stilling the mind. One should try to discard all distractions, but this must be effortless, not strenuous. A good way to realize mind stillness is to concentrate on breathing, trying to forget all else, only being aware of the in and out breathing rhythm, slow and steady (this is a method also recommended in Buddhist meditation). This focus on breathing can be practiced for its own sake, without further ambition besides calming the mind: It helps to overcome stress, and if done in the evening, it promotes dreamless sleep.

• *Stage 3:* One can also go a step further and concentrate on various objects, one's own body, apart from breathing, and, as in the Shang-ch'ing or Mao Shan tradition, on the deities dwelling in one's body. That requires intense concentration. The gods must be visualized as clearly as possible, through mental imagining, according to their descriptions found in the scriptures. Once they appear clearly and distinctly, they must be inspected in all details. This results in fixing the deities inside one's body; if they remain there, the adept has a better chance to attain **immortality**.

One can also concentrate on mental events, such as aspects of Taoist teaching. This may lead to fuller understanding, not just intellectually, but vitally and existentially, so they become part of one's inner being. In all these exercises, the mind remains fully active, although through practice, this may become a natural and easy activity.

• *Stage 4:* Introduces a higher type of meditation in which mental activity is discarded. It is emptying the mind, "fasting of the mind." In the former stages, words are necessary, because one must recite scriptures and read instructions to learn the correct techniques. Once known, words must be forgotten, the mind must be emptied of all thoughts (these thoughts usually express themselves in words, even if only "thought-words"), one must withdraw to a preword condition, where insight is direct or immediate, not depending on the instrumentality of language.

• *Stage 5:* Leads to the pinnacle of inner experience, where everything is forgotten, even one's own subjectivity or awareness of self is lost, and one merges with *Tao*. There is a sense of union, perhaps of "flying" and "wandering" beyond space, a sense of freedom and intense joy. This is the mystical state of trance, so often described by Christian mystics, who interpret their experience as a "divine union," a "spiritual marriage." (This is a natural procedure because one uses the terminology and theological framework of one's own tradition.)

Mystical trance is not restricted to one religious tradition. It is possible that the experiences of Christians, Buddhists, Muslims (Sufis), and Taoists are very similar, except that they are described by each in their own "language." But between Buddhists in China and Taoists, there has been a large amount of mutual absorption, so that to call one method Taoist or Buddhist may be incorrect. It has been said about the methods explained in *Taoist Yoga* that there is hardly anything specifically Taoist about them (N. Sivin, 1979; 319n.27).

One final comment: The Shang-ch'ing method of visualization seems to be very similar to the Buddhist technique of visualization, as explained in various sutras, especially in the *Sutra on Visualizing the Buddha of Infinite Life* (see J. Pas, 1995). Once again, streams of influence may have been operative at that time, although direct evidence has been lost.

(For more details about Taoist meditation, see Robinet, 1979/1993; Kohn, 1987-a & b; Lu K'uan Yu, 1964 & 1970. See also **Yellow Court Scripture, Tso-wang lun, T'ien-yin-tzu.**)

MEN-SHEN See DOOR GODS

MILITARY STRATEGY (*Ping-fa/Bingfa*). As an ideal Taoist ruler governs his country with *wu-wei* (let-do policy), he will go to war reluctantly, only in defense. Military strategy is a corollary of the art of rulership in the *Tao-te ching*. Separate treatises have been written on it, and were very popular in the early Han period. In 1972, archeological excavations in Shantung brought to light ancient bamboo slips with texts, such as the well-known *Sun-tzu/Sunzi* and the previously lost *Sun Ping ping-fa* ("Sun Ping's Military Strategy"). These tombs date from about 134 BCE (A. Rickett, 1985: 23–24).

Without claiming that these two treatises on strategy are of Taoist origin, they have certainly been inspired by Taoism, as well as by yin-yang philosophy. The *TTC* contains several chapters on strategy, not exactly detailing methods of warfare, but expressing general principles on strategy and its moral implications. In Chapter 31 the evil nature of warfare is stated very bluntly:

> Weapons are instruments of ill omen.
> When you have no choice but to use them, it's best to remain tranquil and calm.
> You should never look upon them as things of beauty.
> If you see them as beautiful things, this is to delight in the killing of men. (Chapter 31: 4–7)

If forced to do battle, one should feel regret and even victory should be "celebrated" like a funeral ceremony: "When multitudes of people are killed, we stand before them in sorrow and grief" (Chapter 31: 12, Henricks, 1989: 248)

Those who are advisers to the ruler should use the *Tao* as a guiding principle and oppose the use of weapons to resolve conflicts. The use of force necessarily provokes force, and wherever armies are stationed, the land only produces weeds and thorns: After a war, evil years (of starvation) follow (Chapter 30: 1–4).

If war is necessary, some principles can still be applied to reduce the chances of loss and to gain victory: Do not show off! Don't get angry! A show of force implies underestimation of one's opponent; that is the beginning of disaster. If one loses one's calm and becomes angry, that is often the completion of disaster. Simple but essential rules, not only wise and practical in warfare but also in the practice of martial arts (Chapter 68: 1–3).

The same advice is expressed in other words (Chapter 69): Do not dare to advance, rather, retreat. Hold weapons that are invisible.

"When opposing troops meet in battle, victory belongs to the grieving side" (Chapter 69: 8).

Whenever a new emperor is enthroned or high officials are being installed, let others offer them jade and horses: It is far better to present them with this *Tao* (Chapter 62: 4–5). This will lead the country away from warfare and toward prosperity.

MILLENARIANISM. This is a term borrowed from the Christian apocalyptic tradition, which believes that at the end of time, Christ will return to earth to establish a 1,000-year glorious kingdom. "The term has lost its precision in recent years because of its application to widely disparate utopian or eschatological beliefs, as well as to heterodox, reforming, and insurgent religious movements" (*HCDR*: 718). It is in the latter sense that the term applies to Taoism, because as *Webster* says, a millennium may apply to "any period of great happiness, peace, prosperity, etc.," or to an "imagined golden age."

In China, the second century CE was a period of great apocalyptic expectations. Because of the decay of the Han government, worsened by natural catastrophes and economic collapse, the people had become restless and gladly joined the *T'ai-p'ing* ("Great Peace") movement in Eastern China. In 184 CE, the movement turned rebellious (see **Yellow Turbans**), but was defeated by the Han armies.

The dream of a future time of happiness and prosperity did not die out. Throughout the period of the North-South dynasties, many messianic movements arose, with a Taoist ideological background and belief in Lao-tzu (or **Li Hung**) as the coming messiah. They were suppressed by the government. Although influenced by Taoist ideas, the established Taoist institution did not support them.

In later times, many more messianic movements mushroomed, inspired by Buddhism or by syncretistic speculations, or even by Christian beliefs. An example of the latter was the *T'ai-p'ing* ("Great Peace") Rebellion (1850–64), which threatened to overthrow the Manchu dynasty.

MONASTERY See *KUAN* or TEMPLES

MOTHER OF THE NORTHERN DIPPER See TOU-MU

MORALITY TEXTS (*Shan-shu*). A literary genre in its own right that focuses on moral principles or, more narrowly, on "admonishing" readers to act according to moral standards. The term *shan-shu* (literally "good books") is an abbreviation of *ch'uan-shan shu*, "books admonishing morality." It is a genre of popular literature, based on religious principles, but not confined to Taoism. In fact, they may be inspired by Confucian or Buddhist principles as well, and are most often produced in the context of the Popular religious tradition.

The *shan-shu* genre started during the Sung dynasty. One of the earliest texts, which Taoism claims as its own but is not included in the Taoist Canon, is *T'ai-shang kan-ying p'ien* (***Treatise on Action and Retribution***). It is considered to be a popular religious tract, qualifying as a *shan-shu*. In modern times, starting with the Ming period, *shan-shu* production increased, until the 20th century, when the genre went into mass production. Hundreds of such tracts, all admonishing readers to behave morally and avoid moral evil, are produced every year in Taiwan. They are printed through the generosity of mostly lay donors, who thereby wish to increase their accumulation of merits. They are distributed to almost all the temples in Taiwan, which provide special shelves for their display. Visitors are free to help themselves, free of charge. There are even stands of *shan-shu* in railways and bus stations.

Of course, most of these tracts properly belong to the Popular religion, but some are more specifically Taoist and discuss moral principles from a Taoist religious viewpoint. The boundaries, however, often overlap.

Different techniques are used to produce these tracts. A great number are communicated through direct revelation, called automatic or spirit-writing (*fu-luan*, "Flying Phoenix"). A medium, in most cases a member of a sectarian movement, holds a wooden implement (a bifurcated willow branch) in one hand and awaits the descent of a deity. When the god comes down, he/she moves the medium's hand and writes down a message on a sand-covered board. The message is deciphered word by word and written down by secretaries. This practice of *fu-luan* is probably very old; it is believed that **Yang Hsi** may have received the Shang-ching revelations in this way.

A great number of contemporary *shan-shu* are not the products of revelation, but of ordinary authorship. *Shan-shu* are perhaps the successors of another genre, named **"precious scrolls"** (*pao-chuan*), which flourished especially during the Ming and Ch'ing periods. *Shan-shu* and *pao-chuan*, at first treated with contempt by Chinese literati, are now being actively collected and studied. Several private collections exist in Taiwan, Japan, and North America. They are in many cases excellent documents of sectarian beliefs, but also witness to the syncretistic spirit of Chinese religiosity, which stresses the unity of Taoism, Confucianism, Buddhism, and the Popular religion. (For details about contemporary spirit-writing, see Jordan and Overmyer 1986.)

MOUNT CH'ING-CH'ENG (*Ch'ing-ch'eng shan/Qingchengshan*). One of the famous sacred mountains of Taoism, in fact, the fifth

Grotto Heaven, situated in Szechuan province. The mountain counts 36 peaks, 72 caves, and 108 scenic spots. From a distance, the mountain looks like a city panorama, hence the name "clear city mountain" (the current name is "green city mountain," but "clear" and "green" are homonyms: *ch'ing*). The mountain is famous for its quietness. There is a legend that while **Chang Tao-ling** resided here, he subdued evil spirits. Several spots remain to commemorate this and other wondrous events in Chang's life.

Among the cultural relics preserved here is a stone tablet erected by T'ang Emperor Hsuan-tsung, a T'ang iron cauldron engraved with flying dragons, stone carvings of the Three Sovereigns (*San-huang*), also dating from the T'ang period, and an image of Chang T'ien-shih from the Five Dynasties era (907–960).

Among the temple buildings preserved on Mount Ch'ing-ch'eng are the Chien-fu kung ("Established Happiness palace"), the Heavenly Master Cave, Tsu-shih chien ("Ancestral Teacher temple"), Shang-ch'ing kung ("Great Purity palace"), and Yü-ch'ing kung ("Jade Purity palace"). The Tsu-shih chien and the Heavenly Master Cave are among the most renowned Taoist temples in the country.

During the Ming dynasty this mountain belonged to the Cheng-yi School. During the Ch'ing period, a Ch'uan-chen monk of the Lung-men branch went there from Mount Wu-tang and made it a center of Lung-men Taoism (*CMTT*: 251).

MOUNT CHUNG-NAN (*Chung-nan Shan/Zhongnanshan*). One of the famous sacred mountains of Taoism, located to the south of the ancient capital Ch'ang-an (today Xi'an) in Shensi province. This mountain complex (including the Five Southern Terraces, Chia-feng Peak), was a place of great scenic beauty, attractive to both Taoists and Buddhists, who all went to live there to cultivate spiritual perfection. According to Buddhist records, famous Buddhist monks resided there since the Sui dynasty. Pure Land master Shan-tao (613–681) of the T'ang period was one of them. He stayed there for about six or seven years before he engaged in spreading the Amita-cult in the capital Ch'ang-an.

It is also recorded that Ch'uan-chen founder Wang Ch'ung-yang and other transcendents spent time there in cultivation of the Tao.

MOUNT HO-MING (*Ho-ming Shan/Hemingshan*). Translated as "crane-call mountain," it is one of the sacred mountains of Taoism, situated in Szechuan province. In fact, it is one of the founding sacred sites of the Taoist religion, because it was here that Chang Tao-ling cultivated his spiritual life and received revelations from T'ai-shang Lao-chün (the deified **Lao-tzu**).

During the Sung period, the number of Taoist temples here was increased, and the building and repair works continued through Yuan, Ming, and Ch'ing times. Today three temples are preserved, and the mountain opened for tourism in 1987.

MOUNT HUANG (*Huang Shan*). Name of a sacred mountain of Taoism (and Buddhism) located in Anhwui. Its ancient name, Mount Yi (*Yi shan*) ("black and shining, ebony") was changed to Mount Huang ("yellow") during the T'ang dynasty, because it was believed that the **Yellow Emperor** had practiced inner alchemy on it.

The mountain is famous for its extraordinary scenery: Evergreens of different unusual shapes abound, and the clouds floating around the tops are like an ocean. It is considered one of the ten most scenic places in China, and is world-famous as a tourist attraction.

Most interesting among its features are two lakes, three waterfalls, 24 streams and 72 peaks. Some of the peaks have distinct Taoist names: *lien-tan* (inner alchemy) peak, *Hsuan-yuan* (Yellow Emperor) peak, *hsien-jen* (Immortals) peak, etc.

Since ancient times, Buddhists and Taoists built temples on this mountain. The Tz'u-kuan ke (Bright Compassion Pavilion) below the southern peak and the Sung-ku an (Pine Valley Temple) on the northern side are two well-known Taoist structures (*DBK*: 850).

MOUNT KO-TSAO (*Ko-tsao Shan/Gezaoshan*). One of the renowned sacred mountains of Taoism: the 36th Blessed Spot (*fu-ti*), located in Kiangsi province. Because the mountain's shape is like a pavilion (*ko*) and its color is dark (*tsao*), it was named *Ko-tsao* ("Dark Pavilion Mountain").

A Taoist transcendent (*chen-jen*) resided there to do alchemical experiments. Several temples were built during the T'ang and Sung dynasties. A stone-arched bridge, built in 1117 during Sung times, still exists today (*CMTT*: 251).

MOUNT K'UN-LUN/KUNLUN. Whereas the other Taoist mountains discussed in this work are "real" mountains, Mount K'un-lun is a mythical mountain (although there is also a real Mount K'un-lun, situated in southwest China, that has nothing to do with its mythical counterpart).

Mount K'un-lun, in the mythical tradition, has ancient roots in Chinese literature; it is already mentioned in the classic *Shu ching* (*Book of Historical Documents*), and other ancient texts, such as the *Shan-hai ching* (*Book of Mountains and Seas*). It was considered to be "the early residence of the Celestial Sovereign [T'ien-ti] and the abode of one hundred deities" (M. Kaltenmark in *Mythologies II*: 1012).

In the *Huai-nan-tzu*, Chapter 4, "Kunlun is described in considerable detail . . . it is said that plants of immortality grow on this mountain and that it is there that is found the Cinnabar River [Tan-shui], whose water prevents death if it is drunk. . . But soon it was made the residence of [Hsi-wang mu], **Queen Mother of the West**, who had become queen of the Immortals. Hereafter, Kunlun was a paradise of immortality" (Kaltenmark: 1012–13).

In some other texts, Kun-lun figures as a replica of the mythical Mount Meru, center of the universe in Indian cosmology. In popular stories, the Queen Mother grows an orchard of peaches on the mountain and invites gods and immortals to a banquet whenever the peaches are ripe.

It is possible that the concept of "western heaven" (*hsi-t'ien*), so well known in popular Buddhism as the paradise of the Buddha Amita (*Sukhavati*), has been influenced by the paradise of Mount K'un-lun.

MOUNT LOU-FU (*Lou-fu Shan/Loufushan*). One of the famous sacred mountains of Taoism: the seventh **Grotto Heaven**, located in Kwangtung province. Its main peak is called Fei-yün ting ("Flying Clouds Peak").

During the Eastern Chin period, it was the place of residence of famous master Ko Hung, who did his alchemical research and wrote his treatises here. He also built four (cave) temples named Ch'ung-hsü an (South), Ku-ch'ing an (West), Pai-ho an (East), and Su-lao an (North). The southern temple was his center for alchemy experimentation and for collecting herbs, while a seven-star shrine in the western temple was his place for resting.

During the *t'ien-pao* era (742–755) of the T'ang, the temples were elevated in rank from *an* to *kuan*, and Sung Emperor Che-tsung donated a plaque with the inscription "Ch'ung-hsü kuan" ("Emptiness Monastery"). Inside, there is a Ko Hung memorial hall, as well as his alchemical furnace, for which Su Shih wrote an inscription (*CMTT*: 252).

The current Ch'ung-hsü kuan was rebuilt during the Ch'ing dynasty *t'ung-chih* period (1862–74).

MOUNT LUNG-HU (*Lung-hu Shan/Longhushan* or Dragon-and-Tiger Mountain). One of the famous mountains of Taoism, for many centuries the administrative center of Heavenly Masters or Cheng-yi Taoism. It is located in the province of Kiangsi, and considered the 32nd Taoist Blessed Spot. Its name is derived from twin mountains, one appearing as a rising dragon, one resembling a crouching tiger.

It is not clear at what time Mount Lung-hu became the Heavenly

Masters headquarters. Legend has it that Chang Lu's son, Chang Sheng, moved out there, but this is not based on reliable sources. The move probably took place during the T'ang period. During the Sung era, the Heavenly Masters of Mount Lung-hu were officially commissioned to give out ordination certificates to local Taoist priests. It became a registration center for southern China. It has been reported that Taoist candidates from Taiwan traveled to Mount Lung-hu to receive copies of the Taoist scriptures and to be ordained by the residing master. For instance, the Taoist Lin Ju-mei from Hsinchu city in northern Taiwan visited Mount Lung-hu from 1886–88. He received ordination and ". . . purchased a library of ritual and meditative manuals from the Sixty-first Heavenly Master . . ." (M. Saso, 1978: 73).

In 1949, the 63rd Patriarch, Chang En-fu (1904–1969), left Mount Lung-hu and moved to Taiwan. The PRC's government appointed his nephew, Chang Chin-t'ao, to be in charge of Mount Lung-hu; currently, he is a director of the Taoist Association of China.

MOUNT MAO (*Mao Shan/Maoshan*). One of the sacred mountains of Taoism, located in the southwestern part of Kiangsu province. Its original name was Mount *Chü-ch'ü/Juqu*. It is the eighth of the Ten Great **Grotto-Heavens**. According to tradition, three brothers named Mao went to the mountain to cultivate the Tao during the reign of Western Han Emperor Ching-ti (r. 156–140 BCE). The three peaks were each named after one brother and jointly called Three-Mao Mountain, shortened to Mao Mountain or Mao Shan.

During the Six Dynasties, several famous Taoists settled on Mount Mao: Ko Hsuan/Ge Xuan, Ko Hung/ Ge Hong, Yang Hsi, Hsü Mu, Lu Hsiu-ching, Sun Yu-yueh, and T'ao Hung-ching all chose it as their domain for spiritual cultivation. When T'ao, a patriarch of the Shang-ch'ing school, settled on Mount Mao, the school became known also as Mao Shan Taoism. It remained the most influential school of Taoism until the end of the T'ang period. During the Yuan dynasty, Mount Mao became an important center of Cheng-yi Taoism.

In modern times, Mount Mao was struck with disasters: During the war against Japan, most of the temples were destroyed by fire (in 1939), and during the Ten Years of Chaos ("Cultural Revolution") in 1966, some of the remaining buildings were demolished. In recent years, some of the temples have been restored and some precious artifacts have been recovered. Currently, about 30 Taoist priests live on Mount Mao.

MOUNT WU-TANG (*Wu-tang Shan/Wudangshan*). One of the famous mountains of Taoism, located in the northwest of Hupei province. It is considered the birthplace of the cult of the martial god **Chen-wu**

Ta-ti and owes its reputation mainly to the imperial support of the Ming court.

It has been called "mountain of transcendents" (*hsien-shan/xian-shan*), "Tao mountain," even "first mountain of the transcendents under heaven." The first Taoist monastery was built there during the reign of the T'ang Emperor T'ai-tsung (r. 627–649), but additional constructions continued during the Sung and Yuan dynasties. It was, however, during the Ming period that the mountain reached its peak of fame: The founder of the Ming dynasty, Emperor T'ai-tsu (r. 1368–1398), considered himself the earthly incarnation of the god Chen-wu and undertook great construction works on Mount Wu-tang: He built eight temples (*kung/gong*), two monasteries (*kuan/guan*), 36 convents for nuns (*an-t'ang/antang*), 72 cave temples (*yen-miao/yan-miao*), and, moreover, 39 bridges and 12 pavilions. The mountain covered a large area, including several hamlets.

The famous Taoist monk **Chang San-feng**/Zhang Sanfong is believed to have lived on this mountain.

Because of imperial support, Wu-tang Taoism flourished during the Ming period. But during the Ch'ing dynasty, even Wu-tang Taoism fell victim to the general decline.

After 1979, Mount Wu-tang started to regenerate itself. It has become a training center for young Taoists, it is protected by the state, and preserves some precious cultural relics. It also has become a tourist attraction.

MOUNTAINS. Sacred mountains have played an important function in the religious consciousness of all peoples and of the Chinese people in particular. Several dozen mountains have been designed as "sacred" throughout time and today remain active as centers of spiritual cultivation and attractive as places of pilgrimage. Some mountains are considered Taoist, others are Buddhist, but at least five predate any such designation and are universally Chinese. The Five Sacred Mountains also have been called "Imperial Peaks," although Taoists and Buddhists have built monasteries and temples on their slopes. These five have long been honored by the official state cult: Emperors used to visit them and offer sacrifices to the mountain gods.

Why do mountains fascinate people, religious people in particular? Alpinists find a challenge in them: Because, they are there, they must be conquered. Artists are awed by the majesty of lofty peaks and cannot resist to conquer them on their canvas. But religious people have a different concept. Why is that? There may be several reasons, not the least being that

> As the highest and most dramatic features of the natural landscape, mountains have an extraordinary power to evoke the sacred. . . [they]

embody powerful forces beyond our control . . . (E. Bernbaum,
1990: xiii)

It is possible that in human imagination mountain tops are seen as
closer to "heaven." But, being far away from the "yellow dust" of
cities and the bustle of secular activity, mountains are seen as pure
and clean, free from physical and spiritual pollution. Therefore, they
are attractive as centers of spiritual cultivation and study, or as special
places for vision quests where adepts prepare themselves for vision-
ary revelations of the residing deities.

Another reason mountains are awe-inspiring is that, since ancient
times, people believed that the elevated peaks were sources of water,
and, thus, agriculturally very important. In ancient times, until the
20th century, many villages situated near mountains had temples dedicated to the mountain spirit, where people would go and pray for
rain.

In Taoism, mountains also inspire great respect. But this respect is
not unqualified: Mountains also are seen as dangerous. Malevolent
spirits take up residence there, as well as benevolent ones, and would-
be visitors are warned against attacks from the elements (thunder,
storms, falling rocks, etc.) and from wild animals. One should not
enter the mountains unless one is well protected by specially drawn
talismans. In *Pao-p'u-tzu*, Ko Hung warned against these dangers.
(See also **Talismans**.)

Some of the more renowned "Taoist" mountains will be discussed
in separate entries. Here, Taoist mountains are placed in the perspective of Chinese mountain lore:

First, there are the Five Sacred Peaks (*wu-yueh*), or "imperial
peaks," located in the four directions and the center, corresponding
with the **Five Agents** and other sets of fives:

East: Mount T'ai (T'ai-shan/Taishan), Shantung province
South: Mount Heng (Heng-shan), Hunan province
West: Mount Hua (Hua-shan), Shensi province
North: Mount Heng (Heng-shan), Shansi province
Center: Mount Sung (Sung-shan/Songshan), Honan province

There are also Four Sacred Mountains of Buddhism, spread geographically. Each is the center of worship of a particular *Bodhisattva*:

East: Mount P'u-t'o, Chekiang: Kuan-yin (Avalokiteshvara)
South: Mount Chiu-hua, Anhwei: Ti-tsang (Ksitigarbha)
West: Mount Omei, Szechuan: P'u-hsien (Samantabhadra)
North: Mount Wu-t'ai, Shansi: Wen-shu (Manjushri)

Finally, there are many "Taoist" mountains, each famous for the worship of a particular deity or for being the seat of a particular Taoist school (see also special entries for **Mount Mao, Wu-tang, Chung-nan, Lung-hu, Ho-ming, Huang, Ch'ing-ch'eng, Ko-tsao, Lou-fu**).

MUSIC. The study of Taoist music is still in its infancy, but it is encouraging to note that scholarly attention has been given to it in recent times. Here a distinction will be made between the theoretical foundations and the practical performance of Taoist music. The former has much in common with the theory of Chinese music in general, whereas the latter has close ties with popular music (Chinese opera) and, in earlier times, with court music. There is a need for an in-depth study of Taoist music theory and for recording the various regional performances of the most important Taoist rituals. In fact, this recording process was begun in the 1980s in a Shanghai conservatory studio, where videotapes have been produced of several major rituals (*chiao*), which include Taoist chanting and musical accompaniment.

Taoist music has indeed always been "practical," performed within the liturgy. Its connection with popular music is obvious and also explains the great variety of local customs. Although its roots go back to ancient times, it appears that throughout history many changes have occurred.

It is interesting to see that one of the earliest Taoist texts, the ***Great Peace Scripture*** (*T'ai-p'ing ching*), already discussed the significance of music.

> It regards music as a bridge between man and the cosmos, through which man may provoke corresponding forces in the cosmos. The bridge will link man and the universe together, thus protecting man from evil and calamities. (Jan Y.h. in Tsao, 1989: 15)

This view of correspondence between music and reality is significant: It gives music a metaphysical foundation. But music must also correspond with human emotions and must, in particular, express happiness.

> The relationship is mutual and dialectical. Music is produced by happiness [and] . . . will produce more happiness in turn. (Jan: 16)

All through history, Taoist music has been performed by specialists, usually Taoist priests themselves, because besides musical skills, a performer needs knowledge of Taoist doctrine. Perhaps this is the unspoken reason why learning how to play musical instruments is an important aspect in the training of priestly candidates. In today's *chiao* rituals, many of the musicians are also priests: They exchange places occasionally. Musical performance is indeed part of the ritual itself; it is not only meant to awaken the people in attendance, but also to move (and to entertain) the deities invited to be present.

For centuries, the performance of ritual music was, together with staged operas in the villages, one of the few means of popular education.

With regard to historical documents concerning music, most of the ancient music, Taoist and other, has been lost. It is, however, certain that during some imperial rules, Taoist music was especially promoted at court. That was the case of T'ang Emperor Kao-tsung (r. 650–683), who asked his court musicians to compose Taoist music. During the reign of Emperor Hsuan-tsung (r. 713–755), a mass production of Taoist melodies took place, incorporating folk music and music from Central Asia. During the Sung, this trend continued. There was a publication of 50 musical annotations, titled *Yü-yin fa-shih* ("Manual of Jade Music"), which recorded T'ang and Sung Taoist music and is the earliest surviving musical document; yet, it has not been deciphered so far.

In 1112, Sung Emperor Hui-tsung published the text *Ritual Regulations of the Ling-pao Liturgy of the Golden Register* (*Chin-lu ling-pao tao-ch'ang yi-kui*), of which he distributed 426 copies. Two years later, he summoned ten Taoist priests from various regions to the capital to practice this ritual manual of ceremonial and music. Once the priests had been familiarized with it, they were sent home to teach others. As a result, Taoist music from different regions intermixed and was mutually enriched.

During the Ming period, Taoist ceremonial was simplified and codified or standardized. Ming Taoist music continued from earlier dynasties, and also included patterns from the folk musical tradition (*DSC*: 516–521).

Today's Taoist music continues the older traditions. There are still numerous regional differences. Even in a small area like Taiwan (China's smallest province), regional differences are obvious. Taoists from both North and South Taiwan all claim to belong to the Cheng-yi School (Heavenly Masters Taoism), yet "they do not have a single text in common and their ritual music is equally very different" (Lü/Lagerwey, 1988: 113).

There are various types of vocal recitation: the more solemn, drawn-out chanting, and the staccato-like recitations. These are accompanied, or even guided, by two nonpitched instruments, found on the altars of all temples;

the *ta-ch'ing*, an inverted bowl-shaped bell struck with a mallet; the *mu-yü* [wooden "fish"], a wooden slit drum struck by a stick . . .

the *ta-ch'ing* represents heaven and the male principle, *yang*, while the *mu-yü* represents earth and the female principle, *yin*. (E. Wong, *ER* 10: 198)

• *Musical Diversities:* Taoist music is always connected with the liturgy. But several types of performance can be noted: solo music, orchestral music, accompaniment music. *Solo music* is perhaps not a clear term: It means that sometimes musical instruments are played without chanting, most common by the drummer, but sometimes by several instruments together. This occurs at the beginning or the end of a ceremony, occasionally in the middle, when the drum indicates changes from chanting to recitation, etc. Some exciting drum solos take place during special nonrecitative rituals, as, for example, during the exorcism ritual in the temple, when the grand master chases the offensive demon who has stolen the incense burner.

Orchestral music here means the joint performance of various instruments, accompanying the more solemn chanting of the ritual texts. During any given ritual, there are at least four instruments performing.

Accompaniment music here means when only one instrument accompanies the solo recitation of a text by one Taoist priest, for example, the *Canons of Penance* during the **Cosmic Renewal Festival**.

• *Musical Instruments* (based on Taiwan fieldwork: see Lü/Lagerwey, 1988: 117–8). In Taiwan, the musical instruments used in Taoist liturgy are the same as those of popular music. There are three categories: basic, secondary, and percussion instruments.
• Basic instruments. Four or five kinds: *so-na* (oboe), but with sharp, penetrating tones, different from a Western oboe; smaller *so-na*; two-string violin (*erh-hu*); and the three-string lute, with octagonal soundboard. The oboes are used at the beginning and end of rituals and accompany the major parts of the chant.
• Secondary instruments. "Overseas" lute (*yang-ch'in*); traverse flute (*ti-tzu*) and straight flute (*hsiao*), usually both made of bamboo; a larger size *erh-hu* (*ta-kuang hsuan*); a secondary *erh-hu* (*ho-hsuan*); and, sometimes, the electric guitar. (Not mentioned in Lü's report, but often seen as well, are a sort of horizontal harp and a xylophone.)
• Percussion instruments. Gongs and drums contribute to create the right atmosphere and to mark the rhythm (Lü: 118). They are about the same as in Chinese theater. They are drums (with one or two surfaces), clappers, small and large cymbals, and a variety of gongs (large or small, held in the hand or suspended on a wooden frame (Lü: 118). These percussion instruments listed are

only used in the inner sacred area (*t'an*). Outside the temple, they are replaced by a large gong, a pair of cymbals, and a large drum. (For more information, see the informative summary by Lü/Lagerwey: 118–126.)

MUSICAL INSTRUMENTS See MUSIC

MYSTERY LEARNING (*Hsuan-hsueh/Xuanxue*). This refers to a philosophical movement in early Taoist history (third and fourth centuries CE) usually translated as "Dark Learning," which is not adequate. "Mystery" Learning is preferable, because the focus of study was on three "mysterious" texts (rather than "dark" texts): the *Yi Ching*, the *TTC*, and the *Chuang-tzu*. Others prefer the expression "Profound Learning," because "in Taoist philosophy, the profound or metaphysical aspect is paramount" (W.t. Chan, 1963: 788).

At the time of great political and social changes following the collapse of the Han dynasty, Confucianism, which had been the official educational system of the Han, was greatly discredited. Many younger intellectuals looked for different parameters of intellectual culture. Most famous among them were **Wang Pi** and **Kuo Hsiang**, promising young philosophers who were interested in the scriptures of the Mystery Learning and wrote commentaries on them. Their movement is perhaps part of a wider phenomenon, called "**Neo-Taoism**," a term that has been criticized as meaningless, because, like "Neo-Confucianism," it is a creation of Western sinologists.

MYSTICISM as an extraordinary spiritual or better, psychosomatic experience occurs in a variety of traditions and in multiple forms. The unifying factor is probably the intense personal experience of oneness with a transcendent reality, natural or supernatural. Indeed, as *Webster* states, mysticism is ". . . the doctrine that it is possible to achieve communion with God through contemplation and love without the medium of human reason." This interpretation is, of course, rather culture-bound and unilaterally Christian, but if one grasps the essentials and changes the context, mysticism refers to the belief that communion with a transcendent reality, however defined, is possible. Mystical experience is the personal direct experience of such a communion.

There is no doubt that mysticism is found in the Taoist tradition. B. Schwartz recognizes the "mystical dimension" of the *TTC* and the *Chuang-tzu* (Schwartz. 1985: 192), and several recent publications deal with Taoist mysticism in detail (L. Kohn, 1991 & 1992; J. Paper, 1995). But as was already stated in the **Introduction** ". . . there exists such a thing as natural mysticism . . . [an] ecstatic union with the Tao, not in the theistic [or religious] sense, but as a naturalistic, humanist experience." This applies most clearly to the philosophical writings, *TTC* and *Chuang-tzu*, but not to later mystical texts from the Period of Disunity or the T'ang, such as the Shang-ch'ing tradition. These later writings deal with religious mysticism, which means intimate, even ecstatic, communion with deities experienced as personal beings.

Union with the transcendent Tao is not described in such terms of personal communion. Moreover, mystical trance states are not directly expressed in the *TTC*; they are indirectly hinted at, while the *Chuang-tzu* has some passages that unambiguously describe mystical states.

Two examples from the *TTC* will clarify this point:

From Chapter 16:   Attain complete vacuity,
                      Maintain steadfast quietude.
                      All things come into being,
                      And I see thereby their return.
                      . . .
                      Being kingly, he is one with Heaven
                      Being one with Heaven, he is in accord with
                          Tao.
                      Being in accord with Tao, he is long-lasting.
                      (W.t. Chan, 1963: 147–8, with some minor
                          changes)

From Chapter 10:   Holding onto the oneness of *hun* and *p'o*
                      Can you not let them separate? . . .
                      Purifying your original vision,
                      Can you make it spotless?

From the *Chuang-tzu*'s "Inner Chapters," the following are most eloquent examples of direct mystical states.

Chapter 2 starts with the anecdote of a sage who had "lost himself": his body had become "like a withered tree" and his mind "like dead ashes" (Watson, 1970: 36). Although the description is brief, it clearly refers to a state of trance, during which the mind is in ecstasy, while the body has become lifeless (see J. Paper, 1995: 133).

Chapter 4 narrates a conversation between Confucius and his disciple, Yen Hui, who asks his master's permission to go on a trip to the state of Wei to serve its ruler in government. Confucius warns him of the dangers of serving as an advisor to a king. His ultimate advice is to practice "the fasting of the mind." Puzzled, Yen Hui wants to know what his master means. Confucius says:

Make your will one! Don't listen with your ears, listen with your mind. No, don't listen with your mind, listen with your spirit. Listening stops with the ears, the mind stops with recognition, but spirit is empty and waits on all things. The Way gathers in emptiness alone. Emptiness is the fasting of the mind. (Watson: 57–58)

This passage reminds one of the above-quoted Chapter 16 of the *TTC*: "Attain complete vacuity . . ." It is a common experience in mystical trance that the self is "dissolved" in emptiness and filled with the presence of Tao or, in a theistic context, filled with the presence of the divine.

In Chapter 6, the roles of the master and disciple are reversed: Yen Hui reports to Confucius about his gradual spiritual progress: He has "forgotten benevolence and righteousness," "rites and music," and, finally, "can sit down and forget everything" (*tso-wang*: "sit-and-forget," an expression often used in later religious texts). Startled, Confucius asks what he means. Says Yen Hui: "I can smash up my limbs and body, drive out perception and intellect, cast off form, do away with understanding, and make myself identical with the Great Thoroughfare" (Watson: 90). Ironically, Confucius is impressed and wants to become his student's disciple! The "Great Thoroughfare" can also be translated as "Great Universality" (*ta-t'ung/datong*) (Paper: 134) or "universal thoroughfare" (Graham, 1981: 92) and appears to be a metaphor for Ultimate Reality of Tao.

In a previous episode of Chapter 6, Woman Crookback explains how she tried to make a sage out of someone she recognized as having "the talent of a sage." In summary, this is the progress chart:

first (after three days), he could put the world out of himself;
next (after seven days), he could put things out of himself;
next (after nine days), he could put life out of himself;
then, he could achieve the brightness of dawn;
then, he could see his own aloneness;
then, he could do away with past and present;
then, finally, he could enter where there is no life or death.
(paraphrase of Watson: 82–83)

We can see here a description of a gradual process of transcending the world and even oneself, a very concrete expression of mystical rapture. In none of the above passages, however, is there any allusion to union with a divine entity. It is union with Tao as a Natural, be it a Transcendent Reality. It is also easy to realize the possibility of interpreting such an experience in theistic terms, if one is so inclined, and especially if one has been predisposed to such an interpretation because of one's educational background.

Within the realm of the Taoist religious practice, one would expect to encounter written documents about personal mystical experiences. Apparently, as L. Kohn states, this is not the case: ". . . there are no personal reports on the overwhelming and powerful nature of certain specific experiences that could be compared in compact and importance to their Christian counterpart" (Kohn, 1992: 10–11). Yet, there is an abundance of Taoist religious writings explaining the process, initiating the adepts in the various techniques of meditation and inner visualization that will lead them to mystical states. The experience itself remains elusive, and is better not expressed in words. The state of ultimate bliss, like that of enlightenment in Ch'an Buddhism, escapes all verbalization (see L. Kohn, 1991 & 1992; I. Robinet, 1979/1993).

N

NATURALNESS or **SPONTANEITY** (*Tzu-jan/Ziran*). An important concept in Taoist thinking. It expresses the idea of something appearing or happening out of itself, rather than being caused or created by an outside agent. In that sense, it also means spontaneity. One quote from the *Tao-te ching* will clarify this:

> Humans model themselves after Earth.
> Earth models itself after Heaven.
> Heaven models itself after Tao.
> Tao models itself after itself.
> (*TTC* Chapter 25: 9–10)

Heaven-and-Earth, although verbally divided into two, actually stands for one reality: the cosmos, in which we live. This cosmos, being a creation of Tao, obviously follows its own inner essence, in accordance with Tao. But Tao, uncreated, self-existent, does not follow any other norm but itself. It is the ultimate norm and norm-setter.

The translation of the last line, "And Tao models itself after Nature" (Chan, 1963: 153), is incorrect. "Nature" here is an anachronism. Only in modern times, the Western concept of Nature was translated as *tzu-jan*. But originally *tzu-jan* means "self-so," "out of its own self," therefore "natural, spontaneous."

Applied to human action, *tzu-jan* means what people do spontaneously, not forced by external rules or laws. They just follow their own instincts, their own "nature" (this is the link with "Nature"), as the *TTC* expresses: Great rulers accomplish their work without imposing laws on the people.

Nevertheless, the people say: We have achieved it ourselves! (*TTC* 17: 7)

Naturalness and spontaneity are characteristics of free beings: As with many other good qualities, there is always a danger of running wild. But that is rather against the Tao!

NATURE AND LIFE (*Hsing-ming/Xingming*). Among the many spiritual practices found in the Taoist religion, two in particular gained importance during the Jurchen Chin and the Sung periods; they are expressions of **inner alchemy**. These two focus on two essential aspects of a human being: nature (*hsing*) and life (*ming*).

• *Nature* (*hsing*). Chuang-tzu often talks about "nature" (which B. Watson translated as "inborn nature"). But the meaning of nature in later Taoism appears to be different, and was apparently strongly influenced by Ch'an Buddhism. For them, "nature" was "mind." To cultivate one's nature means to look at one's own mind, which is originally and essentially enlightened but is obscured by various factors. For the Taoists, nature must be cultivated by mind concentration and tranquility; once enlightened, the mind returns to its spirit-like essence (*shen*) and that is the beginning of immortal existence.

• *Life* (*ming*). The term *ming* can be understood either as fate or as life. In the Taoist context, life is the obvious meaning. In contrast with nature, which refers to one's mind, life refers to the physical-psychic base of life, one's vital energy, *ch'i*, or, more narrowly, to the reproductive power of one's body, the *ching* (or *ovum* for a woman). It is probably more correct to explain *ming* here as the vital energy, the *ch'i*, which one is endowed with at birth.

Looking at it this way, the dual emphasis on nature and life is perhaps a parallel with the **Three Primary Vitalities**.

In the Taoist religious tradition, one must obviously cultivate both life and nature. But during the Chin-Sung period, there was disagreement about their priorities. The Southern and Northern Schools advocated dual cultivation of *hsing* and *ming*. Whereas **Wang Che** found it most important to cultivate nature first, others, such as **Chang Po-tuan,** would argue that life comes first, nature next. If there is no life, how can nature subsist? It is interesting to remember that Wang Che was indebted to Ch'an Buddhism, for his own conceptions of spirituality, and for Ch'an Buddhism, the mind (or nature) is the ultimate foundation.

NATURE DEITIES. The Taoist pantheon contains a mixture of gods and goddesses of various origins: mythical creations, deities controlling aspects of nature, deified historical personalities (see also **Pan-**

theon). Here the emphasis is on "nature deities," which, in fact, pre-date Taoism, but were later incorporated into the Taoist pantheon. They are shared with the Popular religion, or with the state cult.

Nature deities are personifications of natural powers or phenomena, and thus belong to polytheism. Another religion in which nature deities are prominent is Hinduism, which is also polytheistic. In China, nature deities are one important group of the pantheon; besides them, the Chinese worship ancestor spirits and apotheosed human personalities, deified after death because of their outstanding merits or effective spiritual power (*ling*).

The nature deities, incorporated into the Taoist pantheon, include the "officials of the weather bureau," stellar deities, the gods of mountains and rivers, some gods of fertility, the god Szu-ming (Controller of Destiny), and the high-ranking triad of the Three Officials (*san-kuan*).

• *Weather deities* include the god of thunder, the mother of lightning, the gods of rain (water) and wind, and, although not listed here, the god of fire. Most prominent is the god of thunder, Lei-kung (Lord of Thunder). It is said that Taoism split him up into several gods, forming the Thunder Bureau (Maspero, 1971/1981: 97).

> He is represented as a man of repulsive ugliness, with a body blue all over, furnished with wings and claws. He wears nothing but a loin-cloth, with one or more drums hanging at his side, and his hands hold a mallet and a chisel. (Ou-I-Tai, 1973: 383)

By orders of heaven, the thunder god punishes those guilty of major crimes that go undetected, and evil spirits who use their powers to harm mankind.

The thunder god is assisted by Mother-Lightning (Tien-mu), the Master of Rain (Yü-shih), and the Earl of Wind (Feng-po) (Ou-I-Tai: 383–4; Maspero: 97–98), all deities having ancient roots, but adopted by Taoism.

Two gods not usually listed as such in the category of weather deities are the god of water and the god of fire. They are not exactly the same as the Master of Rain (water) and the Mother of Lightning (fire), but control water and fire on earth. Both are powerful forces influencing human society, but are ambiguous in their function. They can be both creative and destructive. Therefore, on special occasions, such as the **Festival of Cosmic Renewal**, special rituals are performed by the Taoist priests to exorcise their dangerous potential, hoping that the future will be free from destructive fires and floods or typhoons.

• *Gods of mountains and rivers*. Since ancient times mountains and rivers were believed to be inhabited by divine spirits, and seasonal sacrifices were offered to them by rulers or their representatives (see also **Five Sacred Mountains**). This was one aspect of the official cult, but some of those deities also were absorbed into Taoism. The major mountain god is the Great Emperor of the Eastern Peak, one of the judges supervising the courts of hell. He is directly responsible to the **Jade Emperor** and has an administration under him of 80 offices (Ou-I-Tai: 386–7; Maspero: 102–5).

• *Gods of heavenly bodies.* Foremost among them are the deities ruling over the sun and the moon. Both were worshipped in the official cult; their temples used to be in the eastern and western suburbs of Beijing. Both also had their Taoist gods, "but those were catalogue divinities to whom nobody prayed" (Maspero: 96), except possibly under the names of Yin-god and Yang-god, often encountered in Taiwan temples (see also **Star-deities**).

• *Fertility gods.* In the ancient popular religion, these were the gods of soil and grain, responsible for the fertility of the earth by securing good harvests. Today, the **God of the Soil** is still very popular in the folk religion. But more important is dragon worship. Four dragon kings are responsible for sending down seasonal rain. They rule the four seas surrounding the earth. Their worship was shared by the official state cult, the Popular religion and Taoism. They were directly responsible to the **Jade Emperor**. (See also **Director of Destiny** and **Three Officials.**)

NEI-TAN See INNER ALCHEMY

NEO-TAOISM. As a term, "Neo-Taoism" has been criticized as meaningless, a creation of Western sinologists. Yet it is a convenient way to define a two-dimensional movement during the third and fourth centuries CE, for which there is no equivalent Chinese term. It includes a rational and a sentimental aspect. In Chinese, there are two terms: **Mystery Learning** (*Hsuan-hsueh*) and **Pure Conversation** (*Ch'ing-t'an*). (The situation may be compared with "Neo-Confucianism," also a Western term, which likewise includes two schools of thought: School of Principles, *Li-hsueh*, and School of Mind, *Hsin-hsueh*. A unifying term has its advantages.)

The word Neo-Taoism or new Taoism only points at Taoist philosophy, as Fung Yu-lan states: "This revived Taoist philosophy I will call Neo-Taoism" (Fung 1966: 211). Some scholars criticize the term Neo-Taoism as "highly inadequate," because they think of Mystery Learning (*hsuan-hsueh*) as "a Confucian recasting of early Taoist philosophy. . ." (E. Zürcher 1959: 289). That is a questionable statement, since the most important representatives of the movement,

Wang Pi and **Kuo Hsiang**, did talk metaphysics, which, in Confucianism of the time, had little place.

It is certainly true that Neo-Taoism represents the first emergence of syncretistic speculation, in which Taoists, Buddhists, and Confucians participated, be it in different ways. This whole period, from the end of the Han until the T'ang, was a time of political confusion that had a strong impact on intellectual life. **Confucianism,** the state learning of the Han dynasty, had been discredited with the fall of the Han empire. Many literati felt disaffected with it, and started to explore both Buddhist learning and the old Taoist classics. That sparked a complex network of interactions, which is difficult to reconstruct in its entirety.

Let us look at **Buddhism** first. It arrived in China as a foreign doctrine and religion. To be acceptable, it had to transpose itself into a form that would be intelligible for the Chinese. At first mistaken for a different brand of Taoism, because it had to rely on Chinese terminology to express its own concepts (and Taoist terminology was the one available), it moved away from this strategy after Kumarajiva arrived in China (about 400 CE) and introduced better translation techniques.

However, some of the Buddhist scriptures attracted the attention of Chinese literati; they were mainly the so-called *prajna*-literature ("wisdom" scriptures), circulated and studied by the *prajna* school from the end of the Han until the Southern Liu Sung dynasty. In a translation of a Buddhist scripture it was said that "the perfection of wisdom (*prajnaparamita*) was equivalent to the Tao of the Taoists . . . The term used . . . to designate the ultimate reality or original nature was *pen-wu*, original non-being" (K. Ch'en, 1957: 33). The similarity of Buddhist terminology with Neo-Taoist Wang Pi is striking.

To make a long story short, interactions between Buddhists and Taoists (Buddhist scholars were well versed in Taoist philosophy of *TTC* and *Chuang-tzu*), between Buddhists and Confucians, between Taoists and Confucians stirred dialogue and comparison that enriched them all and produced the Neo-Taoist movement in its two dimensions: **Mystery Learning** and **Pure Conversation** (discussed under separate entries). The most eminent figures of the former were Wang Pi and Kuo Hsiang; representatives of the latter are the **Seven Sages of the Bamboo Grove**.

This period of mutual interactions between the three teachings did not last; eventually, each school returned to its own focus. Buddhism developed its intricate system of philosophy during the Sui-T'ang; Confucianism would recover from its position of weakness and revive as Neo-Confucianism; Taoism would leave the area of metaphysics and turn inward toward spiritual cultivation as exemplified in the

Shang-ch'ing or Mao Shan School. But this early period of mutual contacts was an enriching experience for all three, and the spirit of syncretism would survive.

NONACTION See *WU-WEI*

NONBEING (*Wu*). A concept in Taoist philosophy, the importance of which has often been overstated, at least as a metaphysical concept. There are only three passages in the *TTC* where a contrast is mentioned between *yu* ("what is, what exists") and *wu* ("what is not," "what does not exist"); one passage sometimes quoted to make the distinction between "being" and "nonbeing" was based on a misunderstanding and mistranslation of the text. The Ma-wang-tui text has solved this problem by adding punctuation (the passage is Chapter 1: 5–6. example, Chan, 1963: 139).

In the three relevant passages (Chapters 2: 3; 11: 7; 40: 3–4) "being" and "nonbeing" are contrasted indeed, but in a concrete way, not as abstract metaphysical principles. "Being" means that which exists, "nonbeing" is that which does not exist, or does not yet exist. Each existing thing is produced by something existing previously (each person has his/her parents); or, as in Chapter 11: 7, within existing things, there are aspects of non-existence, there is emptiness. That is what makes a carriage useful. A carriage is made of parts (they exist), but its purpose is to be a vehicle, to carry people or things. This is made possible by the empty space in it. As the text says, both the being aspect of the parts and the nonbeing aspect of space have their usefulness, their function. This is far from metaphysical speculation about being (*être*) and nonbeing (*néant*).

Metaphysics entered into the discussion with Neo-Taoism, probably due to Buddhist influence. "Nonbeing" was compared with "emptiness," nonsubstantiality of all things. Taoist philosophers then started to realize that all that exists, except the eternal Tao, is only a temporary manifestation, but ultimately void of substance. The passages in the *TTC* were then gradually reinterpreted.

NONSTRIVING or not-competing is a basic quality recommended in the *Tao-te ching*. It is one of the numerous facets of **wu-wei**, but it is particularly stressed in the *TTC* as a modality of ruling the country. As the Tao produces all beings and does not compete with them, so the sage (*sheng-jen*) or sage-ruler likewise does not compete with the people and does not encourage competition. He avoids all policies that could stir up competition and strife.

This is certainly a difficult ideal to pursue, both for a ruler and for anyone else. In our society, we are told from childhood to be the best, to beat everyone else, etc. Such an educational device is ambiguous. If it means that we should try our best to develop our potential to the utmost, it is just fine. That is the meaning of "education," which means "to bring out" the potential present in our mental-biological makeup. But if it means ruthlessness in our "competing," trying to "beat" everyone else, it becomes selfish and very negative. The Tao does not strive or compete in such a way. If people would walk this "Way," life would be happier, and many neurotic conditions could be avoided. That is the implied message of the *TTC*.

NORTHERN BUSHEL See BIG DIPPER

NORTHERN SCHOOL (Pei-tsung/Beizong). Refers to the northern branch of the Complete Realization School, in contrast with the **Southern School**. When Ch'uan-chen Taoism was founded in the north by Wang Che, there was no distinction between north and south. It was only after **Pai Yü-ch'an** in the south had started his Southern School that the northern group called themselves "northern school"; it was also called Ch'ung-yang School.

This school emphasizes first "nature" (*hsing*), only then "life" (*ming*). It venerated as its five patriarchs Tung-hua Ti-chün, Ch'ung-li Ch'uan, Lü Tung-pin, Liu Hai-ch'an, and Wang Ch'ung-yang. They were later called the Five Northern Patriarchs. It also venerates Wang Ch'ung-yang's seven disciples as the "**Seven Perfected**" (*CMTT*: 27).

NOURISH BREATH/VITAL ENERGY See *YANG-CH'I*

NOURISH LIFE See *YANG-SHENG*

NOURISH NATURE See *YANG-HSING*

NOURISH PHYSICAL BODY See *YANG-HSING*

NOURISH SPIRIT See *YANG-SHEN*

NUMINOUS TREASURE See *LING-PAO*

NUMINOUS TREASURE TAOISM See LING-PAO TRADITION

O

ORDINATION see PRIESTHOOD

ORTHODOX UNITY SCHOOL see CHENG-YI TAOISM

OUTER ALCHEMY (*Wai-tan/Waidan*). Outer alchemy, or external, operative alchemy ("alchimie opératoire") is a protoscience (pseudo-science?) by which attempts are made to refine ordinary, "base" metals (like lead or copper) into "noble" metals—gold or silver. This process, which J. Needham called "aurifaction" (gold-making) in contrast with the deceptive technique "aurifiction" (gold-faking) (Needham V, 2: 12) probably first emerged in China during the Warring States period, possibly in the circle of Tsou Yen and his School of Naturalism. Gold (and silver in a lesser way) was seen as incorruptible; it does not oxidize and therefore, was considered a symbol of an immortal state, in which the human body does not disintegrate.

Han Emperor Wu (r. 140–87 BCE) was a keen supporter of alchemical research. He funded *fang-shih*, especially **Li Shao-chün**, who claimed to be able to transform cinnabar into gold.

> When this gold has been produced it can be made into vessels for eating and drinking, the use of which will prolong one's life. If one's life is prolonged one will be able to meet the immortals (of the isle) of P'eng-Lai in the midst of the sea. When one has seen them one will be able to make the *feng* and *shan* sacrifices, and after that one will never die. The Yellow Emperor did just this. (Needham V, 3: 31)

The use of gold vessels was supposed to confer longevity to its users: The incorruptible gold would rub off on the adept's body. But the alchemists' claims proved to be futile. Li Shao-chün was unable to come up with lasting results. Other *fang-shih* after him also failed and were executed.

Besides the metallurgical-chemical efforts, other methods were attempted: Foremost, at first, a pharmaceutical-botanical tradition existed, according to which there was a "plant of deathlessness" believed to grow on the mystery islands in the eastern ocean. This mushroom-like plant, *ling-chih*, proved to be too elusive to find. Both the First Emperor of China and Han Emperor Wu sent out expeditions to bring it back: They all failed.

A third method was then used, which Needham called "macrobiotics," and involved

> the belief that it was possible to prepare, with the aid of botanical, zoological, mineralogical, and especially chemical knowledge, drugs or elixirs (*tan*) which will prolong human life beyond old age, rejuvenating the body and its spiritual parts so that the adept can endure through centuries of longevity, finally attaining the status of eternal life and arising with an etherealized body as a true Immortal (*sheng-hsien*). (Needham V, 2: 11)

The above-described methods, except for the *ling-chih*, relied on lab experiments, using an alchemical furnace or cauldron (*ting*). Their expected products, alchemical pills or elixirs, were ingested into the body (that explains the appellation "outer" or "external") with the hoped-for result of physical immortality. Usually alchemy is associated with Taoism, but that is probably only valid for inner alchemy. As N. Sivin says,

> Alchemy did not originate in the Taoist milieu and was never confined to it. (Sivin, 1987, *ER* 1: 190)

After the failure of the "gold rush" in alchemy, other techniques were tried and a variety of materials were used: realgar, orpiment, mercury, gold, silver, alum, malachite, quartz, jade, and mica (I. Robinet, 1986: 381). The list does not include cinnabar, a term turning up all the time in alchemical literature. The reason must be that cinnabar is in fact mercury sulphide (Hg_2S) and was used to prepare mercury. That mercury plays such an important role in alchemy is rather surprising because it is highly toxic and can be harmful to health, rather than immortalize the body. In fact, at least five emperors of the T'ang dynasty died of elixir poisoning.

If the attainment of immortal life is theoretically possible (which is doubtful, because that which has a beginning also has an end!), it appears that outer alchemy did not produce the hoped-for result. Moreover, it was certainly not an option for the great majority of people. **Ko Hung,** who has left behind a number of wonderful recipes promising astounding effects, admitted that alchemy aims first of all at prolonging life through alchemical pills; once long life is achieved (like 300 years), one has an opportunity to experiment further and to produce the pill of deathlessness. It was, however, a very costly process, because the ingredients were extremely rare and expensive. This limited the research to emperors and nobles.

Eventually, *wai-tan* experiments were abandoned. The interest in **immortality** did not fade, but shifted to *nei-tan*: eternal life could be achieved not by externally taken pills, but by using one's own body physiology and combining these practices with the more spiritual-mystical cultivation of Taoism. (See also **inner alchemy**. For more detailed information about alchemy, see the volumes by J. Needham, V, parts 2–5; also, N. Sivin, 1968; *ER* 1: 186–190.)

P

PA-HSIEN See EIGHT IMMORTALS

PA-KUA See EIGHT TRIGRAMS

PAI YÜ-CH'AN/BAI YUCHAN (1194-?). A Taoist master during the Southern Sung and Yuan periods. He became the fifth patriarch of the

Southern School of **Inner Alchemy**. Many consider him to be the real founder of the school.

Born on the island of Hainan (from Fukienese ancestry), he was a precocious boy who passed the civil service examination for children at the age of 12. He was not only versed in the classics, but was also a painter and poet. When he once killed a person out of reaction against injustice, he decided to disguise himself as a Taoist to avoid the authorities. He escaped to Mount Wu-yi, and later roamed south of the Yang-tzu, living a very precarious life.

In 1212, he became a disciple of Ch'en Nan (d. 1213), who instructed him in the secrets of **alchemy**. After his master died the following year, Pai dressed himself in shabby clothes with disheveled hair and traveled (as one of those "crazy monks"!) to various famous mountains: Lou-fu, Wu-yi, Lung-hu, T'ien-t'ai, and Chin-hua. In 1222, he visited the capital Lin-an and submitted a memorial to the emperor to express his views on current state affairs. He was ignored by the authorities and even arrested once for drunkenness.

After this episode, he devoted himself wholeheartedly to the spreading of Taoist alchemy. He attracted a large number of disciples and established religious districts, known as *ch'ing/qing*. His school was officially recognized by the government as a legitimate religious establishment.

After Ch'en Nan, Pai was confirmed as the fifth patriarch of the Southern School. He advocated celibacy (he himself never married) and in his teaching he combined **Confucianism** and Ch'an Buddhism with Taoism. He gave particular attention to one's spiritual-mental well-being. His approach had a tremendous impact on Taoist thought from the Sung period onward. He also was an expert in thunder magic (*lei-fa*), talismans, medicine, and exorcism.

He wrote quite a number of books, published during his life or posthumously by his disciples. Some were included in the Taoist Canon.

PAI-YÜN KUAN See WHITE CLOUD MONASTERY

PANTHEON. Each religion has its own objects of worship, whether it is one God alone, without a second (as in the three monotheistic traditions) or numerous gods and goddesses (as in polytheistic religions, such as Hinduism, Taoism, and the Chinese Popular religion). Besides gods and goddesses, some religions also venerate saints, sages, and heroes, but these are not equal to the supreme deities, although their popular appeal may challenge a high god's supremacy.

The Chinese objects of worship, conveniently called the Chinese pantheon, are a complex matter. Several distinct religious organizations have existed in China, and each had its own set of deities to be worshipped. Often there has been mutual competition and/or mutual absorption. Buddhist cult objects made their way into the folk tradition, and what started as a popular cult object was eventually claimed by Taoism or by the official state religion.

In spite of this confusion, a discussion of the Taoist pantheon is possible. In view of what has been said about the distinction between Taoist philosophy and the Taoist religion (see **Introduction**), it is obvious that the former does not have any gods to worship. The highest reality, the Tao, is an impersonal presence in the universe; it is the universe and is therefore not an object of worship. What we call the Taoist pantheon falls completely under the category of the Taoist religion.

For the sake of clarity, three aspects of the Taoist pantheon will be discussed: first, the appropriation of ancient nature deities by the Taoist religion; second, the creation of what are purely Taoist deities, especially during the Han and Five Dynasties periods; third, the overlap between Taoist and popular deities.

• *Taoist Appropriation of Ancient Nature Deities*

Since very early times, probably during the Shang, the Chinese worshipped several forces of nature, which were personified as distinct and conscious deities (see also **Nature Deities**). Such were the gods controlling the weather, and the gods of geographically important locations or elements. Although these deities existed in the royal and popular cults before Taoism, later Taoists have adopted them as their own and systematized them after the imperial administration model. The celestial "Weather Ministry" included the gods of thunder and lightning, of rain and fire, as well as the gods of the five mountain peaks. Among the fertility gods figure the dragons who control rainfall and harvests, as well as the gods of the soil. Other ministries included the gods of literature, of wealth, of epidemics, medicine, and exorcism. "Each [had] its own presiding officer, with his assistants and his army of subordinates, as earthly ministries had in imperial times" (Maspero, 1981: 92).

Other ancient deities taken over by later Taoism are Szu-ming/Si-ming (**Director of Destiny**, god of the furnace or stove) (Welch, 1957: 100) and San-Kuan (**Three Officials**). Yet, being incorporated into the Taoist divine hierarchy did not stop the people from worshipping them as their own as well. (The problem of the relationship of Taoist and popular pantheon will be resumed below.)

• *The Pantheon Created by Taoism*

The earliest known alchemists and *fang-shih* (magicians) operating during the Western Han, worshipped Szu-ming and introduced a new deity, whose worship they strongly recommended to Han Emperor

Wu: This deity was **T'ai-yi** (Supreme Unity or Supreme Oneness), probably a personification of a metaphysical concept. (The "One" occupies an important place in the *TTC*.) During the Han, he was considered to reside in the pole star, and Emperor Wu worshipped him in his search for immortality.

Soon after the introduction of T'ai-yi, another alchemist, Miu Chi, expanded this cult into the worship of the **Three Ones** (San-yi): T'ai-yi (Supreme Oneness), T'ien-yi (Heavenly Oneness), and Ti-yi (Earthly Oneness). These play an important role in later Taoist worship and ideology, as they relate to the three centers in the human body.

The early alchemists had a special cult for Szu-ming, not only **Director of Destiny**, but also controller of the alchemical furnace. Further, among the Huang-Lao Taoists flourishing during the Western Han, the first distinctly Taoist deities rose to eminence: the culture hero Huang-ti, or **Yellow Emperor**, and the deified *TTC* author **Lao-tzu** or Lao-chün.

The Heavenly Master movement in the second century CE took over the worship of Lao-tzu, who eventually was called **T'ai-shang Lao-chün**, and reintroduced the worship of the Three Officials (*san-kuan*) in their liturgy.

During the Six Dynasties period, when new Taoist movements arose, a proliferation of gods and goddesses took place that Welsh called "mass-production" (Welsh 1957). Buddhist prototypes of bodhisattvas and the supreme model of the *Trikaya* (Triple "Body" or "Modes of Being" of the Buddha) may have been at work here, but the Taoists outdid their model in sheer numbers of new deities. Foremost among them was a new triad and the deities inhabiting the human body.

The new triad, parallel to the San-yi, was headed by Yuan-shih T'ien-tsun (Heavenly Venerable of the Original Beginning), flanked by Ling-pao T'ien-tsun (Heavenly Venerable of the Numinous Treasure) and Tao-te T'ien-tsun (Heavenly Venerable of Tao and Te), another title of the deified **Lao-tzu**. (That Buddhist inspiration was involved here can be inferred from the expression *T'ien-tsun*; the Buddha was often titled *Ti-tsun*, World-Honored One.) A popular equivalent of this triad is found in another triad: the "**Three Pure Ones**" (San-ch'ing), including Yü-ch'ing (Jade Purity), Shang-ch'ing (Upper or High Purity), and T'ai-ch'ing (Supreme Purity). These three supreme gods are believed to reside in the three heavens of the same name.

The gods of the body are a creation of the inner meditation school of early medieval Taoism: Their names and description are found in scriptures created by the Shang-ch'ing school, and must be memorized by Taoist adepts who strive for perfection. This view of the body is literally staggering. The body is divided into three "fields of energy" (*tan-t'ien*), each presided over by one member of the **Three Ones.** In each of the three parts of the body, there are 12,000 deities for a total of 36,000. They are also the gods who control the outside cosmos, thus making the human body a microcosm, a small replica of the cosmos. The gods' presence in the body and their cultivation are crucial for the adept's spiritual progress.

Besides these mostly mythical deities, Taoism also created a whole range of "human" gods, rather legendary or heroic human beings, sages or saints, and "immortals" (to be compared with the Buddhist "saints" or arhats). But they also honored their truly human saints, historical persons, such as founders of new schools. As could be expected, **Chang Tao-ling** is the foremost example, but later personalities include Wang Ch'ung-yang and Ch'iu Ch'u-chi (both of the Complete Realization School), and Chang San-feng, who is credited with the creation of *T'ai-chi* exercises.

• *Taoist and Popular Deities.* The problem of overlap and confusion between both groups is only one symptom of the overall confusion between Taoism and the Popular religion of China. The problem is aggravated by the fact that the Chinese people themselves do not make clear distinctions in this regard. They easily identify the Popular religion as Taoism. Rather than studying all the deities of the Chinese pantheon one by one, which would be an endless process, we can make general statements about some of the more important gods/goddesses in question. Besides the specifically Taoist deities, there are a number of deities that are "shared" by the Taoists, by the Popular religion, and sometimes by sectarian associations and the state. Sometimes one hears one group claim them as their own.

• Shared deities of rather mythic origin, or personifications of nature, or star deities:

- Gods of the five mountain peaks
- Gods of hells
- Gods of the "weather bureau," including fertility gods, dragons, protectors of the local soil (T'u-ti-kung)
- Star gods: Hsuan-t'ien Shang-Ti (Chen-wu), K'ui-hsing, and Wen-ch'ang (gods of literature)

• Shared deities who are historic human beings, whose biographies have developed into hagiographies:

- Kuan-kung or Kuan-ti, often called Kuan-sheng Ti-chün
- Ma-tsu, or T'ien-hou or T'ien-shang Sheng-mu (Holy Mother in Heaven)

- Hsi-wang-mu (Queen Mother of the West), today also named Yao-ch'ih Chin-mu (Golden Mother of the Jasper Pool)
- Pao-sheng Ta-ti (Great Lord Protecting Life)
- Huang-ti (**Yellow Emperor**), more mythical than historic
- Fu-yu Ti-chün, or Lü-tsu, (Lü Tung-pin, foremost among the **Eight Immortals**)

- Deities shared by the state cult and the Popular religion:

- Kuan-kung (see above)
- Ch'eng-huang (city god)

Gods and goddesses, as well as mythical heroes, saints, and immortals, have a protective function in the minds of the people. They also serve as symbols of what is spiritually possible, they encourage one's own efforts toward perfection. For the Taoist adept, the "gods of meditation" are essential in the pursuit of longevity-immortality.

In their liturgy, especially during the *chiao* celebration, Taoist priests worship their own set of gods, which are mostly beyond the scope of popular worship. As a preparation of the great renewal liturgy, they bring their own scrolls of Taoist deities and hang them up on the north wall of the temple, temporarily replacing the temple's deities.

Foremost are the members of the Taoist supreme triad: the Three Heavenly Venerables, or **Three Pure Ones**. On their left side (right side when one faces the altar) is a scroll of Yü-huang Ta-ti (**Jade Emperor**); on their right is the picture of Tzu-wei Ta-ti, Lord of the North Star, sometimes identified as T'ai-yi. Besides these two deities flanking the triad, there sometimes are two more: Chang Tao-ling on the left; Hsuan-t'ien Shang-ti on the right. Opposite to the triad, on the southern wall of the temple, there is the altar of the **Three Officials**, but usually there are no scrolls of them. Most of these deities are worshipped by Taoist priests, but, except for the Jade Emperor and Hsuan-t'ien Shang-ti they are ignored by the common people.

Two final remarks are in order: first, it is obvious from the above description, that many Taoist deities, especially the body gods and goddesses, are impersonal; they have no history, their titles are more important than their names (Robinet, 1991: 24–25). Second, in the Taoist liturgy, the priests are faced with two distinct types of gods: those who must be worshipped and prayed to (the higher ones) and those who can be commanded by them to do their bidding. To enable them to do this, the priests must memorize the gods' names and descriptions as they are recorded in special registers (*lu*). This is an eloquent example of the magico-religious nature of Chinese religion.

PAO-CHUAN See *PRECIOUS SCROLLS*

PAO-P'U-TZU/BAOPUZI. This is the title of a book on **alchemy** written in 317 by **Ko Hung** (283–343/63 CE), who is usually associated with Southern Taoism, but because the identification of alchemy as Taoist is questionable, one may also question Ko Hung's status as a Taoist. His intent was rather "to demonstrate that the pursuit of immortality is a fitting goal for upstanding gentlemen (i.e., for Confucians). Ko actually was not a representative of any form of 'Taoism': he repudiated the classical Taoists and had no use for the T'ien-shih Taoists. He is thus best characterized as "a maverick Confucian" (R. Kirkland, "Historical Outline" of the Taoist Tradition).

Ko Hung is often called, after the title of his book, *Pao-p'u-tzu*, the "master who holds on to *p'u*," almost always translated as "the master who embraces simplicity." But because *p'u* does not just mean "simplicity," this is an unsatisfactory translation (see **p'u**). It is more accurate to translate it as "the master who holds on to wholeness."

The book is divided into an inner and an outer section. The former consists of 20 chapters dealing with alchemical formulas and methods to nourish life and attain longevity; it further lists talismans to protect against evil spirits and avoid calamities. This section is classified as Taoist. The second section, on the other hand, has been classified as Confucian: it consists of 50 chapters, that deal with social and political issues.

The inner chapters contain a discussion of theories on "spirit-immortals" since the Warring States period, from which a systematic theory about immortals is constructed. This section further continues **Wei Po-yang's** theories on alchemical purification; it lists and describes up to 282 kinds of spirit-talismans and contains philosophical discussions about concepts such as "mystery" (*hsuan*), *Tao*, "oneness" (*yi*). It answers questions concerning the origin and end of the universe.

The outer chapters express the author's social and political thinking, particularly his ideal of being a "Taoist inside" (*nei-Tao*) and a "Confucian outside," in action (*wai-Ru*). It shows the intimate connection between the Taoist system of immortalism and Confucian ethical values.

(The *Pao-p'u-tzu* is contained in the *Tao-tsang*, CT 1185 & 1187. For a partial English translation, see Sailey, 1978. See also **Uncarved Wood**.)

PAO-SHENG TA-TI/BAOSHENG DADI ("Great Emperor Who Protects Life"). Listed as a "Taoist God," it is more correct to consider him a member of the community pantheon. Historical sources state that he was born in T'ung-an/Tong'an county in Fukien province during the Sung dynasty. He became a medical doctor of great repute, who once "cured an empress of the Sung dynasty, as well as a tiger whose throat was obstructed by the bones of a woman he had eaten. The grateful tiger became a guardian spirit [in his] temples after [he] had been deified" (Thompson, 1996: 60).

Stories of his miracle cures circulated among the Fukien people, and when a large number immigrated to Taiwan in the 17th and 18th centuries, they took with them images of Pao-sheng Ta-ti and established his cult in their new settlements. Although his cult, unlike Ma-tsu's, remained local, his level of prestige and his reputation in Taiwan remain high today. A recent survey lists 162 temples dedicated to him, mostly located in Southern Taiwan (*TMSC*: 443–454). In some of his temples, one can still find "medical divination slips." People select a numbered bamboo stick, approved by the deity, and accordingly receive a printed prescription, which can be filled in one of the neighborhood drugstores. Diseases are divided into man's and woman's diseases, children's diseases, and eye diseases. The use of this type of "divination for healing" is slowly diminishing in Taiwan.

There is an interesting legend about Pao-sheng Ta-ti. It is said that in real life he knew Ma-tsu as a young girl, fell in love with her, and wanted to marry her, but she refused. As a result, he fostered a long-lasting grudge against her: On his birthday (15th of third lunar month), she makes the wind blow his ceremonial hat off; on her birthday (23rd of third lunar month), he makes sure it rains on her new dress!

PAO-YI See HOLD ON TO ONENESS

PEACH See PLANT SYMBOLISM

P'ENG-LAI/PENGLAI. Land of Taoist Immortals, one of the three mysterious and mythical islands (the others are Ying-chou and K'un-lun) said to be located opposite the northeastern coast of the Eastern Sea. It measures 5,000 li in circumference.

It is the central axis of the Nine Heavens of the Heavenly Emperor (T'ien-ti) and thus very precious. After the Great Yü in ancient times had controlled the floods, he went there to pay tribute to Shang-ti (*CMTT*: 248).

In Taoist lore, P'eng-lai is also the island where the "magic mushroom" or *ling-chih* grows. The **First Emperor of China** sent an expedition there to bring him that plant of deathlessness, but they did not return. P'eng-lai became a symbol of a happy paradise.

PERFECTED See *HSIEN*

PINE See PLANT SYMBOLISM

PLANT SYMBOLISM. Many plants (trees or flowers) are found in Chinese folklore as symbolic expressions of cultural values. That is a phenomenon found in other cultures as well: Everyone knows that the rose symbolizes love, and the lily, purity. The Chinese symbols focus on different values, and the Taoists in particular are fond of symbolism. Among the many flora symbols, only six are chosen here: pine, bamboo, gourd, jujube, peach, and magic mushroom.

• *Pine*: Because this is a tree that grows old, it was a natural candidate to symbolize longevity (and immortality). It is often found in the company of the crane (see **Animal Symbolism**) and the magic mushroom. Pine trees grew in abundance on mountains chosen as retreats by Taoist practitioners, and pine seeds were one of the chosen foods for Taoists who were selective in their diet (see Eberhard, 1986: 237–8).

• *Bamboo*: Another symbol cherished in China. Together with the pine tree, the bamboo is a favorite theme in poetry and painting. It also has been an extremely useful material for making dozens of utensils and furniture; and bamboo shoots are a delicious dish.

The symbolic value of bamboo is twofold: It is an evergreen and, hence, a symbol of old age. Because it is hollow inside, it symbolizes the "empty heart," which is modesty, a most appropriate Taoist symbol (see Eberhard: 28–30).

• *Gourd* or *calabash*: Belongs to a plant family that includes squash, melon, pumpkin, etc. Also called bottle gourd. In the Taoist tradition, the gourd or calabash, in its ornamental variety (not edible), is a cherished symbol, especially the "double gourd" (*hu-lu*), which has the appearance of two globes joined together. It was seen as a symbol of the union of yin and yang, or of heaven and earth, and therefore considered a good omen.

In Taoist mythology, the gourd is related to **chaos** and is seen as an image of "a closed embryonic state," or a state of being before heaven and earth were separated (N. Girardot, 1983: 179).

The gourd used to be a favorite emblem on traditional silver amulets worn around the neck, similar to the many other kinds worn to bring good luck and to protect from evil (see A. Cohen in J. Pas, 1989). Today, double gourds are still attractive souvenirs; they are painted, inscribed with good luck characters, varnished, and offered for sale at many souvenir stands near popular temples in Taiwan. Besides the hoped-for good luck, they are also decorative.

• *Jujube*: An edible, datelike fruit growing in warm climates. Some

Taoist practitioners, intent on inner visualization, followed a strict diet by avoiding the five grains and excluding meat and alcohol. Food items recommended were limited. "Some got down to eating nothing but jujubes" (H. Welch, 1957: 108). Others fed on breath and saliva or preferred the seeds of pine cones (see also **Diet**).

• *Peach*: Both the tree (its wood) and the fruit have symbolic value in Taoism. The wood is of *yang* essence and has the power of exorcism. Taoist priests use peach wood in some of their ritual instruments. As a fruit, the peach symbolizes longevity and immortality. Legend has it that the **Queen Mother of the West** has a peach orchard in the K'un-lun mountains and invites gods and immortals to a banquet when the fruit ripens (see Eberhard: 227–228).

• *Magic Mushroom*: Called *ling-chih* (numinous plant), but considered to be the plant of deathlessness. According to legend, it grows on the mysterious islands of the East, such as ***P'eng-lai***, and several emperors hoped to find it and become immortal. The *ling-chih* has been compared with hallucinogenic mushrooms in other cultures and with the soma plant used during Vedic sacrifices in ancient India. A sort of fungus, popularly called *ling-chih*, grows in some mountain areas of Taiwan, and is sought for its medicinal value (as a tonic, etc.). The *ling-chih* is often found as an art motif in Chinese paintings and sculpture.

P'O See "SOUL"

POPULAR RELIGION and **TAOISM.** Within the various streams of China's spiritual tradition, the Taoist religious stream and that of the Popular religion are running close together and are often confused. The major reason for this confusion is the lack of precision with regard to the essence of each of them. Yet, confusion can be avoided: Both the Taoist religion (hereafter named "Taoism"), and the Chinese Popular religion (hereafter abbreviated as CPR) can be defined in such a way that their particular natures become clear, even if some overlap is unavoidable.

The Taoist religion—as it exists today and during late imperial times—is a social institution with its own priesthood (either married clergy or monastics), its own scriptures, its own liturgy, sometimes its own temples and monasteries. But they do not have any significant constituency or community of believers. The monastic Taoists pursue a life of spiritual cultivation in a monastic setting (they meditate, study the scriptures, perform liturgies, etc.), striving for immortality, whereas the married Taoists, the majority, do not live in communities; they are family men or "fire-dwellers" having their own home shrine (*t'an*), but, although they do not have a "congregation," their services are available to all: individuals and communities. In general, their goals are to bring divine blessings down to earth, to ensure happiness and a peaceful existence during this life. This description of what Taoism is today makes it clear that Taoism is essentially an institutional priesthood: The great majority of the people are not Taoist believers, although in their religious conceptions, Taoist (as well as Buddhist and Confucian) elements are present.

The CPR is the religion of the Chinese people in general. It is a religious system that contains some beliefs, but is essentially expressed in ritual. The major aspects of ritual are the family (or clan) religion of the ancestor cult, and the community rituals centering around the community temples. Those temples are built and run by the community, which, for special occasions, may invite ritual specialists, Taoists or Buddhists, and others, such as mediums and fortune-tellers.

If one includes in the practices of the people more specialized techniques or rituals, such as *feng-shui*, divination, etc., it becomes clear that the word "Popular" in CPR is not accurate any longer. Many (most?) of those practices, as well as those mentioned above, also are shared by the cultural elite (for example, the emperors of China practiced *feng-shui* and followed the yearly calendar of festivals, etc.). In that case, the word "Popular" should be replaced by "Communal": a much wider term, making the Communal Religion of China the true universal religious system of that country. The term "communal" includes all levels of society, but excludes the elite minorities (Buddhism, Taoism, and, in imperial times, the state cult), although among all of them and the Communal religion there has always been mutual interaction.

Once the problem of identities is settled, one can usefully look back into the past to discover how Taoism and the CPR related to each other. There are several clues:

• The CPR existed *before* Taoism. One may call it the ancient matrix, going back to prehistoric times, and eventually giving birth to two daughters: Confucianism and Taoism. The first Taoist religious movement started in the second century CE with the Heavenly Masters School. It adopted many aspects of the ancient religion (shamanism), but also reacted against some of its excesses, such as blood sacrifices.

• During the medieval period (Disunity to T'ang), the relationship between Taoism and the CPR is not clearly defined. Both Buddhism and Taoism appealed to the people and to the imperial house, but Buddhism more so than Taoism (merely looking at the statistics, Buddhism on average was ten times stronger than Taoism). Among the population, some uprisings took place, inspired by Taoist messianism, but official Taoism did not support them, as they favored the support of and by the imperial court.

• The CPR seemed to have come into its own during the Sung period. Although some emperors strongly favored Taoism, it is not known whether this had any major effect on the population.

• In modern times (starting with the late Ch'ing), Taoism and Buddhism were in decline. The CPR and villages became stronger and gained some kind of independence. Many townships constructed community temples, in which they enthroned deities of their own choice (not necessarily Taoist or Buddhist deities). Those community temples, in contrast with other temples run by Taoists, Buddhists or the state, became the centers of community worship, but there were usually no resident priests. However, Taoists and Buddhists continued to serve the spiritual needs of the people, either from their own shrines or monasteries or by invitation in the community temples. Besides them, there are a fairly large number of spiritual practitioners, having a loose organizational relationship with the communities, which they do not administer, but to whom they offer their services (comparable to today's doctors and lawyers, etc.). In other words, the CPR has become independent in its administrative organization, while still availing itself of the spiritual services offered to them by specialists.

• According to the above interpretation, the boundaries or areas of governance between Taoism and the CPR are fairly clear. Confusion occurs because of incorrect identifications. Practical errors have been made by the people themselves, by modern Taoist organizations, and by scholars. Very often, aspects of the Chinese worldview and practice are called "Taoist" erroneously. Examples are the **Yin-Yang Worldview** and the **Five Agents System**: they are essentially Chinese, not Taoist, although Taoism has incorporated them. **Outer alchemy** and Chinese medicine have been called "Taoist," but that again is highly questionable, although Taoists also have engaged in these fields. Organizational ambition often encourages the use of wrong labels. An example is the Taiwan Taoist Association, which has recruited memberships from all interested temple committees, many of the Popular religion. In a great number of large or small temples, one can see the plaque of Taoist Association membership on the temple wall, although these temples are not strictly Taoist. Because the CPR does not have a clear name, it is tempting to affiliate themselves with an organized religious body and thus find their own identity.

If it happens to temples, it also happens to deities worshipped in them. Among the most popular gods worshipped in Taiwan (and elsewhere) today are **Ma-tsu** and **Kuan-kung**, often named "Taoist" deities. This also is incorrect: They are deities of the community religion. There are more examples, and several have been discussed in this volume, although they do not strictly belong here.

Another example of confusion, caused by the Taoists themselves, is the compilation of the **Taoist Canon**. As N. Sivin (1978) pointed out, the *Tao-tsang* is sometimes appealed to in order to prove the oneness of Taoism (as against its multiplicity). That is a false argument: the collectors and compilers of the scriptures were not very discriminating. Included in the Ming edition of the canon are many writings that are not Taoist at all, but the compilers found them "useful" enough to include them. Examples are the text of the Chinese philosopher Mo-tzu (Sivin, 1978: 32), a number of texts that belong to the popular religion (K. Schipper, 1994), and at least seven texts of temple oracles (M. Kalinowski, 1989–90: 85–114).

Other texts must be analyzed and reevaluated (those on **alchemy**, medicine, breathing exercises, etc.); they are not Taoist just because they are included in the **Taoist Canon**.

Some Western or Eastern scholars, in their enthusiasm for Taoism, tend to overstress the importance of Taoism and put on the Taoist "plate" a large number of practices ("dishes") that are shared by all. Some have hardly anything to do with Taoism (for example, M. Saso's little volume on "Taoist" rites of passage. There is hardly anything Taoist in them. See M. Saso, 1990). There may be economic reasons behind this phenomenon. During late imperial and republican times, Taoist priests had to make a living, which was sometimes very difficult. As a result, they would learn and include in their repertoire various popular techniques and rituals that would appeal to the people and increase their revenues. That is a good excuse indeed, but it confused the various identities.

To conclude, Taoism today is not the religion of the Chinese people (it never was), but Taoist ideas have infiltrated the popular worldview, and Taoist practitioners provide their specialist services to community and individuals (see also A. Seidel, 1989–90: 283–286; R. Stein in Welch & Seidel, 1979: 53–81).

POWER See *TE*

PRECIOUS SCROLLS (*Pao-chuan/Baojuan*). A genre of popular Chinese literature, usually written in the vernacular, that are perhaps the precursors of the contemporary **morality texts** (*shan-shu*). Most *pao-chuan* are claimed to be given by revelation, and are produced within sectarian groups, such as the White Lotus Society during imperial times, or the Compassion Society and Yi-kuan-tao in contemporary Taiwan. Precious scrolls discuss religious topics from a Taoist,

Buddhist, or Popular religious viewpoint, and often blend the teachings. These texts are comparable to *ching* (scripture) in that they are revealed by divine beings, very often by means of automatic writing. The content of *pao-chuan* may vary considerably: They can be narratives, often placed in a sectarian setting, they may also focus on salvation or eschatology, or just preach ethical values from a Buddhist, Taoist, or Confucian standpoint.

Like the *shan-shu*, the precious scrolls have drawn the attention of modern scholars of religion, and collectors. They are also discussed in books on Chinese literature, as a particular type of popular literature.

PRIESTHOOD. The terms "priesthood" and "priest" have a wide range of meanings in the various religious traditions of the world. Although applying more strictly to the Judaeo-Christian traditions, the words have been also used in other religious systems, such as Buddhism and Taoism. In the Judaeo-Christian context, priesthood refers essentially to sacrificial or cultic duties, but in the course of time also appropriated other responsibilities, such as the ministry of the word and administrative duties (see the various articles on "priesthood" in *ER*: 11).

The terms "Taoist priesthood" and "Taoist priest" are Western approximations of a Chinese phenomenon, which does not fully coincide with the Western equivalents. (Buddhist "priesthood," again, is another case of using the same terminology with a different content.)

Within the Chinese religious tradition, there is a great variety of spiritual functions and functionaries, which all have religious meaning, although most cannot be considered as "priests" in the technical sense. Taoist priesthood is a category that is very different from other Chinese religious specialists, such as mediums, diviners, ritual masters (*fa-shih*), etc. Taoist priests share one essential characteristic with Judaeo-Christian priests in that their function is essentially ritual. Taoist priests perform rituals for the benefit of the community. Some of those rituals are exorcistic (removal or prevention of evil influences), but others are definitely more positive in that they are intended to bring down divine blessings into the community. (See also **Cosmic Renewal Festival**.)

There are various types of Taoist priests, each type having its own function and chosen set of goals. First, one can distinguish monastic Taoists from secular Taoists. The former live in a communal, monastic setting, are celibate, and strive toward spiritual perfection removed from the world. They may also perform ritual functions for the community, but that is more a sideline of their vocation. They could be compared to Christian monastics (for example Benedictines) whose primary goal is the pursuit of their own spiritual perfection. Ritual services are more or less accidental. Today's monastic Taoists belong mainly to the **Complete Realization Order**, with its major temple, Pai-yün kuan, in Beijing.

The secular Taoist priests live within the community that they serve as ritual specialists. They are called "fire-dwellers" (which means they are married), and their profession used to be hereditary, although in today's economically affluent society (especially in Taiwan), sons do not always wish to follow in their fathers' footsteps.

Among the secular Taoists, one can further distinguish two main groups: official and nonofficial Taoists. These terms are perhaps ambiguous and inaccurate, and need clarification, but are better than "orthodox" and "heterodox." "Official" Taoists are also called "**Blackhead**" **Taoists**, as opposed to the "**Redhead**" popular Taoists.

The Blackhead Taoists of today are members of the **Heavenly Masters School**: The term "official" does not mean government-approved, but refers to a higher more respectable status, and their ability to perform the elaborate rituals of the Chiao festival. The Redheads, on the other hand, are popular functionaries. They are more like the ancient shamans, curing disease and performing various kinds of exorcisms. They are able to perform many rituals both for the dead and the living, but are excluded from enacting the *chiao* liturgy.

In today's society (again mainly referring to Taiwan, where both groups are still very active) Blackheads and Redheads often cooperate, but there is also competition among them. Both types focus on ritual services. Their mission is not to instruct or to be administrators. Formal religious instruction is almost nonexistent in Chinese society (unless one thinks of public lectures organized by Buddhists and sectarian temples, and the mass circulation of religious pamphlets). This is reflected in the training of Taoist priests. Both Blackheads and Redheads start as apprentices of established masters (called *Tao-chang*, in contrast to the more general title, *Tao-shih*, "gentlemen of the Tao," which applies to ordinary priests). They are trained on the spot, in the office of the master or in temples of the community where the master is invited to function on occasion. Training starts with learning to play the ritual musical instruments: metal gong, two-stringed violin (*er-hu*), oboe, and drum. Gradually, apprentices make their way through the various ranks of assistants in the rituals, first as incense attendant (*chih-hsiang*) and group leader (*yin-pan*); next as assistant cantor (*fu-chiang*) and chief cantor (*tu-chiang*). They learn to chant or recite the liturgical scriptures and to perform the various rituals, some of which are rather complex. They are further trained in copying the ritual texts used in the liturgy (they must practice calligraphy) and in copying the standard Taoist sets of **talismans** (*fu*) needed in the liturgy or requested by individuals for various personal needs.

Although some masters add theoretical instruction to the practical on-the-spot training (an example is Master Chuang, reported by Michael Saso, 1978), emphasis on Taoist doctrine seems rather limited in the training of young Taoists. One can often see an expensive bookcase in a master's office with a complete set of the printed *Tao-tsang*, but the case is usually locked! There appears to be a greater interest in Taoist learning among the laity than among the clergy, except on mainland China, where young Taoist candidates, male and female, must attend training sessions in so-called Taoist seminaries (such as are held periodically at the White Cloud Monastery in Beijing). There is no equivalent to this in Taiwan, the reason probably being the exclusive focus of the Taoist clergy on the liturgy.

When the period of apprenticeship is finished, young candidates may apply for ordination. One type of ordination is performed by the current Heavenly Master himself. The candidate, who has copied the ritual texts of his master for his own future use, must present gifts to the master (red envelopes today) and is invested with the powers of priesthood in a special ceremony. The handing over of the seal of office and the ritual texts belong to the essence of ordination. Candidates, moreover, receive an official document as proof of their ordination. From now on, they are entitled to perform rituals independently, they may set up their own home office or shrine (*t'an*), but often continue to assist their master in the more elaborate rituals of the *chiao*.

Although in older times (T'ang and Sung periods) Taoist ranks of priesthood were elaborate, there seems to be little evidence of this today. The only common ranks are *tao-shih* (Taoist priest) and the more dignified title of *tao-chang* (Taoist high priest). It is said that to become a *tao-chang* today (at least in Taiwan), one must perform the rite of "climbing the sword-ladder," which is most likely a remnant of an ancient shamanistic ritual.

P'U See UNCARVED WOOD

PURE CONVERSATION (*Ch'ing-t'an/Qingtan*). A branch movement of **Neo-Taoism** during the third and fourth centuries CE (the other branch is called **Mystery Learning** or *hsuan-hsueh*: It engaged in metaphysical discourse). The *Ch'ing-t'an* branch, by contrast, is considered sentimentalist, even romantic. It started during the closing years of the Han dynasty, when scholars were often persecuted. This situation discouraged them and made them turn away from the political arena to find refuge in freedom.

In order to escape from such intolerable conditions, the men of letters took refuge in poetry, music, wine, or excursions into the Taoist realms of nonbeing. The *Ch'ing-t'an* movement was, therefore, a way of life, tinged with romanticism, in which the followers strove to develop the art of conversation to its highest point; such conversations were in the form of philosophic dialogues or subtle repartee, expressed in the best language and most precise phrases, and held between friends of comparable tastes and intellectual attainments. (K. Ch'en, 1957: 38)

If one remembers the special interest in "nonverbal" communication found in the *TTC* and the *Chuang-tzu,* one starts wondering whether the meaning of *ch'ing* (pure) in *ch'ing-t'an* possibly refers to silence, because

At times, the participants understood each other so well that they just remained silent. (Ch'en: 38)

Indeed, the highest "purity" of conversation is nonconversation, as the *TTC* expresses: "The Sage spreads his teaching without words" (Chapter 2: 9). *Chuang-tzu* makes the same point in a more fascinating way: Four old gentlemen met for conversation and said:

"Who can look upon non-being as his head, on life as his back, and on death as his rump? . . ."

"Who knows that life and death . . . are all a single body? I will be his friend."

The four men looked at each other and smiled . . . [They] became friends.

(*Chuang-tzu*, Chapter 6—Watson, 1970: 84)

A more amusing and paradoxical passage is this:

Words exist because of meaning; once you've gotten the meaning, you can forget the words. Where can I find a man who has forgotten words so I can have a word with him? (*Chuang-tzu,* Chapter 26, Watson: 302).

Is this not conversation at its purest?
(See also **Seven Sages of the Bamboo Grove.**)

PURE TENUITY SCHOOL See CH'ING-WEI SCHOOL

PURIFICATION FAST See *CHAI*

PURITY AND TRANQUILLITY SCRIPTURE (*Ch'ing-ching ching/ Quingjingjing*). The title of a very short (only 391 characters) but popular Taoist text of unknown authorship, but dating from the first half of the T'ang dynasty. It is included in the **Taoist Canon** (*CT* 620; *TT* 341) under the full title of *T'ai-shang Lao-chün shuo ch'ang ch'ing-ching miao-ching*, also abbreviated as *Ch'ing-ching miao-ching*. Several commentaries were written on it, the earliest by **Tu Kuang-t'ing**; others by **Pai Yü-ch'an** of the Sung dynasty and Li Tao-ts'un of the Yuan period.

Because the present text has a postface written by **Ko Hsuan**, he is sometimes considered to be the author. But because of inner criticism (analysis of the contents) it is quite certain that the small scripture could not have been written before the Six Dynasties. The main argument is heavy reliance on Buddhist ideas.

The main theme is how to gain "purity" (*ch'ing*) and "tranquillity" (*ching*). If a person's mind is able to rid itself of all desires, the mind will become tranquil; if the mind can be settled, the spirit will spontaneously become clean. Then the six desires will not arise, and the three poisons will be destroyed. Through inner vision into one's mind, one realizes the no-mind; through outer vision of the body, one realizes the no-body; by looking at things from a distance, one realizes the no-thing condition. If one understands these three, one only sees "emptiness" as the nature of reality; then all delusions and defilements disappear and one reaches the state of everlasting purity and tranquility.

This short text, as popular among Taoists as the *Heart Sutra* among the Buddhists, is often used in recitation, and is still often reprinted for free distribution, together with a short commentary. It is important in Taoist spirituality.

Q

QUEEN MOTHER OF THE WEST (Hsi Wang-mu/Xiwang Mu). An important Taoist goddess whose roots go back to the Han dynasty, and even before, as her name is mentioned in the *Chuang-tzu* (Chapter 6, Watson: 82), and possibly even in the Shang oracle bone inscriptions.

Her paradise is situated in the K'un-lun mountains in the far southwest of China: There, she has an orchard of peach trees, which need 3,000 years to mature. Then she invites deities and immortals to a banquet; eating the peach fruit confers or confirms immortality. Her paradise is one of the abodes of the Immortals (***Hsien***).

In the mid-20th century, a sectarian movement arose in Taiwan, "The Compassion Society," which worships the Queen Mother in her contemporary manifestation as "Golden Mother of the Jasper Pool," whose popular name is Wang-mu Niang-niang or Lao-mu. This sect has been growing steadily since 1950, and many splendid temples have been built for her worship. She is one of several female deities rising to prominence today. (For a detailed study of Hsi Wang-mu, see M. Loewe, 1979, Chapter 4; S. Cahill, 1993; also *ER* 6. For the study of the Golden Mother, see D. Jordan and D. Overmyer, 1986, Chapter 6.)

R

REDHEAD TAOIST (Hung-t'ou Tao-shih or Fa-shih). Refers to a group of spiritual practitioners, perhaps not truly Taoist, but often considered as such, although they are more like popular ritualists. They are active in Taiwan today, but probably originated in the Province of Fukien. They seem to be the modern heirs of the ancient shamans, at least in some of their shamanistic practices. Another group of practitioners with roots in shamanism are the contemporary trance mediums, both male and female, of which there still are thousands active in Taiwan, Hong Kong, Singapore, etc.

To gain more respectability for themselves, it seems that the Redhead Taoists love to imitate the rituals of their more "orthodox" colleagues, the **Blackhead Taoists**. They also occasionally dress in ritual garments resembling those of Blackheads. A. Cohen, who had frequent dealings with a *Fa-shih* (Master of Rites, another name for Redhead) in the Taiwan city of Tainan, reported that Mr. Lin "appears to be a Blackhead Taoist":

> It seems that he wants to convey the appearance of being a Blackhead Taoist—or at least a Taoist of higher status than the ordinary Redhead— either because of his unfulfilled aspiration to achieve such status, or because it would attract a broader clientele and higher fees, or both. (Cohen, 1992: 194–5)

From his personal contacts and observations, A. Cohen states that the Redhead Taoists perform rites of the yang-world related to the living, and some rites of the yin-world related to the dead. The former include rites of exorcism, curing of disease, dissipation of calamities (*hsiao-tsai*), consecration of images (*k'ai-kuang*), rites to improve good luck, and rites related to blessing of new homes (Cohen: 198). But the rite most often performed is "crossing over to salvation" (*ch'ao-tu*) the souls of those who died prematurely, often through a violent death. This ritual is most often performed in the Temple of the Eastern Peak (Tung-yueh chien) in Tainan city by a Redhead Taoist and a trance medium. The climax of the ritual is when the master breaks open the (paper replica of the) Citadel of Wrongful Death to release the soul from its suffering.

The ritual instruments used by a Redhead Taoist are somewhat different from those of Blackheads: sword, bell (hand-bell), horn, and whip. Blackhead Taoists also use a ritual sword for exorcism and various small handbells, but horn and whip are more properly used by the Redheads. As Cohen explains:

> The Redhead tradition asserts that their teachings and rituals originated on mythical Mount Lü (Lü-shan) where True Man Hsü Chia . . . [a young disciple of Lao-tzu and Founding Patriarch of the Lü-shan sect] taught the rituals to Three Matrons named Ch'en, Lin, and Li . . . who then propagated the teachings and rituals . . .
>
> The formal name of the Redhead tradition is Shen-hsiao (Divine Empyrean) sect; it also is commonly called the Lü-shan or San-nai [Three Matrons] sect. (Cohen: 188)

(See also **Blackhead Taoist**; for further information see Schipper, 1985; Saso, 1970 and 1974; McCreery, 1973.)

RESURRECTION. It may seem strange to include this entry in a Taoist work, but recent research into Han religion has brought up the issue. A. Seidel published an article, *"Post-Mortem* Immortality, or the Taoist Resurrection of the Body" (Seidel, 1987). A more recent article by Donald Harper is titled "Resurrection in Warring States Popular Religion" (Harper, 1994). It may come as a surprise that the idea of resurrection is not a uniquely Christian prerogative.

What is resurrection, though? *Webster's* defines it as follows: "a) a rising from the dead, or coming back to life; b) the state of having risen from the dead." But there is an additional sentence: "the Resurrection: 1. the rising of Jesus from the dead after his death and burial; 2. the rising of all the dead at the Last Judgment."

In the Western context, resurrection usually applies to Jesus alone (but is equally applicable to his mother, Mary, who soon after her death was revived and "assumed" or taken up into heaven). What is essential for a correct understanding is that a person has really died. Regaining consciousness after a period of being in a coma, or after a "near-death" experience, does not qualify. Moreover, implied in the Christian concept is a transformation of the physical body: It becomes light and subtle, can move at will, pass through walls, cannot suffer pain anymore, and is eternally alive. It is a spiritualized body. (It is difficult to know whether such a concept is meaningful or self-contradictory and merely mythical.) In any case, persons who returned to life just in their "old" bodies (like Lazarus in the gospel of

John) do not fully qualify for the state of resurrection, only for B-class resurrection.

In Taoism, some of the immortals whose stories are described in legendary accounts (and hence probably purely mythical!), qualify for the strict category of resurrection. They are the "earthly immortals," whose bodies were not yet perfectly purified at the moment of death. But after their burial, the transformation continues and soon their bodies are reawakened and rejoin their spirit to live eternally in some earthly abode of the blessed. When their coffin is reopened, it is found empty, except for a few objects of personal use: a sandal, a sword, or a piece of clothing. (See also **Body Liberation**.)

These immortals may sometimes appear among humans and are reported to be compassionate, but mostly they are invisible, out of reach of mere humans. The extraordinary qualities of their transformed bodies are described in the scriptures (see, for instance, I. Robinet, 1979/1993: 42–48). In general, they are comparable to the glorified state of the post-resurrection Christ.

The interesting case of "resurrection" discussed by D. Harper is, after the fashion of Lazarus, only a B-class resurrection. A man named Tan had stabbed someone and thereupon killed himself. He was buried according to custom, but after three years, he was restored to life. No sage called him to exit from the grave. It was purely a bureaucratic decision communicated between the authorities of this world and the netherworld. But this man's body had not been transformed and glorified; to the contrary, he had a scar on his throat (mark of his suicide by sword) and "his four limbs were useless" (Harper, 1994: 14). This is an interesting case, different from later stories about the revival of near-dead persons, who had died because of a bureaucratic error and eventually were returned to life. But these persons had not been completely dead yet, so resurrection is not involved here. (See also *Hsien*.)

REVERSAL (*fan*) and **RETURN (*fu*)**. The character *fan*, meaning "to turn over, to rebel, to turn back," is often confused with *fu*, which means "to return, to repeat." Both characters occur in the *TTC* in connection with some action of Tao. Example:

> Reversion (*fan*) is the action of Tao.
> Weakness (*jo*) is the function of Tao.
> (Chapter 40: 1–2, Chan, 1963: 160)

This is the only instance in the *TTC* where *fan* is used; there are four other passages where the character *fu* occurs. Example:

> All things come into being,
> And I see thereby their return (*fu*).
> All things flourish,
> But each one returns (*fu kui*) to its root.
> (Chapter 16: 2–3, Chan: 147)

Comparing the two characters *fan* and *fu*, one sees their similarity, which is rather superficial. In a deeper sense, they express very different realities. *Fu* (or *fu-kui*) is a return to one's origin, a return from where one came, as in the biblical saying: You are dust and you will return to dust. It expresses the ephemeral nature of all beings. Created by the power of Tao, beings appear on the stage for a while, then disappear again to make room for new beings.

The term *fan*, on the other hand, expresses the idea of reversal. Things change into their opposites, winter turns into summer, day into night. This is a constant process, a characteristic of all that exists. or it is similar to the yin-yang processes: Yin becomes yang, yang again becomes yin. It is the cyclical motion of history and natural processes, with the implication that things and situations eventually change into their opposites.

Although *fan* and *fu* are different concepts, both are characteristics of the operations of Tao.

RITUAL (or Taoist Liturgy). Although there is a theoretical difference between the terms *ritual* and *liturgy,* in practice they often are used interchangeably in the context of the Taoist religion. Taoist liturgy is perhaps a more general term, encompassing the whole ritual spectrum, whereas ritual seems to signify individual rites more than the whole series. However, there is much overlap. Here the focus will be on rituals, in the sense of individual rites that do not necessarily have mutual connections. Some do not exist anymore, such as rituals of early Heavenly Masters Taoism, but have been recorded in historical reports; others are still well and alive today. This essay is not meant to be comprehensive but to give a general overview of some of the major ritual activities of the Taoists. Among *ancient rituals* will be discussed some rites of T'ai-p'ing Taoism and **Heavenly Masters Taoism**, both flourishing during the latter part of the second century CE. Among *modern rituals* (still performed today) are several kinds that are proper to the modern Heavenly Masters (**Blackhead Taoists**), and others, of which the **Redhead Taoists** are the specialists. Some rituals are performed by both groups. But rather than focusing on the spiritual practitioners who perform the rituals, a more useful distinction is between *rituals for the living* and *rituals for the dead*.

Rituals for the Living (Yang rites). Performed by Taoist practitioners (Blackhead or Redhead Taoists) to pray for various blessings, to ensure good luck and peace (*ch'iu p'ing-an*), which include good health, wealth or prosperity, numerous offspring, success in career or business, longevity. Other rituals are intended to ask for forgiveness from the deities, or to avert various kinds of evil that may threaten the living. Some rituals are for the benefit of individuals or families and may take place at the Taoist's home "office" or shrine (*t'an*) or at the house of the individual(s) involved. Community-oriented (or public) rituals take place at the temple, but in ancient times also in the open, on specially erected platforms. Among the *public rituals* for the living, the following will be briefly described: the "fast of mud and soot," the rituals of the *chiao* (Community Renewal or Great Offering), and the consecration of images. (For the ritual called *ho-ch'i*, see **Union of Energies**.) Among the *private rituals*, curing disease, exorcism, blessing of homes, and various rites to improve one's luck or to attain long life are among the main types (but the list is not exhaustive and does not include wedding ceremonies, which are usually a family affair, only rarely performed by Taoist priests).

• *Fast of mud and soot* (*T'u-t'an chai*). The origin of this ritual is ancient, one of the many held by T'ai-p'ing Taoism and by the Heavenly Masters. It is like "most of these festivals, and particularly the penitence rituals . . . attributed" to the three **Chang Brothers**, chiefs of the **Yellow Turbans** (Maspero 1971/1981: 291). It was not a ritual celebrated at set times in the year, but organized occasionally. Its purpose was confession and purification from moral misbehavior, forgiveness to ward off disease and ensure a long and happy life. After days of preparation through study, prayer, and fasting, the group of individuals who signed up for the rite assembled in the sacred space set up for it, and (as described by Maspero: 385–6), with disheveled hair and face smeared with soot,

> They enter the Sacred Space . . . When all are ready, suddenly the drum resounds; the Instructor [ritual leader] chants a prayer announcing the start of the ceremony . . . twenty-four drum rolls bear the news of the festival to the highest heavens . . .
> . . . the preliminaries accomplished, there comes the chief moment of the festival, that of public repentance. The Instructor, and with him all those taking part, chants the lists of sins and the formulae of penitence, while the band gives rhythm to the recitation, first slow and calm, then more and more lively and noisy. The incense vapors make the air heavy while all, officiating elders and participants, recollect their sins as the prayers roll on and become excited, gripped by repentance and also by the terror of all the maladies that are going to pounce upon them, certain consequence of past faults. Little by little, some of the sinners become agitated, excited by the noise, the perfumes, the emotion; exaltation

seizes them, and suddenly one of them, gripped by religious enthusiasm, throws himself on the ground and starts rolling about in all directions, covering his face with dirt and lamenting. Soon those next to him imitate him, seized by the contagion; the madness grows by degrees, and soon all are sprawling on the ground in a more and more deafening uproar. The throng outside the enclosure also begins to be affected and some of them, who had come simply to watch, cast away their hats, snatch out their haircombs, let their hair fall in disorder, and they too roll on the ground. But the Instructor does not leave them in this condition for a long time, He was chosen from among the educated people, he must know his business and know that, since the ceremony is lengthy, the faithful must not be exhausted on the first day . . . After renewed prostrations, conventional gestures well known to all, a second appeal to the divinities manages to restore order after the paroxysm just preceding . . .

. . . The first session is finished. But there must be more of them at noon, and then again in the evening. The crises will recur more and more violently, as time passes and as the general exaltation, fatigue, lack of food, noise, and the demonstrations of the crowd which presses outside the enclosure stretch the nerves of all. It will begin again the following day if the participants are pious and rich, for the Fasts last two, three, seven, or even nine consecutive days, according to the wish of the devout. And all this time the participants have but a single meal per day, at noon, according to the strict Taoist rule.

This ancient ritual of confession did not survive, probably due to ritual reforms during the Southern dynasties. It is, however, a very interesting phenomenon to see the proverbially "sober and reserved" Chinese people being involved in something like a very strong revival event!

• The *Rituals of the Chiao Festival* are the contemporary remainder of another ancient liturgy, probably based on Han and pre-Han customs, but codified by **T'ao Hung-ching** and **Tu Kuang-t'ing**. Some of the important rituals have been described (see **Cosmic Renewal Festival**) and need no repetition. To witness such rituals, usually lasting three, five, or seven days, one is overwhelmed by the splendor of these colorful events, which must make a deep impression on the people and (hopefully!) on the gods themselves.

• *Consecration of Images* (*k'ai-kuang*). After an image of a deity has been made (mostly out of wood, but also out of stone, clay, metal, and, nowadays, synthetic materials), it still is a dead piece of material. It must be specially consecrated by a spiritual practitioner, either a Taoist priest, Buddhist monk or nun, a spirit-medium or a layperson (*fa-shih*). There are differences in detail, but the overall rite is very much alike in all cases.

The essential part consists of dotting the eyes, ears, nose, mouth, heart, and body of the image with red ink by using a brush. This act (similar to dotting the ancestral tablet in the Popular religion) makes the image the seat of the deity, which means that the deity is believed to be present in it, or, in other words, the image is truly alive, replenished with the god's *ling*, not just a symbol of a deity.

In Taoist rituals, if the image was carved from wood, the Taoist priests would complete the ritual with a formula of apology to the "spirit" of the tree that had been cut down for image making. This is reminiscent of *hsieh-t'u* (apology to earth) rituals when the local soil has been disturbed for temple building or digging a grave.

The *k'ai-kuang* rituals can be public or private, but mostly public, when the statues ordered for a temple are inaugurated.

• *Curing Illness*. In late Han times, the Heavenly Masters and T'ai-p'ing Taoism both performed rituals to cure disease. But because illness was seen as being caused by moral transgression, acts of repentance were a necessary condition for regaining physical health. In the process, the use of talismans (*fu*) and talismanic water (*fu-shui*) was of great importance.

In modern times, faith healing is still practiced in Taoism, but very often the emphasis is on the use of written talismans. Taoist priests have their own register of talismans, inherited from their master, copied by hand before ordination. This register includes a great variety of *fu*, many of them for healing purposes. The patient wears them or burns them to mix the ashes in a cup of water, or uses the ashes while bathing. This is a "supernatural" way to cure illness, since the talisman is basically an order issued to certain deities to expel the evil spirit who caused the disease.

• *Exorcism* is usually a private ritual, but can also involve the community. Like illness, possession is believed to be caused by external evil agents (see **Exorcism** for details).

• *Blessing of Home* is a ritual performed for individual families. The emphasis is more on exorcism (cast out evil influences) than on positive blessing, which would ideally include the invitation of good spirits or deities to descend and dwell in this particular house. It is possible that the consecration of images (see above) is some kind of home blessing.

• *Luck Improving Rites.* Chinese people in general strongly believe in the power of fate (*ming*) as shaper of one's destiny. Yet, they are not resigned to accept fate blindly. If there is a way to get around it, to "soften the blow" of merciless fate, they will certainly try it out. Taoist priests have been willing to assist them in their efforts. There are certain dangers in every person's life, which can be ritually averted. Today, at least in Taiwan, various practitioners offer their services to help people overcome dangers of a spiritual nature. Taoist priests are only one of their possible resources.

• A ritual called *hsiao-tsai/xiaozai* is now universally practiced in Taiwan. It means "cancellation of evil" and takes place around the time of the New Year (Spring Festival). Temples announce every year which persons are subject to "evil influences" (clashes with the year spirit *T'ai-sui*), usually those born in a particular year of the 12-year animal cycle. To counteract and ritually neutralize the lurking danger, special rituals are organized in temples, mostly for large crowds of people. The ritualists are Taoist priests, Buddhists, laymen or women, or mediums. Sometimes the rite is performed for individuals (see J. Pas in Tsao, 1989: 28–35).

• A related ritual, sometimes even identified with *hsiao-tsai*, but named differently, *kai-yün/gaiyun*, is performed to "improve one's luck." That may happen around the New Year, or at other times through the year, and is also performed by a variety of practitioners, usually in the temple. People who are running into a series of bad luck are most anxious to have their luck changed: it can be ritually arranged.

• A ritual named *shou-ching/shoujing* is different from the above two. The literal meaning is "to receive a fright," and is performed upon request by individuals if a person, mostly a young child, is losing his/her energy. This is explained as an attack on the child's vital spirits and if nothing is done about it, the child's health will deteriorate and may result in death. The cause is that the spirits have been "frightened" so that there is loss of appetite, loss of sleep, crying at night, etc. To counteract the evil attack, the "fright" is taken away, or "received." The ritual is performed by Taoists and other practitioners in Taiwan, most often by older women, who specialize in this technique.

• *Prayers for Longevity.* A special minor ritual performed privately for one elder person at a time by a Taoist priest (or other practitioners). As in most rituals, the substance of the rite consists of chanting a text, in this case usually the *Wonderful Scripture for the Prolongation of Life by the Northern Dipper* (*Pei-tou yen-shou miao-ching*). (There are different versions in the **Taoist Canon**: *CT* 45, *TT* 29; *CT* 622, *TT* 341.)

Rituals for the Dead (*Yin rites*). The rituals concerning "disposal of the corpse" are very complex. They involve particular rites surrounding a person's actual disease, a set of rites before, during, and after a funeral, and also memorial and mourning rites (see J. de Groot I-VI). Here only a few rituals will be discussed, rather as samples (even de Groot needed six volumes to discuss the topic in detail!).

• The *Yellow Register Fast* (*huang-lu chai*) is an early ritual performed—posthumously—to liberate the deceased from their suffering in the netherworld. Through penance on their behalf and sacrifices to the netherworld spirits, it was believed that past ancestors up to the seventh generation could be saved and gain access to heaven (see R. Malek, 1985: 200–204).

• *Funeral Rites.* To appease the deceased's spirit, weekly prayer meetings are often organized by families on the seventh, 14th, 21st, etc., day after death until the 49th day. Some families have it done after the third, fifth, and seventh week. Most often, Buddhist nuns, monks, or laypeople are invited: They chant and recite appropriate texts, such as the Pure Land scriptures. During the funeral itself, monks and nuns are usually invited to accompany the coffin to the graveyard. This is, however, also done by Taoist priests today.

The Taoists also have special rites (of exorcism?) in a case when a person died a violent death.

• *Rites of Salvation.* There is a variety of salvational rituals, depending on the time and on the circumstances of death. People who died an "unnatural" (early, violent) death are believed to be imprisoned in the netherworld and are stuck. Their souls cannot be reincarnated unless "liberation" takes place. This can be done ritually by "breaking" the gates of hell and setting the soul free (see, for example, J. Boltz, 1983). This ritual is often seen performed by Redhead Taoists in the Eastern Peak temple (Tung-yueh chien) in Tainan (Southern Taiwan). The ritual is for the benefit of individuals (it is called *ch'ao-tu*: ritual of "crossing over").

A very important community event is the *P'u-tu/pudu* ritual, either a yearly event on the 15th of the seventh (lunar) month, which is the Ghost Festival, or on the last day of a *chiao* (**Cosmic Renewal**) celebration. All families bring their offerings (food and drink) to a designated area near the temple on specially brought tables, usually in the hundreds: on the side there are sometimes hundreds of sacrificial pigs and goats, equally being offered to the main target of the rite: the souls of the "lonely dead," the hungry ghosts.

The performers of this ritual are usually Taoist priests or Buddhist monks dressed in grand robes. They number mostly seven. By chanting ritual texts of salvation and by blessing the offerings, it is believed that the ghosts can be redeemed—set free, in other words—leave the dark hells, and be reincarnated (see D. Pang, 1977; J. Lagerwey, 1987; S. Teiser, 1988).

Within the sphere of Taoist rituals of salvation, one more interesting rite should be mentioned: "ghost marriage." If a person dies young, even as a child, several years later it would have reached marriageable age. Because a normal wedding is hereby excluded, "spirit" or "ghost marriages" are sometimes arranged for the repose of their soul. A living human partner is found (for a fee), and a marriage ceremony is contracted through the services of a Redhead Taoist (very often in the above mentioned Tainan temple). The living party remains free to marry in the normal fashion.

To conclude: Taoist ritual has proven to be very complex. This essay is far from complete (a monograph on Taoist ritual would be welcome!). Some aspects of the Taoist liturgy have not been discussed, but can be found elsewhere: See **Dance**, **Music**, **Ritual Garments**, **Ritual Instruments**, **Blackhead** and **Redhead** Taoists. More information can be found in the numerous publications by K. Schipper. For rituals performed by Complete Realization Taoists in Hong Kong, see B. Tsui, 1991.

RITUAL GARMENTS. If the essence of religion consists in ritual expressions of worship, one may expect that ritual, in any religious system, is carefully designed and well executed. Ritual texts, music, and dance are all planned out. Ritual garments and instruments are an important component of the ritual function. Knowledge of this aspect of religion can be gained only by fieldwork experience. As far as the Taoist religion is concerned, there is apparently no monograph dealing with ritual garments (and instruments). Some field workers have briefly reported on it: de Groot (a century ago), K. Schipper (1982/ 1993) and J. Lagerwey (1987) in recent years, and in many recent publications we can study a number of photographs. Just two examples of Chinese journals that often include photographs of Taoist rituals are *Chung-kuo Tao-chiao/Zhongguo Daojiao* (Chinese Taoism) (Beijing) and *Journal of Taoist Culture* (Taiwan).

Over a hundred years ago, de Groot described some of the ritual garments worn by Taoist priests during their liturgy. He calls it the "religious dress of the Wu-ist priests" (VI: 1264–1268). It must be recalled that his research took place in the south of China, in Fukien, the place of origin of most immigrants to Taiwan. Three types of garments are described by de Groot (they correspond with the recent descriptions by Schipper and Lagerwey).

• *Chiang-yi*, "garment of descent," also called "red garment," or "square garment." It is indeed "a square sheet of silk, which has in the center a round hole for the neck . . . Its form represents that of Earth . . ." (VI: 1264). This garment is only worn by a Taoist high-priest (*tao-chang*) on the most solemn occasions. Today garments are usually made of heavy brocade and decorated with heavy embroidery, which "represents the three levels of the natural universe" (Lagerwey: 291): heaven, earth, and water.

• *Tao-p'ao*, "gown of the Tao," is the standard garment worn by high priests and sometimes by his assistants in first-class rituals. Its basic color is red (sometimes yellow-orange), it is made of silk, has wide sleeves, and has decorations on the back and front of the "eight diagrams" (*pa-kua*), or just of the character *t'ai-chi* ("Supreme Ultimate").

• *Hai-ch'ing*, "sea-blue," is now a black or yellowish orange silk vestment (in older times it used to be plain blue) worn during "negative" rituals, such as chanting the scriptures of penance (Lagerwey: 291). It is often worn by the high priest's assistants while the master himself wears the *tao-p'ao*.

The above descriptions of three garments are based on experience in Fukien and Taiwan. Garments worn today by Taoists in China reveal two different styles: the Lung-men Taoists (as in the White Cloud Monastery of Beijing) and the Cheng-yi Taoists wear ritual robes that are different from those used in Taiwan. But if one studies photographs published recently in China (*Lo-t'ien ta-chiao*, 1993, a small volume on the *chiao* celebration), one sees a basic similarity with the above descriptions: The three types of garments are all represented, although the colors and the embroidery motifs are different. It is possible that other areas in China have their own regional differences.

One final remark on the symbolism of Taoist garments: de Groot (1887/1977 I: 62–63) pointed out that Taoist priests imitated the practices of ancient rulers. When offering sacrifices to Heaven, the king or emperor wore robes with symbols of heaven embroidered on them: sun, moon, stars. Only the ruler was entitled to wear such robes, as he was the sole official representative of heaven. When Taoists wear robes with symbols of the Three Worlds or of the Eight Diagrams, this also has a deep cosmic meaning, implying that Taoists represent the ultimate power of the universe.

Another aspect of Taoist ritual outfit is their headdress, shoes, and apron.

• The head is covered with a black skullcap under which their long, knotted hair is hidden. On the skullcap is a metal crown, called "crown of gold," and on the very top a flame-shaped pin, received at ordination.

The flame, Flower or Gold or Flaming Pearl, illustrates the One energy, the original vital breath (*ch'i*) emanating from the disciple's body. (K. Schipper: 71; see also de Groot, VI: 1267–8)

• The footwear of the high priest are boat-like "court shoes" with thick soles. They are decorated with "cloudpatterns symbolizing his capacity to 'pace the void' and carry messages to heaven" (Lagerwey: 292).

• The apron, a square piece of silk, is wrapped around the priest's waist: It is "embroidered with the emblem of the Cinnabar Field" (Schipper: 70). It is worn out of respect for the gods.

(See also **Ritual Instruments**. For the dress of a Redhead Taoist, see A. Cohen, 1992.)

RITUAL INSTRUMENTS. Besides a set of liturgical texts and **talismans**, which a Taoist candidate inherits from his master (he actually copies by hand his master's collection), he also receives during ordination a number of **ritual garments** and sacred objects that will be his professional instruments during his career as a priest (for all these instruments and garments, as well as for his ordination, the candidate must pay an appropriate fee).

The major ritual instruments of a Taoist priest (at least of the Heavenly Masters School) are a sword, a bowl, an audience tablet, and a seal of office.

• *Ritual sword*, also called "seven stars precious sword" (*ch'i-hsing pao-tao*), is a fairly long steel sword, not usually sharp, with symbolic images of the Big Dipper engraved on both sides of the blade. It is often used during exorcism (as during the **Cosmic Renewal Festival**) to purify the temple premises, but can also be used in private ceremonies of exorcism or blessing. (Mediums also use such a sword, but wound themselves with it during solemn trances.) The Taoist master often uses the sword to write "space" **talismans** in the five directions, as part of the purification ritual.

• *Bowl*. A small copper bowl to hold "holy water" ("lustral" water). The Taoist sips from it during purification rituals and then blows it in fine spray into the five directions.

• *Audience tablet*. A long rectangular and curved piece of material (made from ivory in the past, more recently from wood or plastic) that a Taoist holds in both hands in front of him during certain rituals, probably copied from court officials. During imperial times, whenever an official attended an imperial audience, he had to hold a similar tablet.

• *Seal of office*. Heavenly Masters priests receive a copy of a heavy stone seal (a cube about 8 cm^3), one side of which is engraved with the emblem attributed to Chang Tao-ling. The archaic characters are *Tao-ching shih-pao* ("Treasure of the Master of the *Tao-te ching*"). The seal is used to certify important religious documents. Each Taoist priest has several other seals, often used to validate paper talismans.

• *Ordination certificate*. This is not a ritual instrument, but a document and proof of ordination. Today it is issued by the Heavenly Master (at present, the 64th successor of Chang Tao-ling, who lives in

Taiwan), but in past centuries, "monk certificates" (for Buddhists as well as Taoists) were often issued by the state.

RIVER CHART (or "Yellow River Map") (*ho-t'u/ hetu*) . A cosmological diagram, according to mythology revealed to culture hero Fu Hsi/Fu Xi when a dragon-like horse emerged from the Meng River, a tributary of the Yellow River. From this diagram, Fu Hsi derived the **Eight Trigrams** (*pa-kua*), which became the base of the *Yi ching* in its "Former Heaven" or "Primal" arrangement, which means in their pre-cre-

Pa-Kua
(Former Heaven)

ation, life-bearing order. Later on, King Wen rearranged the *pa-kua* in the order of "Later Heaven" (after creation), which is the arrangement actually found in the *Yi ching*. While the "Former Heaven" order symbolizes the powers of the universe in a rather static manifestation, the "Later Heaven" arrangement stresses change, which is a manifestation of continuous motion and life processes seen in the cosmos.

The *ho-t'u* has been a very important symbol in Chinese history: it was a token of legitimation of power for the ruling class, a symbol of life-giving and protection for the people and for the Taoist priests of the Cheng-yi (Heavenly Masters) tradition, an instrument of religious power, that has been outlined in various scriptures. M. Saso describes it as symbolizing and effectively causing control of seas and rivers and of the spirits of the cosmos, in order to protect life and avert disasters. In ritual use it can effect immortality and bring about union with the *Tao*. It is thus evident

> that the *ho-t'u* cannot be confined to a single definition but is rather a genre of religious or mystical symbols for expressing the unchanging state of the Tao of Transcendence, and the permanent state of beatitude in the heavens. (M. Saso, 1978: 414)

(For a more complete discussion of the *ho-t'u*, see the article by M. Saso, 1978: 399–416.)

S

SALVATION SCRIPTURE (*Tu-jen ching/Durenjing*). It is the longest Taoist scripture, the very first of the **Taoist Canon** (*CT* 1, *TT* 1–13), opening the first section, the *Tung-chen* division. It consists of 61 chapters. Its full title is "Wondrous Book of the Transcendent Treasure, Supreme Stanza on Limitless Salvation" (Strickmann, 1978: 331).

The dates and circumstances of its composition are rather obscure. It is beyond doubt that the first chapter (out of 61) was written by **Ko Ch'ao-fu** at the end of the fourth century CE as part of the original group of *Ling-pao* scriptures. Its existence and authority were recognized during the T'ang dynasty, but still as a single chapter. The other 60 chapters date from the Northern Sung period, during the reign of Emperor Hui-tsung (r. 1101–25), the "Taoist emperor." Very likely, they were composed under the emperor's patronage at court. Claimed to emanate from the highest Taoist deities, the Heavenly Venerable of Original Beginning, the Primordial Lord of the Tao, and the Great Lord of Life Everlasting, their authority was beyond any doubt supreme. And the emperor's prestige was enhanced by the claim, made by Taoists, that he was the earthly incarnation of the Great Lord of Life Everlasting.

As a result, the high respect for these 60 newly revealed chapters was without equal: They were considered to be "the culminating revelation of Shang-ch'ing and so took precedence over all other texts of that most aristocratic of scriptural lineages" (Strickmann: 339). Although originally a *Ling-pao* scripture, that should have been placed within the second section of the *Tao-tsang*, it was placed in the first section at the head of all other texts. The reason was "political expediency," and because the Taoist scriptures were reprinted in the 1120 Sung canon, the court Taoists had the facilities to reshuffle the original order, to accommodate their own and the emperor's religious preferences.

The content of the *Tu-jen ching* is remarkably homogeneous. It claims to contain "the potential for the salvation of all mankind, living and dead. Recitation of the scripture will assure the immortality of one's ancestors and that of the reciter himself" (Strickmann: 340).

Actually, one can divide the scripture into three parts: First, it deals with the origin of the universe, explained in terms of *yin-yang*, five agents, and "three powers" (heaven, earth, and mankind). Second, it discusses methods for exorcism of evil spirits and improving one's bad luck. Third, it explains ways of preserving one's physical body and nourishing one's spirit in order to obtain longevity and become a "transcendent" (perfected). The structure of the 60 added chapters is similar to the original first chapter, except for the addition of talismans, which are absent in Chapter 1.

This scripture is not a philosophical treatise; it was written for use in the liturgy and for recitation. As in other texts, recitation is strongly recommended, because "by invoking the supreme deity, [it] cures the deaf and blind, revives the dead, gives speech back to the mute, movement back to the paralyzed, and rejuvenates the old" (Robinet, 1979/1993: 31). (For a discussion of the historical background, see M. Strickmann, 1979: 331–354.)

SAN-CHIAO See THREE TEACHINGS

SAN-CHIEH See THREE WORLDS

SAN-CH'ING See THREE PURE ONES

SAN-CH'UNG See THREE WORMS

SAN-HUANG CHING See *THREE SOVEREIGNS SCRIPTURE*

SAN-KUAN See THREE OFFICIALS

SAN-YI See THREE ONES

SAN-YUAN See THREE PRIMARY VITALITIES

SAN-YUAN See THREE PRIMORDIALS

SCHOOLS OF TAOISM. There are three Chinese terms used to signify a particular movement in Taoism: *tao, p'ai,* and *tsung.*

The first one, *tao,* should not be understood as the basic term *Tao* of Taoism in its metaphysical dimension. It is rather the common word *tao* meaning a way, a method, a particular path to follow in one's actions (for example, *wang-tao,* the royal way, the correct way of ruling).

P'ai and *tsung* are more specific terms to indicate a particular Taoist movement within the overall context of the Taoist tradition. Whereas *tsung* is usually translated as "school," *p'ai* is translated as "sect," but this gives the wrong impression, because "sect" usually refers to "a small group that has broken away from an established church" (*Webster's Dictionary*). *Tsung* is the word for school mostly used in Buddhism: *Ch'an-tsung,* the Ch'an (or Zen) School; *Ching-t'u-tsung,* the Pure Land School; *Hua-yen-tsung,* the Hua-yen School, etc.

It seems more correct to translate both *p'ai* and *tsung* as "school"; in some cases, it may even be preferable to use the term "order" (as in the Christian context of a religious order: Order of the Franciscans, Order of the Jesuits). This term "order" is most suitable to indicate the three Taoist movements in north China founded during the Southern Sung: the Complete Realization or Ch'uan-chen Order, the T'ai-yi Order, the Ta-tao Order. These three most resemble the Christian counterparts just mentioned.

There is one more term sometimes used in Taoist literature, *chih-p'ai/zhipai*, which means a branch of a *p'ai*; literally, it means "branch-sect," but a better rendering would be "branch-school." This term is commonly used for subdivisions of the Complete Realization School, foremost of which is the Lung-men Branch, the only monastic Taoist institution still active in China today.

Examples follow to indicate how the three terms are used in today's literature (see separate entries for each).

Tao
Huang-Lao Tao (Huang-Lao Taoism)
T'ien-shih Tao (Heavenly Masters Taoism)
Wu-tou-mi Tao (Five Bushels of Rice Taoism)
T'ai-p'ing Tao (Great Peace Taoism)
Cheng-yi Tao (Orthodox Unity Taoism)
Ch'uan-chen Tao (Complete Realization Taoism)
T'ai-yi Tao (Supreme Unity Taoism)
Chen Ta-tao (True Great Tao Taoism)

Tsung
Lung-hu Tsung (Mount Lung-hu School)
Mao Shan Tsung (Mount Mao School)
Nan Tsung (Southern School)
Pei Tsung (Northern School)

P'ai
Tan-ting P'ai (Alchemy "School")
Fu-lu P'ai (Register "School")
Chai-chiao P'ai (Fast and Sacrifice "School") ("School" of Liturgy)
Shen-hsiao P'ai (Shen-hsiao "School")
Lung-men P'ai (Lung-men Sub-"School")
Ch'ing-wei P'ai (Ch'ing-wei "School")
Hua Shan P'ai (Mount Hua "School")
Ch'ing-ching P'ai (Ch'ing-ching "School")

If one reflects on the above listings of *Tao, tsung,* and *p'ai,* another possibility comes to mind: *Tao* and *tsung* are particular Taoist schools, with an institutionalized structure or a social body with a priesthood, temples and scriptures. (*Tao* is perhaps more developed, more impressive than *tsung*.) *P'ai*, on the other hand, are not such organized structures: They are particular techniques, methods of specialization, which could be practiced by one or many schools. That is obvious in the case of *tan-t'ing p'ai*, *fu-lu p'ai*, and *chai-chiao p'ai*, but is perhaps applicable to all *p'ai*.

For example, the Heavenly Masters School specializes in *fu-lu* (**talismans** and registers), as well as in *chai-chiao* (liturgy). The Complete Realization School specializes in *tan-ting*, or **inner alchemy**.

One final remark needs to be made: All the above schools are branches/methods of the Taoist religion. The other aspect of Taoism, its philosophy, is indicated by other terms: *chia/jia* or *hsueh/xue* (school of learning). The most eminent example is *Tao-chia* (Taoist philosophy), but there is also *Huang-Lao Hsueh* (Huang-Lao Learning, a synonym of Huang-Lao Taoism).

SCRIPTURE See *CHING*

SEMINAL FLUID See *CHING*

SEVEN LOTS FROM THE CLOUD BAG See *YÜN-CHI CH'I-CH'IEN*

SEVEN PERFECTED (Ch'i-chen/Qizhen). They are the seven immediate disciples of **Wang Che**, founder of **Complete Realization Taoism** (*Ch'uan-chen*), sometimes also called Seven Perfected of the Northern School or Seven Patriarchs.

They became Wang's disciples when he traveled from Shensi to Shantung in 1167. Four of them returned West with him in 1169, where he passed away in 1170. These are the Seven:

Ma Tan-yang/Ma Danyang (1123–1183)
Tan Ch'u-tuan/Dan Chuduan (1123–1185)
Liu Ch'u-hsuan/ Liu Chuxuan (1147–1203)
Ch'iu Ch'u-chi/Qiu Chuji (1148–1227)
Wang Ch'u-yi/Wang Chuyi (1142–1217)
Hao Ta-t'ung/Hao Datong (1140–1212)
Sun Pu-erh/Sun Bu'er (1119–1182)

Among them, Ma and Sun were husband and wife, who followed Wang Che together. Each of the seven founded their own subbranch: most famous among these is the Lung-men branch, which is still active in China today. Its most famous temple is the **White Cloud Monastery** (*Pai-yün kuan*) in Beijing.

(See also **Complete Realization Taoism**; **Wang Che.**)

SEVEN SAGES OF THE BAMBOO GROVE. This group of eccentrics, a "mixed bag" of Taoism- and Confucianism-oriented scholars, lived during the breakup of the Chinese empire after the Three Kingdom period. Disillusioned because of the political disaster, many of them had no opportunity to serve their country any longer and turned idle or engaged in a new adventure: **"Pure Conversations"** (*ch'ing-t'an*), also called **"Neo-Taoism."** They enjoyed their leisure, lived spontaneously and had probably never felt better in their lives.

> The men in this tradition held themselves disdainfully aloft from unsavory politics and all other mundane matters. Their answer to the social and political disillusionment of the time was to develop their own esthetic sensibilities and give individualistic expression to their every impulse. Typical of such men were the Seven Sages of the Bamboo Grove, a group of wealthy and eccentric recluses, living at the Western Chin capital, who loved to engage in philosophical debate, compose poetry, play the lute, enjoy nature, and drink to excess. A similar but even more eccentric group was the Eight Understanding Ones, who lived at Nanking in the fourth century. (Fairbank, 1973: 84–85)

Although to call these gentlemen Taoists is to simplify the situation, they certainly lived in grand Taoist style, unconcerned about the world of politics, but instead "wandering" through the boundless and relaxing in easy sleep under the useless old tree in the "field of Broad-and-Boundless" (*Chuang-tzu*, Chapter 1). Their appeal to the aesthetic, *wu-wei*-minded gentlemen of later ages has been significant.

SEXUALITY ("Arts of the Bedchamber," *fang-shu*). Some sexual practices advocated by Taoism are considered to be conducive to longevity or even **immortality** and deserve our attention. Together with physical exercises and meditative methods, they are much more than an interesting aspect of an old and weird lifestyle, but contain important clues for us today, if not to reach immortality, then at least to prolong a happy life and make it more meaningful.

In contrast to Western views of sexuality, the Chinese view (especially the Taoist one) is more relaxed and at ease. They do not see the human body as a danger, a source of evil, but as a positive asset. Mind and body are not contrasted or opposed to each other. **Ko Hung** summarizes the importance of sexuality in the Taoist worldview by stating that no one can obtain longevity who ignores the "arts of the bedchamber" (M. Beurdeley, 1969: 11). In other words, as K. Schipper says, to make love is a "happy necessity": abstention is as dangerous as excess (Beurdeley: 18). Whereas excesses can lead to early exhaustion and death, total abstention may be the cause of neuroses of deprivation (see J. Needham, V-5: 190). When Buddhism introduced monastic life and celibacy into China, monks were objects of mistrust and disbelief; women who did not marry except for special reasons were considered to be vampires. On the other hand, the sexual act was compared to the union of heaven and earth: Through their continuous interaction, the myriad things on earth were produced and fostered. By making love, humans become a microcosmic replica of the macrocosmic model and fulfill their natural destiny.

Once the importance and mystical significance of the sexual act have been stated, Taoist authors still emphasize the need for self-control: Man's seminal vitality (*yüan-ching*) is limited and should not be wasted; a woman's seminal *ch'i* is considered to be unlimited. Therefore, in lovemaking, a man should control ejaculation as often as possible (taking into account his age), whereas a woman may reach orgasm without restriction. It is believed that by bringing a woman to orgasm, a man can activate her energy (which is beneficial to herself), and nourish or increase his own vitality. In this way, both partners benefit.

There are, however, different views concerning the benefits of intercourse. Some authors focus on the male's benefit: If he knows the technique, he can exploit young females and pluck their energy without their gaining anything in return. Conversely, if a woman knows the method, she also can tap the energy of ignorant young men and so increase her own longevity (Needham, V-5: 194). This self-centered practice is often criticized as unorthodox and as an abuse and exploitation. In true Taoist fashion, the benefit should be mutual.

The major obstacle to maximizing one's sexual potential is the male's desire to ejaculate. This biological urge, combined with a psychological factor, the male's pride, is not easy to overcome. The power to ejaculate is often seen as proof of masculinity, of adequacy, and also as the only source of sexual joy and fulfillment. These, the Taoist masters say, are prejudices that should be overcome with correct understanding and with practice.

To call ejaculation "the climax of pleasure" is just a habit (Chang, 1977: 21). Chang points out that refraining from emission is, on the contrary, a greater pleasure in the end. By the male's self-control, foreplay can last longer. Caressing and touching, extremely important for emotional balance not only of children but also of adults, can be fully developed and deepen the loving relationship. During actual intercourse, male pride is compensated by the greater delight of his partner. Man is compared to fire, easily aroused and easily consumed; woman is like water, which takes longer to boil. If a man restrains himself, he shows caring and love rather than an urge for quick and selfish satisfaction. This by itself is a great factor that deepens mutual loving (Chang, 1977: 21–23).

R. van Gulik mentions that this technique of self-control was very important for a man in traditional China: If he has a wife and several concubines, he must exert great self-control in order to be physically able to satisfy all the women in his household (van Gulik, 1961: 47). Ejaculation was not absolutely forbidden or discouraged. If conception was desirable, emission of semen evidently was permitted; but through regular self-control, the birth of healthy offspring could be ensured. Moreover, another type of emission was acceptable and was considered to be conducive to health and longevity: the method of "making the semen return" or "guiding of one's semen," already mentioned above. It

> . . . consisted of an interesting technique which has been found among other peoples in use as a contraceptive device . . . At the moment of ejaculation, pressure was exerted on the urethra between the scrotum and the anus, thus diverting the seminal secretion into the bladder, whence it would later be voided with the excreted urine. This, however, the Taoists did not know; they thought that the seminal essence could thus be made to ascend and rejuvenate or revivify the upper parts of the body—hence the principle was termed *huan ching pu nao*, making the *ching* return to restore the brain. (Needham, II: 149–150)

Although the Taoists made a mistake in their physiological explanation, it is still not impossible that this kind of ejaculation control may have had important psychological effects or even produced a greater flow of energy in the body.

What is even more unusual in Taoist history is that such practices were not only taking place in the privacy of the bedroom between single couples, but were occasionally organized as community ceremonies. It is mentioned by J. Needham (II: 150–151) and described in some detail by H. Welch (1957: 120–122). K. Schipper gives an alternative description of the ritual and believes that Taoism had absorbed and adapted ancient festivals into their own celebrations; the sexual festivals, commonly attributed to the Three Changs of the second century CE, are one example.

This "orgiastic ritual," called "Union of Energies" (*ho-ch'i/heqi*), was minutely regulated for the initiates and prepared for through several days of purification, meditation, and prayer. It does not appear as just an orgy to satisfy one's sexual desire, but as a communal effort to reach salvation. On the final day, apparently held on the solstices and equinoxes, there was a protracted ritual dance with prayers and invocations, until the couples undressed and performed sexual union.

The male partner said: "The divine youth holds the passage, the jade girl opens the gate for him; let us join our essences, so that the *yin* may give me its vital force."

The female partner responded: "From the *yin* and the *yang* creation proceeds; the ten thousand beings are born in profusion. Heaven covers and Earth sustains. With your force I want to nourish my body."

(K. Schipper in Beurdeley, 1969: 34)

These celebrations of "Union of Energies" were heavily criticized and ridiculed by Buddhists and Confucians; later, even by some groups of Taoists, like the Taoist movement of **K'ou Ch'ien-chih** during the Northern Wei. Yet, it is said to have survived in secret until modern times. (For an excellent recent treatment of sexuality in Chinese society, see D. Wile, 1992.)

SHAMAN. Refers to a type of spiritual practitioner found in many different cultures in various time periods. In Chinese studies of Taoism (the Taoist Religion), they are often said to be the precursors of Taoist priests. It is worthwhile to investigate briefly whether this is a valid claim.

It is important to have a clear notion of what a shaman (or shamaness) stands for, then contrast/compare it with the notion of priest. *Webster's* definition is not very helpful: A shaman is "a priest or medicine man of shamanism," and the latter is defined as "the religion of certain peoples of NE Asia, based on a belief in good and evil spirits who can be influenced only by the shamans." A more specific definition is given by A. Hultkranz: A shaman is ". . . a social functionary who, with the help of guardian spirits, attains ecstasy to create a rapport with the supernatural world on behalf of his [or her] group members" (Hultkranz, 1973, cited by J. Paper, 1995: 52). From this definition it appears that two activities characterize a shaman: ecstasy and contact with supernatural agencies on behalf of the community.

In ancient China, shamanism was very common. The ordinary character for shaman, *wu*, refers actually to shamanesses, whereas males were called *hsi*. However, gender determination is not certain: *Wu* is defined by Karlgren as "witch, wizard, sorcery, magic tricks [the work of two dancing figures set to each other—a shamanistic dance]" (1923/1973: 363). The etymology of "two dancing figures" is not convincing: It could as well depict one person with flapping arms, as in a dance. The dance aspect is well established: A shaman became entranced by chanting and dancing to drum music.

Besides and beyond the shaman's gender, his/her functions in ancient China appear to be exorcism, dream interpretation, curing illnesses, praying for rain in case of drought. In all these activities, they could use either guardian spirits or be possessed by certain deities. This makes them into magicians rather than priests, as it is characteristic of magical power to control and command spiritual beings,

> While possessed of these spirits' powers, they could command *shen* (deities), kill *kuei* (ghosts), and communicate with specific spirits of the recently dead. In trance, they would perform miracles as evidence of their powers: mutilate themselves without consequence, walk through fire, spirit-talk, or ghost-write. The writing and blood, especially from their tongues, was used to make amulets. (*HCDR,* 1995: 979)

The above description presents a clear picture of shamanistic powers and activities. But when compared with present-day situations, it is obvious that these ancient powers have been divided up and are now within the spiritual repertoire of three different kinds of practitioners:

• Taoist (**Blackhead**) priests are able to summon or control certain deities, according to their personal "register" (*lu*). They are still employed to perform exorcisms and cure illness, but their main responsibility is the liturgy, which was not so much part of ancient shamanism.

• Taoist (**Redhead**) Masters (*fa-shih*) are able to communicate with the spirit-world, especially with the "souls" of the dead, but also perform exorcisms and healing.

• Mediums (trance mediums), *chi-t'ung* or *tang-ki* (Taiwan) are possessed by deities and give advice to their clients about all matters of importance. They may also perform exorcism and healing, and, most spectacularly, mutilate themselves to demonstrate supernatural power.

This means that the functions of ancient shamanism are now being divided, although some functions overlap between the three groups. Their social status is also very different: Blackhead priests, more literate, more dignified than the others, enjoy more social respect than the two other groups. Redheads and mediums are placed much lower in the social hierarchy, but their services are still in great demand today.

Blackhead Taoist priests have a certain contempt for their lower-placed colleagues. They may even punish mediums who intervene during the liturgy (an example is found in M. Saso, 1978: 120). This possibly goes back to very ancient times, when **Heavenly Masters Taoism** reacted against some of the inferior practices of the popular religion, blood sacrifices, and worship of unorthodox ghosts.

This topic of shamanism and its relationship with Taoism is most interesting, but needs further study, not only through textual research, but through actual fieldwork observation in places where old shamanism still survives in some of its manifestations: Taiwan and Southeast Asia. (See also **Blackhead Taoist**; **Redhead Taoist**.)

SHAN-SHU See MORALITY TEXTS

SHANG-CH'ING/SHANGQING SCRIPTURES (Superior or High Purity Scriptures). A collection of Taoist scriptures revealed to **Yang Hsi** between 364 and 370 CE. They became the basis of the first of the three major divisions of the **Taoist Canon** and developed into a major school of Taoism, the Shang-ch'ing or Mao Shan School (see also **Shang-ch'ing Taoism**).

The original revelations to Yang Hsi numbered 31 volumes. They were collected and catalogued by **Lu Hsiu-ching** and **T'ao Hung-ching**. Their focus is not on liturgy but on inner visualization in order to promote one's spiritual and physical health and, ultimately, to reach immortality. Some of the more fundamental scriptures of this collection are the *Yellow Court Scripture* (*Huang-t'ing ching*) and the *Great Profundity Scripture* (*Ta-tung ching*).

SHANG-CH'ING/SHANGQING TAOISM. A school of Taoism established during the Southern Dynasties, as a result of revelations received by **Yang Hsi** between 364 and 370. A century later, **T'ao Hung-ching** took the original manuscripts to Mount Mao (Mao Shan): hence the school is also called Mao Shan Taoism.

The revelations took place during midnight sessions, in which **Lady Wei Hua-ts'un** and a dozen other Perfected Immortals appeared to Yang Hsi and "dictated" to him a number of scriptures from the Shang-ch'ing Heaven (the second highest of Three Heavens, which are Yü-ch'ing or Jade Purity Heaven; Shang-ch'ing or Superior Purity Heaven; T'ai-ch'ing or Grand Purity Heaven). It is believed that the scriptures were revealed to Yang through the technique of *fu-chi* or divination writing, in which the descending deity moves the hand of a human subject through automatic writing; however, this is only a hypothesis. However the revelations were communicated, the result was astonishing: the quality of calligraphy and literary composition was outstanding.

Yang Hsi, who was in the service of the southern aristocratic Hsü family, transmitted the texts to his masters, Hsü Mi and Hsü Hui, who copied them and gradually circulated them among their literati friends. Lu Hsiu-ching catalogued them and included them in the first catalogue of the Taoist scriptures (see **Taoist Canon**). But it was through the efforts of T'ao Hung-ching that the Shang-ch'ing scriptures were brought together and became the foundation of the Shang-ch'ing School of Taoism. In fact, Hsü Hui's son, Hsü Huang-min, had given some of the manuscripts away to other interested parties, and it was through painstaking detective work that T'ao was able to recover a great deal of the original handwritten texts. Meanwhile, the scriptures had become very famous and were in great demand among the literati of the South. Many were recopied, and new texts were forged and circulated as authentic revelations. What made the scriptures so attractive was their excellent calligraphy and elegant writing style. Much of the text was written in "ecstatic verse." As a result, the Shang-ch'ing movement spread widely among the intellectuals of the South, where a reaction had arisen against the lower-class traditions of the Heavenly Masters School, especially against their "blood sacrifices."

With T'ao Hung-ching, the Shang-ch'ing school became well organized, and because T'ao established himself on Mount Mao (Mao Shan), the school also became known as Mao Shan Taoism. During the T'ang dynasty, Shang-ch'ing was the most influential current of Taoism. Several of its patriarchs were invited to the imperial court (Wang, Szu-ma, and Tu) and became advisors of emperors. The most brilliant among them were **Szu-ma Ch'eng-chen** and **Tu Kuang-t'ing**, who wrote many important works, of which a number are still extant and are included in the **Taoist Canon**.

Finally, during the Yuan dynasty (1277–1367), the Mao Shan School disappeared, as it was absorbed into the Ling-pao movement. But its scriptural tradition remains a lasting testimony to the once-flourishing school. (Details about the spiritual practices of Mao Shan Taoism are found in the **Introduction**; see also *Declaration of the Perfected, Yellow Court Scripture, Great Profundity Scripture, Discourse on Sitting-and-Forgetting,* **Meditation**.)

Patriarchs of Shang-ch'ing or Mao Shan Taoism

1st Patriarch & Foundress:	Lady Wei Hua-ts'un (252–334) (Appeared to Yang Hsi 364–370)
2nd Patriarch:	Yang Hsi (330–386)
3rd Patriarch:	Hsü Mi (305–373/6)
4th Patriarch:	Hsü Hui (341–370) (His son, Hsü Huang-min, moves to Shan mountains)
5th Patriarch:	Ma Lang
6th Patriarch:	Ma Han
7th Patriarch:	Lu Hsiu-ching (406–477)
8th Patriarch:	Sun Yu-yo (398–488)
9th Patriarch:	T'ao Hung-ching (456–536) (retires to Mao Shan)

10th Patriarch:	Wang Yuan-chih (528–635)
11th Patriarch:	Pan Shih-cheng (587–684)
12th Patriarch:	Szu-ma Ch'eng-chen (647–735)
13th Patriarch:	Li Han-kuang (683–769)
?? Patriarch:	Tu Kuang-t'ing (850–933)
45th Patriarch:	Liu Ta-ping (wrote a monograph on Mao Shan Taoism about 1317–28)

SHEN See SPIRIT

SHEN-HSIAO/SHENXIAO TAOISM ("Divine Empyrean," highest heaven). A school of Taoism arising at the end of the Northern Sung dynasty. Its founder was a Kiangsi Taoist: Wang Wen-ch'ing (1093–1153), who claimed to have inherited the teaching from T'ang Master Wang Chün. Invited to court by Emperor Hui-tsung, he was given the honorary title of *T'ai-su ta-fu* (great gentleman of "Grand Simplicity") and other titles.

The name *shen-hsiao* ("divine empyrean") refers to the central compass point of nine empyreans or celestial regions; it was ruled by the deity Great Emperor of Long Life (Ch'ang-sheng Ta-ti).

This new school of Taoism is famous for its creation of new **talismans** (*fu*), claimed to have been transmitted by the high Shen-hsiao deity: Yü-ch'ing Chen-wang (True Lord of Jade Purity), also called Ch'ang-sheng Ta-ti of the Southern Pole. These talismans relate to **Thunder Magic** and were welcomed by Emperor Hui-tsung. Very soon, they gained great popularity. Thunder rituals were also performed by other schools, such as the **T'ien-hsin School**, which centered on the use of Thunder Magic: Here the power of thunder is seen as the active power behind the five agents.

Perhaps the most famous of the Shen-hsiao adepts was **Lin Ling-su**, who gained acceptance to the court of Emperor Hui-tsung and proclaimed the emperor to be the earthly incarnation of the god Shen-shiao Chen-wang (True King of the Divine Empyrean). Hui-tsung ordered the construction of Shen-hsiao temples in all *chou* capitals to worship Shen-hsiao Ta-ti. This gave rise to the founding of many branches of Shen-hsiao Taoism. The major focus of the school was the combination of **inner alchemy** and **fu-lu** (literally registers and talismans). The inner alchemy aspect was due to the influence of **Chang Po-tuan**, an eminent Taoist during the Southern Sung. He considered inner purification (*nei-lien*) as the essence, registers and talismans as functions, or as a means to reach the essence. The goal is to develop the original spirit (*yuan-shen*) of one's basic nature (*pen-hsing*).

One of the major insights of Shen-hsiao Taoism is the analogy of the human body as a microcosm, and the physical universe (*T'ien-ti*, heaven-and-earth) as the macrocosm. Moreover, it believes that the thunder method's summoning of thunder spirit-generals, in fact, is an appeal to *ching-ch'i-shen* (vitality, energy, spirit) of one's own person and to the vitality (*ch'i*) of the five agents.

During the Yuan period, the Shen-hsiao school was greatly influenced by Ch'uan-chen Taoism and Confucian learning: It then started to emphasize the practice of virtue and religious discipline and held to loyalty and filiality as primal virtues (*CMTT*: 21. See also Saso, 1978: 51–57).

Some contemporary Taoist masters still practice Thunder Magic in their rituals; although the school itself has ceased to exist, its methods have not.

SHEN-HSIEN CHUAN See *BIOGRAPHIES OF SPIRIT-IMMOR-TALS*

SHIH-CHIEH See BODY LIBERATION

SILK MANUSCRIPTS (*po-shu/boshu*). In 1973, the Institute of Archaeological Research in the PRC excavated an ancient tomb dating from the early Han, situated near Changsha, Hunan. This is the **Mawang-tui** site. Many funerary artifacts, 51 items, were discovered, among them a great number of texts written on silk, contained in a lacquered wooden trunk. All these texts, consisting of 120,000 Chinese characters, date from before 168 BCE, date of the funeral of the tomb's occupant.

For the study of Taoism, the Huang-Lao manuscripts are very significant, but even more so are the two versions of the *TTC* (A and B): From the presence or absence of certain taboo characters in the texts (taboo characters are those which are part of a ruling emperor's name), it is clear that version A dates from before 206 BCE, while version B dates from between 206 and 194 BCE.

It is surprising that the silk manuscript texts do not differ much from the transmitted text, although they occasionally throw light on some previously unclear passages and have a number of variant readings. The major difference is that the *TTC* of the silk manuscripts is divided into two parts: on *Te* and *Tao*, in that sequence, which is the reverse of the traditional sequence. (For more details, see ***Tao-te Ching***: Historical Study; also see Jan, 1977, and Henricks, 1989.)

SONGS OF THE SOUTH See CH'U TEXTS

"SOUL" (*Ling-hun, hun, p'o, shen, kui*). (Quotation marks are used to indicate that the Taoist/Chinese concept of "soul" is not identical to the English term, but then, there is no other more suitable equivalent. Quotation marks should be used throughout, but will be omitted for the sake of convenience.)

The Taoist concept of soul is practically identical with the overall Chinese concept in its theoretical framework. It is possible, however, that its practical applications in Taoist spirituality are divergent.

The Chinese concept of soul is very complex: There is no unified understanding of its nature, and even less of its destiny. Several terms relate to soul: *ling-hun*, *hun*, *p'o*, *shen*, *kui* must all be clarified and correlated, but whether or not a clear and logical system will follow is questionable.

In earliest times, going back to prehistory, there was no formulation of any soul-theory. There were only ritual practices in the context of ancestor cult and funerary customs, which implied certain concepts about the afterlife. From those, deductions (assumptions) can be made, with caution. Those customs, with certain changes, were continued through the Chou dynasty. During this period, some theorizing took place, but the emphasis still remained on the practice, rather than on theory.

When Buddhism was introduced into China (second century CE), the whole scenario changed: The concept of soul and the afterlife underwent a thorough transformation, which occasioned new ritual practices, some of which continue today. Once again, the ritual customs are one thing; the theoretical concepts implied in them are something else. One cannot expect logic in this area ("logical" theories about the soul are not found in any religious tradition!). Because this is a "huge" topic, on which no monographs exist so far, only a brief outline will be presented here, and aspects that are important in the Taoist tradition will be highlighted.

During Shang times, belief in a dual soul was implied in two important religious practices: consultation of the ancestors through divination ("bone oracle") and funeral customs. Royal Shang tombs, excavated in modern times, have brought to light many artifacts buried together with the corpse. This implies that Shang people believed in life after death as a continuation of earthly life. Texts engraved on oracle bones attest that the royal ancestral spirits were believed to live in heaven (in the constellations?) together with all the other *Ti* (deified ancestors) and even *Shang-ti* (supreme ancestor? supreme deity?).

This twofold practice continued during Chou times, but toward the end some formulations were made, in which two kinds of soul-principle were distinguished: *hun*, identified with yang, and *p'o*, identified with yin. Each soul had its own function during life, and its own destiny after death. The *hun* rises up, returns to its origin, heaven, and becomes a **shen** (spirit); the *p'o* descends into the grave, its origin in earth; here, it disintegrates gradually with the corpse. In cases of violent death, the *p'o* may turn into a *kui*, an evil spirit or ghost, which can return to earth to harm the living.

Toward the end of the Warring States period and all through the Han, concepts of immortality changed the outlook. Some funeral texts discovered in Han tombs state that both *hun* and *p'o* descend to the netherworld, to be judged by spirit-officials. But immortality of the body with the soul seems one possible destiny. This hope was taken up by early Taoism, which promised its adepts physical immortality as a result of a virtuous life. One special type of immortality could be reached through **body liberation** (*shih-chieh*).

The arrival of Buddhism changed all that. Gradually, new concepts of the afterlife made their way into the popular and Taoist traditions. Reincarnation and its motive force, *karma*, became permanent features of all Chinese religions, together with beliefs in paradises and hells. As a result, the belief in a soul and in its fate after death became even more complex. New rituals were devised to save ancestral souls from the pains of hell and to liberate the numberless ghosts who do not have descendants to save them. Buddhists devised special rituals for the dead to mitigate their painful condition and to ensure a better reincarnation.

The situation became complex because the old belief in a continued soul existence somewhere in the netherworld was not abandoned. The outcome was a belief (explicit or implicit) in multiple souls: a soul that rises to heaven (*shen*), a soul that descends into the grave (*p'o*) (Yellow Springs), a soul that goes to the netherworld for judgment and punishment (Buddhist influence), and a soul enthroned in the home in the ancestral tablet. The *p'o* soul descending into the grave can be of two kinds: It either disintegrates with the corpse or it continues a kind of physical existence in a special area of the netherworld. All together, it means there are *five* soul principles. This is confusing and even implies contradictions. And the rituals also imply those contradictions. For instance, the practice of praying for the dead (toward a better reincarnation) is not logically compatible with the practice of burning "spirit-money." There are other inconsistencies, but it appears that the people are not bothered by it.

What is important for the Taoist practitioners is twofold: First, an elite of adepts, full-time practitioners, hope to achieve immortality, mostly by the practice of **inner alchemy.** The body is then expected to become immortal and remain united with the soul (*shen*). Second, common believers, even Taoists, foster hopes similar to Buddhist expectations: a future reincarnation, and eventually a rebirth in a Taoist heaven. But that seems to be immortality of the soul only. Taoist priests are instrumental in guiding the soul through the netherworld and in some cases save adepts from the clutches of hell. In Taoist philosophical writings, immortality is not an issue, it is rather an illusion. Life is the coming together of particular energies (*ch'i*); death is their separation. To long for eternal life as a continued individual existence is an empty dream and pretentious at best. Chuang-tzu's skull would frown severely!

SOUTHERN SCHOOL (Nan-tsung/Nanzong). Refers to the southern branch of the Complete Realization School, in contrast with the **Northern School**. When Wang Che founded his new Taoist school in the north, a similar movement arose in the south, focusing on **inner alchemy** and claiming to have Lü Tung-pin and Chung-li Ch'uan as their founding patriarchs.

It is claimed that after Chang Po-tuan of the Northern Sung had obtained the golden cinnabar (*chin-tan*) method from Ch'uan and Lü, he transmitted it to Shih T'ai, Shih T'ai transmitted it to Hsieh Tao-kuang, then to Ch'en Nan, next to **Pai Yü-ch'an**. These five were later revered as the Five Southern Patriarchs. This Southern School was not very strong and, not receiving any support from the Yuan rulers, they merged with Complete Realization Taoism.

In their spiritual cultivation, this southern school stressed first "life" (*ming*), then "nature" (*hsing*). Pai Yü-ch'an was the most famous of the patriarchs; he wrote several books, in which he was influenced by the Neo-Confucian "School of Principle" and by Ch'an Buddhism.

After the Yuan period ended, the southern and northern branches were united (*CMTT*: 26–27).

"SPIRIT" (*Shen*). The term "spirit" in the English language is almost as ambivalent as the Chinese *shen*. "Spirit" may refer to an external agent (spiritual entity), as well as to an internal aspect of human nature (similar to but different from the term "soul"). In Chinese philosophy and religion, including Taoism, *shen* has even more meanings, all commonly used and not always clearly defined.

First, *shen* may refer to supernatural beings, gods/goddesses, or deities. For example, the **City God**, spiritual magistrate of all major cities in China, is called Cheng-huang *shen*, the God of Moats and Walls. But even without the term *shen* added to their name, all deities belong to the *shen* category, in contrast to evil spiritual beings or ghosts, which are called *kui*. The *shen* are benevolent, intent on assisting and protecting human beings; *kui* are malevolent, looking for ways to harm humans. The supreme "spirit," the "God" of the Western tradition, has been sometimes translated as *shen* (although more often as *Shang-ti,* "Lord-on-High," or *T'ien-chu,* "Lord of Heaven").

In the second place, *shen* refers to the "spirits" of ancestors, at least one's own, in contrast to those of other families, which are sometimes called *kui*. The ancestral *shen* is the yang "soul" of an individual who has died. One aspect of "soul" rises to heaven as *shen* and/or resides in the ancestral tablet in the home shrine; this tablet is called s*hen-wei* or *shen-chu*, "spirit seat" (or tablet).

The third meaning of *shen* is even more complex: It is the spiritual component of each living human being, sometimes confused with the yang "soul" or *hun*, in contrast to *p'o*, which is the yin "soul" (for a detailed discussion, see "**Soul**").

In Taoism, the concept of *shen* in the third meaning is more technical. It is the spiritual vitality of each individual, one of the three vitalities received at birth: *ching, ch'i, shen*. The goal of spiritual cultivation is to transform all other vitalities into *shen*. Once that goal is achieved, one becomes an immortal, a spiritualized person, who will continue living forever in celestial or terrestrial paradises. This process of spiritual transformation is the objective of **inner alchemy**, especially according to the Shang-ch'ing School of Taoism. (See also "**Soul**" and **Three Vitalities**.)

SPONTANEITY See NATURALNESS

STAR DEITIES. Taoism worships a variety of divine spirits believed to inhabit and control particular stars. There are several groupings: the seven luminaries, the 28 lunar lodges, the 36 heavenly generals, the 72 earthly generals, the 60-year stars, the six *ting* and six *chia*, and other divine beings believed to reside in particular stars or constellations.

The Seven Luminaries (*ch'i-yao hsing-kuan/qiyao xingguan,* literally, the executives of the seven luminaries) are the spirits controlling the sun, moon, and five planets, correlated with the five agents.

wood planet:	Jupiter
fire planet:	Mars
earth planet:	Saturn
metal planet:	Venus
water planet:	Mercury

The 28 Lunar Lodges (*erh-shih-pa hsiu/ershiba xiu*) are the spirits controlling 28 constellations situated around the equator. Divided into four directional segments, each segment is ruled by one of the four mythical animals.

East:	Green Dragon
South:	Vermilion Bird

West: White Tiger
North: Black Warrior (Turtle?)

During the *chai* and *chiao* rituals, Taoist priests often summon the 28 heavenly generals to descend in order to control and subdue demons. The 28 Lunar Lodges also figure on the geomantic compass in one of the outer circles.

The 36 Heavenly Generals (*san-shih-liu t'ien-chiang/sanshiliu tianjiang*) are also called *t'ien-kang/tiangang*, although the term *kang* applies strictly to the four stars of the Big Dipper. They are believed to be subject to the authority of the god **Hsuan-t'ien Shang-ti**. During *chai* and *chiao* rituals, Taoist priests invoke them to descend to control ghosts.

The 72 Earthly Assassins (*ch'i-shih-erh ti-sha/qishier disha*) seem to have an ambiguous role: They are described as star generals inhabiting the stars of the Big Dipper, invoked by the Taoists to control evil spirits. But they are also believed to be evil influences on earth causing misfortune and disease.

The 60-Year Stars (*liu-shih yuan-ch'en/liushi yuanchen*) are also called 60 *chia-tzu/jiazi*. Taoism considers them spirits of fate, destiny, which create good luck and dispel misfortune. They do not have real names, but are indicated by the combination of cyclical characters: ten **heavenly stems** and twelve **earthly branches**. The first one is *chia-tzu/jiazi* (first of the stems plus first of the branches). In fact, they are personified or deified cyclical characters, each ruling one year in succession of the 60-year cycle. The spirit of the year in which a person is born is thus that person's destiny spirit (*pen-ming shen/ benming shen),* who is able to protect and guarantee that person's happiness. An alternative name is *T'ai-sui/Taisui*.

Painted images of these 60 spirits have been preserved in the Beijing White Cloud Monastery (*Pai-yün kuan/Baiyun guan*). Statues or at least wooden or paper tablets of the 60 are now also found in some Taiwan temples. In a few cases, new side chapels have been erected to house the 60 statues (for instance the Yü-huang Temple in Tainan, Southern Taiwan).

Paper **talismans** of the particular year-spirit are found in the folk almanacs, published in Taiwan before each New Year (or Spring Festival).

The Six Ting and *Six Chia* (*liu-ting/liuding* and *liu-chia/liujia*) are 12 martial spirits or armies of spirits, whose names are derived from combined stems and branches: *chia* is the first heavenly stem, *ting* is the fourth.

chia-tzu	ting-ch'ou
chia-yin	ting-mao
chia-ch'en	ting-szu
chia-wu	ting-wei
chia-shen	ting-yu
chia-hsu	ting-hai

It is believed that the six *ting* spirits are female: They are of yin nature; the six *chia* are male and belong to yang. They are all subordinate to the authority of Chen-wu Ta-ti. They control the thunder and spiritual beings. During *chai* and *chiao* rituals, Taoist priests often summon them by means of talismans to bring good fortune and exorcise evil spirits.

In TT 84 or 37, there are reproductions of 60 *liu-chia* talismans (Taiwan reprint, 1977: 1620, ff.).

Popular talismans and Taoist "cosmic talismans" often represent the *liu-chia* and *liu-ting*.

STEP(S) OF YÜ (*Yü-pu/Yubu*). A particular ritual performed during Taoist liturgy that had its origin in a shamanistic dance, going back to Yü the Great, ancient culture hero, who controlled the floods in China and prepared the land for agriculture.

According to a mythical story, a giant turtle emerged from the Lo River with a mysterious diagram on its back, "translated" into a magic square whose lines of numbers in all directions add up to 15. (See also **Lo River Writing**.)

> Yü the Great was said to have divided the nine provinces of Central China on the basis of the *Lo-shu* . . .
>
> One of the ritual dances performed by the Taoist, called the "Steps of *Yü*," which are thought to imitate the lame pace of *Yü* as he walked throughout the nine provinces stopping the floods and restoring the order and blessing of nature, is modeled on the *Lo-shu*, from 1 through 9, arriving before the gods of Prior Heavens, and ordering nature as *Yü* did in controlling the raging waters of the flood. (Saso, 1972: 59)

As Ed Schafer explains, the "step of Yü" (also called "shaman's step") represents a walk among symbolic stars and injects supernatural energy into the practitioner. By pacing the nine stars of the Dipper, the Taoist priest is able to summon the polar deity **T'ai-yi** ("Grand Monad") to receive his power for blessing the community (Schafer, 1977: 283–9).

In present-day rituals, the step(s) of Yü are performed by the master to walk up through the stars for an audience with the Supreme Triad of Taoism, to receive its blessings into his own body, and to communicate them alchemically to the community.

SUN EN (?-402 CE). A Taoist priest of the Eastern Chin dynasty (317–420). His family, originally from the present Shantung, moved to Kiangsi. It was believed that he was born in a commoner's family, but recent studies tend to agree that he was born in a lower-ranking aristocratic family. For several generations, his forebears had been followers of the Heavenly Masters School. His uncle, Sun T'ai, propagated the school's teachings among the lower classes, but he also cultivated good relations with the aristocracy. His family intermarried with some upper-class families.

In 398, Sun T'ai believed that the Chin dynasty's good fortune was running out. He started a rebellious movement to replace it. Sun En joined his uncle. However, the uprising failed, and Sun T'ai was executed. Sun En himself escaped capture and settled for a while on the Chu-san Island, near Chekiang, vowing revenge.

In 399, Sun En took advantage of widespread discontent about misgovernment and overtaxation. He launched a seaborne invasion, and had great initial successes. He called himself "General of the Eastern Expedition" and his followers "People of Eternal Life" (*Ch'ang-sheng jen*). Their opponents were treated with extreme cruelty. The rebel army was defeated by the famous Gen. Liu Lao-chih (d. 402) and retreated back to its offshore island base. In 402, Sun En attacked Lin-hai (in Chekiang), but was again defeated. In despair, he drowned himself. Many hundreds of his followers and their female companions followed suit. They were later on called "water immortals" (*shui-hsien*).

The remaining rebels then rallied around Lu Hsun (d. 411), Sun En's brother-in-law. In 410 they marched their army north, but once again were defeated. Lu Hsun escaped to present North Vietnam. But realizing this was the end, he poisoned all his female relatives and then committed suicide by drowning. This was the end of a 13-year rebellion, the first major uprising since the **Yellow Turbans Rebellion** in 184 CE. It was heavily influenced by Taoist ideology.

After this, the Heavenly Masters School rapidly declined. The backwardness, the barbarism and the darker side of the Taoist mass movement started off a series of reform efforts among the Taoists, especially those of the upper classes. As a result, new Taoist movements appeared, tailored to the wishes of the ruling class. It was more submissive and willing to cooperate with the ruling house.

SUN PU-ERH/SUN BU'ER (1119–1182). A priestess of the **Complete Realization School** of (Ch'uan-chen) Taoism during the Jurchen-Chin Dynasty (1115–1234). She was a native of Shantung province and wife of Ma Tan-yang, a priest of the same Taoist order. She became initiated into the priesthood by Founder Wang Che in 1169, together with her husband. After her initiation and instruction in the methods of cultivation, she lived alone in a quiet room, facing the wall and meditating.

After seven years of practice, she had perfected the Tao. She then moved to Loyang, where she passed away in 1182. She was the foundress of a sub-branch of Complete Realization Taoism, named Purity-and-Tranquillity Sect (*ch'ing-ching p'ai*) (see also **Seven Perfected**).

SUN SZU-MIAO/SUN SIMIAO (581–682). An eminent Taoist, physician, alchemist, and author of the T'ang dynasty who became very famous through his works on medicine and alchemy, but of whose life very little is known. He was born near the western capital of Ch'ang-an in Shensi. Starting his schooling at age seven, by the time he was 20, his knowledge was extensive and included the Taoist works by Lao-tzu and Chuang-tzu, as well as some Buddhist texts. He went into seclusion on Mount T'ai-po (Chung-nan mountains). He became friends with the eminent Buddhist scholar Tao-hsuan (596–667), author of the continuation of *Biographies of Eminent Monks* (*Hsü kao-seng chuan*) who also lived in the Chung-nan mountains.

Two emperors invited Sun to court: Sui Emperor Wen (r. 589–604) and T'ang Emperor T'ai-tsung (r. 627–649). Twice Sun declined, but when Emperor Kao-tsung (r. 650–683) invited him in 659, he did accept the invitation and "he remained in the emperor's retinue for fifteen years in some informal capacity" (U. Engelhard, in L. Kohn; 1989: 267).

After his death, legends arose, making him into an immortal the people called *yao-wang* ("king of healing"); they worshipped him in many temples dedicated to him. But his greatest merit lies in his numerous works on medicine, health practice, and alchemy.

Two of his works, *Ch'ien-chin yao-fang* and *Ch'ien chin yi fang* (see below),

> are among the most important sources for Chinese traditional therapeutics and are still being used in the training of traditional physicians in China today. Both works bear witness to Sun [Szu-miao's] broad medical knowledge and his gift of exact observation. They document his ability to integrate his various clinical experiences with medical theory and his concern for medical ethics and the social responsibilities of the physician. (Engelhardt: 278)

In typical Taoist fashion, Sun emphasized the essential unity of mind and body. Medicine for him is a combination of "nourishing nature" with various techniques, such as gymnastics and guiding one's *ch'i*, which are preventive rather than therapeutic. In this framework, he also stressed the need to control one's emotions and to be moderate in all one's desires. Through some autobiographical material in his works, it is known that Sun traveled to a great extent, collecting prescriptions from folk medicine and consulting other physicians. He has summarized in his works the whole of medical theory and practice up to the T'ang period. His contribution to medicine and pharmacology cannot be overestimated.

Ute Engelhardt makes a very interesting comparison between Sun and another Taoist master of the T'ang era: **Szu-ma Ch'eng-chen** (647–735). She comments:

> It is curious to note that Sun [Szu-miao], the famous physician, places primary emphasis on mental discipline, while [Szu-ma Ch'eng-chen] the Taoist master concentrates most strongly on the medical and physical aspects of the undertaking. Sun . . . claims that no progress is possible without an awakened mind. (Engelhardt: 291)

Although Sun's works are fundamentally Taoist in nature, he has a definite syncretistic outlook, and some parts of his opus bear a clearly Mahayanist Buddhist imprint. In his *Ch'ien-chin yao-fang,* he remarks that "nobody who has not read Buddhist texts will ever be a good physician" (Engelhardt: 278).

Among the methods most recommended for immortality figure: preserving the essence, guiding the *ch'i,* and the taking of drugs. Sun stresses above all the importance of guiding the *ch'i*: It "supposedly cures all kinds of diseases and even epidemics" (Engelhardt: 287).

Here follows a list of some of Sun Szu-miao's works (the standard histories of the T'ang list 32 works, but apparently more have been discovered. Some works have been lost):

- *Ch'ien-chin yao-fang/Qianjin yaofang* ("Essential Prescriptions Worth a Thousand Ounces of Gold"), written around 650. Stresses the importance of preventive methods or the healing of "latent diseases."
- *Ch'ien-chin yi-fang/Qianjin yifang* (revised edition of former work).
- *She-yang chen-chung fang/Sheyang zhenzhong fang* ("Pillowbook of Methods for Nourishing Life").
- *Ts'un-shen lien-ch'i ming/Cunshen lianqiming* ("Inscription on Actualization of the Spirit and Refinement of *Ch'i*").
- *Chen-chung chi/Zhenzhong ji* ("Pillowbook Record").
- *Fu-shou lun/Fushou lun* ("Treatise on Happiness and Longevity").
- *Pao-sheng ming/Baosheng ming* ("Inscription on Preserving Life").

- *Tan-ching yao-chueh/Danjing yaojue* ("Essential Formulas of Alchemical Classics"). Sun's authorship has not been universally acknowledged, but is strongly confirmed by N. Sivin.

(See U. Engelhardt in L. Kohn, 1989: 263–296; N. Sivin, 1968.)

SUPREME ONE See T'AI-YI

SUPREME ULTIMATE (*T'ai-chi/Taiji*). A Chinese philosophical term commonly used in several systems, especially in Taoism and Neo-Confucianism, but with different connotations. It also served as the base of a certain type of martial arts: ***T'ai-chi ch'uan***, although here the philosophical significance is not obvious.

The etymology of *t'ai-chi* refers to the ridgepole of a building, that which holds the structure together, but its extended meaning is the ultimate principle that holds the universe together. It embraces yin and yang as a totality of creativity and is represented by the circle in which both yin and yang find their relative positions. That is the Taoist understanding of *t'ai-chi*.

In Neo-Confucianism, especially in the system of the great synthesizer Chu Hsi (1130–1200 CE), it has a different significance. Chu Hsi's interpretation of reality is based on the distinction between *ch'i* ("matter," primal material) and *li* (principle). The nature of all things is determined by their *li*, but *li* needs embodiment, which is provided by *ch'i*. The totality of all *li* or principles, for Chu Hsi, is *t'ai-chi*: The supreme ultimate principle of all that exists. This is an interesting theory, somehow similar to the distinction in Aristotelian philosophy of "being" and "essence." But whereas for Chu Hsi this is a purely metaphysical explanation, for the Taoists, *t'ai-chi* is an active, creative reality, also metaphysical (nontheistic), yet very dynamic: one could even say it is the dynamic aspect of the Tao.

SZU-MA CH'ENG-CHEN/SIMA CHENGZHEN (647–735). A Taoist priest, scholar, and 12th patriarch of the Shang-ch'ing School during the T'ang Dynasty. He was a native of Wen County in present-day Honan. He received his training from the 11th patriarch of Shang-ch'ing Taoism, P'an Shih-cheng (587–684). Later, he went to live as a recluse on **Mount Wu-t'ai** and became associated with many scholars and famous poets of the period, such as Li Po, Wang Wei, and Ho Chih-chang. Empress Wu (r. 684–704) summoned him to the capital and personally wrote an imperial edict praising him for his personal and religious achievements.

In 711, Emperor Jui-tsung (r. 711–713) invited him to his palace and asked him about the yin-yang theory, the Taoist arts of divination, and the correct method of ruling the country. Szu-ma answered that the yin-yang theory and the arts of divination were heretical doctrines, unworthy of the emperor's attention. As for the way of ruling the country, the emperor should concentrate on *wu-wei* ("nonaction") as the basic principle. The emperor was pleased with Szu-ma's answers.

In 721, Emperor Hsuan-tsung (r. 713–756) sent an envoy to summon him to the palace. Later, the emperor was initiated into the Taoist order by Szu-ma personally. In 727, Emperor Hsuan-tsung invited him again to his palace to ask for his advice. Because of the long distance between Szu-ma's residence and the capital, the emperor asked him to choose a site on Mount Wang Wu to build a residence closer to the capital, so that consultation could be more frequent.

Szu-ma was a good calligrapher. Emperor Hsuan-tsung asked him to copy the *Tao-te ching* in three calligraphic styles and had them all carved onto stone tablets. In his thinking, Szu-ma was influenced by **Confucianism** and **Buddhism.** He adopted the Confucian concepts of sincerity and the rectification of the mind, as well as the Buddhist practice of meditation, known as *samatha* ("calming" of the mind) developed by T'ien-t'ai Buddhism. He incorporated and developed Lao-tzu's and Chuang-tzu's ideas into an integrated system of Taoist cultivation. In his opinion, the potential to become an immortal (or transcendent, *hsien*) was inborn. As long as one follows one's nature in spiritual cultivation, one eventually will achieve immortality.

Ch'ing Hsi-t'ai/Qing Xitai and others point out that Szu-ma Ch'eng-chen was a pioneer moving away from external alchemy (*wai-tan*) to internal alchemy (*nei-tan*) as a more suitable method of cultivation in the search for longevity and immortality (see Ch'ing's *Chinese History of Chinese Taoism*, vol. 2).

Szu-ma had a tremendous impact not only on Taoism but also on Neo-Confucianism, which took over his concept of "calming the mind" as a method of self-cultivation.

He has left behind several important books: besides ***Tso-wang lun*** and ***T'ien-yin-tzu***, he also wrote *Secret Essentials of Cultivation* (*Hsiu-chen mi-chih*), *Discussion of the Nature of Tao* (*Tao-t'i lun*), and other texts.

SZU-MING see DIRECTOR OF DESTINY

T

TA-TAO CHIAO See GREAT WAY TAOISM

TA-TUNG CHING See *GREAT PROFUNDITY SCRIPTURE*

T'AI-CHI See SUPREME ULTIMATE

T'AI-CHI CH'UAN/TAIJICHUAN. A form of usually nonaggressive **martial arts**, rather physical exercises in slow motion, sometimes called "meditation in motion." There are many different styles of *T'ai-chi ch'uan*, named after the creator of a particular form. The Ch'en and Wu styles are well known today, but the most popular form is the Yang style. Each style consists of a series of stereotyped slow movements, which the student must learn by heart: Once he or she has mastered the whole set, the movements become smooth, elegant, almost effortless. This kind of exercising is very beneficial to one's mental and physical health. It is not strenuous and is suitable for elderly people. It helps one to relax and concentrate, while at the same time it exercises all the parts of the body, including the inner organs. Breathing in and out follow the rhythm of the movements. The results of this slow, smooth exercising can be amazing. Some masters have said that it had helped them to overcome serious health problems; others have accumulated a vast store of energy (*ch'i*), which can be communicated to others for healing purposes.

Although the origin and early development of the *T'ai-chi ch'uan* are not clearly known, one Taoist master is usually considered as one of its founders; **Chang San-feng**, but that is considered to be purely legendary.

Although *T'ai-chi ch'uan* is often considered to be a Taoist creation, that statement must be qualified. It has certainly made use of Taoist principles and was often practiced in Taoist monasteries, yet there is a quality to it that makes it more universally Chinese. The name itself, *t'ai-chi* and *ch'uan* poses some problems. *T'ai-chi* is a central concept in Neo-Confucianism, especially in Chu Hsi's system, where it means the sum total of all principles (*li*). If one goes one step back in history, *t'ai-chi* means the ridge pole of a house, the central beam that holds the roof together. A possible connection with the *t'ai-chi* practice, which may have inspired the founders, is that the *t'ai-chi* of the human body is the spinal column, the major channel of energy flowing through the body. In *t'ai -chi ch'uan* (as well as in meditation), the spinal column must be kept straight to allow the maximum flow of energy. (A note: in the term *t'ai-chi/taiji*, the character *chi/ji* is different from the term *ch'i/qi*, meaning vital energy or breath. Often, the two are confused in popular writings.)

T'AI-HSI See BREATHING EXERCISES

T'AI-P'ING CHING See *GREAT PEACE (EQUALITY) SCRIPTURE*

T'AI-P'ING TAO See GREAT PEACE TAOISM

T'AI-SHANG KAN-YING P'IEN See *TREATISE ON ACTION AND RETRIBUTION*

T'AI-SHANG LAO-CHÜN/TAISHANG LAOJUN ("Highest Venerable Lord" or "Very High Old Lord"). The history of the Taoist religion starts when **Chang Tao-ling** in 142 CE received revelations and a spiritual mission from the deified **Lao-tzu**, named T'ai-shang Lao-chün, who was also believed to be the embodiment of the Tao (L. Kohn, 1993: 3).

It is the same supreme god of the Tao, T'ai-shang Lao-chün, who again appeared to **K'ou Ch'ien-chih** in the fifth century, ordering him to reform the depraved practices of contemporary Taoism.

One can see here a clear development in the conception of Lao-tzu: From the legendary author of the *TTC*, he became the exalted sage-advisor to kings (in **Huang-Lao Taoism**), appearing on earth in numerous human incarnations, and was finally declared to be the creator of the universe. This is an interesting transformation, parallel to the gradual elevation of the Buddha in Buddhism. Indeed, from a historical viewpoint, the first time the Buddha/Lao-tzu appear in human history, it is as extraordinary teachers of humanity. As time goes on, however, it is believed that Buddha and Lao-tzu often appear when a special need arises. But ultimately, speculation leads both Buddhists and Taoists to recognize that the historical figures of Gautama and Lao-tzu are only apparitional bodies (transformation bodies), but that the true and absolute Buddha is the *dharma-kaya* ("body of essence") and the real Lao-tzu is only an incarnation of the transcendent Tao. The effect of this revolutionary shift in "theology" was that the original teaching of the Buddha was changed from a nonreligious spiritual path to a religious movement, and ditto for the original teachings of Lao-tzu, expressed in the *TTC*. It is even probable that these changes in Taoist "theology" were influenced by the Buddhist prototype.

An example of the Highest Venerable Lord, the personified Tao, creating the universe, is found in a T'ang dynasty text *Scripture on The Highest Venerable Lord's "Opening" (Creating) of the Universe (T'ai-shang Lao-chün k'ai-t'ien ch'ing)* (*CT* 1437, *TT* 1059). (For a detailed discussion, see L. Kohn, 1993: 35–43.)

In the Taoist traditions of the South (Shang-ch'ing and Ling-pao Taoism), the position of the Highest Venerable Lord changed considerably. He lost his preeminence in favor of the newly created (mythical) **Yuan-shih T'ien-tsun** (Heavenly Venerable of the Original Beginning), and became the third member of the new trinity, renamed *Tao-te T'ien-tsun* (Heavenly Venerable of the Tao and Its Power).

According to Maspero, T'ai-shang Tao-chün (Very High Lord of Tao) refers to the same divine being as T'ai-shang Lao-chün (Maspero, 1971/1981: 275). But this Venerable Lord should not be confused with **Huang-Lao Chün**, who was the cult figure of Huang-Lao Taoism (see also **Lao-tzu Deified** and **T'ien-tsun**).

T'AI-YI/TAIYI (Supreme One or Oneness, Great Unity, Grand Monad). One of the foremost gods of Taoism, whose cult presents a strange riddle: what came first, the worship of a real deity, or the philosophical concept of "Oneness" found in Taoist philosophical writings and eventually personified into a deity? It has even been suggested

> that the T'ai [Yi] of the shamans and the T'ai [Yi] of the philosophers came into being independently and that they were united at the hands of the magician Miu Chi [about 122 BCE]. Whatever the truth is, [Emperor] Wu eventually became enthusiastic about T'ai Yi and sacrificed to him on several occasions. (Welch, 1957: 103)

The philosophical origin of T'ai-yi seems to be the better choice: The name T'ai-yi, itself an abstract principle, has nothing in common with the ancient nature gods, nor with Shang-Ti (Lord-on-High), but has some links with the *TTC*, Chapter 42:

Tao produced the One
The One produced the Two
The Two produced the Three, etc.

A later text almost paraphrases these lines, but is more specific:

T'ai Yi produced the Two forms,
The Two Forms produced *yin* and *yang* . . . (Welch: 103).

Once the abstract principle had been personified and adopted by Taoism, the road lay open for further growth: The One became the Three, or T'ai-yi became the highest member of a triad, with *T'ien-yi* (Heavenly Oneness) and *Ti-yi* (Earthly Oneness) as companions. These deities were believed to inhabit the cosmos (the stars and/or paradises), but also to dwell in the body of each individual (see **Three Ones**).

This has been an interesting process: From abstract principles, concrete, living deities were projected. This is the opposite process of a more common one: the deification of historical persons, or human beings apotheosed into divinities. (For a further discussion on T'ai-Yi, see Robinet, 1979/1993: 134–138.)

T'AI-YI TAO See GRAND UNITY TAOISM

TALISMANS (*Fu***) AND MAGIC FORMULAS** (*Chou/Zhou*). One of the major technical devices used in the Taoist religion are the production and ritual applications of "talismans." The Chinese term *fu* has no exact equivalent in modern Western languages, but "talisman" or "charm" are the better approximations. The writing of *fu* by Taoist specialists must be accompanied by the recitation of a magic formula (*chou*), like a mantra, to empower it with magical potency.

In pre-Han times, *fu* already existed, but had only a secular meaning: They were documents providing evidence of a contract between two parties. They were divided into two halves: Each party kept one as a token of the contract. These tokens could be made of various materials, including wood or metal.

During Han times, the use of *fu* was extended, especially in the Heavenly Masters School: *Fu* now became tokens of a "contract" between divine spirits and human beings. If they were drawn up, signed, and sealed by religious power-holders, *fu* were considered to be promissory notes of divine protection and assistance guaranteed to the carrier. They were used by the early Taoists as promises of forgiveness of sins and as guarantees of healing. Tradition holds that **Chang Tao-ling**, founder of **Heavenly Masters Taoism**, was the actual creator of a great number of *fu*, which are still currently used by Taoist priests. Today, they are usually written on paper slips.

For a long time, *fu* were transmitted from generation to generation of Taoist priests: Disciples had to copy their master's scriptures as well as their sets of *fu*, as part of their inheritance before they would be ordained. Even today, Taoist priests copy sets of talismans as consultation manuals for their own reference.

Taoist *fu* often combine excellent calligraphy and secret symbolism. The **Taoist Canon** has incorporated hundreds of *fu* in some of their technical manuals or scriptures. They are often very simple, yet mysterious. Some are extremely complex and one may wonder if there is anyone left today who is able to understand their meaning. Fortunately, some texts in the Taoist Canon are rather friendly in that respect: They not only analyze and dissect the *fu* into their component parts, but also explain the significance or symbolism of each part. Moreover, they tell the practitioner the correct sequence of each stroke (similar to the writing of Chinese characters: Here, too, one must follow a correct sequence of strokes).

During the medieval period and late imperial China, *fu* were reproduced by block printing. Today, they are often mass-produced by ordinary printing techniques. But to be very powerful, they should be drawn—by brush—on an individual basis. During the writing, the Taoist must recite the correct formula (*chou*), while he is mentally concentrated. The power of *fu* depends on the spiritual energy (*ch'i*) of the person who creates them.

Once the drawing is finished, a sign of authority (*fu-tan*, "liver of the *fu*"), plus an official stamp in red wax, must be affixed to give the *fu* effective power, which means to execute the order expressed in the text. It is said that Taoist talismans resemble imperial prescripts: they are written in black ink on yellow or vermilion paper, and contain divine orders delegated by higher deities to lower-ranking gods to bring about a certain effect. The popular religion has adopted the use of talismans: Almost every temple in Taiwan, Hong Kong, Singapore, and elsewhere produces its own brand, with a divine mandate issued by the main temple deity. These temple talismans are for "general protection": An order is issued by the supreme deities to, for example, the goddess Ma-tsu or the god Pao-sheng Ta-ti to bring peace to home and community or to drive away evil influences.

Most of the Taoist *fu* are very specific and could be called "specific mandate talismans." They have a very special purpose—for example, to cure sickness (there is an appropriate *fu* for almost all diseases), to promote health, to assist women in childbirth, for purification, and for particular kinds of protection, such as for those who want to enter the mountains. Other *fu* are used while in meditation, and a great number are still currently produced for ritual purposes, such as various rites of the *chiao* or **Cosmic Renewal Festival**, or during ceremonies to improve one's fate or to cancel out dangerous calendar clashes. (See also **Ritual**.)

Talismans can be used in several ways: One can hang them up in the home in particular rooms, or one can fold them and wear them around the neck or, more often, one can burn them and mix the ashes in water, tea, or wine. This is considered strong medicine to cure illness or to obtain protection against evil spirits.

The popularity of paper talismans has become so great that Buddhists also create their own; moreover various spiritual practitioners (mediums, ritual masters, etc.) always make them on the spot during their sessions or seances.

While many of those popular ones sometimes are mere scratches of ink, other Taoist *fu* are masterpieces of calligraphy.

TALISMANS AND REGISTERS See *FU-LU*

T'AN/TAN ("Sacred Area," "Sacred Space," Shrine, Altar). The term is used in at least two different meanings, either as a sacred area, circumscribed for Taoist rituals, or as a small sanctuary, rather an office, used by Taoist priests (and mediums) at their own home, where they perform rituals for individuals or small groups of people on a private basis. Setting up a *t'an* is for a Taoist priest similar to a medical doctor establishing a private practice in an office.

A variation of shrine-*t'an* is the temporary structure built for the

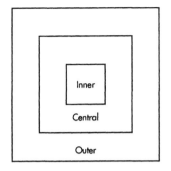

Figure 1: Older T'an Model

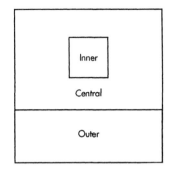

Figure 2: Contemporary Model

Cosmic Renewal Festival. These structures—built of bamboo poles tied together and wood panels painted in vivid colors, some of them multileveled pyramid-shaped—are imitations of temples and house various deities. The most commonly enshrined deities are the **Jade Emperor**, Bodhisattva Kuan-yin, Heavenly Master **Chang Tao-ling**, **Queen of Heaven Ma-tsu**, etc.:

> Each of the wealthier families of the community sponsors a *T'an* in the visiting deities' honor. The more *T'an* constructed, the greater the merit and praise for the *Chiao* festival in the eyes of the surrounding villages, and the more abundant are the blessings won from the gods. (Saso, 1972: 33)

The more esoteric kind of *t'an* as sacred area is the space in the temple where the rituals are performed. There are several models that can be followed, but mostly there is an inner *t'an*, a central *t'an* and an outer *t'an* all situated in the temple (see figures 1 and 2).

The inner *t'an* (of figure 2) is where most of the rituals are performed, just before a central altar. This is like "home base," where the Taoist priests most often stand or kneel chanting or reciting the scriptures. The central *t'an* is the northern half of the main temple hall: On the northern wall, the Taoists hang their scrolls of the Three Supreme Deities (**Three Pure Ones** or Heavenly Worthies), the gods of "Prior Heaven," which temporarily replace the temple's own statues of the patron deity and other gods of "Posterior Heaven." The temple gods are removed to the southern wall or to side walls and, in more recent times, placed on specially constructed shelves on the side walls or in adjacent areas (the number of statues, mostly "visiting guests," can be exorbitant!).

Besides the scrolls of the Three Supreme Deities, there are scrolls of other high-ranking deities, the Jade Emperor, Tzu-wei Ta-ti, etc., and scrolls of the Three Realms (heaven, earth and water). Near the southern temple door (locked for the duration of the festival), a special altar is erected in honor of the **Three Officials** (San-kuan), of highest dignity in the second century CE, but later eclipsed by the Three Supreme Deities.

The outer *t'an* contains paper-and-bamboo images of Kuan-yin and from four to ten marshals, riding their mythical mounts. This is an interesting aspect of folk art: The colorful images are excellent handicraft products, but must be burned on the last day of the festival.

The outer *t'an* is the area where some of the rituals take place, which may be attended and witnessed by the community.

TAN-T'IEN/DANTIAN ("Fields of Cinnabar," "Energy Field(s)"). The Taoist view of the human body is very particular and unique. It is divided—but not in an absolute way that would separate—into three fields of energy, like three spheres of influence: the head, the chest, and the abdomen. Each has a focus point, the exact location of which is described in the texts.

- The upper field, or upper *tan-t'ien*, is located inside the head, between the eyebrows. It is the residence of the Infant.
- The middle *tan-t'ien* is located in the Crimson (or Scarlet) Palace in the heart. It is the residence of the Perfected.
- The lower *tan-t'ien* is located in the lower abdomen, three inches below the navel. It is the residence of the Immortal Embryo (L. Kohn, 1993: 209).

These three fields of human vitality are also the seats of the supreme cosmic deities, hence also called "Three Palaces": the **Three Ones** are *T'ai-Yi*, Supreme One (Supreme Oneness), residing in the upper field; *T'ien-Yi*, Heavenly One, residing in the middle field; *Ti-Yi*, Earthly One, residing in the lower *tan-t'ien*.

Originally, it appears that only one field, the lower one, was recognized and, even now, among the three fields, the lower *tan-t'ien* is still the crucial one, because it is the source of life:

The [lower] Cinnabar Field is the root of the human being. This is the place where the vital power is kept. The five energies [of the Five Agents] have their origin here. It is the embryo's home. Here men keep their semen and women their menstrual blood. Meant for the procreation of children, it houses the gate of harmonious union of *yin* and *yang*. Three inches under the navel, adjacent to the spine, (the Cinnabar Field) lies at the base of the kidneys. (K. Schipper, 1982/1993: 106)

The Taoist texts deal extensively with the three *tan-t'ien*, but not all is clear and unified. The exact nature of each field is not described unanimously. For instance, the *tan-t'ien* in the head consists of "three palaces" or of "nine palaces." The three are named Hall of Light, Grotto Chamber, Niwan Palace (Kohn, 1993: 209). (The term "niwan" is derived from the Sanskrit Buddhist word *nirvana*.)

If there are nine, they are described as forming two rows, one above the other: five and four "houses." The five below are called Hall of Government (at the entry), Chamber of Secrets, Cinnabar Field, Palace of the Moving Pearl, Palace of the Jade Emperor; the four above are named Heavenly Court, Palace of the Great Pinnacle Reality, Palace of Mysterious Cinnabar, and Palace of Great Majesty (Maspero, 1971/1981: 268).

The middle *tan-t'ien*, located near the heart, is also divided into compartments, one of which is the Yellow Court, another the Purple Chamber (gall bladder), which is inhabited by deities, such as the Master of Southern Cinnabar and the God of Radiance Solid.

The most enigmatic of the three *tan-t'ien* is the lower one; it is also the most crucial. Near the navel, called Central Summit, and also near the kidneys are located various important centers: Ocean of Energy (*ch'i-hai*), Gate of Destiny (*ming-men*), Root of Life (*sheng-ming ken-yuan*).

The three original vitalities with which humans are born (*ching, ch'i, shen*) are also associated with the three *tan-t'ien*. By forcing one's *ching* to the brain and by circulating one's *ch'i* throughout the body, the mysterious embryo can be generated, which will eventually become the new emerging person, the immortal.

TAN-TING P'AI See GOLD CINNABAR TAOISM

TAO (The Way). The central concept of the Taoist tradition (philosophical speculation and Taoist religion), from which the terms Taoism and Taoist are derived. Because this is a central article, attention will be focused on the following: etymology of the term Tao, its general meaning, its specific meaning in Taoist philosophical speculation, its specific meaning in the Taoist religion.

• *Etymology*. The structure of the *Tao* character is interesting and revealing: the upper and right part signify "head"; the left part is the radical for "walking feet." The total image suggested is a head (looking ahead) with feet carrying the head (or person) in a certain direction. A road is indeed made by walking feet under control of an agent; by mere walking it is created as a road. By extension, a road can mean a certain direction of life, of action, or intention. As the character structure indicates, the "head," or thought agent, is the main factor, the feet are only the servants.

• *General Meaning of Tao.* Before Taoism, other schools used the word *tao* in their vocabulary. It could mean just a "way" of doing things, a "way" of ruling (like in *wang-tao*: the king's way), but eventually it became a little more specific, as in the teaching of Confucius: the correct "way" of action, the right way to behave ethically, the right way to rule the country based on moral principles. This perhaps led to a more abstract notion—the "way" of life, as is suggested in one of Confucius's sayings: "In the morning, hear the Way; in the evening, die content" (*Analects* 4: 8, Chan, 1963: 26).

When Buddhism started to spread in China, they needed Chinese terms to express Buddhist concepts. A term of great significance for them was "Eightfold Noble Path"; it summarizes for them the correct way toward enlightenment. The obviously available term was *tao*. Then, the Buddhist *tao* has a specific meaning within the overall Buddhist worldview: a spiritual path to follow in search for nirvana. It is yet different from the Taoist "Way."

Within Taoist philosophical writings, *tao* sometimes appears as a term expressing some kind of action, but not yet in the special meaning of *the* Way. Examples are found in the *TTC*: the "way of Heaven" (*T'ien-tao*), as in Chapter 9: 5, "To withdraw when the work is done, is the way of Heaven"; Chapter 47: 2, "Without looking through the windows, one can see Heaven's way"; and Chapter 79: 5, "Heaven's way has no personal affections, (yet) it is on the side of good people." In these instances, heaven is portrayed as the natural cosmos (as in "**heaven-and-earth**"), yet not identified with the *Tao* itself. It resembles more the heaven of Confucianism: a powerful and moral conscience that appears to control nature and human fate.

• *Special Meaning of Tao in Taoist Philosophy.* The nature of Tao in the *TTC* is discussed in the entry **Tao-te ching: Themes**. Here is the most relevant passage:

Tao is the eternal reality beyond, but also within, the visible universe. It is the Ultimate. It is creative force, not in the sense of a creator-god, but as an impersonal energy that creates and transforms without interruption. Its presence is everywhere, not as a spiritual being, but as the basic stuff, the *ch'i*, out of which all things have issued. It gives life to all living beings and maintains them, dispassionately, with no likes or dislikes.

This *Tao* is deepest mystery: it cannot be grasped by the rational mind only, but intuitively, if the mind is still and desires are controlled. That must be done through spiritual cultivation, through contemplation. Only those who are able to gain a deep insight into the nature of *Tao* are entitled to rule the country.

This analysis raises a serious problem: Is the Tao, which produces the universe, to be understood as a separate being, distinct from the universe? The answer is no! Rather, Tao is a self-transforming process. Tao is reality, but reality understood as a continuous process of becoming, changing, beginning, and ending. To separate Tao from the created universe is to falsify the Taoist view with extraneous concepts, found in other systems of thought, where Creator and creation are set apart from each other. Even when the *TTC* mentions "something undefined and yet complete, which existed before Heaven and Earth" (Chapter 25: 1), it points to the Tao itself in an early phase of self-transformation. In other words, the visible and continually changing universe *is* the Tao, but if one wants to make distinctions, one can say that the universe, including our own planet earth, is the visible expression of the Tao. It is the Tao in a momentary self-manifestation. Yet the Tao is also something beyond: It is the inner power, the eternal *ch'i*, that makes the universe appear in visible forms, while being at the same time distinct from it, meaning that the visible forms are not the complete Tao.

One thing is certain, the 10,000 beings are not separate from the Tao, even if some *TTC* passages seem to make such a statement. For instance, Chapter 51: 1 says: "Tao gives them life" (or "Tao generates [all things]").

All things are partial expressions of an eternal Tao: Tao brings them into existence, cares for them (gives them a chance to grow and mature), and lets them return to their origin. It is like an eternal play of becoming and ending, an eternal fireworks of short moments of brightness then reabsorbed into the darkness of nonbeing. If a special term is needed to express this concept of Tao, "pantheism" is the one that comes closest.

The ***Chuang-tzu*** talks about the Tao in many passages, but only occasionally takes the risk of explaining it. As in the *TTC*, language fails to express what is by nature inexpressible. Indeed: "The Great Way is not named . . . If the Way is made clear, it is not the Way." (Chapter 2, Watson, 1970: 44). Talking about Tao is a paradoxical attempt, because

> The Way has its reality and its signs but is without action or form . . .
>   you can get it, but you cannot see it.
> It is its own source, its own root.
> It was born before Heaven and earth, and yet you cannot say it has been
>   there for long . . . (Chapter 6, Watson: 81)

In the fascinating chapter "Knowledge Wandered North," it says:

> The Way cannot be heard; heard, it is not the Way.
> The Way cannot be seen; seen, it is not the Way.
> The Way cannot be described; described, it is not the Way.
> That which gives form to the formed is itself formless—
> can you understand that? There is no name that fits the Way. (Chapter 22, Watson: 243)

If inexpressible, it follows that the Way cannot be transmitted to others, unless there is already a potential for understanding inside the receiver's mind (Chapter 14, Watson: 161). But the receiver must have the right mind, open and receptive:

> You can't discuss the ocean with a well frog—he's limited by the space he lives in . . . You can't discuss the Way with a cramped scholar—he's shackled by his doctrines. (Chapter 17, Watson: 175–6)

Yet the Tao, transcending everything, is also everywhere, even in the lowest things that we despise, such as "shit and piss" (Chapter 22, Watson: 241). It infuses life into all beings; they could not exist without the Tao, which

> is the path by which the ten thousand things proceed. All things that lose it, die; all that get it, live. (Chapter 31, Watson: 352)
>
> In other words, as time cannot be stopped, the Tao cannot be obstructed (it will get its own way!).

Get hold of the Way and there's nothing that can't be done; lose it and there's nothing that can be done (Chapter 14, Watson: 166).

Whoever follows the Tao, will succeed in life, not perhaps in the "ways of the world," but where it really counts: spiritual perfection.

> He who holds fast to the Way is complete in Virtue; being complete in Virtue, he is complete in body; being complete in body, he is complete in spirit, and to be complete in spirit, is the Way of the sage. (Chapter 12—Watson: 135)

• *Special Meaning of Tao in Taoist Religion.* The first truly Taoist religious movement to arise was the Heavenly Masters School in the second century CE. Although this movement had no historic connections with the Taoist philosophical stream, there was one element that contributed to link them together: belief in **Lao-tzu**, now deified as a divine being, T'ai-shang Lao-chün. This process of transformation had probably already started earlier, within **Huang-Lao Taoism**.

With a truly religious cult, deities became necessary: The divine Lao-tzu became a central cult figure, while other gods were adopted from earlier popular cults—nature deities, the Three Officials, the Controller of Destiny.

Lao-tzu deified remained an important object of worship; he was even seen as the incarnation of the eternal Tao (see **Lao-tzu Inscription**). Yet, eventually, his importance in the Taoist religious movement somehow was eclipsed with the creation of new deities, especially the **Three Heavenly Venerables** or the **Three Pure Ones**. This triad was indeed a personification of the Tao; out of an impersonal concept, mythic deities were projected and offered for worship. The original Tao was said to transform into *yuan-ch'i* (primordial *ch'i* or energy): The triad mentioned was seen as the triple manifestation of this *yuan-ch'i*. (Buddhist influence in the form of the *Trikaya* or Triple Embodiment of the Buddha may have been at work here.)

As a result of this "mythologization," Tao became invested with qualities of a real supreme being, a Creator God, that must be worshipped, which controls the course of history. These qualities are consciousness, omniscience, omnipotence, creativity, all-loving kindness, etc.

This evolution of the Tao concept is probably the key for solving the riddle of "One Taoism, or Plural Taoism." The original "abstract, impersonal, philosophical" concept of Tao was "pulled down" to a practical, human level, available for worship. Tao philosophy became Tao theology.

TAO-CHANG See PRIESTHOOD

T'AO HUNG-CHING/TAO HONGJING (456–536). A famous Taoist scholar and alchemist from the Six Dynasties, best known as a patriarch of Shang-ch'ing or Mao Shan Taoism, and collector-editor of the basic Shang-ch'ing scriptures. He was born in an aristocratic family in present-day Nanking, in Kiangsu province. As a young boy, he was precocious. At the age of ten, he read the *Biographies of Spirit-Immortals* (*Shen-hsien chuan*) by Ko Hung and started to foster the desire to preserve good health. At the age of 15, he wrote *Hsün Shan chih* (*Records of Mount Hsün*), in which he expressed his wish to live the life of a recluse.

At age 20, he was invited to court by Ch'i Emperor Kao to become a tutor of the royal princes. In 492, he resigned from government service and, a year later, he withdrew as a recluse to Mount Chü-ch'ü (later renamed **Mount Mao** or Mao Shan), in Kiangsu province, where he received training in drawing **talismans** and diagrams, as well as in chanting the Taoist scriptures.

Although he was in retirement, the court of the Liang Dynasty still sought his advice in political matters; as a result, he was known as the "Prime Minister from the Mountains."

Although strongly influenced by **Lao-tzu**, **Chuang-tzu** and **Ko Hung**, T'ao advocated the synthesis of the **Three Teachings**. He was even initiated into the Buddhist order in Ningpo. In his Mount Mao refuge, there were two halls, one Taoist and one Buddhist. T'ao rotated his worship rituals on a daily basis.

T'ao is probably most famous for his efforts in collecting the Taoist scriptures, following in the footsteps of **Lu Hsiu-ching**. In his famous book *Declaration of the Perfected* (*Chen-kao*), he narrates the story of his recovery of the Shang-ch'ing scriptures, as well as the origin and transmission of these texts. He also drew up the first Taoist pantheon, arranged in hierarchical order (see H. Maspero, 1971/1981: 358–360). Moreover, T'ao further developed the theory of Taoist cultivation, emphasizing the inner discipline of the mind, as well as the importance of chemical and herbal remedies and drugs as a support system in the quest for immortality. He was most instrumental in raising the spiritual level—and the reputation—of the Shang-ch'ing or Mao Shan school of Taoism (see also M. Strickmann, 1979).

TAO-SHIH See PRIESTHOOD

TAO-TE CHING/DAODEJING: **THE TEXT.** The often used title *Lao-tzu's Tao-te ching* (*TTC*) reflects the Chinese attribution of the text to **Lao-tzu**, probably a legendary sage, later deified in the Taoist religion. The true authorship and the circumstances of composition are still a historical riddle, although in recent years great progress has been made toward solving it.

The *TTC* is a very short text (about 5,000 Chinese characters) and has been extremely influential in China. Since the 19th century it has enjoyed a surprising popularity in the West. So far, about 250 translations into Western languages have been listed, of which about 85 are in English.

Not all these translations are of superior quality. A number are the work of amateurs who did or do not know Chinese. But more disturbing is the fact that a great number of translators used the text as a vehicle to propagate their own world-view, such as idealist philosophy, Christian theology, theosophy, scientism, feminism, and romanticism (Zürcher, 1992: 287). A correct translation must attempt to render the original intention of the author as faithfully as possible. This is a difficult enterprise, because this text was written more than 2,000 years ago, in a cryptic, dense language, and in circumstances which are not immediately evident. Study of the ancient language and of the historical context are therefore extremely important and must be accompanied by a detached attitude in the mind of the translator. The numerous commentaries written in China may be consulted, but should be handled with caution: Instead of interpreting the text, they may also falsify the author's intention or reinterpret the text in the light of their own biases.

• *Text History and Transmission*

Traditionally, a person named **Lao-tzu** is credited with the composition of the *TTC*. The Lao-tzu legend is narrated in Szu-ma Ch'ien's *Shih-chi/Shiji* ("Historical Documents") of around 90 BCE. (See E.M. Chen, 1989: 4–22; Henricks, 1989: 263; Welch, 1957: 1–17 for details on authorship.) The name "Lao-tzu" is not a real name, it simply means "Old Master" and could suggest a legendary figure whose name was used by those who actually composed the text.

Until modern times, it was believed that the *TTC* was written in the sixth century BCE. The *Shih-chi* legend narrates Confucius' (ca 550–480 BCE) visit to Lao-tzu to inquire about the rites (*li*). But this legend, as well as all the others, including Lao-tzu's departure from China riding an ox, must be held for what they really are: interesting legends with no historical base at all.

Who then wrote the *TTC*? Most scholars today believe that the text was written around 300 BCE or even later, around 250 BCE. Some light has been thrown on the issue of origin with the discovery of the so-called silk manuscripts in 1973. The excavation of a nobleman's tomb located in Ma-wang-tui (province of Hunan) brought to light a considerable number of old manuscripts, two of which contained the *TTC*. This was a very important discovery. One manuscript has been dated to a time before 206 BCE, the other one to between 206–194 BCE. That these manuscripts were considered important enough to be buried with the corpse implies that they had already been circulated for some time and gained popularity. (For more details, see **Silk Manuscripts.**)

Recent studies have suggested that the TTC may have been composed within a circle of scholar-gentlemen, called *shih*, perhaps patronized by the ruler of one state after the model of the Chi-hsia Academy in the eastern state of Ch'i, active during the life of the Confucian master Mencius (371–289 BCE?). This particular group of *shih*, named "Laoist" school, since they are assumed to have produced the *Lao-tzu*, were idealists who felt alienated from the social-political order of their day, but still had "a strong sense of social responsibility" (Lafargue, 1992: 192). *Shih*-idealists had two principal concerns: (1) cultivating moral/spiritual excellence in their own persons and (2) reforming the practice of contemporary Chinese politics" (LaFargue, 1994: 48). That double concern explains the twofold theme clearly expressed in the *TTC* (see below).

The Laoist school, although mildly interested in politics of their time, had no predominant influence on political decisions. This was a hard time for the rulers of states, threatened by powerful neighbors. A "soft" government was considered to lead to defeat. Neither Taoist idealism nor Confucian emphasis on virtue and virtuous rule found any sympathy among leaders intent on conquest or defense of their own state.

By the middle of the third century, the political climate in China must have been very tense with the conquest by the Ch'in armies of some states. The crisis escalated between 230 and 221 BCE, when Ch'in annexed one by one the states of Han, Chao, Wei, Ch'u, Yen, and, finally, Ch'i. This period of intense chaos and brutal conquests was certainly not conducive to Taoist or any other speculation, and does not find an echo in the *TTC*. Therefore, it is plausible to accept a time between 300 and 250 BCE as the approximate date of composition.

If the *TTC* was a joint product of several scholar-gentlemen (Laoist *shih*) circa 300 BCE or slightly later, it would explain several important authorship problems: first, the obvious incoherence of the text. There is no way to explain away the multiplicity of topics covered in the text or even the abrupt changes of topics in separate chapters. One must be blind or prejudiced to believe that the *TTC* is a coherent text. Although by stating this the authorship question is not solved, at least this recourse to inner text criticism allows the exclusion of one single author. Reading the *TTC* carefully, one cannot escape the conclusion of multiple topics: There is philosophical speculation about the nature of Tao and its action; many passages deal with ethical principles; there is a serious concern about government and military strategy; many chapters deal with the figure of the sage (and not necessarily the sage as ruler); there are some anti-Confucian passages; quite a few chapters deal with spiritual cultivation and often have mystical overtones; of course, the topic of *Te* (power, virtue) is important; many paradoxes or aphorisms appear, which do not easily fall into any of the above categories; and, finally, almost as a fluke, there is one chapter that reflects an utopian primitivist worldview. Although it is not impossible that later editors have manipulated the text, even to the point of creating more incoherence, it is more likely that the original version was already affected by a lack of topical structure.

The *TTC* has gone through a curious history of textual transmission. For the longest time, Chinese commentators and Western translators had only access to one or two versions: The "transmitted" or "received" text, established and commented upon by neo-Taoist philosopher **Wang Pi** (226–249), and also commented upon by **Ho-shang kung** (probably later than **Wang Pi**, although some scholars believe it was earlier).

Between the composition of the *TTC* and Wang Pi's time, there is a gap of about 500 years. Where did Wang find his text? It has been suggested that his text was perhaps the same as the one that Fu Yi (555–639) of the T'ang edited, and although "now lost, predated the Ma-wang-tui (MWT) texts by about twenty or thirty years" (Chen, 1989: 44).

What is most remarkable however, is that the MWT texts do not differ considerably from the transmitted text: "there are no chapters in the Ma-wang-tui texts that are not found in later texts and vice versa, and there is nothing in the Ma-wang-tui texts that would lead us to understand the philosophy of the text in a radically new way" (Henricks, 1989: xv). A minor puzzle concerns the order of the chapters. At one time, the *TTC* was divided into two parts: *Tao-ching* and *Te-ching*, which may even have existed as separate texts. In the transmitted version, the chapters on *Tao* come first, 1–37; those on *Te* follow, 38–81. In the MWT manuscripts, the order is reversed. (That is why Henricks' translation is titled: *Te-Tao ching.*) The reason for this reversal is not clear. Was it a deliberate choice or just a historic accident? There is no definite answer for this, although it has been suggested that it may reflect the worldview of legalism and Huang-Lao Taoism, which was more interested in *Te* (power?) than in speculation on Tao. Whatever caused the reversal, it is not certain that this *Te-Tao* sequence was the original one.

The transmitted text is divided in 81 chapters. This is most likely because of the symbolic value of 81 ([3x3]x[3x3]). The MWT text is not yet divided. It is possible that the division took place around 50 BCE (Henricks 1989: xvii), but it is rather artificial and confuses in many cases the meaning of particular chapters.

• *Text Criticism and Standards of Translation*

Although the theory of multiple authorship explains a number of incoherences in the *TTC* text, it is also certain that the text has further been corrupted in later times. Comparing the MWT manuscripts with the transmitted text, it appears that corruptions already took place before 200 BCE: As a result, "a critical study of a text, which is obviously corrupt, is indispensable" (Duyvendak, 1954: 3).

Most translators have written chapter-by-chapter translations of the transmitted text without altering the sequence or without transferring verses of one chapter to another. Yet, such an operation is sometimes necessary. Moreover, sometimes single characters in the present text do not seem to make sense; they violate the principle of intelligibility.

Therefore, variant readings must be considered, although with great caution.

Some translators have been troubled by the incoherence of the text. The earlier mentioned division into a *Tao-ching* and a *Te-ching* does not offer much assistance, because both parts have no clearly defined content. Topics such as the nature of **Tao**, or speculation on *Te*, or passages on government and strategy, and so on, occur indiscriminately in both parts.

Translators often misrepresent, even betray, the original text and the reasons may vary, from prejudice to ignorance or merely lack of linguistic skills. To translate technical works, good language skills and an understanding of the field are necessary and sufficient. To translate literary and artistic works, one needs, moreover, literary gifts and inspiration. It is not easy to find those talents combined in one individual; therefore, high-class translators are a rare species.

No wonder that some of the *TTC* translations do not pass the test of excellence, not even the test of simple goodness. But being such a short text, just over 5,000 characters, and having a reputation for inspiring religious and mystical speculation, many individuals tried their hand at it. Perhaps some underestimated the difficulties inherent in this terse and deceivingly simple text. As a result, what we have today is a huge assemblage of various translations of uneven quality, some made by amateurs, some by well-trained scholars-specialists, and some by poets who had more inspiration than linguistic skills.

What is a good translation supposed to be? Several criteria or standards must be met that would apply to most kinds of translations, but here we are particularly interested in translations of the *TTC*. These are the basic standards:

(1) know the language, understand the historical context;
(2) be faithful to the author's intent;
(3) imitate the style and the flow of the original.

• *Principles of Interpretation*

Going one step beyond translating the *TTC*, there is the problem of interpretation. Most classical texts, and religious documents as well, have been subject to reinterpretation throughout the centuries by groups or communities that cherish them and use them as an inspiration for living. The Bible is a well-known example of rereading or reinterpreting ancient texts (Old Testament) in the light of later events and later revelations (New Testament). The Koran, in turn, reinterprets parts of the Bible in the light of their own religious experience. One cannot not question the legitimacy of such a procedure, but it must be stated that this happened and continues to happen. In the Christian churches, it developed into a new branch of Bible study: exegesis, which is the "exposition, critical analysis, or interpretation of a word, literary passage, etc.," of a text, even of a whole book.

Exegesis goes beyond translation, but is closely linked with it, sometimes confused with it. Translation should bring forward the author's intent, or the literal sense of a text. Interpretation may grow out of it, but at best only presents a derived or applied meaning. That, per se, is not wrong, if the distinction is acknowledged. The purpose of (re)interpreting a text seems to be the need of making an old text of certain authority meaningful to new situations or an inspiration for new social or religious bodies. Waley makes the distinction of "historical" and "scriptural" translations (Waley, 1934: 13).

In the context of Bible research, many examples could be cited. Just to mention one case, there is the "Song of Solomon," one of the Old Testament books. Its literal sense is the poetic expression of intense feelings between lovers; it is love poetry. But in the eyes of the religious leaders who decided to include it in the Bible, it became an allegory: It "implies" (or symbolizes) the love story between God and his chosen people, Israel.

The history of Chinese commentaries on the *TTC* is one of reinterpretation. One of the earliest attempts in this regard was the "religious conversion" of the book by the Heavenly Masters School of early Taoism. The *TTC* was "forced" to say what religious Taoists wanted it to say. One of the results of this process of appropriation was the blurring of two aspects of Taoism: the philosophical and the religious, and it still haunts modern scholarship.

That does not mean that texts such as the *TTC* do not lend themselves to wonderful speculation. The *TTC* does inspire a richness of applications, meaningful for life in the 20th century.

TAO-TE CHING/DAODEJING: **THEMES.** In the **Introduction**, several basic themes have already been briefly discussed; other themes are analyzed under separate entries: *Tao, Te, wu-wei,* **human perfection, uncarved wood, weakness, water, military strategy**. Because the *TTC* is so well known in the West, and often misunderstood, a more detailed analysis of its basic concepts is indeed a necessity. In spite of dozens of modern translations, there are few specialists who have risked to produce an in-depth study of the *TTC*'s worldview. Popular books such as the *Tao of Pooh* are charming and able to whet a reader's appetite, but after *Pooh*, where does one go?

Here, some fundamental themes and concepts of the *TTC* are presented and analyzed. An attempt is made to discover first of all the intention of the author(s), or, in other words, the "literal" meaning of the text. However, for us living in the 20th century, soon welcoming the 21st century, there may be other meanings hidden in the ancient text. We could call them "secondary" or "applied" meanings, showing what values an old text could have for us now.

As was discussed in the **Introduction**, there was once a twofold division in the text: *Tao* and *Te* (in the Ma-wang-tui manuscripts: *Te* and *Tao*). It would be ideal if this division was logically and consistently followed, but it is not the case. Otherwise, it would be an excellent device to identify the two major concerns of the *TTC* with *Tao* and *Te*: *Tao* would deal with personal cultivation through a deep understanding of the reality of the Way; *Te* would deal with the down-to-earth techniques of Taoist government. As the book is arranged today, the two themes are somewhat unsystematically scattered all over the text.

The themes chosen for discussion here, although not exhaustive, present the basic concepts of the *TTC*: They are *Tao* and *Te*, symbols of *Tao*, the sage and the government of the sage, and spiritual cultivation (other themes are discussed separately).

Tao is the eternal reality beyond, but also within, the visible universe. It is the Ultimate. It is creative force, not in the sense of a creator-god, but as an impersonal energy that creates and transforms without interruption. Its presence is everywhere, not as a spiritual being, but as the basic stuff, the *ch'i*, out of which all things have issued. It gives life to all living beings, and maintains them, dispassionately, with no likes or dislikes.

This *Tao* is deepest mystery, it cannot be grasped by the rational mind only, but intuitively, if the mind is still and desires are controlled. That must be done through spiritual cultivation, through contemplation. Only those who are able to gain a deep insight into the nature of *Tao* are entitled to rule the country.

The "One" (or Oneness) occurring several times in the *TTC* is perhaps a synonym of the *Tao*: It created the two, understood as yin and yang, or as heaven and earth. Heaven and earth, a compound of two concrete ideas, together become an abstract: Here, the universe, or nature (although "heaven" by itself also stands for what is natural, given, or nature). Nature, the inner essence of all things combined, but also of all individual things, is the visible expression of *Tao*.

A paradox in the *TTC* is that, on the one hand, *Tao* is creative and nurturing, symbolized by the concept of "motherhood," but on the other hand, heaven and earth (the world in which we live) is not "kind" (Chapter 5), it has no affections, it is rigidly impartial, and treats all beings alike, without favoritism. The *Tao* is not like a "divine providence," actively promoting the well-being of all (besides, the "providence" of some religious systems is more mythical than real). The best we can say is that *Tao* is indeed impersonal: It creates an environment wherein living beings can flourish, but it is not consciously engaged in promoting their state of well-being. It is up to all beings themselves to take nourishment from the *Tao*.

Te is then the inner and outer power bestowed on each being by *Tao*, or all the qualities for action inherent in the nature of each being, which gives each being a way to maintain itself, to grow and flourish. By extension, *te* also means "virtue," but that word is ambiguous and is often understood in the sense of "moral virtue" imposed on humans externally. True "virtue" comes from within, and has a power of its own. For instance, "true love" is powerful, it is able to achieve miracles and influence others. "True wisdom" is likewise powerful. It is the basic quality of a ruler, his special *te*, without which he cannot bring order to the world. The ruler's *te* is also charismatic power, by which he is able to achieve things without actually ordering them, just by his mere, magical presence. It further means that *te*, as "power," is the opposite of "force": A good ruler may stimulate action, but without using force (political, or even spiritual, force such as meddling with people's conscience).

The *TTC* often suggests that real *te* looks as its opposite: Real eloquence may be hidden in poor speech; real wisdom may be concealed in a humble person, etc. The image of an infant is an eloquent example: Powerless in appearance, its vitality is unimpaired; its persuasive power on adults is invincible: who can ignore the crying of a baby?

Among the symbols of *Tao* found in the *TTC* are "water," "female-mother," "valley," "emptiness," "infant," "uncarved wood." They also appear occasionally in the text, often rather casually. As concrete symbols of the *Tao*, they have the power to evoke what *Tao* is, better than any abstract reasoning. One must keep in mind that symbols point out one aspect of the symbolized only, or that "each comparison limps"; other qualities of the symbol do not apply.

"Water" is a rich symbol used in many traditions. It sometimes symbolizes "spiritual cleansing," or life-giving power. In the *TTC*, water symbolizes the *Tao* in several ways: It is humble (runs to the "lowest" places); it is adaptive, flexible; it goes around obstacles; it is weak, yet possesses great power in that it erodes rock; it is, above all, beneficial to all living things, but does not demand anything in return. A multisymbol dear to the Taoist heart!

The "female" and/or "mother" is another rich symbol in the *TTC*. In other traditions, the supreme being is represented as a "male" (which is nonsensical, but a result of language). Here, the *Tao* is represented as "female" (it does not mean that the *Tao* is female; this would also be nonsensical!). But the *Tao* has qualities/energies that we usually ascribe to the female and/or to the mother: humility (she is "below the male." This has sexual connotations, but in fact, she—

most often—controls the male); and fertility (she bears children and nurtures them, which is seen as degrading by some females today, but not by the *Tao*!). It is interesting that the *TTC* chooses the female as a symbol of the *Tao*; also interesting that yin comes before yang in the language: one has suggested that the roots of Taoism lie in a matriarchal society. In Chinese history, Confucianism is more male, Taoism more female. The symbolism is well chosen.

The "valley," like the "female," is a symbol of humility and fertility. Being lowly, it attracts the waters flowing down the hills and mountains; being well watered and receiving sunshine, it generates life. "Valley" is also a yin symbol, in opposition to "mountain," which in its harshness and pride is rather of yang nature.

The use of "emptiness" as a symbol of *Tao* is maybe inept, because the word is an abstract. But the *TTC* chooses concrete objects with "empty space" in them as symbols. A vehicle (of any kind) must be put together with many parts. The technical skill and the parts (the "being" aspect) are important; otherwise, there is no vehicle. But, in the end, it is the "empty space" (the "nonbeing" aspect) of a vehicle that makes it usable: It carries people and things to various destinations.

The "infant" as a symbol of *Tao* has already been mentioned. But the *TTC* goes further. At birth, an infant is flexible, its bones are soft. Infants often fall without getting hurt. They are a symbol of life. In death, everything becomes stiff and rigid. This, at first, points to a physical phenomenon, but it equally applies to spiritual realities. Young children are malleable, old people tend to be conservative. But whatever cannot bend anymore is doomed to die. The infant resembles the *Tao*, ever young and flexible.

The symbol "uncarved wood" refers to nature, to all beings, in their original state of oneness, the state of wholeness. (The common translation of "uncarved block" is not as suggestive as "uncarved wood.") The symbolism refers to the *Tao* as a unifying super-reality that has been broken up by divisiveness and selfishness (see also **Uncarved Wood**).

Taken together, one after another, those symbols are very enriching, inspire poetry, and can be a first step in our spiritual understanding of the elusive *Tao*.

The next theme: the sage and sage government, is one of the central foci of the *TTC*. After all, spiritual cultivation, important for oneself (like in the *Chuang-tzu*) must go beyond and find expression in actual government. Basically, Taoist government, at least in the *TTC*, should be a laissez-faire ("let do") type of governing, the middle way between "absolute nondoing" (anarchy) and absolutism or dictatorship. A "let do" policy means that a ruler lets his people do as much as possible themselves. This is the meaning of **wu-wei**, not only advocated in the *TTC*, but also in other Taoist writings.

Many chapters in the *TTC* advocate the correct government of the sage ruler. To start with two particularly significant passages, we should read Chapters 29 and 60.

Chapter 29: 1–2.   If anyone wants to grasp the country and manipulate it,
I see that he cannot succeed.
The country is a "sacred (spiritual) vessel," it cannot be manipulated.

Chapter 60: 1.   To govern a country is like frying small fish.

Both these texts emphasize that political leadership must be based on deep respect for the people and express itself in cautious and careful action. Trying to "manipulate" is "overdoing" it, will be counterproductive, and is doomed to failure. By being in tune with one's people, being responsive to their needs, a ruler will be successful.

The sage ruler manages without action, teaches without words; does not take possession and does not claim merits (Chapter 2:9–13); he is selfless and thus realizes his own self (Chapter 7:6); he avoids all extremes (Chapter 29:8) and is moderate in his demands; not overtaxing the people (Chapter 75:1) and being frugal in his personal life (Chapter 59:1), he leads the people to a life of simplicity (Chapter 57:12).

Indeed, the ideal ruler avoids contention among his people: By not exalting the worthy, by not displaying great wealth (Chapter 3), by not multiplying unnecessary laws, he brings peace and contentment to his country. A good ruler fills the people's bellies, empties their desires (Chapter 3:4). He does not encourage learning, because smart people become crafty (Chapter 3:6–7). Staying in the background, he makes the people feel that they do all themselves. Indeed, the best ruler is he that the people hardly know (Chapter 17:1) .

These are only a few examples of sage rule; the basic underlying principle is the all-embracing **wu-wei** (good government is also expressed in **military strategy**).

Although it appears that almost half of the chapters discuss some aspect of sage rule, the other basic theme, spiritual cultivation, is also in evidence. The two themes are like woof and warp in weaving. There are, however, no direct instructions on methods of meditation or principles of spirituality. But there is a wealth of suggestions to guide the reader in the right direction.

Foremost, there is a need for stillness and control of desires; what kind of desires are meant is left vague, but it probably includes physical desires and striving for fame and power. If one is driven by desires, one cannot penetrate to the deeper essence of the *Tao*, one can only touch the periphery (Chapter 1). Stillness of body and mind means to turn off one's sense impressions ("Block the passages, shut the doors," Chapter 56), it means to unlearn all the (useless) things one has learned, to empty oneself, to return to Primal Wholeness (*p'u*). This leads to primal "harmony," which is the constant, the eternal. To know the eternal is enlightenment (Chapter 55: 8). Ultimate wisdom is to understand the impermanence of all things: They all return to their root (their origin); in this there is peace, and fulfillment of destiny. To know the constant is enlightenment (Chapter 16: 3–5).

If a ruler can live up to these ideals of spiritual self-cultivation and deep understanding of the reality of *Tao* and how it operates, he will not seek self-glory and power, he will be aware of his own mortality, so that the people will live in contentment and also fulfill their own destiny. Is that not what human life is all about?

TAO-TE T'IEN-TSUN/DAODE TIANZUN (Heavenly Venerable of the Tao and its Power). Title of the third-highest deity of Taoism, within the triad of **T'ien-tsun**, Heavenly Venerables, also called **Three Pure Ones.**

His full name is T'ai-ch'ing (Supreme Purity) Tao-te T'ien-tsun, but his former appellation was T'ai-shang Lao-chün; he is, in fact, a transformation of the deified **Lao-tzu**, and, indeed, in the iconography of this triad, the third member, seated at the right hand of Yuan-shih T'ien-tsun, is the only one with recognizable human features: an old man with white hair and a white beard, similar to the representations of Lao-tzu as an independent figure.

The cult of Lao-tzu, although integrated into the triad of Heavenly Venerables, remained an independent movement as well. Not all schools accepted the worship of the triad. Lao-tzu deified kept his independent status and was honored with great titles by several emperors.

One may wonder why Tao-te T'ien-tsun occupies the *third* place in the supreme Taoist trinity, and Buddhist influence is certainly a possibility. The Taoist trinity was a creation of Ling-pao Taoism, which of all early Taoist schools was most affected by Buddhism. If one thinks of the Buddhist Trikaya ("Triple Body") concept, it is very clear that Lao-tzu's appearance in the world, as counselor to kings and savior of humanity, is very similar to the *third* body (embodiment) of Buddhism, the *nirmanakaya* or body of transformation, which is the historical figure of Siddharta Gautama, descending to the world to save mankind from its eternal frustration. The parallelism is too obvious to ignore (see also **T'ien-tsun**).

TAO-TSANG See TAOIST CANON

TAO-TSANG CHI-YAO See *EPITOME OF THE TAOIST CANON*

TAO-YIN See GYMNASTICS

TAOIST CANON (*Tao-tsang*). The collected scriptures of Taoism or the Taoist Canon are called *Tao-tsang* (*ching*)/*Daozang(jing)*. The extant Chinese collection (of which few individual texts have been translated) is a reproduction of the *Cheng-t'ung Tao-tsang* published during the Ming dynasty in 1444–45 and contains more than 1,480 titles (see also **ching** and **tsang**). The present essay is divided into three parts: the history of the Taoist Canon; an analysis of its contents or organization; the use and significance of Taoist scriptures in religious life.

• *History of the Taoist Canon*

The first systematic catalogue of Taoist scriptures is the work of Six Dynasties Taoist master **Lu Hsiu-ching** (406–477). Scriptures of various kinds had already circulated before, such as the Taoist philosophical writings, the Han text *T'ai-p'ing ching*, and works attributed to Chang Tao-ling and his disciples. But up to the fifth century, no effort had been made to collect and collate all the existing scriptures. In fact, except for the philosophical texts and some commentaries, the bulk of early scriptures was only written between about 290–400 CE.

Liu Hsiu-ching's first catalogue of Taoist scriptures was completed in 471. It was done by imperial decree. This pattern of imperial involvement in the cataloguing, collection, and printing of the Taoist scriptures would be continued up to the Ming dynasty. There have been all together seven editions of the Taoist scriptures. (See chart below.)

During the Sung, three compilations of the Taoist scriptures were made, but due to frequent warfare and foreign invasions, they did not survive. The Chin (Jurchen) edition was made from old woodblocks, but a number of new ones were carved. The limited number of copies were mostly destroyed in the subsequent warfare of the Mongol conquest.

The Yuan (Mongol) edition was compiled by Taoist masters of **Complete Realization** Taoism in 1244, but soon Khubilai Khan ordered its destruction (in 1281).

The Ming edition was ordered by Emperor Ch'eng-tsu in 1406; it was based on fragments of the Yuan and earlier editions. This canon was a limited edition, not easily accessible to interested readers and scholars. With the assistance of the Chinese government, a reproduction was made by the Commercial Press in Shanghai in 1923–26. A Taiwan reprint appeared in 1962. Then, finally, a more manageable reprint was made in Taiwan in 1977 (60 vols.), so that at the present, access to the *Tao-tsang* has become rather easy. This has been an important factor in the growth of interest in Taoist studies, in Asia as well as in the West.

Compilations of Taoist Scriptures
(see J. Boltz 1987: 4–7)

Dynasty	Compiler	Title	No. of Scrolls	Date
Liu-Sung	Lu Hsiu-ching	*San-tung ching-shu mu-lu* (not a collection of scriptures, just a catalogue)	1,200	471
T'ang		*San-tung ch'iung-kang* (Emperor Hsuan-tsung)	3,700 (7,300?)	748
Sung	Wang Ch'in-jo	*Pao-wen t'ung-lu*	4,359	1016
Sung	Chang Chun-fang	*Ta Sung t'ien-kung pao-tsang* (Emperors T'ai-tsung & Chen-tsung)	4,565	1019
Sung		*Cheng-ho wan-shou Tao-tsang* (Emperor Hui-tsung)	5,400	1120
Chin	Sun Ming-tao	*Ta Chin hsuan-tu pao-tsang*	6,455	1192
Yuan	Sung Te-fang & Ch'in Chih-an	*Hsuan-tu pao-tsang*	7,000 (7,800?)	1244
Ming	Chang Yü-ch'u & Shao Yi-cheng	*Ta Ming Tao-tsang ching (Cheng-t'ung Tao-tsang)*	5,318	1444–45
		Supplement: *Hsü Tao-tsang ching*	240 (180?)	1607

• *Organization or Contents of the Tao-tsang*

It is a well-known fact that the *Tao-tsang* is a "very mixed bag"; in an eloquent way, it symbolizes the heterogeneous nature of Taoism itself. The extant Ming edition (reproduced in 1977 in 60 volumes) contains 1,487 titles (in 5,318 scrolls) and

> gathers together works by philosophers like Lao-tzu and Chuang-tzu; pharmacopoeial treatises; the oldest Chinese medical treatise; hagiographies; immense ritual texts laced with magic; imaginary geographies; dietetic and hygienic recipes; anthologies and hymns; speculations on the ideograms of the *I ching*; meditation techniques; alchemical texts; and moral tracts. One finds both the best and the worst within the canon. (Robinet, 1979/1993: 1)

Other types of writings should also be mentioned: collections of talismans (*fu*) and incantations (*chou*); works on divination; and tracts of the popular religion (see Kalinowski, 1989–90, and Schipper, 1994). This indicates the mutual borrowing processes that went on between Taoism and China's Popular religion. (See also **Popular Religion and Taoism**.)

The present organization of the *Tao-tsang* yields some interesting insights into the origins of the canon; combined with historical information from later Taoist writings, one can form a fairly accurate picture of the canon's genesis. The *Tao-tsang* is divided into three major sections, named *tung*, and four supplements of later date, named *fu*. *Tung* is usually translated as "grotto, cave, cavern"; modern scholars usually refer to it as "Three Caverns," but it is unlikely that, originally, *tung* had that special meaning of cavern; it indicated only that the three major scriptures had each "*tung*" in their title. In other words, rather than indicating "Three Caverns," *san-tung* referred initially to three *tung* scriptures. Indeed, *tung* also means "profound, mysterious" (Chavannes, 1919). This means that the translation "Three Caverns" is based on a misunderstanding. Therefore, an alternative way of naming the triple division of the canon is preferable. M. Strickmann suggested: *Perfection, Sublimity,* and *Divinity* (Strickmann, 1979: 333, note 10), but these titles do not translate *tung*. If this term translates as "profound, mystery," then the following naming could be proposed: *Profound Perfection* (*tung-chen*), *Profound Mystery* (*tung-hsuan*), and *Profound Divinity* (*tung-shen*).

The term *san-tung* was first applied by Lu Hsiu-ching to scriptures from three streams of Taoism:

> The Shang-ch'ing tradition (School of Great Purity), later identified with the Mao Shan school. The central scripture *Ta-tung chen-ching* (True Scripture of Great Penetration) gave rise to the abbreviated term *tung-chen*: "profound perfection." (*Tung* in the title does not mean "cavern.")

The Ling-pao school had produced many scriptures which had *tung-hsuan* as a prefix in their title: "profound mystery."

The *San-huang* scripture gave rise to the *tung-shen* division: "profound divinity," since the major text was once titled *Tung-shen san-huang ching*. (Ofuchi, 1979: 256–7)

The expression *san-tung* (three *tung* scriptures), first used by Lu Hsiu-ching to organize the texts he had collected from three different traditions, is said to have been in existence before him. Lu belonged to the Ling-pao School and yet put the *Shang-ch'ing* scriptures in the first place. This indicates that the triple division derived from the Shang-ch'ing School and was already well established in Lu's time.

It is now commonly accepted that this triple division was made in imitation of the Buddhist model. It did not follow the Buddhist Canon, the Tripitaka or Triple "Basket" (Treasury), but the Buddhist ranking system of "Vehicles" (*yana*). The Buddhists had arranged their texts into three groups: *sutras* (sermons pronounced by the Buddha), *vinaya* (rules of monastic discipline), and *abhidharma* (treatises on the teachings). The Taoist division is quite different in that the three divisions embody the texts of three independent schools of Taoism, parallel to the Buddhist division of three *yanas*: the "vehicles" of the auditors (*sravakayana*), the self-made or self-styled Buddhas (*pratyekabuddhayana*); and the Bodhisattvas (*Bodhisattvayana*). Because these three are further identified with the Lesser, Middle, and Greater vehicles of Buddhism, the Taoist division implies a value judgment of superior, middle and lesser *tung* (Ofuchi, 1979: 261).

Some important inferences can be made: If the expression *san-tung* was created by the Shang-ch'ing School, it implies that they considered their own scriptures (and school) as superior to all the others, the Ling-pao as second, and *San-huang* as the lowest. Indeed, not much is known about the history of the *San-huang* tradition, and it seems that no lasting school of Taoism grew out of it. But why these scriptures were included, while those of the Heavenly Masters School were not, is still a riddle, about which one can speculate and make reasonable guesses.

The **Heavenly Masters School** (or *T'ien-shih Tao)* was founded in the second century CE and presided over by the Three Changs. Chang Lu had submitted to Wei general Ts'ao Ts'ao in 215. He was rewarded for his submission, yet, to break his power and political threat to the regime, Ts'ao Ts'ao "forced several tens of thousands of believers to leave Shu [Szechuan] and move . . . near modern Xi'an, thus placing them under the close scrutiny of his government" (Kobayashi, 1992: 17). The result was the disintegration of the Heavenly Masters (HM) movement. What happened next is rather unclear, but it is said that many families in the north converted to HM Taoism, and that, after 311 CE, the HM Tao spread all over China. It particularly moved to the south, where the imperial house and many court officials had taken refuge (Strickmann, 1979: 167). A new Taoism developed in the south as a result of the merging of HM Taoism with the practices and beliefs of the south. It is stated that the HM School was very influential in the south during the Six Dynasties period. Yet there is reason to doubt this: Their scriptures were not included in the first catalog of the Taoist Canon in 471. That is a serious problem.

Could it be that the Shang-ch'ing School (Mao Shan Taoism), which created the *San-tung* division of scriptures, was too elitist (intelligentsia-oriented) and had no interest in the more "popular" ritual tradition of the HM School? Did they perhaps look down on this "lower class" Taoism, which specialized in rituals of confession and exorcism? Whatever the reasons for ignoring the HM scriptures in the first canon, it would take another century or so for their inclusion into the Four Supplements.

While the three *tung* were being collected and edited, a parallel development took place with regard to the Taoist pantheon: the creation of the **Three Pure Ones** (*San-ch'ing*). Each section of the canon was credited to the inspiration or revelation of one member of the triad, in descending order. This confirms the ranking of the three sections as superior, middle, and lower, parallel with the ranking of the three deities.

San-Tung and *San-Ch'ing*

Shang-ch'ing scriptures (*Tung-chen*)	Yuan-shih T'ien-tsun = Yu-ch'ing
Ling-pao scriptures (*Tung-hsuan*)	Ling-pao T'ien-tsun = Shang-ch'ing
San-huang scriptures (*Tung-shen*)	Tao-te T'ien-tsun = T'ai-ch'ing

An interesting comment on this table is the fact that Tao-te T'ien-tsun, the equivalent of the more popular deity T'ai-shang Lao-chün, which is the personified or deified **Lao-tzu**, is placed third, on the lowest level. Indeed, most "philosophical" texts, the commentaries on the *Tao Te Ching* and *Chuang-tzu*, are found in the third *tung*, the *Tung-shen* division of the canon. In the 1977 Taiwan edition, *TTC* commentaries are, except for three, in volumes 19–24, all together, 52 commentaries. In the minds of the earliest compilers, those "philosophical" texts did not reflect the elitist stand of the Shang-ch'ing and Ling-pao schools, and were therefore relegated to the "Lower Vehicle."

Twelve Subdivisions of the Three Sections

Buddhist influence on the organization of the Taoist canon has been mentioned already. Its influence on the composition of particular texts, especially those of the Ling-pao tradition, has also been established (Zürcher, 1980).

A further parallel between the two Canons can be seen in the subdivision of the three sections into 12 literary genres (this subdivision is not found in the Four Supplements). Buddhist influence made the Taoists choose their own 12 genres, but what is copied is the principle and the number 12; the contents are different, as the following table shows.

Comparison of 3 *Tung* with Buddhist Canon

Twelve-fold Division of 3 tung	Twelve genres in Buddhist Canon
1. *pen-wen* (original revelations)	1. *sutra* (Buddha's addresses)
2. *shen-fu* (talismans)	2. *geya* (song, repeating prose)
3. *yü-chueh* (exegesis, instructions)	3. *gatha* (song, hymn)
4. *ling-t'u* (sacred diagrams)	4. *nidana* (sutras written upon request)
5. *p'u-lu* (history, genealogy)	5. *itivrttaka* (previous lives of disciples)
6. *chieh-lu* (conduct codes)	6. *jataka* (birth-stories)
7. *wei-yi* (ceremonial)	7. *adbhuta-dharma* (miracle stories)
8. *fang-fa* (rituals)	8. *avadana* (stories, parables)
9. *chung-shu* (techniques)	9. *upadesa* (treatises, Abhidharma)
10. *chi-chuan* (records, biographies)	10. *udana* (spontaneous statements)
11. *tsan-sung* (hymnody)	11. *vaipulya* (fuller explanations, Mahayana)
12. *piao-tsou* (memorials)	12. *vyakarana* (predictions)

It is obvious that the Taoist genres have greater variety than their Buddhist counterparts. This is because the Buddhist division relates only to the *sutra-pitaka* (the sermons of the Buddha). It does not include rules of conduct, nor historical records, liturgies, or techniques. This is another indication that the Taoists did not take the Buddhist *Tripitaka* as their own model for dividing the scriptures, but, as was already said, the triple *yana* division.

The Four Supplements (*szu fu*) were added to the canon about one hundred years after Lu's first catalogue circa the beginning of the sixth century (Ofuchi, 1979: 267). Others believe it was after the first half of the sixth century (Liu, 1973: 112). But no evidence of a collection of texts between 471 and the T'ang edition of 748 seems to be at hand.

The four supplements are called: *T'ai-hsuan*; *T'ai-p'ing*; *T'ai-ch'ing*; and *Cheng-yi*. The three former ones were meant to supplement the three *tung* in their respective order:

Tung-chen, Profound Perfection	supplement: *T'ai-hsuan*, *Great Mystery*
Tung-hsuan, Profound Mystery	supplement: *T'ai-p'ing, Great Peace and Equality*
Tung-shen, Profound Divinity	supplement: *T'ai-ch'ing, Great Purity*

The fourth supplement, the *Cheng-yi* scriptures, stands alone. It had no precedent in the earlier *san-tung* canon and, in fact, contains the scriptures of HM Taoism, finally recognized as an important school of Taoism. It probably reflects the reorganization and the social acceptance of the Heavenly Masters.

The addition of the four supplements did not occur in a systematic way: the earlier rules of organization were bent, and the result is "the comparatively chaotic collection that the Taoist Canon is today" (Ofuchi, 1979: 267).

• *Taoist Scriptures in Religious Life*

Scriptures have an important function in the religious life of all religious communities, either as an inspiration for individual believers or as sacred texts to be chanted, recited, or sung in various types of liturgical services. Scriptures are also the basis of theological interpretations and serve as sources of moral ideals.

Before the modern publications of the *Tao-tsang,* very few individuals had access to the Taoist writings, except for works of "philosophical" nature, such as the *TTC* and the *Chuang-tzu* and some others, also included in other collections or published as separate works.

Yet, the Taoist scriptures of each school were significant in the school's life and activities. Let us take the Heavenly Masters as a concrete example. This school operates in Taiwan today and has been studied in some detail. When a master accepts students, they must go through years of training or apprenticeship. They learn on the job. Mastering the various musical instruments is a first step, but gradually they are involved in the liturgy, until they have a close relationship with the master and are ready to receive ordination. One of the young candidate's duties or privileges is to make handwritten copies of the master's scriptures. Each master has an extensive set of scriptures used in his rituals. They are guarded with caution and not allowed to be handled by outsiders. Even today, the Cheng-yi priests of Taiwan use these handwritten texts, bound in Chinese fashion and often executed with a high degree of calligraphic skill. Some texts preserved today go back many generations.

Most of the Taoist rituals performed during a *chiao* festival consist of reciting and chanting these sacred texts. In contrast with other religions, such as Judaism and Christianity, Taoism does not hold community gatherings, during which the scriptures are read and commented upon for the instruction and edification of the congregation. Buddhism, on the other hand, used to hold lecture meetings, sometimes for large audiences of lay people, and eminent monks would lecture on some of the most important *sutras*.

Besides this communal aspect of scripture usage, some texts were also read and studied individually. Each school of Taoism had its own selection, and individuals could read them and meditate on them. Among the few texts of Taoism that have gone beyond the boundaries of China and have gained a tremendous appeal abroad are the *Tao-te ching* and the *Chuang-tzu* (in translation). While most of the scriptures found in the *TT* have a limited and local appeal, these two texts enjoy a truly international reputation, and are tremendous sources of inspiration in modern times.

TE/DE. After Tao, this is one of the most central concepts in Taoism, at least in its philosophical stream. Its meaning is even more elusive than the meaning of Tao. The dictionary translations of *Te* already express the problem and indicate the variety of possible meanings: virtue; moral excellence; goodness; conduct, behavior (not always good); energy, power.

Translations of the *Tao-te ching*, where *Te* is part of the title and must therefore express a crucial theme of the whole text, diverge in their renderings of *Te*. Most commonly, it is translated as "virtue," sometimes as "power." An original way of translating is "integrity" (V. Mair, 1990). Checking out 12 recent translations of the *TTC*, one obtains these results. *Te* is rendered as:

"virtue": five times
"power": one time
"te" (not translated): three times

"integrity": one time
"life": one time
"attainment": one time

An analysis of the character etymology is not very helpful. It is complex in structure and to find meaning in the parts is only partially useful. The left part and radical evokes the principle of motion or action; one element in the right part is *hsin* (mind, heart) (E.M. Chen, 1973: 460). But that remains too vague to draw any conclusions. The best way to solve the difficulty is to see how *Te* is used in various ancient contexts. M. LaFargue found that in three pre-Taoist texts, the term *Te* is used as follows:

In the *Book of Documents* (*Shu ching*), it refers to awe-inspiring charisma in a ruler, which gives rise to political power.

In the Book *Mencius*, *Te* relates to a moral ideal, to virtues (*jen, yi, li*), or the virtuous character of the *shih* (gentlemen) deserving respect.

In the *Nei-yeh* (part of *Kuan-tzu*), *Te* is internal force as the result of self-cultivation. That means that *Te* is understood differently in different systems of thought.

The best way of finding a suitable English equivalent (at least one that approximates the Chinese term) is by elimination. First of all, *Te*, not translated but transliterated, does not solve much. It is different from the term *Tao*, which has a good English equivalent in "way" (besides, *Te* is hard to pronounce if one doesn't know Chinese and is usually mispronounced).

Then comes "virtue," which has several meanings. Taking *Webster's* as a guideline, virtue can mean: general moral excellence, goodness or morality; a specific moral quality (as in "cardinal virtues"); chastity; excellence in general, merit; effective power or force, efficacy, potency; strength, courage. A lot to choose from. What is interesting is that all these meanings can be reduced to two basic concepts: moral virtue and power. These are the two meanings implied in the basic Latin word, *virtus*. However, actual usage puts much more emphasis on moral virtue than on the aspect of power. Therefore, to render the Taoist *Te* by "virtue" is not a good strategy, because it would mislead unaware readers.

In other Chinese schools, "virtue" would be more acceptable, especially in the Confucian context, in which "virtue" most commonly refers to particular moral qualities, such as benevolence or humaneness (*jen*), righteousness (*yi*), loyalty (*chung*), filial piety (*hsiao*), etc. But it is against just such Confucian virtues that the *TTC* and some chapters of *Chuang-tzu* react (see *TTC*, Chapters 18–19). Their "preaching" is a sign of their absence. That they appeared in the first place was the cause (and a sign) of the darkening of the Tao. Therefore, "virtue" as a rendering of *Te* would not do.

Moreover, and this is a positive argument, there are better terms to render *Te*. The most suitable one is "power" at least if one can do away with one wrong association of this word: its possible reference to physical power or violence. That too goes against the basic meaning of the texts. Rendered as "power," it becomes also clear that *Te* is the direct result of *Tao*, as *TTC* Chapter 21: 1 expresses:

The manifestation(s) of great power follow uniquely from the Tao.

This appears to mean that Tao is the generator of *Te*. If Tao is the overarching reality and cosmic energy, *Te* is what all beings receive from Tao; it is their own nature, with its specific talents and potentials, that enables them to act in their own way as if by their inner compulsion. This concept has nothing to do with "moral virtue" or "goodness" (Tao itself is not virtuous in that sense, because virtue is a human quality). In other words, *Te* is the power of Tao, individualized, as, for example, in a seed, which has the inner potential and unfailing power to sprout and grow into a preprogrammed plant or tree.

In the *TTC*, which addresses itself to rulers, *Te* is elevated to an even higher level; it is the power to rule, not through physical force, but through inner charisma, which may be a natural talent, but also must be cultivated. There are humans who have this special power, personal charisma, possibly based on physical appearance, but more so emanating from the inner, spiritual self, almost magical in nature. This kind of power to rule does not exclude "moral virtue" in its ordinary sense, but goes beyond it. It is also expressed in other leadership qualities: deep knowledge and wisdom, even moral virtues, such as goodness, compassion, sincerity, honesty, integrity. Perhaps the Confucian "sincerity" (*ch'eng*) comes closest to the concept of *Te*, since it also has a metaphysical foundation.

A ruler who possesses *Te* in its fullness has the natural authority needed to lead the people, without showing his power. He nourishes his people, without self-seeking. True *Te* manifests itself in **wu-wei** and in other qualities related to it: **weakness**, **naturalness**, holding on to wholeness.

TEMPLES. The most appropriate title for a Taoist monastery is *kuan/guan*, observation post, belvedere (ex. Pai-yün kuan or "White Cloud Monastery" in Beijing); very often one also encounters the title *kung*, literally "palace" (ex. Pa-hsien kung or "Eight Immortals Palace" near Xi'an). Today, besides these two, a great variety of appellations exist for different kinds of temples, including Confucian temples, Buddhist and Taoist monasteries, and temples of the Popular religion. There is no consistency in their actual use. But in general, *kuan* and *kung* are the most current appellations for Taoist places of worship and/or monastic life.

It would be very difficult to point out what differentiates Taoist temples/monasteries from their Confucian and Buddhist counterparts. Architectural styles of temple building are distinguished more geographically (northern and southern styles) than denominationally. The earliest Taoist temples were constructed during the Period of Disunity (third to sixth century), modeled after Buddhist monasteries, which, in turn, borrowed from the official architecture of the imperial palaces. Even today, building styles overlap to a great extent.

Taoist temples/monasteries that have survived until the present number about 40 in China. In Hong Kong, there are only half a dozen major ones and in Taiwan their exact number is not known, for the simple reason that most temples of the popular cult call themselves "Taoist" and that is certainly confusing (see **Popular Religion and Taoism**). Yet, a few distinctly Taoist temples exist in Taiwan: the Chih-nan kung ("South-Pointing Palace") in the suburbs of Taipei, and the Tao-te yuan ("Hall of Tao and Te") in Kaohsiung are clear examples.

Taoist temple architecture generally follows the patterns of Chinese temple architecture: Monasteries are built along a North-South axis (facing South) and consist of several halls separated by courtyards. Richly ornamented roofs (in the South) and sober roofs (in the North) are supported by stone columns ("dragon pillars") and attached to them by a complex system of brackets.

What differentiates temples of various systems is more the images placed in them than the building styles. Taoist temples obviously hold images of Taoist deities: mostly the **Three Pure Ones** and famous founders, such as Wang Ch'ung-yang and Ch'iu Ch'u-chi. Occasionally, there is an image of T'ai-shang Lao-chün (**Lao-tzu deified**) and the popular **Eight Immortals**.

Most of the temple paraphernalia are shared by all religious buildings: architecture, images, sculpture, worship tools, etc. The Confucian temples are more soberly built and do not contain statues/images of their sages: They are represented by wooden tablets.

A recent report says that there are about 600 Taoist temples and monasteries in China today (compared to 9,500 on the Buddhist side: one to 15!), of which 21 are listed as "key" temples.

A few samples: on Mount T'ai in Shantung, Pi-hsia tz'u. ("When Chavannes studied T'ai Shan at the beginning of the twentieth century, more than 250 Taoist temple halls or shrines were located there"

(*ER* 14 [1987]: 381). One wonders whether they are all strictly Taoist.)

Other famous mountains are also the location of renowned—and still active—temples: Mount Lao in Shantung, Mount Mao in Kiangsu, Mount Lung-hu in Kiangsi, Mount Lou-fu in Kuangtung, Mount Ch'ing-ch'eng in Szechuan, Mount Wu-tang in Hupei, Mount Sung in Honan, Mount Hua in Shansi, Mount Ch'iang in Liaoning (see T. Hahn, 1989: 79–101; and 1988: 145–156).

THIRTY-SIX HEAVENS See THREE WORLDS

THREE AGENTS See THREE OFFICIALS

THREE CHANGS See CHANG BROTHERS

THREE CORPSES See THREE WORMS

THREE OFFICIALS (San Kuan/Sanguan) (also called "Three Agents," "Three Rulers," "Three Officers"). This refers to a triad of Taoist deities whose worship goes back to antiquity and was very prominent in the early **Heavenly Masters School**. Their full name is *San-kuan Ta-ti*: Three Agents, Grand Emperors, sometimes also called *San-chieh Kung*, Lords of the Three Worlds (see **san-chieh**), and sometimes also identified as *san yuan*. They are "the lords in charge of the three offices of heaven, earth, and the waters under the earth" (Lagerwey, 1987: 19). The Heavenly Masters instituted three festivals in their honor, celebrated on the days called *san yuan*:

> the 15th day of the first lunar month: heavenly *kuan*
> the 15th day of the seventh lunar month: earthly *kuan*
> the 15th day of the tenth lunar month: water *kuan*

They rank very high in the Taoist pantheon, just below the **Jade Emperor**, and possess great authority:

> To each of them is attributed the power of bestowing a particular favor. The Agent of Heaven gives happiness; the Agent of Earth pardons sins; the Agent of Water protects from misfortune. (Maspero, 1971/1981: 158)

The Heavenly Master Taoists worshipped the Three Officials during rituals of confession or repentance. Illness was explained as the result of moral wrongdoing ("sin"); therefore to regain one's health, one had to make a confession and admit one's wrongdoing to the Three Officials. Prayers for pardon were written on three slips of paper: The one addressed to the Ruler of Heaven was burned (or placed on a mountaintop); the one addressed to the Ruler of Earth was buried in the ground; the one addressed to the Ruler of Water was submerged in a watercourse.

The cult of the Three Agents spread among the people since the fifth century CE, and even today the community religion celebrates their festival days. In Taiwan, about 80 temples are dedicated to their worship, and on their festival days, the premises are crowded with a continuous flow of devotees.

The Three Agents have been identified with three mythical culture heroes: Shun, Yao, and Yü. The latter, Yü the Great, is the hero who brought the floods under control and is naturally identified with the Water Agent.

In popular folklore, the Heavenly Official is most prominent: one sees his picture on many New Year's greeting cards and special posters. He is believed to bring happiness and good fortune to his worshippers (see *TMSC*: 342–349).

THREE ONES (*San-yi/Sanyi*). This is an important concept in the meditation methods of the Great Purity School (Mao Shan Taoism), related to the concept of the One. It is a very complex concept, referring to a trinity of deities, as well as principles. It is said that the ". . . Three Ones basically refers to the fundamental trinity of the universe, the first division of the primordial unity, The Way . . . [The term] is also applied to the manifestations of this fundamental trinity or subsequent levels of existence. (P. Anderson, 1980: 22). These manifestations are three celestial gods residing in the *T'ai-wei* heaven ("Supreme Subtlety") and the three (identical) gods also dwelling in the three vital centers of the human body (**tan-t'ien**).

From macrocosmic divine beings, the Three Ones also become the microcosmic vital principles of human life, and thus refer to three vital forces or energies within the human body: *ching* (seminal, essence), *ch'i* (breath, energy), and *shen* (spirit). From this parallelism, it is obvious that it is very crucial for the Taoist adept to cultivate the Three Ones: by concentrating on them and obtaining an inner visualization, their presence inside the body will be maintained and strengthened. If they "become clearly visible in a permanent way, immortality has been achieved" (Anderson: 27). If the vision stops, their presence diminishes; if exhausted, death is the result.

Meditation on the Three Ones is explained in several Taoist scriptures (for details, see Anderson, 1980; I. Robinet, 1979/1993; L. Kohn, 1993: 204–214). (See also **Hold on to Oneness**.)

THREE ORIGINALS See THREE PRIMORDIALS

THREE PRIMARY VITALITIES (*san-yuan, san-chen*). If the underlying principle of **outer alchemy** is to speed up the natural processes of nature, **inner alchemy** attempts to reverse the natural processes of aging and "bring about a reversion of the tissues from an aging state to an infantile state" (J. Needham V, 5: 25). Expressed differently, it was an attempt to recover or replenish the vitalities that one was born with and that gradually are consumed by living. Indeed, Taoism believed that every living being, at birth, is endowed with three primary vitalities, called *san-yuan* (three originals) or *san-chen* (three true things). These *san-yuan* should not be confused with another set of *san-yuan*, written in the same way, but meaning something very different (see **Three Primordials**). The endowment of *san-yuan* is called "prior heaven" (*hsien-t'ien*) and signifies what is given to an embryo before it leaves the womb.

The three primary vitalities are *yuan-ching, yuan-ch'i*, and *yuan-shen* (Needham V, 5: 26):

> • *yuan-ching* is primary seed vitality, which degenerates into seminal essence, seed or sperm during sexual intercourse. The sources are not clear about the female equivalent: Woman's seminal energy is the "menstrual blood" (more likely the ovum), which is also limited, yet the Taoist view considers her seminal energy as unlimited (see **Sexuality**).
> • *yuan-ch'i* is primary *ch'i*, which degenerates into respiratory breath, inhaling and exhaling (see ***Ch'i***).
> • *yuan-shen* is primary spirit, which degenerates into mental activity, anxiety, and worry (see **Spirit**).

> The first of these vitalities was correlated with the peripheral parts of the body as a whole, the second with the heart [mind] (*hsin*) or the thorax in which it centered, and the third with the mind (*yi*). (Needham V, 5: 26)

By performing the correct practices, the processes of degeneration could be reversed and longevity attained. But because these correct practices are all internalized, i.e., taking place within a person's body-mind unit, there was a need for a new term to express this new "elixir within." Needham coined this new term "enchymoma," a pouring into the body, from its own resources, of vital humors or energies, that would stop the aging process and lead to rejuvenation. Needham does not further explain this process, but it would not be presumptuous to relate the following Taoist practices to the threefold revitalization: The *yuan-ching* can be strengthened by retention of semen or, as in exceptional situations not advocated by all Taoist schools, by "dual cultivation" or the "union of energies" of man and woman. The *yuan-ch'i* can be strengthened by special breathing techniques, such as "embryonic breathing," whereas the *yuan-shen* can be regenerated and brought to ultimate spiritualization through meditative practices: stilling of the mind, inner visualization, and **"Holding on to Oneness."**

Through constant and single-minded effort, the adept would then be able to convert his *ching* into *ch'i*, and his *ch'i* into *shen*, pure spirit. This is sometimes concretely expressed by images of the adept, sitting in meditation, with a new infant inside his body. This is most likely a symbol of the new life generated inside oneself, which, ultimately, once fully grown, will be released and become the immortal body (*hsien*).

Because these practices demand great effort and must be accompanied by proper diet, only a very small number of humans can hope to achieve this. Ordinary mortals continue to use up their three vitalities, and when they run out, death ensues. Still, this is much more desirable than to die in mid-stream, when the vitalities are not yet exhausted. Such people are believed to turn into vengeful ghosts (*kui*) and lead a restless existence.

Whether this Taoist view of Three Vitalities is based on solid scientific knowledge, especially physiology, is a question that needs further investigation. Another question is whether the principles are consistent internally. When it is said that primary *ch'i* degenerates into respiratory breath, it does not seem correct, because *ch'i* is not only breath but vital energy. These and other aspects of Taoist **alchemy** need critical examination.

THREE PRIMORDIALS (*san-yuan*) (also called "Three Originals," "Three Primes," "Three Origins"). They are the three supreme deities and/or primordial *ch'i*, that "created" the cosmos and issued the scriptures of Shang-ch'ing Taoism. Moreover, within the body, they inhabit the three cinnabar fields or *tan-t'ien*. It appears that the Three Originals are identical with the **Three Ones**, both in their cosmic and their human-body dimensions. They further are seen as announcers of the three basic scriptures that constituted the three sections of the **Taoist Canon**.

The *san-yuan* are thus supreme deities as well as supreme creative energies; they have also been transformed into principles and periods of time, in as far as three days in the year are specially consecrated to them. The three "days of origin"—*shang-yuan*, (first *yuan*), *chung-yuan* (middle *yuan*), and *hsia-yuan* (last *yuan*)—coincide respectively with the 15th day of the first, seventh, and tenth months: On these days, the **Three Officials** or Agents (***san kuan***) are worshipped. These days are therefore also called Heaven Festival, Earth Festival, and Water Festival. The first one coincides with the more popular Lantern Festival (first full moon of the new year), whereas the second one (*chung-yuan*) coincides with the Ghost Festival, due to Buddhist influence. This Ghost Festival, during which a ritual for Universal Salvation (*p'u-tu*) takes place, is not a Taoist affair but is a celebration of the community religion.

THREE PURE ONES or **THREE PURES** (*San-ch'ing/Sanqing*). Names of the highest deities of Taoism. The epithet "Pure" refers to the three heavens in which they are believed to reside:

> The Jade Pure (One) resides in the heaven of Jade Purity (*Yü-ch'ing*), the highest level of the three;
> The Higher Pure (One) resides in the heaven of Higher Purity (*Shang-ch'ing*);
> The Grand Pure (One) resides in the heaven of Grand Purity (*T'ai-ch'ing*).

Because these three heavens of Taoism are products of mythical creation, so likewise are the Three Pure Ones mythical deities, who have no basis in the natural world, in contrast to the deified powers of nature (or **Nature Gods**).

The creation of the Three Pure Ones are the end products of a gradual development, starting with the deification of **Lao-tzu**, who was at first called T'ien-shang Lao-chün, or *Chiao-chu*, "Lord of the (Taoist) Teaching." In his *Pao-p'u-tzu*, Ko Hung called Lao-tzu by the title of *Yuan-chün* ("Original Lord" or "Lord of the Origin").

During the Southern Liang dynasty, T'ao Hung-ching, who was the first to draw up a hierarchical chart of the Taoist pantheon, elevated Yuan-shih T'ien-tsun ("Heavenly Venerable of the Original Beginning") to the top of all the gods, even higher than Lao-tzu.

It was during the T'ang period that the triad of Three Pure Ones came into existence: They were then called T'ai-shang Tao-chün ("Grand Lord of the Tao"), Yuan-shih T'ien-tsun (adopted from T'ao Hung-ching's pantheon), and T'ai-shang Lao-chün ("Grand Lord Lao-tzu").

A final regrouping and renaming resulted in the triad, still worshipped by Taoists today:

Yuan-shih T'ien-tsun
Ling-pao T'ien-tsun (new title for T'ai-shang Tao-chün)
Tao-te T'ien-tsun (new title for T'ai-shang Lao-chün)

These three were identified with the Three Pure Ones. It was also believed that the **Jade Emperor** (Yü-huang) was the younger brother of Yuan-shih T'ien-tsun.

In today's Taoist rituals, especially during the **Cosmic Renewal Festival**, Taoist masters bring their own painted scrolls of the Three Pure Ones or Three Heavenly Worthies to the temple and hang them up on the northern wall, normally reserved for the lower-ranking deities of the local temple. During the whole celebration, the Three Pure Ones receive the worship and offerings of the priests and the community; they are indeed the ones who have the power of cosmic renewal.

In some Taoist scriptures, the Taoist triad is said to be the transformation of the one original *Ch'i*, out of which the whole cosmos issued forth.

In other texts, the three are also said to preside over the three sections (*san-tung*) of the **Taoist Canon**, of which they are the respective original creators.

In Taoist monasteries and temples, since T'ang and Sung times, there was always one hall (San-ch'ing chien) dedicated to their worship. But they are not worshipped by the common people.

THREE RULERS See THREE OFFICIALS

THREE SOVEREIGNS SCRIPTURE (*San-huang ching/Sanhuang-jing*). A Taoist scripture of unknown authorship, yet important, because it was a basic text in the triple division of the **Taoist Canon**; in fact, the leading scripture of the third or *Tung-shen* section.

The Three Sovereigns refer to the three sovereign powers, **heaven, earth** and **humanity** (also called Three Powers, *san-ts'ai*). It is said that this scripture was revealed to Pao Ch'ing of the Western Chin (265–317 CE) while he was practicing the Way on Mount Sung, around 300 CE. He, in turn, transmitted it to Ko Hung, who transmitted it to Lu Hsiu-ching, the first organizer of the canon.

The main contents of the text have to do with summoning spiritual beings, with methods of talismanic charts and concentration.

T'ang Emperor T'ai-tsung ordered the text to be destroyed in 646, so the old version has been lost. Two scriptures included in the present Taoist Canon with *san-huang* in their title (*CT* 855, *TT* 575, and *CT* 856, *TT* 575) are not the original *San-huang* text, but have preserved some of its original ideas.

THREE TEACHINGS (San-chiao/Sanjiao). Because Taoism is one of the Three Teachings or Three Doctrines (not Three Religions), a discussion of its meaning and uses must be included.

Chiao/jiao by itself means "teaching, doctrine, culture," but because the Western term "religion" was in modern times translated as *tsung-chiao/zongjiao*, *chiao* by itself was mistakenly also translated as religion. As a result, *san-chiao* was rendered as "Three Religions" (of China). Another aggravating circumstance was that *chiao* was often combined with other terms, which gave rise to *Tao-chiao* (Taoist religion), *Fo-chiao* (**Buddhism**), and, occasionally, even *Ju-chiao* (**Confucianism**). All these terms distinguish *chiao* from *chia/jia*. The latter means school of thought or philosophy, a term coined already during the Han dynasty (pointing to the "hundred schools" of learning competing for success during the Warring States period).

The translation of *san-chiao* as "Three Religions" is inadequate, because China does not have just three religions. These "three" are elite schools of learning and practice, but the overwhelming majority of the people are not much affected by it. They follow their own beliefs and especially their own sets of religious practices, better called the community religion or "communal" religion. Even the elite participated in many of these traditions.

The term *san-chiao* was an elite creation. They looked at Confucianism, Taoism, and Buddhism as systems of thought rather than as religions. Even as early as the Six Dynasties period, adherents of the three met for discussion and confrontation. Later, during the Northern rule of the Chin (Yurchen) when the South was ruled by the Southern Sung, the new school of **Complete Realization** Taoism was very much interested in seeing and practicing the oneness of the three. This set a pattern for later generations, and many famous literati would in their own ways embody the unity of the three teachings: In spite of different verbal expressions (specialized jargon), the three schools ultimately tend to reach a similar goal, the highest degree of human perfection. Whether it is called sagehood, *hsien*-ship or enlightenment, the deeper essence was seen as the same. This notion is a far cry from the mistaken western idea of "Three Religions," which are seen as divisive and competitive, not as a unifying ideal.

THREE WORLDS (*San-chieh/Sanjie*). Taoism has several sets of three worlds or three realms, either referring to cosmic time, cosmological space or structure of the universe, or to spiritual cultivation.

- *Cosmic Time*: refers to the evolution of the universe in cosmic periods. They are the "Ultimateless World" (*wu-chi chieh*), the

TA-LO T'IEN
3 Heavens of Purity
4 True Believers' Heaven
4 World of Formlessness
18   World of Form
6   World of Desire

"Great Ultimate World" (*t'ai-chi chieh*), and the "Present World" (*hsien-shih chieh*).

- *Cosmic Space*: in terms of spatial differentiation of the universe, there are two sets, which have roots in ancient times. Distinguished are heaven, earth, mankind, and heaven, earth, and water. The latter are prominent in the Taoist religion, and it is believed that these three worlds are ruled by the **Three Officials** (*san-kuan*), worshipped since the second century in **Heavenly Masters Taoism**.
- *Cosmology*: a very different division of space is derived from Buddhism, but has been adopted by the Taoists, at least in some of their scriptures. This cosmological map divides the universe into 36 "heavens." Of these, 28 make up the Three Worlds: the world of desire (lower six), the world of form (middle 18), and the world of formlessness (higher four).

Above the Three Worlds are the Heavens proper. They are specifically Taoist, and are eight in number: four Heavens of True Believers (or Brahma Heavens), and the Three Heavens of Purity

(Clarity) in which resides the heavenly hierarchy. The highest heaven is called *Ta-lo t'ien* (Great Network Heaven): "It contains the Jade Capital of Mystery Metropolis . . . From here, the heavenly venerables of the Three Worlds rule and administer the universe" (L. Kohn, 1993: 70).

A Taoist scripture says the following about the Three Worlds:

> The Three Worlds are beautiful places where people can be upright and develop their strength. Once above the World of Desire, human life is extended considerably. On these higher levels, the ground is made of yellow gold . . . people in these worlds still have not yet transcended the cycle of life and death.
> This happens only above the Three Worlds . . . (Kohn, 1993: 69)

- The *Three Worlds of the Immortals* (*hsien*): the same as the ones described under cosmology, but they are seen here as stages in spiritual cultivation (or inner alchemy):

> When the mind forgets conscious deliberation and thoughts, it goes beyond the World of Desire. When the mind forgets all the states of mental projection, it goes beyond the World of Form. When the mind does not manifest even a vision of emptiness, it goes beyond the World of Formlessness.
> Leaving the Three Worlds, the pure spirit dwells in the realm of immortals and sages. Inner nature resides in the heaven of Jade [Purity].
> (From a text of **Complete Realization Taoism**, translated by L. Kohn, 1993: 92.)

THREE WORMS (*San-ch'ung/Sanchung*) or THREE CORPSES (*San-shih/Sanshi*). Among the practices to attain **immortality** performed by individual adepts during the early centuries CE (in particular from the fourth to the sixth century), the choice of a correct diet was crucial. The rationale was different from 20th-century ideas about a healthy, nutritious diet; it was rather based on a particular view of the body as a microcosmic replica of the great cosmos.

It is the Taoist belief that the body is divided into three centers of vital energy (*tan-t'ien* or "fields of cinnabar"). In each of them, there resides one of the **Three Ones**, supreme deities. Correct treatment of these gods and constant meditation on them leads to immortality. If the gods would leave the adept's body, he would gradually decline and die.

Meditation, however, is not sufficient, for in the three centers there also lives an enemy, who wishes the adept's early death. These three are called "worms" (a symbol of devitalizing processes) or "corpses" (to indicate the end result if they go unchecked). In fact, they are a sort of demon, who have funny but scary names ("Old Blue, White Maiden, Bloody Corpse"), but mean business: They eat away the vitality of each center and, moreover, adding insult to injury, spy on the adept's actions and report all his evil deeds to heaven. Accordingly, his/her life will be shortened.

The worms or corpses are generated and fed by the intake of cereals. This already takes place before birth, and is sped up as each person grows older. To hope for immortality, the intake of five cereals (*wu-ku*: rice, millet, wheat, oats, beans) must be stopped because

> The Five Cereals are the most harmful of food, that which prevents the obtaining of immortality. "The Five Cereals are scissors that cut off life, they rot the five internal organs, they shorten life. If a grain enters your mouth, do not hope for Life Eternal!" (H. Maspero, 1971/1981: 333)

If one keeps eating the five cereals, the worms become stronger and sap the adept's energy: The worm in the upper field makes people blind and deaf, causes baldness, makes the teeth fall out, and causes bad breath. The worm in the center causes heart trouble, asthma, and melancholy. The worm in the lower field twists the intestines, dries out the bones, causes rheumatism, weakens the will, makes the spirit waste away and creates confusion (Maspero: 332).

This is not the end of the story! Besides avoiding cereals, one must also abstain from wine (liquor) and meat, and plants of the five strong flavors (garlic, onion, etc.). One must maintain cleanliness of the body and clothing. The reason for this is that the Three Ones and other gods in the body hate the smell of liquor and resent meat, which smells of blood. If the adept keeps consuming them, the gods will leave and life will be shortened.

There is not much left for a healthy diet! Fruit and vegetables are not on the forbidden list, although pure breath and jujubes are most recommended. Moreover, many drugs are recommended to help destroy the three worms (they are described in Maspero: 335–338). Ideally, these rather negative methods of purification should be combined with another exotic practice: **embryonic respiration**. (See also **diet**.)

THUNDER MAGIC (*Lei-fa*). A particular Taoist magical technique that consists of using the power of thunder in order to stimulate the five agents (hence, one speaks of "Five" Thunder magic). This technique developed and flourished during the Sung dynasty. M. Saso lists five "sects" having thunder magic in their repertoire: the Ch'ing-wei sect, the T'ai-yi School, the Shen-hsiao School, the Cheng-yi Heavenly Masters School, and the Pole Star sect (Saso, 1978: 56).

The difference between these various styles depended on the distinctive "register" (*lu*) owned by each school. In general, thunder magic was considered to be very powerful, but should be used only for helping people. It was, occasionally, abused for evil purposes, when evil spirits were invoked and black magic performed (Saso: 56).

Many **talismans** (*fu*) and rituals used in thunder magic have been incorporated in the voluminous *Corpus of Taoist Ritual* (*Tao-fa hui-yuan*) (*CT* 1220, *TT* 884–941). (See J. Boltz, 1987: 47–49.) A fairly detailed discussion of thunder magic as practiced by a contemporary Taoist master in northern Taiwan is found in M. Saso's Chapter 6: "Thunder Magic: Neo-Orthodoxy of the Sung" (1978: 234–266).

TI-CHIH See EARTHLY BRANCHES

T'IEN See HEAVEN

T'IEN-HSIN/TIANXIN TAOISM ("Heavenly Mind"). A Taoist school that developed as a branch of the Cheng-yi School during the Sung period. Its name is based on a new kind of *fu-lu,* called "orthodox method of heavenly mind." This revelation was discovered by Jao Tung-t'ien in 994. After Jao, Wang T'ai-ch'u used this method to control evil spirits and specters; his reputation spread widely and reached the court. One Taoist was summoned to the palace to heal the empress's illness. Later, the school branched off into two: a southeastern branch and a western branch (in Szechuan).

The school's major deity is the Northern Ultimate in Heaven (T'ien-shang Bei-chi). Later on it adopted meditation methods from Shang-ch'ing Taoism, stressing the principle that inner cultivation must come before healing practices.

The scriptural tradition of this school had a tremendous influence on sacred and secular literature; for example, on the classical novel *Shui-hu chuan* (*The Water Margin*) and the mythical storybook *Feng-shen yen-yi* (*Metamorphoses of the Gods*). In both works, the exorcism of demons is a central theme. (See J. Boltz, 1987: 33–38.)

T'IEN-KAN See HEAVENLY STEMS

T'IEN-SHANG SHENG-MU See MA-TSU

T'IEN-SHIH TAO See HEAVENLY MASTERS TAOISM

T'IEN-TSUN/TIANZUN. A title given to the three highest deities of the Taoist pantheon. *T'ien* means "heaven," *tsun* means "honorable, venerable, honored, respected, worthy." The compound then signifies "heavenly venerable one," "heavenly worthy," or "respected in heaven," etc. It seems to be a parallel of one of the titles of the Buddha: *Ti-tsun/Dizun*, "World-honored One," and was perhaps created to show the superiority of Taoism over Buddhism.

The creation of the three "Heavenly Venerables" seems to date from the Six Dynasties period. This triad eventually replaced any other supreme beings of Taoism, including T'ai-shang Lao-chün (deified **Lao-tzu**), and was identified with another triad: the **Three Pure Ones** (*san-ch'ing*). Yet, probably because of Lao-chün's established authority, he was transformed into the third member of the triad: Taote T'ien-tsun (see also separate entries for **Yuan-shih T'ien-tsun, Ling-pao T'ien-tsun, Tao-te T'ien-tsun**).

During Taoist rituals today, Heavenly Masters Taoists hang their painted scrolls of the three T'ien-tsun on the northern wall of the temple where they celebrate their liturgy. This indicates the superiority of this trinity ("Prior Heaven" gods) over all other deities ("Posterior Heaven" gods). Only in Taoist monasteries is there a special hall where the Three Pure Ones are worshipped.

T'IEN-TI See HEAVEN AND EARTH

T'IEN-TI-JEN See HEAVEN, EARTH, MANKIND

T'IEN-YIN-TZU/TIANYINZI. This is a Taoist text, named after an unknown Master T'ien-yin, and recorded by T'ang Taoist **Szu-ma Ch'eng-chen** (in the **Taoist Canon** *CT* 1026, *TT* 672). This short text is a meditation guide, similar to the *Tso-wang-lun*, but instead of seven steps, it presents a method of union with *Tao* in five stages. Although "not a meditation manual in the strict sense . . . [it] gives a general outline of the methods to be practiced, explaining their usefulness and application in a simple . . . manner." (L. Kohn, 1987-b: 3). More than the *Tso-wang-lun*, "it shows the physical and mental actions to be undertaken" (Kohn: 3).

A most interesting detail is its implied concept of immortality: Here, it "refers to the liberated state of mind and body as it lives in this world" (Kohn: 3), but as "a necessary prerequisite and guarantee for the attainment of immortality in the other world" (Kohn: 4).

Although the text consists of eight sections, the first three are preliminary. The five basic steps are as follows:

- *Fasting and abstention* are immediate preparations to regulate body and mind.
- *Seclusion* is understood in two ways: physical separation from

life in society in a lonely place, and the calming of the mind, free from involvement in daily affairs.

- *Visualization and imagination* concern the seeing of the deities living in one's body. This also extends to visualizing the viscera and circulating energy through them and, ultimately, making ecstatic excursions to stars and paradises.
- *Sitting in oblivion* does not mean just forgetfulness, but entering a state of mind in which personal consciousness is totally dissolved. It is the final preparation for mystical rapture.
- *Spirit liberation* in Chinese (*shen-chieh*) is a difficult concept: does it mean liberation *of* the spirit or *by* the spirit? Perhaps both meanings are implied: The spirit is set free, emancipated, but it is achieved by the spirit itself. It is the attainment of the *Tao*. (For a fuller discussion, see L. Kohn, 1987-b.)

TORTOISE See ANIMAL SYMBOLISM

T'OU-LUNG See DRAGON THROW

TOU-MU/DOUMU (Mother of the Northern Dipper). A Taoist goddess. The character *tou* signifies the stars of the Northern Dipper. Other names are T'ien Mu (Heavenly Mother) or Tao Mu (Mother of Tao).

Her origin has a connection with Buddhism. Chinese Buddhists call her Goddess of Light. Her full Chinese title is Yuan-ming tou-lao yuan-chün. According to legend, she was born in India, where she married the king of the northern realm of Chou-yü. They had nine sons: The oldest two are high-ranking deities—T'ien-huang Ta-ti and Tzu-wei Ta-ti. The other seven sons are the seven stars of the Northern Dipper.

Tou-mu occupies in Taoism a position similar to Kuan-yin's in Buddhism: Possessing supernatural powers, she is also motivated by compassion for suffering humanity. Together with her husband and sons, she was invited by Yuan-shih T'ien-tsun to reside in heaven. "He placed her in the palace Tou-shu, Pivot of the Pole, because all the other stars revolve around it . . . Her husband inhabited the same palace, her nine sons having their palaces in the neighboring nine stars . . ." (Werner, 1932/69: 511).

In iconography, Tou-mu is represented with three eyes, four heads, and eight arms, two of which hold the sun and the moon. She is also pictured with 18 arms, like some images of Kuan-yin. This would indicate a definite Tantric influence. (See Werner, 511–512; *CMTT*: 81.)

TRANSCENDENT See *HSIEN*

TRANSFORMATIONS OF LAO-TZU SCRIPTURE (*Lao-tzu pien-hua ching/Laozi bianhuajing*). This is an early popular Taoist scripture, dating from the second century CE, that had been lost but was discovered among the Tun-huang manuscripts (Stein manuscript 2295).

The *Transformations Scripture* probably originated in a popular sect and leads to the assumption that, by the end of the second century, **Lao-tzu** had become a popular deity. Although the text has been corrupted and is often unintelligible,

It invests Lao-tzu with transcendent qualities, but also reports his apparitions over the centuries as the counselor of emperors. He transformed himself many times to teach the art of ruling and of becoming an immortal. The parallel with the **Lao-tzu ming** is quite striking.

It is possible that popular movements of the second century took over the political concepts of Huang-Lao Taoism and infused them with their religious messianic expectations. It was perhaps their hope to establish a theocratic rule on earth, but their expectations were crushed with the Yellow Turban defeat. From then on, the Heavenly Masters were prepared to cooperate with the government and become the "heavenly teachers" of the emperors. But the great dream of unity had not been realized:

> This is a phenomenon whose importance for the history of Taoism cannot be overstressed: What failed at the end of the Han is the great effort to make the religious administration coincide with the official administration of the empire. (Seidel, 1969: 118)

TREATISE ON ACTION AND RETRIBUTION (*T'ai-shang kan-ying p'ien/Taishang ganying pian*). A short and extremely popular Taoist text dating from the 11th century CE. Many reprints have been made, and a number of commentaries were written. Although it is not included in the **Taoist Canon**, it has been claimed that its "editions exceed even those of the Bible and Shakespeare . . ." (Carus & Suzuki, 1906 & 1950: 3). Some of the commentaries appear in the *Tao-tsang* (*CT* 1167; *TT* 384–839, a commentary by Li Chang-ling) and in the *Tao-tsang chi-yao*, (vol. 6, nos. 2271 and 2304).

This booklet is a treatise on ethics and the results of following or not following the moral laws. It is like a Taoist version of the very popular Buddhist tract *Yin-kuo lun* (*Treatise on Cause-and-Effect*). The Taoist equivalent is *kan-ying*, which means "responsiveness" and expresses in a more metaphysical way what the Buddhist said in a legalistic way. The practical result is the same as the tract repeats over and over: Good actions attract a reward, evil actions end up in punishment. This is what the introductory verses express:

> Curses and blessings do not come through gates, but man himself invites their arrival. The reward of good and evil is like the shadow accompanying a body . . . (Carus and Suzuki: 51)

The short text (only 1,284 characters, which is not even a third of the *TTC*) is followed by moral tales, a genre which in modern times has often been imitated by authors of "**morality texts**" (*shan-shu*). There seems to be only one complete English translation, made by D. T. Suzuki and Paul Carus and first published in 1906.

TS'AN-T'UNG-CH'I See *KINSHIP OF THE THREE*

TSANG/ZANG. Pronounced as *Ts'ang/cang*, this character literally means "to hide, to conceal, to hoard"; pronounced as *tsang*, the same character means "storehouse, treasury." It is the latter meaning that applies here. This is to say that the complete title, *Tao-tsang ching/ Daozangjing*, signifies "Treasury or Storehouse of Taoist Scriptures." Abbreviated as *Tao-tsang/Daozang*, it means "Treasury of Taoism" or "Treasury of the Tao."

The term *tsang* has been borrowed from **Buddhism**: The collected scriptures of Buddhism, called *Tripitaka* in Sanskrit, were rendered as *Ta-tsang ching/Dazangjing* in Chinese, which literally means "Great Treasury (or Storehouse) of Scriptures."

The most commonly used abbreviations are *TT* for *Tao-tsang* and *T* for the *Taisho* edition of the Buddhist *Tripitaka*.

TS'AO KUO-CHIU/CAO GUOJIU (*Emblem*: castanets). One of the Eight Immortals. Believed to be the younger brother of the Empress Ts'ao of the Sung dynasty, he is represented in official court robes with the headdress of an official. A pair of castanets are his emblem: They are said to be derived from the court tablet, authorizing free access to the palace, to which his birth entitled him.

According to one legend, he met the immortals **Lü Tung-pin** and **Chung-li Ch'uan.** Asked what he was cultivating, he said: "I cultivate the Tao." They asked: "Where is the Tao?" Ts'ao pointed to heaven. "Where is heaven?" they asked again. Ts'ao pointed to his heart. The two laughed and said: "Your heart is one with heaven, and heaven is one with Tao. You have indeed understood the Way" (Lai, 1972: 29). Recommended by all seven immortals, he became the eighth.

TSO-WANG LUN   See *DISCOURSE ON SITTING-AND-FORGET-TING*

TSOU YEN/ ZOU YAN (305–240 BCE?). Commonly regarded as the leading thinker of the Naturalist School (or Yin-Yang and Five Agents School) during the pre-Ch'in or Late Warring States period (before 221 BCE). (For details, see also **Yin-yang Worldview** and **Five Agents System**). Aspects of yin-yang and five agents thinking may have existed before Tsou Yen, but he combined them into an integrated system of metaphysical and cosmological theory. The two had separate origins, however, and even in Tsou Yen's system, there is something artificial in their combination. Yet the new system was very successful and was accepted by all schools of philosophy. Taoism adopted it, as well as Confucianism. Tsou Yen's own writings have been lost, but his ideas have been preserved in other books.

It is believed that Tsou Yen was an important thinker of the Chi-hsia Academy, founded in the state of Ch'i during the fourth century BCE. A century later, this academy's tradition was maintained and extended in Huainan, at an academy patronized by Liu An, prince of Huainan. The *Huai-nan-tzu* continued to elaborate the principles of Tsou Yen's naturalist school (J. Major, 1993: 2).

One of the basic ideas of the Five Agents theory, as formulated by Tsou Yen, is the mutual generation and mutual overcoming of the five. But one of the most important consequences of the theory is the

> . . . cyclical philosophy of history on the one hand and the mutual influence between man and Nature on the other. Just as the seasons rotate, so does history; since man and Nature correspond to each other, they are expressions of the same force and therefore can influence each other. (Chan, 1963: 245)

TU KUANG-T'ING/DU GUANGTING (850–933). A famous Taoist master and scholar from the end of the T'ang period through the Five Dynasties. He was a native of Ch'u-chou, in present-day Chekiang province.

As a young man, he studied Confucian learning and became widely versed in the classics and in the schools of philosophy. He participated in the state examinations, but was not successful. Realizing the ups and downs of human fortune, he went up to Mount Wu-t'ai and studied Taoism.

When T'ang emperor Hsi-tsung (r. 874–888) heard about his reputation, he invited him to court and conferred the "purple robe" on him (a mark of great distinction). Tu stayed at the court from 875 to 881 as imperial advisor to the young emperor. In 881, Emperor Hsi-tsung fled the capital due to rebellion and escaped to Szechuan. Tu accompanied him in exile. In 885, the court returned to the capital.

Tu traveled extensively in Szechuan, collecting scriptures and writing his own works. In his later years, he withdrew to Mount Ch'ing-ch'eng near Chengtu to cultivate the Way. He died at the age of 83.

Tu's influence on later Taoism was profound. He researched various areas of Taoism, the ritual tradition, methods of spiritual cultivation, Taoist doctrine, etc. His study of the *TTC* is especially remarkable: He reviewed and collated more than 60 previous commentaries on it and divided them into five groups. He personally admired T'ang Emperor Hsuan-tsung's commentary on the *TTC* and expanded the imperial commentary further into 50 chapters. The central idea of the *TTC* in Hsuan-tsung's and Tu's view was "inner self-cultivation" and "outer ordering of the country." Altogether, Tu Kuang-t'ing wrote more than 20 books, greatly contributing to our understanding of Taoism (*CMTT*: 133–4; see also the monograph by F. Verellen, 1989).

TU-JEN CHING See *SALVATION SCRIPTURE*

T'U-TI KUNG See GOD OF THE SOIL

TUN-HUANG/DUNHUANG. Name of an ancient Chinese city in modern Kansu, situated on a crossroads to Central Asia: the beginning of the "Silk Road" (road used by traders since the Han to transport Chinese silk to the West, even as far as Rome). In Tun-huang, a Buddhist community started to excavate caves as a monastic residence (in pre-T'ang times). They added a large number of painted frescoes and cut thousands of sculptures out of the rock walls. Moreover, they built an extensive library in the caves covering manuscripts from the southern dynasties until late T'ang. During the war years at the end of the T'ang, the grottoes were sealed off for protection, and the whole treasure was forgotten.

It was only in the late 19th and early 20th century that Tun-huang was rediscovered. British scholar Aurel Stein and French scholar Pelliot "bought" important manuscript collections and placed them in the British Museum and the Louvre. The discovery has been of extreme importance for the study of medieval China (comparable with the discovery of the Dead Sea manuscript collection for Bible studies).

The frescoes and sculptures are important for an understanding of medieval Buddhist art, whereas the manuscript cache is a great source of information about not only Buddhism but Taoism and other religions, as well as for social history. Many Buddhist and Taoist manuscripts, otherwise long lost, have resurfaced in the Tun-huang collections.

TUNG-T'IEN See GROTTO-HEAVENS AND BLESSED SPOTS

TZU-JAN *See* NATURALNESS

U

"UNCARVED WOOD" (*P'u/Pu*). The Chinese term *p'u* is found several times in the *TTC* and its translation as "uncarved block" has become stereotyped, but needs to be challenged. The idea implied in it comes closer to "wholeness," which is also contained in "uncarved block," except that "uncarved block" has been reified. As a result, what was an excellent analogy of the Tao has become sterile and counterproductive.

Since the Southern Dynasties, *p'u* has become immortalized in a book written by **Ko Hung/**Ke Hong, *Pao-p'u-tzu*. This is in fact the pen name of the author, and has been rendered in English as "the master who embraces simplicity." That, too, has become a stereotype in Taoist scholarship, although a more accurate rendering would be "the master who holds on to wholeness." (How would one "embrace" simplicity anyway?)

Because the terms "uncarved block" and "the master who embraces simplicity" have become almost standard expressions in Taoist writing, it is worthwhile to have a closer look at the original meaning of *p'u*. Both "uncarved block" and "simplicity" are translations of the same *p'u*. Is that justified?

When Ko Hung adopted "Pao-*p'u*-tzu" as his pen name, it was a clear reference to *TTC* 19:6, a verse translated in very different ways by modern English translators. In its most literal sense, the verse reads as follows:

> manifest plainness (*chien su*) hold on to wholeness (*pao p'u*).

(Other occurrences of *p'u* in the *TTC* are 15:7; 28:6–7; 32:1; 37: 3–4; 57:12.)

In this verse, *su* and *p'u* are quasi-synonymous. It is important to check on the basic meanings of the two terms.

First, *p'u* is translated as "wood that has not been worked on; simple, without ornament, without disguise" (Couvreur, 1890/1966: 475-a); or "wood in its natural state, not worked: rough, plain, natural, simple" (Karlgren, 1923/1973: 231). From these two texts, it is obvious where the expression "uncarved block" came from, but the addition of "block" is an interpretation. The term means "plain wood," "uncarved wood."

Next, *su* means "a piece of silk of natural color, simple, without ornament . . . of natural color, of white color; raw silk, plain" (Couvreur: 87-c); or "white silk, in a natural state; white, plain, simple; valueless, empty, ordinary" (Karlgren, 244). The term then means "plain silk," or silk that has not been dyed for human use yet. The common denominator of *p'u* and *su* is "plainness, in a natural state of being, authentic." It reminds of the primitivist *Chuang-tzu* chapters, which discuss basic human nature in its state of naturalness, unspoiled by ethical impositions. In other words, *p'u* and *su* are metaphors for a state of being before culture brings in divisions and strife, a state of society in which people behave ethically in spontaneity, not coaxed or coerced, following their inborn good nature.

In Wing-tsit Chan's *TTC* translation, he translates Chapter 19:6 as follows: "Manifest plainness, Embrace simplicity." Is that perhaps the source of the "master who embraces simplicity"? (Sailey, 1978). Indeed, *p'u* could mean "simplicity," better still, "natural simplicity" (Duyvendak, 1954) or "primal simplicity" (Wu, 1961) or "the simple" (*su*) and "the primal" (*p'u*).

To conclude: The use of metaphors may be misleading. One must be careful about the precise intention of a metaphor. In the *TTC* context, *p'u* is a symbol of the natural state of humanity, plain, not artificial, authentic, primordial unity.

UNION OF ENERGIES See SEXUALITY

V

VIRTUE See *TE*

VITAL ENERGY See *CH'I*

W

WANG CHE/WANG ZHE (1112–1170). His religious name is Wang Ch'ung-yang. He was the founder of **Complete Realization** (Ch'uan-chen) Taoism during the foreign rule of the Jurchen-Chin Dynasty (1115–1234). He was born in Hsien-yang in Shensi province to a landlord family.

As a young man, he loved reading as well as archery and horsemanship. During the reign of the Ch'i puppet regime (1130–1137), he took part in the civil service examination, but failed. Under Emperor Hsi-tsung (r. 1135–1148), he tried his hand at the military service examination, which he passed. Confident that he would enjoy a distinguished military career, he was in fact, merely a petty government official for many years. As a result, he became disgusted and resigned his position.

In 1159, he left home and his family and went touring the neighboring regions. At Kan-ho township (Hu county, in Shensi), he met an extraordinary person, believed to be the reincarnation of the Immortal **Lü Tung-pin**, who taught him the method of spiritual cultivation. He then realized the Tao and became a Taoist priest. In Nan-shih village, he lived for more than two years in a cave, which he called "tomb of the living dead."

In 1167, he left Shensi and moved to Shantung to spread his teaching and recruit disciples. Among them, seven became known as the **"Seven Perfected."** Each of them later founded their own school.

Wang named his residence in Ning-hai, Shantung *Ch'uan-chen* (Complete Realization). Therefore, his followers were known as *Ch'uan-chen* priests. In 1169, Wang Che took four of his closest disciples (Ma, Tan, Liu, and Ch'iu) back to the West. He passed away the following year in Ta-liang (present-day Kaifeng in Honan) and was buried in his birthplace in Shensi: Liu-chiang village in Hu county. His later followers regarded this place as the sacred site of their Grand Patriarch.

Wang Che's "theology" was a combination of Confucian and Buddhist elements with Taoist doctrine. He advocated the equal treatment and study of these "three teachings" (*san-chiao*). As basic texts for study, he chose the *Tao-te ching*, the Buddhist *Heart Sutra*, and the Confucian *Classic on Filial Piety* (*Hsiao ching*).

He considered the discipline of the mind and the elimination of desire the basic conditions to reach the Tao. To nourish one's nature (*hsing*) was his first priority, whereas to maintain one's physical health and well-being was the second. Whoever wants to cultivate the Tao should abandon sexual desire and the craving for wealth, as well as the emotions of love and hatred and all other worldly concerns. Then, even if one lived in the mundane world, one's mind would be still and tranquil, one would be able to reach out for the Tao and the realization of spiritual perfection.

Recent scholarship has pointed out that the success of the Complete Realization School was due to the fact that most of Wang Che's early disciples were from the educated gentry landlord class. They helped the school with financial support and intellectual leadership, unavailable to other Taoist schools of the period (see Ch'ing Hsi-t'ai and others, *History of Chinese Taoism*—in Chinese—vol. 3).

WANG CH'UNG/WANG CHONG (27–100?). A bright and original philosopher during the Later Han period. Although he was not a Taoist, he was not a Confucian either, as he attacked several Confucian teachings. It is said that, because of his critical and rational spirit, he "prepared the way for the revival of Taoism that came one century later" (Fung, 1966: 211).

His book *Balanced Inquiries* (or Critical Essays) (*Lun-heng*) was preserved and has been translated into English by A. Forke, 1962. (See Chan, 1963: 292–304.)

WANG LING-KUAN/WANGLINGGUAN ("Spirit Official Wang"). A deity worshipped by the Taoists, also named T'ien-chün (Heavenly Lord Wang), "Lord Benefactor" Wang. There is little worship of him as a separate deity, but he is sometimes found in the group of Five Lord Benefactors. His image is frequently posted at the entrance to sacred mountains as a guardian spirit. (See also **Director of Destiny**; and *TMSC*: 430.)

WANG PI/WANG BI (226–249). A well-known philosopher during the Wei dynasty, considered to be a Taoist, but not uniquely, as Wing-tsit Chan says:

> Like philosophers of the Han, they are syncretic. While they are Taoistic in their metaphysics, they are Confucian in their social and political philosophy. (Chan, 1963: 316)

This wave of syncretic thinking has been called **Neo-Taoism**. Besides Wang Pi, another well-known member of the group was **Kuo Hsiang**.

Wang Pi became famous at a young age. He loved discussing Confucian and Taoist principles. A friend of his, Ho Yen (d. 249), praised him highly for his awesome intellect and analytical abilities. Wang died very young: he was only 24.

He is best known for his commentaries on the *TTC* and the *Yi ching*. He also annotated the *Analects* of Confucius, but only segments of this work have survived. Wang's main contribution to Neo-Taoism was his theory that Tao, or Nonbeing (*wu*), was the origin of all things in the universe. Nonbeing is ultimate reality and "transcends all distinctions and descriptions" (Chan: 136). Or, in other words, he made the distinction between the fundamental or substance (*t'i*), which is Nonbeing, and the incidental or function (*yung*), which is Being. This is only one of the dichotomies that Wang Pi postulated and that he applied to society and political reality. Other contrasting pairs were movement (*tung*) and tranquillity (*ching*); the one (*yi*) and the many (*to*); language (*yen*) and ideas (*yi*); nature (*tzu-jan*) and morals and institutions. He advocated that human morality and institutions are derived from nature and were necessary for the smooth operation of human society.

Following the pattern of Taoist reasoning, he stated that language could not adequately express or explain ideas of the mind. (See also **Neo-Taoism**; the best edition of his collected works is *Wang Pi chi chiao-shih*, edited by Lou Yü-lieh in 2 vols, 1980.)

WAY See *TAO*

WEAKNESS (*Jo/ro*). This concept expresses one of the many paradoxes of Taoism: Tao is the ultimate "power" in the universe, yet it works in "weakness." As *TTC*, Chapter 40: 1–2 says:

> Reversion is the action of Tao.
> Weakness is the function of Tao.
> (Chan, 1963: 160)

The term "weakness" is reflected or implied in other concepts: *wu-wei* is the one coming to mind first of all. But also the concept of yielding, bending. The ability to yield, to bend is a sign of life, as the *TTC* 76 clearly states:

> When man is born, he is tender and weak.
> At death, he is stiff and hard.
> . . . the stiff and the hard are companions of death.
> (Chan: 174)

There are other associations related to this: In the *TTC*, woman is a favorite symbol of the Tao. In her (proverbial) weakness and ability to yield to male "power," she actually overcomes the male strength. And so the "balance of power" is restored.

The Taoist concept of weakness has found a rich field of applications in the martial arts. One art form in particular is based on it: *Judo*, which in Chinese is *Jo tao:* the "way of weakness." The central idea is to yield to one's opponent: Let his own aggressive force turn into his defeat.

Is this an echo of the Beatitudes: "The meek shall inherit the earth"?

WEI HUA-TS'UN See LADY WEI HUA-TSUN

WEI PO-YANG/WEI BOYANG. An alchemist and author about whose life not much is known. He lived during the Later Han Dynasty (25–220 CE), and probably flourished between 100 and 170 CE. He was a native of Chekiang province. In Ko Hung's **Shen-hsien chuan**, it is recorded that Wei went into the mountains to pursue alchemical research. In the same volume, there is a delightful story about him sharing his elixir of immortality with one of his three disciples and a dog (see Needham V, 2: 295).

Wei Po-yang is best known for his authorship of the first still-extant book on **alchemy**, **Kinship of the Three** (*Ts'an-t'ung-ch'i*), which had a tremendous impact on all later alchemy. It was written around 142 CE; it gained Wei the reputation of the ' "father of alchemy."

WEN-CH'ANG TI-CHÜN/WENCHANG DIJUN. Listed as a "Taoist deity," it is more accurate to consider him a god of the communal religion, although he was also specially worshipped by Confucian scholars hoping to be successful in the imperial examinations. Indeed, Wen-ch'ang is the god of literature and scholarship.

Historical sources state that he was born during the T'ang period. He went to live in Szechuan, and was known as a brilliant writer, later canonized by the T'ang court. During the Sung and Yuan dynasties, the court bestowed on him various honorary titles (Werner, 1969: 555). Several legends have been created, making an exact historical account more difficult.

Obviously, he became a very important figure in the Chinese pantheon, because it was believed that he and K'ui-hsing, a star deity, "presided over the examinations and were dispensers of examination degrees" (Yang, 1970: 270).

Many temples were built in China with Wen-ch'ang as the major deity, with other minor literary gods placed on side altars. The god's birthday was an occasion for scholarly meetings and literary contests (Yang: 271).

In Taiwan, there are about 20 temples dedicated to him, but in many other temples, there are side altars enshrining his statue. Today, his role has been changed slightly: Because the imperial examination system no longer exists, students go to pray at his shrine for success in the grueling university entrance exams. In some temples, one can see placed on the altar in front of his image photocopied identification papers with photographs of students praying for his assistance. His birthday is on the third of the second lunar month. (For a more detailed study, see T. Kleeman, 1994.)

WESTERN ASCENSION SCRIPTURE (*Hsi-sheng ching/Xisheng jing*). A Taoist text written in the fifth century CE that became very popular during the seventh and eighth centuries. By Sung times, there existed nine independent versions of the text, demonstrating the high esteem it enjoyed.

The expression "western ascension" in the title refers to the legendary background of the text: From Lao-tzu's biography in Szu-ma Ch'ien's *Historical Records,* it was assumed that **Lao-tzu** wrote the *TTC* when he was on his way out to the West, at the request of the guardian of the border pass, Yin Hsi. Further legend builders claimed that Lao-tzu went to India, where he reappeared as the Buddha, to convert the "barbarians." (See **Conversion of Barbarians Scripture** or *Hua-hu ching.*)

The *Hsi-sheng ching* contains the essence of Lao-tzu's teachings to Yin Hsi; it was strongly influenced by the *TTC,* but is more religiously oriented. The scripture consists of 39 sections, which can be grouped in five cycles of about seven sections each. Section 39 relates Lao-tzu's ascent into heaven. As L. Kohn explains in her monograph on the text, the cycles are titled: Tao knowledge (1–7); Tao Practice (8–14); Cosmization (15–22); The Sage (23–30); The Return (31–38); The End (39) (Kohn, 1991: 43).

The story of Lao-tzu's excursion to the West, started in a book of history, was amplified in the *Hua-hu ching* for apologetic reasons. Here, the same narrative provides a framework for Lao-tzu's complementary instructions on Taoist doctrine and practice. The story is a legend, but the teaching stands by itself. Because of its mystical overtones, it was cherished by Taoist spiritual practitioners.

L. Kohn's work provides both an interpretation and a translation of the text (Kohn, 1991).

WHITE CLOUD MONASTERY (Pai-yün kuan/Baiyunguan). One of the most famous Taoist monasteries, located in Beijing. It also has one of the largest premises: estimated at six hectares or 15 acres, with 150 structures, large and small.

Its affiliation is with **Complete Realization Taoism** (Ch'uan-chen) in its Lung-men branch, founded by Wang Che's disciple, **Ch'iu Ch'u-chi** (1148–1227).

The temple was first built by T'ang Emperor Hsuan-tsung in 739. Its name then was T'ien-ch'ang monastery (*kuan*). In 1203, under the foreign rule of the Chin, its name was changed to T'ai-chi temple (*kung*). During the Mongol administration, it changed names again, this time called Ch'ang-ch'un temple (Ch'ang-ch'un was the religious name of the Lung-men founder).

When Patriarch Ch'iu died in 1227, his disciples buried his body at the Wai-shun hall on the temple premises. This hall became an active Taoist center during the Ming period, from 1403–1424. New structures were added. In 1443, the temple's name changed again, taking its final name, which is still used today, Pai-yün kuan (White Cloud Monastery). Many of the old buildings, reconstructed during the Ch'ing dynasty, still exist today. On the central axis, North-South, are the major shrines: Three Pure Ones Hall, The Founder's Hall (Ch'iu-tsu tien), the Lao-tzu Hall, and the Jade Emperor's Hall. The Founder's Hall contains an image of Founder Ch'iu, and below it is his grave. Besides these central buildings, there is also the Hall of the Seven Patriarchs, the Ling-kuan tien, and the Ordination Platform.

The monastery is famous for its unique set of the Ming edition of the **Taoist Canon**: It served as the base for a modern edition in the 1920s. There is also a great number of engraved stone tablets, which are a precious source of information about Taoist history.

A ground plan of the whole compound is found in an article by Yoshioka (1979): It was drawn up during his visits to the temple in 1940–46.

The temple was totally restored and redecorated in the early 1980s, and its reopening was celebrated in 1983. It serves today as the headquarters of the Taoist Association of China, and has become an attractive tourist target (*CMTT*: 259).

WOMEN IN TAOISM See FEMINIST PERSPECTIVE

WU See NONBEING

WU-FU HSÜ See *FIVE TALISMANS SCRIPTURE*

WU-HSING See FIVE AGENTS SYSTEM

WU-SHANG PI-YAO See *ESSENTIALS OF SUPREME SECRETS*

WU-T'OU TAO-SHIH See BLACKHEAD TAOIST

WU-WEI ("Nonaction"). A very crucial term in Taoist philosophy, but not that important in the context of Taoist religion. It is apparently a simple term, yet its deeper meaning is hard to fathom.

The Chinese character *wu* is a negation, whereas *wei* means to act, to do; therefore, literally, *wu-wei* expresses the idea of "not to act." It does not mean to do nothing at all, it emphasizes restraint from certain actions, which are seen as conflicting with the Tao.

Various translations have been presented, especially in the context of the *Tao-te ching*, where the concept often appears. Among the clearest instances are Chapters 3:8; 43:3; 47:6; 48:3; 57:9–12; 63:1. Taking Wing-tsit Chan's translation as a modern representative, one can get a feeling for what *wu-wei* actually means.

- By acting without action, all things will be in order. (Chapter 3:8)
- . . . the advantage of taking no action. (Chapter 43:3)
- . . . The sage . . . accomplishes without any action. (Chapter 47:6)
- No action is undertaken, and yet nothing is left undone (Chapter 48:3)
- The sage says:
  I take no action and the people of themselves are transformed.
  I love tranquillity and the people of themselves become correct.
  I engage in no activity and the people of themselves become prosperous.
  I have no desires and the people of themselves become simple [naturally genuine]. (Chapter 57:9–12)
- Act without action, Do without ado (Chapter 63:1)

The most striking of these paradoxes is probably in the fourth quotation: *wu-wei erh wu pu-wei*, which literally means: "do not do (act) and (yet) there is not(hing) not done." It is obvious that the author of these verses wanted to impress some important principle on his readers, and therefore took such a strong stand. One often exaggerates to bring a point home. But behind the paradoxes, there is some principle of action that a Taoist would approve of (even the author "acted" when he wrote these verses!).

Other translations are "inactivity" (Waley); "not doing" (E. Chen); "do nothing" (Henricks); "does nothing" (Lau); "nonaction" (Mair); "doing nothing" (LaFargue); "non-doing" (Addis & Lombardo); "No-Ado" (Wu).

Although these five quotations from the *TTC* try to make a point by extravagant language, the context of the whole work has more clues as to the correct understanding of "acting without action." Seen in context, *wu-wei* can be interpreted correctly in several ways, each way stressing one vital aspect, but always within the basic message of the text, which is the right political action seen in the light of the Tao. Thus *wu-wei* can mean any or all of the following: acting naturally, spontaneously, effortlessly; acting modestly, governing by laissez-faire, without undue interference in the people's lives or, expressed in a more positive way, leaving the people as much freedom as possible, without demanding too much from them, either in taxes or in imposed corvee. That means royal *wu-wei* is not calculating, not selfish (after all, the only rationale for there being a ruler is to serve the people), a good ruler performs his task and does not wait for recognition. He holds his own interests in check, and by being generous, noncalculating, his own interests are served the best.

Realizing that his people are prone to selfishness, he does not encourage it. He avoids fostering ambition for titles, high honors, and high salaries, because that will necessarily end up in strife; he avoids the display of wealth, since that will stir greed and desire; he will avoid promulgating too many laws, since too many laws create resentment and lawbreaking. Above all, a ruler practicing *wu-wei* does not meddle with his people's minds.

In warfare, a Taoist-inspired leader will avoid aggressive action as much as possible, only attack when forced, and not take any vindictive action (see **Military Strategy**).

After the *TTC*, other Taoist writers continued to embroider on the theme of *wu-wei*. *Chuang-tzu* does not use the term that often, but the principle of *wu-wei* is clearly implied in many passages. *Wu-wei* is spontaneous, natural, not calculated, not forced action (as exemplified in stories about the butcher, the artist, the swimmer, the cicadacatcher). *Wu-wei* also means action without ulterior motive, as exemplified in the anecdote of the boy playing with gulls. The birds did not fear him and came down to play. One day his father asked him to catch one for him, but the gulls did not come down again. They sensed his intention.

The *Huai-nan-tzu* has much to say on the subject of *wu-wei*. In this context, J. Needham stresses how wrong many western sinologists have been when they translated *wu-wei* by "nonaction" or "inactivity." The *HNT* understands *wu-wei* as "refraining from activity contrary to Nature," which means

> . . . going against the grain of things, from trying to make materials perform functions for which they are unsuitable, from exerting force in human affairs when the man of insight could see that it would be doomed to failure, and that subtler methods of persuasion, or simply letting things alone to take their own course, would bring about the desired result. (Needham, 1956: II, 68)

Although in Taoist philosophical thought, *wu-wei* is first of all a matter of correct government, one can easily sense its great potential of applications to nonpolitical areas of life. By simply letting things take their own course, many artificially created problems can be avoided. By not unduly interfering in the lives of others, especially of those closest to us, one leaves them free to express themselves spontaneously, not forcing them to be different from what their basic nature really is. Of course, this type of *wu-wei* does not mean indifference for the well-being of others. On the contrary, self-development of those near us is encouraged and stimulated, yet not forced. This kind of detached patience, together with positive encouragement, promises the best results in human relationships, as well as in education, business, and other kinds of employment. This is ultimately one of the most profound statements of Taoist philosophy, transcending time and space, universally applicable.

As mentioned at the outset, this worldview/attitude is not part of Taoist religion, where action is most necessary and efforts in self-cultivation, etc., are indispensable to reach the goals of longevity and immortality. Yet here, too, a solid dose of *wu-wei* may yield better results than nervous, strenuous action. Taoist recluses combine the *wei* and *wu-wei* into a great harmony, leading to contentment and oneness with the Tao.

Y

YANG-CH'I/YANGQI ("Nourish Breath" or "Vital Energy"). This is the first (in alphabetical order) of five types of "nourishing" discussed in the texts of the Taoist religion. To "nourish" means to "feed, support," or to "increase." Vital energy is given to all living beings at birth, but its supply will run out, and that is the end of life. Taoists believe they can prevent exhaustion by various exercises, physiological and spiritual. (See also **Breathing Exercises**; **Three Vitalities**.)

YANG CHU/YANG ZHU: THE PERSON. A hedonistic philosopher who was probably a contemporary of Mencius (371–289 BCE?) and was fiercely attacked by him because of his selfish desires. He is sometimes portrayed as a Taoist or a proto-Taoist, but this is not a correct interpretation. It is true that there is a "Yang Chu Chapter" in the Taoist book *Lieh-tzu*, but this material juxtaposition is not a solid reason to call Yang Chu a Taoist. His ideas are far from Taoist, and have only a superficial similarity with the Taoist worldview. It is like Taoism gone crazy.

However, what Yang Chu has to say stimulates reflection. His outlook on life and death makes some sense if applied in moderation. Life *is* short, death *is* unavoidable; why not make the best of it and enjoy life to the fullest? Many religious preachers would attack this view violently, but still practice it secretly! If Yang Chu was a crook, he was not a hypocrite.

YANG CHU/YANG ZHU: THEMES. In the book *Lieh-tzu*, there is one chapter (Chapter 7), titled "Yang Chu," which does not belong there. Superficially, there is some similarity with Taoism, such as spontaneity or naturalness, acceptance of death as an unavoidable fact, and "caring for life." Yet, here these very Taoist principles are applied to an extreme degree (Taoism "gone crazy"!).

Spontaneity for Yang Chu means to follow all one's sense cravings without restrictions; acceptance of death is seen as a permit for wild passionate living, since death is the end with only "rotten bones" left; and caring for life means to indulge completely and absolutely. Taoism, on the contrary, advocates restraint and moderation. Life may and must be enjoyed, but the life energy should be spent sparingly.

Two themes of the Yang Chu chapter are of particular interest. The first one because it was the ground for Confucian attacks against Yang Chu's hedonism (in the *Mencius*); the second one for its extreme view of life and death and its resulting action.

Mencius accused Yang-chu of extreme selfishness: If he could save the world by sacrificing only one hair, he would refuse to do it. However, it is not certain that this is a correct appraisal of Yang's position. It might rather be that if he could gain the world (become the world's ruler) at the expense of just one hair, he would not do it. In other words, becoming a king does not interest him. Why look for trouble and heart disease, if life is so short?

That leads to the second Yang Chu motif, expressed in very realistic language: life is short, 100 years at the most (but not one in a 1,000 lives that long). Suppose one lives 100 years:

Infancy and senility take nearly half (40%?)
Sleep, wasted time, take 30%
Pain, sickness, sorrow, loss, anxiety 15%
Of the rest (15%—perhaps only 12%): times of contentment, without
    care, "it does not amount to the space of an hour."
(Chapter 7, Graham: 139)

Maybe there is poetic exaggeration here, but to be realistic and honest, most of our lives are indeed spent in anxiety and psychosomatic discomfort. Why not try to enjoy the rest of it in pleasure?

. . . where is [man] to find happiness? Only in fine clothes and good
food, music and beautiful women. (Graham: 139)

This desire becomes more urgent if we consider the end of life: In death, all people are the same. Cleverness, wealth, reputation, etc., do not affect the dead any longer. What remains is

. . . stench and rot, decay and extinction . . . saints and sages die, the
wicked and the foolish die . . . in death, they are rotten bones. Make

haste to enjoy your life while you have it; why care what happens when you are dead? (Graham: 140–141)

YANG HSI/YANG XI (330–386 CE). In the service of the southern Hsü family, he received divine revelations during the years 364–370. During a series of midnight visits, about a dozen "perfected beings" (*chen-jen*) came down from the heaven of Great Purity to transmit to him their instructions and scriptures (Strickmann, 1981: 82). These revelations became the nucleus of a body of texts, later called "Great Purity Scriptures." They were the basis of the new Taoist school, **Great Purity Taoism**, also called Mao Shan Taoism, because the school settled on Mount Mao.

One of the principal "spirits" to descend was **Lady Wei Hua-ts'un** (who had died in 334 CE), a libationer (*chi-chiu*) in the Heavenly Masters School. Other "perfected beings" were Han immortals, local saints, and the three Mao brothers.

Yang Hsi's revelations were written in an elegant style and praised by **T'ao Hung-ching** for their high literary quality. There has been some speculation about the method in which these divine revelations were received: Was it through "automatic writing" or through divinely inspired illumination? Opinions are divided. Yang's elegant style seems to exclude the possibility of automatic writing. It was rather like revelations received in other religious traditions: St. John's Book of Revelation, the Koran, and the visions of Swedenborg (Robinet, 1991: 120).

Yang Hsi became the second patriarch of Shang-ch'ing Taoism (after Lady Wei, who was considered to be the foundress).

YANG-HSING/YANGXING ("Nourish Nature"). Refers to the cultivation of one's nature, and includes *ching*, *ch'i* and *shen* (the **Three Vitalities**). Or it can be understood in the sense of one's spiritual nature only, one's mind (*hsin*), in the Buddhist sense, as opposed to life (*ming*). Among the Northern and Southern Schools of **Complete Realization Taoism**, there was controversy as to the priority of the two, but it was agreed that both need to be cultivated (see also **Nature and Life**).

YANG-HSING/YANGXING ("Nourish the Physical Body"). This character *hsing* is different from the previous one; here it means one's physical makeup, one's body and its health. Most Taoists agree that the body must be "nourished," not only by eating healthy food, but also by exercises (gymnastics, etc.), so that it becomes an effective instrument for mind cultivation. A minority would recommend physical hardships (fasting to the extreme), but one may wonder about the results of such endeavors.

YANG-SHEN/YANGSHEN ("Nourish the Spirit"). At birth, each person is endowed with original spirit (*yuan-shen*), which is dissipated in life by thinking, worries, etc. Through inner cultivation, this process can be reversed to the point where all one's vitalities are transformed into spirit. Then longevity, even immortality, follows, as a Han dynasty text, *Wen-tzu*, says:

> It is most important to nourish the spirit, it is of secondary importance to nourish the body. The spirit should be pure and tranquil, the bones should be stable. This is the foundation of long life. (Quoted by Y. Sakade in L. Kohn, 1989: 6)

YANG-SHENG/YANGSHENG ("Nourish Life"). This practice is almost identical with *yang-hsing* ("nourish the physical body"). To promote one's physical health was the basis for all spiritual practices. "Life" can be nourished by physical exercises (diet, gymnastics, breathing, etc.), but also by meditation, as, for example, visualizing the inner organs and encouraging the protection of the indwelling deities.

YELLOW COURT SCRIPTURE (*Huang-t'ing ching/Huangtingjing*). One of the oldest Taoist texts, existing before the Shang-ch'ing revelations, but eventually incorporated into them. It had a great influence on later Shang-ch'ing texts, dealing with meditation.

This scripture does not provide technical methods of meditation, but it must be recited while the adept visualizes the inner gods dwelling in the body.

Apparently, the text as it is today consists of two versions, one called esoteric (*nei-ching*), which is most likely the earlier version. It is addressed to initiates, since it gives the names and appearances of the deities to be visualized. The other version, called exoteric (*wai-ching*), is meant for noninitiates; it does not list the names of deities. Which one was the earliest version is still not clear: Textual comparison does not lead to any definite conclusion.

Although the text is difficult to understand, two important themes are clearly discernible: visualization of the viscera, and circulation of *ch'i*. By interior vision, one "must learn to see the form and function of the entrails and inner bodily organs, as well as the spirits that inhabit the body" (Robinet, 1979/1993: 60). As correlations of the Five Agents, the Five Viscera connect the microcosm of the body with the macrocosm:

liver	wood	East
heart	fire	South
spleen	earth	Center
lungs	metal	West
kidneys	water	North

It is extremely important for one's physical as well as spirtual well-being to keep the viscera in good health, for if the viscera are injured, the indwelling spirits will leave. Moreover, only if the adept enjoys good health can he make progress in his search for the *Tao*. In order to be able to visualize the inner organs and their indwelling spirits, the organs must be made luminous, transparent. There are various methods to achieve this: magical herbs, absorption of the outflow of stars, the use of magic mirrors. Luminosity is a sign of good health.

Among the most effective means to maintain and increase good health is the circulation of *ch'i*, or circulation of *ch'i* and *ching*, translated by Robinet as "breath" and "essence" (Robinet: 83). The *ch'i* are the airy elements of the body, the *ching* (and saliva) are the watery elements. They operate like *yang* and *yin*. Through their union, a spiritual embryo may be born, leading to the creation of *spirit* (*shen*) and immortality.

(For an excellent analysis of the *Yellow Court Scripture*, see I. Robinet, 1979/1993: 55–96.)

YELLOW EMPEROR (Huang-ti/Huangdi). Name of a mythical ruler of antiquity, as well as of an important Taoist deity. His name literally means "Yellow" (*huang*) and "emperor, monarch, thearch, god." The traditions about this deity are complex, the roles ascribed to him vary, but his popularity since Chou times until today remains strong.

As a celestial deity, he was one of the Five Emperors, ruling the four directions of space and the center, all worshiped by the feudal lords of the Chou kingdom.

A strong belief prevailed that Huang-ti's reign was the actual realization of a golden age of peace and equality (*T'ai-p'ing*). This belief in him as the ideal ruler would later become an important aspect of **Huang-Lao Taoism**. On what perceptions this belief was built is not easy to say. It could be that at first the royal family of the state of Ch'i considered him to be their clan ancestor (this is based on an inscription dating from the mid-fourth century BCE) (Jan, 1981: 118). In the second century BCE, "the majority of feudal clans claimed Huang-ti as their ancestor" (A. Seidel, 1987, *ER* 6, 484–5). Even today, he is considered to be the common ancestor of all Chinese.

His claim to fame is not only based on being an ancestor, however.

He is also a cultural hero, to whom various discoveries have been credited: invention of the calendar, first planting of crops, construction of houses and weaving of clothes, arranging of funerals, building of ships and carts, making of musical instruments, introducing of medicine. He is also credited with learning and applying the arts of the bedchamber, and thus contributing to the formation of immortality techniques. The list of credits vary, but they are all impressive.

Finally, his name has been connected with the first Taoist politico-religious movement: Huang-Lao Taoism. "Huang" stands for Huang-ti; "Lao" for **Lao-tzu**. Together, they symbolize perfect rulership: the sage king and the sage advisor.

In the *Chuang-tzu*, the Yellow Emperor is often cited—all together in 14 episodes. Sometimes he is presented as a sage; even the outlaw Robber Chih admits that "There is no one more highly esteemed by the world than the Yellow Emperor" (Chapter 29, Watson: 328). Yet, at the same time, he is criticized for bringing decline to a perfectly peaceful society, for plunging the world into the worst confusion.

In other passages, the Yellow Emperor appears to be a sage who, after receiving the Tao, "ascended to the cloudy heavens" (Chapter 6, Watson: 82). These different evaluations are obviously related to the particular stream of Taoism each author belonged to. In the *Lieh-tzu*, Chapter 2, titled "The Yellow Emperor," there is an anecdote about the Yellow Emperor's political career. At first self-indulgent, he started to govern for the benefit of the people. Then he "retired to live undisturbed in a hut . . . where he fasted to discipline mind and body and for three months had nothing to do with affairs of state" (Graham, 1960: 34). Once in a dream, he visited the country of Hua-hsü (utopia land). From then he started to rule his country with *wu-wei*. "After . . . twenty-eight years, when the Empire was almost as well-governed as the country of Hua-hsü, the Emperor rose into the sky [became an immortal]. The people did not stop wailing for him for more than 200 years" (Graham: 35).

Today, the Yellow Emperor, under a different but also ancient name, *Hsuan-yuan*, has become the focal deity of a new religion, *Hsuan-yuan chiao* ("Yellow Emperor Religion"), founded in Taiwan in the mid-20th century. This new religion has its own temples and has designed its own rituals and ritual garments (yellow in color). It ". . . teaches a mixture of Taoist, Confucian, and Moist [Mohist] ideas and labors for a renaissance of Chinese culture and for the reunification of the empire" (Seidel: 485).

YELLOW TURBAN REBELLION. A Taoist uprising against the Han dynasty in 184 CE. The middle of the second century CE was a period of political instability and palace intrigues, aggravated by natural disasters, bringing the country to the verge of collapse. A messianic movement arose in Eastern China, based on the vision of the **Great Peace Scripture** (*T'ai-p'ing ching*). Three brothers, named Chang, (see **Chang Brothers**), established a theocratic state that spread fast throughout eight eastern provinces. (See **Introduction: Healing Cult in Eastern China**.) The Changs assumed titles of the Lords General of Heaven, Earth, and Men:

> . . . under their orders, they had a whole hierarchy of leadership whose functions were simultaneously military, administrative, and religious. (J. Gernet, 1982: 155)

The year 184 was the first of a new 60-year cycle: a good omen for a revolutionary new beginning and the establishing of a Kingdom of Great Peace and Equality. In that year, the T'ai-p'ing Tao movement had 360,000 men under arms. They wore yellow strips of cloth around their heads, hence the name of Yellow Turbans given to the revolt. The color "yellow" was chosen with intent: "green" was the color of the Han dynasty, which was doomed to destruction. "Yellow Heaven" would be established in the year 184.

Once determined to attack the weakened Han dynasty, the rebel armies planned to start in the city of Yeh (Hopei province). They had support from the eunuchs and palace guards in the capital city of Loyang. However, about ten days before the target date, the plot was betrayed by an inside informer, and the government took action. Many rebels were captured and executed. The date of rebellion was advanced, but to no avail. The leader Chang Chueh died of illness, and his two younger brothers were captured and executed in 184. Because of the strong military action taken by generals such as Ts'ao Ts'ao, the rebellion was suppressed, although some groups remained active for the next 20 years. Ts'ao Ts'ao, now rising to power, incorporated most of the rebel armies into his own elite troops, which helped him to unite the north. Although the Yellow Turbans did not succeed in overthrowing the Han dynasty, they weakened its power so badly that it never recovered. The dynasty finally came to an end in 220 CE, to be followed by the Three Kingdoms, with Ts'ao Ts'ao in the North founding the Wei Dynasty.

YI CHING/YIJING (*Book of Changes*). It is one of the five ancient classics of the Chinese tradition, inaccurately called "Confucian" classics (since they are pan-Chinese). The *Yi ching* is one of these oldest classical texts. Its beginnings go back to early Chou times, but its completion is much later: Warring States or Han period.

At first it was a technique of divination, used by the early Chou people together with the older Shang method of using animal bones (scapulomancy, osteomancy). This new Chou method, called *Chou Yi* ("Changes of the Chou"), was initially very simple. Milfoil or yarrow sticks were placed in a container; a bundle were removed at random, the remainder was counted. An odd number meant "lucky": the action contemplated would be successful. An even number meant "unlucky": action to be avoided. As time went on, results of each consultation were marked by symbols: a whole line ——— symbolized "lucky" (odd number, "one," etc.); a broken line — — meant "unlucky" (even number, expressed by "two," etc.).

The next step was to record the results of three consultations: One wanted to make sure the correct answer was given, so consultations could be repeated. The resulting symbols of three lines can be only eight in number, as follows:

| (1) | (2) | (3) | (4) | | (5) | (6) | (7) | (8) |

The *trigrams* or *pa-kua* (symbols made of three lines), originally the records of a triple divination, were gradually interpreted in philosophical terms. They were seen as symbols of cosmic reality and human reality: (1) and (8) referred to heaven and earth; the intermediate ones were interpreted as symbols for thunder (2), water (3), mountain (4), lake (5), fire (6), and wind or wood (7). This stresses the cosmic aspect of the *pa-kua*. Human reality was superimposed on them: The original pair also mean father (1) and mother (8), the intermediate ones are three sons (2–4) and three daughters (5–7). Human characteristics were further added: father (1) stands for the creative, strong; mother (8) is the receptive, yielding; the six children are also opposing but matching pairs:

- first son (2), thunder, is the arousing inciting movement; first daughter (7) is the gentle, penetrating.
- second son and second daughter, as water and fire, are the abysmal or dangerous (3), and the clinging, light-giving (6).
- third son and third daughter are symbols of quietude, the mountain is keeping still, restful (4), third daughter, the lake, is the joyous, joyful (5).
    (Wilhelm/Baynes, 1950: l-li)

These eight graphics, with their rich symbolism, constitute the basic energies that operate both in the cosmos (nature) and in the human world, as physical as well as psychic realities (They somehow are parallel to the **Five Agents**, some are duplicates, like *water* and *fire*.)

At a later stage still, the eight trigrams were multiplied by themselves, each one superimposed on all the others, thus forming a total of 64 symbols, called **hexagrams** (graphics consisting of six lines). These 64 were then interpreted as graphic expressions of the whole of reality, including the human world of action and all situations that could arise in life.

When the yin-yang philosophy emerged, it was also applied to the *Yi ching*: a whole line was seen as *yang*; a broken line as *yin*. Trigram (1) was seen as full *yang* (three whole lines); trigram (8) as full *yin* (three broken lines). This addition of *yin-yang* philosophy enriched the *Yi ching* commentaries (called 'Ten Wings'), the sacred book (*ching*) was complete.

Far from being a divinatory oracle, it had now become a book of deep wisdom that could be consulted for appropriate action in each difficult situation. One can either throw three coins (six times) to obtain a particular hexagram or use milfoil (yarrow) sticks in a more complicated manner to obtain the same result. Once an answer is obtained (a particular hexagram), one reads and studies the commentaries, and finds an answer to one's doubt or question. Because the text is often mysterious, one must be mentally still and meditate on it. But the results can be surprisingly accurate.

Both Confucians and Taoists have evaluated the *Yi ching*. The commentaries contain both Confucian (ethical) viewpoints and Taoist (cosmic) interpretations. Today, Taoist priests use the classic for private consultation with their clients; in Western circles, each individual can perform a personal ritual for guidance in the complex situations of life. Publications of the *Yi ching* and interpretations are numerous. One of the best translations now available was written by Wilhelm, translated into English by C. Baynes (see Wilhelm/Baynes, 1950).

YIN-FU SCRIPTURE (*Yin-fu ching/Yinfujing*). A short Taoist text of unknown authorship and uncertain date, that had, however, a great influence on the Taoist tradition. Its full title, as recorded in the **Taoist Canon** (*CT* 31, *TT* 27), is *Huang-ti Yin-fu ching*. It is included in the first part of the canon, in the *Tung-chen* section. It consists of about 400 characters, divided into three parts. The canon contains 20 commentaries on it.

Although the author is unknown, there has been much speculation about the authorship and the time of its composition: Some have said it dates from the Warring States period, others prefer the Chin dynasty (265–420); others believe it was written by **K'ou Ch'ien-chih** of the

Northern Wei, or during the T'ang period. It appears that inner criticism is not helpful in settling the matter.

Therefore, it is better to focus on the contents, for that is what attracted so much attention. In summary, it says that in the revolution of heaven and earth, the transformation of yin and yang, and in human affairs, there is a relationship of mutual generation (stimulation) and mutual control. The sage must carefully observe the Way of heaven and follow heaven's action in order to grasp the inner mechanism of heaven and humanity's correspondence. Then, in ruling the country and nourishing life, all will obtain their benefits: This is the firm foundation of the ten thousand transformations. All through history, both Taoists and Confucians have had a high regard for this text, comparable with the *TTC* and the *Chuang-tzu* (*TTTY*: 29).

***YIN-YANG* WORLDVIEW.** It may also be called a philosophical system, because it sets out to interpret reality and its operations in terms of two polar concepts, *yin* and *yang*, which are not only mental concepts, but also powers inherent in all things. Both as mental categories, by which reality is categorized, and as inherent powers in things or energies constituting things, *yin* and *yang* are polar extremes, competing and harmonizing in continuous transformation, but ultimately blending into harmony.

The creation of these two terms, *yin* and *yang*, is one of the most genial expressions of the Chinese mind. Whether derived from observation of natural phenomena or arrived at by abstract speculation, their universal acceptance into all domains of knowledge and practice had a unifying effect on the overall Chinese worldview. Being the brain child of the *Yin-Yang* School of **Tsou-yen** (third century BCE), it was eventually accepted by and incorporated into all systems of Chinese thought, Confucianism and Taoism alike. What the  Taoists especially liked in it is its similarity to and compatibility with its own view of cosmic transformation. An example is found in the *TTC* (Chapter 40): The Tao or the One produced the Two, etc. One can see the easy identification of the "Two" with *yin* and *yang*, which in turn give birth to the myriad beings. All things are produced by the interaction of *yin* and *yang*. They are also made of *yin* and *yang* energies. That shows the complexity of the system and, as will be shown later, the infinite possibilities of application.

The terms *yin* and *yang* are used to categorize the universe by arranging all things into two polar camps. That, of course, is a rationalization, but it helps to create order in our minds when we try to understand the origin, constitution, and operations of the world in which we live.

One wonders how it all started. Although the system was finalized by Tsou Yen and his School of Naturalism (which also developed the **Five Agents System**), the elements of *yin* and *yang* were certainly present in much earlier culture, perhaps already in the beginning of the Chou kingdom.

It is most likely that the *yin-yang* dualistic worldview started as a simple pair of opposites, gradually gained momentum, and finally "conquered" all aspects of Chinese thought. The exact historical process of development is impossible to reconstruct, but at least the starting point seems to be clear.

Originally, *Yin* signified: dark, shady, cloudy.
Originally, *Yang* signified: light, bright, sunny.
The first extension was geographic:
Yin is the dark, shady side of a hill (north side) or the dark bank of a river (south side);
Yang is the bright side of a hill (south side), or the bright riverbank (north side).

Further extensions embraced heaven (bright), its generative power, the sky; and earth (dark), its life-giving power, the soil. The pair sun and moon was a natural result.

Since heaven and earth were seen as the cosmic pair of generation and production, it was an easy step to apply this to the human pair: father-mother, husband-wife, male-female. Further: ruler, king, superior (son of heaven), and subject, official, inferior.

New extensions related to natural phenomena: *Yang* was summer and spring (bright seasons), sunshine, heat, dryness, but also activity, movement. *Yin* was winter and fall (dark seasons), rain, coldness, wetness, but also rest and tranquillity.

What is bright (*yang*) is also high, manifest, open, visible, public, and full; it is rationality, reason. What is dark (*yin*) is low, hidden, mysterious, closed, invisible, private, and empty; it is emotion, feelings, intuition. Here we see the *yin-yang* dualism applied not only to natural phenomena, but to the human psyche as well; a new, especially Taoist, confirmation of macro- and microcosm interaction.

Further extensions related to the physical body, health and medicine: distinctions are made between *yang* sickness (fever) and *yin* disease (cold), *yin* and *yang* pulses, *yin* and *yang* medicine, *yin* and *yang* food.

Perhaps most important in Taoist practice is the distinction of *yin-ch'i* and *yang-ch'i*, two types of vital energy vitalizing body and mind. Applied to the concept of soul, there is a *yin* soul (*p'o*) and a *yang* soul (*hun*), each responsible for different aspects of human life, physical and/or mental, spiritual.

Applied to the "spirit" world: the realm of the gods/goddesses and ancestral spirits is *yang*, the realm of the dead, the residence of "dead" souls, is *yin*. Finally, *yang* is the realm of life, is good; *yin* is the realm of death, and because most humans hate death, it is seen as *bad*. But that is a popular interpretation only; originally, *yin* and *yang* were both equally good; only an imbalance between the two is seen as not good.

In Taoist spirituality, it is often claimed that practitioners attempt to transform their *yin* energy into *yang* energy in order to reach immortality. But that is ambiguous, because it implies that *yin* energy is not good and an obstacle to progress.

The *yin-yang* worldview has its applications in all fields of human knowledge and human action, yet *yin* and *yang* are relative concepts, never to be taken in an absolute sense. The two are in continuous interaction and change into each other, like night and day are in ceaseless motion, as winter and summer, rest and activity continue to rotate. Except for their application in the area of religious concepts, *yin* and *yang* are both essentially good, equally necessary to bring balance to the world, the human body and mind. If "man" is categorized as *yang* and "woman" as *yin*, this is not in an absolute sense: Both man and woman need *yin* and *yang* qualities to reach harmony and perfection.

Often one sees comparisons of *yin* and *yang* as "negative" and "positive." This is as misleading as the good-and-evil dualism. If *yin* and *yang* are dualistic, it is not in an absolute sense. They are relative to one another, as two extremes of one continuum. Combined, *yin* and *yang* are the Supreme Ultimate, the oneness that combines all opposites. (See also **Five Agents System**.)

YÜ CHI/YUJI. Name of a famous *fang-shih* at the end of the Han dynasty. He was a native from present-day Shantung. According to a record in the *Hou-Han shu* ("Latter Han History"), he obtained a "spiritual book" in 170 scrolls (chapters) at a place named Ch'ü-yang. The title was *T'ai-p'ing ch'ing-ling shu*, and the book is an early version of the important *Great Peace Scripture*. It is said that his disciple, Kung Ch'ung, took it to the capital and presented it to Emperor Shun (r. 126–144 CE).

There is a report about (another?) Yü Chi from the Three Kingdoms period who lived in east China. He burned incense and studied Taoist books and made talismanic water (*fu-shui*) to cure illness. He had a great following in the southern kingdom of Wu; many chose him as their spiritual master. One day he went to the headquarters of Sun Ts'e, the ruler of Wu, where a great number of officers believed in him: They left the banquet table and went to pay their respects to Yü Chi. Angry with spite and jealousy, Sun Ts'e had him executed, his head was put on public display as a warning. Although Yü Chi was no threat to Sun Ts'e's political authority, he was probably seen as some kind of personal threat.

The story is not finished yet. After his execution, his followers continued to worship him and to pray to him to intercede for their good fortune, saying: "The Master Yü Chi is not dead! His mortal flesh has decomposed and he has become [an immortal] "sylph"! (Tsukamoto/Hurvitz, 1985: 473–4). (The parallel with Jesus' execution and resurrection is fascinating!)

YÜ-HUANG CHING See *JADE EMPEROR SCRIPTURE*

YÜ-HUANG TA-TI See JADE EMPEROR

YÜ-PU See STEP(S) OF YÜ

YUAN-SHIH T'IEN-TSUN/YUANSHI TIANZUN (Heavenly Venerable of the First Origin, or of the Original Beginning). Title of the Supreme deity of Taoism, the highest of the triad of **T'ien-tsun** or **Three Pure Ones**.

He is also called Yü-ch'ing (Jade Purity) Yuan-shih T'ien-tsun. His emergence in Taoist scriptures is later than that of T'ai-shang Lao-chün (**Lao-tzu deified**), whose cult goes back to the second century CE. Even as late as the time of **T'ao Hung-ching**, Yuan-shih T'ien-tsun had not yet reached the top position. In T'ao's pantheon, he is the foremost deity of *middle* rank.

Yuan-shih T'ien-tsun is believed to have existed before the creation of the universe and its 10,000 beings. He is eternal, imperishable, whereas the universe goes through cycles of creation and destruction. When a new creation of the universe takes place, he descends to earth to reveal to mankind the secrets of the Tao.

His residence is above all the heavens, at the top of the **Three Worlds** (*Ta-lo t'ien*), called "mysterious city jade capital." It is built of marble; its palaces consist of seven jewels. Those who dwell in this city are immortals of various ranks who do not perish whenever the universe comes to an end.

Yuan-shih T'ien-tsun is not worshipped in isolation, but always as the central member of the trinity. Statues of these three are found only in **Three Pure Ones** temples of Taoism. The **Taoist Canon** contains several scriptures on Yuan-shih T'ien-tsun (*MDC*: 71).

YUEH-FEI YUAN-SHIH/YWEFEI YUANSHI (Primal Teacher Yueh-fei). A famous Sung general, deified after his death and enthroned in the Chinese pantheon, he is also being worshipped by the Taoists, sometimes together with Kuan-kung, Lü Tung-pin, and others, as the Five Lord-Benefactors.

In the service of the Sung dynasty, he battled against the invading Chin and Mongol armies, until he became the victim of a jealous prime minister; he was jailed and executed when he was only 39 years old. His cult spread among the people during the Ming and Ch'ing dynasties, and even today, 11 temples are dedicated to his worship in Taiwan, especially in the counties of Chiayi and Tainan. In some temples, one can see murals representing his mother tattooing on his back four characters: "single-minded loyal, dedicated to the country" (see *TMSC*: 32).

YÜN-CHI CH'I-CH'IEN/YUNJI QICIAN (*"Seven Lots from the Cloud Bag"*). An important Taoist compendium (or collectaneum), in 122 chapters, compiled by Taoist master Chang Chün-fang (fl. 1008–1029) during the Northern Sung. Although still published today as a separate work, it has also been included in the Ming **Taoist Canon** (*CT* 1032, *TT* 677–702, in the *T'ai-hsuan* supplement).

Chang Chün-fang was in charge of the new edition of the Sung Taoist Canon, published in 1019, but on orders of Emperor Chen-tsung (r. 993–1022), he prepared the *Yün-chi ch'i-ch'ien* as a personal reference work to provide "bedtime reading" for the emperor (J. Boltz, 1987: 230). However, the collection was only finished in 1028 or 1029, and was then presented to Emperor Jen-tsung (r. 1023–1063).

This compendium is not exactly an abridged version of the Taoist Canon (the texts on liturgy are missing), but is an invaluable source of information on earlier texts (Six Dynasties and T'ang periods) and thus gives insight into the "founding years of early revelatory traditions" (Boltz: 231).

Besides the opening chapters, dealing with cosmogony and scriptural transmissions, the subjects covered are "cosmology (Chapters 21–22), astral meditation (Chapters 23–25), topography of sacred space (Chapters 26–28), birth and destiny (Chapters 29–31), hygiene, diet, and physical therapy (Chapters 32–36), codes of behavior (Chapters 37–40), ritual purification (Chapter 41), techniques of visualization (Chapters 42–44), additional instructions on the cultivation of perfection and miscellaneous applications (Chapters 45–53), control of the vital forces of the body (Chapters 54–55), embryonic respiration (Chapter 56–62), *chin-tan/nei-tan* (Chapters 63–73), prescriptive pharmaceuticals (Chapters 74–78), talismans and diagrams (Chapters 79–80), *keng-shen* lore (Chapters 81–83), *shih-chieh* or corpse liberation (Chapters 84–86), theoretical issues, such as whether divine transcendence can be learned (Chapters 87–95), selections of verse (Chapters 96–99), chronicles (Chapters 100–102), and hagiography (Chapters 103–122)" (Boltz: 231).

This rich work of Taoist literature deserves translation, but it would be an arduous task. Instead, it is often quoted in scholarly studies, and shorter extracts have been translated. (For a further discussion, see J. Boltz, 1987: 229–231.)

Bibliography

During the last decennia, the study of Taoism in all its aspects has resulted in a remarkable increase in publications, both in Western languages and in Chinese and Japanese. The availability of the Taoist Canon was one of the major factors stimulating scholarly research. The study of the philosophical texts, especially the *Tao-te Ching* and the *Chuang-tzu*, had been going on long before the interest in the Taoist religion and Taoist liturgy developed in the West.

Today, it is hard to catch up with the continuous flow of new publications. Chinese and Japanese scholars flood the academic "market" with important reference works and scholarly treatises. Those who are able to handle Chinese sources, will find a recent listing of Chinese publications on Taoism in *Great Encyclopedia of Chinese Taoism (Zhonghua Daojiao da cidian)*, edited by Hu Xuechen and published in Beijing, 1995. The publication list is found on pages 1771–1807. It covers the years 1900–1993. Other recent reference works are listed at the end of *Abbreviations*. Besides dictionaries and encyclopedias, it is important to mention *Tao-tsang t'i-yao (Essentials of the Taoist Canon)*, which discusses all the texts contained in the Ming edition of the *Tao-tsang*: their date of origin, authorship, and a summary of their contents. For those who know how to read Chinese, it is a good reference work.

Those who do not read Chinese will have to wait a little longer, until the *Tao-tsang Project (Projet Tao-tsang)*, started in Paris in 1979, is published. This grand project is being coordinated by K. Schipper in cooperation with some 30 European scholars. It will provide a comprehensive catalogue of all the texts contained in the Taoist Canon. In the meantime, a very useful reference work is available: Judith Boltz, *A Survey of Taoist Literature, Tenth to Seventeenth Centuries*. (See category *Taoist Literature, general works*.)

Bibliographies on Taoism in Western languages also have been produced (see *Bibliography* below, first section *Bibliographies*). The long review article by Anna Seidel (*CEA*, 1990) is especially recommended. The Thompson volume (1993) is also very useful for the study of Taoism, although it covers all other aspects of Chinese religion. The Walf volume (1992) is useful for the study of Taoism, but overshoots its target: It includes too many titles on the Popular religion of China. My own *Select Bibliography on Taoism*, first published in 1988, has been revised and augmented, and was published in 1997.

The bibliography that follows only lists books and articles in Western languages, mainly in English, but occasionally in French and German. A division into categories seems to be the most appropriate way to make such a bibliography practical, although in some cases a clearcut assignment of a book or article to a particular category is difficult. Readers may wish to consult related categories in some cases. The selection proposed here is not complete, but is representative. The more important publications have been included, and works of special interest to nonspecialists have been marked by an asterisk (*).

The categories listed below are fairly adequate, but some overlap is unavoidable, especially within categories 7, 8, and 9. Category 11 lists works that are quoted in the *Dictionary*, but are not strictly or uniquely Taoist: They refer either to Chinese history or to other religious traditions in China beside Taoism. This is to show that Taoism as a uniquely Chinese phenomenon cannot be isolated. It must be studied within the context of Chinese cultural and religious history. Its relationships with Chinese Buddhism, Confucianism, and the Popular religious tradition must always be considered in order to have an integrated understanding of the Taoist tradition.

Contents

1. General Works on Taoism
2. Taoist Philosophy
3. History of Taoism
4. Taoist Literature
5. Taoist Religious Life: Private Dimensions
6. Taoist Religious Life: Public Dimensions
7. Taoism and Society
8. Taoism and Chinese Culture
9. Taoism and Other Traditions
10. Study of Taoism
11. Supplementary References

General Works on Taoism

1.1 Bibliographies

AU, Donna and Sharon Rowe. "Bibliography of Taoist Studies," *BTS-I*, (1977), 128–148.

COHEN, Alvin P. "Western Language Publications on Chinese Religions, 1981–1987," *TT: RCT* (1989), 313–345.

PAS, Julian. *A Select Bibliography of Taoism*. Saskatoon: China Pavilion, 1997. (Enlarged edition).

*SEIDEL, Anna. "Chronicle of Taoist Studies in the West 1950–1990," *CEA*, 5 (1990), 223–347.

*THOMPSON, Laurence G. *Chinese Religions: Publications in Western Languages 1981 through 1990*. Ann Arbor, Michigan: Association of Asian Studies, 1993.

THOMPSON, Laurence G. compiler. *Chinese Religion in Western Languages. A Comprehensive and Classified Bibliography of Publications in English, French and German Through 1980*. Tucson, Arizona: University of Arizona Press, 1985. (Published for the Association for Asian Studies)

WALF, Knut. *Westliche Taoismus-Bibliographie (WTB) Western Bibliography of Taoism*. Essen: Verlag Die Blaue Eule, 1992. (First published in 1986).

YU, David C. "Present-day Taoist Studies," *RSR*, 3 (1977), 220–239.

1.2 Collections of Articles

CHAPPELL, David W., ed., *Buddhist and Taoist Studies 2 (BTS-2): Buddhist and Taoist Practice in Medieval Chinese Society*. Honolulu: University of Hawaii Press, 1987.

History of Religions, 9 (1969–1970), "Symposium on Taoism."

History of Religions, 17 (1978), "Current Perspectives in the Study of Chinese Religions."

LEBLANC, Charles & Rémi Mathieu. *Mythe et philosophie à l'aube de la Chine impériale. Etudes sur le Huainan zi*. Montréal: Presses Universitaires de l'Université de Montréal, 1992.

MAIR, Victor H., ed., *Experimental Essays on Chuang-tzu*. Honolulu: University of Hawaii Press, 1983. (*Asian Studies at Hawaii,* No. 29).

MAIR, Victor H., ed., *Chuang-tzu: Composition and Interpretation*. Symposium Issue of *JCR*, 11 (1983).

MASPERO, Henri. *Taoism and Chinese Religion*. Frank A. Kierman, Jr. trans. Amherst: University of Massachusetts Press, 1981. (French ed.: 1967).

SASO, Michael and David W. Chappell, eds., *Buddhist and Taoist Studies 1 (BTS-1)*. Honolulu: University Press of Hawaii, 1977.

SHINOHARA, Koichi & Gregory Schopen, eds., *From Benares to Beijing. Essays on Buddhism and Chinese Religion*. Oakville, ON: Mosaic Press, 1991.

STRICKMANN, Michel, ed., *Tantric and Taoist Studies in Honour of R.A. Stein (TTS)*. Vols. 2–3. Brussels: Institut Belge des Hautes Etudes Chinoises, 1983. (*Mélanges Chinois et Bouddhiques,* vols. 21–22).

*WELCH, Holmes and Anna Seidel, eds., *Facets of Taoism (FT)*. New Haven & London: Yale University Press, 1979.

WERNER, E.T.C. *A Dictionary of Chinese Mythology.* New York: Julian Press, 1961. (First published in 1932).

WOLF, Arthur P. (ed.). *Religion and Ritual in Chinese Society. (RRCS)* Stanford: Stanford University Press, 1974.

1.3 Short Introductions to Taoism in General

*CREEL, H.G. "What is Taoism?", *JAOS,* 72 (1956), 139–152.

EICHHORN, Werner. "Taoism," R.C. Zaehner, ed., *Concise Encyclopaedia of Living Faiths.* (New York: Hawthorne Books, 1959), 384–401.

RAGUIN, Yves. *Leçons sur le Taoïsme.* Taipei: Publications de l'association française pour le développement culturel et scientifique en Asie, 1981 & 1985.

ROBINET, Isabelle. "La Pratique du *Tao.*" In *Mythes et croyances du monde entier,* vol. 4. (Paris: Lidis, 1986), 381–398.

SCHIPPER, Kristofer. "Taoïsme," *Encyclopaedia Universalis.* (Paris: Encyclopaedia Universalis France, Editeur à Paris, 1973), vol. 15, 738–744.

*SCHWARTZ, Benjamin I. "Ways of Taoism," *The World of Thought in Ancient China.* (Cambridge, Massachusetts and London: The Belknap Press of Harvard University Press, 1985), 185–254.

SEIDEL, Anna and Michel Strickmann. "Taoism," *Encyclopaedia Britannica,* vol. 28 (1988), 394–407.

SEIDEL, Anna. "Taoïsme—Religion non-officielle de la China," *CEA* 8 (1995), 1–39. Farzeen Baldrian-Hussein (translator from the German).

SMITH, Huston. *The Illustrated World's Religions. A Guide to our Wisdom Traditions.* San Francisco: Harper, 1994 (first published 1958). (Chapter 5: "Taoism": 122–143).

THOMPSON, Laurence. "What is Taoism? (With Apologies to H.G. Creel)," *TR,* 4.2 (1993), 9–22.

1.4 Monographs on Taoism

BLOFELD, John. *The Secret and Sublime. Taoist Mysteries and Magic.* New York: E.P. Dutton, 1973.

BLOFELD, John. *Taoism: The Road to Immortality.* Boulder: Shambhala, 1978.

COOPER, J.C. *Taoism: The Way of the Mystic.* Wellingborough: Aquarian Press, 1972.

*GIRARDOT, Norman J. *Myth and Meaning in Early Taoism: The Theme of Chaos (Hun-tun).* Berkeley: University of California Press, 1983.

HARTZ, Paula. *Taoism.* Oxford: Facts on File, 1993.

*KALTENMARK, Max. *Lao Tzu and Taoism.* Roger Greaves. trans. Stanford: Stanford University Press, 1969.

LAGERWEY, John. *Taoist Ritual in Chinese Society and History.* New York: Macmillan Publishing Co.; London: Collier Macmillan Publishers, 1987.

*MASPERO, Henri. *Taoism and Chinese Religion*. Frank A. Kierman, Jr., trans. Amherst: University of Massachusetts Press, 1981.

*NEEDHAM, Joseph. "The Tao Chia (Taoists) and Taoism," *Science and Civilization in China 2. (*Cambridge: Cambridge University Press, 1956), 33–164.

NI, Hua-ching. *The Taoist Inner View of the Universe and the Immortal Realm.* Malibu, California: Shrine of the Eternal Breath of Tao, 1979.

*SCHIPPER, Kristofer. *The Taoist Body.* Karen C. Duval, trans. Berkeley: University of California Press, 1994.

*WELCH, Holmes. *Taoism. The Parting of the Way. Lao Tzu and the Taoist Movement.* Boston: Beacon Press, 1957.

1.5 Articles on Taoism

*SIVIN, Nathan. "On the Word Taoist as a Source of Perplexity. With Special Reference to the Relations of Science and Religion in Traditional China," *HR*, 17 (1978), 303–330.

WELCH, Holmes. "Bellagio Conference on Taoist Studies," *HR*, 9 (1969–1970), 107–136.

1.6 Popular Works

DENG, Ming-dao. *Chronicles of Tao. The Secret Life of a Taoist Master.* San Francisco: Harper, 1993.

HOFF, Benjamin. *The Tao of Pooh.* New York: Penguin Books, 1983.

HOFF, Benjamin. *The Te of Piglet.* New York: Penguin Books (Dutton), 1992.

PAYNE, David. *Confessions of a Taoist on Wall Street.* New York: Ballantine Books, 1984.

SMULLYAN, Raymond M. *The Tao Is Silent.* San Francisco: Harper, 1977.

WONG, Eva, trans., *Seven Taoist Masters: A Folk Novel of China.* Boston: Shambhala Press, 1990.

Taoist Philosophy

2.1 General Works

CHANG, Chung-yuan. "The Concept of Tao in Chinese Culture," *RR*, 17 (1952–1953), 115–132.

CHANG, Chung-yuan. "Tao: A New Way of Thinking," *JCP*, 1 (1974), 137–152.

CHEN, Ellen Marie. "Nothingness and the Mother Principle in Early Chinese Taoism," *IPQ*, 9 (1969), 391–405.

HANSEN, Chad. *A Daoist Theory of Chinese Thought: A Philosophical Interpretation.* New York: Oxford University Press, 1992.

IZUTSU, Toshihiko. *Sufism and Taoism: A Comparative Study of Key Philo-sophical Concepts.* Berkeley: University of California Press, 1984.

JANG, Paul Y.M. "The Ineffability of Tao in Chinese Thought," *JOSA,* 12 (1977), 5–15.

KASULIS, T.P. "The Absolute and the Relative in Taoist Philosophy," *JCP,* 4 (1977), 383–394.

NEEDHAM, Joseph. "Tao: Illuminations and Corrections of the Way," *Theol-ogy,* 81 (1978), 244–252.

PEERENBOOM, R.P. "Cosmogony, the Taoist Way," *JCP,* 17 (1990), 157–174.

RAWSON, Philip and Laszlo Legeza. *Tao, The Chinese Philosophy of Time and Change.* London: Thames & Hudson, 1973.

THIEL, Joseph. "Der Begriff der Tao im Tao-te-ching," *Sinologie,* 12 (1971), 30–108.

WATTS, Alan and Al Chung-Liang Huang. *Tao: The Watercourse Way.* New York: Pantheon Books, 1975.

WU, Yao-yü. *The Literati Tradition in Chinese Thought.* Laurence Thompson. trans. Gary Seaman, ed., *San Chiao Li Ts'e, part 2.* Los Angeles: Centre for Visual Anthropology, USC, Ethnographics Press, 1995.

WU, Yao-yü. *The Taoist Tradition of Chinese Thought.* Laurence Thompson trans., Gary Seaman, ed., *San Chiao Li Ts'e, part 1.* Los Angeles: Centre for Visual Anthropology, USC, Ethnographics Press, 1991.

2.2 Antecedents: The *Yi Ching* and *Yin-Yang* Philosophy

BLOFELD, John. *The Book of Change. A New Translation of the Ancient Chi-nese I Ching.* London: Allen & Unwin, 1965. New York: E.P. Dutton, 1968.

COOPER, J.C. *Yin and Yang. The Taoist Harmony of Opposites.* Wellingbor-ough: Aquarian Press, 1981.

FORKE, Alfred. *The World-Conception of the Chinese: Their Astronomical, Cosmological and Physico-Philosophical Speculations.* London: Probsthain, 1925.

GRAHAM, A.C. *Yin-yang and the Nature of Correlative Thinking.* Singapore: Institute of East Asian Philosophies, 1986.

PAS, Julian F. "Yin-yang Polarity: A Binocular Vision of the World," *Asian Thought & Society* (Oneonta), 8 (1983), 188–201.

RUBIN, Vitaly A. "The Concepts of Wu-Hsing and Yin-Yang," *JCP,* 9 (1982), 131–158.

WALEY, Arthur. "The Book of Changes," *BMFEA,* 5 (1933), 121–142.

WILHELM, Hellmut. *Change: Eight Lectures on the I Ching.* Cary F. Baynes. trans. New York: Pantheon Books, 1960 (*Bollingen Series,* no. 62). New York: Harper Torchbooks, 1964. Princeton: Princeton University Press, 1973. (Orig-inal German edition: Peking, 1944.)

WILHELM, Hellmut. *The Book of Changes in the Western Tradition, A Selec-*

tive Bibliography. Seattle: University of Washington, Institute for Comparative and Foreign Area Studies, 1975.

WILHELM, Hellmut. *Heaven, Earth and Man in the Book of Changes.* Seattle and London: University of Washington Press, 1977.

*WILHELM, Richard, trans., *The I Ching or Book of Changes.* Cary F. Baynes (trans. from German). New York: Pantheon Books, 1950 (*Bollingen Series,* no. 19): 2 vols. Princeton: Princeton University Press, 1961 (2 vols. in 1).

2.3   The *Tao Te Ching (Lao-tzu)*

2.3.1   *English Translations*

ADDISS, Stephen & Stanley Lombardo, trans., *Lao-Tzu Tao Te Ching.* (Ink paintings by Stephen Addiss). Indianapolis & Cambridge: Hackett Publishing Co., 1993.

BYNNER, Witter. *The Way of Life According to Laotzu. (Capricorn Books).* New York: The John Day Co., 1944 & 1962.

*CHAN, Wing-tsit. *The Way of Lao Tzu, a Translation and Study of the Tao-te Ching. (The Library of Liberal Arts,* no. 139). Indianapolis, New York: Bobbs-Merrill, 1963.

*CHEN, Ellen M. *The Tao Te Ching. A New Translation with Commentary.* (A New Era Book). New York: Paragon House, 1989.

CH'EN, Ku-ying. *Lao Tzu: Texts, Notes and Comments.* Yang Yu-wei and Roger Ames. trans. San Francisco: Chinese Materials Center, 1977.

CH'U, Ta-kao. *Tao Te Ching. A New Translation.* London: The Buddhist Lodge, 1937.

DREHER, Diane. *The Tao of Inner Peace.* New York: Harper, 1990.

*DUYVENDAK, J.J.L. *Tao-te Ching: The Book of the Way and its Virtue.* Translated from the Chinese and Annotated. London: J. Murray, 1954.

ERKES, Eduard. *Ho-shang-kung's Commentary on Lao-Tse.* Ascona: Artibus Asiae Publishers, 1958.

FENG, Gia-fu and Jane English. *Lao Tsu Tao Te Ching.* New York: Vintage Books, 1972.

GRIGG, Ray. *The Tao of Being. Lao Tzu's Tao Te Ching Adapted for a New Age.* Atlanta: Humanics New Age, 1989.

*HENRICKS, Robert G. *Lao-tzu Te-Tao Ching: A New Translation Based on the Recently Discovered Ma-wang-tui Texts.* New York: Ballantine, 1989.

HOFF, Benjamin. *The Way of Life. At the Heart of the Tao Te Ching.* New York and Tokyo: Weatherhill, 1981.

*LAFARGUE, Michael. *The Tao of the Tao Te Ching. A Translation and Commentary.* Albany: State University of New York Press, 1992.

*LAU, D.C. *Lao Tzu Tao Te Ching.* Baltimore: Penguin Books, 1963.

*LAU, D.C. *Tao Te Ching.* Hong Kong: The Chinese University Press, 1982.

LIN, Paul J. *A Translation of Lao Tzu's Tao Te Ching and Wang Pi's Commen-*

tary. Ann Arbor, MI: Monographs in Chinese Studies, no. 30, University of Michigan Center for Chinese Studies, 1977 & 1983.

LIN, Yutang. *The Wisdom of Laotse, with Introduction and Notes.* London: M. Joseph, 1958.

*MAIR, Victor. *Tao Te Ching. Lao Tzu. The Classic Book of Integrity and the Way.* New York: Bantam Books, 1990.

MILES, Thomas H., trans., *Tao Te Ching. About the Way of Nature and its Powers.* Garden City Park, NY: Avery Publishing Group, 1992.

REN, Jiyu. *The Book of Laozi.* He Guanghu e.a. trans. Beijing: Foreign Languages Press, 1993.

WALEY, Arthur. *The Way and its Power: A Study of the Tao Te Ching and its Place in Chinese Thought.* London: G. Allen and Unwin, 1934, 1942, 1949.

WU, John C.W. *Lao Tzu Tao Teh Ching.* Chinese text with English translation by John C.H. Wu. Paul K. Shih, ed., New York: St. John's University Press, 1961. (*Asian Institute Translations,* no.1)

2.3.2 French Translations

DUYVENDAK, J.J.L. *Tao-te King, le livre de la voie et de la vertu.* Paris: Librairie d'Amérique et d'Orient, Adrien-Maisonneuve, 1953.

ETIEMBLE, René. *Tao tö King.* Paris: Gallimard, 1967.

JULIEN, Stanislas. *Lao Tseu Tao Te King. Le livre de la voie et de la vertu.* Paris: Imprimerie Royale, 1842.

JULIEN, Stanislas. *Lao Tseu, Tao Te King. Le livre de la voie et de la vertu, traduit en Français et avec le texte chinois et un commentaire perpétuel.* Paris: Cercle du Livre Précieux, 1967.

LARRE, Claude. *Tao Te King. Le livre de la voie et de la vertu.* Paris: Desclée De Brouwer, 1977.

LIOU, Kia-hway. *Tao tö King: Traduit du Chinois.* Paris: Gallimard, 1967.

2.3.3 German Translations

COLD, Eberhard. *Laotse, Tao Te Ching. Das Buch des Alten Meisters vom Tao und der Demut.* Königsten: Sophia, 1982.

JERVEN, Walter. *Das Buch vom Weltgesetz und seinem Wirken.* München-Bern: O.W. Barth, 1986.

KOPP, Wolfgang. *Das heilige Buch vom Tao und der wahren Tugend.* Interlaken: Ansata, 1988.

OPITZ, P.J. *Lao-tzu. Die Ordnungs-Spekulationen im Tao-te-Ching.* München, 1968.

ULENBROOK, Jan. *Lau Dse, Dau Dö Djing.* Bremen: Carl Schünemann, 1962.

WEIGLAND, Jörg. *Lao-Tse, Weisheiten.* München: Heyne, 1982.

WILHELM, Richard. *Lao-tse Taote king. Das Buch des Alten vom Sinn und*

Leben. Jena: Diederichs, 1937 und 1941. Düsseldorf und Köln, 1957. Bern und Stuttgart: Huber, 1958.

WÜPPER, Edgar. *Laotse—der alte Mann und die Sprüche.* Kiel: Chiva, 1985.

2.3.4 *Other*

DEBROCK, Guy and Paul B. Scheurer *Tao: De Weg van de Natuur.* Nijmegen: Katholieke Universiteit Nijmegen, 1986.

2.3.5 *Studies About Lao Tzu and/or Tao Te Ching*

BOLTZ, Judith M. "Lao-tzu," *ER,* 8 (1987), 454–459.

CHEN, Ellen Marie. "The Meaning of *Te* in the *Tao Te Ching*: An Examination of the Concept of Nature in Chinese Taoism," *PEW,* 23 (1973), 457–470.

HOMANN, R. "Die Laozi-Diskussion in der Volksrepublik China nach den Funden von Ma-Wang-dui," *AS. Etudes Asiatiques (Schweizerische Gesellschaft für Asienkunde)* 30 (1976), 79–113.

JAN, Yün-hua. "Problems of Tao and *Tao Te Ching*," *Numen,* 22 (1975), 203–234.

JAN, Yün-hua. "The Silk Manuscripts on Taoism," *TP,* 63 (1977), 65–84.

*LAFARGUE, Michael. *Tao and Method: A Reasoned Approach to the Tao Te Ching.* Albany, NY: State University of New York Press, 1994.

PONTYNEN, Arthur. "The Deification of Laozi in Chinese History and Art," *OA,* 26 (1980), 192–200.

ROBINET, Isabelle. *Les commentaires du Tao To King jusqu'au VII siècle.* Paris: Collège de France, Institut des Hautes Etudes Chinoises, 1977. (*Mémoires de l'Institut des Hautes Etudes Chinoises,* vol. 5)

TU, Wei-ming. "The Thought of Huang Lao: A Reflection in the Lao Tzu and Huang Ti's Texts in the Silk Manuscripts of Ma-wang-tui," *JAS,* 39 (1979), 95–110.

2.4 The *Chuang-tzu*

2.4.1 *Translations*

FENG, Gia-fu and Jane English. *Chuang Tseu: Inner Chapters.* New York: Vintage Books, 1974.

FUNG, Yu-lan. *Chuang-Tzu. A New Selected Translation with an Exposition of the Philosophy of Kuo Hsiang.* New York: Paragon Book Reprint, 1964. (First published in Shanghai, 1933)

GILES, Herbert A., trans., *Chuang Tzu, Mystic, Moralist and Social Reformer.* Shanghai and London: Bernard Quaritch, 1926; reprint, Taipei: Ch'eng Wen Publishing Co., 1969.

*GRAHAM, A.C. "Chuang-Tzu's Essay on Seeing Things as Equal," *HR*, 9 (1969–1970), 137–159.

*GRAHAM, A.C. *Chuang-Tzu: The Seven Inner Chapters*. London: George Allen & Unwin, 1981.

LEGGE, James. *The Texts of Taoism*. Part 2: *The Writings of Chuang Tzu (Books 18–33). The T'ai Shang Tractate of Actions and their Retributions (Sacred Books of China 40)*. New York: Dover Publications, 1962 (first published by Oxford University Press, 1891)

LIOU, Kai-hway. *L'Oeuvre complète de Tschouang-tseu: Traduction, Préface et Notes*. Paris: Gallimard, 1969.

MAIR, Victor, trans., *Wandering on the Way: Early Taoist Tales and Parables of Chuang Tzu*. New York: Bantam Books, 1994.

WALEY, Arthur. *Three Ways of Thought in Ancient China*. London: Allen & Unwin, 1939; reprint, Garden City, NY: Doubleday, 1956. ("Chuang Tzu," 2–79)

*WATSON, Burton, trans., *The Complete Works of Chuang Tzu*. New York and London: Columbia University Press, 1970.

2.4.2 Studies

CHANG, Chung-yüan. "The Philosophy of Taoism According to Chuang Tzu," *PEW*, 27 (1977), 409–422.

GRAHAM, A.C. "How much of 'Chuang Tzu' did Chuang-tzu write?," H. Rosemont and B. Schwartz (eds.), *Studies in Classical Chinese Thought*, Thematic Issue of *JAAR*, 47 (1979), 459–502.

KOHN, Livia. "Kuo Hsiang and the Chuang Tzu," *JCP*, 12 (1985), 429–447.

MAIR, Victor H. "Chuang-tzu and Erasmus: Kindred Wits," V.H. Mair (ed.), *Experimental Essays on Chuang-tzu*, 85–100. [see 1.2]

MAIR, Victor H. "Wandering in and Through the *Chuang-tzu*," V.H. Mair (ed.), *Chuang-tzu: Composition and Interpretation, JCR*, 11 (1983), 106–117.

MAJOR, John S. "The Efficacity of Uselessness: A Chuang-tzu Motif," *PEW*, 25 (1975), 265–279.

RAJNEESH, Bhagwan Shree. *The Empty Boat. Talks on the Stories of Chuang Tzu, compiled by Ma Krishna Priya*. Poona, India: Rajneesh Foundation, 1976.

ROBINET, Isabelle. "Chuang-tzu et le taoïsme 'religieux'," V.H. Mair (ed.), *Chuang-Tzu: Composition and Interpretation, JCR*, 11 (1983), 59–105.

ROTH, Harold. "Who Compiled the Chuang-tzu?," *CTPC*, 79–128.

THIEL, J. "Das Erkenntnisproblem bei Chuang-tzu," *Sinologica*, 11 (1970), 1–89.

WATSON, Burton. "Chuang-tzu," *ER*, 3 (1987), 467–469.

2.5 Huang-Lao Taoism

JAN, Yün-hua. "Human Nature and its Cosmic Roots in Huang-Lao Taoism," *JCP*, 17 (1990), 215–233.

TU, Wei-ming. "The 'Thought of Huang-Lao': A Reflection on the Lao Tzu and Huang Ti Texts in the Silk Manuscripts of Ma-wang-tui," *JAS*, 39 (1979), 95–110.

2.6 Huai-Nan Tzu

2.6.1 *Translations*

AMES, Roger T. *The Art of Rulership. A Study in Ancient Chinese Political Thought. Huai Nan Tzu*, Book Nine: "The Art of Rulership" (translation, 165–209).

KRAFT, Eva. "Zum Huai-nan-tzu, Einführung. Ubersetzung (Kapitel 1 und 2), und Interpretation," *MS*, 16 (1957), 191–286; 17 (1958), 128–207.

LARRE, Claude. *Le traité VII du Houai Nan Tseu. Les esprits légers et subtils animateurs de l'essence. (Variétés Sinologiques,* No. 67) Taipei: Ricci Institute, 1982.

LARRE, Claude, Isabelle Robinet and Elisabeth Rochat de la Vallée, trans., *Les grands traités du Huainan zi.* Paris: Institut Ricci & les Editions du Cerf, 1993 (Variétes Sinologiques, no. 75).

*LEBLANC, Charles. *Huai Nan Tzu, Philosophical Synthesis in Early Han Thought.* Hong Kong: Hong Kong University Press, 1985.

*MAJOR, John. *Heaven and Earth in Early Han Thought: Chapters Three, Four and Five of the Huainanzi.* Albany, NY: State University of New York Press, 1993.

MORGAN, Evan. *Tao, The Great Luminant; Essays from Huai-nan-tze.* London: Kegan Paul, 1933.

WALLACKER, Benjamin E. *The Huai-nan-tzu, Book Eleven: Behavior, Culture and the Cosmos.* New Haven: American Oriental Society (Monograph Series, 48), 1962.

2.6.2 *Studies*

*AMES, Roger T. *The Art of Rulership. A Study in Ancient Chinese Political Thought.* Honolulu: University of Hawaii Press, 1983.

LARRE, Claude. *Le traité VII du Houai Nan Tseu. Les esprits légers et subtils animateurs de l'essence. (Variétés Sinologiques,* No. 67) Taipei: Ricci Institute, 1982.

LEBLANC, Charles. *Huai Nan Tzu, Philosophical Synthesis in Early Han Thought.* Hong Kong: Hong Kong University Press, 1985.

LEBLANC, Charles & Rémi Matthieu, eds., *Mythe et philosophie à l'aube de la Chine impériale: Etudes sur le Huainanzi.* Montréal & Paris: Les Presses de l'Université de Montréal, 1992.

ROTH, Harold D. "The Concept of Human Nature in the Huai-Nan Tzu," *JCP*, 12 (1985), 1–22.

ROTH, Harold D. *The Textual History of the Huai-nan Tzu.* Ann Arbor, Michigan (AAS Monograph Series 46), 1992.

WALLACKER, Benjamin E. *The Huai-nan-tzu, Book Eleven: Behavior, Culture and the Cosmos.* New Haven: American Oriental Society, 1962. (*American Oriental Series,* vol. 48)

2.7   Lieh Tzu

FORKE, Anton. "Yang Chu, the Epicurean in his Relation to Lie-tse, the Pantheist," *Journal of the Peking Oriental Society,* 3 (1893), 203–258. (Also published separately as: A. Forke, *Yang Chu's Garden of Pleasure.* London: John Murray, 1912)

GILES, Lionel. *Taoist Teaching from the Book of Lieh Tzu.* Translated from the Chinese, with Introduction and Notes. Second edition. London: J. Murray, 1959.

*GRAHAM, A.C. *The Book of Lieh-tzu.* New York: Grove Press, 1960.

GRYNPAS, Benedykt. *Le Vrai Classique du Vide Parfait par Lie-tseu.* Paris: Gallimard, 1961. (*Connaissance de l'Orient*)

2.8   Other Ancient Texts

KANDEL, Barbara. *Wen Tzu: Ein Betrag zur Problematik und zum Verständniss eines taoistischen Textes.* Bern: 1974.

KOHN, Livia. *Taoist Mystical Philosophy: The Scripture of Western Ascension.* Albany: SUNY Press, 1991.

REITER, Florian C. *Der Perlenbeutel aus den drei Hölen. Arbeitsmaterialen zum Taoismus der Frühen T'ang-Zeit.* Wiesbaden: Otto Harrassowitz, 1990.

RICKETT, W. Allyn. *Guanzi: Political, Economic and Philosophical Essays from Early China. Vol. 1.* Princeton: Princeton University Press, 1985.

YANG, Hsiung. *Tai hsuan ching. The Elemental Changes: the Ancient Chinese Companion to the I ching. Text and Commentaries.* Michael Nylan (trans.). Albany, NY: State University of New York Press, 1994.

2.9   *Hsüan-hsüeh* and "Neo-Taoism"

BERGERON, Marie-Ina. *Wang Pi, Philosophe du "non-avoir."* (*Variétés Sinologiques,* no. 69) Taipei: Ricci Institute, 1986.

CHAN, Alan Kam-Leung. *Two Visions of the Way: A Study of the Wang Pi and the Ho-shang Kung Commentaries on the Lao-tzu.* Albany: State University of New York Press, 1991.

CH'EN, Kenneth. "Neo-Taoism and the Prajña School during the Wei and Chin Dynasties," *CC,* 1 (1957), 33–46.

HOLZMAN, Donald. *La vie et la pensée de Hi K'ang (223–262 Ap. J.C.).* Leiden: E.J. Brill, 1957.

HOLZMAN, Donald. *Poetry and Politics: The Life and Works of Juan Chi, A.D. 210–263.* Cambridge: Cambridge University Press, 1976.

KNAUL, Livia. "The Winged Life: Kuo Hsiang's Mystical Philosophy," *JCS,* 2 (1985), 17–41.

SAILEY, Jay. *The Master Who Embraces Simplicity: A Study of the Philosopher Ko Hung, A.D. 283–343.* San Francisco: Chinese Materials Center, 1978.

The History of Taoism

3.1 General Works

KALTENMARK, Max. "Ling-pao: note sur un terme du taoïsme religieux," *Mélanges publiés par l'Institut des Hautes Etudes Chinoises,* 2 (1960), 559–588.

*ROBINET, Isabelle. *Histoire du taoïsme des origines au XIVième siècle.* Paris: Editions du Cerf, 1991.

ROBINET, Isabelle. *Taoism: Growth of a Religion.* Trans. Phyllis Brooks. Stanford: Stanford UP, 1997.

SEIDEL, Anna. "Imperial Treasures and Taoist Sacraments," *TTS-2,* 291–371.

STEIN, R.A. "Religous Taoism and Popular Religion from the Second to Seventh Centuries," *FT,* (1979), 53–82. [see 1.2]

3.2 Antecedents: Roots of Taoism

ALLAN, Sarah. *The Shape of the Turtle: Myth, Art and Cosmos in Early China.* Albany: State University of New York Press, 1991.

DEWOSKIN, Kenneth, trans., *Doctors, Diviners and Magicians of Ancient China: Biographies of* Fang-shih. New York: Columbia University Press, 1983.

DEWOSKIN, Kenneth. "A Source Guide to the Lives and Techniques of Han and Six Dynasties *Fang-shih.*" *SSCRB* 9 (1981), 79–105.

PEERENBOOM, R.P. "Naturalism and Immortality in the Han: the Antecedents of Religious Taoism," *CC,* 29 (1988), 31–53.

3.3 Huang-Lao Taoism, the *T'ai-p'ing ching* and Han Thought

BALAZS, Etienne. "La crise sociale et la philosophie politique à la fin des Han," *TP,* 39 (1949–1950), 83–131.

EICHHORN, Werner. "T'ai-p'ing und T'ai-p'ing Religion," *Mitteilungen der Deutsche Akademie der Wissenschaften,* 5 (1957), 113–140.

JAN, Yün-Hua. "The Change of Images: The Yellow Emperor in Ancient Chinese Literature," *JOS,* 19 (1981), 117–137.

*KALTENMARK, Max. "The Ideology of the *T'ai-p'ing ching*," *FT*, (1979), 19–52.

LEVY, Howard S. "Yellow Turban Religion and Rebellion at the End of Han," *JAOS*, 76 (1956), 214–227.

PEERENBOOM, R.P. *Law and Morality in Ancient China: The Silk Manuscripts of Huang-Lao.* Albany, NY: SUNY Press, 1993.

*SEIDEL, Anna. "The Image of the Perfect Ruler in Early Taoist Messianism: Lao-Tzu and Li Hung," *HR*, 9 (1969–1970), 216–247.

SEIDEL, Anna. *La divinisation de Lao Tseu dans le taoïsme des Han.* Paris: Ecole Française d'Extrême-Orient, 1969.

STEIN, Rolf A. "Remarques sur les mouvements du taoïsme politico-religieux au 2ème siècle ap. J.C.," *TP*, 50 (1963), 1–78.

TU, Wei-ming. "The Thought of Huang Lao: A Reflection in the Lao Tzu and Huang Ti's Texts in the Silk Manuscripts of Ma-wang-tui," *JAS*, 39 (1979), 95–110.

3.4 Early Taoist Movements and the "Heavenly Master" Tradition

GROOT, J.J.M. de. "On the Origin of the Taoist Church," *Transactions of the 3rd International Congress for the History of Religions.* (Oxford: Clarendon Press, 1908), 138–149.

KOBAYASHI, Masayoshi. "The Celestial Masters Under the Eastern Jin and Liu-Song Dynasties," *TR*, 3.2 (1992), 17–46.

LEVY, Howard S. "Yellow Turban Religion and Rebellion at the End of the Han," *JAOS*, 76 (1956), 214–227.

*MATHER, Richard. "K'ou Ch'ien-chih and the Taoist Theocracy at the Northern Wei Court," *FT*, (1979), 103–122. [see 1.2]

MICHAUD, Paul. "The Yellow Turbans," *MS*, 17 (1958), 47–127.

TSUKAMOTO, Z. *A HIstory of Early Chinese Buddhism from its Introduction to the Death of Hui-yüan (2 vols.).* L. Hurvitz. trans. Tokyo: Kodansha International Ltd., 1985 (Japanese edition: 1979). (In Chapter 3, part C is titled: "Buddhism and the Rise of Dark Learning Under the Wei": 123–133).

3.5 Six Dynasties Taoism

HENRICKS, Robert G. *Philosophy and Argumentation in Third-Century China: The Essays of Hsi K'ang.* Princeton: Princeton University Press, 1983.

HOLZMAN, Donald. "Les sept sages de la forêt des bambous et la société de leur temps," *TP*, 44 (1956), 317–346.

SAILEY, Jay. *The Master Who Embraces Simplicity: A Study of the Philosopher Ko Hung, 283–343.* San Francisco: Chinese Materials Center, 1978.

3.6 The Shang-ch'ing Tradition

ROBINET, Isabelle. *La révélation du Shangqing dans l'histoire du taoïsme.* Paris: Ecole Française d'Extrême-Orient: Dépositaire, Adrien Maisonneuve, 1984.

STRICKMANN, Michel. *Le Taoïsme du Mao Chan, Chronique d'une Révélation.* Paris: Institut des Hautes Etudes Chinoises, Collège de France, 1981. (*Mémoires de l'Institut des Hautes Etudes Chinoises,* vol. 17)

STRICKMANN, Michel. "The Mao Shan Revelations: Taoism and the Aristocracy," *TP,* 63 (1977), 1–64.

3.7 T'ang Taoism

BARRETT, Timothy. *Taoism under the T'ang. Religion and Empire during the Golden Age of Chinese History.* London: Wellsweep Press, 1996.

BARRETT, Timothy. "Taoism under the T'ang," Denis Twitchet (ed.), *The Cambridge History of China, vol. 4: Sui and T'ang China, part 2.* (Cambridge, Cambridge University Press, forthcoming).

BENN, Charles David. *Taoism as Ideology in the Reign of Emperor Hsüan-Tsung, 712–755.* Ann Arbor: University of Michigan, 1977.

EBREY, Patricia Buckley and Peter N. Gregory (eds.), *Religion and Society in T'ang and Sung China.* Honolulu: University of Hawaii Press, 1993.

HERBERT, Penelope. "Taoism and the T'ang State," *Proceedings of the first International Symposium on Church and State in China: Past and Present.* (Taipei, 1987), 59–68.

KIRKLAND, Russell. "From Imperial Tutor to Taoist Priest: Ho Chih-Chang at the T'ang Court," *JAH,* 23 (1989), 101–133.

KIRKLAND, Russell. "Huang Ling-wei: a Taoist Priestess in T'ang China," *JCR,* 19 (1991), 47–73.

KOHN, Livia. "The Teaching of T'ien-yin-tzu," *JCR,* 15 (1987), 1–28.

SCHIPPER, Kristofer M. "Taoist Ritual and Local Cults of the T'ang Dynasty," *Proceedings of the First International Conference on Sinology.* (Taipei: Academia Sinica, 1980), 101–115.

VERELLEN, Franciscus. *Du Guangting (850–933), taoïste de cour à la fin de la Chine médiévale.* Paris: Collège de France, 1989.

3.8 Sung Taoism

BOLTZ, Judith M. "Not by the Seal of Office Alone: New Weapons in Battles with the Supernatural," P.B. Ebrey and P.N. Gregory (eds.), *Religion and Society in T'ang and Sung China.* (Honolulu: University of Hawaii Press, 1993), 241–305.

CAHILL, Suzanne E. "Taoists at the Sung Court: The Heavenly Text Affair of 1008," *BSYS,* 16 (1980), 23–44.

EBREY, Patricia Buckley and Peter N. Gregory, eds., *Religion and Society in T'ang and Sung China*. Honolulu: University of Hawaii Press, 1993.

3.9   Taoism and New Movements During the Conquest Dynasties

CHEN, Yuan. *The New Taoism in the Northern Provinces at the Beginning of the Southern Song. [Nan-Song chu hebei xin Daojiao kao]*. Beijing, 1941. J. Pas and M.K. Leung trans. (in preparation).

JAGCHILD, Sechin. "Chinese Buddhism and Taoism during the Mongolian Rule of China," *JMS*, 6 (1980), 61–98.

THIEL, Joseph. "Der Streit der Buddhisten und Taoisten zur Mongolenzeit," *MS*, 20 (1961), 1–81.

TSUI, Bartholomew P.M. *Taoist Tradition and Change. The Story of the Complete Perfection Sect in Hong Kong*. Hong Kong: Christian Study Centre on Chinese Religion and Culture, 1991.

YAO, Tao-chung. *Ch'üan-chen: A New Taoist Sect in North China During the Twelfth and Thirteenth Centuries*. Doctoral Dissertation; University of Arizona, 1980.

3.10   20th-Century Taoism

HAHN, Thomas. "On Doing Field Work in Daoist Studies in the People's Republic of China—Conditions and Results," *CEA*, 2 (1986), 211–217.

HAHN, Thomas. "New Developments Concerning Buddhist and Taoist Monasteries," *TT:RCT*, (1989), 79–101.

JAN, Yün-hua. "The Religious Situation and the Studies of Buddhism and Taoism in China: an Incomplete and Imbalanced Picture," *JCR*, 12 (1984), 37–64.

MacINNES, Donald E. *Religion in China Today: Policy and Practice*. Maryknoll, NY: Orbis Books, 1989.

WELCH, Holmes. "The Chang T'ien Shih and Taoism in China," *JOS*, 4 (1957–1958), 188–212.

Taoist Literature

4.1   General Works

*BOLTZ, Judith. *Survey of Taoist Literature: Tenth to Seventeenth Centuries*. (Institute of Asian Studies). Berkeley: University of California Press, 1987.

LOON, Piet van der. *Taoist Books in the Libraries of the Sung Period: A Critical Study and Index*. London, Ithaca Press, 1984.

STRICKMANN, Michel. "Taoist Literature," *EB, (Macropaedia)*, 17 (1974), 1051–1055.

4.2 The History and Nature of the *Tao-tsang*

ANDERSEN, Poul. "The Study of the Daozang," *SCEAR,* 3 (1990), 81–94.

CAMPANY, Robert F. "Buddhist Revelation and Taoist Translation in Early Medieval China," *TR,* 4.1 (1993), 1–30.

KOHN, Livia. "Taoist Scriptures as Mirrored in the *Xiaodao Lun,*" *TR,* 4.1 (1993), 47–70.

LIU, Ts'un-yan. "The Compilation and Historical Value of the Tao-Tsang," Leslie, MacKerrar and Wang, *Essays on the Sources for Chinese History.* (Canberra: Australian National University Press, 1973), 104–119.

OFUCHI, Ninji. "The Formation of the Taoist Canon," *FT,* (1979), 253–268.

4.3 Studies of Texts

BOKENKAMP, Stephen R. "Sources of the Ling-pao Scriptures," *TTR-2,* (1983), 434–486.

CHANG, Po-tuan. *The Inner Teachings of Taoism.* Thomas Cleary. trans. Boston: Shambhala, 1986.

CHANG, Po-tuan. *Understanding Reality: A Taoist Alchemical Classic.* Thomas Cleary, trans., Honolulu: University of Hawaii Press, 1988.

CHAVANNES, Edouard. "Le jet des dragons," *Mémoires concernant l'Asie Orientale* (Paris), 3 (1919), 53–220.

CLEARY, Thomas, ed., *Vitality, Energy, Spirit: A Taoist Sourcebook.* Boston: Shambala, 1991.

KANDEL, Barbara. *Taiping Jing: the Origin and Transmission of the "Scripture on General Welfare." The History of an Unofficial Text.* Gesellschaft für Natur- und Völkerkunde Ostasiens, 1979.

KEEGAN, David J. *The Huang-ti Nei-ching: The Structure of the Compilation; the Significance of the Structure.* Doctoral Dissertation, University of California, 1988.

*KOHN, Livia. *Seven Steps to the Tao. Sima Chengzhen's Zuowanglun.* Nettetal, Monumenta Serica Monograph Series, vol. 20, 1987.

KOHN, Livia. *Taoist Mystical Philosophy: The Scripture of Western Ascension.* Albany: State University of New York Press, 1991.

KOHN, Livia. "The Teaching of T'ien-yin-tzu," *JCR,* 15 (1987), 1–28.

LAGERWEY, J. *Wu-shang pi-yao. Somme taoïste du VIième siècle.* Paris: Ecole Française d'Extrême Orient, 1981.

REITER, Florian C. *Der Perlenbeutal aus den drei Höhlen (San-tung chunang). Arbeitsmaterialien zum Taoismus der Frühen T'ang-Zeit.* (Asiatische Forschungen, vol. 112). Wiesbaden: Otto Harassowitz, 1990.

STRICKMANN, Michel. "The Longest Taoist Scripture," (Book of Salvation, *Tu-jen ching*), *HR,* 17 (1978), 331–354.

THOMPSON, Laurence G. "Taoism: Classic and Canon," Frederick M. Denny and Rodney L. Taylor, eds., *The Holy Book in Comparative Perspective.* (University of South Carolina Press, 1985), 204–223.

VEITH, Ilza. *The Yellow Emperor's Classic of Internal Medicine.* Berkeley: University of California Press, 1966 (1st published in 1949).

WARE, James R. *Alchemy, Medicine and Religion in the China of A.D. 320: The Nei-p'ien of Ko Hung (Pao-p'u-tzu).* Cambridge, Mass.: Massachusetts Institute of Technology Press, 1966.

4.4 Translations of Texts

CLEARY, Thomas. *Understanding Reality: A Taoist Alchemical Classic by Chang Po-tuan, with a Concise Commentary by Liu I-ming.* Honolulu: University of Hawaii Press, 1987.

DREXLER, Monika. *Daoistische Schriftmagie: Interpretationen zu den Schriftamuletten "Fu" im "Daozang".* (Münchener Ostasiatische Studien, 68). Wiesbaden: Franz Steiner Verlag, 1994.

KEEGAN, David J. *The Huang-ti Nei-ching: The Structure of the Compilation; the Significance of the Structure.* Doctoral Dissertation, University of California, 1988.

SEIDEL, Anna. "Le sutra merveilleux du Ling-pao suprême, traitant de Lao tseu qui convertit les barbares." In *Contributions aux études du Touen-houang,* edited by Michel Soymié, 3 (1984): 305–52. Geneva: Ecole Française d'Etrême-Orient.

WILHELM, Richard, trans., *The Secret of the Golden Flower: A Chinese Book of Life.* New York: Causeway Books, 1974 (first publication London, 1931).

WONG, Eva. trans. *Cultivating Stillness: A Taoist Manual for Transforming Body and Mind (T'ai Shang Ch'ing-ching ching).* Boston: Shambhala Publications, 1992.

4.5 Themes in Literature

DESPEUX, Catherine. *Taoïsme et le corps humain: le xiuzhen tu.* Paris: Editions Maisnie-Trédaniel, 1994.

DREXLER, Monika. *Daoistische Schriftmagie: Interpretationen zu den Schriftamuletten "Fu" im "Daozang".* (Münchener Ostasiatische Studien, 68). Wiesbaden: Franz Steiner Verlag, 1994.

KOHN, Livia. "Taoist Visions of the Body," *JCP,* 18 (1991), 227–252.

ROTH, Harold. "The Early Taoist Concept of *Shen:* A Ghost in the Machine?" Kidder Smith, ed., *Sagehood and Systematizing Thought, 11–32.*

YU, David C. "The Creation Myth of Chaos in the Daoist Canon," *JOS,* 24 (1986), 1–20.

The Taoist Religious Life: The Private Dimensions

5.1 Taoist Concepts of Life and Death

BODDE, Derk. "The Chinese View of Immortality: Its Expressions by Chu Hsi and its Relationship to Buddhist Thought," *RR,* 6 (1942), 369–383.

CHEN, Ellen Marie. "Is There a Doctrine of Physical Immortality in the *Tao Te Ching?*" *HR,* 12 (1973), 231–249.

HU, Shih. "The Concept of Immortality in Chinese Thought," *Harvard Divinity School Bulletin,* (1946), 23–43.

KOHN, Livia. "Eternal Life in Taoist Mysticism," *JAOS,* 110 (1990), 622–640.

LIEBENTHAL, Walter. "The Immortality of the Soul in Chinese Thought," *Monumenta Nipponica,* 8 (1952), 327–397.

*LOEWE, Michael. *Ways to Paradise, the Chinese Quest for Immortality.* London: G. Allen & Unwin, 1979.

SCHIFFELER, John W. "An Essay on the Traditional Concept of Soul in Chinese Society," *CC,* 17 (1976), 51–56.

SEIDEL, Anna. "Post-mortem Immortality or the Taoist Resurrection of the Body," Shaked Shulman, & G.G. Strousma (eds.), *Essays on Transformation, Revolution, and Permanence in the History of Religions.* (Leiden: E.J. Brill, 1987), 223–237.

YU, Ying-shih. "Life and Immortality in the Mind of Han China," *HJAS,* 25 (1964–1965), 80–122.

5.2 Taoist Self-Cultivation

5.2.1 *Taoist Spirituality and Practices*

BLOFELD, John E.C. *Taoism: The Quest for Immortality.* Boston: Unwin Paperbacks, 1979.

CHIA, Mantak. *Awaken Healing Energy Through the Tao. The Taoist Secret of Circulating Internal Power.* Huntington, NY: The Healing Tao Press, 1983.

CHIA, Mantak. *Chi Self-Massage. The Taoist Way of Rejuvenation.* Huntington, NY: The Healing Tao Press, 1986.

CHIA, Mantak. *Taoist Ways to Transform Stress into Vitality.* Huntington, NY: The Healing Tao Press, 1985.

CHIA, Mantak and Maneewan Chia. *Healing Love Through the Tao: Cultivating Female Sexual Energy.* Huntington, NY: The Healing Tao Press, n.d.

CHIA, Mantak and Michael Winn. *Taoist Secrets of Love: Cultivating Male Sexual Energy.* New York: Aurora, 1984.

DONG, Y.P. *Still as a Mountain, Powerful as Thunder: Simple Taoist Exercises for Healing, Vitality and Peace of Mind.* Boston: Shambhala Publications, 1993.

GRIGG, Ray. *The Tao of Relationships: A Balancing of Man and Woman.* Aldershot, Hants: Wildwood House, 1989.

NAN, Huai-chin. *Tao and Longevity, Mind-Body-Transformation.* York Beach, Maine: Samuel Weiser, 1984.

ROTH, Harold. "Psychology and Self-Cultivation in Early Taoistic Thought," *HJAS,* 51 (1991), 599–650.

WU, Jing-nuan (trans.). *Ling Shu or the Spiritual Pivot.* Washington, D.C.: Taoist Center, 1993. Distributed by University of Hawaii Press.

5.2.2 Outer Alchemy

BERTSCHINGER, Richard. *The Secret of Everlasting Life (Can Tong Qi).* Rockport, MA: Element Books, 1994.

BOEHMER, Thomas. "Taoist Alchemy: A Sympathetic Approach Through Symbols," *BTS-1,* (1977), 55–78. [see 1.2]

COOPER, Jean C. *Chinese Alchemy; the Taoist Quest for Immortality.* Wellingsborough: Aquarian Press, 1984. New York: Sterling Publishing Co., 1990.

DREHER, Diane. *The Tao of Peace. A Modern Guide to the Ancient Way of Peace and Harmony.* London: Mandala (Harper-Collins Publishers), 1990.

*NEEDHAM, Joseph. *Chemistry and Chemical Technology.* Part 2: "Spagyrical Discovery and Invention: Magisteries of Gold and Immortality." *Science and Civilization in China,* vol. 5. Cambridge: Cambridge University Press, 1974.

NEEDHAM, Joseph. *Chemistry and Chemical Technology.* Part 3: "Spagyrical Discovery and Invention: Historical Survey, from Cinnabar Elixirs to Synthetic Insulin." *Science and Civlization in China,* vol. 5. Cambridge: Cambridge University Press, 1976.

*NEEDHAM, Joseph. *Chemistry and Chemical Technology.* Part 5: "Spagyrical Discovery and Invention: Physiological Alchemy." *Science and Civilization in China,* vol. 5. Cambridge: Cambridge University Press, 1983.

ROBINET, Isabelle. "Sur le sens des termes *waidan* et *neidan,*" *TR,* 3.1 (1991), 3–40.

*SIVIN, Nathan. *Chinese Alchemy: Preliminary Studies.* Cambridge, Mass.: Harvard University Press, 1968. (*Harvard Monographs in the History of Science*)

STRICKMANN, Michel. "On the Alchemy of T'ao Hung-ching," *FT,* (1979), 123–192. [see 1.2]

5.2.3 Inner Alchemy

BALDRIAN-HUSSEIN, Farzeen. "Inner Alchemy: Notes on the Origin and Use of the Term Neidan," *CEA,* 5 (1989–1990), 163–190.

BALDRIAN-HUSSEIN, Farzeen. *Procédés secrets du joyau magique. Traité d'alchimie taoïste du XIième siècle.* Paris: Les Deux Océans, 1984.

DESPEUX, Catherine. *La moelle du phénix rouge: santé et longue vie dans la*

Chine du XVIe siècle. (Translation of *Chih-feng sui*). Paris: Editions Maisnie-Trédaniel, 1988.

HUANG, Jane, in collaboration with Michael Wurmbrand. *The Primordial Breath. An Ancient Chinese Way of Prolonging Life Through Breath Control.* Torrance, Calif.: Original Books, 1987.

*KOHN, Livia, ed., in cooperation with Yoshinobu Sakade. *Taoist Meditation and Longevity Techniques.* (Michigan Monographs in Chinese Studies, 61). Ann Arbor: University of Michigan Center for Chinese Studies, 1989.

LU, K'uan-yu (Charles Luk). *Taoist Yoga. Alchemy and Immortality.* New York: Samuel Weiser, Inc., 1973.

ROBINET, Isabelle. "Metamorphosis and Deliverance from the Corpse in Taoism," *HR,* 19 (1979), 37–70.

ROTH, Harold D. "Psychology and Self-cultivation in Early Taoistic Thought," *HJAS,* 51 (1991), 599–650.

5.2.4 *Meditative Practices*

ANDERSEN, Poul. *The Method of Holding the Three Ones: A Taoist Manual of Meditation of the Fourth Century A.D.* (*Studies on Asian Topics,* No. 1). London and Malmo: Curzon Press, 1980.

BOLTZ, Judith M. "Opening the Gates of Purgatory: A Twelfth Century Taoist Meditation Technique for the Salvation of Lost Souls," *TTS-2,* (1983), 487–511.

CHU, Wen Kuan, trans., *Tao and Longevity. Mind-Body Transformation: An Original Discussion about Meditation and the Cultivation of Tao. (From the Original Chinese by Nan Huai-Chin).* York Beach, Maine: Samuel Weiser, 1984.

KOHN, Livia. *Seven Steps to the Tao. Sima Chengzhen's Zuowanglun.* (Monumenta Serica Monograph Series, vol. 20). Nettetal (Germany): Steyler Verlag, 1987 (1987-a).

KOHN, Livia. "The Teaching of T'ien-yin-tzu," *JCR,* 15 (1987), 1–28 (1987-b).

KOHN, Livia. "Taoist Insight Meditation: The Tang Practice of *Neiguan,*" *TMLT,* (1989), 193–224.

KOHN, Livia, ed., in cooperation with Yoshinobu Sakade. *Taoist Meditation and Longevity Techniques.* (Michigan Monographs in Chinese Studies, 61). Ann Arbor: University of Michigan Center for Chinese Studies, 1989.

LUK, Charles (Lu K'uan-yu). *The Secrets of Chinese Meditation.* London: Rider, 1964 & 1984.

ROBINET, Isabelle. *Taoist Meditation.* Julian Pas and Norman Girardot. trans. Albany, NY: State University of New York Press, 1993.

5.2.5 *Mysticism*

HUGHES, Catharine, ed., *Shadow and Substance: Taoist Mystical Reflections.* New York: Seabury, 1974.

*KOHN, Livia. *Early Chinese Mysticism: Philosophy and Soteriology in the Taoist Tradition.* Princeton: Princeton University Press, 1992.

KOHN, Livia. "Eternal Life in Taoist Mysticism," *JAOS,* 110 (1990), 622–640.

KOHN, Livia. *Taoist Mystical Philosophy: The Scripture of Western Ascension.* Albany: State University of New York Press, 1991.

NAN, Huai-chin. *Tao and Longevity. Mind-Body Transformation. An Original Discussion about Meditation and the Cultivation of Tao.* Translated by Chu Wen Kuan. York Beach, Maine: Samuel Weiser, 1984.

ROBINET, Isabelle. "Taoïsme et mystique," *CEC,* 8 (1989), 65–103.

5.3   Taoist Biographies

CORLESS, Roger J. "T'an-luan: Taoist Sage and Buddhist Bodhisattva," *BTS-2,* (1987), 36–45.

KIRKLAND, J. Russell. "The Last Taoist Grand Master at the T'ang Imperial Court: Li Han-kuang and T'ang Hsüan-tsang," *TS,* 4 (1986), 43–67.

KOHN, Livia. "Chen Tuan in History and Legend," *TR,* 2.1 (1990), 8–31.

PORKERT, Manfred. *Biographie d'un taoïste légendaire; Tcheou Tseu-yang.* Paris: Collège de France, Institut des Hautes Etudes Chinoises, 1980.

SEIDEL, Anna K. "Chang San-feng, A Taoist Immortal of the Ming Dynasty," W.T. de Bary, ed., *Self and Society in Ming Thought.* (New York: Columbia University Press, 1970), 483–531.

VERELLEN, Franciscus. *Du Guangting (850–933). Taoïste de cour à la fin de la Chine médiévale.* [A Court Taoist in Late Medieval China]. Paris: Collège de France, 1989. Mémoires de l'Institut des Hautes Etudes Chinoises, vol. 30.

5.4   Tales of Immortals and Sages

DESPEUX, Catherine. *Immortelles de la Chine ancienne. Taoïsme et alchimie féminine.* Puiseaux: Pardés, 1990.

HO, Kwok Man & Joanne O'Brien, eds. and trans., *The Eight Immortals of Taoism. Legends and Fables of Popular Taoism.* Martin Palmer (intro.). New York: Meridian, c1990.

HOLZMAN, Donald. "Les sept sages de la forêt des bambous et la société de leur temps," *TP,* 44 (1956), 317–346.

KALTENMARK, Max. *Le Lie-sien tchouan: Biographies légendaires des immortels taoïstes de l'antiquité.* Peking et Paris: Publications du Centre d'Etudes Sinologiques de Pekin, 1953.

KIRKLAND, Russell. "The Making of an Immortal: The Exaltation of Ho Chih-Chang," *Numen,* 38 (1991), 201–214.

LAI, T.C. *The Eight Immortals.* Hong Kong: Swindon Book Co., 1972.

LING, Peter C. "The Eight Immortals of the Taoist Religion," *JNCB RAS,* 49 (1918), 53–75.

WERNER, E.T.C. *A Dictionary of Chinese Mythology.* New York: The Julian Press, 1979 (first published in Shanghai, 1932).

WONG, Eva, trans., *Seven Taoist Masters: A Folk Novel of China.* Boston: Shambhala Press, 1990.

YANG, Richard F.S. "A Study of the Origin of the Legends of the Eight Immortals," *OE,* 5 (1958), 1–22.

YETTS, W. Perceval. "The Eight Immortals," *JRAS,* (1916), 773–808.

YETTS, W. Perceval. "More Notes on the Eight Immortals," *JRAS,* (1922), 397–426.

5.5   Concepts of Sages and Immortals

CHING, Julia. "The Ancient Sages *(sheng)*: Their Identity and Their Place in Chinese Intellectual History," *OE,* 30 (1983–1986), 1–18.

ROBINET, Isabelle. "The Taoist Immortal: Jesters of Light and Shadow, Heaven and Earth," *JCR,* 13–14 (1985–86), 87–105.

ROTH, Harold D. "The Concept of *Shen* in Early Taoism: Ghost in the Machinery?," Kidder Smith Jr., ed., *Sagehood and Systematizing Thought in Warring States and Han China.* (Brunswick, Maine: Bowdoin College, 1990), 11–32.

ZIA, Rosina. "The Conception of 'Sage' in Lao-Tze and Chuang-Tze as Distinguished from Confucianism," *Ching-chi hsüeh-pao,* 5 (1966), 150–157.

The Taoist Religious Life: The Public Dimensions

6.1   General

FUKUI, Kojun. *Fundamental Problems Regarding the Schools of Religious Taoism.* Tokyo: Maruzen, 1959.

KALTENMARK, Max. "Le taoïsme religieux," Henri Puech, ed., *Histoire des Religions,* (Paris: Editions Gallimard, 1970), vol. 1, 1216–1248. [*Encyclopédie de la Pleiade*].

KIRKLAND, Russell. "The Roots of Altruism in the Taoist Tradition," *JAAR,* 54 (1986), 59–77.

SASO, Michael R. *The Teachings of Taoist Master Chuang.* New Haven: Yale University Press, 1978.

6.2   Taoist Temples and Holy Places

CHAVANNES, Edouard. *Le T'ai-chan. Essai de monographie d'un culte chinois.* Paris: E. Leroux, 1910; reprint, Taipei: Ch'eng-wen Publishing Co., 1970.

GOULLART, Peter. *The Monastery of Jade Mountain.* London: J. Murray, 1961.

HAHN, Thomas. "The Standard Taoist Mountain and Related Features of Religious Geography," *CEA*, 4 (1988), 145–156.

LAGERWEY, John. *Le continent des esprits: la Chine dans le miroir du taoisme*. Maisonneuve & Larose, 1993.

SWANN, Anne Goodrich. *The Peking Temple of the Eastern Peak. The Tung-yueh Miao in Peking and its Lore*. Nagoya, Japan: Monumenta Serica, 1965.

6.3   Taoist Ritual

ANDERSEN, Poul. "The Practice of Bugang," *CEA*, 5 (1989–1990), 15–53.

BELL, Catherine M. *Medieval Taoist Ritual Mastery: A Study in Practice, Text and Rite*. Ph.D. Dissertation; University of Chicago, 1983.

BELL, Catherine M. "Ritualization of Texts and Textualization of Ritual in the Codification of Taoist Liturgy," *HR*, 27 (1988), 366–392.

BOLTZ, Judith M. "Opening the Gates of Purgatory: A Twelfth-century Taoist Meditation Technique for the Salvation of Lost Souls," *TTS-2*, (1983), 487–511.

CHAVANNES, Edouard. "Le jet des dragons," *Mémoires concernant l'Asie Orientale*. tome III (1919), 53–220 (5 planches).

DEAN, Kenneth. "Field Notes on Two Taoist Jiao Observed in Zhangzhou, December 1985," *CEA*, 2 (1986), 191–209.

DEAN, Kenneth. *Taoist Ritual and Popular Cult in South-East China*. Princeton: Princeton University Press, 1993.

*LAGERWEY, John. *Taoist Ritual in Chinese Society and History*. New York: Macmillan Publishing Company; London: Collier Macmillan Publishers, 1987.

MALEK, Roman. *Das Chai-chieh Lu. Materialien zur Liturgie im Taoismus*. [Materials Concerning Taoist Liturgy]. Frankfurt am Main, Berne, New York: Peter Lang, 1985. (*Würzburger Sino-Japonica*, Band 14)

PAS, Julian. "Rituals of Cancellation of Evil (*Hsiao-tsai*)," in Tsao Pen-yeh and D. Law, eds., *Studies of Taoist Rituals and Music of Today*. (Hong Kong: Chinese University of Hong Kong, 1989): 28–35.

PAS, Julian. "Symbolism of the New Light. Further Researches into Taoist Liturgy, Suggested by a Comparison Between the Taoist Fen-Teng Ritual and the Christian Consecration of the Easter Candle," *JHKB RAS*, 20 (1980), 93–115. (Published in 1983)

SASO, Michael R. *Taoism and the Rite of Cosmic Renewal*. Pullman: Washington State University Press, 1972. (2nd Edition 1990)

SASO, Michael R. "What is the *Ho-t'u*?" *HR* 17 (1978), 399–416.

SCHIPPER, K.M. *Le fen-teng: rituel taoïste*. Paris: Ecole Française d'Extrême-Orient, 1975. (*Publication de l'Ecole Française d'Extrême-Orient*, vol. 103)

SCHIPPER, Kristofer. "The Written Memorial in Taoist Ceremonies," *RRCS*, (1974), 309–324.

SCHIPPER, Kristofer. "Vernacular and Classical Ritual in Taoism," *JAS*, 45 (1985), 21–57.
STRICKMANN, Michel. "Therapeutische Rituale und das Problem des Bösen im frühen Taoismus," *RPOA*, (1985), 185–200.
TEISER, Stephen. *The Ghost Festival in Medieval China*. Princeton: Princeton University Press, 1988.

6.4 Taoist Monastic Life and Priesthood

BENN, Charles D. *The Cavern-Mystery Transmission: A Taoist Ordination Rite of A.D. 711*. Honolulu: University of Hawaii Press, 1991.
COHEN, Alvin P. "Biographical Notes on a Taiwanese Red-Head Taoist," *JCR*, 20 (1992), 187–201.
ESKILDSEN, Steven. "Asceticism in Ch'üan-chen Taoism," *B.C. Asian Review*, 3/4 (1990), 153–191.
LAGERWEY, John. "The Taoist Religious Community," *ER*, 14 (1987), 306–317.
ROBINET, Isabelle. "Nature et rôle du maître spirituel dans le taoïsme non liturgique," M. Meslin, ed., *Maître et disciples dans les traditions religieuses*. (Paris, 1990), 37–50.

6.5 Taoist Deities

CAHILL, Suzanne. *Transcendence and Divine Passion. The Queen Mother of the West in Medieval China*. Stanford: Stanford University Press, 1993.
FENG, Han-chi. "The Origin of Yü Huang," *HJAS*, 1 (1936), 242–250.
GAUCHET, L. "Recherches sur la Triade Taoïque," *BUA*, série 3, 10 (1949), 326–366.
HARLEZ, de, Ch. *Le Livre des esprits et des immortels. Essay de mythologie chinoise d'après les textes originaux*. Brussels: Mémoires de l'académie royale des sciences, des lettres et des beaux-arts de Belgique, vol. 51, 1893.
LeBLANC, Charles. "A Re-Examination of the Myth of Huang-ti," *JCR*, 13–14 (1985–86), 45–63.

6.6 Taoist Mythology

*GIRARDOT, Norman J. *Myth and Meaning in Early Taoism: The Theme of Chaos (Hun-tun)*. Berkeley: University of California Press, 1983.
YÜ, David C. "The Creation Myth of Chaos in the Taoist Canon," *JOS*, 24 (1986), 1–20.

6.7 Taoist Music

JAN, Yün-hua. "The Bridge between Man and Cosmos: the Philosophical Foundation of Music in the *T'ai-p'ing ching*," in Tsao Pen Yeh and D. Law (Hong Kong: 1989): 14–27.

LÜ, Ch'ui-k'uan. "Enquête préliminaire sur la musique taoïste de Taiwan." (Summary in French by J. Lagerwey of a Chinese article by Lü Ch'ui-k'uan), *CEA*, 4 (1988), 113–126.

Taoism and Society

7.1 Taoism and Government

*AMES, Roger T. *The Art of Rulership. A Study in Ancient Chinese Political Thought*. Honolulu: University of Hawaii Press, 1983.

CHEUNG, Frederick Hok-ming. "Religion and Politics in Early T'ang China: Taoism and Buddhism in the Reigns of Kao-tsu and T'ai-Tsung," *JICS*, 18 (1987), 265–275.

GROOT, J.J.M. de. *Sectarianism and Religious Persecution in China*. 2 vols. Amsterdam: Johannes Muller, 1903–1904. Taiwan reprint (2 vols. in 1), Taipei: Ch'eng-wen Publishing Co., 1969 and 1976.

HSIAO, Kung-chuan. *A History of Chinese Political Thought*. F.W. Mote. trans. (Vol. 1: From the Beginnings to the Sixth Century A.D.). Princeton: Princeton University Press, 1979.

LEVY, Howard S. "Yellow Turban Religion and Rebellion at the End of the Han," *JAOS*, 76 (1956), 214–227.

MICHAUD, Paul. "The Yellow Turbans," *MS*, 17 (1958), 47–127.

SEIDEL, Anna. "The Image of the Perfect Ruler in Early Taoist Messianism," *HR*, 9 (1969–1970), 216–247.

STEIN, Rolf A. "Remarques sur les mouvements du taoïsme politico-religieux au IIième siècle après J.C.," *TP*, 50 (1963), 1–78.

7.2 Women and Taoism

CAHILL, Suzanne E. "Performers and Female Taoist Adepts: Hsi Wang Mu as the Patron Deity of Women in Medieval China," *JAOS*, 106 (1986), 155–168.

CAHILL, Suzanne E. "Practice Makes Perfect: Paths to Transcendence for Women in Medieval China," *TR*, 2.2 (1990), 23–42.

CLEARY, Thomas. *Immortal Sisters: Secrets of Taoist Women*. Boulder, Colo.: Shambhala, 1989.

DESPEUX, Catherine. *Immortelles de la Chine ancienne. Taoïsme et alchimie féminine*. Puiseaux: Pardés, 1990.

DESPEUX, Catherine. "L'ordination des femmes taoïstes sous le T'ang," *EC*, 5 (1986), 105–110.

KIRKLAND, Russell. "Huang Ling-wei: a Taoist Priestess in T'ang China," *JCR*, 19 (1991), 47–73.

NEEDHAM, Joseph. "Feminity in Chinese Thought and Christian Theology," *CF*, 23 (1980), 57–70.

OVERMYER, Daniel. "Women in Chinese Religions: Submission, Struggle, Transcendence," in Shinohara and Schopen. (Oakville, Ontario: Mosaic Press, 1991): 91–120.

7.3   Taoism and Ethical issues

GIRARDOT, Norman J. "Behaving Cosmogonically in Early Taoism," Robin W. Lovin and Frank E. Reynolds, eds., *Cosmogony and Ethical Order.* Chicago: University of Chicago Press, 1985,

KLEEMAN, Terry. "Taoist Ethics." John Carman & Mark Juergensmeyer, eds., *A Bibliographic Guide to the Comparative Study of Ethics.* (Cambridge: Cambridge UP, 1991), 162–194.

KOHN, Livia. "Taoist Visions of the Body," *JCP,* 18 (1991), 227–251.

WU, Kuang-ming. "Deconcentration of Morality: Taoist Ethics of Person Making," *HHYC:CS,* 1 (1983), 625–654.

7.4   Taoism and Sexuality

BEURDELEY, A., a.o., *Le jeu de la pluie et des nuages. L'art d'aimer en Chine.* Paris: Bibliothèque des Arts, 1969.

CHANG, Jolan. *The Tao of Love and Sex. The Ancient Chinese Way to Ecstasy.* London: Wildwood House, 1977.

CLEARY, Thomas, trans. and ed., *Immortal Sisters: Secrets of Taoist Women.* Boston: Shambhala, 1989.

*GULIK, Robert H. van. *Sexual Life in Ancient China.* Leiden: E.J. Brill, 1961.

HARPER, Donald John. "The Sexual Arts of Ancient China as Described in a Manuscript of the Second Century B.C.," *HJAS,* 47 (1987), 539–93.

ISHIHARA, Akira and Howard S. Levy. *The Tao of Sex: An Annotated Translation of the 28th Section of the Essence of Medical Prescriptions (Ishimpo or I-hsin-Fang).* New York: Harper & Row (*Harrow's Books*), 1970.

*WILE, Douglas. *Art of the Bedchamber. The Chinese Sexual Yoga Classics including Women's Solo Meditation Texts.* Albany, NY: State University of New York Press, 1992.

7.5   Taoism, Medicine and Healing

BLOFELD, John. *Gateway to Wisdom: Taoist and Buddhist Contemplative and Healing Yogas Adapt.* London: Allen & Unwin, 1980.

DESPEUX, Catherine. *Prescriptions d'acupuncture valant mille onces d'or.* Paris: Guy Trédaniel, 1987.

ESKILDEN, Steven. "Early Quanzhen Daoist Views on the Causes of Disease and Death," *B.C. Asian Review,* 6 (1992), 53–70.

HUARD, Pierre and Ming Wong. *Chinese Medicine.* Bernard Fielding (translation from French). New York and Toronto: McGraw-Hill Book Co., 1968.

KOHN, Livia. "Medicine and Immortality in T'ang China," *JAOS,* 108 (1988), 465–469.

PALOS, Stephen. *The Chinese Art of Healing.* New York: Herder and Herder, 1971; New York, Toronto & London: Bantam Books, 1972.

PORKERT, Manfred. *The Theoretical Foundations of Chinese Medicine.* Cambridge: Massachusetts Institute of Technology Press, 1963.

SIVIN, Nathan. *Traditional Medicine in Contemporary China.* Ann Arbor: University of Michigan, 1987.

STRICKMANN, Michel. *Tao und Medizin: Therapeutische Rituale im Mittelalterlichen China.* Munich: Kindler Verlag, 1986.

UNSCHULD, Paul U. *Medicine in China: A History of Ideas.* Berkeley: University of California Press, 1985.

7.6 Taoism and the Physical Sciences

CAPRA, Fritjof. *The Tao of Physics.* Berkeley: Shambala, 1975.

SIU, R.G.H. *The Tao of Science: An Essay on Western Knowledge and Eastern Wisdom.* Cambridge, Mass.: M.I.T. Press; New York: Wiley & Sons, 1957.

7.7 Taoism and Ecology

AMES, Roger T. and J.B. Callicott. *Environmental Philosophy: The Nature of Nature in Asian Traditions.* Albany, NY: State University of New York Press, 1988.

AMES, Roger T. "Taoism and the Nature of Nature," *Environmental Ethics,* 8 (1986), 317–350.

IP, Po-Keung. "Taoism and the Foundations of Environmental Ethics," *Environmental Ethics,* 5 (1983), 335–343.

PEERENBOOM, Randall P. "Beyond Naturalism: A Reconstruction of Daoist Environmental Ethics," *Environmental Ethics,* 13 (1991), 3–22.

Taoism and Chinese Culture

8.1 Taoism and Literature

DESAI, Santosh. "Taoism: Its Essential Principles and Reflection in Poetry and Painting," *CC,* 7 (1966), 54–64.

HAWKES, David. *Ch'u Tz'u: The Songs of the South.* Oxford: Oxford University Press, 1959.

LI, Wai-yee. "Dream Visions of Transcendence in Chinese Literature and Painting," *AAr,* 3 (1990), 53–78.

LIU, Ts'un-yan. *Buddhist and Taoist Influence on Chinese Novels.* Vol. 1, *The Authorship of the Feng Shen Yen I.* Wiesbaden: Harrassowitz, 1962.

MITSUDA, Masato. "Taoist Philosophy and its Influence on T'ang Naturalist Poetry," *JCP,* 15 (1988), 199–216.

PALANDRI, Angela Jung. "The Taoist Vision: A Study of T'ao Yuanming's Nature Poetry," *JCP,* 15 (1988), 97–120.

RUSSELL, Terrence C. *Songs of the Immortals: The Poetry of the Chen-kao.* Ph.D. Dissertation, Australian National University, 1985.

SCHAFER, Edward H. "The Cranes of Mao-shan," *TTS-2,* (1983), 372–393.

SCHAFER, Edward H. *Mirages on the Sea of Time: The Taoist Poetry ot Ts'ao T'ang.* Berkeley: University of California Press, 1985.

SCHAFER, Edward H. "The Snow of Mao-Shan: A Cluster of Taoist Images," *JCR,* 13–14 (1985–86), 107–126.

WALEY, Arthur. *The Poetry and Career of Li Po, 701–762.* London: Allen & Unwin; New York: Macmillan Co., 1950, 1958.

YEH, Michelle. "Taoism and Modern Chinese Poetry," *JCP,* 15 (1988), 173–196.

8.2   Taoism and the Fine Arts

CHANG, Amos Ih-tiao. *The Tao of Architecture.* Princeton: Princeton University Press, 1981. (First title, 1956: *The Existence of Intangible Content . . .*)

CHANG, Chung-yuan. *Creativity and Taoism: A Study of Chinese Philosophy, Art and Poetry.* New York: Julian Press, 1983.

EICHENBAUM KARETZKY, Patricia. "A Scene of the Taoist Afterlife on a Sixth Century Sarcophagus Discovered in Loyang," *ArA,* 44 (1983), 5–20.

GIESELER, G. "Les symboles de jade dans le taoïsme," *RHR,* 105 (1932), 158–181.

HOFFMAN-OGIER, Wayne H. "Dragonflight: Chinese Calligraphy and the Mystical Spirit of Taoism," *SM,* 6 (1983), 3–43.

LEE, Wayne. "The Painter Immortal: Wu Tao-tzu," *ACQ,* 11 (1983), 27–40.

LEGEZA, Laszlo. *Tao Magic. The Secret Language of Diagrams and Calligraphy.* London: Thames and Hudson, 1975.

LEGEZA, Laszlo. "Chinese Taoist Art," *Arts of Asia,* 7, no. 6 (1977), 32–37.

LITTLE, Stephen. *Realm of the Immortals: Daoism in the Arts of China.* The Cleveland Museum of Art, distributed by Indiana University Press, 1988.

PAPER, Jordan. "Riding on a White Cloud: Aesthetics as Religion in China," *Religion,* 15 (1985), 3–27.

POWELL, James N. *The Tao of Symbols.* New York: Quill, 1982.

REITER, Florian C. "The Visible Divinity. The Sacred Icon in Religious Taoism," *NDGNVO,* 144 (1988), 51–70.

SHAW, Miranda. "Buddhist and Taoist Influences on Chinese Landscape Painting," *JHI,* 49 (1988), 183–206.

8.3   Taoism and Health Exercises

DESPEUX, Catherine. "Gymnastics: The Ancient Tradition," *TMLT,* (1989), 225–262.

GALANTE, Lawrence. *T'ai Chi. The Supreme Ultimate.* York Beach, Maine: Samuel Weiser, 1981.

LIU, Da. *Taoist Health Exercise Book.* New York: Links Books, 1974.

8.4   Taoism and Chinese Philosophy

COLEMAN, Earle J. "The Beautiful, the Ugly and the Tao," *JCP,* 18 (1991), 213–226.

DAHLSTROM, Daniel. "The Tao of Ethical Argumentation," *JCP,* 14 (1987), 475–485.

LIN, Tung-chi. "The Taoist in Every Chinese," *T'ien-hsia Monthly,* 11 (1940–1941), 211–225.

LIU, Xiaogan. "Wuwei (Non-Action): From Laozi to Huainanzi," *TR,* 3.1 (1991), 41–56.

8.5   Taoism and Chinese Culture

DAWSON, Raymond, ed., *The Legacy of China.* Oxford: Oxford University Press, 1971. (First published by Clarendon Press, 1964)

HAAS, William S. *The Destiny of the Mind, East and West.* New York: Macmillan Co., 1956.

HOU, Cai. "The Contents of the Daoist Religion and Its Cultural Function," *CSP,* 22 (1990–1991), 24–42.

*KIRKLAND, Russell. "Person and Culture in the Taoist Tradition," *JCR,* 20 (1992), 77–90.

LIN, Tung-chi. "The Chinese Mind; Its Taoist Substratum," *JHI,* 8 (1947), 259–272.

LIU, Da. *The Tao and Chinese Culture.* New York: Schocken Books, 1979.

WEI, Francis C.M. *The Spirit of Chinese Culture.* New York: Scribner's Sons, 1947.

Taoism and Other Traditions

9.1   Taoism and Buddhism

BLOFELD, John E.C. *Beyond the Gods: Taoist and Buddhist Mysticism.* London: George Allen and Unwin, 1974.

BLOFELD, John. *Gateway to Wisdom: Taoist and Buddhist Contemplative and Healing Yogas Adapt.* London: Allen & Unwin, 1980.

CAMPANY, Robert F. "Buddhist Revelation and Taoist Translation in Early Medieval China," *TR,* 4.1 (1993), 1–30.

CH'EN, Kenneth K.S. *Buddhism in China: An Historical Survey.* Princeton: Princeton University Press, 1964.

CH'IEN, Edward T. "The Concept of Language and the Use of Paradox in Buddhism and Taoism," *JCP,* 11 (1984), 375–400.

FRANKE, Herbert. "The Taoist Elements in the Buddhist Great Bear Sutra," *AM,* 3 (1990), 58–87.

GRANT, Beata. *Buddhism and Taoism in the Poetry of Su Shi (1036–1101).* Ph.D. Dissertation, Stanford University, 1987.

HSU, Sung-peng. "Han-shan Te-ch'ing: A Buddhist Interpretation of Taoism," *JCP,* 2 (1975), 417–428.

JAN, Yün-hua. "Cultural Borrowing and Religious Identity: A Case Study of the Taoist Religious Codes," *CS,* 4, no. 7 (1986), 281–294.

JAN, Yün-hua. "The Religious Situation and the Studies of Buddhism and Taoism in China," *JCR,* 12 (1984), 37–64.

*KOHN, Livia. *Laughing at the Tao. Debates among Buddhists and Taoists in Medieval China.* Princeton: Princeton University Press, 1995.

LIU, Ts'un-yan. *Buddhist and Taoist Influences on Chinese Novels.* Wiesbaden: Harrassowitz, 1962.

POO, Mu-chou. "The Images of Immortals and Eminent Monks: Religious Mentality in Early Medieval China (4–6 century A.D.)," *Numen,* 42 (1995), 172–196.

SASO, Michael R. "Buddhist and Taoist Notions of Transcendence: A Study in Philosophical Contrast," *BTS-1,* (1977), 3–22.

VERELLEN, Franciscus. "Evidential Miracles in Support of Taoism: The Inversion of a Buddhist Apologetic Tradition in Tang China." *T'oung-pao,* 78 (1992): 217–263.

WU, Yi. "On Chinese Ch'an in Relation to Taoism," *JCP,* 12 (1985), 131–154.

*ZÜRCHER, Erik. *The Buddhist Conquest of China.* Leiden: E.J. Brill, 1959.

*ZÜRCHER, Erik. "Buddhist Influence on Early Taoism," *TP,* 66 (1980), 84–147.

9.2 Taoism and Confucianism

ALMEDER, Robert. "The Harmony of Confucian and Taoist Moral Attitudes," *JCP,* 7 (1980), 51–54.

AMES, Roger T. "The Common Ground of Self-Cultivation in Classical Taoism and Confucianism," reprinted from *Tsing Hua Journal of Chinese Studies* (Dec. 1985), *TR,* 1 (1988), 22–55.

CHANG, Chung-Yuan. *Some Basic Philosophical Concepts in Confucianism and Taoism.* New York: Bulletin Missionary Resources Library, 1955.

CHAO, Paul. "The Chinese Natural Religion: Confucianism and Taoism," *CC,* 24 (1983), 1–14.

FUNG, Yu-lan. "The Rise of Neo-Confucianism and its Borrowing from Buddhism and Taoism," Derk Bodde. trans. *HJAS,* 7 (1924), 89–125.

LIN, Yü-sheng. "The Unity of Heaven and Man in Classical Confucianism and Taoism and Its Philosophical and Social Implications," *Proceedings of the*

31st International Congress of Human Sciences, Tokyo: Vol. 1 (1984), 258–259.

LIU, Ts'un-yan. "Lu Hsi-hsing: A Confucian Scholar, Taoist Priest and Buddhist Devotee of the Sixteenth Century," *AS,* 18–19 (1965), 115–142.

LIU, Ts'un-yan. "Lin Chao-en (1517–1598): The Master of the Three Teachings," *TP,* 53 (1967), 253–278.

LIU, Ts'un-yan. "The Penetration of Taoism into the Ming Neo-Confucianist Elite," *TP,* 57 (1971), 48–50.

MUNRO, Donald J. (ed.) *Individualism and Holism: Studies in Confucian and Taoist Values.* Ann Arbor: University of Michigan Press, 1985.

POLITELLA, Joseph. *Taoism and Confucianism.* Iowa City: Sernal, 1967. (*Crucible Books*)

ROBINET, Isabelle. "La notion de *hsing* dans le taoïsme et son rapport avec celle du confucianisme," *JAOS,* 106 (1986), 183–196.

WEBER, Max. *Confucianism and Taoism.* M. Morishima (abridg.), M. Alter and J. Hunter. trans. London: London School of Economics, 1984.

YEARLY, Lee. "Hsün-tzu on the Mind: His Attempted Synthesis of Confucianism and Taoism," *JAS,* 39 (1980), 465–480.

ZIA, Rosina C. "The Conception of 'Sage' in Lao-tze as Distinguished from Confucianism," *Chung Chi Journal,* 5 (1966), 150–157.

9.3 Taoism and Popular Religion

CHAN, Wing-tsit. "Taoist Occultism and Popular Beliefs," Wing-tsit Chan et al., eds., *The Great Asian Religions.* (London: Collier-Macmillan, 1969), 162–178.

*DEAN, Kenneth. *Taoist Ritual and Popular Cults of Southeast China.* Princeton: Princeton University Press, 1993.

HOU, Ching-lang. *Monnaies d'offrande et la notion de trésorerie dans la religion Chinoise.* Paris: Collège de France, 1975. (*Mémoires de l'Institut des Hautes Etudes Chinoises,* vol 1).

KALINOWSKI, Marc. "La littérature divinatoire dans le *Daozang,*" *CEA* 5 (1989–90): 85–114.

SASO, Michael R. *Blue Dragon, White Tiger: Taoist Rites of Passage.* Washington, D.C.: The Taoist Center, 1990. Distributed by the University of Hawaii Press.

SCHIPPER, Kristofer. "Sources of Modern Popular Worship in the Taoist Canon: A Critical Appraisal," in *Proceedings of International Conference on Popular Beliefs and Chinese Culture.* (Taipei: Center for Chinese Studies, 1994), 1–23.

STEIN, R.A. "Un exemple de relations entre taoïsme et religion populaire," *Fukui Hakase Shoju Toyo Bunka Ronshu. Oriental Culture. A Collection of Articles in Honor of the Seventieth Anniversary of Dr. Kojun Fukui.* (Tokyo: 1969), 79–90.

9.4 Taoism and Other Religions

CHRYSSIDES, George D. "God and the Tao," *RS*, 19 (1983), 1–11.
KÜNG, Hans and Julia Ching. *Christianity and Chinese Religions*. New York: Doubleday & Collins, 1989.
LEGGE, James. *The Religions of China Compared with Christianity*. London: 1880; Folcroft, Penn.: 1976; Philadelphia, Penn.: 1978.

9.5 Taoism and Philosophy (Comparative Philosophical Issues)

DECAUX, Jacques. "Taoist Philosophy and Jungian Psychology," *CC*, 22 (1981), 95–110.
EBER, Irene. "Martin Buber and Taoism," *MS*, 42 (1994), 445–464.
FREIBERG, J.W. "The Dialectic in China: Maoist and Daoist," *BCAS*, 9 (1977), 2–19.
FU, Wei-hsun Charles. "Creative Hermeneutics: Taoist Metaphysics and Heidegger," *JCP*, 3 (1976), 115–144.
KASULIS, T.P. "The Absolute and the Relative in Taoist Philosophy," *JCP*, 4 (1977), 383–394.
PARKS, Graham. "Intimations of Taoist Themes in Early Heidegger," *JCP*, 11 (1984), 353–374.
PARKS, Graham. "The Wandering Dance: Chuang Tzu and Zarathustra," *PEW*, 33 (1983), 235–250.
ROSS, R.R.N. "Non-Being and Being in Taoist and Western Traditions," *RT*, 2 (1979), 24–38.
TOMINAGA, Th. T. "Taoist and Wittgensteinian Mysticism," *JCP*, 9 (1982), 269–290.
WU, Kuang-ming. "Dream in Nietzsche and Chuang Tzu," *JCP*, 13 (1986), 371–382.
ZHANG, Longxi. *The Tao and the Logos. Literary Hermeneutics, East and West*. Durham & London: Duke University Press, 1992.

The Study of Taoism

10.1 Academic Study Today

"Some Recent Asian Publications on Taoism," *TR*, 2.1 (1990), 95–112.
BARRETT, Timothy H. "Taoism: History of Study," *ER*, 14 (1987), 329–332.
BELL, Catherine. "In Search of the Tao in Taoism: New Questions of Unity and Multiplicity" (review article), *HR*, 33 (1993), 187–201.
KANDEL, Barbara. "A Visit to the China Taoist Association," *SSCRB*, 8 (1980), 1–4.

LEUNG, Man Kam. "The Study of Religious Taoism in the People's Republic of China (1949–1990): A Bibliographical Survey," *JCR,* 19 (1991), 113–126.
YÜ, David C. "Present-Day Taoist Studies," *RSR,* 3 (1977), 220–239.

10.2   Contemporary Taoism

BOLEN, Jean Shinoda. *The Tao of Psychology: Synchronicity and the Self.* New York: Harper and Row, 1979.
PORTER, Bill. *Road to Heaven: Encounters with Chinese Hermits.* San Francisco: Mercury House, 1993.

Supplementary References

11.1   Chinese History

The Cambridge History of China. Cambridge: Cambridge University Press. Vol. 1 (1986) *The Ch'in and Han Empires* (D. Twitchet & M. Loewe, eds.). Vol. 3 (1979) *Sui and T'ang China* (part 1) (D. Twitchet, ed.)
EBERHARD, Wolfram. *A History of China.* Berkeley: University of California Press, 1977 (1st publication, 1950).
FAIRBANK, John, E.O. Reischauer and A.M. Craig. *East Asia. Tradition and Transformation.* Boston: Houghton Miflin Co., 1973.
GERNET, Jacques. *A History of Chinese Civilization.* J.R. Foster, trans. Cambridge: Cambridge University Press, 1982.
LIN, Yutang. *The Gay Genius. The Life and Times of Su Tungpo.* New York: John Day Co., 1947.
WATSON, Burton, trans., *Records of the Grand Historian of China.* Translated from the *Shih Chi* of Szu-ma Ch'ien (2 vols). New York: Columbia University Press, 1971.
WRIGHT, Arthur and D. Twitchet, eds., *Perspectives on the T'ang.* New Haven: Yale University Press, 1973.
WRIGHT, Arthur. *The Sui Dynasty. The Unification of China, A.D. 581–617.* New York: A. Knopf, 1978.

11.2   Chinese Religion and Culture

The Arts of China. Horizon Book. New York: American Heritage Publishing Co., 1969.
BERLING, Judith. *The Syncretic Religion of Lin Chao-en.* New York: Columbia University Press, 1980.
BERNBAUM, Edwin. *Sacred Mountains of the World.* San Francisco: Sierra Club Books, 1990.

BONNEFOY, Yves, compiler, *Mythologies* (2 vols). Chicago & London: University of Chicago Press, 1991.

CHAMBERLAIN, Jonathan. *Chinese Gods.* Hong Kong: Long Island Publishers, 1983.

COUVREUR, F.S. *Dictionnaire classique de la langue chinoise.* Taichung: Kuangchi Press, 1966 (first published in 1890).

EBERHARD, Wolfram. *A Dictionary of Chinese Symbols* (trans. from the German by G.L. Campbell). London: Routledge, 1986.

ELLWOOD, Robert. *Many Peoples, Many Faiths.* Englewood Cliffs, N.J.: Prentice-Hall, 1982.

FUNG, Yu-lan. *A History of Chinese Philosophy* (2 vols.) Derk Bodde, trans. Vol. 1, Peking, Henri Vetch, 1937; Princeton University Press, 1952. Vol. 2: Princeton University Press, 1953.

GROOT, J.J.M. de. *Les Fêtes annuellement célébrées à Emoui (Amoy). Etude concernant la religion populaire des Chinois.* First published Paris: E. Leroux, 1886. Taiwan reprint: San Francisco: Chinese Materials Center, 1977 (2 vols.).

KARLGREN, Bernhard. *Analytic Dictionary of Chinese and Sino-Japanese.* Paris: P. Geuthner, 1923. (Taiwan reprint) Taipei: Ch'eng-wen Publishing Co., 1973.

KUBO, Noritada. *Dokyoshi (History of Taoism).* Tokyo: 1977. (In Japanese)

MATHEWS, R.H. *Chinese-English Dictionary.* Cambridge: Harvard University Press, 1969 (11th printing) (first published in Shanghai, 1931).

OU-I-TAI. "Chinese Mythology" in *New Larousse Encyclopedia of Mythology.* (London: Paul Hamlyn, 1959/1973), 379–402.

OVERMYER, Dan. "Women in Chinese Religions: Submission, Struggle, Transcendence," in K. Shinshara & G. Shopen, eds., *From Benares to Beijing. Essays on Buddhism and Chinese Religion.* (Oakville, Ontario: Mosaic Press, 1991), 91–120.

PAS, Julian. *Visions of Sukhāvatī. Shan-tao's Commentary on the Kuan wu-liang-shou-Fo ching.* Albany, NY: SUNY Press, 1995.

PAS, Julian, ed., *The Turning of the Tide. Religion in China Today.* Hong Kong: Hong Kong Branch of the Royal Asiatic Society & Oxford University Press, 1989.

PAUL, Diana. *Women in Buddhism: Images of the Feminine in Mahayana Tradition.* Berkeley: Asian Humanities Press, 1979.

REPS, Paul. *Zen Flesh, Zen Bones: A Collection of Zen and Pre-Zen Writings.* New York: Anchor Books, n.d. (before 1969).

SCHAFER, Edward. *Pacing the Void. T'ang Approaches to the Stars.* Berkeley: University of California Press, 1977.

SMITH, Jonathan, ed., with the American Academy of Religion. *Harper-Collins Dictionary of Religion.* San Francisco: Harper, 1995.

SMITH, Richard. *Fortune-Tellers and Philosophers. Divination in Traditional Chinese Society.* Boulder, Colorado: Westview Press, 1991.

TILL, Barry and Paul Swart. *Chinese Jade, Stone for the Emperors.* Victoria, BC: Art Gallery of Greater Victoria, 1986.

WALEY, Arthur, trans., *The Analects of Confucius.* New York: Vintage Books (Random House), 1938.

WILLIAMS, C.A.S. *Outlines of Chinese Symbolism and Art Motives.* Shanghai, 1932 (2nd revised edition, New York: 1960).

YANG, C.K. *Religion in Chinese Society.* Berkeley: University of California Press, 1970.

Appendix

Centers of Taoist Study and Practice Today

The following information is very incomplete: It can be used for what it is worth (it is hoped that readers worldwide will be motivated to send us more information, to be included in a second edition of the *Dictionary*).

The study of Taoism has become a worldwide movement. Its land of origin, China, is paying increasing attention to it, both as a religious way of life and as a subject of scholarly study.

China

As a *religious organization*, there is in the PRC a national body, called Taoist Association of China (TAC), originally founded in 1957, but revived in 1979 (after the "Ten Years of Chaos"). Its goal is to strengthen the Taoist heritage in the homeland through publications, including a quarterly journal (*Chung-kao Tao-chiao/Zhongguo Daojiao*) and by organizing training sessions for young candidates. Many provinces have branch organizations.

Study centers focusing on Taoism are established in many Chinese cities. The more important ones are in:

- Beijing, Chinese Academy of Social Sciences, Institute for the Study of World Religions, which has a separate unit for research on Taoism.
- Shanghai, Academy of Social Sciences, with a special unit researching Taoism. They publish a quarterly journal, *Shanghai Tao-chiao*. One of the most active scholars there is Ch'en Yaot'ing/Chen Yaoting.
- Szechuan province has strong centers for Taoist studies in Chengtu, both at the Szechuan University, Department of Religious Studies, and at the Academy of Social Sciences. Several internationally known scholars are active there: Ch'ing Hsi-t'ai/Qing Xitai; Li Shu-yuan/Li Shuyuan.

A recent assessment of the state of Taoism in the PRC is found in the journal *China Heute* (*China Today*), published in Germany. See vol. 14 (1995), 108–110: "Daoismus oder die Lehre des Laozi." (See also **Introduction: Taoism in Modern Times**.)

Taiwan

The *ritual practice of Taoism* in Taiwan is foremost in the hands of the Taoist clergy (see entry **Popular Religion and Taoism**). Yet there also is an independent religious organization, calling itself *Chung-hua Tao-chiao hui* (Taoist Association of China/Taiwan). It has local chapters in all major cities.

The *study of Taoism* is encouraged by several bodies: the International *Lao-Chuang Society*, the *Yi-ching Society*, and, more recently, by a new organization strongly influenced by Taoism, the *Ling-chi hsieh-hui* (Association of "Mediums"). (See *JCR,* 24, 1996.)

Several well-known scholars are members of the Academia Sinica in Taipei. One of their ongoing projects is investigating the relationship between Taoism and the Popular religion. There are also plans for the founding of a Taoist university in Taiwan in the near future.

North America and Europe

The study of Taoism is being actively promoted in various academic institutions. In Europe, Paris has a long history of sinology with special focus on Taoism. In most of the larger universities of the United States and Canada, there are programs in Asian Studies or Religious Studies, with an emphasis on Taoism.

Journals publishing in the area of Taoism are *Journal of Chinese Religions*, *Taoist Resources*, and *Cahiers d'Extrême-Asie* (Kyoto). For more detailed information, especially concerning bibliographies on Taoism, see **Bibliography** in this volume.

About the Author

JULIAN F. PAS (S.T.D. and S.T.L., University of Louvain, Belgium; Ph.D., McMaster University, Hamilton, Ontario, Canada), was professor emeritus of religious studies at the University of Saskatchewan, Saskatoon, Canada. His prior books include *The Turning of the Tide: Religion in China Today* (1989); *Taoist Meditation,* translated with Norman Girardot from the French *Méditation Taoïst* by Isabelle Robinet (1993); *Visions of Sukhāvatī: Shan-tao's Commentary on the Kuan wu-liang-shou-Fo ching* (1995); and *A Select Bibliography on Taoism* (1988), a second enlarged edition of which came out in 1997.

He published several dozen professional articles and book chapters on Chinese Buddhism, Taoism, and the Popular religion of China in such journals as *History of Religions, Monumenta Serica, Journal of the Royal Asiatic Society* (Hong Kong Branch), *Journal of Chinese Religions, Field Materials, Institute of Ethnology, Academia Sinica.*

He was the editor of *Journal of Chinese Religions* (vols. 15–20, 1987–90), and was also the vice president of the Society for the Study of Chinese Religions.

Julian Pas passed away on June 12, 2000.